The Memoirs of André Trocmé

The Memoirs of André Trocmé

The Pastor Who Rescued Jews

André Trocmé

Edited by Patrick Cabanel

Translated by Patrick Henry and Mary Anne O'Neil

Plough

Published by Plough Publishing House
Walden, New York
Robertsbridge, England
Elsmore, Australia
www.plough.com

Copyright © 2025 by Plough Publishing House
All rights reserved.

Original French edition copyright © 2020 by Labor et Fides.
This translation published by arrangement with Labor et Fides.

ISBN 978-1-63608-159-5
29 28 27 26 25 1 2 3 4 5

A catalog record for this book is available from the British Library.
Library of Congress Cataloging-in-Publication Data

Names: Trocmé, André, 1901-1971 author | Cabanel, Patrick editor | Henry, Patrick (Patrick Gerard) translator | O'Neil, Mary Anne, 1945- translator
Title: The memoirs of André Trocmé : the pastor who rescued Jews / André Trocmé ; edited by Patrick Cabanel ; translated by Patrick Henry and Mary Anne O'Neil.
Other titles: Mémoires. English | Pastor who rescued Jews
Description: Walden, New York : Plough Publishing House, [2025] | Original title "Mémoires" published in French in 2020. | Includes bibliographical references. | Summary: "André Trocmé's personal memoirs reveal the formative experiences that led him to stand up to Nazis, save Jews, and become an international peacemaker"-- Provided by publisher.
Identifiers: LCCN 2025010455 (print) | LCCN 2025010456 (ebook) | ISBN 9781636081595 print | ISBN 9781636081618 ebook
Subjects: LCSH: Trocmé, André, 1901-1971 | Righteous Gentiles in the Holocaust--France--Le Chambon-sur-Lignon--Biography | Protestant churches--France--Clergy--Biography | World War, 1939-1945--Jews--Rescue--France--Le Chambon-sur-Lignon | Holocaust, Jewish (1939-1945)--France | Trocmé, Magda, 1901-1996 | Le Chambon-sur-Lignon (France)--Biography | LCGFT: Autobiographies
Classification: LCC D804.66.T76 A313 2025 (print) | LCC D804.66.T76 (ebook) | DDC 940.53/44--dc23/eng/20250520
LC record available at https://lccn.loc.gov/2025010455
LC ebook record available at https://lccn.loc.gov/2025010456

Printed in the United States of America

Contents

Introduction

Patrick Cabanel

WE HAVE WAITED a long time for the publication of the memoirs of André Trocmé (1901–1971). I am delighted now to present them to the public. For the most part, they were written in 1955, but Trocmé worked on them again in 1962 and completed his work in 1967. They remain unfinished, however, since they only give us a continuous narrative up to the early 1950s.

It is important to point out that the original typed manuscript belongs to the Magda and André Trocmé archives in the Swarthmore College Peace Collection and that a photocopy of the original has been deposited in the archives of the Ecumenical Council of Churches in Geneva. These copies have been fully accessible to scholars, who have used them and quoted from them over the years. But this text has never been accessible to the public at large, even though its existence was well known. Originally, the Trocmé children, Nelly and Jacques, did not envisage publishing the integral text before 2025. However, as the only surviving child, Nelly Trocmé Hewett authorized me to publish this annotated edition in French in 2020.

Trocmé was the pastor in Le Chambon-sur-Lignon (in the Haute-Loire region of France) from 1934 to 1950. The role this village's people played in the rescue of hundreds of Jewish children and adults in the 1940s has become one of the most beautiful pages in the history of France or, more generally, in the history of European Christians faced with the genocide of the Jews. Since the end of the 1970s, a wave of memorials – historiographical, editorial, and even cinematographic, musical, and political – has submerged the village of Le Chambon-sur-Lignon and the high-altitude plateau that surrounds it. Several dozen people from the area have been designated "Righteous Among the Nations," with André and Magda among the first to be so named. It would take too long to establish the chronology and bibliography of the process that led to this international recognition of the village and the plateau, especially in Israel and the United States. The attention given to the area has not let up in forty years, and there are perhaps as many books and articles written about this exceptional history in English as there are in French.

Yet one text, this memoir, has been glaringly absent from the public record. We should consider it an important source because it was written very soon after the events, before anyone paid much attention to what had happened on the plateau. Furthermore, this text was composed by the principal actor, or at least one of the principal actors, in the events. In fact, excerpts from the memoirs have been circulating for a long time without the family's knowledge. These extracts, which dealt with the 1940s, provoked lively and heated debate some thirty years ago on the very soil where the events took place. The countryside has since returned to its natural serenity.

It appears that the major problem raised by the fragments circulated from André Trocmé's memoirs (roughly 18 percent of the text) is that they reduced a book and a life to a few years. These were certainly important years, but the memoirs in their entirety are at once much less than the portrait of a human community under Vichy rule (they are only the story of an individual) and much more, since we can consider them a formidable document regarding the history of French Protestantism (or even of France itself) during the first half of the twentieth century.

I would like to insist on this double perspective that views the memoirs as both larger and smaller than the story of Le Chambon-sur-Lignon. I have not concentrated on the psychological history of the man because, to do so, I would need an in-depth knowledge of psychology and psychiatry that I simply do not have. But such specialists will read the opening pages of these memoirs with great profit. Here we find the description of an upper-middle-class, industrialist Protestant family from the north of France (but also from Germany) and, above all, its irreparable heartbreak: the death of a mother witnessed by her ten-year-old son in a car accident caused by his father. An aged father, suddenly a widower, with many offspring. A timid child, the youngest, closed in on himself, insecure about his talent and shattered by a sense of guilt.

Taken as a whole, the memoirs depict the importance of the father ("Papa" is always written with a capital "P") and of a family sure of its place and prestige, a typical upper-middle-class family and probably a typical upper-middle-class Protestant family. Without a doubt, it would be difficult to find in the Trocmé family, beyond their obvious Puritanism, a very Calvinist sense of predestination, a form of pride that comes less from "class" than from "grace." André's entire destiny, despite his timidity, would be to become independent at the ideological and denominational levels. He became a socially aware pastor who took the side of the workers, not the bosses (which could be interpreted as a liberating rejection of his milieu), then a pacifist and a conscientious objector who opposed the patriotism affirmed by his family. Finally, he married a woman who was not Protestant (as did his brother Francis). The fact that Magda was a foreigner (Italian) whom he met in the United States was not a problem for a family that had a cosmopolitan side to it, since André's mother was German. His mother had, however, been the daughter of a pastor. Magda was not Protestant, in either sense of the word for a French Protestant of the time: by belief and practice on the one hand, or by her family origin on the other. The spouse of Pastor André Trocmé and daughter-in-law of Paul Trocmé, the president of the Committee of the Northern Christian Society, was not Protestant and never wanted to become Protestant. This love marriage was both a sign and a condition of a series of breaches that André and, later, the couple were capable of, breaches that risked both ecclesiastical and social solitude.

For the moment, I will skip over the period of World War I, a decisive time for André, to continue with the question of Protestantism. Readers for whom the name Trocmé evokes only the rescue of Jews in Le Chambon-sur-Lignon between 1940 and 1944 may be stunned by these memoirs. Certainly, these readers will know that Trocmé was a pastor, along with his colleague Édouard Theis. They may also know that Trocmé's and Theis's church was a major center of dissent in the local community and that from the pulpit the two men pronounced the famous June 23, 1940, declaration on resistance using the "weapons of the Spirit." But, to some degree, this is only superficial knowledge.

One reason we forget what constituted Trocmé's profound pastoral identity is that his sermons were not recorded; he only made outlines of them. But these memoirs compensate in their own way for the absence of the sermons. They remind us that Trocmé was, from the beginning and throughout his career, a *pastor* – a minister of the Holy Gospels, as was said in days past. He was a man whose vocation (in the elevated sense of the word, a life's choice) was to spread the gospel and try to live and take seriously everything in the Gospels that is disturbing and revolutionary (in the socialist sense and in the sense of Saint Francis of Assisi and others), especially the scandal of the cross.[1]

Young André grew up in a Protestant milieu suffused with practice and piety, with a father who conducted the family prayer services. This was an inherited faith, a mimetic faith. "A religion of forms," a "routine," wrote André after the fact. He went through what he calls "revivals" (*réveils*), using the typical Protestant word designating a personal conversion to Christ when one already considered oneself "Christian," what Americans call "born again." But he also experienced the phenomenon of collective outpourings when conversions occur by the dozens, or even by the thousands, as in the great historical revivals of the nineteenth and twentieth centuries. Trocmé went from revival to revival. He made a list of them: the Young People's Christian Union in Saint Quentin, Plaisance, and Clamart; the Northern Group and the parish of Sin-le-Noble. At first, he was a follower; later he became a leader.[2] Throughout his life, he was nostalgic about the revivals, long after the initial dynamism had dissipated.

We learn a lot in these memoirs about the history of French Protestantism in the twentieth century, which remains poorly known even among its few specialists. If the settling of the Baptists in the north, the actions of the Brigade in the Drôme, and the somewhat charismatic figure of Henri Nick are all well known, it's not quite the same for the Northern Group, the generation of the "friends" (*copains*), the former students at the School of Theology in Paris who wanted to evangelize the proletarian milieus and who resembled both the Drôme Brigadiers and the worker priests. Some of the friends went into Pentecostalism, which was establishing itself in France at the time. Trocmé hosted Douglas Scott in his presbytery in Sin-le-Noble. He describes the first Pentecostal groups, the speaking in tongues, and the pre-Taizé atmosphere created in Charmes-sur-Rhône in Ardèche by his former theology classmate, Louis Dallière. Here we have some astonishing pages written by a man who is

1 In this regard, see André Trocmé, *Jesus Christ and the Nonviolent Revolution* (Plough, 2014).

2 He hoped to have a revival in Le Chambon but it never took place.

neither an opponent nor an outside observer, but rather a Christian who has himself undergone a rebirth experience, who "speaks the language" of this deeply believing milieu, and who, after reporting its excesses and failures, is fully capable of analyses that one would think were written by historians or sociologists of religion.

You will read a letter in this collection that was never published by Trocmé. Dated October 1943, when Trocmé was in hiding far from his family, it announces the founding of an order of "Servants," a men's group that would be recognized by the "small chain" around their neck. This type of third order was not some whim completely out of touch with the Reformed tradition. It was rather an echo of the third order tradition of the "Watchmen" (*Veilleurs*), made popular some twenty years earlier by Pastor Wilfred Monod, not to mention the nascent Taizé movement.

Another curious point, earlier and better known, is the young theologian's stay in New York for an additional year's study from 1925 to 1926 after completing his degree at the School of Theology in Paris. New York City is not only where he meets the love of his life, the beautiful Italian of Russian origin, Magda Grilli di Cortona, and encounters a typically American Protestant form of student internationalism, but also where he tutors the Rockefeller children (as Édouard Theis, his future co-pastor, had done just before him). The memoirs contain pages about a railroad and automobile cross-country vacation trip taken by this extraordinarily rich family. As in other moments, André is both an outsider and an insider, an often uncomfortable situation but one that allows for astute observation.

When he becomes the pastor of a rural parish, Le Chambon-sur-Lignon, Trocmé turns into an ethnologist of this milieu so foreign that he doubts it will ever appeal to him. He came from an urban world and only wished to leave the North to go to the Parisian suburbs. Here is how he describes the plateau, the peasants, and his village: "When, in the North, I pronounced the word 'God,' I brought a revolution, because, in the heart of slavery, of poverty, and of working in the mines, God appears as a liberator. But here, God is Nature, Destiny, the Unknowable One who, with chance shots, dispenses death, birth, sickness, health, sunshine, and frost. Faith consists in bowing before these arbitrary decrees. That's what religion is."

One would be mistaken to see in these analyses a lack of understanding or a sense of self-importance. Here two directly opposed cultural universes confront each other, and the initial feeling of strangeness slowly gives way to friendship. "It was in Le Chambon, from 1934 to 1944, that Magda and I were truly happy," writes André. Magda confirms this view in her own memoirs.

To finish with what one might call "Le Chambon before it became Le Chambon" (before the 1940s), we should say a word about the 1937 founding of the École Nouvelle Cévenole, later known as Collège Cévenol.[3] The Collège became famous because it welcomed Jewish students and faculty during the war, but it had been created for the local population, and for the pastors who had many children[4] and great ambition for their scholarly success. Undoubtedly, the Collège was the most useful present the pastor gave his parish and the people of the plateau.

The memoirs give additional information on the history of Protestantism internationally. This international aspect is not surprising, not only because Trocmé had strong connections with the United States, especially after World War II, but because, since the end of the eighteenth century, the small French Protestant community had always kept abreast of theological developments, often introduced by missionaries coming from other countries. It also experienced the influence of various revivals, as well as the increasing critiques of religion emanating from German universities in the nineteenth century. Pentecostalism is an example of these international currents.

More intriguing for those familiar with the spiritual resistance in the different branches of European Protestantism during the years 1930 to 1940 is Trocmé's relation to the Swiss theologian Karl Barth. Barth, who dominated this period and years afterward as well, is almost completely absent from these memoirs. Trocmé did not remember, or did not find it useful to remember that, in early September 1937, he participated in the pastoral meeting organized around the works of Barth at the Saint-Jean-Chambre in Ardèche. When Barthianism appears in these memoirs, it is presented in a critical and perhaps false light, as it had been initially by the adherents to the social Christianity that Trocmé

3 The institution was first called the École Nouvelle Cévenole, the adjective *nouvelle* indicating its pedagogical ambition and linking it to the École des Roches, which was well known to the Trocmés, and to the École Beauvallon, founded at the same time in Dieulefit by the Protestant Marguerite Soubeyran. The name Collège Cévenol was adopted after the war.

4 Trocmé had four children and Theis had eight girls. The school was coed from its beginning.

inherited. In their eyes, Barthianism was a new form of Pietism that refused all Christian commitment to the community. Trocmé denounces the "barrenness of Barthian theology behind which many took refuge to avoid commitment," and reproaches it for defining conscientious objection as "an act of spiritual pride." Obviously, the pacifist Trocmé was hardly able to recognize himself in the famous letter that Barth wrote to the Czech theologian Josef Hromádka in September 1938, on the eve of the conference in Munich. Every Czech soldier who fights, wrote Barth, "will also do so for the church of Jesus Christ."

It is astonishing to see how two radically opposed theologies (that were also political stances) could come together a few years later to reach a common attitude of spiritual resistance and help the persecuted Jews. This enigma found its source in the universality of the Christian message and in the anti-Christian and anti-humanist hatred nourished by the Nazis and the challenge it presented to Christianity. There is, besides, an important link between the German Confessing Church with its Barthian stamp and the pacifist "nest" in Le Chambon. According to Trocmé's memoirs, it was in Le Chambon that Édouard Theis and an Austrian Jewish refugee named Hilde Hoefert, who also taught at the Collège Cévenol, translated Johan Maarten's German novella *Village on the Mountain* (1939), which deals with Christian resistance.

The question of conscientious objection also separated Trocmé from the American theologian Reinhold Niebuhr[5] and led him to become one of the directors of the Fellowship of Reconciliation. This is one of the great contributions of the memoirs, a contribution to the history of Christian pacifism and conscientious objection, which was relatively unknown at the time and seriously divided not only Protestantism but French society more generally at the beginning of the 1930s. A handful of future pastors (whom their church refused to ordain) – Henri Roser, Philippe Vernier, Jacques Martin – went from the courtroom to military prisons, and Trocmé himself was almost prevented from becoming a pastor, while a virulent anti-pacifist patriotism surged in right-wing French Protestantism.

5 Reinhold Neibuhr (1892–1971), as Trocmé writes, converted to a "pragmatic neo-Calvinism, typically American, which allowed the church to tell young soldiers: individuals can conduct themselves morally, but societies cannot. You must choose the lesser of two evils: let Hitler do what he wants or wage war against Hitler. The lesser of the two evils is obviously to wage war against Hitler because Christians, as responsible citizens, must accept to dirty their hands."

The memoirs relate a decisive encounter between young André and a German soldier in the occupational army in the north of France during World War I. The soldier was living, as were others, in the Trocmé mansion in Saint-Quentin. The soldier offered André bread (which he at first rejected) before explaining that he was a Christian who refused to bear arms. This fellowship was Trocmé's initial encounter with Christian pacifism. His account of the rest of World War I and the German occupation in the north from 1914 to 1918 should hold the reader's attention: the sight of wounded German soldiers, the mistreatment of Russian prisoners of war, the evacuation of the population of Saint-Quentin into Belgium. All this marked André. Too young to be drafted, he nonetheless understood the meaning of total warfare, experiencing it as a civilian living between occupation and forced displacement. Although in September 1921 he agreed to do his military service, he refused the corporal stripes that were then forced upon him. Later, named to the army's Geodetic Service and sent to Morocco, where certain zones were not yet peaceful, he discreetly left his rifle and cartridges in the weapons closet in the barracks and told his lieutenant that he refused to kill. One easily understands his admiration for his friends Henri Roser, Philippe Vernier, and Jacques Martin, who refused to serve at all and spent long portions of the 1930s in prison.

Once he entered the School of Theology in Paris, Trocmé became a lifelong Christian pacifist. He was close to Wilfred Monod, the great advocate of social Christianity, pacifism, and ecumenism. Immediately after World War I, he struggled to decide between two rising Christian pacifist networks: the Universal Alliance for International Friendship through Churches, spearheaded by Monod and Pastor Jules Jézéquel, and the Fellowship of Reconciliation. A "desire for the absolute" led him to choose the latter. His second baptism into Christian pacifism came about when the Englishman Oliver Dryer, general secretary of the International Fellowship of Reconciliation, visited the School of Theology in Paris. This was Trocmé's other "vocation," which was fully espoused by Magda – perhaps even more so than by her husband! His full-time pastoral duties in Sin-le-Noble and Le Chambon left him little free time, but things changed in 1945 when he only served as a half-time pastor in Le Chambon. His other half-time commitment was as European Secretary of the International Fellowship of Reconciliation, a function that became full-time in 1950 when he left Le Chambon and moved into the vast, decrepit, bourgeois house that he rented in Versailles. This next-to-last stage in his life – he would once again assume a parish in Geneva in 1960, which is only sketched out in the final pages of the memoirs – offers us invaluable commentary on the hesitant recognition of Nazi culpability by postwar Germans and a moving passage about the camp named Dora and what an ex-member of the Hitler Youth heard and saw there.

Of course, the years 1940 to 1945, spent in Le Chambon, are prominent in the memoirs. Trocmé does not pretend to be writing a history. He simply records his memories, often in intimate fashion, undoubtedly to exorcize two accidental deaths that wounded him for life, that of his mother and of his oldest son. He forgets to record many important things as well, among them the famous declaration that he and Theis made in June 1940 on the "Weapons of the Spirit."

The present edition of the memoirs offers a document with gaps and excesses, subjective assertions, and verifiable truths. It is annotated because, not having been written for publication, the author did not prepare a formal manuscript. It was up to the historian to group facts and narration with equally valid personal reflections.

Just as André and Magda were extraordinarily united throughout their lives, they remain together in their autobiographical practices. After the death of her husband, Magda wrote and then recorded her memories on cassettes during the second half of the 1970s. They are as remarkably well written as those of her husband and appear in two volumes: *Souvenirs d'une jeunesse hors normes* (2017) and *Souvenirs d'une vie d'engagements* (2021).[6] These two volumes, like those written by André, tell of a bourgeois childhood, the lack of a mother, the encounter of a lifetime, and a shared life together. The writings of the two spouses do not, however, duplicate one another. It is a rather stunning exercise to read them one after the other, or in conjunction. It is one of the privileges of this story that it has had two quality writers to relate it.

Apart from that, I decided to insert into the body of the memoirs a few documents written by André Trocmé or concerning him, often never published before, that seem appropriate to read at the same time as the memoirs themselves.

6 Magda Trocmé, *Souvenirs d'une jeunesse hors normes*, ed. Nicolas Bourguinat and Frédéric Rognon (Presses Universitaires de Strasbourg, 2017); Magda Trocmé, *Souvenirs d'une vie d'engagements*, ed. Frédéric Rognon, Patrick Cabanel, and Nicolas Bourguinat (Presses Universitaires de Strasbourg, 2021).

One can read these memoirs for the chapters that cover the 1940s in Le Chambon, and I suppose many readers will begin by doing so. One can also read them for their strictly pastoral and Protestant dimension. This volume is undoubtedly situated at the intersection of these two possible readings. We are dealing with a Protestant story (which is absurd at the statistical level since Protestants were not even 2 percent of the population) and at the same time a national story, even a universal one, whether we are talking about revival meetings in Christianity or spiritual resistance against totalitarianism. This coming together of a minority and the universal is not a first. The Calas Affair,[7] to cite but one example, offers a paradigmatic illustration, as does the Dreyfus Affair, with a Jewish and Judeo-Protestant echo.[8] Classifying the Cévennes as a World Heritage Site for Protestant resistance and the rescue of Jews could furnish another. Reading the memoirs from the angle of the role of minorities in world history will, perhaps, yield their greatest profit.

7 Jean Calas was a Protestant merchant living in Toulouse who was tried, tortured, and executed for the murder of his son on March 10, 1762. He had continuously proclaimed his innocence, even during horrific torture intended to make him confess. The Enlightenment French writer Voltaire intervened, and Louis XV had the decision overturned. As Jean Calas had always maintained, his son, Marc-Antoine, had committed suicide.

8 Alfred Dreyfus, a Jew, was wrongfully convicted of treason and condemned to life in prison. That decision divided the country from 1894 until it was rectified in 1906. Once again, a French writer, Émile Zola, led a campaign to have the decision overturned.

1

Childhood

LIKE ALL SMALL CHILDREN, I thought my childhood home was normal. To this day, I tend to judge houses and people by comparing them to the house and people of my life before 1914.

First, the huge house: eighteen rooms not counting the kitchen and utility rooms, including twelve bedrooms. It was so big for a small boy that I only got to know it gradually. The third floor, for example, remained mysterious until 1914. It was not a very cheery-looking house. Built by Papa around 1895 to provide for his large family (he had nine children with his first wife, Marie Walbaum), its address was 156 Boulevard Gambetta in Saint-Quentin, Aisne. Papa's business was prospering. Boulevard Gambetta was a wide street bordering Les Champs-Elysées, a long, dreary promenade. The trunks of the trees that lined it were green with moss. In the old days, they were painted up to eye level with tar to save the leaves from caterpillar infestations. When I think of my childhood, I can still see, through the tight grid of tree branches, a melancholy sunset stretching out above the houses, over there, "on the other side of Les Champs-Elysées." It seemed so far away.

Behind the house there was a walled garden, a rather poorly tended lawn with a locust tree covered with ivy at its center. Every time I travel and find myself in a dwelling situated between a garden and a public walkway, I feel at home.

My early childhood unspooled in the front bedroom on the second floor that connected to my parents' bathroom. On the wall, there was an advertisement for thread with the name "J. Thiriez Père et Fils."[1] I didn't understand what it meant until I learned to read.

1 The "Julien Thiriez Father and Son" business, founded in 1857, was one of the major textile firms in the north of France.

My mother, who died in an automobile accident when I was ten years old, did not leave me with any very tender or precise memories. I remember her as a stocky woman squeezed into a fitted corset, as was fashionable at the time, with her hair in a bun that came to a point and nose-clip eyeglasses. I know I loved to be close to her, but there were too many maids involved in our upbringing. I remember Mathilde, whom I called to wipe me, and Marie, whom my children knew, an excellent but easily startled creature who bathed me on Saturdays before putting me to bed (with eggnog and rice pudding, whose bland sweetness I still crave today). "There you go, clean as a new penny," she would say as she dried me.

Three memories of my mother stand out. In the first, I am in someone's arms, probably my mother's. The shutters are closed, but we can see through the slits. It's still daylight. I must be sad, because a voice is trying to comfort me by showing me a strange, jolting machine below. "Chug, chug, chug, chug," says the voice. The machine is my older brother Maurice's car. I think that the spectacle must have consoled me since I still remember it.

Here's another memory: I am standing in the bathroom in front of my mother. I am wearing my first real boy's suit made of velour. It has a turned-down white collar and a floppy, loosely tied scarf as a necktie. I have long blond curls that fall to my shoulders. The women on Les Champs-Elysées greatly admire my curls. "What beautiful hair," they say. But I am a big boy, gauche and timid, and their compliments bother and humiliate me. I have never lost this character trait. I experience the same feeling today when American women tell me, "I enjoyed your sermon so much."

One day when I was seriously ill with either measles or the flu (I was often sick and coughed a lot, as did my children later), my parents took me into their bedroom. I have kept a very sweet memory of this moment. The wallpaper had a rather somber, bronze color to it. Golden rain fell at a slant onto bouquets of flowers. In my feverish imagination, this gold covered me little by little, transforming me into a beautiful and happy being. This transfiguration must correspond to a profound yearning in me that later expressed itself in my religious sensibility.

Aside from these three precise memories, I only remember my mother as someone who was always there. I didn't need to think about her because she was part of the normal order of things. I wasn't a precocious child. I awakened slowly from the drowsiness of an overprotected childhood.

My mother was Papa's second wife. That's why my half-brothers and I called her *Mère* and not *Maman*. I wonder if this was not an error on Papa's part. I noticed quickly that all the children called their mother *Maman* except us. In the somewhat solemn atmosphere of our house in Saint-Quentin, the title *Mère* seemed normal to me. My mother was not the mother of my older brothers and sisters, who were much older than I was. Maurice, Louise, Albert, and Francis could have been my parents. I think that Mère tried hard not to show a preference for her own children, Pierre and me. Duty was the key to all attitudes on the Boulevard Gambetta. A duty that restricted the expression of feelings, dreams, and impulses. It seems to me that my own impulses washed away like water over smooth pebbles on a barren shore. The united front presented by my father, mother, and brothers drained me of resistance. But, as I said, I was timid and not the least bit assertive. Perhaps my memory is playing tricks on me.

My memories of visiting Germany are very different. Could it be that, finding herself back home with her German family in an atmosphere much less tense than that of Saint-Quentin, my mother relaxed? There was my charming little grandmother, and my funny aunt Louisa, whom we called "Aunt Lou." I remember our departures, very late, very drowsy, from the Saint-Quentin train station. Maternal warmth reigned in the second-class carriage. We woke up several times in Belgium to the sonorous calls of the customs officers and the foreign railway workers. I remember the enormous train station in Cologne, the cathedral with its twin towers, and the magnificent river glimpsed through the arches of the famous bridge. Then there was the German countryside with neat houses, the hills along the Weser River, and the hearty noise of the train wheels on the bridges and between the embankments.

There was the poetry of Petzen, a city in Lower Saxony not far from Hanover, with its old presbytery and its Romanesque church; the odors of the parlor (coffee, rye bread, ham, and the tobacco from *Grossvater*'s long pipe); the rustic joys of the *grosse Diele* (a barn with a brick floor adjoining the house); the comfort of *Kaffee trinken*; the enormous, sugared cakes (the *Zuckerkuchen* was so large you needed a baker's oven to cook it). All that left me with a memory less staid and less artificial than that of Saint-Quentin and Saint-Gobain,[2] where I spent most of my childhood.

2 The Trocmé family had a summer home in Saint-Gobain, twenty miles from Saint-Quentin.

I recall my grandmother, still pretty under her black lace headdress; my grandfather, silent and huge in his wing chair, who every evening chased *der Bösewicht* (the demon) from my body and my soul by laying his enormous hands on my head; Aunt Lou, who sent me off to look for eggs on Easter Day along the footpath that led to the forest, eggs hidden by *der Osterhase* (the Easter Bunny); the coachman who let me ride in the front seat of my grandfather's carriage with him; the women from the village, in red skirts and black bodices, with their curious headdresses adorned with pearls under which they swept up their blond hair. All this formed an idyllic tableau in my mind that Saint-Gobain never succeeded in creating.

Why? I think I understand. A vaguely romantic heritage, which found no expression in the lucid and critical atmosphere of the Trocmé family, lay dormant in my soul. Later, when my grandfather died (in 1907, I think), I returned to Germany. The rustic carriage with the shaky glass windows that smelled like manure did not come to get us at the station. But I found my grandmother in a small apartment in Bückeburg, and I visited all the aunts (there were seven of them). I slept in large bedrooms furnished with wooden beds and enormous white, puffy, down quilts. Their windows opened onto orchards. I shot marbles with kids in short leather pants. I offered my hand to Uncle Heinrich and to Pastor Sprenger, a tall, thin man with an energetic profile, strapped into a tailored morning coat. I exchanged, as he did, a sonorous *Guten Abend* (good evening) with the peasants in the village. It was the Empire. It was order, respect, work, cleanliness, whereas Saint-Quentin was the Republic, the mocking mask of the factory workers, sneaking a look at the "rich kids" that we were, from behind the curtains of their hovels. At Saint-Gobain, the sputtering automobile already separated us irreversibly from the wheelbarrow pushers going to their gardens.

On a spring day, one of my cousins – Thea Sprenger, I think, a tall girl with black hair and dark eyes – opened her window and clapped her hands when she saw an apple tree filled with flowers right up against the house. "*Wie entzückend!*" (How charming!), she cried out, and all her family exclaimed along with her. Why would the "How charming!" of my French family before the apple trees in bloom in the valley of Saint-Gobain never evoke the same echo in my heart? I don't know. Perhaps the shade cast by the death of my mother in 1911 was so penetrating that our hearts were no longer able to leap as naively as those of my German cousins. Perhaps it was simply what I said earlier: I was an enthusiastic child. I was happy around other enthusiastic people, as I still am today.

The death of my mother was an unbelievably sudden and brutal tragedy. One Sunday in June 1911, Papa decided that we would go spend the day at Saint-Gobain because the weather was so beautiful. We were used to these "departures for Saint-Gobain." Our car, a "limousine," had a closed space behind.[3] The roof came forward above the front seats. To get out, the driver and his front-seat companion detached a small, low door made of oilcloth. The children and any luggage went in the back. Since the luggage and blankets fit so tightly around us, I had the impression that I was planted like a small tree: my legs were the roots, my arms the branches, and my head a piece of fruit.

But on that Sunday, we were not planted. Saint-Gobain was only twenty miles from Saint-Quentin, so we were going to return that same evening. I can still see the car, parked next to the sidewalk, leaning decidedly toward the house, because the pavement bulged noticeably. Right after passing the train station, Papa branched off to the right to avoid the monotony of the Route de La Père that we always took. He wanted to take us for a ride. Later, why did this decision, which led to the catastrophe, always appear to me as a "moral error" on Papa's part? I don't know, but even today when I don't take the direct route, I am assailed with scruples as if I were threatened with misfortune. It is true that, thirty-three years later, Magda and I also contributed to an irreparable tragedy because we did not return home as quickly as possible. So be it.

The road chosen by Papa was narrow, dusty, and poorly maintained. Under the Origny railroad bridge, Papa noticed that his horn wasn't working. He was going at a moderate speed, when a small, open car passed him. Papa was very proud of his powerful car, and he couldn't bear this humiliation. He took off after the other car with the intention of passing it. Pierre, Annette, and I were behind, very shaken and frightened by the bumpy ride. The car in front of us was casting clouds of dust into our faces which made it impossible to see the road clearly. I saw Mère, half up in her seat, touch Papa's hand and cry out: "Paul, Paul, we are going to have an accident!" These were her last words. Papa was driving on the far left to pass the car. Through the dust, I suddenly saw a pile of stones intended for

3 A "limousine" was an enclosed automobile with an open driver's seat. It was supposedly called a limousine because the driver's roof resembled the cloak-hood worn by the shepherds in the region of France called Limousin.

roadwork. Our left wheel hit it. We were going very fast. An indescribable chaos ensued. There was a dreadful noise of twisted metal and broken wood. Then silence interspersed with the frightened cries of children. I found myself outside, standing, and unharmed but trembling from shock. Papa was walking like someone in great pain, holding his broken right wrist in his left hand. Mère was not there. Papa began calling for her and looking for her. She was lying on the roadway twenty yards behind us and no longer appeared to be alive. She had rolled in the dust and was lying on the road facing the sky with a trickle of blood coming from the corner of her mouth. Peasants arrived and carried her to the embankment. The car we were pursuing had turned around and left for town in search of help. An ambulance came to get Mère. We followed in a taxi. Torrents of childish love, bursts of trusting prayers arose indistinctly from my heart toward my mother and God, but my deepest instincts told me it was all over. As soon as I saw her on the road, I understood that there are ruthless events one cannot fight against, decisive moments that no one, not even God, can undo. One cannot go back in time. The minutes and hours flow mercilessly, and we learn that those who were once part of our lives belong to a past that will never bring them back.

Mère lay dying for three days. The first night, Pierre and I, who were staying in the room next to hers, heard the noisy breathing of the dying. Then I was placed in a different room. A surgeon came from Paris and operated right in her room. The operation failed.

On the third day, Papa appeared in the hallway like a ghost, holding his broken wrist. "My children, your *Maman* is no longer with us." He was sobbing. I had never seen him cry. I hugged him with all my strength and said to him: "Papa, promise me you will never own another car." That, I remember clearly. Apparently, I also said: "Why are you crying, since Mère is in heaven?" but I don't remember having said it.

A "funeral chapel" was set up in the study, now draped in black. It was a big funeral because Papa was well-known in Saint-Quentin. All my brothers and sisters came to comfort Papa. The next morning in the dining room, Papa wanted to worship as we normally did. But once again he was in deep despair. "I killed her, I killed her," he cried out, sobbing uncontrollably. Robert, the youngest of my half-brothers, was holding him. Anyone who knew Papa and his incredible fortitude will understand to what extent this spectacle impacted me. Papa, on whom everyone counted, on whom everything rested, was a broken and repentant man.

He nonetheless recovered quickly. Papa was always very sure of himself. I don't know whether it was in his temperament or whether he had constructed, by sheer will, an impenetrable rampart around himself which gave him his incredible authority. He taught us that if we do our duty, we will never be mistaken, and we saw him as a man who never made mistakes. Very quickly, a few months after the accident, as soon as his broken wrist permitted, he bought another car and got back behind the wheel. He drove until he was ninety-two or ninety-three and always drove fast. When, having become drivers ourselves, my brothers and I objected to his fast driving, he responded without hesitating: "Be quiet. I know what I am doing. I have never had an accident!" We were silent, stunned. You didn't argue with Papa.

Since then, I have often reflected on his self-assured answer. I think he didn't know he was lying. Now that I have known a grief comparable to his, I know that there are unthinkable memories, horrors that you cannot evoke without fear of losing your mind. You must banish the very thought of having been responsible for them, even indirectly. Papa, responsible for Mère's death, was only able to maintain his sanity by eliminating the memory of the accident. I am not reproaching him in the least. I am grateful to him for having quickly reestablished his incredible moral strength and for having been able to assume once again his role as an unshakeable rock upon which we, his children, constructed everything.

As for Pierre and me, we were young. Wounded more deeply than we thought, we went back to our games. I hear Papa's voice reproaching us one day: "My children, do you still remember your mother? You must always think about her." We didn't answer. How would I have been able to speak? I had discovered my mother the day I lost her. I had to grow up carrying in my heart a huge amount of never-expressed feeling, an unsatisfied desire for love that had been crushed and only blossomed very slowly as time went by, in the form of profound impulses, sad and religious.

After Mère's death, the house on Boulevard Gambetta became gloomier. My older half-sister, Louise, widow of Pastor Paul Dumas and mother of two children – Yvonne, a year older than me, and Étienne, six months younger than me – left her home on the Rue de L'Est to take charge of Papa's household. Louise spoke very little. She was distant, even from her own children, and had an aristocratic nature: intelligent, firm, and lucid. She became very close to Papa, whom she greatly resembled. But under her direction, the house didn't acquire any demonstrable warmth. Did Louise find herself facing the same problem that Mère did? Did she want to avoid showing her own children more tenderness than she showed me and Pierre, who no longer had their mother? I remember our visits to Louise's home before Mère died. I didn't feel any freer there than I did on Boulevard Gambetta. Pierre, Yvonne, André, and Étienne formed, between 1911 and 1914, a quartet of three brothers and a sister under the direction of German governesses, whose attitudes and games marked my early adolescence and my years attending lycée, the public secondary school.

There were three successive governesses: Miss Winter, Miss Kalcher, and Miss Wiegand. Whereas Papa and Louise used the small living room called the Petit Salon, where we were only admitted very briefly between 1:00 and 1:30 in the afternoon or after dinner and before bedtime at nine "if we had all our homework done," the study was our world unto ourselves. An austere world: an immense, black, double-leafed table desk with six compartments where we stowed our books by raising the roll-top; a cupboard where each one of us had a shelf for books and a few personal treasures; a big, glass-doored bookcase, always locked, containing yellow paperback books "for adults"; a blackboard and Vidal de La Blache wall maps.

We did not go up to our rooms during the day. It was forbidden. Our days were regulated as if we were in a convent: up at 7:00, bell for breakfast at 7:30, school at 8:00, back at noon, two bells between which we washed our hands, lunch at 12:15, walk between 12:50 and 1:30. A quick recitation of our afternoon lessons, school from 2:00 to 4:00, back at 4:15, snack (bread, chocolate, and a glass of milk) in the garden until 5:00. Homework from 5:00 to 7:00, dinner at 7:00 (two bells), short visit to the living room from 7:45 to 8:00. Homework from 8:00 to 9:00. (When we got older, it was from 8:00 to 10:00.) There were exceptions on Thursday afternoons: walk until 4:00, then homework; and on Sunday afternoons: walk until 4:00, followed by free time. In fact, we only had two hours to ourselves each week: Sunday evenings from 5:00 to 7:00. The rule was the rule; there were no exceptions.

We were practically never invited out (except at Christmas to Aunt Marie's and on New Year's to Aunt Alice's). I remember two or three invitations to Gérard and Gilbert's and an afternoon spent with my friends, the Gillets. Otherwise, I didn't know any other house but ours. The Trocmés were supposed to be sufficient unto themselves. There had been the de Saint-Affrique family of my sisters-in-law, but they had left Saint-Quentin. So, we had virtually no friends. Later, Papa explained to me that this isolation was part of his educational system: children were not capable of distinguishing between true and false or good and evil. It was therefore necessary to imprint on their nature ideas and habits that would last a lifetime. As a result, no primary school until the age of ten. After that, we could go to the lycée but without mixing with others. No casual strolling; a precisely timed return home by the most direct route, and homework. Walks were for health (we really racked up the miles!). I only kicked a soccer ball once, on the turf of Saint-Quentin stadium with my Gillet friends and their priest uncle, who was their tutor. I remember this as an inexpressible joy but a decidedly common one that was never repeated.

Everything that was outside of this strict framework imposed by Papa and reinforced by the German governesses, like going through the Grand-Place when the most direct route home from the lycée skirted the "Fontaine aux Grenouilles," going into a shop, or even strolling and looking into a display window, appeared sinful to me. When the Saint-Quentin fair, which lasted a month, built its gingerbread houses along the Grand-Place, the temptation was much greater. But I couldn't fall into temptation because I didn't have any money. It was only in Brussels at the age of seventeen that I had pocket money for the first time. However, one Thursday a year, we were given a very small amount of money to spend at the fair, following the guidance of the governess. I remember a boat costing nineteen sous that I wanted badly for months. It was red inside and white on the outside with four small, wooden sailors in the back stuck on benches. Since it was neither my birthday nor Christmas, the dream of owning this boat remained unsatisfied until the day when Marguerite, the wife of Maurice, took me to the Grand-Bazaar on Rue de la Sellerie (where I had never been before) and bought the boat for me. Marguerite was warm-hearted and had the brilliant idea of presenting "consolation gifts" to those invited to birthday parties who weren't celebrating their birthdays. In my hands, the four little sailors in the boat had many adventures on the high seas: shipwrecks, shark encounters, rescues, and battles with lead soldiers.

When my mother was alive, Christmas was an extraordinary feast inspired by German Christmases. We celebrated it in the Billiard Room, the large room added to the house behind the Petit Salon. Aunt Walbaum had it built for my older brothers and gave them the gift of a billiard table when they were adolescents. Papa had never been very enthusiastic about this worldly game, and the billiard table was taken down when my brothers left. Papa didn't even want anyone to call this room the Billiard Room. He preferred that we call it the Game Room. But for our generation, which had never known billiards, it was always the Billiard Room anyway.

The Billiard Room, always empty and usually cold, became animated with warmth and life at Christmas time. The mystery for us was complete. We had the right to make "Christmas wishes" using catalogs from large department stores, Sears Roebuck–type catalogs that have disappeared from France now that we have become a poor country. On the days before Christmas, we were not allowed to run to the door to see what had arrived. Consigned to the study, we waited. We never saw anyone go into the Billiard Room. Preparations must have taken place when we were asleep.

On the evening of the 24th, we were allowed into the Petit Salon. A window, veiled by transparent blinds, separated the Petit Salon from the mysterious room. Through it, we watched the lighting of the candles, one at a time, on the Christmas tree.

We entered in a procession. The caroling, recitations, and reading of the Christmas story lasted too long for our taste. We had our eyes on the immense tables covered with tablecloths and presents that filled two sides of the room. Everyone was seated at the table according to age. When the ceremony ended, we found our place and sat down in contemplation. To tell the truth, I don't have a very precise memory of the presents I received, but, strangely, I remember exactly the presents Pierre received. He was two years older than I was and "very mature for his age." He got older boys' presents, whereas everyone persisted in giving me toys. "In two years, when you are as old as Pierre is now, you'll get the same presents," they told me. But that promise, two years later, was of course forgotten. As children with a good memory do, I counted my two years. When I entered the Billiard Room, my eyes locked on the promised object, and when we had finished singing the carols, I discovered that it was "not at my place."

Thus, Pierre got a Peugeot bicycle and I, as a consolation for waiting, a hoop. Pierre got a Kodak camera and I, the following summer, a square box with a hole in it but without a lens. It had belonged to Francis when he was young. I used it once, but the photographs were so faint that I lost interest. When Pierre received a gold watch from his godfather (Henri from the École des Roches) – engraved gold, mind you – I got a silver chain with a whistle at the end "to hang a watch on in two years." I got my first watch when I began studying theology at the university. I was nineteen years old, and the watch was copper. When Pierre received a chemistry set, they promised me wonderful future gifts that I never got, and when we *both* got a real microscope, it was understood that its use was reserved for "the older" of us. Sometimes "the older" would let me look through the eyepiece so I could see the slides of diatom algae that he had prepared. My turn to use the microscope never came.

These small pedagogical errors had a significant effect on my future. As a sensitive and proud child, I reacted by deciding that "none of that stuff interested me." My mother was dead, and those charged with my education were taken in by my response. Neither music (Pierre took music) nor drawing (Pierre drew well) interested me.

I was considered rather dumb, and I took refuge in imaginative games that I shared with Étienne Dumas. We inherited a good number of lead soldiers that had belonged to my older brothers. One great day, Aunt Pauline, while she still lived in Saint-Quentin, gave us a giant model train, an extraordinary and marvelous mechanical object whose tracks covered almost the entire surface of the Billiard Room. We took the roof off one of the train cars and found tables and seats in a dining car. Étienne and I, left to ourselves in the Billiard Room during the week between Christmas and New Year's, transformed the tile floor into an imaginary country: streets, bridges, mountains, oceans, boat trains, soldiers, and battles. Lost in our games, we groaned when the governess pulled us away at mealtimes. Kneeling on our dark stockings (little boys had short pants, with stockings attached to a kind of stiff vest under a navy-blue sweater), we got holes in them so quickly that Papa had leather kneepads made for us that we strapped on above and below the knee. On these leather patches, propelling ourselves with our arms at top speed, we played among the toy soldiers, sailors, and villages.

After New Year's Day, inexorably, the governess closed the Billiard Room, which fell back into its glacial mystery until the following Christmas. By doing so, our educators acted wisely. The Billiard Room would have lost its charm, as would the model trains (which we weren't allowed to set up elsewhere) if we had been able to use them all year long. By only opening them up for a dozen or so days a year, the adults created a world of dreams for us, a world of anticipation, and gave us the sense of sacrifice, austere duty, and renunciation. It's true, however, that their calculations probably didn't have such profound motives. For them, it was more a question of saving money on heating and not giving us any temptation to play when it was time for homework or lessons.

We had to go out into the garden between 4:15 and 5 p.m. whenever the weather permitted. Miss Wiegand sent us there with a resoundingly military "Get outside," which allowed for no discussion. It took only five minutes to consume the prescribed bread and chocolate. Then we were directed toward the gazebo, whose walls were made of a tight network of small glass diamonds. Many of the small panes were missing. We took great pleasure in "accidently" pushing out other panes and then using the end of a broomstick to knock away any shards still stuck in the putty.

The inside of the gazebo was a chaos of mismatched toys: children's wheelbarrows, deflated soccer balls, hoops, carts, garden hoses, shovels, and sprinklers. It was there that we got the materials we needed for our games. The garden itself was limited: a circular lawn with an ivy-covered locust tree at its center; a "grotto" in the back on the left; a simple entrance to a cellar whose door, surrounded by loose stones, frightened us somewhat. The "Petite Montagne" (small mountain) leaned against the wall of the garden and had a cement platform that we reached by mounting a short staircase. It lost a good deal of its mystery when Papa cut out half of it to build a garage for his car. There was also a dark path behind the kiosk, where the moss grew better than the grass. Our games consisted of unrelentingly going around the lawn while pushing a hoop with a wheelbarrow or a cart. The gravel on the pathways bounced under our steps. That was how we measured our speed. It was forbidden to get gravel on the lawn, in the flower beds, or on the tiled sidewalk in front of the house. If we did, the head of the governess, the cook, or our sister or father would pop out scoldingly from one of the windows of the house. The call from the adult calmed the yelling children, who moved toward another part of the garden where they could engage in less visible mischief.

Most of all, Étienne and I played war. When we read Caesar, we made a catapult from a stone and a piece of twisted string that we stuck between the sides of a wooden box. A cardboard tube set between two wheels was our canon when we studied Napoleon, our voices furnishing the resounding booms of explosions. Gravel supplied our never exhausted munitions; the glass windows of the gazebo constituted all the vulnerable targets we could desire. Around 1912, we started to use paper planes and even a plane with a propeller that we wound up with a rubber band. Étienne and I filled the garden with our heady cries of victory. Elsewhere, the sound of real heavy artillery echoed our childish cries of "Charge!" This was the age of General Lyautey,[4] the Balkan conflict, and the Italo-Turkish War. We belonged to a breed of men and a social class whose privileged position had never been questioned.

One day, I made a frightening discovery. Above the wall, from atop the small mountain, we had already seen women without hats on the other side of the garden wall.[5] They passed by four times a day with their pointed buns, their curly hair (made so with a curling iron) that fell in front of their ears, their impertinent laughs, their camisoles, and their black shawls. They were the workers at Décaudin et Béguin,[6] the main competitors of Paul Trocmé et Fils. They obeyed the whistle call: eight a.m. to noon, two to seven p.m. We knew there was a similar troop of workers in Papa's factory. When they talked about these people in the Petit Salon, the adults referred to them as "the salt of the earth," except when they called them imbeciles or bird brains. It had never occurred to me that such people could have feelings, aspirations, and thoughts like ours. This was the real downside of the education that Papa gave us. It provided us with a keen sense of our honor, responsibility, and duties, but it formed us into the Trocmé clan, a separate people, different from the rest of humanity.

In short, we lived in the garden as if in a vacuum, but one day we discovered it was not airtight. Every autumn, a professional gardener came to put some order into the garden. He pruned the laurel trees and ivy and spaded the flower beds. He never came through the house but through the convenient iron door in the wall on the street side. Étienne and I, after reading Viollet le Duc's *Histoire d'une forteresse*, called this door "the

4 Louis Hubert Lyautey (1854–1934) was a French Army general and colonial administrator. After serving in Indochina and Madagascar, he became the first French Resident-General in Morocco from 1912 to 1925.

5 At that time, in the bourgeois world, it was unacceptable for women to go outside without a hat and gloves.

6 A pillow-lace factory which later combined with the Trocmé factory and other firms to form La Cotonnière de Saint-Quentin.

postern."[7] On this day, although we didn't know it, the gardener forgot to lock the postern. Our imaginary war was going full blast, probably so loud that one could hear it on the street. Suddenly, the postern opened. The creaking of the rusty hinges drew our attention. In the gateway stood what in 1912 we would have called a "pale hooligan," in a flat cap, short jacket, and bell-bottom pants, with a pallid face and a cigarette stuck in the corner of his mouth. He looked at us for a long time silently, bitterly, sardonically. He took in the garden and the house and nodded. Our cries and gestures had frozen; our outbursts caught in our chests. For the first time, we understood that the Trocmé world was perhaps not the only "normal" world. Then the "pale hooligan" cast a pitying eye on us, sneered, and said, "Bunch of assholes." He left, closing the door behind him.

This event, which I never recounted to anyone until I became an adult, changed the entire course of my thinking. Henceforth, I was no longer able to play war with complete conviction or feel like the master of the world simply because I controlled a garden. I now knew that others heard, looked, and judged, and that all my life I would have to bear their scrutiny and compare my ideas with theirs. Being taken for a moron did me the greatest good.

As I write these lines now, I realize that, of the four who formed our generation, two – Étienne and Yvonne – have died. I will never be able to sit down with them and share these memories. The "pale hooligan," whose image I will take to the grave with me, was only seen by me and Étienne. Thus, he belongs entirely to the past. I can evoke him to sit here at my side, as a member of my family, one of the mysterious inhabitants of my brain that I can conjure up and put back to sleep as I wish. Go, "pale hooligan," rest until I call you back. You revealed to me the problem of class antagonism and I am truly grateful to you. You did a good deed without knowing it, with the help of an insult common to the world in which you lived. I had never heard these words before. I learned them from you and have often pronounced them silently in reference to myself and to all those "absurd people" who take no account of the other human beings around them.

The garden was the scene of many other games. It offered a sneaky way of communicating with the "outside world" and of playing with it that we never would have dared do in the street. I was afraid of the street. I was tall, fat, and awkward, and had a terrible fear of being mocked because

7 A secondary door or entrance in the stone wall of a castle or fortress.

my fat thighs stuck out of my short pants and my over-long arms came out of my narrow sleeves. In the street, I would have liked to be a turtle that, from under its shell, could watch others with its tiny, observant eyes. The garden wall was the shell I wanted. The "Petite Montagne" put us six feet higher than the passersby; the drooping branches of the hazelnut trees allowed us to see without being seen.

Our play with the "outside world" began with a few simple games like throwing moss on the brims of hats. I can still feel the freshness of the moss under my nails. It was hit or miss. We wondered what the hats' wearers would say when they got home.

Once Pierre "pulled off" a master stroke on a woman's hat. We smothered our triumphant laughter in our throats. At four p.m. we were brought back down to earth when we had to appear before the "Petit Salon" tribunal: the drawing teacher from the girls' lycée, Yvonne's school, had given Yvonne a letter of complaint. A short young man with glasses, whom she had seen clearly through the branches, had deliberately soiled her brand-new, beautiful hat. Papa and Louise couldn't understand the humorous aspect of our games. We lowered our heads pitifully and exchanged sideway glances. Pierre kept the nickname "short young man with glasses." When no one was watching us, our games with the "outside world" continued until the German occupation [of World War I].

I'll skip over the stories of old wallets that only contained phony bills placed under the feet of passersby, or the biography of Aristopompe Beauclair, the inventor of mechanical marvels, whose great, imaginary achievements we documented on a small play typewriter to disseminate on the street. I will simply relate the story about the fishing line. Étienne and I (especially Étienne, who had much patience) had a great interest in fishing in the canal. But it was now under German occupation. Confined to the narrow city limits by barbed-wire barriers, we no longer went to Saint-Gobain. Our parents encouraged us to find some innocent entertainment, and we had fishing gear. We quickly grew weary of fish. We wanted to catch people. A solid fishing line used to catch pike, with a cork attached, passed over a branch of the hazelnut tree. We put bait at the end of it: an old harmonica, a wallet, a worthless toy, and we let it hang at a man's height. Then we waited. This game taught us a lot about human behavior. There was "the woman who saw nothing." Dignified, she avoided the object as she passed, without even looking to find out what it might be. Then there was "the little, old, distrustful man," who stopped on the spot, examined the object knowingly, looked up at the string, saw the red cork, saluted us, and went off laughing. Above all, there was "the naive person." Ah yes! He was our favorite victim. He approached the harmonica with admiration, his mouth opened as if to play it, and he looked around to make sure no one could see him. Then he reached out his hand to take the present that came to him from the heavens. But before he was able to grab it, we pulled in the line with loud sneers: Haha! Haha! Hehee! Hehee! He blushed from ear to ear and ran away.

The day came when we lost our harmonica. Up the street, there was an army post of German Red Cross soldiers. They had spotted our games. One day one of them, pretending to pass by our fishing line without noticing it, suddenly grabbed it with a quick gesture. We jerked the cord as hard as we could but couldn't save our property. All four of us were soon hanging on to the cord, which was rubbing against the ledge of the wall. The German had called his comrades to the rescue. Without seeing each other, amid cries and laughter, we all began a pulling match. The cord broke! The Germans carried off the harmonica. We were slightly ashamed of playing with the Germans. For as long as their post remained on our street, we never again played "fishing for men."

Our three governesses were quite different from one another. I vaguely remember Miss Winter, a small young woman with a reddish complexion who wore gold-rimmed glasses. She was clumsy and one day dropped a tea tray at the door of the "Petit Salon." This event, which took place during the boring prewar period, sufficed to mark her: Miss Winter! Ah yes, that nice young girl who dropped . . . etc. Some people only leave behind memories of their blunders.

Miss Kalcher was the one we really loved. She was Silesian and loved to talk about her family's nobility. I can still see her Greek profile and her mass of ash-blond hair. She was intelligent and won over our entire family, except for my sister Louise. She knew how to laugh, nicknamed Papa "Vice-Papa," and expressed affectionate, filial sentiments toward him that were too intimate for Louise's taste. As a result, much to the great despair of the children who adored Miss Kalcher, Louise opposed her spending a second year on Boulevard Gambetta.

Yet Miss Kalcher knew how to win us over. She was a pedagogical genius. She had us call her "Mutter Akka." Akka was Akka de Kebnekaïse from Selma Lagerlöf's novel *Nils Holgersson*. Miss Kalcher had another book, a kind of German *Jungle Book*, in which animals speak. Miss

Kalcher read us this book in German. In Saint-Gobain during the summer vacations, she made this novel come alive for us. The boring walks in the forest, in single file on muddy paths under a swarm of mosquitoes, were replaced by adventurous and mysterious expeditions. We were equipped with hatchets, hammers, dishes, and a saucepan that we loaded onto our "German tank." It was forbidden to tell the adults what we were doing.

We were building a hut out of branches, stuffing moss into the cracks. Pierre and Yvonne were studying Greek, so the hut was named Hydropolis (Water City). It was situated in a marshy area deep in the forest; we had to jump over several ditches full of water to get there. We were convinced that our hut couldn't be found. Yvonne named the streams after rivers in Australia. Pierre built an oven with bricks. I insisted on planting a garden of field horsetails. At that time, I was going through the vegetal phase of my childhood. I tried hard, but with no success, to transplant small oak trees with two leaves growing from rotten acorns in our garden in Saint-Gobain.

When Hydropolis was ready, we invited the adults. The day, as might have been expected, turned into a disaster. The Trocmé family never appreciated what the children were doing. From their very first steps into the forest, cries and reproaches arose: It's too far! It's too hot! Above all, it was Rose, Francis's Russian wife, who complained. We had to jump over muddy streams and her shoes were paying the price. When we got there, there was no place to sit. "Is that it, your hut? You can't even stand up inside." In fact, a photograph, now lost, later revealed to me that my childish imagination had greatly exaggerated the splendors of Hydropolis. The semolina pudding, cooked the night before for our guests, had been nibbled by a field mouse whose two small rodent teeth had left their dainty marks on the surface. That was enough for the adults to declare that it was "disgusting," and they refused to "share their snack with rats."

When it was time for Easter vacation, we rushed into the forest to find Hydropolis. The bare woods of April held no more mysteries for us. We had a hard time finding the spot because the forest rangers had destroyed our hut, leaving only a small bundle of branches. We felt great sorrow and anger. Papa explained that we were actually lucky, and that it was against the law to cut down young trees in the forest. The rangers had certainly discovered our previous summer's toils but had turned a blind eye. Thus, the veil of mystery and poetry that enveloped a summer of our childhood was torn asunder. The austerity of manmade laws and the total lack of imagination that characterized adults chilled our blood. I remember that one day, in the parlor of Saint-Gobain, I screamed at the rigid and skeptical assembly of adults. The Trocmé men never said a word or only talked about the scenery and the distance from one place to another. The women did all the talking (but about what?). I yelled out, "When I get older, I won't be like you. You don't play anymore because you are afraid to look ridiculous. I will continue to play my whole life." And I have kept my word. I've never learned to amuse myself like other adults and am still perfectly capable of getting down on the floor and playing with building blocks for as long as my solitary imagination enjoys it.

To finish the story of Miss Kalcher, I want to evoke a memory from our days in Saint-Quentin. She had discovered a bench placed against the house in the garden. We children had never thought of this bench as a place to sit because our father's orders were very precise – you went into the garden to run. The rest of the time we belonged in the study, where we worked, even during the long June evenings, until it was bedtime. Inexorably, bedtime was nine o'clock, even though sometimes it was still light outside. Miss Kalcher taught us the value of idleness. I never studied with as much pleasure as I did when she was with us. She sat in the middle of the bench, and we gathered around her. We were allowed to cuddle and, as the sun set, she told us stories from her inexhaustible stock. We could also interrupt her with our own stories. That's where I first experienced the comfort of a motherly lap. I remember one evening when I fell asleep on her lap while the others were telling jokes. I had missed the gentleness that emanates from a mother since my mother's death, but Miss Kalcher knew how to supply it. An adult voice woke me with a reproach to Miss Kalcher, something like "Come on, sit up straight. Don't sprawl over one another." I rose quickly, feeling guilty. This incident, along with several others, contributed to my fear of immoral contact with women. The fear protected me but also clouded my adolescent years and made me into a timid boy who blushed in front of women.

Miss Kalcher taught us to play "ghosts," a hide-and-seek game for big children. We did so in Saint-Gobain, at dusk, when the leaves in the orchard took on shades of brown as the summer sky darkened above us. One of us was the ghost and disappeared behind the bushes that protected the flower beds. The other children went looking for it. When one of us passed near enough, the ghost jumped out and chased its victim, trying to grab it. We ran toward the house. We had to touch it, screaming "*Geist, Geist!*" (ghost, ghost) before we were grabbed. These mad dashes at nightfall left me with the memory of strong emotions – fantastic falls, exaltation in danger – that I can't forget. One day Miss Kalcher caught her neck on a wire that had been stretched between two apple trees for a clothesline. This accident left her with a scar for a long time, so the game was forbidden. We could simply have moved the wire elsewhere, but that kind of thing never happened in our house.

Miss Kalcher introduced us to scouting before it existed in France. I was ready to become a scout when the first troop was established in Saint-Quentin in 1913. There was going to be a scout camp in Pommery, an old-age home on a large estate. I asked permission to take part in it. The department store catalogs sold scout uniforms. I already imagined myself starting on a great adventure. But Papa was opposed, even though he probably didn't seriously investigate what scouting was. It was new. Scouts slept in a tent and risked catching a cold and being corrupted by vulgar comrades. Besides, we had a place in Saint-Gobain, and that was enough.

Every day in Saint-Quentin, between 12:45 and 1:30 p.m., we had to take walks with our governess. That's where my physical characteristics took shape. I had the muscular legs of a tireless walker, but my athletic prowess stopped at the waist. My arms have never been strong enough to lift me off the ground.

We had three walks: "The White Mill," "The Burnt Mill," and "Around the Canal." The "White Mill" was the shortest. Near the canal there were houses of painted brick. In winter, I liked seeing their colors through the branches of the poplar trees. The "Burnt Mill" was much longer and monotonous. On the right, the road dipped past an estate with big trees and then ascended between banks of clay soil adorned with a fringe of thick, green grass. It passed next to a brick chateau and descended toward the canal where, if there was time, we could watch a boat going through the lock. As the lock keeper manually cranked open the valves, the water churned against the hidden doors that were eaten away by green moss. A little dog barked at us. Very slowly, the boatman worked his hook. The horses, tensed in exertion, pulled the heavy barge, and set it in motion. After that, we had to hurry back to the city, shake the clay dirt from our shoes, grab our books, and run to the lycée that smelled of dirty aprons, chalk dust, and wet dogs.

I have painful memories of sleepy afternoon classes during which the teacher's voice rose and fell in my ear like the barking of a sad dog. My legs and butt, and especially my head, which had been buffeted by wind on our walk, tingled unpleasantly as the blood rushed back into them.

Thursday was reserved for the "Around the Canal" walk. This was a slow, monotonous walk along muddy canal banks pitted with puddles. We walked through the brush and in the fog next to the yellowish water of the endless canal, listening to the crows croaking in the trees. Once we were able to skate on a stagnant marsh at the canal's edge. We always had to go up the slope leading to the "Burnt Mill." We grabbed the governess's arm to be dragged home, where we knew the only reward we would receive on arrival was bread, chocolate, and homework, always homework.

Our third governess, Miss Wiegand, who came after Miss Kalcher, had no luck with us whatsoever. She was stiff, thin, wore glasses, pursed her lips, and wore a green hat that looked like a cake mold. We took an immediate dislike to her. Yvonne called her "the police officer in petticoats." Pierre sketched her image on his notepads. Dozens of paper effigies of her were scattered everywhere, even in the toilets. We put camphor and pepper in the purse where she had to stick her pointy, red nose to retrieve her *Strich* notebook because she was near-sighted. She had brought with her from Germany a mathematically fair system for grading our work and our obedience. Any failing merited one *Strich* (small vertical line). Five *Striche* merited punishment. Ten *Striche* got you a visit to the Petit Salon where, with our strict Papa watching, you received a warning. But Miss Wiegand started to sneeze uncontrollably every time she plunged her nose into her purse, and we couldn't control our sniggering. We also set up a complicated arrangement of strings going from the door to objects on top of the bookcase in the study. It caused catastrophes whenever Miss Wiegand entered. One day she didn't show up. Everything was in disarray. Louise came down from her room and told us reproachfully that she had found Miss Wiegand in tears over her failures. Poor thing! My memories are so colored by my childish callousness that I can't manage to feel pity for her retrospectively. If I remember correctly, she didn't finish her time with us and was not replaced. The family authorities decided that we were old enough to take care of ourselves. I was thirteen years old.

Miss Kalcher visited us in Le Chambon before the war with her husband, Mr. von Wersebe. It was a disappointing visit. She was certainly intelligent but so imbued with a sense of German superiority that her visit was upsetting. She was surprised that there were forests in France. She described Saint-Quentin as a sad, mean city whose narrow-minded inhabitants dressed in black and led boring lives. Some of what she said was true, but I didn't like hearing her say it. That's the kind of thing you prefer to discuss with family members, if you dare.

PAPA WAS THE INDISPUTABLE HEAD of the Trocmé clan. He was already fifty-six years old when I was born, so I only knew him with gray, and then white, hair. He lost his hair and teeth late in life and maintained his astonishing mental vigor well into old age. He was very thin and upright. Never did his shoulders or his back curve with age or from the many ordeals that assailed him. The only sign of physical weakness (which I inherited) was in his knees, which he could never straighten out completely. When he got old, he dragged his feet a bit when walking and often stumbled.

Papa was neither handsome nor terribly tall, yet he carried himself with an air of nobility that impressed everyone. No one addressed him with familiarity as an equal, whether in the city, at Saint-Gobain, at the synod, or in business matters. He was essentially a man one consulted, who always had the last word. Toward the end of his life, his authoritarianism became trying. He got angry easily and not always with good reason. But in the prime of life, which for him lasted up to his eightieth year, he rarely needed to raise his voice to impose his views. His desires were orders. Like all authoritarians, he didn't know that he was one. "My system," he loved to say, "is to insist on very few rules but to allow for no exceptions. Rules are made to be obeyed." I realize retrospectively that life in Saint-Quentin and Saint-Gobain consisted of one rule after another. But since we always obeyed these rules, they became unconscious and unquestioned habits for us children.

Papa had a high, glowing forehead. His admirably shaped head was more impressive than his face, shoulders, and body. He had sparse eyebrows. His small eyes, under their slightly puffy lids, were brown, intelligent-looking, and penetrating. They were a bit like the eyes of God, eyes which encompassed everything. A rather large moustache and a carefully trimmed white beard gave him the indisputably aristocratic air that we all knew.

We liked to caress Papa's extremely fine hair. That was the only familiarity he allowed. I could get on his lap when he sat in the big armchair of the Petit Salon until I was twelve. He didn't speak and would gently pat us. These signs of tenderness didn't last long, and he never confided in us. Still, we got up from his lap reassured, feeling protected and encouraged by this affectionate contact with the rock of our family.

Papa loved to tell stories from the past, and we listened to them without tiring, even if they were repeated so many times that we knew them by heart. It would take too long for me to repeat them all, so I'll just note a couple.

There was the story of Trocmé-Bouton-d'or (Buttercup), who wore a royal-blue overcoat in the style of the First Empire and shuttled between Hargicourt and Saint-Quentin on market days by asking for rides in the carts of peasants who were better off than he was. One day he complained, in local Picardy dialect, of *"eun tiote benque dans min sole"* (a little something in my shoe). When he got to the Saint-Quentin town square, he took off his shoes and found a fork in one of them.

There was also the story of my grandfather, Eugène Trocmé, and his wedding in 1843 (Papa was born in 1845). These were my father, Paul Trocmé's, exact words:

> In the past, before the Revolution, when Protestants in the north of France wanted to marry, they had to go to Tournai in Belgium. In fact, in France, only Catholic priests could perform legally recognized marriages. If Protestants refused the blessing of a priest, they were considered to be living out of wedlock and their children were illegitimate.
>
> But King Louis XIV, who used Protestant Swiss and German soldiers, had given their chaplains permission to hold church services. Thus, in Tournai, there was the Church of the Gate, where Protestant families went to baptize their children and get married. That's why, André, the marriage records of your ancestors are in Tournai.[8]
>
> Your great grandparents married in Tournai. It took two days to get there from his village of Hargicourt. They left early in the morning in carts and stopped half-way through the trip at a hospitable Protestant farm near Saint-Armand-les-Eaux called 'Le Rosult.'
>
> This farm passed from father to son in a family of rich farmers, the Davaines. When my father, Eugène, reached twenty-five years of age, my grandfather, who was a weaver, the mayor of Hargicourt, and an important person in the village, said to him: "Eugène, you

8 Unfortunately, the Tournai library was destroyed by German fire in 1940.

have reached marrying age, and I don't see anyone around here who would be a suitable match for you. But I remember the Davaine family from Le Rosult, where we stayed a long time ago when I went to Tournai to marry your mother. We'll take the cart to Saint-Amand tomorrow to see if we can find a fiancée for you."

They left early the next morning and arrived in Le Rosult in the late afternoon. Like all the farms in the north of France, the buildings of Le Rosult were arranged around a large, square, paved courtyard with the manure pile at its center. You entered through an archway. The home was at the back of the courtyard.

In the old days, when strangers came to the door of a bourgeois home, if there were any young ladies in the greeting room, they were not allowed to remain in the presence of the men. They had to leave. The secret code in the Davaine household was "Young ladies, go sort the apples in the attic!" There were two girls of marrying age in the Davaine family and, while grandfather Trocmé and his son attached the horse to the hitch post, Grandmother Davaine clapped her hands and pronounced the magic words: "Young ladies, young ladies, go sort the apples in the attic!"

The girls got up. One of them disappeared rapidly. The other had sprained her ankle a few days earlier and dragged her feet. Or maybe she slowed down on purpose? In any case, at the very moment when Eugène and his father entered through one door, she disappeared through the other. But not so quickly that they didn't exchange glances. Bang! That was it. It's because of that glance, André, that I came into this world and that you did after me.

Papa was an excellent student at the Collège des Bons Enfans (later named the Lycée Henri-Martin) on whose benches all the Trocmés of Saint-Quentin were educated. He competed for the top prizes in math and sciences with a certain Édouard Branly, a professor's son. Later, when Branly became famous as one of the inventors of wireless telegraphy, Papa wrote to him recalling their youthful camaraderie. Branly never responded and Papa was offended.

My grandfather, having left Hargicourt, settled in Saint-Quentin as a fabric merchant on the Rue du Gouvernement. He bought woolens, hand-made by the inhabitants of villages, and sold them to Parisian retailers. His business prospered. Papa vaguely remembered his father in the impressive National Guard uniform under King Louis-Philippe before the 1848 revolution! The Eugène Trocmés had four children: Paul, Alphonse, Alice, and much later, Pauline.

When he got good grades in composition, which happened often, Paul got a franc (a good amount for the time). If his grades dropped, they withdrew a sum from the kitty. But this rarely happened.

When Papa was about to finish his religious instruction, his stash contained an impressive sum, and he had plenty of ideas on how he would spend his money on materials in experimental chemistry. But his father took him aside:

"Paul, soon you will make your First Communion."

"Yes, Papa."

"You must have thought about showing your gratitude to your pastor, who went to so much trouble for you . . ."

"Er . . ."

"Have you noticed how shabby his cassock looks? Well, it's in bad shape."

"Ah?"

"Your mother and I were thinking that it would be appropriate for you to withdraw enough money from your funds to buy a new cassock for your pastor."

"OK, Papa."

My father's savings were all spent on that cassock. He told us this sad story when we complained about the rigor of his method of education.

The Trocmé family was the only well-to-do family in the church in Saint-Quentin, and they were very religious. A large oil painting in the living room on the Boulevard Gambetta revealed a distinguished Eugène Trocmé, majestic and sad. The war of 1870 completed the gradual ruin brought on by the invention of weaving machines. Eugène Trocmé believed in handmade fabrics and thought that cloth made on mechanical looms would never compete with them. He was sadly mistaken. His business declined; an associate swindled him. He was completely ruined and died at the age of sixty of heart disease, just before the war of 1870. His large property, Bellevue, to the east of Saint-Quentin, was barely saved. Grandmother Trocmé-Davaine continued to live there for a few years. Those were lean years. Papa served as head of the family for his mother, brother, two sisters, and his seven living children. They ended up subdividing the property.

2

The Family

IT IS NOW TIME for me to talk about my half-brothers and half-sisters from Papa's first marriage.

Around 1875, at the age of thirty, Papa decided to get married. At this time, marriages were arranged. Papa was presented to Miss Marie Walbaum from Reims. From the time of their first meeting, he filled her with admiration by speaking to her, if I remember correctly, about squaring the circle. Papa loved to tell this story which proved two things: Miss Walbaum's keen intelligence and the usefulness of a good scientific education for a young man. Miss Walbaum, who was born and raised in Reims but was of German origin, had had a French education. Her family had come from Schaumburg-Lippe in Lower Saxony at the invitation of their relatives, the Heidsiecks, founders of the famous champagne house of that name. The type of life one led in Reims in no way resembled the austerity of life in Saint-Quentin. My brothers and sisters were often invited to grandmother Walbaum's house in Pontavert near Laon. Francis had unforgettable memories of these visits. But Papa didn't want his children to discover Reims's luxurious living style. He always taught them that the Trocmés were from modest circumstances and would have to work hard to earn their living. Papa had nothing but tremendous energy and the memory of a family that once had a comfortable existence, but Marie Walbaum brought with her a considerable dowry for the time, about 100,000 francs.

With this dowry, Papa went to England and bought mechanical looms for making lace fabric called guipure. Factories in Calais were already producing this lacy, transparent cloth so popular for sheer curtains. He bought property on Rue Quentin-Barné and launched the lace-weaving business that would determine the industrial fortunes of Saint-Quentin. The factory was built in a U shape. The steam engine, topped with a high chimney, took up one of the branches of the U. During my childhood, the other branch and the base were made up of workshops two floors high. The lace looms were enormous; those made after 1918 were over twenty yards long! Above them, a second, small machine, suspended from the ceiling, spread out hundreds of yellow threads over the looms like a tent. The noisy looms were controlled from above by jacquard punched cards. These jacquard looms seemed as intelligent as the human brain and turned out enormous spools of curtain material with floral or Greek designs.

I rarely went to the fabric factory. Like everything that surrounded me on Boulevard Gambetta, it was cloaked in an almost terrifying mystery. There was Papa's office, as well as Maurice's, men dressed in gray work coats who were always rushed and hardly spoke, workers dressed in blue with greasy hands and yellowish features drawn with fatigue. At the time when Robert was doing his apprenticeship as a weaver, after having been to the Technische Hochschule in Hanover and to London to study business, I once saw him also dressed in blue. It never occurred to me that I could one day aspire to be like him. Doctors, engineers, professors, manufacturers, even weavers, all seemed to me like demigods who understood things that I would never understand and who accomplished difficult and superior actions that I would never be able to imitate.

I wasn't a bad student in the lycée; I was even a rather good one. But my mother was dead, and no one ever gave me the least encouragement. Instinctively, I considered myself at the low end of the scale. I still do today. I tremble before professors, manufacturers, and well-known church authorities as if I were a street kid caught in the act, and when I sometimes perceive that I know as much or even more than they do, it's too late. They too have already judged me, and I can't remove the label they have given me. This lack of self-assurance is probably equally due to a system of education that always made us (especially Étienne and me) feel that we were at the bottom of the heap and that we had no voice in the process. Yvonne and Pierre were, however, treated much better. On the other hand, it was fortunate that I had no wish to take over the business in Saint-Quentin. The factory had been constructed with Marie Walbaum's dowry, and, by an oral agreement between Papa and Maurice, who had become Papa's associate, neither Pierre nor I had any claim to the factory because we were the sons of another woman.

Maurice was the eldest in all senses of the term. He resembled Papa in intelligence and energy and, like Papa, was born to take control. He was an excellent businessman but could get angry and loud-mouthed, as we learned from Jeanne, our cook, and Marie, our chambermaid. However, under his direction, the factory prospered. I loved his wife Marguerite, who was pretty and affectionate to us children.

From 1875 to 1895, Papa was content with a simple life. He rented a modest house with a garden in the back. It was only around 1895, after raising seven children, that he considered moving. His business was prosperous. It grew until 1914, so that, by a strange irony, my mother, who had come into the marriage with nothing but had married under the law of joint property, automatically acquired – and left me and Pierre – a good-sized inheritance, whereas the mother of my seven brothers and sisters, who furnished the money for the factory, left them a much more modest sum. Papa suggested that Pierre and I rectify this injustice. We willingly did so once we reached legal age: an accounting trick I never fully understood allowed us to transfer our inheritance to a common fund that gave all the children an equal sum after Papa's death. By suggesting this, Papa fostered an amicable atmosphere among the children. I think he certainly did the right thing. It would have been unbearable for me to become rich with the Walbaum money. I hope that this Trocmé tradition, never to quarrel over money, will be carried on from generation to generation, as well as those other, no less important traditions, such as chastity before marriage, conjugal fidelity, and sobriety. Those are the major inheritances, far more important than receiving several million francs.

As regards Maurice, his opinion of me improved with time. He was intelligent and observant, and though he never adopted my ideas about nonviolence, he listened and understood my spirit of independence. We loved to play in his old, poorly designed house with its galleries, terrace, and garden. There, we felt no strict, burdensome rules weighing us down and had the freedom to play with all our hearts. Marguerite gave us kisses, something I badly needed.

Maurice's house was destroyed and pillaged during World War I. He decided to leave Saint-Quentin. Furthermore, the Paul Trocmé et Fils business disappeared in 1918 when it became part of La Cotonnière de Saint-Quentin, which, for a time, had an entire office building in Paris. Maurice, his wife Marguerite, and their family moved to Eaubonne, a suburb north of Paris, and then to Enghien, where Maurice dedicated his life to rebuilding the factory that had been leveled by the war. He became distant and hardly talked.

Maurice's demise was sudden and sad. At the age of sixty, he had a heart attack and died within minutes in Enghien. Marguerite died in 1954, old but still good-natured. She had featured in some of the most enjoyable parts of my childhood.

Louise came right after Maurice. Among her giant brothers, she appeared short and pale. She spoke little but wrote a lot and well. Her husband, Paul Dumas, was a pastor from the South. A scrupulous fundamentalist, he wore himself out and contracted tuberculosis, a disease they didn't know how to cure at the time. He was a pastor in Saillans, in southeastern France; he convalesced in Die and died in 1907 in Saint-Gobain. He was a mild-mannered, calm person whom I admired greatly. After his death, Louise got us together from time to time with their children, Yvonne and Étienne, to reminisce by reading letters written years before. She prayed with us on these occasions in a less formal manner than we did during our morning services. These get-togethers did me a world of good. Every day now, I regret that I did not find time to arrange similar moments with my own children. I could have evoked both the memory of our deceased loved ones and a beautiful family tradition.

Louise remained with Papa from mother's death until 1917. In 1918, she came again to share Papa's life – and therefore ours – in Judlin Square and then on Rue Jacob in Paris, where we lived after our return from Belgium. I was studying to become a pastor. Her daughter Yvonne wanted to become a missionary. Louise was very pious and very taken by the Young Women's Christian Association where she worked. During my military service, I wrote to her often. Our affection for one another manifested itself more easily in writing. Louise suffered from horrible migraines. They were never able to determine what caused them. She, who was so controlled in her actions, was forced to flee the daylight and close herself up for hours, sometimes even days on end, in her bedroom. She died of heart disease when I was in Morocco, the result of a poorly treated childhood case of scarlet fever. Her son Étienne, my playmate and friend, died exactly like his mother, of the very same cause but at a much younger age.

Albert was the third of the first line of Trocmés. He was extremely tall and had a slight limp because of a fall from his bicycle. His slow movements, his voice, and his pastoral tone all impressed me greatly during my childhood. Under this rather forbidding appearance, Albert hid a warm, lively, and restless heart. With only a few brief and ironic remarks, he showed that he completely understood everything. His religious faith was profound and enlightened. I remember solemn and sad services that he led in Saint-Gobain during vacations that were so different from Papa's optimistic services. Often anguish gained the upper hand over Albert's faith. He eventually had to renounce his parish ministry. His capacity for sympathy was such that the sorrows of others hopelessly overwhelmed him. Twice, he spent time in mental hospitals. His wife Juliette, dignified, calm, and even-tempered, supported him with perfect discretion.

Francis was the most original of my brothers. As far back as I can recall, he was already bald and had small, piercing eyes behind pince-nez glasses, a thin moustache, and an often tense mouth. His ears stuck out. Yet he was handsome and distinguished – another one of the inscrutable Trocmés with whom you never discussed anything. He simply dropped ironic remarks that were often so accurate that they left you speechless, judged, and furious. Nevertheless, Francis was astute, noble, and had a beautiful soul. As he grew older, he showed his family what his patients already knew well: his profound attachment to those he loved, his faithfulness, and his sensitivity. He could have become a great doctor. He had the vision, the ability to diagnose, and an unquestioned sense of authority. But Francis always suffered from timidity and a pride that wouldn't allow him to betray himself to succeed. He could very well have become an intern in a Paris hospital, but certain of having failed the written exam, he never showed up for the oral. In fact, he had passed the written exam. Nonetheless, he never tried again. Francis had an adolescent crush on a sister of my mother, Aunt Cölli, an intelligent, energetic, and good woman. Aunt Pauline and Papa opposed the marriage on the grounds that there were already enough Germans in the family. As often happens after a disappointment, Francis soon fell in love again, this time with a ravishing Russian Jew, Rose Grossmann. She was so different in every way from those in our milieu that I still remember her arrival in Saint-Gobain, her hair and dark eyes, her exclamations, and her accent as a pleasant but somewhat unsettling intrusion. Rose could never have children, and that clouded Francis's happiness.

From Calais, Francis and Rose moved to Paris. After the house on Boulevard Gambetta, their apartment at 15 Rue Lagrange became the longest maintained address of the Trocmé family and the rendezvous site for the nephews and nieces. Francis and Rose never dared move to a better residence. The provisionary became definitive. In the apartment, patients filled up the living room, which served as a waiting room. On the other side of a glass door in a living room/kitchen, we chatted in low voices and had tea. Francis's bald head and glasses sometimes appeared above the small curtains on the hallway door. He glanced to see who was there. The hospitality of Francis and Rose at the time when I was finishing my theological studies was indispensable yet troubling, generous yet sparing. Was Rose a miser? Or was she generous? She gave, but with commentary. She complained about what she gave, as they say in Le Chambon-sur-Lignon. She could not at all understand my idealism, my pacifism, or my somewhat unorthodox religious faith. She had lived in sophisticated Jewish and Russian circles and was unable to grasp the mysticism that provided the stability of my radical opinions. Francis tended to be ironic. I nonetheless felt that they understood me. Why? I don't know. Elsewhere in the family, I hit stray balls that were never returned. In Francis's household, there was at least a religious, political, and moral dialogue, and I needed that.

Ever since settling in Versailles, we have seen them often. Rose's illness, the onset of which we witnessed in Saint-Gobain, and Francis's surgery have brought us closer together. A sick doctor needs affection. The little brother that I was is now an adult who enjoys giving and receiving affection. But above all, the two foreigners, Rose and Magda, who didn't come out of a super-Protestant milieu, understand, love, and support one another. When they get together, they don't feel the stigma of being different from others. Rather, they are more spontaneous and freer than the others. Rose tries desperately to be more French than the French while Magda remains herself. Their friendship is rich and full of fun.

The fifth child of Paul Trocmé and Marie Walbaum was Madeleine, who has been dead for a long time. Papa always mourned her, as he did his two other children who died very young: Pierre and Yvonne, who died at the age of four. Above all, I remember Madeleine because she taught me to read. She was more patient than Mère, who once gave me a slap that raised me off my seat and made me fall over! I probably deserved it. When I didn't know a letter, my mouth watered, and if I opened my mouth, the spit got all over my book!

I still remember Madeleine at home. She was tall, intelligent, and curious about theological and philosophical problems. She married an older man, Julien Hutter, a maritime engineer and the first intellectual whose well-stated, numerous theories I admired. Madeleine lived for a time in Paris at 10 Rue Poussin on the fourth or fifth floor of a new building with an elevator. I was invited to her home in 1912, I think, and saw Paris for the first time: the metro, Eiffel Tower, Louvre, and Trocadéro. Naturally, I especially remember the fifth-floor balcony where, with Pierre, we spit into the street. It was two years later, just after giving birth to Roger, that Madeleine arrived one day at our home from Paris. I still see her standing in the hallway of our house on Boulevard Gambetta. "Papa," she said, "I have diabetes." I don't know if she said it in front of me, but I know that I was astonished that this word, *le diabète*, was masculine but had a feminine ending. Diabetes was then an incurable disease; they hadn't yet discovered insulin. The only remedy at that time was a strict diet, which did not prevent the sick person from wasting away, falling into a diabetic coma, and then dying. Madeleine died in 1915 during the German occupation.

Along with my full brother Pierre, Eugène is the quietest of my brothers. Papa said that I resemble him physically. Robust and calm, with angular features, Eugène is exceedingly modest. He finished the École Polytechnique and the École des Mines without difficulty. I remember when he was a student at the École des Mines. I also remember a visit he made to Saint-Gobain during his military service in the artillery at La Cère. He was my godfather. He had written me a card that I kept with pride for many years in which he told me that he had two horses: Pancarte and Ligature, names that meant "Label" and "String." He entered the garden in Saint-Gobain and had "Label" and "String" trot along the upper paths of the garden. Eugène married Madeleine de Saint-Affrique, the daughter of a former pastor from Saint-Gobain, a tall, charming, and smiling person. Madeleine was always welcoming. Eugène rarely spoke. He liked maps, photography, and writing poetry. They have the best marriage I've ever known. Eugène was decorated for his military service in 1914. In 1940, he lost his military unit in a debacle and was almost shot as a spy by an overanxious soldier.

There remain only two brothers to describe: the one closest to my heart and the one closest to my flesh. The one who lives in my heart is Robert. Papa decreed that he would work in industry. He obeyed but remained a poet. Distinguished, affectionate, less conventional than the other Trocmés, he lived for a long time in our home on Boulevard Gambetta. The younger children were drawn to him.

There was a bedroom above the kitchen that Robert transformed to his liking. He installed a closet at his own expense, and a washroom with running water while we were still using pitchers and basins. He had brought back lots of books from Germany and England and spoke and read German and English fluently. He used to call my brother Pierre and my cousin Yvonne into his room and read *Alice in Wonderland* to them aloud in English. Étienne and I, the youngest, weren't invited because we didn't know English. But beautiful fragments were transmitted to us by Yvonne, who was very maternal to us.

Robert had a romantic adventure. A beautiful young woman came to spend time in our home on Boulevard Gambetta. She was Hildegarde Schwerdtmann, the daughter of my uncle Johannes, whom we called "the Bishop of Hanover." Robert had spent time in my uncle's home during his studies in Germany and had slowly fallen in love with Hildegarde. She loved him too. Papa and Aunt Pauline, applying the dogma that "there are already too many Germans in the family," opposed the marriage. Papa thought Robert was too "scattered" and worldly. Furthermore, Robert had progressive ideas, and there were rather heated discussions between him and Papa that I never quite understood. There was tension in the air. World War I came along and Robert, in spite of his love for Germany, left to fight for France as if with a death wish. He was decorated and came home transfigured by the authentic patriotism of the trenches. Hildegarde took care of wounded German soldiers and died of tuberculosis and grief.

Robert suffered a terrible chest wound in the Battle of the Somme. He was left for dead by the Germans who had captured him. He found himself all alone in a sheltered spot in the middle of the battlefield. Despite his crushed chest and pierced arm, he crawled toward the French trenches, guiding himself by the light of the rockets. He was spotted by the Germans, recaptured, and hospitalized.

Saint-Quentin was situated inside the German lines about eighteen miles from these events. We saw soldiers along the roads, terrorized, exhausted, bloody prisoners. Comrades of Robert shouted to the civilians: "Tell the Trocmé family that their son is wounded and a prisoner of the Germans." Eight days of anguished searching in German hospitals produced no results. Several weeks later, we learned from a letter that came via Switzerland and Germany that Robert was alive but seriously wounded.

As a child and adolescent, I had always prayed for Robert. He probably never suspected it. This habit was so fixed in my soul that, even after the war, I continued to pray for him. Still today, in moments of deep anguish, a short phrase will come to mind: "My God, save Robert." That phrase sums up my attachment to Robert and my admiration for him, as well as my faith in a God who can save anyone. Today it is for the moral salvation of my loved ones that I pray to God. We retrieved Robert in Brussels in 1916. He was one of the first French officers allowed to enter the liberated city of Saint-Quentin in 1918. There was a reception in his honor at the home of the actress Mrs. Rooman, who appeared dressed in blue, white, and red. An exalted patriotism crystallized in me because of my brother. At the same time a painful, religious pacifism struggled in the depths of my soul. Like night and day, these impulses would never be reconciled. I'll speak more about this later.

When we lived in Paris on Rue Jacob, Robert discovered that neither Pierre nor I knew how to shave, and that at ages seventeen and nineteen, we were dressed like shabby refugees. He also understood that we were musically, literarily, and artistically unsophisticated. To compensate, he did something absolutely extraordinary by Trocmé standards: he established the "Fund for Artistic Growth." "Buy books you want to read," he said to us. "Not textbooks but novels. Go to concerts and the theater. Let me know whenever the cash register is empty, and I'll fill it right back up again."

Can you imagine that? In just a few minutes, Robert revealed ideas of which we were totally ignorant: (1) There are values in life other than strict duty. (2) One can read simply for pleasure. (3) When you are having fun, you are learning on your own. (4) Beauty exists.

Yes, beauty. One day, Robert took me to the Louvre. From time to time, Pierre and I went to the museum in Brussels, and it was there that I came to love the first of my painters – Bruegel. But what drew me to him was the anecdotal quality of his paintings; I still didn't know what beauty was.

Robert insisted that I visit the Italian Primitive Painters Room at the Louvre. The collection was minimal. He explained the pure and simple gesture of Fra Angelico's angel, on its knees in adoration with a flame on its forehead. I immediately loved this angel. I bought a black and white photograph, which remained for a long time above my student desk. Robert explained the beauty of an aesthetic discovery when it comes to life. Therein lies the inimitable ingenuity of the Italian Primitive painters. After them, the Classical Italians would attend art schools and their works always show it. The Primitives, however, drew feelings and gestures from the depths of their souls with total sincerity and freshness.

Robert himself was absolutely sincere when he told me about his relationship with Hildegarde, his desire to die, his flirtation with death, and about the deathly wounds that one gives and that one receives. He will never know how much he did for me. I was a young boy caught between my puritanical education reinforced by my adolescent struggles, on the one hand, and on the other, my thirst for the absolute, my religious enthusiasm, and my somewhat Germanic romanticism. Robert taught me about physical and moral beauty. He prepared the road that would one day lead me to Magda – my own authentic, creative Florentine primitive.

Everyone wanted to marry Robert. He hesitated for a long time and finally chose Germaine Pacquement, whom I found interesting and befriended. I was somewhat dazzled, of course, by her milieu. Her father, a rich fabric broker, sponsored the Vieux Colombier,[1] talked a lot, spoke elegantly, and lived on the Boulevard Malesherbes in an apartment filled with choice paintings. He had been a friend of Fantin-Latour and owned many of his works.

At their marriage ceremony in the Oratoire du Louvre church, I was an awkward and blushing groomsman, giving my arm for the first time to a young lady, Suzon Pacquement. Later, Germaine would have liked me to marry this rather extravagant girl who was in the theater and became the wife of a much older actor. She died early of cancer. Her brothers, Jean and Robert, one handsome, the other ugly, though both refined and worldly, simply stunned me. I would have loved to break free of my dull, satisfied, provincial chrysalis and flutter along with them. But for someone like me who was obsessed with poverty, chastity, and total renunciation, that was sinful. Besides, the door to these opportunities hardly opened. Papa always lived "beneath his means" and made us live a life of poverty on Rue Jacob. When I left for the United States at age twenty-four, I wore an overcoat donated to a secondhand store for the benefit of poor students in theology! I never imagined that I would be able to frequent Germaine's upper-class milieu on an equal footing. I never really had a good time, despite the "Fund for Artistic Growth." Just a few poems

1 This was the famous theater founded by Jacques Copeau in 1913 in the sixth arrondissement in Paris.

by Vildrac, a handful of concerts in a dilapidated hall on the Rive Gauche where it didn't cost much to hear an interesting but miserable string quartet. I simply wasn't up to it. I belonged to another world, the world of needy students, the YMCA, the poor, the world of duty and faith. Robert's wedding went by like a breach in the clouds, opening suddenly onto the scintillating, worldly life of the wealthy section of northwest Paris. My Paris wasn't even the Latin Quarter's Boulevard Saint Michel, which I passed with hurried steps to get to the Sorbonne, forging my way through the crowds of half-students and pseudo-intellectuals. My Paris was the Theological Seminary and the suburbs, the workers and rank-and-file clerks. I felt right at home with them. I had something to tell them, and they had something to teach me.

Germaine wasn't at all worldly; she wasn't committed to that brilliant way of life. She was religious and serious, and gladly moved into 134 Boulevard Gambetta. Whenever I stayed in Saint-Quentin, I loved to visit and chat with her and Robert. The inside of their home was decorated in fashionably modern style. They had woodwork painted in vivid colors, handsome furniture, and some watercolors. Robert and Germaine listened to my somewhat radical points of view. Germaine was very patriotic, and Robert ever remained the Reserve Officer, but they let me speak my mind. They responded objectively; they understood and were warm toward me.

Now, I finally come to Pierre, my 100 percent brother, whom I resemble physically to such an annoying degree that he has occasionally been congratulated for my sermons, while others mistake me for him.

I lived for twenty-one years in the same room as Pierre without ever getting to know him. He was always the same: studious, precise, quiet, pedantic, issuing brief judgments without conviction, often correct but ironic and humorless. Side by side, on foot, we explored the streets of Saint-Quentin and Brussels and exchanged thousands of small pleasantries about things and people. But there was never any closeness between us. Never could I catch the slightest glimpse of struggle, languor, doubt, or desire in him. In our Saint-Quentin home classroom, he was the leader, the best student among us. He was always the top student in the lycée. One day, he needed a wheelbarrow to bring home all the books he received as prizes for the best grades! At fifteen, like a true scientist, he made use of the microscope we had both received as a present. In the bedroom that he, Étienne, and I shared on Rue Jacob in 1920, he memorized his anatomy book without allowing himself to be distracted by anything. He became a hospital intern and was promised a brilliant professorial future by his superiors. He married Aline de Saint-Affrique, Madeleine's sister. This marriage was easily arranged because Aline came often to our home on Rue Jacob and wanted to marry him.

Aline lived with Pierre on Rue Pestalozzi in Paris. During an entire winter, I was frequently their guest and became the godfather of their oldest son, Étienne. Pierre worked hard, and they lived very modestly. With scientific confidence and a preordained certainty of success, they then moved to La Rochelle, where Pierre is still a consulting doctor, specializing in the heart and lungs. He established and expanded a private clinic, is recognized by the medical community as an authority, and travels and lectures widely. Because he has had a weak heart since his youth, once a year he vacations alone either in Spain or Sicily. He was a member of the council of elders of the church in La Rochelle but resigned for lack of time. Conservative and patriotic, he played an important role in the Resistance, was arrested, and released. He did not want to see our German family between the two wars and dealt harshly with them more than once in his letters. However, today his youngest daughter exchanges homestays with the children of our cousin, Irmela. Pierre waited until after the war to reestablish good family relations, whereas I always tried to balance my pacifist views and my family attachments.

The house at 52 Rue Chaudrier in La Rochelle, under the direction of Aline and Pierre, resembled life as it had been on Saint-Quentin's Boulevard Gambetta. The same study room, the same relations between brothers and sisters and even with governesses when they had them. Aline was a remarkable educator who raised her brood perfectly. Her letters were "official announcements," always somewhat conventional, praising the success of her children. She had six good children, and I was always a wee bit jealous because of their "consistent" successes.

Étienne, my godchild, was as intellectually impeccable as his father, with an unfailing memory. He was more eloquent than his father but basically just as mysterious. After brilliantly completing his studies at the École des Chartes, he suddenly decided to go into the ministry. Did my example influence him? I would be most proud if it did. In any event, he spent a year living in the home of my friend Pettengill in Los Angeles and met a young English woman named Ann, whom he married. They live today in Strasbourg. Everyone steered him toward becoming a theology professor; his slightly inaccessible nature would have created difficulties for him in parish ministry. At first, he was a historian of the city of La Rochelle, but after a few years he became a New Testament scholar and editor of *La Revue du Christianisme Social.* Yet he isn't really a man of the Left and wouldn't want to be confused with me. I suspect him of being conservative like his father – an intelligent conservative, who understands and analyzes everything without needing to express an opinion, and for whom established institutions are above reproach, so there is no need to defend them. I (almost) envy these fortunate people who, like Étienne and Pierre, never doubt conventional values.

BEFORE RETURNING TO MY OWN story, I have to talk about Papa's brothers and sisters: my aunts, Alice and Pauline, and Uncle Alphonse. Aunt Alice lived for a long time in a modest house in Saint-Quentin on Rue Richard Lenoir. She never got married and, in her later years, lived with Aunt Pauline. I only remember her vaguely as someone joyful and calm. She died tragically from cancer in her neck. Aunt Pauline was the "queen mother" of the family. Younger than her brothers and sisters, she nonetheless dominated them. Papa talked to her as an equal; in fact, she was the only person who made him nervous. Aunt Pauline had married Gustave Viala, an engineer from the École des Mines with a strong Southern accent. He became director of the mining firm Compagnie de Liévin and was very wealthy. They had no children. Above all, Aunt Pauline was a Great Lady. Was she intelligent? Yes, undoubtedly, because she dominated people and things with a penetrating lucidity and even stood up to Papa. No, because her horizons were desperately narrow and bourgeois. She had her friends, her judgments, her aphorisms, and her manner of looking at you through a pair of glasses mounted on a handle. She was very much like a Marquise from the seventeenth century – not the eighteenth century, not Pompadour – very Madame de Maintenon.

Aunt Pauline's nephews, on the Paul and Alphonse side of the Trocmé family, were assiduous in their attendance at her Sunday get-togethers – extraordinarily assiduous. Meeting place: Rue Michel-Ange, Sundays from three o'clock to six o'clock.

"Bonjour, Jean; bonjour, Madeleine, how are your children doing?"

"They're doing well, thank you. And you, Aunt Pauline, how are you feeling?"

"Not too bad, thank you."

There was tea, little cakes, and chocolate around New Year's Day. Sometimes the conversation would rise above generalities. People would complain about the tough times and then others started to leave. No one said where they were going. Those who went to the theater or to concerts said nothing. Civilities were over; duty accomplished.

Duty? Certainly. I am positive that none of these nieces or nephews were looking for an inheritance. We knew well in advance that absolute justice would reign in the Trocmé family. Aunt Pauline had endowed a few nieces whom she liked, but that was it. An effusion of affection? Not that either. When Aunt Pauline died, no one, in truth, experienced any deep grief, except perhaps Jean Trocmé, the son of Uncle Alphonse, who was in some ways her adoptive son. What was it then? Convention? No. Faithfulness, that's the word. Aunt Pauline was the family, and the family was everything. Everything for Papa. He, who was so austere in his needs, would immediately spend money if it was a matter of bringing the family together. God and the family were paramount. An astonishing remnant of the tribal instinct well into the twentieth century. The great transformation that we are now experiencing is not the mechanization of life or automobiles. It's the appearance of a new form of life: pleasure and work with your companions of choice, without your parents, without your aunts and cousins. That's the revolution.

In the midst of this revolution, Papa, Aunt Pauline, Jean, Pierre, and the other Trocmés refused to enter this new world. The family was still the law. Faithfulness to the family was the alpha and omega of their religion. It was this philosophy that made families great, nations too perhaps. Whatever it might cost me to say this, for me, who received everything from his family, this outlook is no longer sufficient to rebuild the world or even the church. In today's world, there are requirements other than duties to the state, one's job, one's country, or one's family. This is what I discovered at the age of twenty from the German invasion, the war, and my comrades at the School of Theology, who came back from the frontlines boiling over with anger. Will my children know how to hold on to this broader vision? I want them to know, *first*, that family virtues are the basis of all well-balanced lives. But then to discover and keep the expanded vision of their parents.

Uncle Alphonse was the hedonist of the Trocmé family. An artist, that's what he was. He drew very well without having gone to school, but my grandparents stood in the way of his vocation. How could one be a painter or a sculptor? It wasn't serious. Alphonse didn't have the strength to get beyond their roadblock. Who in his place would have had the strength? He became a *raté*, a failure. But who among us would have suspected that he was a failure? The secret was so well guarded by the adults that I only learned it much later, from Papa himself, when I too was an adult. Alphonse was considered odd. For the young ladies of the Reboul boarding house, he drew caricatures of their professors. He was Papa's business partner and almost drove him to bankruptcy. He was given the capital to create a shipping-case factory on the Place de Remicourt, and devoured the funds and benefits. There was only one solution: marry him off. They found a Christian Alsatian woman for him: Marie Becker, the delightful daughter of a notary from Strasbourg. She had money and was very thrifty. They lived their entire lives together solely on their annuities.

I knew them when they lived in a modest home on Rue Bénézet in Saint-Quentin. He made a great impression on me. I found him good looking, always dressed in light-colored suits, very much like Edward VII, with his handsome beard and his tobacco-stained moustache. He had a carnation in his buttonhole and joined in with our play, which was something Papa never did. He would then disappear to the back of the narrow garden into a greenhouse arranged as a studio, where I sometimes followed him. The smell of clay wrapped in wet rags permeated the greenhouse. There were busts and medallions just about everywhere. Alphonse made bas-relief medallion portraits for all the members of the Trocmé and Saint-Affrique families. Some of them are still around, like the one of my mother that looks very much like her.

We made fun of him in the family. We told the story of the medallion of Marthe de Saint-Affrique as a child dressed in a little smock that the Saint-Affriques had accepted with affectionate gratitude. They placed it on a very unstable pedestal in the middle of a hallway until it fell and broke. We also told the story of Uncle Alphonse's copy of the Mona Lisa, a medallion whose eyes had the virtue of following you everywhere. Uncle Alphonse presented it to the Salon, the official art association in Paris, for its yearly exhibit. They, of course, refused it. There was something pathetic about how the family that had brought this artist into the world scorned him. Even if Alphonse didn't have the ability to be a great sculptor, why make fun of him? Because he didn't come out of the family mold. Who knows? He might have become an artist if they had sent him to the Quentin-de-La-Tour School in Saint-Quentin that many artists attended. Some of them were later awarded the Prix de Rome. Many of the Trocmés had a gift for drawing: Papa, Maurice, Robert, Pierre, me, Étienne, and above all Alphonse's granddaughter, who was awarded the Prix de Rome. But in the hyper-ironic atmosphere of Boulevard Gambetta, talents were not made to flourish. Once, when I briefly sensed the temptation to draw and even successfully completed a few portraits, I refused to show them to anyone because I had already learned that it was shameful not to be like everyone else, which means not to be like all the Trocmés. They were first in class, serious, chaste, modest, and cultivated the supreme virtue: doing one's duty. To draw was not one's duty.

Aunt Marie set up wonderful Christmas trees and gave modest gifts with kindness, with a slightly quivering voice even before she was old. She had three sons, one of whom, Henri, would establish himself at the École des Roches and marry Ève Rist. Henri was austere in his behavior and had far-reaching literary and moral ideas.[2]

2 Henri Trocmé was the assistant director of the École des Roches in Verneuil-sur-Avre in Normandy. He was notably the father of Daniel Trocmé, whom we will meet later in Le Chambon-sur-Lignon.

3

First World War

NOTHING REMAINS STATIC. Things began to happen on Boulevard Gambetta and in Saint-Gobain with Papa, the governesses, Pierre, Yvonne and Étienne, and my older brothers and sisters who came and went, got married and had children. There were so many that Papa had to add to the house. It had become too small to host his children's families.

In 1911, three months after Mère's death, a new reality entered my life: the lycée. I already mentioned that Papa didn't send us to school before the age of ten. I learned to read with Madeleine and my mother, and then I took piano lessons with Miss Devred at the age of seven. After about six months, they decided that I had no musical talent. Like Étienne and Yvonne, I learned grammar with a Miss Guille, whose sharp voice, according to Yvonne, resembled that of "the butcher in Die." Then there was Mr. Eugène Poëtte (a witness at my marriage), the director of our elementary school, whom I liked a lot. He taught us in our study hall at home, but I also went to the elementary school for lessons, which were held in a curious, hexagonal hallway that smelled of gas. At the age of ten, I started going to the lycée.

How strange that I am obliged to explain to my American grandchildren what a lycée is. They will only come to know entirely different school systems that strike me as completely unstable institutions. The lycée is stable; it is eternal. All the lycées are the same. The one in Saint-Quentin hasn't changed since 1855, when it was called the Collège des Bons Enfans (without the "t") and Papa went there! In a city in France, the lycée is like the train station, the town hall, the hospital, the cemetery, the cathedral, the museum, the army barracks, the main square – there's only one. We speak about it in the singular, as we do about the prison.

It sat on a rectangular site, with a statue of Henri Martin[1] and a partially open, covered entrance. Inside were a guard post, the superintendent's quarters, a courtyard surrounded by arcades, a chapel (transformed into a gymnasium because we are in a secular republic), and impeccably ordered classrooms: 6th, 5th, 4th, 3rd, 2nd, 1st (rhetoric), philosophy. On the other side of the courtyard: English, German, the restrooms. On the second floor: physics, chemistry, natural history. Léon, the laboratory assistant, was also the drum major. At 8 a.m. the drums rolled, students stopped yelling, and the boarding students in dirty smocks emerged from a mysterious hallway like caterpillars.

In the sixth level I had Mr. Jay, who was young and kind, and for German, Mr. China (Medrzeski), a Polish German with a good accent whom my brothers already had for a teacher. But the following year I had Mr. Dumont, so hideous that he inspired fear. He squinted and removed the dirt from his pen with such a frightening grimace that one day I peed in my pants because I didn't dare ask him to leave the room. A real puddle, a pond! I can still feel my frozen underwear sticking to my rear when I returned home in humiliation. Fortunately, no one in the class noticed since I was seated so far up in the bench tiers, which were nothing but a narrow band of wood that caused uncontrollable itching on my poor, huge backside.

I remember classes in winter when the stove in the classroom didn't work very well and our hands were numb. I remember, above all, classes in June, in the early afternoons, when the professor's voice droned on in my head like a meaningless bell ringing. A blue fly crashed into the window, and when a tree branch, above the frosted glass panes, dared to sweep across the colorless sky, we only saw it in sections because of the diagonal, poorly furled blinds.

I loathed Dumont. He frightened me no end. Never in my imagination have I killed a man so often. It was always with a bomb that came in through the window or the door, rolled along, stopped snugly against the podium, and exploded, leaving nothing of Mr. Dumont and his beard and twitches but powder and smoke. "Trocmé" is a piercing name, which awakened and spread panic in me when I was called upon to explicate a paragraph of *De viris illustribus urbis Romae*. I was not paying attention because I was plotting the annihilation of the professor.

1 Henri Martin (1810–1883) was a historian born in Saint-Quentin whose writings on the history of France brought him great renown. He supported progressive causes and became a mayor and a senator.

My beginnings at the lycée were difficult. I didn't like Latin or math; I only liked history, geography, natural history, and German. But our history and natural history professors were terrible. The first one dictated until he ran out of breath. He's the one responsible for my poor handwriting. I needed hours at home to decipher the pages of unreadable scribblings from class. My German governess completely lost it trying to recreate the history of France. Louise gave it a try, but her regular scolding, tears, and punishments didn't work very well on me either.

Mr. Dubois was the worst of all. He was fat and sluggish and arrived in class with a denture that he put into a jar in the adjoining laboratory. He then came back into the classroom thick-lipped, slobbering, and ready to strike. I had the good fortune not to be his whipping boy. I loved natural history and did good drawings in my notebook, which satisfied the insatiable Mr. Dubois as far as I was concerned.

But Costeux! He was obviously stupid. Lanky, with a hanging jaw, he was invariably questioned by Dubois:

"Costeux, talk to me about echinoderms."

"Huh?"

"Don't you know your lesson?"

"Somewhat."

"Somewhat or not at all?"

"I don't know, sir."

"Ah, you don't know! You don't know if you know! What kind of an answer is that?"

Having created the situation, Dubois left Costeux standing, turned toward the class and began slobbering without his teeth: "Gentlemen, human stupidity is unfathomable. But among all the idiots, all the cretins, all the blockheads that I have seen parade through this classroom, I have never seen anyone as stupid as Costeux."

As Costeux, on the verge of tears, lowered his head and blushed, Dubois continued: "Stand up straight, Costeux, when I talk to you. Yes, that's it. That's how you stand when you talk to a professor. You are adding impoliteness to stupidity. You will do four hours of retention on Thursday. That's what you get for being an idiot!"

The whole class trembled. Any one of us might have become the object of Dubois's persistent hatred. In our natural history class, we worked not from love but from terror.

How did Dubois get like that? It's easy to explain. Students didn't take natural history, physical education, or drawing seriously. If these professors of secondary subjects can't win over the students with their charm or just let things go, they often become brutal, like Dubois.

Another source of my terror was Sirugue, the vice principal. One day, after receiving my first retractable ink pen, I discovered that I could use its cap as a whistle. Often alone during recess, I whistled in the courtyard behind one of the pillars of the arcades. That day, the vice principal passed by and took this blast of the whistle as a personal attack. He pounced on me, scolded me terribly, and confiscated my pen. But I didn't have to go to detention. In fact, I never in my life had to go to detention. I was an obedient student, too big for my age, with my pudgy legs squeezed into the short trousers of the well-worn "sailor suit" inherited from my German cousins. I considered this outfit ridiculous, especially among my classmates, one of whom only came up to my shoulder. They already sported long pants and men's jackets.

Among my classmates, Leroy was my great enemy. He was the nephew of a famous general and the leader of the games in the schoolyard. He was brutal, not very bright, and always picked on the weaker boys. Among the weak was Lefèvre. What had happened to him? Polio maybe? I don't know. In any event, his legs were malformed, his calves leaned inward and rubbed against each other when he walked, and only his toes touched the ground. Although I was tall and strong, I hated the violent games played by my schoolmates. I hung around with Lefèvre, who had the typical sarcastic mindset of the weak. Anyway, we took the same route home after school.

Lefèvre was Leroy's punching bag. Sturdy and fast, Leroy would push him into the gutter, knock the books out of his hands, and steal his scarf. I would try to defend Lefèvre, who thrashed his arms about uselessly in the air, and fell outlandishly amid the sniggering of Leroy's pack. Then I too felt Leroy's fists and came home several times with a bloody nose.

I called on Pierre to help me. He was two classes ahead of me and tall. He walked under the arcades with his friends, who were all too old to play games. Pierre ignored the issue, but Papa ordered him to defend me if I were attacked.

Pierre had a system: he pumped his forearms and fists like a powerful lawnmower, thus terrorizing those who confronted him. But Leroy gave him a vicious headbutt in the stomach, and Pierre turned away disgusted, saying that he refused to get involved in these "childish quarrels."

Things reached their peak when Leroy founded the "hard shits," whom he chose from the toughest guys around, those who supported his dictatorship. He then furnished his gang, who hated coats, with thick woolen scarves about two meters long that they wrapped around their necks. The two ends hung down their backs. Leroy invented a kind of heavy club by twisting the scarf repeatedly. He wielded it like a nightstick. The "hard shits" waited until the end of the school day and, on the Place Henri Martin, used these clubs to beat their victims, whom they referred to as the "soft shits."

The "hard shits" reigned from the Rue de Fervacques, past the Palais de Justice, right up to the doors of the Institut Saint-Jean, our rival Catholic lycée. One day, using barbed wire, they even locked the sleeping oyster merchant in her market stall.

We had to defend ourselves, so I organized and became the leader of the "soft shits." Rolling up our scarves, we, the "soft shits," burst forth in tight ranks and took the offensive. There were fights and bloody noses. Then the vice principal forbade all these practices. Leroy's dictatorship ended, but he continued to hate me. Through him, I came to detest all things military.

IT WAS IN THE FOURTH LEVEL, at age fifteen, that I began to emerge from my childhood apathy. I had been a mediocre student up to that point. Now I became a good student in French, history, geography, and German, though I was still average in Latin and weak in mathematics.

It was my teacher Dodancourt who got me going. He had a certain literary sense and knew how to communicate it to his students and gave us interesting homework, requiring us to describe nature and people. Nonetheless, Mr. Dodancourt was also responsible for my inhibitions during the following years. One day, he gave us as a writing assignment: "A Winter Day." I knew those winter days well because of the daily walks that I described earlier. For the first time in my life, I gave myself over to inspiration. I spoke about the gray sky, the mud, the ashen-colored canal, the squawking of the crows. I remember relighting my lamp at night, after lying down, to add to my draft on the night table a more personal impression, a more sincere one from the banks of the canal. For the first time in my life, I was alive. I was writing; I was expressing my true self. I was certain that I was going to get a good grade.

The day arrived when Dodancourt returned our papers. I hung on his every word. He began by returning the best ones first. I wasn't called. My paper was among the last returned. He read passages from it, ridiculing them: "Cliché," "Where did you find that?" "You didn't write this." "Who helped you?" I was brimming with shame and anger. Never again, for as long as I was in the lycée, did I let my soul overflow onto the page. I did as the others did: "What does the prof want us to say?"

Home and school now worked in tandem to reduce me to their level. A vast level, to be sure: the Classics and lots of them. The Romantics, not so much. I had to learn school jargon, had to discuss "passions in the plays of Racine" or "Boileau's aesthetics." My soul almost died from it. At the heart of my being, my enthusiastic soul wanted to love and be loved, wanted to love the sky and the grass, the forests, and people, and to be loved by a mother who would perhaps understand me. The real me was inside the fat, sluggish boy who was enormously bored in class, who never had a teacher to reveal to him what he was looking for: the true poetry of life. In class, I continued to dissect, learn by rote, recite, analyze, translate, prepare, take daily tests, take notes, and discipline myself.

I nonetheless liked Dodancourt. Thirty years later, my son Jean-Pierre had the same experience. He had to write an essay on "Springtime" for Miss Wavre at the École Nouvelle Cévenole. In my view, it was a masterpiece, but it received a bad grade. "Clichéd" was the professor's opinion. We were so indignant, Magda and I, that we showed the assignment to one of our friends, the General Inspector of Secondary Education, without telling him who wrote it or what grade it received. He really took to this text, claiming that he was able to see true literary talent in it despite inevitable adolescent naiveté. He thought the author was about sixteen years of age, but our son was only twelve at the time. Jean-Pierre was knocked around by his teachers in the school that I had founded in hopes that my children wouldn't have the disastrous experiences I had during my youth. When he died, one of his professors, whose name I'll withhold, said to us as a kind of funeral oration: "Yes, he was certainly intelligent, but not at all scholarly."

Jean-Pierre left notebooks of childish poems that he kept to himself. He, at least, dared to write. His professor is still alive, dried up and washed out. One should appoint poets, not accountants, as professors of literature.

FROM THE FOURTH LEVEL onward, my life changed completely: the 1914–1915 school year began under the German occupation. The school buildings had been requisitioned by the Germans. Before the evacuation of the city in the spring of 1917, we had to relocate two or three times, first into scattered locales in the city, then into an abandoned factory, halfway between the Grand-Place and the train station. Classes were greatly reduced in size and often interrupted. A certain intimacy developed between professors and students, who all shared the same anxieties. I was growing up, and little by little I became aware of a world beyond the narrow periphery of my schoolboy preoccupations.

During all these years, I was under the iron rule of Mr. Marchand, an old acquaintance of our family whom we nicknamed "Macaque." As far back as the time of Miss Kalcher, Marchand's daughter came to our house on Boulevard Gambetta to play music. Marchand crossed the Champs-Elysées with a strange, vacillating step, as if he were going to fall on his face but somehow recovered his balance at the last moment. He moved his arms in a strange manner. The little conversations he carried on with himself *mezzavoce* in front of the students were interspersed with exclamations such as "Ooooh! What! Hum!" Whether you were reciting a lesson or stumbling through a translation, Marchand's facial expressions followed one after another without any necessary correlation to your mistakes or strong points. Sometimes he interrupted us, and his remarks were pertinent, often witty. Everyone loved and respected him. He was a good prof.

Marchand had progressive ideas. For one thing, he was antimilitary. Before the war, it wasn't rare to see, written on the blackboard and addressed to him, some patriotic phrase, like "Long live the Army" or "Death to Traitors." He treated these incidents with scorn. During the occupation, he became more cautious. Too dissident a comment would have labeled him a "*Boche*" or "*Kraut*" and had him blacklisted. Furthermore, while the Germans were there, everyone was patriotic. I sometimes took private tutoring lessons from Marchand, who explained things well. I met with him again in Belgium for a while. You might suppose he had an influence on my ideological development, but I don't think so. He learned how to become cautious when he had to be.

I gradually became a good student, not a brilliant one. I had a sketchy memory and still do today. But facts, conversations, and things in general were well ordered in my mind. I now thought more actively and listened closely to conversations in the Petit Salon. I worked hard. When I daydreamed, I liked nothing better than arranging my desires, ambitions, inner dialogues, and hopes, which emerged softly like bubbles just above the surface of my adolescent meditations.

IN JULY 1914, the war broke out. We were in Saint-Gobain. I was thirteen years old and did lots of cycling (always in a group; we weren't allowed to go out alone). We visited extraordinary historical landmarks, such as the cathedral of Laon. There were no more visits from German relatives. We needed passports to get from place to place and a special permit for our car. We touted in advance our victory in eastern France and the reconquest of Alsace, but the Germans came through Belgium, that is, from the north. Pierre got back just in time from camp on the Île d'Oléron, where he was spending the summer. Because of a train breakdown, Papa drove the Marchand family to Vailly. On the way, we crossed the Chemin des Dames, a road in the middle of fields. We didn't know then that tens of thousands of men would give their blood for us to maintain possession of it.

My sister Madeleine was worried. She wanted to join her husband in Paris. The newspapers were optimistic, and Papa was always reassuring. One day, he left in his car to go to Saint-Quentin to get money out of the bank. Madeleine panicked, and with good reason. Papa didn't return that evening. He didn't get home until the next day. He arrived, very upset, with a car mechanic and a second car. A great battle had taken place around Charleroi in Belgium, and it didn't turn out to our advantage. The "Prussians" were advancing. (Papa, who had fought in the 1870 war, still called the German soldiers "Prussians.") A sense of alarm pervaded the house. The people in Saint-Gobain claimed that machine guns had been set up in the forests. I went to the garden across from our house and climbed my favorite apple tree. I attached a tri-colored French flag to the highest branch. By this striking action, I wanted to show that I was courageous and ready to defend my country. Papa saw the flag from the terrace, called me, and bawled me out: "If the Prussians saw that, they would shoot all of us. Go take down your flag." Frightening stories circulated about German atrocities in Belgium. The sacking of Dinant was unfortunately true, but the rumor about children with their hands chopped off that haunted all of us proved false. "Barbarians, barbarians, that's what they are," people repeated with fright, as an enormous exodus of the panicked population choked the highways. We were packed into two cars, child-bundles among the bundles of covers and down quilts returning to Saint-Quentin. I left Saint-Gobain without looking back, unaware that I would next see it in ruins. I was turned toward tomorrow, toward what was going to happen, toward adventure. Adolescents are so hungry for adventure that they are hopeful as they pass through events their parents consider tragic.

After the flag incident, I thought about another grandiose scheme. Since it was dangerous to advertise one's patriotism because the Germans were barbarians about to burn Saint-Quentin and massacre the population, we had to try something along the lines of the woman in Jericho in the Bible (Joshua 2), who had attached a scarlet cord to her window. I would go before the Germans with a white handkerchief and tell them: "Stop, my mother was German." They would spare us. This is what I was thinking about as the car rolled straight ahead on the highway. After Vendeuil, we passed British canons and trucks painted red, shiny, brand new, retreating toward the south. The men were laughing and waving branches. "What a phony war," we thought. I hadn't yet learned that all wars were phony and that some men laughed while others a few miles away died drenched in their own blood.

We arrived in Saint-Quentin at dusk. The city was astonishingly calm. Optimism reigned. The proper authorities were in charge. There were no soldiers. Trains were operating. In the distance you could hear dull rumblings intermittently. Some people claimed it was cannon fire, but no one really believed them. "They are being pushed back; they're retreating," everyone repeated. A defeat of the French was unthinkable. This time we were ready! Not like in 1870. Now we had the Russians and the English on our side – the English, with their red trucks who laughed as they fled.

In fact, Saint-Quentin was like a city returning from vacation – an early return, since it was August 27 and not September 30. On August 28, however, the city was empty, as if in a state of suspense, and we could hear definite cannon fire. Papa hastened to a meeting in the city. A committee of the Musée de La Tour that he was on was gathering at the home of one of the members. Padded trucks came from Paris to transport the famous eighteenth-century pastels. At noon, Papa announced the bad news: a huge battle was taking place near Busigny. Passenger trains going toward Paris were no longer running.

In the afternoon, while Papa was at his meeting, things picked up speed. The mayor, Doctor Muller, fled the city. Being Alsatian, he feared the worst. He was replaced by a courageous deputy, Mr. Gibert. Something happened suddenly around five o'clock. On the other side of the Champs-Elysées, on the Rue de Baudreuil, where something was always happening (unlike our street, which was quiet by comparison), gray-uniformed troops were parading. We could distinctly hear the shrill sound of their fifes. It was the English, or perhaps the Scots with their bagpipes. Before Louise could grab us, we three boys took off to meet the soldiers on the other side of the Champs-Elysées. Halfway there, a young man running the opposite way warned us: "Where are you going? Run away – it's the Prussians!"

For the first time in my life, I panicked. Seeing that other fellow fleeing, without another thought, I scampered toward the house, where Louise crammed us into the basement. The blinds on the ground floor were lowered. Where now was my heroic project with the white handkerchief? On that evening, our basement, which later sheltered us so often during air-raid alerts, brought together a small herd of trembling women and children, while outside the noises of war raged: intermittent shots, then bursts of machine gun fire, and soon thereafter, hatchet blows on the doors along the avenue, when the residents refused to open to the invaders. The next day, we learned that there had been no resistance in Saint-Quentin, but that French soldiers, having escaped from a bloody battle to the north of Saint-Quentin, tried to find refuge among the locals and exchange their uniforms, which would have betrayed them, for civilian clothes. They could then pass for members of the village with the complicity of their provisional hosts. The Germans, fearing isolated guerrillas posted in houses or on street corners, systematically cleaned out the village by demanding that each family open its door. They smashed in the doors with hatchets when residents refused to do so. Louise and Madeleine negotiated in German with the soldiers who showed up at 136 Boulevard Gambetta. I can't remember if they even took the time to search the house.

Nighttime came and the sounds of war died out. As they always did, Louise and Madeleine had carefully hidden from the children the anguish gnawing at them when Papa had not returned from his meeting. Papa finally came home. Safe and sound, a bit wild-looking and dusty, he explained his great adventure. The committee had been holding a serious meeting to discuss the delicate operation of transporting the La Tour pastels to Paris. The trucks that finally arrived to do so were waiting in the courtyard when one of the committee members, hearing a noise, cried out: "The Prussians are here, downstairs."

Papa then rushed down into the street to join his endangered family. He was picked up by a German patrol: "*Zivil! Zivil!*" For hours, he was dragged from street to street with women and children to serve as a living shield between the invaders and any possible French guerrillas. Against his will, he had thus been at the frontlines of several skirmishes but without anything happening to him. Finally liberated, he was seized by another patrol and unable to get home until ten in the evening. His excited account, his outrage at the cowardly methods of the German soldiers, which were contrary to the "laws of war," his joy in being alive amid his loved ones, all these evoked waves of strong emotion in me. I felt danger, hatred, the humiliation inflicted on my father, and a deep desire for vengeance all mixed with the instincts of a thirteen-year-old boy for adventure and combat.

By the next morning, the Germans had moved into our house. Some slept on the third floor. They were everywhere. How would we be able to go out? I remember one beautiful, sunny day when the troops were camped on the Champs-Elysées. On the doors which had been opened for their searches, the soldiers of the city had marked in chalk in Gothic script: *Gute Leute, bitte schonen!* (Good people. Please spare them!). At the corner of Rue Charles-Picard, from atop a balcony, an officer called out his decree in a cordial voice which suddenly transported into France the Germany of my youth.

The following days witnessed the German army rushing south. A regiment of uhlans passed right under our windows.[2] They wore green-gray uniforms – one of the many surprises in this well-prepared war. They literally fell from their exhausted horses with their lances that sported a white and black flag and stretched out on the grass of the promenade without the strength to take another step, even if only to get water or food. To our great astonishment, for the first time we saw automobile convoys. Here, too, the Germans had prepared for "the war of the future." In these hundreds of identical, iron-gray trucks, provisions for the invading troops arrived with unheard of speed, completely surpassing the much slower movements of the French, who were still operating on foot.

2 Uhlans were Lithuanian, and later Polish, light cavalry units primarily armed with a lance.

In the beginning under the occupation, life pretty much returned to order. There were supplies of food, fuel, and clothing. A local journalist wrote a book about these events: *The City That Died: Saint-Quentin 1914–1917.*[3] In fact, this city of 55,000 inhabitants died slowly between September 1914 and February 1917, when it was completely emptied of its population by the German army. These two and a half years were the most important ones of my adolescence. I was thirteen when the war began and sixteen when it ended. It began when I was a child; when it ended, I had become a man.

Madeleine died in 1915. It had become more and more difficult to find the food needed by diabetics. Papa and Louise took care of her as best they could. This drama unfolded in front of the children, who could not grasp its meaning. We knew that Madeleine had been separated from her husband, Julien Hutter, by the front, and that it had been a real hardship for her to see herself fading away without him as her hopes of ever seeing him again waned. The grown-ups understood this; the children only picked up bits and pieces.

Our world was the lycée, held in abandoned factories because the Lycée Henri-Martin had been requisitioned and made into a hospital. Hadn't I already seen wounded French soldiers arriving, lying on the straw of huge farm wagons drawn by four horses? Our world was the world of rapidly decreasing food rations that could never satisfy our adolescent appetites. My personal world was still, for a few months, the world of prolonged childhood: self-centered, playful, jealous of the special meals prepared for Madeleine. Diabetes is a sickness you don't see. Madeleine came down for meals and stayed in the Petit Salon. I did not have a sense of her growing weakness, nor did I share my father's worries, until the day when – one of those images that will never leave me – she was so weak that she had to go up to her room slowly, leaning against Papa on the stairway. A few days later, she was dead, and I suddenly understood the hideousness of my culinary jealousies. I followed her casket just as I had followed my mother's casket four years earlier.

The events that ensued painfully forced me out of my irresponsible childhood.

There was the story of the stolen cookies. I lived at a time when parents got cakes and children didn't. Papa loved Petits Beurres LU cookies. He ate them with his coffee at noon and in the evening with tea. As

3 Marc Ferrand, *La ville mourut. Saint-Quentin 1914-1917* (La vie universitaire, 1923).

everything became rare before the war, the children begged a little and sometimes got a Petit Beurre. But during the war, they had to be satisfied by looking at them from a distance. Nevertheless, I knew where the cookie box was situated in the buffet in the dining room. Before going to bed, I used to take a stroll around the dining room and slip one or two of them into my pocket. As I undressed, I placed my loot under my pillow. As soon as I thought my roommate, Pierre, was asleep, I tasted the fruits of my sin. Oh, the delicious taste of the corners of the rectangular Petit Beurre that slowly melted in my mouth! But one day, I was called before Papa. Jeanne, the cook, was there, pale with outrage, full of vengeance, brandishing a Petit Beurre. "Look, Monsieur, what we found under André's pillow! So now he's a thief!"

I stood there, filled with terror and desperation. Evidently, I had fallen asleep the night before, forgetting that I had a Petit Beurre under my pillow.

Before I could speak, Papa said: "Is it true that you steal cookies?"

Frozen in my tracks, I lied: "No, I didn't do it."

"Then how did the cookie get under your pillow?"

I lied a second time and this time without any plausibility: "Perhaps someone else put it there."

I must explain the situation here. Madeleine's son, Jean, was much younger than I, very intelligent but hard to deal with. Probably for the first time, Papa's inflexible will came up against a will craftier than his own. Whenever Jean misbehaved, he was severely punished. When Jean was punished, he would then punish his grandfather. Once he slashed the precious Vidal de La Blache wall maps in the study with a metal ruler. Another time, he went out into the garden and broke a mercury thermometer Papa treasured.

Papa decided to clamp down on Jean and accused him of doing many misdeeds that he never committed. My despicable lie immediately seemed likely to Papa: "We must believe André, *he never lies*," he claimed. He dashed out of the room. I heard Jean's howls: Papa was spanking him. I should have intervened at that moment and confessed my vile cowardice. But I didn't budge, and the following weeks found me in agony. I now knew that I passed for a truthful boy who "never lied." I knew I wasn't worthy of this trust, and I blushed in shame, the shame of passing for what I was not. I learned that some people – the weak, the innocent, and children, as in the case of Jean – were punished and scorned in place of the guilty ones, who adroitly withdrew in their dignity. I knew – and this was the most painful knowledge – that I didn't have, that I would never have, the courage to admit my cowardice. I was too much of a coward to admit publicly that I was a coward. This discovery of the profundity of my sin made me an unhappy, blushing boy, who thought he always saw in the eyes of others a silent accusation and lowered his own appropriately.

There was also a lie I told to my professor, Mr. Marchand, to excuse myself from a tutoring session in Latin that I had skipped. And I had cheated on a geography test by looking at notes I had written on slips of paper. I came out first in the class, but came away once again with the conviction that I was a usurper, a usurper with a good reputation that I didn't deserve.

One year later, I had a profound religious experience I'll talk about later. Jean was no longer living with us. When I was "convinced of my sinful nature," I went to my father and confessed my horrible sin to him. Papa, who vaguely remembered the incident, passed it off lightly. He pardoned me much too easily. Still today, I regret that he didn't punish me. I should have suffered to reestablish my moral equilibrium.

When I saw Jean after the war in Saint-Gobain, he was sixteen years old. I told him my story. He laughed about it. He didn't recall it at all. He had no bitterness toward Papa for coming down hard on him. On the contrary, it appears, from what his wife Margaretha claims, that he was devoted to Papa and carried that devotion to the grave with him.

THE WAR TURNED ME into a staunch, young patriot. An uncomplicated nationalism that I picked up in school superimposed itself on my dreams of the "white handkerchief" and an alliance with the Germans, whom I secretly admired for their discipline, order, and cleanliness. I ridiculed everything concerning the enemy, who quickly became tyrannical and hated. The arrogance of German officers who forced civilians off the sidewalks when they encountered them and demanded that the gentlemen of the city, such as Papa, salute them in the street, ironically caused them to be hated by the whole population. The requisitions piled up: wine, copper, supplies of cotton (that Papa fought against the best he could; he was vice president of the chamber of commerce), wheat, beets, and sugar. And when the Battle of the Somme took place in 1916, the troops that went up to the front sacked the countryside of everything it contained: cattle, poultry, cereals. Not only the city but the countryside also died, and the entire nation sank into profound despair. Without bread (the daily ration fell to 125 grams of a black, sticky mass), and without firewood, we were in desperate straits. Only the ever-fluctuating hope of liberation upheld our spirits. When the Germans began to smash the weaving looms in our factory with sledgehammers to extract the copper combs, Papa protested so fiercely that he was almost deported several times. The killings of French "patriots" by firing squads increased significantly. They were accused of spying, although they rarely gave themselves over to such dangerous activities. If the Germans simply found a hunting rifle in a barn, the owner would be executed.

We knew that Robert, Eugène, and Maurice were fighting in the French army and risking their lives every day to deliver us. Then Verdun and the Somme happened. The Battle of the Somme began twenty miles from Saint-Quentin near Péronne on July 1, 1916, with rounds of artillery fire that lasted several days and nights. At night, the horizon was illuminated by continuous explosions. During the day, the windowpanes in our houses shook. It was at this time that Robert was seriously wounded, as I related earlier, and that we searched in vain for him among soldiers in his depleted unit who had been taken prisoner by the Germans.

You can understand why I was so patriotic: Robert had become my idol, my good luck charm. But before this feeling reached maturity, I passed through a period of childish behavior. Pierre, Étienne, and I became fond of collections. I remember dreaming of a marvelous but difficult feat: getting hold of a German pointed helmet, hiding it until the end of the war, and then exhibiting it as a trophy. In the meantime, I made do by going at dusk to tear down the still fresh German notices announcing orders or executions. We stuck them together again at home and before the evacuation of the city, we buried them in sealed bottles at the back of our garden. Oh, what a paradox! We found them all intact after the war, whereas our family silverware, which we children didn't care much about and which was also buried at the back of the garden next to our bottles, was destroyed by a shell!

The poster game we were playing was dangerous: people who slashed them were punished with prison. We were chased once or twice by big German policemen dressed in green, but we easily escaped because we knew all the ins and outs of the old part of town.

Thus, while our parents were living in anguish for the future, carefree and vindictive, we waged the children's war. The noise of the explosions thrilled us. Allied planes often flew over Saint-Quentin looking to strike the train station, which was full of troops and munitions. Twice they succeeded, and the lower part of town was ravaged by frightening explosions of land mines that were being transported by German trains. There were deaths, roofs blown off, and cracked walls. The second time, Étienne and I were almost caught in the disaster. We had gone to gather shrapnel for our collection, but the planes returned. We scampered off like madmen amid broken windows and falling plaster. We returned from these expeditions with a sense of being crowned with glory. The useless risks we were taking were not, however, appreciated by Papa and Louise.

Our most successful adventure had to do with the "liberation of Saint-Quentin." The city was cut off from any news and saturated with rumors that circulated by word of mouth. Mostly, they carried hopes that were soon dashed. Pierre and I planned to spread a false rumor. On a toy typewriter, we composed a redundant message signed by General Joffre: "People of Saint-Quentin, in a few days, the hour of your liberation will have sounded. The victorious arms of the Republic, after a devastating offensive, will plant the flag of our country in front of your city hall," etc.

We waited patiently for the arrival of a French plane, and after having judged its altitude, we wrote in pencil with a trembling hand: "Thrown from an altitude of three thousand meters" and signed it "Lieutenant-aviator Moreau." Then at dusk, we set out like conspirators and threw our papers in the deserted streets. The effect was overwhelming. Early the next morning, a highly excited butcher boy rang the bell. He brandished a deformed copy of our announcement, rife with spelling errors: "This time, it's true. They are coming!"

At the lycée, we were greeted by cries of joy: "Have you read General Joffre's proclamation?"

"No," we responded, pretending to be astonished.

"What?" they answered, "It's amazing. In a few days, we will be liberated, the flag replanted at city hall."

Decidedly, our farce was reaching exaggerated proportions. We became terribly embarrassed by the credulity of these good people, mostly of the professors who commented in class about the big news. The most comical thing in the whole business was that a Moreau family in Saint-Quentin thought they recognized their son's writing on the announcement.

Only one man didn't join in the parade – Papa! He read the text of the butcher boy, shrugged his shoulders, and said the most obvious: "If General Joffre was preparing an offensive, he wouldn't tell the Germans about it. The style is ridiculous and pompous." (This remark lightly ruffled our egos.) "No, this is the work of a fraud." The butcher boy shrugged and said: "But it's signed by General Joffre." Nothing helped; Papa couldn't be convinced. In our hearts, we were proud to have such an intelligent father.

The rumor, like so many others, had no sequel, and with good reason. Those who had proclaimed the forthcoming liberation were discreet, allowing others to forget that they had been duped.

One day, we told Papa that we had been the authors of the document. He refused to believe us. In that, he was certainly less insightful.

Another element helped to dissipate our adolescent patriotism. It was the occasional visits of certain German cousins – Werner Seebas, among others, and his brother Paul, who was later killed near Reims – as well as the more regular visits of German deaconesses.

The cousins greatly annoyed us. Suddenly, they were there at the door: Werner with his war-style glasses for his myopic eyes, attached behind his ears with elastic bands we thought were ugly. They arrived, those cousins, as naive as only Germans could be, conquerors in flat caps, so happy to see their dear "Onkel Paul" and their dear cousins. Papa received them coolly. We boys were terribly embarrassed by them. Werner asked me to show him the beautiful sights in town. It was a real ordeal for me. How could I admit to my friends that this hideous Kraut was my cousin? I walked very slowly or picked up my pace whenever I saw a friend or a prof or someone I thought I knew. Werner, who did not understand the torture he was putting me through, was astonished at my strange behavior.

We received the deaconesses more warmly. They belonged to the Henriettenstift order.[4] My uncle, the "General Superintendent," was their director. This uncle, a kind of Bishop of Hanover before they had Lutheran bishops in Germany, was famous and conservative. He was the one who had forbidden my mother to take communion in the Reformed Church. She went over his head to get permission. The deaconesses arrived carrying letters full of concern from our aunts in Germany. In

4 An important community of Lutheran deaconesses (religious nurses) founded in Hanover in 1860.

the beginning, they even brought us some food and Christmas packages with the cinnamon gingerbread that I liked so much. The hard part was convincing them to take letters to our relatives in France. This was *streng verboten* (strictly forbidden), and we quickly became acquainted with the spirit of discipline among the Germans, who are incredibly scrupulous about not disobeying any order, even when they are certain that the action is harmless.

One of the sisters, Else, was more courageous than the others. She directed the *Kasino*, the mess hall, of the German officers. Louise, who had a solid knowledge of German, wrote her messages in German, making her letters as sharp as possible. These letters were taken to the military post by Sister Else, just as if they were letters from German soldiers. They were addressed to an aunt in Germany who would forward them to relatives in Switzerland. Our Swiss correspondent would translate them into French to avoid the suspicions of the French censors. In a month, sometimes in only three weeks, we would get news from our relatives. This was how the story of Robert, wounded, left to die, and convalescing, was recounted in such a way that the German censor believed the soldier was German!

Sister Else often arrived with a military chaplain, Mr. Depuhl, whom she married after the war. He was in no way her equal. Always bowing and clicking his heels, he trembled before the authorities and dissuaded Sister Else from doing anything he thought was subversive.

One day, Papa, noticing the chaplain's holster, asked him abruptly: "What do you have in there, Mr. Depuhl?"

"My revolver," responded the chaplain proudly, showing it to him.

"As long as you, a minister of God, have that thing in your holster, I ask you not to come into my home."

The next day, Mr. Depuhl returned without his revolver.

Papa lacked prudence when it came to the Germans. He decided not to let his home be invaded by the officers that the *Kommandantur* sent with accommodation tickets. German soldiers had the right to third-floor bedrooms, but not to those on the second floor. One day, a high-ranking officer came to the door.

"I want to see the best bedroom in the house," he said.

Papa showed him his bedroom.

"I'll sleep here tonight," said the officer.

"No, sir, I'm old," responded Papa. "I won't give you my room."

“Then show me another one.”

“Here’s my young sons’ room. I need to watch over them. You can’t sleep there.”

They did a tour of the entire floor in this fashion. At each bedroom, Papa found another decisive argument and, with his lofty air that allowed for no discussion, imposed his will on the officer.

As Papa was firmly showing him the staircase to the third floor, the officer had had enough.

“You didn’t open this door,” he cried out, indicating Madeleine’s bedroom.

“My daughter Madeleine died in that bedroom a few weeks ago. You will not sleep in that room, sir,” responded Papa in the same tone of voice.

The officer yielded, but as he finally went to the staircase, Papa showed him the last door which had remained closed.

“Here’s a door that you didn’t have me open yet, sir,” said Papa. Turning the doorknob, he invited the officer to enter: “You can sleep here this evening,” he said.

It was the toilet.

Ashen, the officer ran down the staircase. We heard him slam the door behind him as he left the house. Cheerful as can be, Papa rubbed his hands together. We adored Papa; we wanted to be just like him.

But chaos reigns in the adolescent soul. I remember conversations in the Petit Salon in German when Sister Else or her companions visited. I listened in silence. Here was the world of the “Aunties,” of the family, services rendered, and friendship. We “buttered up” the deaconesses a bit because we depended on their good will. Then the German sisters left, and the normal tone of anger took over once again: the stories of requisitions, resistance to the requisitions, wishing misfortunes on the Germans to punish them for their crimes, accounts of atrocities committed by them. It was all black and white; these two worlds came and went but never met. I knew that all this didn’t hold together, that there was, under these political and familial decors, a gross error that I would discover one day. I knew that, to say the least, the adults were mistaken. Within myself, I protested with all my soul.

IT WAS RELIGIOUS FAITH that suddenly brought light to my inner darkness. Everything in me was tension and conflict. I didn’t like my schoolwork. I found it superficial. I didn’t like our home. I felt sad there, stifled. I didn't like myself. My ennui, my first sexual awakenings, and the lies I told horrified me.

But I felt great admiration for our pastor, Mr. Kaltenbach. He wasn't a handsome man: small, always rushing about, his myopic eyes hidden behind thick glasses. He had a funny, childish mouth under a Fu Manchu moustache and above a tiny chin. He spoke with a sentimental voice that was a bit tremulous and poorly pitched. But what he said was clear, well thought out, and profound. He had studied for a year in America and told us many interesting things. He was affectionate and direct, paid attention to our group, and had a personal comment for each one of us. I must have learned later that he had attended Mr. Nick's school. Mr. Nick was a remarkable preacher from northern France who had communicated his vision of the kingdom of God and the evangelization of the world.

I took Mr. Kaltenbach's course in religious instruction to prepare for membership in the church at the age of sixteen. Papa wanted me to do this before the baccalaureate exam, so that nothing would interfere with my preparation for that fiercely competitive exam. Mr. Kaltenbach's class was exciting, but that wasn't where I had my sudden revelation. Catechism, family services, Sunday school belonged to the routine religion in which I had been raised. Much later, when I was a man, seated next to Papa in the rebuilt Petit Salon in Saint-Quentin, I learned from his own lips that, for him as well, faith was not a routine: he too had experienced a religious conversion. He had even thought about becoming a pastor. The devout lay person he became as an adult expressed his convictions in our daily devotions so strongly that we couldn't doubt their religious origin. We had a short prayer service at breakfast: a reading from the Bible, a reading of a meditation, a prayer that was always basically the same ("Teach us to do our duty"), and the recitation of the "Our Father" by one of the children. There were prayers before meals at noon and in the evening before sitting down at table. On Sundays, we had church services (my older brothers went to church twice on Sundays!). The children had Sunday school in church, led by Papa, of course, who began his fiery exhortations with, "My dear children . . .," which I can still hear resonating in my ears fifty years later.

I learned the religion of duty, of prayers before going to sleep. I learned my lessons well. Without any effort, I was "first" in catechism, because my comrades, who were older than I was, had only received basic instruction. I recall the rather silly pride I took in reciting my lessons correctly among boys and girls who stumbled through the "Our Father" in local dialect.

Kaltenbach was aware of my academic talent, but he didn't set me apart from my fellow students. I am grateful to him for very different reasons. He invited me several times to his home where, in unforgettable, intimate discussions, he implored me to give myself to God and to practice purity, truth, love, and self-abnegation, placing my entire life and will in the hands of a God who would save lost humanity.

I am not sure that I entirely understood the second part of his appeal at that time because, despite my efforts, I didn't feel that I was lost. My comrades repented for huge sins: thefts, adultery, drunkenness. I had nothing but a meager inventory to present – a few lies, misbehaving in class, laziness. What won over my conviction was Mr. Kaltenbach's allusion to a lost world, the lost world of the war, full of monstrous and absurd human crimes that I saw every day. "You should put the family heritage you have received to the service of others," he told me. "Shouldn't you become a pastor or a missionary?"

I would have liked to become a preacher like Mr. Kaltenbach, but I didn't feel at all capable of doing that. So, I simply blushed, as was my wont.

One day, I addressed Papa, trembling. Why trembling? Not because I was afraid of a negative response, but because I doubted myself and my intellectual and moral abilities. To preach like Mr. Kaltenbach seemed like an unreachable ideal. Furthermore, it wasn't easy to speak to Papa, even about a serious matter. "Papa," I said to him, swallowing my saliva, "I think I want to become a pastor."

"Ah, good," said Papa. "I'm happy to hear it. It's a very noble goal. You will have to learn how to speak more distinctly." In Papa's presence, I often stammered because he intimidated me. In class, too, I was "weak" in recitation. "If your mother were able to see you, she would rejoice in your decision," continued Papa. "The day of your birth, Easter Day 1901, we both consecrated you to God, in the hope that one day you would become a pastor. I never told you, because I never wanted to influence any of my sons. But, since you have decided, let me say that I am very happy with your decision." He added yet another memory that touched me deeply: "It was because you were born on Easter Day that we gave you the middle name "Pascal." After you were born, your mother asked that the windows of the bedroom be opened wide, so that the sun of

Easter morning and the sound of the bells from the basilica could fill the room."

THIS WAS HOW I MOVED from a routine religion, the only one I knew, to the religion "of spirit and truth." My faith was still stagnant when, one day, coming out of church service, I was approached by Arthur Meunier, a classmate in religious instruction who was a lot older than I was. "Hey, André, why don't you come to the Union next Sunday afternoon?"[5] He addressed me in the familiar *tu* form, which startled the staid petit bourgeois I was at the time. Pierre was also invited, but he declined. He was already too "old," too sure of himself, and too "Trocmé." I replied: "I'm not sure if I can; I have homework from the lycée; I'll ask my father."

I asked Papa. With a simple gesture of his hand, he swept away the proposition: "The Unionists? They do nothing but stupid things like turning over benches and breaking windows. The hall concierge complains about them at every one of our elders' meetings. You'll only pick up detestable words and bad behavior with them. No, my answer is no." I didn't argue; you didn't argue with Papa. I simply passed on my father's negative answer to Arthur Meunier.

Then, something unbelievable happened. The following Sunday as I left church, I saw Meunier, a simple, tongue-tied worker, walk right up to Papa, an important gentleman whom workers normally approached to ask for employment, and begin a lively conversation. I only heard bits and pieces of it.

"Mr. Trocmé," said Arthur, "the old Union is dead. We agreed with Mr. Kaltenbach and dissolved it. We began all over again. We pray; we try to serve God. I assure you that it will do André good to join us."

Papa didn't answer right away. I think he had to question Mr. Kaltenbach (in whom he had great confidence) about the truthfulness of Arthur Meunier's account. Mr. Kaltenbach's response was along these lines: Six young people got together to pray that God would transform their lives, a remarkable thing. The young people's inspiration was founded upon complete faith in the possibility of putting absolutes into practice – purity, love, truth – all of which were later emphasized by the

5 The "Union" was the Union chrétienne de jeunes gens (UCJG) or Young Men's Christian Association (YMCA). It was founded in London in 1844 and spread widely throughout the world.

Moral Rearmament movement.[6] They were certain God answered their prayers. They were freed from their sins. Great enthusiasm reigned among them. One can speak here of a true religious revival.

"Since this is the case," Papa said to me a few days later, "I'll allow you to go to the Union."

Since then, I have often participated in revivals (above all at the Union in Plaisance, Clamart, and Sin-le-Noble) and I have sensed God's presence in them.

Our first meeting took place in the upper room of the church in Saint-Quentin. It was a strange, dilapidated room located above the church entrance, lit by an immense, Gothic glass roof with small diamond-shaped panes set in lead. It had a table and some benches. There were about forty boys, almost all of them older than I, speaking French tinged with the local patois. They were putting on a play, *The Aviator of Mars*. I can still remember the actors: Pierre Blondin, today the very worthy vice president of the Mézières-Charleville council of elders, and André Bonnedame, who turned out badly. It was a poorly written, mediocre skit that I found hysterical. As far as theater was concerned, I was only familiar with Louise's minor attempts in Saint-Gobain to have us put on Maeterlinck's *The Blue Bird*. I hadn't understood a single word of that one. I was dressed up as the "Pleasure of the Forest" and had a few lines to say, but was so grotesquely decked out with apple-green trimmings of crepe paper sewn at the last minute on the back of my three-piece suit, I refused to go on stage. But here things were different. We were all young; the actors and the audience were running wild. They made faces, exchanged jibes, and I laughed heartily among companions who called me André and whom I called Tutur (for Arthur), or Robert, using their first names. (In school, students addressed one another only by their family names.) When the play was over, Tutur suddenly got up on the table. It was no longer to clown around, but to quiet us down. "Now we are going to hold a service," he said, "and a prayer meeting." I was dumbfounded, because services for me consisted of adults reprimanding young people. But now I saw one of my catechism classmates, known for his awkwardness, open a Bible, read a few verses, and lead a meditation about which I have retained nothing, except that it was simple and sincere.

6 *Le Réarmement moral* (Moral Rearmament) was founded in 1938 by an American Lutheran pastor named Frank Buchman. He emphasized the transformation of the individual as the indispensable component of the transformation of society.

Then everyone got down on their knees. I didn't know that you got on your knees to pray. I stood up, looked at all those bent-over backs, blushed, and knelt like everyone else. Their prayers were real prayers. They spoke to God as to a living person right there with us. What did they speak about? All the current problems I was having. One of them asked to be saved from lying, another confessed to fits of anger. The third, in tears, asked God to deliver him from sins of impurity. Others thanked God for having already delivered them. They all rejoiced at having found so much illumination and joy. They asked God to increase their love for one another, and they prayed for a companion who had fallen back into alcoholism.

They all spoke up. Only I remained silent, stunned but happy. For the first time, I learned that the tensions secretly tearing me apart were not the sign of a special, unique curse that fell solely on me. I also learned that I could be delivered from them, that I could confide in others, have friends, and open myself up, and that we could truly love one another as God has loved us. Unbelievable! Thus, the precautions that I had continuously taken to hide myself from the view of others, the control I exerted upon my words and feelings, this mute and monotonous life, the constant suppression of my aspirations and my enthusiasm, all that was false!

I seemed to enter directly into a paradise on earth. Led perhaps more by the contagious example of my new friends than by a truly personal faith, I entered into the marvelous world of religious experience.

Today, I realize that my faith was then more attached to men than to God himself. I "believed in the Union" more than in the power of a personal and living God. Isn't that almost always the case with converts? One day, don't they have to discover weaknesses in those in whom they thought they had found divine perfection? Don't we all have to learn to separate what really comes from God from the jumble of mediocre assumptions the best of us struggle with, even during a period of religious revival?

Be that as it may, I returned home transfigured. A light shone around me, a fire burned inside me: everything was possible, everything had meaning. I began to deplore, with perhaps too much pride, Pierre and Étienne's indifference. They too had attended the sessions at the Union. Strangely, the same causes had not produced the same effects.

Several weeks after my entrance into the Union, Tutur asked me, in the most natural way possible, if I wanted to give the meditation on the following Sunday. That was how I made my debut in religious eloquence. I chose, strangely given my age, the text of Matthew 6, on anxieties: "Don't worry about tomorrow, for tomorrow will take care of itself." Oh, the obliviousness of youth! At an age when I was ignorant of life's heavy burdens, I gave a speech about worries and proposed solutions. It's true that preparing this short piece of eloquence caused me many worries. I asked Papa and Louise for help. I suppose that what I said didn't make a great impression on my comrades because they never asked me to speak again. Many years later, I gave a practice sermon in the School of Theology. Éric Barde, a pastor today in Nîmes, later told me that I had spoken in a monotone voice, with my eyes lowered and my elbows stuck to my body. He said he never would have guessed that under this mask was the André Trocmé who would later address hundreds of people in Le Chambon and elsewhere, in French, German, English, and even Italian! Please remember the education I received: the "Speak distinctly" that my father yelled at me across the table as soon as I opened my mouth, my literary failures with Dodancourt, and the conviction I had formed of being totally incapable and wrong to try to raise myself above my condition. Only a vocation, each day more firmly established, gradually saved me from the oppressive timidity from which I was suffering.

It was also at the Union that I discovered girls. Not that the Union was coed. God forbid! But from time to time during religious instruction, we were together. A religious awakening had also spread among the girls. Some relationships that would end in marriage began there. For the first time, at sixteen years of age, I noticed the curve of a female neck, the curly hair at the nape, the characteristic look that sought your eyes and made you blush, and the shame of having let your eyes fall upon the forbidden object.

This obsession of "not looking at a woman lest you covet her" pursued me until my marriage. Already before the war, Papa, noticing the first signs of adolescence in Pierre and me, had silently placed in our hands a frightening red brochure which described the horrors of immorality. It described everything in the same way: to have sex with a woman outside of marriage invariably contaminated you with syphilis, canker sores, gonorrhea, or early dementia. Masturbation was described in a no less frightening manner: it led to insanity and hell. Now, at the Union, my comrades openly confessed to terrible sins, the very names of which were unknown to me. I was incapable of distinguishing between my small-time childhood experiences that led me little by little to discover my sexual nature and the tragedies suffered by these eighteen- to twenty-year-olds who, for the most part, had not been protected by their working-class families from the pursuit of the vulgarity of the streets and the workshops.

Furthermore, my comrades supposed in me vices comparable to the ones they had before their conversions. Because of them, I became a Puritan, that is, a man horrified by a simple allusion to evil. I maintained this tendency until my military service and never departed from the austerity that constituted my strength against temptations. What was regrettable was that it completely spoiled any natural and friendly relations that I might have established with members of the opposite sex. I never abandoned these reservations until I got engaged. Looking back now, I can see that, fortunately, Providence kept me from the errors that my ignorance could have caused. This interior repression regarding everything female made me into a frightened adolescent who, at the same time, was in love with everything feminine. I recall how, to get rid of sinful thoughts, I used to repeat incessantly: "After all, a girl is only a skeleton dressed somewhat differently than a man." Nonetheless, my frenzied combat against the flesh had a positive result: it charged me with intellectual, spiritual, and ideological energies far more than my friends. Later, I was often astonished by the moral apathy most of them exhibited. The great combat for purity that certain adolescents fight can have a terribly artificial and dangerous side to it. But its effect is to bind the will and prepare it for courageous action, whereas indulgent attitudes are rarely creative.

My best friend at the Union was Robert Jospin.[7] He was only a bit older than I, but taller and more mature, with long arms, broad gestures, and an inextinguishable eloquence that emerged from a full-lipped mouth. He belonged to the Jospin tribe, about whom the Trocmé family spoke only with scorn. The Jospins were all descendants of a poor ancestor, the father of many children. They were ambitious, proud, and intelligent. They competed with the timid Trocmé sons and often outshone them in parish activities. From this competition, there

7 Robert Jospin (1899–1990) was the son of a sales representative and the nephew of Pastor Héliodore Jospin. He was a director of the UCJG and studied theology for two years before becoming a teacher, a militant socialist, and a pacifist. He is the father of the politician Lionel Jospin.

developed a disdainful jealousy that I was delighted to throw overboard as soon as I became Robert's friend.

Robert came to our house, and I went to his. Another guy joined in our conversations, a shy, blond fellow like me, Marcel Capiomont. Robert assumed a prophetic tone and was somewhat protective toward us. He read widely on all topics, and his rather vague mind produced grandiose visions in which he played the role of an inspirational figure who converted the masses. "You will see, André. We are going to do great things after the war," he told us.

After the war, Robert and Marcel began their studies together at the École Préparatoire de Théologie. Marcel never took his baccalaureate exam and became an insurance agent. Robert passed his baccalaureate brilliantly, obtained a degree in humanities, got married, abandoned his pastoral projects, got divorced, and remarried. I have seen him since then. He's still a visionary, still sententious, a pacifist like me, but secular, even antireligious. He finished his teaching career as the director of an institution for at-risk children. When I saw him one day in class and told him that I had become a conscientious objector, he responded: "Ah, you finally made it." That describes him perfectly. In Saint-Quentin, Robert always had a good influence on me. He woke me from my slumber and paraded before my eyes visions of peace and social justice inspired by his Socialist family, to the great chagrin of the Trocmés. I got very inspired when I was with him, though perhaps with no tangible results. Like all adolescents trying to find themselves, I suffered from restlessness at home. I also judged the narrowness of my family's views harshly and unjustly.

Inspired by the Holy Spirit (I am not afraid to use this word because I believe that God inspires those who pray in common), the Saint-Quentin Union made one discovery after another, all in the space of a few months.

1. *Concern for Salvation:* Concern for the soul of one's neighbor; praying for one's comrade until he gives himself to God; the celestial joy that envelopes those who repent – all this filled our Sunday meetings. Expanding beyond the borders of our small Protestant group, the Union reached dozens of other young boys. The situation was conducive to evangelism. Unemployment hit the city hard, and all businesses voluntarily ceased to operate so that they wouldn't be working for the enemy. The municipality distributed paper money to the needy – and two-thirds

of the population was needy. The sole value of the money was as credit granted by shopkeepers at the rate of forty centimes a day. People were suffering everywhere. The Union went looking in the cafés to attract new members among the desperate. Papa never gave me permission to join these salvationist teams. Had I done so, I could have given myself an unforgettable apprenticeship in my future ministry.

2. *Christian Communism:* Like a concentration camp, the city was surrounded by barbed wire. The German sentries guarded the exits by means of barriers that cut off the roads. To leave, you had to get a special pass from the *Kommandantur* by specifying a precise reason. Papa was never able to get one to go to Saint-Gobain. The official food provisions were completely inadequate. A good part of the unemployed population "went through the wall" by passing under the barbed wire barriers between the German patrols. They brought back bread, potatoes, meat, or butter from the country. (Butter had disappeared completely from the official market.) The scammers who got caught spent weeks in German prisons. When one considers that military requisitions exhausted the country, it's easy to understand that no one attached any sense of guilt to the black market. It was resistance, that's all, and those who passed under the barbed wire made the rich (among whom were the Trocmés) pay for the risk they took by charging a higher price for their goods.

At this time, on Sunday afternoons at the Union, a strange market was established: a free black market. Those who had "gone through the wall" during the week brought their supplies and put them on a table. "Take some if you are hungry, or if there are hungry mouths at home. Don't be embarrassed. It's there for you." And those in need took home bread, potatoes, and sometimes milk or butter. This distribution was not organized by chance. It was in prayer that my good friends found the answer to the food problems that many were experiencing. But I neither brought anything nor took anything home. We were much too conformist at home to dare to "crawl under the barbed wire." We bought what we needed at a very high price from clandestine suppliers. I was never allowed to bring anything at all to the Union. But the generosity of the working class made a profound impact on me. I learned that there are other virtues besides abstaining from sin and avoiding obscene words and misdeeds. Some of my buddies, Hoche Bourlet, for example, ended up in the bistro business in Paris. "He lost his faith," we said after the war, "he quit the Croix Bleue."[8] But good Hoche, with his toothless mouth extending from ear to ear and his freckles, was the most skillful and generous supplier among us. "Do you think I'm going to make you pay?" he said in his Northern dialect. "Go ahead, take what you want, it's for you. Eat if it makes you happy."

3. *Defense of the Human Person:* Sometime in the fall of 1916, the Union discovered that there was greater suffering nearby than that of the general civil population. For some reason, after having countered the Allied attacks on the Somme, the Germans prepared a strategic withdrawal along the lines of defense going from Cambrai to Saint-Quentin and Noyen. They undertook the construction of extraordinary underground fortifications capable of withstanding the heaviest bombardments. Sixty-foot-deep shelters were dug into the ground. Machine guns and retractable canons ascended from the depths once it appeared that everything had been destroyed by enemy artillery. That line was later called the Hindenburg Line and served as a model for the Maginot Line in World War II. Only in 1918 did newer tanks succeed in breaching such obstacles.

To carry out this enormous endeavor, the Germans brought in thousands of Russian prisoners, who lived in barely habitable camps in the city and surrounding areas. We saw them going to work in the mornings, in long, pitiable processions, dressed in tattered yellow uniforms and burlap. The Germans, who themselves had begun to experience hunger, hardly fed them. It was not uncommon to see one of these unfortunate Russian prisoners fall in the street from starvation. A German petty officer would kick him to get him to stand up. If he didn't get up, a gunshot to his temple put an end to his suffering.

Outraged and powerless, the people of Saint-Quentin witnessed these horrors. Compared to the suffering of the Russians, we were rich and well-nourished. It's a strange thing, but even though it was strictly forbidden to give anything at all to Russian prisoners, pity won out over prudence and people tried to help them anyway. The Union bought an enormous cooking pot and began collecting vegetables. Thanks to a certain German guard, more easily moved to pity than the others, every day designated members of the Union brought food into the Russian prisoner camp on the sly. Pierre, Étienne, and I stuffed our pockets with

8 La Croix Bleue (The Blue Cross) was a Protestant association that fought against alcoholism. It was founded in Switzerland in 1877 by Pastor Rochat and advocated complete abstinence. The drinker was assisted by a member of the organization, either a former drinker or a supportive member.

leftover bread and musty cigars that we found in the lower part of the bookshelves in our study. We brought them to the Russians, passing these things to them through barbed wire as if at a zoo. The struggle that took place between these unfortunate souls for a crust of bread or a handful of tobacco would have been comical in our youthful eyes if we had not already experienced in our own empty stomachs what it feels like to be starving. We returned home from these expeditions completely shaken and racked with hatred for the occupiers. On Sundays, it would happen that a Union comrade was absent: he was locked up in the cellars of the *Kommandantur* for eight days for communicating with Russian prisoners. The guards had been changed.

4. *Christian Pacifism:* I was the unwitting intermediary of the Union's discovery of Christian pacifism. The constantly changing flow of German soldiers and officers who lodged on the third floor of our home didn't interest us. We only crossed paths with these men in the stairwell. They wore heavy boots and exuded a strange odor of leather and sweat, tobacco and soiled sheets. The Battle of the Somme was in full swing. After the first hopes of liberation, a somber aloofness and a profound hatred descended upon the population. The entire city was transformed into a hospital. An odor of carbolic acid, and sometimes of gangrene, hung over everything. At night, entire trains loaded with bodies returned from the front to the rear guard, where they incinerated their dead. The full horror of war was revealed to me one day when, coming back home from the train station, I ran into a lamentable column of wounded German soldiers. The means of transportation, by automobile or on horseback, had become so rare that all those who could still walk had to get themselves on foot to the hospitals they were assigned to. In the first row, I saw three men, all wounded and bandaged. Instead of a head, the one in the middle had an enormous gauze ball. He certainly couldn't see, because he stumbled and, held up by his comrades, dragged himself along with great difficulty. When he got close to me, I saw with horror that his lower jaw was missing; in its place were mushy linens full of blood clots. It broke my heart. I had not yet realized that war was like that. The illusions of young people are such that they inevitably think of war as a heroic duel, a kind of boxing match, where courage sends one's adversary to the mat. One day, all young people must confront a scene like the one I have just described to understand: "Look what you have done to your brother." This condemns all those who take part in the great abomination that is war.

As a result, I was no longer able to hate this man without a face, and I went home sickened and disgusted.

Several days later, I met a German on the staircase in our home. He stopped, looked at me kindly, and touched my arm with his hand.

"Are you hungry?" he asked me, and he awkwardly handed me a quarter loaf of black bread. It was the famous *Kommisbrot*, marked with a K, that signified *Kartoffelbrot* (potato bread), that we mockingly called "KK bread" (pronounced "caca" in French, that is, "shit bread").

"No," I responded to him in German, "I'm not hungry, but even if I were, I wouldn't take your bread because you are the enemy."

"No, no, I am not your enemy."

"Yes," I retorted, "you are my enemy. You wear this uniform, and tomorrow you may perhaps kill my brother who is fighting against you to rid us of your presence. Why did you come into our country; why did you bring war, suffering, and misery?"

"I'm not what you think," he responded. "I am a Christian. Do you believe in God?"

My face lit up. I understood this language which permeated my whole life.

"We found Christ in Breslau," he continued, "and have turned our lives over to him."

Thereupon, he told me in detailed fashion that he belonged to a church whose name I have forgotten.

"Men can do nothing against those who have placed all their confidence in God," he said. "One day, a man who hated the work we were doing came into our assembly hall to kill the leader of our group. His pistol misfired, and we all saw in this a sign from heaven."

"I won't kill your brother," he went on, "nor any Frenchman. God revealed to us that a Christian must not kill, ever. We never carry a weapon!"

"But what do you do?" I replied. "You are a soldier."

"Well, I explained to the captain what I believe, and he allowed me to come along without carrying a weapon. Normally, radio operators like me carry a pistol or a dagger. I have neither. When I am in danger, I sing a hymn and pray to God. If he decides to save my life, he will. If not . . ."

I was deeply impressed. This man's sincerity was obvious. For the first time, I found myself face-to-face with what we would later call "a conscientious objector." If he had been a Frenchman, I would have been indignant: "What? You refuse to defend your country which has been invaded and trampled upon by an enemy?" But I was dealing with a German, with a man who refused to be part of this filthy business. His courage and his faith were evident. I confided in him without hesitation. I had met a true Christian, the type of Christian we should all resemble, just as God had revealed to us at the Union.

My friendship with Kindler (that was the name of this fine young fellow) brought me the solution to the contradictions that the adults demonstrated and that had poisoned my soul. All at once, my nationalism and my militarism collapsed. I saw war for what it was: a dreadful chaos, where all the belligerents – offenders and victims in turn – disobeyed God, taking justice into their own hands and using cannon fire to do so.

Without thinking deeply about the consequences, I invited Kindler to the Union the following Sunday. He accepted my invitation. Once again, I had to cross the entire city with a German soldier at my side.

My Union friends were surprised when I introduced a German soldier to them. Several were standoffish, with a distrustful reserve. But when I explained that Kindler was a true Christian who, to obey Christ entirely, refused to kill, he was accepted by our group. He said a few words that I translated. He taught us a short hymn that I still remember. Some of our new members giggled while listening:

"Hallelujah! Hallelujah! A-a-a-amen! A-a-a-amen!"

At least the lyrics were easy to remember, and soon everyone joined in with the good-natured Kindler.

As was our custom, we knelt to pray. In the distance, the rumblings of battle never stopped: men out there were killing one another. Here Frenchmen and Germans opened their eyes onto the tangible reality of the unique reign of God. Kindler prayed in German. I think that this was one of the first times that I, too, offered without reticence my intimate thoughts out loud to God.

Kindler left for the front a few days later. He took me up to his room. We prayed together. Then he gave me a few papers and photographs, cutting pliers and a roll of adhesive tape.

"Keep these until I return," he said. "You will be able to see when my regiment comes back from the front. If I'm not there, it means that I'm either wounded, a prisoner, or dead. If I'm either wounded or a prisoner, I'll get in touch with you. If you don't hear anything from me, well then, that means that God found this the right time to take me to him. In this case, kindly send these things to my wife, at the address I've written on this paper."

I never heard anything from Kindler. After a month, I sent the things to his wife, and that was that.

Many years later, as a student in theology, I heard about Christian pacifism, and once again I had the same immediate insight I had with Kindler: "Of course! You must refuse to shoot. That is the gospel of Jesus Christ and any attempts to water it down come from the devil!"

4

Refugees in Belgium

THE EVACUATION OF the civilian population began in early February 1917. It proceeded street by street. Every day, two or three thousand people went down to the train station surrounded by German soldiers. It was forbidden to take more than thirty kilograms of luggage and more than a small sum of money with you. After the people were searched, they were bunched into cattle cars. Their houses remained empty.

Then the pillaging began! Outdoing one another in greed, the Germans and the French civilians who remained in Saint-Quentin rushed into the abandoned houses, opened the drawers, snatched the linens, and turned everything upside down in hope of finding some valuable object. The Germans, leaving for the front a few days later, and the French, waiting to be evacuated in their turn, would all have to surrender their loot. That didn't matter! The primitive instinct to pillage was stronger than that. On our daily walks, Étienne, Pierre, and I went to see these pillaged houses and reported the scandalous sight of these sad spectacles to those at home.

The shopkeepers brought out of their hiding places the supplies they had been jealously guarding. Store windows suddenly were overflowing with products. We bought things that we thought we would need in our place of refuge. "Take what you want," said the shopkeepers. "There's no reason to pay us. We can't take our money with us." I got a pair of folding scissors that was completely useless anyway.

Some German-Jewish shopkeepers, looking like undertakers around the house of a dying person, made their appearance. They rang at our door and offered good money for the furniture and paintings in our large living room. "They are going to pillage it anyway," they said. Papa kicked them out of the house.

Rather than let his property be pillaged, one of our friends, the notary, Labouret, set his house on fire.

Certain houses that were considered chic, like ours, were reserved for the greed of officers. The Germans are an orderly people. A small sign was hung on the doors of houses designated for the officers: *Nur für Offiziere*. One day, when we had taken refuge in the Petit Salon – German officers had invaded our entire home – we heard yells typical of officers bawling out soldiers outside our door. We heard the words *Unverschämtheit, Schande!* (Outrageous! Shame on you!), which passed in German for the height of indignation. What had happened? Some enlisted soldiers had come into our house and were carrying out the magnificent Louis XIV clock from the dining room! Bravo, we thought, there's an honest officer! Alas, the officer was only indignant because the soldiers had dared to enter a house marked *Nur für Offiziere*!

Very secretively, Papa had a mason dig a hiding place in the basement for his fortune, with a vertical hole in the clay soil, a horizontal opening in the foundational wall, and a hole in the earth outside of the house. After placing his treasure in the hole, the wall was carefully redone, the soil in the basement put back in place and covered with dust. This work shook the house with dull blows. Each of us in turn had to stand guard to warn Papa and the worker of the unforeseen return of our unwanted guests. The hiding place was a good one; we found everything intact in 1919.

The lycée was no longer operating. In this surreal atmosphere, we enjoyed a strange freedom. One day, Papa discovered all three of us – Pierre, Étienne, and me – hunched over a large map of Saint-Quentin. What were we doing? We were carefully marking the sites of the underground shelters and batteries built by the Germans. For three weeks on our walks, we carefully recorded these constructions in notebooks we kept in the palms of our hands. "My boys, have you lost your minds? You are going to get us all shot. If the Germans find this, they will think we are spies!" He was right. But youth is heedless, and it was not without distress that we saw the flames in the fireplace consume the results of our efforts.

During the last weeks we spent in Saint-Quentin, the Allies – French or English – greatly increased nighttime aerial attacks on the city. These were no longer the days of those innocuous incursions from the beginning of the war, when a small plane with a blue, white, and red insignia exchanged machine gun bursts with a German plane bearing a black iron cross. At that time, everyone came outside on the sidewalks to wager on these skirmishes. "Zingzingzing" went the French machine gun; "zapzapzap" responded the German guns. After a few passes, the planes went their own ways. Once we saw a French plane perish in flames on the horizon, and we shrieked and wept.

Now things were completely different. The planes came at night and flew high. There were many of them. Their droning filled the houses like the pealing of bells. German alarm sirens increased in number and lowered their anguished wailing. Then it was the "cannon concert," whose muffled sounds were followed by sonorous bursts of shrapnel in the sky. We rushed half-dressed into the basement, where we shivered less from the cold than from nervous fear. Immense rumblings shook the earth, and sinister cracking sounds made it seem like everything was going under. We heard windows shatter on all the floors of the house, and plaster rained down like hail. When the all-clear was given, we returned to our beds in a freezing, dust-filled house. The next morning, we sealed the windows that were missing. Pierre, Étienne, and I went off looking for the string of craters left by the bombs. Our neighbor's house was hit directly but didn't cave in. The piano, which looked like it had been hacked into matchsticks by a maniac with a hatchet, gaped in the middle of the interior ruins. Our neighbor was alive, but the flames had burned his beard and hair. His bald head was colored lemon from picric acid. He walked around the rubble, completely distraught.

As for us, we continued our shrapnel collection. I still have the cap of a German shell that fell next to me one day and made a hole in the ground. I dug it up with my hands while it was still hot and made it into an inkwell. When we had to evacuate, I left behind many useful objects, but without saying anything to anyone, I put my precious inkwell in my bundle, which could only weigh 30 kilograms. The inkwell weighed a kilo and a half all by itself.

No one thought we would be gone for long. Mr. Kaltenbach, who was evacuated before us, said his goodbyes warmly to a German chaplain – "his Kraut," as we said in those days – who committed himself to caring for the house until Kaltenbach returned. After arriving at the train station, Kaltenbach realized he had forgotten his Bible. He got permission from the German guard to go back and get it. He arrived at his home forty-five minutes after he had left it. The chaplain had already overturned everything, looking for valuable objects. Confronted with the unexpected appearance of the owner, he blushed from ear to ear and stammered a few confused words. “I never would have believed this of you,” exclaimed an indignant Mr. Kaltenbach. “*Ach!*” responded the chaplain on the verge of tears. “What do you expect? We’re all crazy; war is war.”

The night before we left, we boys went to the train station to look for a convenient vehicle to transport our luggage the following day. In front of the station, there was a strange and unforgettable fleet of vehicles: wheelbarrows, carts without horses, wagons, hand carts, all abandoned by those who had already left. We got hold of a pretty, sky-blue wagon that had belonged to a candy maker. It became our property for twelve hours, then we abandoned it as the others had done. Papa and Louise were sad, but we, the young, were ready for adventure wherever the wind might take us. Nothing displeases adolescents more than routine!

Our departure was uneventful. When all our gear was loaded on the wagon, we turned around to take one last look at Boulevard Gambetta. Our house still looked great. It was intact, with its curtains at the windows and its air of bourgeois discretion. At the last moment, Papa went back, turned the key and locked the front door. Too bad for our officers! They’ll make do. We wouldn’t see our house again for two years. Then, we would find it shot through by shells, windows and doors ripped out, emptied of its contents, the floors destroyed (to make a fire), but still standing. When the house was repaired in 1922, it once again looked like it had in the past, though nothing on the inside reminded us of our childhood except the layout of the rooms.

We waited a long time on the freezing platform. It had snowed. Then the cattle cars pulled up and we all got in. Later, after arriving in Belgium, I drew from memory our departure scene. To this day, I am rather proud of my artistic effort.

A German guard awaited us in each train car. The doors were closed and darkness settled in. We were forbidden to look outside. The train began to roll slowly. It advanced a short distance, stopped, went backward, and then took off again for our unknown destination. The guard, when asked, said he didn’t know where we were headed. It got colder. The German lit a few small pieces of wood, but the smoke soon made us choke. Once or twice, the train stopped in the open countryside. Men, women, and children dashed into a ditch to relieve themselves. It was then that we learned that an old woman had died in another train car.

Shivering from the cold, we endured the trip, which lasted all night and half the next morning. Those who were unable to hold back relieved themselves in a corner reserved for this.

Finally, after twenty-four hours, the train came to a stop and the doors opened. We saw neat rows of brick houses and called to those who looked in at us curiously: "Where are we?"

"In Belgium," they answered.

Our procession moved through the streets of the city, between hedges of compassionate onlookers. "Those poor people," we heard them say. It's true that with our three-year-old clothing and our various bundles, we must have looked pitiable. On the walls we could read signs: "Appeal from the Mayor," which called on local people to welcome French refugees into their homes. The word "refugee" bothered us. We were not "refugees," but rather "evacuees" whom the Germans kicked out of their homes. They led us into a religious school whose floor was covered with straw. The Catholic nuns served us soup that reinvigorated us.

Locals began to appear in the doorway. They questioned the refugees, asking about the size of each family, choosing the ones they liked or who corresponded to the space they had at home.

Little by little, the schoolroom emptied. Several people took an interest in our family but hesitated when Papa stated proudly that there were nine of us (Papa, Louise, Pierre, Étienne, me, Jeanne, Marie, our cousin Marcel Trocquemé, and Mr. Christol, a distressed missionary who had joined our group) and that there was absolutely no question of separating our family. We remained alone at the school as night fell and we got ourselves ready to spend the night on the straw.

Suddenly, a very loud voice rang out: "Any refugees still left?"

"Yes," responded the nun, "but there are nine of them and they refuse to split up."

"Yeah, yeah, we'll see about that," replied the newcomer.

We saw a middle-aged, average-sized man appear, wearing rather elegant yellow boots and dressed in a short coat like the ones horse traders wear. He sported a flat cap and a large moustache. He held a whip in his hand. We could see that he was drunk.

"So that's it," he said. "No one took you."

"No, as you can see," replied Papa.

"Well, there's a good number of you. The boss won't be happy, but we can't leave you there, can we?"

"There's one sickly woman with us," said Papa. It was true that Louise had already fallen into a bad state of health.

"Not a big deal," he said. "She can ride in the carriage with me, and she'll sleep in the chateau."

In the chateau! Our eyes widened. We would have the good luck of being lodged in a chateau! That calmed Papa's worries. He'd now have us all together in one place. We took off into the night, following the red lantern on the carriage. Louise was on the seat next to the coachman. Part of our luggage had been loaded into the carriage. We had backpacks and walked. We walked for half an hour. We had left that small city behind us a long time ago. We followed the badly paved road straight ahead. It went on forever into the night. We were exhausted and groaning. Papa, despite his 72 years, revived our flagging energy.

We walked for three-quarters of an hour, an hour. Finally, in the dark countryside, where we were only able to distinguish patches of old, dirty snow, our pathetic procession turned to the right onto a road full of potholes. The carriage stopped in front of a one-story detached home. Our guide knocked at the door.

The door opened and a heavy-set woman appeared. "What's going on?"

"You can see for yourself," replied our guide. "I brought some refugees to you."

"How many are there?"

"Nine."

"Jesus, Mary, and Joseph! Mr. Ségard, what have you done?"

We subsequently learned that Ségard, a somewhat rich landowner who didn't do manual labor, lived in a house called "The Chateau" because it was not a farmhouse. He was famous for his drunkenness and his escapades that often caused Homeric battle scenes with his wife.

We were Ségard's latest escapade.

We all entered the vestibule and Mr. Christol, who wanted to bear witness to Jesus Christ, affirmed: "We are Protestant."

"Protestants!" cried out the poor woman. "You don't believe in God. That takes the cake!" In a barrage of conflicting statements, it turned out that Mrs. Ségard had only one extra bed, and it was in a small room in the attic, right behind the bedroom where the farmhand slept. Louise was so exhausted that she was given that bed.

What about the rest of us? "Go out and look on the road," declared Mrs. Ségard. "There are other houses!"

It was probably around eight o'clock. People were already half asleep. With Papa leading the way, we knocked on closed shutters. Étienne, Marcel, and Mr. Christol were the first ones to find lodging in Monier's bistro. Then Jeanne and Marie in the house next to the bistro. Finally, Papa in an opulent-looking farmhouse. That left only me and Pierre. "Go to the Demulders," they said, "They're not rich, but they have a spare bedroom." We went to see the Demulders on the other side of the road. They lived in a brick hut, as we found out the next morning.

We had to enter through the stable, passing through the main room, where the parents and their young son slept, to get to the shabby, cold bedroom. Pierre and I were completely exhausted and had to share the same straw mattress in a large, rickety bed. Over the next few days, we exited through the window, which was close to the ground, so as not to bother the parents and the cows.

We were spread out over more than a quarter mile along the Pavé d'Ath, far from any urban area. Every day, the family got together in a room offered to us by Papa's hosts. Our new life got organized quickly.

Our new life! Only gradually did we become aware of how far we had fallen! In Saint-Quentin, we were among the rich, the sons of Mr. Paul Trocmé, manufacturer of lace curtains, vice president of the chamber of commerce. Our house on Boulevard Gambetta alone ranked us favorably. Here we were nothing! Just a group of refugees who inspired pity. Papa was an elderly gentleman, to be sure, but without any prestige. He had brought a very small amount of money with him. We were poor, and that poverty manifested itself in a thousand small humiliations.

The inhabitants of the village of Marcq generously organized a soup kitchen for the refugees. We went across the fields in turn, two by two, to get the soup in the village. We had to pay strict attention not to spill a single drop of this precious liquid – one ladle per person, no more, no less, to keep everyone happy.

This soup was the basis of our nourishment. Three times daily, we would get together at a round table in Papa's hosts' house, to eat our soup with bread. After our soup, we were sent out two by two to the farms to buy potatoes. We didn't get them very often. Our hosts found various pretexts to refuse us: "We don't have enough for ourselves. How can we give some to you?" Once they told us the harsh truth: "How are we going to fatten up our pigs if we give them to you?"

But they never refused us the beets they fed their cows. We even got them for free. We ate these beets in every possible form and grew familiar with their earthy, sweetish taste in the community soup that they thickened to make it go further; as warm vegetables, with a bit of melted, rancid lard from the officially distributed rations; and as a salad, cold, mixed with dandelions that we gathered in the meadows as soon as the snows melted.

Our menu got somewhat better in the spring with the arrival of the "American supplies" from Herbert Hoover.[1] We ate huge quantities of corn flakes that the Belgians scorned and gave us. There was also a kind of artificial honey, lumpy and tasteless, that young people were crazy about. When the farmers began to thin out the beet plants, there were, above all, young beet leaves that made an excellent dish of greens, especially when combined with nettle tips that we gathered along the brick walls of the farms.

Pierre and I had fallen in with the poorest of the poor and the best people of all. The others tried to take advantage of us by selling eggs and bread from the black market at the highest possible prices. The Demulders, on the other hand, had nothing to sell. Mr. Demulder was called Pol. His real name was Leopold, like the father of King Albert I. He would hitch up the pants that his thin hips couldn't maintain by themselves and sniff noisily, then wipe his nose with the back of his hand and spit out the black juice from his plug of tobacco. His wife, Florence, was disheveled and sluggish and dragged herself from the kitchen to the stable in wooden clogs. Clément, their three-year-old son, swore colorfully in the Belgian manner of stringing together Flemish curse words. His father ran after him and spanked him for this naughty habit. While he administered the punishment, he let out the same string of expletives. When entering the house, you had to hurry past the scrawny rumps of the three cows because their specialty was to discharge their dung without any warning on the wall behind them. One night, Pierre and I were awakened to help Pol with a calf that was being born. Surrounded by blood and dung, we pulled on a rope tied around the calf's hooves. We came away nauseated but with knowledge of the reproductive physiology of animals.

1 During World War I, Hoover, an engineer with a Quaker background who would later be President of the United States, played a decisive role in supplying food provisions to Belgian civilians and people from the occupied north of France in the framework of the Commission for Relief in Belgium.

Our life in Pol's house wasn't a picnic. The bed was broken down and oat barbs pierced the canvas of the straw mattress, scratching our tender skin. But each evening when we tiptoed across the main room of the house where Pol, Florence, and Clément snored away, we found on the "fire" – that is, the Flemish stove – two plates of "buttermilk," a kind of soup made with rice and whey, sour yet sweet, whose taste I have never forgotten. The poorest of all our hosts were the only ones who freely gave, not from a surplus of goods, but from what they themselves needed.

A long time later, after World War II, when Magda, Jispa,[2] and I went by car to see Pol and Florence, they had aged but were just as poor and just as generous. Despite our protests, they forced us to take home gifts of a kilo of sugar and coffee.

The other hosts were a lot less considerate. We did our homework at the Ségards' in a rather comfortable vestibule of the "chateau." Behind the Ségard home there was a pond. It was there, in April, for the first time in my life, that I discovered the wonders of spring. At the edge of the pond, I found a large tub for doing the laundry. By getting astride a washboard that I laid across the tub, I made myself a wobbly boat. I first propelled myself with my hands, then I made myself a paddle with a strong branch and a board nailed on each end. In this manner, I navigated the pond and daydreamed. Frogs were so numerous that the green water seemed thick with them. I watched them mate and lay their eggs; their ecstatic croaking ceased only with the thump of my paddle. Every day the sun climbed higher in the sky. The grass and the wheat, at first stunted and struggling to emerge from the hardened soil, suddenly assumed such vigor that the crust of the earth seemed to burst open from their thrusts. The woods and the embankments covered with bushes were in a festive mood; the birds, intoxicated with joy, celebrated with their music this marriage of the earth and the heavens. The more practical Marcel Trocquemé showed us the paths of the quadrupeds at the foot of the bushes and laid down traps in which we sometimes found a small rabbit.

2 "Jispa" was the Trocmé nickname for Alice Reynier (1894–1989), a teacher and later a member of the young Pomeyrol community. She came to help the Trocmé family at Christmas in 1942, when Magda was completely exhausted. She planned to stay for three months but never left. She moved to Geneva with André and Magda, and to Paris with Magda after André died. She gave herself the name Jispa which stood for "Joie de Servir dans la Paix et l'Amour" (The Joy of Serving in Peace and Love) to remind herself of her purpose in life. Nelly Trocmé-Hewett says that Jispa was her grandmother and the mother neither of her parents had. Her final days were spent with Magda.

Once, he even caught a wood pigeon with bluish feathers that was already dead and cold when we found it. As soon as the month of June came, we went swimming in the canal next to the water mill. (We had already learned how to swim in the Saint-Quentin canal.) The water was cold and the space limited, but the local kids and the village policeman came and watched us, exclaiming in their local accent: *"V'là, c'est comme ça qu'on nache"* (That's it; that's how you swim).

My religious preoccupations had not died out. Far from it. Papa began Sunday services in the Monier bistro, and other evacuated Protestants joined us. Often some Belgian Catholics showed up out of curiosity. But that wasn't enough for me. I got back together with three of my Unionist friends, Arthur Meunier and André and Maurice Delaporte, who were staying in a neighboring village, Saint-Pierre-Capelle. Along with them, Étienne, Marcel, and I resumed our Union meetings, thinking at first that nothing had changed. One day, I went with Arthur, André, and Maurice to visit some other "brothers" in a place called Deux-Acren, near Lessines, in a countryside known for its immense quarries of bluestone. We were received by a family of converts with whom we spent the day in prayer. Their name was Pévenage, and I'll talk more about them later.

On our return, after Arthur, André, and Maurice had left me in the dark of night, I had to cross a lonely wood. My footsteps echoed in the darkness. For the first time, I found myself alone in the country at night. I was afraid, so I sang at the top of my voice the hymns we had practiced earlier in the day. When I finally arrived at the Demulder home, everyone was asleep. I slipped in through the open window, got undressed, and stretched out, reassured and joyful, on the straw mattress where Pierre was already asleep.

Another time, we decided to go visit other members of the Union and Mr. Kaltenbach, who was living near Charleroi. It was impossible to go there by train: French evacuees had to get a special pass (which was always refused) to leave their place of residence. Pierre, Étienne, and I decided to go there on foot. It was a long way off: twenty-five miles or about eight hours' walk. That was hardly enough to quell our youthful spirit. We set off proudly and got to our destination in less than seven hours.

I found lodging with Hoche Bourlet, the future tavern owner with a sunken mouth, in the garret of a house owned by working-class people.

I still remember the bare, rectangular, curtainless window that opened onto a night of glowing steelworks. I recall the loud ticking of the big alarm clock and the jingling of its bell calling my friend to work. Hoche had become a miner, and he made us go down half a mile into tunnels so low that they scraped my vertebrae. We went to church in Marcinelle. In the afternoon, almost the entire Union got together with Mr. Kaltenbach. It was the last time we would do so. Fate would now separate us more completely.

When I look back on these months spent in Marcq, I realize to what extent they stripped away the petit bourgeois that I still was. It was like a cleansing bath, this plunge into the people, of whom I became a component just like everyone else because the barriers of money and prestige no longer stood between us.

Ever since then, I have aspired to return to that working-class milieu. The bourgeois, the pastor, the Protestant in France always lives among a few handpicked friends in a world of rarified air difficult to breathe. In Hoche Bourlet's attic, I could feel the complicated and laborious life of the workers pulsing all around me, and could believe myself one of them. I too could have gone down into the mine to earn my bread, and was ready to do so. I was not yet what one would call an intellectual; I was a member of the Union, that's all, and I could believe, pray, laugh, and feel like my worker friends.

When I tried to return nine years later, after education had made me sophisticated, it was too late. Neither the workers in Maubeuge, nor the peasants in Le Chambon ever took me for one of them, and I never found my Charleroi soul again.

My weeks of semi-liberty in Marcq, alas, were quickly over; my petit-bourgeois obligations, such as studying, soon took over. We discovered, to my dismay, that Mr. Marchand, my professor, was now living in Enghien! Three times a week, Étienne and I walked the two miles that separated us from Enghien to resume our preparation for the baccalaureate exam. A short time later though, I was alone; Louise, Étienne, Marcel Trocquemé, and Mr. Christol obtained passage on a German train that repatriated some evacuated people by way of Switzerland. The Germans were well aware of their diminishing food supplies and were ridding themselves of all "useless mouths." There was no way that Pierre, who was of military age, or I, who was almost at that age, could have taken advantage of that same convoy. Papa, Jeanne, and Marie stayed to watch over us, so five of us remained.

Our studies soon got us into a curious situation. One day, returning to Papa's house, I found him in a lively discussion with two priests.

"We learned of your presence here. We are French like you, Jesuits exiled in Belgium by the laws against religious congregations. Our superior sent us to see if you need anything."

"Thank you," my father replied stiffly. "We're managing just fine."

"We heard that you have two older boys ready to prepare for their French baccalaureate. The programs are so different that your sons won't get any help from the courses in Belgian schools. Although we don't have a teaching institution in Enghien, we would be happy to teach your sons. We would be happy to tutor them and do so free of charge."

"Gentlemen," responded Papa, "I must tell you that we are Protestant."

"We know, we know," they replied pleasantly, "but that makes no difference to us!"

"My children are young," Papa replied, "and might be influenced by a priest's knowledge." He suspected that the Jesuits wanted to convert his sons to Catholicism.

"Our superior asked us to let you know that the priests would be forbidden to raise religious questions with your sons."

"If that's the case," my father responded, "let your superior know that I accept his offer with gratitude."

That is how, on the three days of the week when I didn't go to Mr. Marchand's, I reported to the Jesuit monastery for classes in mathematics, physics, and chemistry.

Mathematics bored me terribly, but theology interested me greatly. I slyly distracted the attention of the priest teaching me at the blackboard in an empty classroom so I could lead him into a discussion of the Virgin Mary or the Mass!

One day, during our math lesson I asked the priest so many questions that he brusquely donned his three-cornered biretta with a pompon and said: "Young man, I have promised my superior never to discuss religion with you. I cannot answer your questions. If you are not willing to do math, I will have to leave." He then disappeared through the door, red with anger, leaving me shamefaced.

When he came back about ten minutes later, I obediently learned formulas.

Papa became friends with the Jesuit superior, a rather famous priest, Michel d'Herbigny, who was a favorite of the pope. After the war, he attempted a reconciliation between Rome and the Eastern Orthodox Church, which had been persecuted during the Russian Revolution. Father d'Herbigny showed Papa the chapel and the library that contained all the famous Protestant books. He seemed so liberal that Papa said to him: "I don't see any images in your church. You speak to me like a Protestant. Are the Jesuits Protestants without knowing it?"

"It's you, Mr. Trocmé, whom we consider a Catholic who doesn't know it because you never had the opportunity to know the truth. You therefore belong to the soul of the church. It is true that there is no salvation outside the Catholic Church. But you are part of the church without knowing it. You will be saved."

Papa came home exhilarated from these discussions.

Things gradually deteriorated with Mrs. Ségard, who was extremely superstitious. She forbade me to sail on her pond and even to go behind the house, because, she said, "one of my pigs died from a bloody fit. Who can prove to me that you, the Protestants, didn't put a hex on him?"

She left for two days on a pilgrimage to Saint Antoine to pray for the protection of the other pigs from our fatal influence. When we learned of the reason for her trip, we laughed a great deal about her folly, and Papa went back to see Father d'Herbigny. "How can it be," he asked the priest, "that you profess such a pure religion, yet you tolerate these superstitions?"

"It's absolutely true," responded the priest, "that Belgian Catholics are very superstitious, but that corresponds to their mindset. You don't want to deprive them abruptly of their traditions."

"I think I would do so," replied Papa.

"Ah, that's exactly where you Protestants are wrong," retorted the priest. "You take faith away from the people and replace it with abstract conceptions that are way beyond them. We need a religion for the people."

"But, after all," Papa replied, "what are you doing with the truth? If Jesus returned, he would once again chase all the merchants from the temple, all those who profit from popular superstition."

"Not at all, not at all," said the Jesuit. "He would understand everyone. Look how he welcomed Mary Magdalene, the repentant sinner. He let her anoint his feet with perfumes. He looked into her heart and found it full of love. Will God reject the candle that an old woman burns in front of a statue? We Jesuits know that the candle is superstitious, but the sincere sacrifice made by the woman goes directly to God's heart."

Papa came back indignant from this conversation: "So, there are several Catholicisms," he said, "and such a contradiction doesn't frighten the church in the least!"

After one particular incident, Papa's relations with the Jesuits cooled off for good. Marie Lécuyer, our faithful maid, had been married in Saint-Quentin. But her husband treated her disgracefully, and she left him three days after the wedding. Fortunately, she wasn't pregnant!

A young Belgian, Joseph, not knowing about her past, fell in love with her and asked her to marry him. He was a nice young man and Marie loved him greatly. As a good Catholic, she told him the truth.

At this time, the newspapers reported that the prince of a royal house had had his marriage annulled by the Sacra Rota, an ecclesiastical tribunal in Rome. Papa, who knew that d'Herbigny was a favorite of the pope, went to see him and explained Marie's situation.

"Can't one obtain an annulment," he asked, "for a marriage that only lasted three days when one of the parties behaved in a sadistic and shameful manner?"

"Let me look into it," said the priest. "Have Mrs. Lécuyer come see me in a week."

A week later, Marie returned home, her face puffy with anger and in tears. Marie was a sweet creature but not too bright. We were stunned to see her in this state. Here is what she told us:

"Was the marriage really consummated?" asked the priest.

"Yes, Father, but . . ."

"There are no 'buts.' If the marriage has been consummated, nothing, alas, can be done. I consulted all the canonical books."

"But," objected Marie, "that prince was married for several years, and his marriage was annulled!"

"I'm not familiar with the details of that case, Madam," said the priest, "but the Sacra Rota never grants annulments to marriages that have been normally consummated."

"But my marriage was abnormal! I'll pay, if necessary," replied Marie. "I'll give everything I've saved to do so. I love Joseph. My life's happiness is at stake."

"Madam, how can you insult the church by believing that money has any weight whatsoever in decisions made by the ecclesiastical tribunals?" replied the priest.

"In that case," Marie declared fittingly, "there's nothing more for me to do here." She got up to leave.

"Wait a minute, wait a minute," said the Jesuit. "Sit back down. The church is not as strict as you might think. There is a way out here."

"How?" begged Marie, still clinging to the hope of a solution.

"You can accept Joseph's marriage proposal, and after obtaining your civil divorce, marry him in a civil ceremony. As far as the church is concerned, you will not be legitimately married. But your confessor will understand your circumstances. He will be indulgent and welcome you among the faithful."

"But if I am not married in the church," replied Marie, "I am in a state of mortal sin and I can't receive absolution or go to communion."

"Naturally. Of course you can't go to communion."

"But I really want to go to communion," said Marie, "and what will happen on my deathbed? I will die in a state of mortal sin, and I will be refused extreme unction!"

"Not at all," replied the Jesuit. "Here's what you should do. When you call the priest, tell your husband, I mean your partner, 'Go away; go into the other room, or better still, leave the house.' This way, you can tell the priest that you have broken with your partner, and he can give you absolution and extreme unction."

"What?" said Marie. "I should confess as a sin living with the husband I love, to whom I will have given everything, and who will have given me his all? And buy my absolution at the price of a lie?"

"There is no other solution," replied Father Michel d'Herbigny.

When she returned home, Marie said: "I am a better Catholic than he is."

The next day, renouncing her love, she explained the cause of their break-up to Joseph. They both wept a great deal.

On Sundays, she went to Mass often.

Until the end of Papa's life, she served him faithfully. Without complaining, she remained a good Catholic and a good housekeeper. She died of lung cancer after World War II.

Gallant Marie!

IN AUGUST, WHAT WAS LEFT of the Trocmé tribe emigrated to Brussels.

Two or three times, Papa was able to get passes from the Germans for the capital, where he contacted former clients who loaned him money. We were no longer so poor. Moreover, thanks to a distant cousin, Mrs.

Hilgenstock, and to the Saint-Quentin actress, Mrs. Rooman, Papa established relations with a highly placed official in the Royal Court of Belgium, a Mr. Mahillon, who found us a house!

The house was situated in a suburb of Brussels, Schaerbeek, on the beautiful Avenue Voltaire. It belonged to a Belgian stockbroker, Mr. Bracke, who had remained in Paris after fleeing from the 1914 invasion. Mr. Mahillon was happy to house "refugees" to avoid having the house requisitioned and pillaged by the Germans.

I still remember when we moved in and the strange impression we had of entering the home of a family that had only left the day before. Jeanne and Marie came upon the clothing of the two Bracke girls in the closet, and we began to mock their low-cut silk dresses, so different from the drab, austere clothing the Trocmé women normally wore. Only Papa's authority was able to stop us from touching all these things that didn't belong to us. I think that Mrs. Bracke and her daughters, who came back home in 1918, at the time of short, flounced dresses, must have had a good laugh when they found their tight-fitting, out-of-style sheaths from 1914 that went all the way down to their ankles.

We reestablished our Saint-Quentin habits in Brussels: the lycée, which was called l'Athénée de Schaerbeek, and mandatory walks, on which we were forbidden to go to the center of the city or far away to the country. I played "right, right; left, left" with Pierre: after picking a starting point randomly, we turned at every street corner, twice to the right, then twice to the left. This led us into unexpected places and provided meager amusement for pedestrians forced to take walks.

Cousin Hilgenstock, wanting to please us, invited us to a chic club in town and offered us her sons' flannel clothing, tennis shoes, and rackets. We rejected her offer, thinking it would be ridiculous to play Romeo with the young women of Brussels. I sometimes think of what might have happened to me had I accepted. I would have learned how to speak to girls. I might have fallen in love. I might have learned to dance. Papa, judging that we were capable of distinguishing between right and wrong at our age, was not against this. It was Pierre and I who declared we were not going. I was a member of the Union Chrétienne des Jeunes Gens and considered these frivolities sins.

On Sundays, I went to the Union in Brussels on Ernest-Allard Street, in a beautiful space with an auditorium that in no way resembled the shabby upper room in the Saint-Quentin church. On the first day, I nearly choked with astonishment: around a long oval table covered with a green tablecloth sat about twenty fellows. The youngest were around twenty-five, while the oldest, Mr. Buyssens and Mr. Boeykens, were in their fifties and cheerfully sported beards. There was also the secretary-general, Mr. Van Duynen, a bad-tempered fellow who spoke through his nose and smelled of garlic.

My zeal was immediately obvious, and I was put in charge of a scout troop. That provided me boisterous and exhausting Sunday afternoons with lots of scolding from Mr. Van Duynen, who didn't like us to make noise. In the spring, we went camping and swimming in the ponds in Haren. They were former sand quarries filled with water, whose shores were strewn with human excrement that we had to clean up with a shovel before we could set up our tents. We didn't wear uniforms; it was forbidden by the Germans.

On Sundays when the Union was not open, Pierre and I took walks. Papa gave us a few francs a week for pocket money, which allowed us to go to museums and take the streetcars. To supplement this money, I collected old corks that I found in the ditches along the streets. The thrift shop owners paid a good price for them: a penny a piece. It was wartime, and cork oaks didn't grow in Belgium.

On Sunday evenings, we were invited by the Wagners, the family of a French banker. Papa and Mr. Wagner would talk; we remained silent, as young boys should around their father.

At l'Athénée de Schaerbeek, I was a good student, especially in the humanities. My professor, nicknamed "Jesus Christ" because of his red beard, resembled the self-portraits of Van Gogh. He was a sophisticated person, and in his classes I began to appreciate classical literature more than I ever had with Mr. Marchand. My rival was a fellow from Brussels named De Geynst who had an Egyptian profile, was somewhat dissolute, and made fun of my prudish reserve. Today, he is a journalist who writes for *Le Soir* in Brussels. The superintendent, a jaundiced, irritable, and unhappy guy, was nicknamed "Piss and Vinegar." I'm afraid I told my sons this once, and they might have applied this same nickname to a certain professor at the Lycée de Versailles thirty-five years later.

Since Pierre had earned his baccalaureate, he went to the Lycée d'Ixelles, where he took special classes in science. He had already decided to study medicine. Neither he nor I enjoyed the pugnacious vulgarity of the Belgians. It was hard to believe that all these boys, aged sixteen to twenty, had had the adventures with women that they related – or had eaten so many delicious things and drunk so many strong beers.

Our menu at home was austere. We were reduced to eating official rations. However, Pierre and I often went to the country to buy potatoes and wheat, which we ground in the coffee grinder. The trick was to avoid getting caught by the German police who searched passengers on the streetcars from the suburbs. I remember an enormous woman who descended quickly from one end of the streetcar just as the Germans entered at the other end. Somehow, she punctured the sack of potatoes that had provided her with a false rump under her skirt. She escaped into the street, dropping her potatoes and becoming thinner, while the Germans laughed and forgot about arresting her.

Papa had made a cardboard box with five sections: 360°÷ 5 = 72°. He applied that to the coarse cake Jeanne baked with our ground wheat. Papa had a mathematical sense of justice, and the least injustice gave rise to fights between us.

One day, I got diphtheria. Looking at my throat that morning, Papa said to me: "Does your throat hurt? Spit out the mucus in the back of your throat. How can I tell if your throat is red or not!" And he sent me to school. "Come on, come on, don't act so lazy."

In the middle of that morning, I came down with a terrible fever and dizziness. I asked to return home. It normally took me twenty-five minutes to get home from school. That day it took me two hours. I sat down on the steps of houses when I could no longer see clearly. When I arrived home, Papa finally panicked. The doctor, who made an emergency visit, told us that I had a serious case of diphtheria with signs of poisoning. Fortunately, there were a few vials of serum at the Pasteur Institute in Brussels. Otherwise, I would have left this earth in 1918! Perhaps it's because of this sickness that I sometimes drag my leg behind me when walking.

In the spring of 1918, the Germans ran out of energy trying to break through the Allied front. Twice, they succeeded in doing so, but they were exhausted, and twice, the gap was closed again. On one occasion, near Montdidier, Robert was there. His soldiers panicked and began to flee, but he got them together and had them do rifle drills until reinforcements arrived and the situation turned around.

Beginning in July, General Foch's famous offensive overthrew the Germans, who slowly retreated. In November, they were defeated on the

Belgian border, and we perceived signs of disorder in the troops crossing Brussels. But nothing made us suspect what was in store.

One Sunday, as usual, I walked to the Union. As I was passing the square called Le Petit Sablon, I witnessed an incredible event: a hundred, no, a thousand voices were singing "La Marseillaise"! It was coming from the lower part of the city and was getting closer and closer. I stopped and saw German soldiers emerge, eight abreast, in close ranks. In the first row, one of them held an enormous red flag, to his right, there was a French flag, to his left a Belgian flag. They were the ones who were singing the old revolutionary song in a heavily accented German.

What in the world was going on? At the sound of their voices, the windows opened. People leaned out of their windows and cried out. As if by magic, huge black, yellow, and red Belgian flags draped the balconies. A woman came out and added her splendid voice to that of the Germans, who applauded her enthusiastically. I forgot all about my Union and began to follow the group, which now numbered several thousand. They marched to the ministerial building, the seat of the German government in Belgium, and occupied it without firing a shot. It was Sunday, and all the offices were empty!

Soldiers and sailors appeared on the main balcony. Below, thousands of soldiers and some civilians had gathered.

A sailor began to shout out a speech. He announced sensational news: the German Kaiser had fled; the Republic of Soldiers and Workers had been proclaimed. He stopped every twenty words or so to wait for applause. "Hurrah, Hurrah, Hurrah," the soldiers cheered three times and not more, exactly as I had heard them on the "Champs-Elysées" in Saint-Quentin when the Kaiser visited. Then a civilian announced the coming end of hostilities because Germany had asked for an armistice and proclaimed the end of censorship and the reconciliation of all nations committed to freeing themselves from the bloody tyrants and capitalists who exploited them and set them against one another.

I had witnessed a revolution! It was one of those great historical events that changed the destiny of nations. I returned home out of breath and related what I had seen. Papa couldn't believe his ears. The divine punishment that he had so often demanded for the Germans was now being meted out.

Pierre and I went back down into town after dinner. The famous Grand'Place of Brussels was boiling like a kettle. Orchestras were playing at the tops of staircases. Germans, with stripes, ranks, and decorations torn off their uniforms, sported red rosettes and danced with Belgian girls. Everyone was embracing.

School was out the next day and for several days. Pierre and I walked from street to street observing astonishing scenes. Coming from their villas in the suburbs, the German officers, who didn't know about or had misunderstood the events of the day before, came as usual to work in the government offices. As they got off the streetcars, they were approached by picket lines of soldiers wearing red rosettes, who saluted them and explained the revolution to them: "The Kaiser has fled (he escaped to Holland). The Republic of Workers and Soldiers has been proclaimed. Kindly hand over your regalia. We represent the new government." Meekly, most of the officers did as they were told. They ripped off their Iron Crosses, their decorations for "meritorious duty," their stripes, and their epaulets and gave them to the soldiers who pinned a red rosette on their chests. This was an extraordinary scene for those who remembered the insolence of the German officers in the imperial army with their monocles and corsets that made their waists thinner.

Only one of them rebelled. He listened to the end of the revolutionaries' sales pitch, turned pale, took a few steps forward, made a menacing gesture with his riding crop, and proclaimed, "I recognize only one government – the kingdom of my leader, the Kaiser, and King William II. Get out of my way! Step back!" Far from jumping on top of him, the revolutionaries came to order, stood at attention, clicked their heels, and saluted him. He walked away quickly. What a strange morning! Frenchmen in their place might have gotten drunk and lynched the rebel.

DURING THE FOLLOWING DAYS, things degenerated. Some of the revolutionaries got their hands on trucks and went hunting for "reactionaries" in the streets of Brussels. One day, Pierre and I almost walked into a series of machine-gun bursts in a street and barely had time to throw ourselves into the doorway of a carriage entrance.

From that day onward, the Germans began to beat their retreat in large, undisciplined waves without provisions, pillaging in order to eat or selling weapons for bread. They blew up trains full of provisions in the Haren train station. The famished population rushed in to loot the trains. Many were killed by the explosions, but the lure of plundering won out over the fear of death.

One day, amid a great assembly in town, Pierre and I saw two motorcyclists whom everyone was cheering and embracing. They were French. The armistice had been signed, and they had broken through the permeable German lines and pushed on as far as Brussels – the first swallows of spring! In the crowd, a scruffy German with a flat cap and a woman hanging on his arm looked on. A week earlier, these men would have been killing one another.

I said earlier that we had an exceptional protector. Mrs. Rooman was originally from Saint-Quentin, the daughter of two modest shopkeepers. But she didn't share her parents' simple tastes. When she was young, she left to act in the theater in Paris. Her career eventually took her to Belgium. She was no longer very young nor very pretty when we got to know her. She had married a Mr. Rooman, a tall, fat, bearded, and talkative guy from Anvers who was the General Secretary of the Belgian Society for Authors and Composers of Music. With great verbosity, he related fantastic tales in which he always played the starring role. His wife corrected him gently and then spoke about all the adorable, marvelous, generous, and delightful people she had known, including King Albert and Queen Elizabeth.

The Roomans lived in a beautiful Flemish-style home on the edge of the Cambre Woods, the chic section of Brussels. They often invited us to dinner, and it was always with great demonstrations of friendship, offers to help, and an extraordinary culinary display. Even Papa seemed dazed and amused, so much so that he, who normally dominated the discussion, often appeared timid before the fireworks of the Rooman couple.

During our meals, they gave us very good wines. In Saint-Quentin, we were forbidden to sip a glass of wine before the age of fifteen. Papa would put an ounce or so into a glass and then dilute it with water. During the war, he had to do without it, as did we. As a result, our first contact with wine took place in the Roomans' home. A server leaned toward us and murmured the magic formula: "Saint-Emilion 1912," and at dessert: "Château Latour Blanc." All this made me and Pierre laugh. Nonetheless, when we were leaving the Rooman house one evening, I had the strange impression that the ground was elastic under my feet. I didn't say anything to anyone, but the next time we were there, I categorically refused the wine they offered. My experience with tobacco lasted just about as long as my experience with wine. I have since abstained from both and never regretted it.

I bring up the Roomans because, at the time of the liberation, they were the ones who organized a reception in honor of Robert.

Robert arrived home one day out of the blue in November 1918, and it was as if he had never left. Yet he was thin, sallow, exhausted, and hardly recovered from two machine-gun bullets that had cut through his chest and his arm. He remained short of breath. That evening, when he undressed, he showed us his scars. They were hardly visible in the front, but in his back he had a nasty hole, which indicated the seriousness of his wound. He was tall, thin, and upright. In his captain's uniform studded with decorations, he was incredibly handsome. We were proud to go out with him on the streets of Brussels.

Alas, these streets didn't offer a gratifying spectacle. Around November 25, the king and the queen, mounted on white horses and followed by Belgian, English, and French troops, crossed the city. The French looked strange. We remembered them in their caps, navy-blue tunics, and red pants. Now they appeared in helmets, completely dressed in sky-blue, including their leggings. We cheered the parade and cried when we saw the flags that had liberated us. Unconsciously, I connected this parade with Jesus's entrance into Jerusalem and the cries of "Hosanna." My religiosity had idealized France, the country of chivalry, nobility, and virtue.

That same evening, I went back down to the Grand'Place to join the public jubilation. But a horrible spectacle awaited me. Instead of noble, patriotic ceremonies (there were, of course, several renditions of "La Marseillaise," "La Brabançonne," and "Le Chant du départ"), I met an overflow of vulgar pleasures. The Belgians had taken out of their wine cellars all the good bottles they had hidden from the Germans. Everyone – men, women, Belgian, French, and English soldiers – was hyperexcited and drunk. I fled. Passing the Gare du Nord, where several days before I had seen German soldiers making out with women of the night near shady hotels, I now saw the same establishments under siege by soldiers – French for the most part – indulging in the same orgies with women who had passed from the arms of the Germans into those of the French. At seventeen, I still had no idea of what debauchery was, nor did I know what diversions World War I infantrymen engaged in between their brushes with death and their return to the heat of battle. Nothing could have allowed me to feel sympathy for these men who, coming out of a nightmare alive, tried to forget – through wine or in the arms of the first woman they met – the horrible fear that had possessed them for four years and four months.

I had imagined beforehand that liberation would be like heaven, but it was hell on earth. I have not yet gotten over this disappointment. I have always tended to believe that there is a better world somewhere else on this earth (Germany during my childhood, Free France from ages fourteen to eighteen, England when I discovered the Fellowship of Reconciliation, America, where I lived during the time of Prohibition), while at the same time knowing that I was deluding myself. Each time I discover the truth, as I do today at age fifty-four faced with an America that can't hide its materialism, debauchery, and militarism, I experience the same disappointment I did that evening on the streets of liberated Brussels.

Mrs. Rooman lived in her artistic dreamworld and made Robert's reception unforgettable. We had been waiting a while in the Gothic dining room of her house, standing near a massive table loaded with food, when she appeared on a kind of elevated stage at one end of the room. She was draped in a dress with a red, white, and blue train and wore stage makeup. Extending her arms toward a stunned Robert, she exclaimed in passionate tones, "I salute you, Monsieur France!" and recited patriotic verses from an author we didn't know. Then, with a gait worthy of a sovereign, she solemnly descended the few steps that separated her from us and gave Robert a long embrace. She wept with heartfelt tears and embraced each of us in turn.

A few days earlier, I probably would have been deeply moved by this ceremony. But with the disappointment I carried in my heart, I experienced it more as an embarrassment, almost ashamed. It seemed false, hypocritical, misplaced. Ever since, during official ceremonies where pomp and disingenuous speeches combine, I have had similar reactions.

5

School of Theology

AFTER ROBERT LEFT, we hurried to return to France. Saint-Quentin was in ruins. Robert advised Papa to settle in Paris temporarily so I could prepare for the first part of my baccalaureate exam, which was on hold and becoming more urgent. Special classes were being held for students from the "liberated regions," as they called us.

Transportation was impossible: there were few surviving railroads or roads. It wasn't until December 11 that we secured a place on the first train from Brussels to Paris. It passed through Zeebrugge, Dunkirk, Calais, and Amiens, an interminable voyage of about fifteen hours that crossed bleak regions ravaged by the war.

Louise awaited us. She had rented a furnished apartment for the family in Judlin Square, near the Champs de Mars and the Cambronne metro station. The square was a somber dead end. The apartment was cramped but equipped with "modern conveniences." I unpacked my treasures and washed the shell base that I had picked up in Saint-Quentin. I dropped it and made a hole in a porcelain basin, earning a terrible scolding. What a singular beginning to our stay in Paris! Alas, the classes for students from the liberated regions had started a few days earlier, leaving me no other option but to begin my studies for the baccalaureate all over again for the third time.

I left every morning on foot for the Lycée Buffon, a mile from our home. It was the first time I had lived in a big city. The elevated metro, lots of cars, the great Babel of soldiers of all colors and nationalities being demobilized – all this intoxicated me. I was seventeen years old, tall, and heavy. A photograph from that time depicts me with angular and thick features, stuffed into a too-tight blue jacket cut from a lycée cape dating back to the prewar years in Saint-Quentin.

My comrades were all younger. In the courtyards of the lycée, they engaged in endless, noisy soccer games. They had seen nothing of the war and hadn't suffered. When I tried to speak to them about my experiences, of the tragedy of losing everything, suffering from hunger, and living under frequent bombings, they responded without even listening: "Where we lived, it was much worse!" Each of them then launched into a boasting session that quickly turned me off. I decided not to speak about the war anymore. I was dealing with children.

Two professors did me a world of good. The humanities professor, a strange guy whose name I have forgotten, had a goatee, an eternal cold, and a running nose, and wore a knitted red scarf around his neck. But when he spoke about Jean-Jacques Rousseau or the Romantics, the magic of his words fascinated us. I got good grades in his classes, and that encouraged me. There was also Mr. Sauvage, a disheveled, red-haired English teacher. He had been in the war and had come out of it disgusted with violence, a real revolutionary. His passionate words resonated deeply in me.

Papa had principles. On Sunday morning, we went to services in a small church in the fourteenth arrondissement, called Plaisance, because Papa had a prejudice against those "*messieurs de Paris*." Papa, who had seemed so bourgeois in Saint-Quentin, didn't like the big bankers of the churches on the Right Bank whom he had met at church congresses.

The pastor, Mr. Édouard Sautter, was a very active, bearded, eloquent man overflowing with affection. He was one of those rare pastors truly loved by their parishioners. He connected me with the Unionists of Plaisance. That's how I ended up for the first time in two years among young people I liked. The president, a tall boy named Vassaux, was honest and loquacious and had a hollow chest and a face marked with acne. There was also Avouac, a typical Parisian street urchin with a protruding chin, who was subject to fits of enthusiasm followed by somber periods of discouragement. I never accepted any official position at the Plaisance Union, but I successfully brought them the "Saint-Quentin message." We had meetings with fervent prayers and ardent and sincere hymns. We spoke a lot about purity, perhaps a bit too much.

I recall coming home alone from the Union late on Sunday evenings along the Boulevard Pasteur. Celebrations were in full swing under the metro overpass: shooting galleries, carrousels, freak shows, lottery wheels. Guys my age were hugging shop girls or seamstresses, who let out cascades of laughter. Girls came up to me. I walked quickly, my neck stiff, without stopping, confusing pure vice and innocent amusements in fear and equal condemnation.

Papa told us: "I know that I can have confidence in you now." How right he was! Life was pure in church, at the Union, and on our outings in the Meudon woods, but dark in the movies, at the circus, and in houses of prostitution. In any event, the great, dissolute Babylon had not rubbed off on me.

On Sundays when we had no Union, I went with the whole family to Aunt Pauline and Aunt Alice's. I've described these gloomy family get-togethers already, encounters where the youngest owed everything to the oldest and the oldest owed them nothing except a cup of tea and some cookies. But this was part of our family rituals. In the aunts' living room, the assembled family criticized – without being unkind of course – all those "good" boys and girls who were not in the family's direct line. When the original and whimsical Henri des Roches's family was absent, they were hung out to dry like anybody else. Woe to those who were only second or third cousins! They were all either "characters" or "failures." Let's not even talk about those who were not related to us. They didn't exist. If we discussed the pastors, look out! They were in for a world of hurt! The "excellent" Henri Monnier, the "unrealistic" Wilfred Monod, the "hothead," Henry Dartigue, etc. I have no idea what the relationship was between these conversations and the morning church services. One day, I blew up and left, slamming the door, because Aunt Pauline expressed her astonishment that "those women without hats, those working girls, now dared to buy chicken." My visits to the aunts became less frequent, and the family classified me as a fanatic, a socialist.

At the end of the 1918–19 school year, I took and passed the first part of my baccalaureate. This was the regular exam, not the watered-down one given to those from the liberated regions. I didn't perform brilliantly and did not receive honors. The strangest thing was that I almost failed the oral exam in one of my strongest subjects: English!

The examiner measured the strapping guy I was and said to me: "During the war, you frequently encountered English and American soldiers. They told you about their experiences in the trenches. Tell me about your conversations with them." Timid and tongue-tied as I still was at the time, I didn't dare say that, on the contrary, I had encountered

Kindler, several other German soldiers, my German cousins, and the deaconesses. I stammered out a couple of sentences, then came up short and began to cry. At eighteen years of age, I had absolutely no idea how to say the English words "trench," "rifle," "cannon," "cartridge," "crater," or "tank."

Furious at first, the professor chastised me: "If you don't know English, what are you doing here? What have you been doing in class?" I managed to say: "David Copperfield." With a groan, he showed me a page and made me read and translate it. While reading, I got my confidence back, and I translated satisfactorily. "How is it," the examiner asked me, "that you don't know spoken English?" I told him that I came from the liberated regions, and we left on pretty good terms.

This was the last incident caused by my incredible timidity. A comrade helped me get over it: Jacques Diény.

At the Lycée Buffon, I had two friends, one named Zuber, the other Dieterlen, who got me involved with the Fédé Lycéenne (Federation of Protestant lycée students). Dieterlen, or Diény, was a slight, nervous fellow with dazzling eyes and glasses, motivated by a limitless religious enthusiasm. He was brilliant, and his head swarmed with prophetic visions and grandiose plans. In him, I recognized a more disinterested and cultivated Robert Jospin.

One day our Fédé group met, and I gave the *laïus* or introduction (the Fédé was crazy about slang). I spoke about "How to Use Vacation Time" and, as I generally did, I tried to say things clearly and simply (advice tirelessly repeated by Papa, for which I am grateful). Diény, like a jack-in-the-box, moved about in his chair, his cheeks on fire. I stuttered from time to time, fearing I would be rebuffed.

When I finished, Diény opened the discussion. When we were leaving, he took me aside: "Hey, your thing was so good," he said, "I need it for *Notre Revue*."

Notre Revue![1] I have kept a few yellowed copies of it. It's a thin review, about sixteen pages per issue, for Christian high-school students, directed by Fédé general secretary Albert Meyer, nicknamed the "High Priest." He signed his columns Coco Cocovitch, and we admired that. For me, *Notre Revue* was the Holy of Holies in which only VIPs had a right to publish. I have always instinctively believed, and still do, in the importance of a "group of leaders." It was only slowly, very slowly, that I came to understand

1 Founded in 1910, *Notre Revue* later combined with *Le Semeur*.

that these groups of leaders are like everyone else. The only difference is that these groups are composed of, at best, willing, hard workers who understand their responsibilities; at worst, ambitious men who know how to hide their ambition behind a façade of disinterested activity. Perhaps the very worst are men who say yes to everyone and never make any compromising decisions for fear of making someone unhappy.

In short, my article appeared in *Notre Revue*, and I was filled with astonishment and pride, whose sweet taste I can still savor. So, I wasn't a dumbbell after all. Our leader Diény had encouraged me.

More astonishment followed. Diény warmly invited me to go with him to Camp Domino. This really made Papa happy. He had already sent Pierre to Domino in 1914. It was an inexpensive vacation and did us a world of good. With the help of the war, Papa had slightly broadened his horizons: he now allowed us to sleep in tents. Furthermore, at Domino, the supervision was excellent.

Camp Domino was on the Île d'Oléron, off the west coast of France near La Rochelle. It sat between wide dunes and small white farms on two acres of sand. A long, low warehouse served as kitchen and refectory. In the small pine woods were a dozen conical tents called "marabouts." Imagine the young refugee from Saint-Quentin who always wore a tie and high, laced-up shoes. I remember the first pair of low shoes I ever bought, and the guilt I felt for such frivolity. At Domino, we walked around half-naked, in bathing trunks, and got sunburned. We engaged in uproarious behavior. We were in contact with the VIPs, or, as we called them, The Oils (because they rose to the top): curates who played basketball with us, poets and writers, camp officials and preachers. Then there was Jacques Babut with the hairy chest. On the day the director imposed a fine of one franc to be given to the missions on anyone who said a swear word, Babut made us cry out together at lunch a resounding "*Merde!*," which brought in 90 francs for the missions. The fun and scandal were such that for the rest of our stay, we said "m—ission" every time we wanted to swear. It cost us nothing and meant what we wanted to say.

Also at Domino were André Nick and his brother, Pierre. We had literary and theological coteries. Above all, I remember Albert Léo, a man with deep eyes and an eagle's profile who, during our services held on the dunes, gave us talks about "Jesus the Man" that I have never forgotten.

We engaged in scout-like maneuvers, which also took place on the dunes, with their small mountains of sand and deep valleys that facilitated crawling. Finally, there was bathing in the ocean that rolled over us in huge waves along the beach. Only the best swimmers crossed the sandbar; it knocked the others down. At low tide, we collected small oysters from the rocks. At sunset, we prolonged our evenings with song, beginning with "Le Chameau," "Gentille Batelière," and "Les Crapauds," and ending with the Psalms and a prayer.

For the first time in my life, I was learning to have a good time.

It was at Domino that Diény said to me: "Hey, Troc, next year I'm leaving for my military service. I'm counting on you to replace me as regional leader of the Fédé and at the Union in Clamart." To be honest, the Union in Clamart wasn't much, only seven or eight boys between the ages of sixteen and eighteen who got together in the sacristy of a tiny church in the south Parisian suburbs. Diény had such a strong influence on me that I accepted without hesitation. Furthermore, I was proud of these sudden promotions. Just a few months earlier, I had still considered myself completely inept.

In September, when I came back from Domino, I found that my family had relocated. Papa had bought some furniture and rented a fourth-floor apartment at 30 Rue Jacob in the middle of the Latin Quarter. The apartment had low ceilings, and the rooms were arranged one behind another without any hallway. Louise and Yvonne, now back with us, had to pass through Pierre, Étienne, and my bedroom to get to the salon/dining room. At the other end, Papa had to go through Robert's bedroom to get to the salon. It was also through Robert's bedroom that Jeanne and Marie, who slept in a bedroom overlooking the courtyard, brought the plates for our meals!

Despite the lack of comfort, the apartment on Rue Jacob left me with warm memories. I had finally broken out of my shell, going from one extreme to the other. In 1919–20, I was accepted, exceptionally, into the first year of theological studies (Greek, Hebrew, etc.) at the School of Theology of the Sorbonne without having completed the second part of my baccalaureate, which I was still preparing for by taking a philosophy course (logic, morals, and psychology) at the famous École Alsacienne. At home, I studied the other subjects (natural history, cosmography, German, and English) on my own. At the same time, I was the regional leader of the Fédé for the Parisian region (with visits to Rouen and Le Havre) and was charged with finding a meeting place for the Union in Clamart.

In July, I got the mumps two days before my baccalaureate exam and stayed in bed because of complications. But I passed the exam in October, with honors in philosophy. In 1920–1921, I dropped the presidency of the Fédé and resumed a more moderate and sensible life.

Let's take a more detailed look at this decisive year.

The room I shared with Pierre and Étienne afforded a view of Rue Jacob. This narrow and picturesque street was not lined, as it is today, with antique dealers. It still echoed with the cries of the street merchants: glaziers, rag dealers, scrap-metal vendors. On the corner of Rue Bonaparte, a strange shop exhibited the handmade fabrics of Raymond Duncan, the brother of the famous dancer Isadora Duncan.[2] He dressed in ancient Greek fashion, encircled his forehead with a golden band, and conversed with his admirers around a loom we could see from the outside. He had a handsome face and a short beard, only one of the hundred or so eccentrics of the Latin Quarter in those days. Its streets resonated with the poetry of the Dada Movement recited by Adonis-like youths in pants that billowed at the knees and narrowed at the ankles. Once a year, for a week, the Quarter was filled with the "Four Arts Ball." The School of Fine Arts was only a few hundred yards away on Rue Bonaparte. Until eight in the morning, drunken students and half-dressed girls filled our street with noise. Then the police came to remove the stragglers.

If we turned to the right on Rue Bonaparte, we soon came to the quays of the Seine across from the Louvre, right where the *bouquinistes* (booksellers) sold their wares from stalls anchored to the walls lining the river. I liked that. Once, for five francs, I bought a seventeenth-century Bible, annotated by a persecuted Huguenot. Another time, I bought an old map of Paris from before the Revolution and before Baron Haussmann.

When we went up Rue Jacob, we found ourselves at the picturesque Bucy intersection, where Jeanne and Marie did their shopping. Still further, we emerged onto narrow streets leading toward the French Institute or Saint-Séverin church. From there, we came to Rue Lagrange, where my brother Francis and his family lived. My customary route, however, led me to the École Alsacienne and the School of Theology. I covered this route on an old bicycle to avoid the cost of the metro. The streets at this

2 Isadora Duncan (1877–1927) was one of the creators of modern dance. Her brother, Raymond Duncan (1874–1966), was a philosopher and a poet.

time on the Left Bank were hardly dangerous, and I loved the lightning speeds I could get to by standing on my pedals, then braking to slow my pace to that of the cars around me.

I went to the Sorbonne by way of Saint-Germain-des-Prés for my classes in Hebrew and Church History. Crossing Saint-Germain amid the crowd of exotic students, I examined the displays in the bookstore windows, without ever buying anything.

In our room, crowded together, Pierre, Étienne, and I worked at the same table covered with a green cloth. Pierre, in his first year of medical school, studied anatomy. Étienne, at the School of Public Works, studied electricity and chemistry. In my preparatory year of theology, I worked on philosophy, Greek, and Hebrew. We spoke very little and never argued. Pierre was the most focused, Étienne the most complaining, and I the most irregular because, depending on the needs of the moment, I went through successive phases of intense study or outside activities.

At the École Alsacienne, I took Mr. Péquignat's classes. A mediocre philosopher but an excellent teacher, he delivered admirable summaries that helped me pass my baccalaureate exam. At the School of Theology, my professors were Henri Monnier, a talented orator who paraded before us all the church's successive dogmas without ever revealing his own beliefs, and Wilfred Monod, who used one metaphor after another to pose the question of goodness as he touched lightly on practical theology. Finally, Maurice Goguel methodically shredded the New Testament texts by employing the infallible methods of textual and extratextual criticism.

At the Sorbonne's École des Hautes Études Religieuses, we had Adolphe Lods, who was incredibly knowledgeable in Hebrew and merciless on exams. His monumental work and historical reconstructions commanded our respect. We also had Eugène de Faye, a tormented man, who read the Church Fathers fluently, especially Origen of Alexandria. He had lost his son Alexander in the war and lived in constant suffering. Through him, I learned to hate war. I also learned that the first Christians suffered persecution because they refused to serve the Roman Empire, bear weapons, or offer libations to Caesar.

I often remained at school for lunch and became familiar with the pitiful dining hall that smelled so sour. On special days, they served us half an artichoke each because provisions were still meager in the wake of the war.

Some of my comrades were much older than I, since the war had interrupted their studies. Between classes, in the halls, they discussed knowingly and passionately the consequences of the horrors they had lived through on the frontlines. They spoke of Charles Grauss, a former Fédé leader who was killed in battle, and of the Protestant author Henri Barbusse. They cited the famous authors Charles Péguy and André Gide, and professed social and political radicalism that was entirely new to me, still the silent novice who simply listened.

There was also the postwar generation, as well as the Chéradame brothers, Robert and Daniel, whose vocations were born on the frontlines. They constituted the "Northern Group," a team that advocated "social Christianity" and spoke a lot about evangelizing workers. Their hero was Henri Nick, the "saint of Fives-Lille." I was admitted as one of the youngest members of the Northern Group by Diény. I presented a study on the "eighteen times the North was invaded," which forced me to spend long hours in the Sainte-Geneviève Library. Between my morning and afternoon classes, we dropped in at Diény's house, my home away from home. At five o'clock, we went to one or the other's room, got down on our knees, and prayed fervently.

In 1919, after the war, there were violent strikes that rocked Paris, hyped by public opinion and provoked by the Chambre Bleu Horizon, a right-wing, military movement, and the candidacy of Georges Clemenceau to the presidency of the Republic. He was defeated.

The Sorbonne theological school was simmering. Dallière and Diény sported wide, red woolen belts. In the courtyard, students sang "The Internationale," and the voices of the prisoners of the adjacent Santé Prison joined those of the future pastors. The police felt obligated to intervene and take down the red Communist flag that a zealous student had floated on the roof of the old and peaceful Sorbonne.

One day, a short English fellow with a soft voice came to see the students. About twenty of us gathered around him. Roser, a student at the Maison des Missions, was there. Oliver Dryer[3] spoke simply: "Some of us have discovered that it's possible to live the Gospel of Jesus Christ. We can love our brothers and sisters. That's why Jesus came down to earth. Many of us have gone to prison rather than kill in the war. The International Fellowship of Reconciliation has just been

3 Oliver Dryer would serve as Secretary General of the International Fellowship of Reconciliation from 1921 to 1928.

founded in Bilthoven in Holland. There will be a second meeting in Nyborg in Denmark."

"This is true Christian radicalism," I told myself as I listened. I thought of Kindler and of my own 1917 epiphany that I had somewhat forgotten in the giddiness of the liberation. The "left-wing ideology" of my classmates still frightened me, but I had been born again. I was on my way and could no longer stop.

A few months later, I learned that Roser, whom I knew only casually, had sent back his military papers and been relieved of his post as reserve officer. The Maison des Missions also felt obligated to reject him as a candidate for the missions. Most of my classmates at the theological school were traditionalists and spoke out strongly against him. They disapproved of Roser and heartily condemned conscientious objection. I still see myself, somewhat scandalized, trying to discern in this much too heated debate what was true and solidly based in Christianity.

Alas, what remains today of all that idealism?

Robert Chéradame, Deschamps, Ducros, Diény, and Babut have all repudiated their pacifism, not vociferously but in roundabout ways. Dallière and Morel became Pentecostals and fell for an extreme mysticism that they haven't yet recovered from. Cornier and Heuzé died.[4] Those who didn't become important in the ecclesiastical hierarchy became ministers in well-known parishes. Apparently, a whole generation went through turmoil for nothing. Their extremism transformed itself into revivalism, then for some into Pentecostalism, which developed into Barthian intellectualism, which in turn became a much more narrow and conservative ecclesiastical spirit than that of the teachers we had pilloried.

It was the next generation, that of Jacques Martin and Philippe Vernier, that furnished men ready to live out fully the faith that animated them. In the final analysis, it's to these men that I feel closest, even though I am their elder. In 1919, 1920, and 1921, I was still one of those mute, admiring students.

The School of Theology was rife with romance. Babut, who had founded a "Misogyny Club" and let it be known that a true pastor should renounce married life, was one of the first to venture into the

4 Marcel Heuzé (1897–1945) was a friend of Henri Nick. He served as pastor in Lens and Marseille. He was a resister and a rescuer of Jews, many of whom he sent to Le Chambon-sur-Lignon. Denounced and arrested in 1943, he was sent to Dora and then Ravensbrück concentration camps, where he died from exhaustion just before the liberation of that camp.

newly founded School for Women Ministers. He married Linette Fabre, our classmate Émile's sister, a ravishing Southerner. I was vaguely touched by Yvonne Dejarnac's classic profile until Cornier, blushing with emotion, announced that he was engaged to her, thus saving me from a strangely listless woman. She was the daughter of a former pastor in Saint-Quentin and we had played together as children. Then Heuzé and Daniel Chéradame got engaged, and Diény fell in love with Yvonne Dumas. I was somewhat interested in Diény's sister and spoke to him about it. He was the one who discouraged me: his sister, he claimed, didn't love pastoral poverty or God enough to be the wife of a pastor.

I ENTERED THE SORBONNE as a student of Goguel, Lods, Henri Monnier, and Wilfred Monod: quite an impressive professorial team! They are all dead now. Gone with them is their honest, clear, and objective spirit, their sense of reality, and their sincere faith in a living God and in a prophetic and inspirational Christ alive within us. Barthianism[5] and Niebuhrism[6] passed this way too: I am always struck by the rabbinical dryness of those pastors who have been influenced by them. If the church proclaims the impossibility of attaining good, faith will find refuge outside of the church with the "citizens of the world," with the Communists or the Moral Re-Armament. Why must the church become skeptical at the very moment when the world thirsts for an absolute? Is the church definitively outmoded, or is this only a temporary crisis?

In 1920 the church had not yet become skeptical. President Wilson had launched the League of Nations and then died. Romain Rolland published the first biography of Gandhi. Saint Francis of Assisi became extremely popular. People also believed, after defeating the German Empire, that they had overcome the tendency toward violence.

I began to frequent the Fellowship of Reconciliation circles, and my classmates from the Sorbonne who had returned from the war cried out: "Barbusse is right, Remarque is right!" Henri Barbusse and Erich Maria Remarque, a Frenchman and a German, had written two novels, *Under*

5 Karl Barth (1886–1968) was an influential Swiss Calvinist theologian known for his seminal commentary on The Epistle to the Romans, his involvement in the Confessing Church, and above all his *Church Dogmatics*.

6 Reinhold Niebuhr (1892–1971) was an American Reformed theologian, ethicist, and public intellectual.

Fire and *All Quiet on the Western Front*, that exploded onto the scene as the definitive condemnations of war.

As for me, I was wearing myself out in too many diverse activities. I was regional president of the Fédé and traveled as far as Rouen and Le Havre "to check things out." There I met young bourgeois types flirting with left-wing ideas.

On Pentecost 1920, I visited the Désert de Retz[7] which then belonged to the Passy family, who were Christian Socialists. I had come to Chambourcy for a high-school camp that had cost me lots of effort and fatigued me terribly. We walked from the Saint-Germain train station all the way to Chambourcy, about three miles. We were very cold in an uncomfortable barn. A hen had made her nest in the toilet bowl, so we had to relieve ourselves outside. I still remember the impassioned speeches I gave to my classmates, without knowing whether Walter and Pintard, my two poised and reasonable disciples, would accept my Saint-Quentin-style Christian radicalism. It was a bit fragile intellectually. We held one more camp at Montmorency, and that was it.

I tried to frequent the university student federation. There I heard, among others, a brilliant speech by André Philip, about whom people said: "He'll go far." I heard about his trip to Nyborg with Samuel Cornier for a Fellowship of Reconciliation conference. They both returned engaged, André to Mireille Cooreman,[8] Samuel to Yvonne Dejarnac. All this took place without my realizing it. My activities were devouring me; I wasn't spending enough time studying. I was far too impressed by the self-assurance of my slightly older classmates and their loquacious speeches. I thought I was far more stupid than I was, and I never allowed myself to compete with the brilliant ones who led the university student federation. A year ago, in 1955, I met one of them, now a pastor in Lyon, and was astonished at his superficiality.

I attended several conferences organized in public halls. The popular orator at that time was Albert Dartigue, a disciple of the pragmatist William James and of Henri Bergson. Dartigue filled the halls, and his

7 *Le Désert de Retz* is an Anglo-Chinese garden created at the end of the eighteenth century that belonged to the political figure Frédéric Passy (1822–1912) who, with Henry Dunand, was the first recipient of the Nobel Peace Prize in 1901. His son, Paul Passy, converted to the Baptist faith.

8 Mireille Cooreman was known by her married name, Mireille Philip. A resister who was named Righteous Among the Nations, she lived in Le Chambon-sur-Lignon during the war.

eloquence provoked passionate discussions. I had loved my philosophy class, and, in this electrifying atmosphere where essential problems were raised, where philosophy, theology, and ethics came together, I finally felt comfortable. I nonetheless contented myself with admiring Dartigue from a distance, never imagining that either he or Pierre Maury, the secretary general of the federation, might look my way. I behaved in the same manner at the following three conferences: in Paris (1919), Montpellier (1920), and Lyon (1921). Today, I regret that I didn't immediately make the most of everything I learned in these circumstances. I didn't begin to "think out loud" like my classmates were doing. I was satisfied just accumulating knowledge.

At Clamart, though, I began to sparkle.

Clamart was a petit-bourgeois suburb of uncomfortably small grit stone houses with garden patches in front stretching all along Moulin de Pierre Street. The street ended at Meudon Woods. It was shabby and littered with greasy paper and broken glass.

On the right side of the street, there was a small church, also made of grit stone, with a few benches. Just enough to seat a minimal number of old women and Mr. Damiron, a sad Alsatian gentleman who took care of the finances of this pastorless annex.

There were also four young men, four young women, and Jacques Diény, who envisioned the town of Clamart converted to the gospel by its youth. An extravagant vision, to be sure! Clamart, however, had no desire to be converted. When we went peddling our ideas from door to door, we found frightened, distracted, or distrustful housewives who exclaimed: "Don't bother. We know all that already!" As for the youth group, it was composed of Coutris, Gautier, Chabrut, and Laly. Coutris spoke too much, and when he did, he made little bubbles at the corners of his lips and sputtered. Gautier didn't have much energy. One Sunday at eight a.m., I came from Paris to take part in an outing and found him in bed with the shutters closed. I beat on the shutters and his mother never forgave me. Chabrut was the most original of the four. A small-time printer, he was destined to become the son-in-law of the director of a newspaper, the *Quotidien*. After it flopped, he supported his ruined in-laws. A tireless handyman, he founded the workers' cooperative in Le Chambon-sur-Lignon and a circulating bookstore, part of the Evangelical Contact Center. Always broke but always bouncing back, this warm-hearted, naive, but handy man is one of my best friends.[9] As regards Laly, he was a charming and impassioned Catholic, the most cultured of the four. He died very young.

Diény's vision necessitated having a place to meet, and thus, some land. An old woman loaned and then gave our group an empty lot to the left of the church. The government was selling decrepit barracks that had housed refugees after the war. You had to break them down and transport them yourself, which we did. Then Diény left to serve his required two years in the military, leaving the situation in my hands: a pile of boards sitting on a nondescript piece of land.

We got together on Wednesday evenings in the upper room of a café across from the train station. It smelled of beer and stale cigarettes. We came with the Bible, prayer, subjects to be discussed, and the vision bequeathed to us by Diény. On Thursdays and Sundays, to the great displeasure of our parents, who thought we were neglecting our studies, we erected our shack. The upright beams lay across the lawn between the pillars. The trusses were raised, fingers were crushed, foreheads sweated under the summer sun, hands went numb with cold in the winter. In June, the shack was ready, but on the eve of the inauguration we realized that Laly, in his haste, had ordered ninety windowpanes an inch too short! We couldn't buy others, so we compensated by nailing scraps of boards over the empty spaces. It didn't look pretty.

I had to give the inaugural address. I began speaking in front of what seemed an immense crowd before yielding the floor to my inexperienced colleagues. My speech was full of "Diény's vision." After a few minutes, some disturbing cracking sounds could be heard. The startled audience calmed down after a reassuring word from me. Worried, I continued, when a loud noise of broken beams shook the shack! The middle of the floor had caved in under the weight of the crowd. People stood up screaming as panic set in. "Don't worry! Rest assured, it won't get any worse!" I cried out, trying to be heard above the noise. Fortunately, my gratuitous affirmation came true. The walls and the roof held up. The beams that broke were at ground level. The end of the ceremonies unfolded in a strange manner: half of the audience leaned to the right, the other half to the left. The two halves supported each other, preventing

9 Gilbert Chabrut moved to Le Chambon-sur-Lignon during the 1940s. He was the secretary of the church council and the printer of André Trocmé's *L'Église de neige* and of the collective brochure *Le visage et l'âme du Chambon-sur-Lignon* (1943).

anyone from falling. Everything worked out fine. Having turned out well, the adventure became an unforgettable memory. We inexperienced builders had omitted the step of constructing brick supports for the floor trusses, which could have caused even more serious problems.

We disassembled the floor, built the supports, and put the trusses back in place. Several years later, the shack itself was replaced by a rather ugly "solid" building. Diény's vision never came about – Clamart was never converted. Nonetheless, Protestant families and proselytes came together around the adventurous youths who believed in God. A small but living church was born in Clamart. Today, Raymond Coutris is the national president of the YMCA. In 1933, the people of Clamart asked me to be their pastor, and I accepted with joy. It was a period when pastors had to promise not to campaign for conscientious objection. I'll tell you what happened later.

ADMITTEDLY, IN 1920–21, many theology students were experiencing a crisis in the course of their studies, provoked by their discovery of the relative character of biblical revelation. Our professors approached the Bible not only through historical criticism but also shone a spotlight on religious experience from the equally troubling points of view of sociology (inspired by Durkheim), psychophysiology (Is there a soul?), and pragmatism (religion is good for you; therefore, religion is good; therefore, religion is true).

Probably more than others, I was immune to doubt. My faith had a pietistic origin, not a rationalist one. Even when stripped of certain dogmatic frameworks, it subsisted without difficulty. On the other hand, I have always lived in a lucid and critical atmosphere, the one that Papa created around us. As a result, I was rendered immune to the poisons of negativism by having taken small doses of it. Finally, my older brothers, who had completed their studies before 1914, had lived in a euphoric atmosphere, comparable to that which reigns in the United States today, where religion seems secondary and useless. In between these periods, my adolescence had known war, the postwar period, the undermining of traditional values, the temptation of total nihilism, and its counterpart, an act of faith in a God who transcends society and is a personal savior. So, my faith persisted without difficulty.

I remember, in my courses at the Sorbonne with Maurice Goguel and Charles Guignebert, applying critical, historical principles (no repetition, no contradictions, etc.), not to the Gospel texts they were shredding but to their own hypotheses. There, too, nothing much remained because they couldn't avoid building their hypotheses about Jesus on other nonverifiable hypotheses. This fact allowed me to conclude that, at the very least, the only thing they had managed to prove was that they didn't know anything. The naive traditions of the Bible, even if they give us distortions, exaggerations, contradictions, and legendary elements, present us with the living presence of the person of Jesus. The neutral hypotheses of the historians, on the other hand, were no longer sufficient to explain the birth of Christianity.

During that same period, there was the salutary appearance of a man we must consider a comedian, Dr. Couchoud, a nonhistorian who wrote a short and simplistic book in which he concluded that Jesus had never existed but was part of a divinity invented by a brilliant mystic, Saint Paul. After Saint Paul, supposed biographies were composed in the form of the four Gospels, and Christians began to believe that Jesus had existed. In a flash, historians woke up and found themselves all in the same camp: the atheists like Guignebert and the believers like Goguel. At the Union, I attended a magnificent debate, during which Couchoud was demolished and ridiculed by these outraged historians. Jesus, once again, had the right to exist!

I've said it before: my crisis didn't emanate from these issues. Enamored of a moral absolute from my days at the Union in Saint-Quentin and having worn out my physical and emotional strength, I asked myself constantly if my moral state, which I considered in bad shape, qualified me for the pastoral life that I greatly esteemed. All around me were older classmates who spoke with confidence. I was part of the "Northern Group" consisting of the orthodox Chéradame brothers, Cornier the saint, Babut the bishop, Heuzé the inspired one, who were all well-fortified with austerity, scholarly success, prayers, and peremptory confirmation of their calling. As for me, I lived on Rue Jacob in my highly bourgeois family, between Pierre and Étienne, under Papa's prying eye and Louise's silent gaze. I was exhausting myself at Clamart, my only act of Christian witness. I was a mediocre student, not in the least bit passionate about my studies.

My older classmates referred to their experiences in the war and their understanding of human beings. I was troubled by pacifism, which struck me as a necessary attribute of sanctity but out of my reach.

It was at this point that I experienced the first great crisis in my life. I was twenty years old, and my intellectual horizon was expanding under the influence of my professors. I wanted to excel in either knowledge or sanctity, but I was getting nowhere. I nonetheless felt called in other directions. I spoke German and English and had taken part in several Fellowship of Reconciliation conferences, one of which, held at Bad Boll in Bade-Wurtemberg, had put me in contact with Henri Roser, Mr. Nick, Siegmund-Schultze, and an English Labour deputy, Sir Walter Ayles, who made a big impression on me.

I was a Christian pacifist, at least in principle. I began to scrutinize the Protestant church with a critical eye. I considered the Protestant leaders too narrow in their thought and language. Pastor Dürrelmann, for example, an eloquent, bearded fellow, had just founded an evangelical movement called "The Cause," which brought together a great zeal for proselytizing and a naive patriotism that posed such questions as: "Was Joan of Arc Protestant?"

Roser, at this point, had already found his place. Helping alcoholics in the Croix Bleue, distributing religious pamphlets, evangelizing, and speaking out for conscientious objection formed the core from which he would never deviate. With Jacques Martin and me, he established a small group of the Fellowship of Reconciliation that Cornier and André Philip often frequented with some non-Protestant, unconventional characters. We met on Avenue Victoria in a narrow room on the second floor also used by Parisian Quakers. Through them, I first heard of Romain Rolland and his recent book on Gandhi.

I began to listen to voices from outside of the traditional Protestant school of thought: those of Auguste Sabatier, Eugène Ménégoz, and Wilfred Monod. Monod, at the same time that he took a stand against Roser's radical pacifism, founded, along with Siegmund-Schultze, Söderblom, and others, the International Friendship Through Churches, whose secretary general was Pastor Jules Jézéquel.[10] I attended one of the conferences of this movement in Lille that initiated the first "Life and Works" seminar, one of the groups from which would emerge, in association with "Faith and Order," the Ecumenical Movement of Non-Catholic Churches. The Lille meeting was too conservative and too church-oriented for my tastes, so I turned completely to the International

10 In 1920, Jules Jézéquel co-founded The French Universal Alliance Committee for International Friendship Through Churches. He was named Righteous Among the Nations in 2001.

Fellowship of Reconciliation, whose clear principles based on the Gospels satisfied my desire for an absolute. I never played an important role there because I wasn't self-confident.

The battles I waged for chastity and sexual purity that should have been less important still took first place in my religious life. I wanted to be pure and couldn't do it. Today I realize that I was at an impasse. Deprived of a mother, I hadn't known feminine tenderness during my entire adolescence. Women for me were temptations, not friends. With posters, the cinema, even conversations, Paris relentlessly attacked the fortress where I hid. I resisted as best I could by fleeing the company of girls, who all seemed equally dangerous. I couldn't tell you if they were pretty or ugly because I didn't dare look their way. I chased the very thought of woman from my mind. I understood later that I was living in the same deceptive world Martin Luther resisted in his monastery. For me, this was the middle of Paris on the Left Bank, where sexual license and the extravagances of Dadaism had free rein.

In hindsight, I think it was these inner struggles more than anything else that made me wonder if I had faith. If I had faith, I told myself, I would win this battle. Since I couldn't win, I didn't have faith. I admired one or the other of my classmates who seemed to have victory written all over their faces while defeat was written on mine.

Biblical criticism certainly played a part, but only secondarily. I had too critical a mind to believe in criticism. I inherited a powerful tendency from the Trocmés to take nothing as absolute, not even the revelations of textual criticism. I could tell how fragile and uncertain they were.

I decided I was too young, that I needed to acquire the experience of an ordinary man. So, I gave up my military deferment and did my two years of service starting in September 1921, that is, only six months after my military number had been called.

6

In the Army

I HAD ASKED TO BE PLACED between Paris, where my family resided, and Saint-Quentin, where they planned to return shortly. Instead, I was assigned to the Fifty-Fourth Infantry Regiment in Compiègne, to the Royallieu barracks.

Royallieu was a modern barracks, that is, it was a plain swept by the cold, covered with mud or burned by the sun according to the season! As a hygienic measure, the toilets were located a hundred yards from the living quarters, which meant that in the winter any soldiers who wanted to urinate during the night had to do so in the sinks or in metal boxes under their beds that sometimes got knocked over.

I was sent to the First Company, commanded by Captain Queyroi. I learned immediately that this was a disciplined company. Queyroi was a former jockey who had been promoted during the war. He was a hero and a ruthless fellow. To top it off, there were not enough students with deferred military service to fill a barracks room, much less a unit. The "toughs" of the First Company immediately disapproved of us and gave us a hard time, as did the junior officers charged with instructing us.

Finally, because we were students, we were destined to become officers. That went without saying. I remembered Papa, who had refused officer stripes in 1870, and I explained my troubled conscience to the officer in charge of instruction. He seemed sympathetic: "Continue your basic training," he told me. "We'll see about things later." The sergeant responsible for our training learned about my objection. He taunted and insulted me and decided to "get me in line." This meant that during maneuvers he made me descend, fully equipped, three times into the "bear pit," whereas my pals only had to go down once. One day I refused to obey him and he threatened me with a court martial. I stood my ground. He did nothing: my fellow soldiers would have turned against him.

The platoon's main amusements were simple. They played cards in the barracks and, at five p.m., billiards in the café. The city was two miles away and there was no transportation, so you couldn't be picky about where you sought refuge. On Saturday, if you had money, you pigged out at the Hôtel de la Cloche, and if you managed to land permission to stay out until midnight or overnight, you could get smashed and hit the whorehouse. I had wanted to learn about human nature and it looked like I would get much more than I bargained for.

I tried to make friends with the men who seemed most decent. There were Isaac and Casella, one Jewish, the other Corsican. I soon found Casella's language unclear and licentious. There was Amos, a Protestant from the East, whose parents sent him 2000 francs a month – a kingly sum! He was vain and stupid. Isaac, Casella, and their circle of junior officers sensed that he had money and courted him. He took them all to restaurants, movies, and of course, more seedy places, and spent his entire allowance in two weeks, like a spoiled child unable to be content with the commonplace. Then the others would abandon him.

When I went to Paris on leave, I brought back cartons full of ham, butter, and saucisson. I, too, was spoiled by a father who didn't want me to lack anything. I was frugal and measured out my food so that it lasted me a whole month. That was when Amos would come to me. I can still see his whimpering face begging me to give him "just one little piece of gingerbread." I gave it to him grudgingly. Other friends who were poorer than Amos asked for nothing.

There was Potel. He wasn't a student but a poor, illiterate wretch who somehow landed among us. A first-class clown, without father or mother, he had a gift for buffoonery and entertained the whole barracks with his tomfoolery after curfew. I liked him and he knew it, but he wouldn't leave me alone to pursue my favorite activity, reading. While the barracks table echoed with the muffled sounds of a card game and two guys engaged in an endless discussion of the relative merits of this or that race cyclist, I lay on my bed trying to concentrate on a difficult book. That's when Potel bombarded me. He threw a sock, a pinecone, then came the heavy artillery: an army boot that tore my book, sent it sailing, and hurt my hand.

I tried patience, protestations, warnings, menaces, but nothing worked: Potel was having fun and was quite adroit, the rascal! One day I couldn't take it any longer: "If you do that again, I'll dump you," I told him. French army beds are composed of heavy metal frames resting on a headboard and a footboard. To dump someone meant that while the person was sleeping, you turned over the frame, mattress, and man. If the move was successful, the victim found himself on the ground under the mattress and heavy metal frame, unable to see who was bullying him.

Potel usually played innocent whenever he bombarded me. Stretched out on his bed, he pretended to sleep. Of course, he did it again! I pounced on him, grabbed the bottom of the box springs where he lay, and turned him over. My flip worked so well that I could hear Potel's head hit the cement.

Then nothing – no gesture, no scream, no movement. I was overtaken by fear and called out "Potel, oh, Potel!" No answer. "That does it," I thought. "I took him out. That's just my luck. I, who never heckle anyone, kill a man the first time I try."

I lifted the box springs, the mattress, and the disorderly sheets. Potel lay on the floor, immobile. He didn't look like he was dead. I leaned toward him and realized he was crying like a child. Not because he was hurt, even if the shock had been great. He cried from sadness, maybe loneliness. I helped him get up. He told me his life story: he was the illegitimate child of an unknown father and had been raised by public welfare agencies. He had never had money to buy a tie or socks. He was all alone in life.

I told him, "OK, everything's all right, we're buddies, but in the future leave me in peace. I like to read. If you do it again, I'm going to buy you some fries." And I assumed my most menacing expression.

Faced with such an awful threat, Potel stayed calm for half an hour and then . . . he started up again. Once again, my book flew away. I bounded out of bed: "Get up," I said, looking furious. He got up. "Get dressed to go out. We're going to settle this now!"

"But what do you want from me," said Potel, pale with fear.

"Get dressed to go out," I said, "I'll do the same, and we'll settle this outside."

He got dressed. So, did I. Across the road there was a little bistro where you could buy a meal different from our usual fare. With my teeth clenched, I dragged Potel there. "Sit down," I told him. Stunned, he sat down. He was served steak and fries, as was I. "What are you waiting for?" I asked. "Eat. Use your knife, fork, and napkin." Obviously Potel had never used a napkin. He ate in silence like a child being punished, but heartily. We didn't exchange a single word. "Are you coming with me?" I asked when we had finished. Potel never again bombarded me. We were friends, but couldn't talk to each other. He had nothing else to tell me, and he wasn't interested in what I had to say.

There was also Poirier, a good Catholic who had black hair and was tall and slightly hunched. He was the one who brought me into the Catholic Circle that was only a few hundred yards from our barracks and open to all those who wanted to read or play billiards. At least it had a calm, clean, atmosphere. But three days later, Sergeant Major Mangin (supposedly, he was the general's nephew) called me to his office.

"Trocmé," he said, "aren't you a student of Protestant theology?"

"Yes," I answered.

"We've noticed that you spend time at the Catholic Circle."

"Yes, it's a clean, pleasant place."

"Well," (he cleared his throat), "we're obliged to ask you not to step foot there again."

"What?" I thought I had misunderstood him. "I'm not doing anything wrong."

"No, but you could talk to Catholic soldiers and cause them to doubt their faith."

"I promise not to do that," I said. "It would be wrong for me to take advantage of your hospitality to try to convert them to Protestantism."

"I believe you, but your presence could create doubt in the minds of these young Catholics, many of whom don't even know that Protestants exist."

"Very well," I answered. "I won't go there again, but I'm surprised at your lack of confidence in your religion."

Times have changed. Catholics are no longer afraid of Protestants. Now they court them!

I didn't smoke or drink; I didn't curse or like pornography. Naturally, I was on the receiving end of my barrack-mates' taunts. I went on the offensive, and this had both positive and negative consequences. It caused Poirier, Crépin, and Potel to support me, but earned me the hostility of the junior officers: Casella, Isaac, and their bunch. Poirier and I often went to a bistro where we played a game of billiards and drank coffee or lemonade. Our fellow soldiers came and went, joined or quit our core group.

One Saturday, Poirier came to see me. He had a mysterious look. "Trocmé," he said,

"The gang has decided to get you tonight. They're coming to the bistro to play billiards and they're going to buy you a beer in which the bartender will put something strong. You'll get drunk because you're not used to drinking. Then they'll make you drink more and take you to the brothel. They plan to have a good laugh when they see you act like them."

I thanked Poirier for warning me. What he predicted happened. The gang arrived at the bistro; they were cordial and noisy. "Troc," they said, "don't sulk. We want to buy you a drink. What do you want?"

"Coffee," I answered.

"Coffee doesn't count. We're all having beer."

As I stood next to the counter, I saw the bartender fill the beer glasses and take out, from behind the counter, a spiked beer for me.

"Cheers!" they toasted.

"No thanks, I'm having coffee."

"Come on, for once in your life, have a beer."

"I said no."

"OK, OK. What do you want in your coffee, a little rum?" They winked at the bartender.

"Just black coffee."

I drank my black coffee, and to be polite, I paid another round. They returned to the barracks in the early morning, noisy and drunk, recounting their great sexual exploits in disgusting terms. I pretended to sleep.

I have often thanked Poirier for his kind intervention. I shudder to think what would have happened if I had fallen victim to the plan. There's no greater pleasure when one is impure, I've heard, than to deflower an innocent man, especially a religious one. I remained a virgin till I married.

I saw Poirier a year later. Without me to support him, he had let himself be dragged into the gang. He moaned to me in a cowardly way: "What do you expect? One must be like everybody else. It happens to all of us."

Crépin wasn't my friend yet, but he was a good guy. I met a few like him in the regiment: restrained, overly cautious, sensitive by nature, and a bit egotistical. They had passed through the stormy adolescent years without much difficulty.

I was so disgusted by my inability to enjoy a minute of peace that I rented a little room with Crépin above the bistro that served fries. There I could keep a few books, had time to pray, and could invite friends into "my" ambiance.

At Camp de Sissonne, where we practiced using live ammunition with rifles, grenades, and machine guns, some of these friends began making fun of two seminarians, who defended themselves rather poorly. Their tormentors attacked the Catholic Church, mocking all the supposedly impotent and perverted priests, the Mass and its mumblings in Latin. To support their claims, they told juicy stories in which the clerics and the nuns played risqué roles.

I could hardly defend a religion I didn't believe in, but I decided to try. One by one, I invited my friends to the mess hall. I had some juice. They preferred a shot of white wine. Then I went on the offensive.

"So, you're a nonbeliever?"

"Oh yes. The priests told me so much rubbish when I studied catechism."

"That's not what I asked you. Suppose that the church didn't exist, that there were no priests, nuns, bishops, or pope. If you got rid of all that, do you think you could get rid of God?"

"God is nothing but an invention by priests so they can exploit the common people's gullibility. The priests get fat and don't do a fucking thing."

I interrupted once again: "Suppose you were alone on an island and in danger. Then would you swear there is no God?"

"Oh, I know there is something above us. The world didn't make itself. And then, everything that happens to us, it isn't by chance."

The answer, always the same, came at the end of five or ten minutes of calm conversation. Some of my anti-Catholic pals even said, "I know there is certainly someone above us," and showed me a medal of the Virgin that their mothers had given them when they left for the regiment. But, above all, they didn't want to seem naive, so they joined the herd and ranted against the church.

Atheism provides a framework for the scholar's refusal to believe, but how can it do that for the simple person ruled by emotions? He obeys his instincts more willingly than his reason. In the herd, he espouses unbelief to liberate himself from the Catholic Church's domination. But in private, he isn't an unbeliever; he submits to his fate. Such fatalism seems like the natural religion of humanity. Throughout history, this religion has found expression, such as in the belief in predestination so strongly rooted in Southern French Protestants. This type of religious sentiment is the most dangerous enemy of evangelical Christianity, as well as Marxism's most intransigent adversary. This is the religiosity that Marx and Engels justifiably denounced as "the opium of the masses."

I tried my best to bear witness to a revolutionary Christ capable of changing society and the individual, but I fear that my words sounded too foreign to the ears they fell upon. Since then, I've learned that even in a Protestant parish it takes years of courageous teaching to prepare and initiate a movement of true faith. Captain Queyroi relaxed his earlier severity toward me, and thanks to Crépin, who had been named our company's secretary, I often obtained a 24-hour leave. Since it went from five p.m. on Saturday until midnight on Sunday, I had the pleasure of going to Paris, where I changed into civilian clothes and visited my family.

I still couldn't reconcile my experience with the world, the barracks, and the street, on the one hand, with that of the church of Jesus Christ, the Clamart Union, and theology school on the other. My experience at home didn't bring me much comfort. I hated the barracks, but my family life was stifling. I wondered if I could ever decide to shut myself up for good in a vacuum like that. The Protestant girls I saw from afar didn't seem to want anything more than to copy the ideas they had received from the previous generation.

My relations with my officers suddenly became tense at the end of my military training. I refused a corporal's stripes. I was written up in a detailed report: I was a good student and would make an excellent corporal. My commanding officer's entreaties didn't succeed in convincing me. I was summoned by the colonel, a narrow-minded, brutal man.

"So, you're the young man who's refusing a corporal's stripes?"

"Yes, sir, Colonel."

"Why, may I ask?"

"I'm a theology student. With God as my witness, I have sworn never to kill. Thus, I can't teach others to kill."

"I couldn't care less about your personal convictions. They're all the same to me. I am an officer, and I bear the responsibility for my men, period! If you refuse, I'll instruct your superiors and they'll find a way to charge you for refusing to obey an order. There'll be a court martial. Ah, you understand, don't you? Obey the order or beware!"

Somewhat cowardly, I accepted, but my conscience wouldn't stop bothering me.

I was named to the toughest company, the First Company, under Captain Queyroi. Queyroi knew my history and picked on me as much as possible. I was the leader of our barracks room. This former junior officer took pleasure in descending on us any time of the day or night to find us in violation. Personal effects poorly folded? Wham! They flew into the air. Trashcan unemptied? He kicked it across the room and ordered: "Bring that back to me!" If a guy was asleep on his bed and didn't answer the corporal's warning, he got a week in the guardhouse, sanctioned by the corporal.

I couldn't stand telling the recruits I was supposed to teach: "Those are *les Boches* (Krauts) – aim at the heart," while pointing to targets in the shape of male bodies.

Morally exhausted, I spoke to Crépin, who had a cushy job in the company's office. "Hey," I said to him, "if the office ever receives a request for a secretary, put my name in. We'll see what the captain says."

And Crépin did it.

One day, I was on maneuver with the regiment when the colonel asked if there was anyone who could draw. I introduced myself and made an enlargement of a chief-of-staff's map using a grid system that was easy to apply.

Despite my subversive ideas, another time Queyroi proclaimed before the entire company that I was the best corporal. Alas, it was no use moderating my zeal for the military; I was still the best educated, the one who most easily imposed my authority without yelling, the one with intelligence and a sense of duty.

A few days after this humiliating glory, the company was again assembled to hear the Colonel's Report, that is, the decisions he had made. The sergeant-major was reading in a monotone when suddenly he read: "Corporal Trocmé of the First Company is posted to the Army Geographic Service. He will leave for Barracks X, Amiens, in three days carrying the following equipment . . ."

Shock among the ranks! I was taken completely by surprise, the captain too. Furious, he headed toward me: "So, you pulled some strings! Congratulations."

"But, Captain, sir, I knew nothing about this!"

"Oh, come on, don't lie! That's just not going to happen. I'll go see the colonel. You better watch out; do you hear me?"

He went to see the colonel and came back crestfallen. I left three days later and bid farewell to the atmosphere of fear and anger to which Queyroi had subjected us.

What had happened? Crépin had seen a request for a secretary from the Army Geographic Service in the company's notebooks and had taken a chance and given my name. That night the captain had been "sampling the fruit of the vine," as he did from time to time. He signed the order without looking at it, thus, officially, *he* was the one who had given my name to the colonel.

Besides, the colonel remembered the map I had enlarged and said to himself, "That's our man." Crépin got bawled out, but Queyroi couldn't deny that he had signed the order.

The morning I left, I stayed in bed until seven. Queyroi, who normally didn't come into our room until eight, stormed into the barracks threatening me with every possible prison sentence. I snickered to myself. He no longer had any power over me.

Before I relate my cartographic campaigns, I'll tell you another funny story. Before I was made corporal, Queyroi had decided to "get my goat." Instead of using me in the office, as was the tradition for future corporals, he assigned me the hardest chores along with the guys who were being punished and spent the night in the police yard. Overseen by the corporals, we spent the day doing disagreeable tasks: cleaning toilets, sorting out dusty uniforms in a dirty attic, carrying mattresses into town, picking up 50 kg potato sacks at the train station, and delivering 50 kg of coal to the homes of noncommissioned officers. Covered in black soot, I provoked a disgusted reaction from their wives that was totally justified. They offered me a tip, which I refused in a dignified manner, or a glass of wine, which I gave to my companion.

I found it interesting, for the first time, to be treated as a "nonspecialized worker" by people without an education who couldn't see that I was a student. I never tried to set them right.

One day, when I went to the station to pick up potatoes, I was seated on the front seat of a horse-drawn regiment vehicle without springs. My companion at the time was a farm boy who asked me, "What do you do in civilian life?"

"I'm a student in theology."

"What?"

"I'm studying to be a minister. That's a kind of Protestant priest, a married priest."

"That doesn't seem very useful."

"Is what you do useful?"

"Of course, I take care of horses!"

"Why do you take care of horses?"

"So they can pull carts."

"And what good is a cart?"

"As you can see, to pick up potatoes."

"And what good are potatoes?"

He looked at me as if I were an idiot. "Uhh, to eat."

"Why eat?"

"To be strong, to work."

"And what work do you do?'

"I said that I take care of horses!"

"Why do you care for horses?"

He looked at me in horror as if I had opened an abyss at his feet.

"What I'm trying to tell you," I continued, "is that ministers are the ones who explain why we live and work."

"Ah, I see," he said.

I had the impression that he hadn't seen a thing. Besides, we had arrived at the train station. We had to load the springless vehicle with one 50 kg sack after another while the horses pawed the ground.

FOR EIGHTEEN MONTHS, I had to travel with two different Army Geographical Service units we called the Geodetic Brigades, up and down the north of France, where the map had to be redrawn after the war's destruction, and across Morocco, where everything had to be done from scratch. It was a very rustic life under a tent. It was easy to get supplies in France and difficult in Morocco, but there we were put in contact with the indigenous peoples. The countryside is monotonous in France, but often magnificent in Morocco. In France, after sleeping on the ground in the beginning, I made myself a good enough bed with the help of a stretcher used for wounded Germans that I found in a trench and nailed a canvas on. I left for Morocco with a regular camp bed that I bought at American Supplies.

In France, I experienced the soft life of soldiers on subsistence allowance: charged with special functions, they had a right to meals and a bed from a military unit that wasn't theirs. They had to be present for roll call at night; that's all. Their only hardship was making their own bed.

An intelligent, grumpy captain, a former student at the École Polytechnique, informed the thirty or so men brought together by chance of their new responsibilities. "The war destroyed so many forests, houses, and villages in this area," he said, "that the geological survey maps are no longer valid. We must start from scratch with triangulation. We will replace the destroyed geodetic points. We will surmount them with a 10- to 20-meter ladder like the masts you see raised on the radio transmitter posts visible from a distance. We leave for Sailly-Saillisel in three days. Here are our trucks and our vans. The drivers will go to the train station tomorrow to pick up the shipment of tents and materials sent from Paris. As for the rest of you, do what you want."

From that point on, I heard this "do what you want" often. There was no reveille for the Geodetic Brigade; you simply had to be there for work. But where could we go? The geodetic points are almost always out in the country. All around us were villages in ruins strewn with corrugated metal panels. Passes were rare, since the captain was afraid that the men wouldn't return on Mondays, and he didn't enjoy the usual leverage that military leaders had – prison or detention. I spent my free time reading – lots of reading, while my comrades did all they could to find girls by making the rounds of village dances. One of my comrades danced with a woman with a wooden leg without ever noticing it. The others had a good laugh at his expense. Sundays were sleepy. Officers disappeared by Saturday afternoon to reach town, where they had their amusements – and often, their women.

We traveled around the area of Noyon in the hills overlooking Bruay-en-Artois in the North. There were destroyed villages, muddy streets bordered with corrugated metal, questionable bistros where they served us *bistouilles* (coffee with a nip). Once they refused to serve me a "black coffee" for the same price. "That's not done here!" said the indignant waitress.

I was occasionally left in charge of the camp. This inevitably caused a quiet struggle with my comrades, often of a higher rank than I was, who did their best to take a van into town to have some fun. One day, the van didn't come back. Some of my inebriated fellow soldiers had had an accident. I was almost severely punished and sent back to my unit. Fortunately, I was able to prove that the guilty soldier had taken the vehicle without my authorization. He was the one who got punished, and he swore eternal hatred for me. Luckily, he was sent back to his unit shortly thereafter.

One Sunday and the following night, alone in my tent, I guarded a comrade who had suddenly gone mad and tried to kill me. With great relief, I saw an ambulance arrive on Monday morning. Since we were miles from any village, it had been impossible to telephone during this long, solitary Sunday.

These incidents taught me a great deal about humanity and how, for the first time in my life, to judge my own ability to deal with unexpected events.

Knowing that I spent my Sundays in the region around Amiens, my father had his friends, the Carmichaëls, invite me to visit them. I went to their home, a big house made of black bricks in Ailly-sur-Somme, two or three times. From the windows of the large living room, you had an excellent view of the textile factories and dismal mining settlements that covered the valley floor.

The Carmichaëls became rich during the war by furnishing the army with sacks of soil for the trenches. They had a son, Robert, a giant with pale skin whom I had met at Domino. Today he's a leader in the Moral Re-Armament in France. They also had a daughter married to a guy named Vandeventer, whom I had known a while back when he was poor. Their second daughter, tall and heavy, sat quietly at the table when I was invited. The Carmichaëls were traditional Protestants destined to occupy a significant place in the church in northern France. Mrs. Carmichaël, especially, was pious and good. Mr. Carmichaël belonged to the ecclesiastical committees Papa presided over. Papa treated all his colleagues casually but showed a certain deference to Mr. Carmichaël. Honor where honor is due.

I attended these dinners with a growing sense of discomfort without knowing why. Having lived as a refugee for so many years, I had completely forgotten the fact that I belonged, by virtue of my family, more to the Carmichaël milieu than to the milieu of the employees and workers I frequented in the Unions.

Furthermore, I felt embarrassed in my ridiculous military uniform with a sky-blue cap whose two corners pointed to the heavens. I hardly took part in the conversations except with Vandeventer, who had been a

Unionist like me. The idea never even occurred to me to enter this rich milieu by marrying, as did Vandeventer, a young woman with a vast inheritance.

In any event, our brigade soon left the region around Amiens, and the dreary Sundays in Ailly-sur-Somme came to an end. It was only two years later that Papa confided to me that he and Mr. Carmichaël had arranged for me and Miss Carmichaël to meet in this manner. "She is a very good person and pious like her mother," Papa said to me. "Furthermore, she has money, which isn't a bad thing. Why don't you try to renew these encounters?" I pushed back on this suggestion with indignation: "I have seen her, and she is of no interest to me. Besides, I have resolved not to marry a woman for her money and not to fall prey to a bourgeois family. Mr. Carmichaël has reactionary ideas." Papa was sorry that I had passed up a marriage he thought was magnificent and advantageous from all angles. But what could he do about it? Much more than my older siblings, I had already escaped from the empire of his will.

Miss Carmichaël married a missionary of Czech origin and became the beloved and devout Mrs. Mikolacèk. I only saw her again in Le Chambon when she was a mother. I had escaped a loveless marriage and a hardly reputable return to the golden prison of "high Protestant society."

The Geodetic Brigade had operated for six weeks around Amiens, then around Noyon. The work was monotonous and of a purely physical nature: loading and unloading trucks, erecting and taking down ladders. My talent in drawing was of no use to me. At Vermandovillers, a village destroyed by the war, Robert and Germaine visited me. Collapsed trenches still cut a groove in the soil. Robert had a great deal of difficulty recognizing the place where he had been seriously wounded and had crawled to get back to the French trenches. We had a picnic together, and I was very proud to introduce my comrades to my brother who drove a Vermorel Torpedo. This would make people laugh today, but at that time it indicated that its owners were wealthy.

Autumn arrived, and we went back to Amiens and its somber brick barracks. There, the brigade was to be disbanded. Our own captain took down the names of those who volunteered for a winter campaign in Morocco, where the Geographic Service was establishing the first geological survey map. For fear of having to go back to Compiègne, I signed up. A few weeks later, in September, I was ordered to Rabat.

I got a short leave that allowed me to go to Paris and say goodbye to my family. I exulted in my new adventure, but Louise seemed in such bad shape that I was afraid I would never see her again. We exchanged numerous letters. She died of heart disease in the spring of 1923, while I was stationed in Morocco and unable to return to the house in Saint-Quentin that Papa, after receiving his war claims, restored to give Louise more comfort.

THIS GEODETIC CAMPAIGN in Morocco was one of the greatest experiences of my life. After a week in Compiègne, where I was reunited with my unit, the Fifty-Fourth Infantry, and Poirier, now lapsed and debauched like the others, I left for Bordeaux. There we shipped out to Morocco. My orders read: "Corporal Trocmé must be on [such and such a date] at the port of Zaër, in Rabat, supplied with the following equipment: [. . .] and a carbine rifle [. . .] with 250 cartridges."

Because of this rifle and the cartridges, I almost gave up my trip to Morocco. I knew that in 1922, Morocco was not a particularly calm spot. (The Rif rebellion, led by Abd el-Krim, would take place the following year). I had vowed not to kill anyone during my military service nor to teach anyone how to kill. Yet there I was, avoiding training recruits in Compiègne only to be sent armed to Morocco.

I arrived at the train station in Bordeaux on a beautiful day in September. I was welcomed by Brigadier Corporal Sabatou, wearing an elegant uniform. He had a sophisticated vocabulary. "I have already been part of a Geodetic Brigade to Morocco," he said to the five or six of us who were shipping out with him. "Let me take care of things. I'll begin by inviting you to dinner." Like a great lord, he took us to the Grand Théâtre brasserie, a change from our ordinary regiment fare.

"We have a *per diem* of 7 francs 50 to spend as we see fit," he added. "On that sum, we'll manage fine and eat well too."

Our orders had specified: "On September 1, by nine p.m., you must be at the Dépôt des Isolés barracks in Bordeaux."

As is always the case in the military, our freedom was of short duration: from the time of our descent from the train until nine that evening.

"You're not going to go to the Dépôt des Isolés," Sabatou said to me. "It's overrun with bed bugs. Only the idiots go there. You'll be holed up there for three days."

"We have to be present for roll call or else we will be punished," I replied.

"We'll see about that," declared Sabatou. "You don't know how to go about this. Come, we'll make a phone call."

He led us to a phonebooth, asked for the Dépôt des Isolés, and spoke in the bluntest, most distant, and coldest military tone possible: "Hello! Give me the commanding officer of the depot. Good. Ah! It's you, Captain. I'm Commander Figaret, head of the Geodetic Brigade. Tell me, Captain, I have my men here: Brigadier Sabatou, Corporal Trocmé, Cavalryman Babolat, etc. I absolutely need all of them for embarkment preparations. Yes. So, don't count on their arrival tonight. No. They'll sleep in town. OK."

He hung up. "All taken care of," he said. "Now off to find some broads!" Clearly, he intended to take us for a highly questionable night on the town. As usual, I put a damper on things. I suggested we look for a hotel. We did so. Evening came and things were calm.

The next day, we had a meeting at nine a.m. with the real Commander Figaret, who struck me as the typical, worn-down "Old Colonial" type. Sabatou gave him his best Saint-Cyr salute.

"Commander, sir, yesterday, in your name, we made a false statement."

"Ho!" protested the commander. "Imitated my signature, did you?"

"No, sir. Not your signature, your voice."

Sabatou was a personable, handsome guy, the only one among his comrades who had some good breeding. Along with Thélinge, a violinist with round eyes and a bouncy step, it was inevitable that we three would form a close group. It was also inevitable that I would agree to lend Sabatou a hundred francs. He assured me he was going to pick up a check from his parents as soon as we arrived in Casablanca.

In any event, we shipped out aboard the *Volubilis*, a small, old boat that kept us bouncing for four days on the Atlantic. I got to know the steerage, the hammocks that tortured our lower backs, the red beans and "monkey" [something like Spam] cooked in a sour wine sauce. I also learned that I didn't get seasick, because all the other passengers were sick and I wasn't.

Once we were on the open sea off Cape Saint-Vincent, the extreme tip of Portugal, good weather took hold. I still remember, thirty-five years later, the marvelous colors that morning when the foam of the waves breaking at the foot of the cliffs appeared to reflect the whiteness of the lighthouse high above, while the sea echoed the blue sky. Dolphins frolicked in our wake.

At this moment, Brigadier Sabatou, who had disappeared two days earlier, chose to reappear. Impeccable in his officer's uniform, a smile on his lips, he smoked a cigarette with a golden holder. "How's it going in there?" he asked. With their waxy complexions, messy hair, and crumpled uniforms, my comrades gave him hostile looks.

"And you, where have you come from?" I asked.

"You don't really think that I'd sleep in such a stable, do you? You really must learn to cope."

He spoke in the same tone as he had that first night in Bordeaux when he said: "You're not really going to sleep in the Dépôt des Isolés – it's a fleabag!"

"I'm gravely ill," added Sabatou. "I have a medical prescription from the assistant physician on board: rest, isolation, and a private room in the infirmary."

His healthy complexion proved that he was lying.

"What else?"

"You idiot! The first night, I got the assistant physician drunk in the officers' bar. He signed all the prescriptions I wanted."

I was furious: "It was with the money I lent you . . ."

"Of course," replied Sabatou. "Unfortunately, there's no more room in the infirmary, but I'll pay you back in Casa."

And he did! At that time, the port of Casablanca didn't yet exist. Ships had to anchor a kilometer out in the open sea in the shelter of a rudimentary dike. Big, old barges, steered by Moroccans and aided by the winds, came to the side of the ships, and the passengers descended on a ladder. Of course, soldiers were meant to get off last, preceded by civilians and officers.

"Follow me," Sabatou said to me, "take your gear, and do what I tell you!"

We descended the ladder and took our place in the second or third old tub. Sabatou's uniform produced its usual effect. The policeman who was supervising the boarding let him pass.

"And who's that?" asked the policeman, seeing my second-class uniform.

"He's with me," said Sabatou, and I got through.

The old tub took to the open sea. Bad news! Another policeman checked our papers. Sabatou showed his orders, and I showed mine. "You are corporals," exclaimed the policeman.

"Yes," said Sabatou.

"But how did you get through?" roared the policeman. "This boat is reserved for officers."

"We walked down the ladder," said Sabatou with the most innocent of looks.

"And my colleague let you pass!"

"Yes," said Sabatou.

It was all true. The policeman had to swallow his anger. He couldn't make the boat turn around. He let us off coldly on the quay and spoke to us as if we were morons: "There you are. In half an hour the other soldiers will get here. You must go to the Dépôt des Isolés as a unit. You don't know where it is? OK, wait right here! Do you understand? They'll come looking for you."

Hardly had the boat turned around when Sabatou hailed a horse-drawn cab! "We're free," he yelled to me. "They won't see us until roll call this evening at nine. You can't go to Casa without visiting the city."

That went without saying! It was nine a.m. We had a magnificent day. Casablanca at that time was a strange city. It rose from the red dust under a brilliant sun. Right next to the old indigenous city was a city of barracks, brand-new apartment buildings, administrative palaces, luxurious shops, and market stalls where shish kebab sizzled. The Arab crowds, splendid in their tattered robes, rubbed elbows with colonists who were seeking their fortune.

With my money, Sabatou wanted to drag me into the demimonde neighborhoods. He couldn't understand my reasons for abstaining from such behavior. He invited me to sit outside on the terrace of the most beautiful café on the Place de France; I let him down by drinking only lemonade. He was an artist, too, and showed me some remarkable watercolors he had brought from an earlier trip. He was a keen observer and already knew Morocco, so we weren't bored for a moment. My presence even prevented him from drinking too much, and he was grateful for that. Around 8:30 p.m., another cab took us two miles outside of the city to an army base composed of white barracks: the Dépôt des Isolés. No one had noticed our absence. At roll call, we answered proudly: "Present."

Our comrades listened with envy to the story of our escapade.

I had hoped for a true friendship with Sabatou, but he was transferred to a different brigade. I only saw him twice thereafter, between campaigns, at Meknès. The first time, Sabatou sparkled like a young

Apollo. He had himself stationed at Meknès by Commander Figaret, under whose protection he became a member of the Officers Circle. "I play tennis and flirt with heiresses," he said. "I offer them flowers and buy presents for them. But it's expensive, you know. They quickly grow tired of my watercolors. So, I go down to the commercial area to get some money."

"The shop owners give you money? That's unlikely," I replied.

"Not right away," responded Sabatou, "but soon enough. Take the hairdresser, for example. I arrive the first day. I get a haircut and a scalp massage. It's expensive. I pay cash on the spot. Two days later, I return, if possible, with the friendly daughter of an officer. Manicure and scalp treatment. Always the most expensive. I look around and spot the hairdresser's daughter in the women's salon. Ugly as can be, but it makes no difference. I give her the eye. The family is blown away. The third time, they invite me for coffee. I tell them a bunch of tall tales. I make the young girl dream. I buy her a bouquet and tell her that I'm waiting for a money order. I pulled it off. Just as I did with you. They advance me the money, and I begin all over again. They are still paying me, hoping for an eligible bachelor for their daughter. When that doesn't work out, I'm out of there. I play the role of the offended one, disappear, and begin all over again at the dairy at the top of the street. You have no idea how much money this brings in."

I was astonished and tried to reprimand Sabatou. "I know that this can't go on forever," he admitted. "I have to get my life in order someday, but not right now."

The second time I was spending a few days in Meknès, I discovered a crestfallen Sabatou. His uniform had lost its freshness, and his eyes were sad. "I drink too much," he said. "I know. I am also woman-crazy. I started hanging around with prostitutes and was seen in their company, so I had to quit the Officers Circle. Merchants won't let me into their places of business anymore."

"Take the Croix Bleue pledge along with me," I told him. He agreed to pledge for a week and felt pretty good after three days. "You're right. I'm going to continue," he said.

But the next day, drunk as a lord, he told me, "Let me fall by the wayside. I'm screwed. I know it. I'm completely debt-ridden. What I need is women and alcohol. Anyway, come meet me at the canteen this evening. I'll show you how I pay my debts. I wasn't born yesterday."

Curiosity got me to the canteen that evening. At the bar, a heavy-set lieutenant with a flushed face, obviously smashed, was holding court. As soon as Sabatou entered, he called out to him: "Ah ha, Brigadier Sabatou, you've come to pay your debts! It's not a bit too soon either!" Holding up a fistful of dirty papers, he cried out, "I have IOUs signed by you for the sum of 850 francs! Either pay up or I am going to file a complaint."

For a few weeks, Sabatou had been hanging around with this rather naive lieutenant. They had been living it up together, and Sabatou had extorted some money from him!

Sure of himself, Sabatou came forward. One after the other, he verified each slip of paper. "That's correct," he said, "I owe you 850 francs."

"Hand them over," growled the lieutenant.

"Wait a second," said Sabatou. "Not so fast. Have you forgotten that you also owe me money?"

"I don't owe you a penny," groused the lieutenant.

"Look here," said Sabatou calmly, "On December 15, I lent you 100 francs. There's your signature."

"Not at all possible," murmured the victim. "That's my signature all right, and the date, both written in my hand. But these are counterfeit."

"How will you prove that?" asked Sabatou, and he calmly displayed the other IOUs. They were all written in Sabatou's hand but dated and signed by the lieutenant.

"Outrageous," screamed the lieutenant. "It's not possible. I was drunk when I signed those."

"Yes," replied Sabatou, as he quickly put the documents back into his pocket. "You were drunk when I had you sign these blank pages. We were buddies then. Now, since you are being mean to me, I'll do the same to you. It's strange, isn't it. These too add up to 850 francs. If you don't immediately tear up my IOUs, I will take yours to your superiors. Go ahead, make a good move, burn them."

All it took was the flame from Sabatou's cigarette lighter to burn the two little piles of papers that formed a single pile of ashes on the floor. Without a word, the lieutenant left and slammed the door behind him. "There you have it," said Sabatou, raising his eyes to heaven, "One friend lost. Plenty more where he came from."

That night, I didn't try to preach to him. We only exchanged our Paris addresses in case we might need one another after our return to civilian life. You never know. In fact, when I returned to the School of Theology in Paris, I received a note written in his great artistic hand. He asked for my help, and what I saw went beyond anything I might have imagined.

Sabatou lived on the sixth floor of 2 Avenue de la Grande Armée, in an immense painter's studio that overlooked the Arc de Triomphe. He received me in the casual dress of a fashionable painter: silk-lined pajamas and a cigarette. On the walls, on the easels, on the floor, casually but deliberately arranged, were his works, some gouaches. As usual, just sketches. "Don't look so surprised," he said to me smiling. "This place is nothing less than the workshop of Luc-Olivier Merson.[1] You can see that a few of his paintings are still hanging on the walls. Alas, I don't owe all this to my talent but rather to a woman. I am the lover of a charming woman, for whom I feel great admiration but not love. She married a very rich man. They welcomed me graciously into their home. I'm a friend of her husband and their three children. She's crazy about me and believes that I have true talent. She's the one who pays for all this luxury. I'm a kept man. By the way, I asked her to drop by. You'll get to meet her. But, for God's sake, play dumb, don't make any allusions to what I am going to tell you now."

"I promise," I told him.

"Her husband," Sabatou continued, "is beginning to suspect something. He's extremely jealous and has been carrying on badly. She threatened to leave him and the children if he continued to do so. I have my scruples: Should I allow this woman, whom I don't love and whom I will never make happy, to separate from her husband and her children, where her duty calls her? I'm telling you this is not a loose woman. Her passion for me is spiritual. She imagines me to be someone I'm not. It's my fault too. I told her a bunch of stories the way I do with everybody. But that's not all. Two days ago, I let her know that I wanted to break up, that we would have a miserable life together, because I don't want to be poor, and I know that my talent is mediocre. She began to sob. She said she would kill herself if I left her. I know her; she's serious. So, I called you, a pastor. Give me your advice. You must know how someone can get out of a terrible predicament like this."

For the first time, I saw Sabatou as he really was: weak, without willpower, hungry for wealth and sensual pleasures, but basically an honest soul.

1 Luc-Olivier Merson (1846–1920) was a popular painter and illustrator before the tsunami of Fauvism and Cubism.

The doorbell rang. Sabatou went to open the door. I saw a thin, pretty woman enter, dressed in a close-fitting suit that looked good on her. She had dark eyes and a serious look about her. Sabatou had not deceived me.

She made tea for the three of us. While I was there, nothing was mentioned about their difficulties. After a half-hour or so, I slipped away. The next day, I telephoned Sabatou and told him that I thought he should break up with her. I offered to mediate and soften the shock of breaking up. "Keep me abreast of events," I told him.

I never again heard from Sabatou. When I later tried to get in touch with him, I found out that he had left Luc-Olivier Merson's studio without giving a forwarding address.

What happened? Did he take off with his mistress? Did he find the courage to break off the relationship? Did the lady do something crazy? I never learned the conclusion to this tragedy, but it opened my eyes to a truth that I confirmed later: it's at the very beginning of an adventure that people make mistakes. After that, they get caught up in a spiral that carries them forward despite themselves. They often maintain a moral conscience in the midst of chaos, but it's of no avail. They can never turn back and set foot on firm ground. Beyond a certain point, all their decisions will necessarily be bad.

LET'S RETURN NOW TO CASABLANCA, where I had just gotten off the ship with Sabatou. At nine p.m., the Dépôt des Isolés closed its doors on us, and I became acquainted with bed bugs, a fever that required anti-typhoid serum, and a sandstorm that, despite the closed shutters, crossed through our windowless barracks and glued miniscule, red grains of the desert to my unshaven, sickly, moist face.

At Rabat, a few days later, I found myself among the dozen or so cone-shaped tents, the horses, the military vehicles drawn by mules, the Moroccan soldiers, and the three French secretaries that made up our brigade. The whole camp was planted at the foot of the long wall of crumbling adobe that surrounded the capital of Morocco. Beyond that was the backcountry, which looked to me like a red desert sprinkled with tufts of stunted palm trees. It was the end of September; we were waiting for the first rain. All the vegetation was burnt to a crisp.

Lieutenant Tardy, who was to command our brigade during our six-month campaign, was thin, of average height and reddish complexion, precise, intelligent, and close to his men. He was basically a kind man under a brusque exterior. He was passionate about cartography and would later become the head of the National Geographic Service. For the first time, I had a leader whom I could respect. He found in me a secretary who could think, and decided that I would do the preliminary calculations for his observations.

There was nothing difficult about those calculations, but, alas, I've always been a weak mathematician, subject to moments of forgetfulness. Tardy found monumental mistakes in my work that made him scream at me in a high-pitched voice. Finally, he gave up on me and replaced me with Thélinge, a funny little guy with a red nose who waddled when he walked but whose calculating mechanism worked impeccably. As for me, the lieutenant sent me on horseback, under the protection of two or three *Moghaznis*[2] lent by a local caid, to repair broken signals. The Moroccan villagers had stolen the wood to make fires.

My relationship with Tardy was complicated by an act of rebellion I committed at our departure for Rabat. I had come to Morocco to make maps, not war. But the only review that we were subjected to before our departure was an inspection of our weapons. Commander Figaret came to tell us: "You are leaving for the Central Atlas Mountains with your lieutenant. Beyond a line controlled by our troops, the unsubdued backcountry extends. There, certain Berber tribes live who have refused to make peace. Your brigade will not enter any territory considered dangerous, but it can always be attacked by a group of Chleuh.[3] That's why you were given a rifle when you left France." He then carefully examined our rifles and cartridges.

I had a very bad night. Hadn't I tried to escape from the obligation of forming young recruits in the art of warfare? And that was only for a hypothetical war. Now, here I was, facing the possibility of killing another man in an actual conflict. No, I couldn't possibly do that! The next morning, I spent quite a while greasing my carbine rifle. Then I bound it like an injured body part with a bandage. I took my cartridges, packed them up, and tied them to my rifle. I went to the barracks where we lived. Because of frequent thefts of rifles, soldiers were advised not to walk alone with their weapons but to house them in each company's arms

2 Generally speaking, the *moghaznis* were members of the irregular French army during the Algerian conflict. Here the term refers to auxiliary soldiers, some on horseback, some on foot.

3 The French term for the Shilha, a Berber ethnic group that lives mainly in the Central Atlas Mountains of Morocco.

depot. My doing so was perfectly normal. The arms depot took my rifle and gave me a receipt. Of course, I said nothing about this to Tardy and left for the backcountry unarmed but with a relieved conscience.

Weeks went by before we reached the invisible line separating the "conquered" backcountry from the "rebellious" part. I can still see the place: low hills covered with sparse vegetation. The lieutenant made us fall in line and called for an arms inspection. "From tomorrow onward," he said, "there's a chance of walking into an ambush and, despite our wishes, having to fire our weapons." I was standing in the back of the line at attention.

"Where is your rifle?" said Tardy as he stood before me.

"I don't have one."

"They didn't give you one before we left France?"

"Yes, they did, sir."

"So, it was stolen from you?"

"No, sir. I left it in Rabat, at the company's arms depot." Then I showed him my receipt.

"What, you're crazy! Didn't you understand the commander's instructions?"

"Yes, sir, but I don't want to kill. I am a student of Protestant theology; I'm trying to be a Christian. How can I teach young people Christian ethics if I have blood on my hands?"

The other soldiers listened with curiosity, and the lieutenant was annoyed. "Come into my tent," he said to me. "At ease," he said to the troops.

Inside the tent, Tardy sat me down and offered me a cigarette, which I refused. "Listen, Trocmé, there's something I don't understand. You're a volunteer in this brigade, aren't you?"

"Yes, sir."

"Your scruples are certainly a credit to you, but there are only twenty-five of us here. Tomorrow we will be isolated from any help, just like the crew on a ship at sea. Would you refuse to participate in a maneuver if the ship were in danger?"

"No, sir."

"If tomorrow we come under attack, the absence of one rifle in our defense system could change the outcome of the battle. If everyone thought like you, we would all be massacred."

"I understand, sir."

"Well, then, do you know what they call that? Refusal to obey an order in the presence of the enemy. That can lead you to the firing squad. Do you understand?"

"Yes, sir."

"I should give you a serious prison sentence and send you back under guard to Rabat, but we are too far away, and I can't afford to let three men take you there." He scratched his head and continued. "I know what I'm going to do. I'm going to ignore your case. After all, I don't care whether you have a rifle or not while we are not under siege. But if one day we are attacked and as the officer responsible for the unit I give the order to fire, and you, for any reason whatsoever, disobey my command, I will have you court-martialed. Your case will be serious. Do you understand?"

"I do, sir."

I started to get up, but he held me back. "I am a good Catholic," he said. "I sympathize with your scruples, but don't you see, my young friend, that if one doesn't accept the rules of the game before getting on the ship, it's only fair to say so in advance. When you were drafted, you should have told the authorities 'I don't want to kill' and accepted the prison term that results from refusing military service."

I had to agree completely with what the lieutenant said because his words defined precisely what conscientious objection was. "In the future," I thought, "I will refuse to allow myself to get conscripted." The news from France at that moment echoed exactly what the lieutenant had said. A teacher in Lille, a pioneer in conscientious objection, had refused to put on an army uniform. He was court-martialed and given a heavy prison sentence.

From then on, I prayed every night that we would not be attacked. Not having yet undergone the tragic hardships that since have taught me that prayer consists, above all, in putting our will in accord with God's wishes, it still seemed to me that by my fervor I might influence the course of events. In a certain way, I was carrying the Geodetic Brigade on my shoulders so that it might not be attacked. I put all my faith in this endeavor, without forgetting for a moment that my personal destiny was seriously tied up in the result!

The brigade was never attacked except for one evening in Aïn Leuh. It was the only time that we took refuge behind the dry-stone walls of a small fort erected by the Foreign Legion. The night was so dark that we never saw our adversaries. We only heard their rifles and their bullets hitting the walls or whizzing past our heads. Weapons in hand, my comrades waited next to the slits in the wall for the order to fire. That order never came. Why waste ammunition on an invisible enemy that hadn't even tried to mount an assault? Before long, the shots became less frequent, and silence soon filled the night. The lieutenant kept his word. Not having received the order to fire, I wasn't guilty of disobeying an order. He pretended not to know why.

I enjoyed this life of adventure immensely: Camping out on the ground in the backcountry, opening my camp bed in the evenings, laying out my few household goods among the stones and the gray grasses, taking a book out of my backpack and reading by candlelight, while outside packs of jackals howled, and horses and mules whinnied in fear. Falling asleep to the sound of a village tom-tom, waking up at dawn to the lieutenant's call. Covering up in woolens because of the cold, and soon thereafter, seeing the golden sun rise on this immense earth unsullied by roads, telegraph poles, and landmarks. Feeling my body warm up gradually, stripping myself of all layers of clothing, offering myself to the sun's warmth. All of that was new and true and took me away little by little from the human and moral problems that had possessed my life up to that point, making me into a kind of pagan.

Whoever has not known the joy of galloping on horseback, compass in hand, across a country without maps and roads; of losing and then finding again, at the whims of the ravines, one's Berber guides with their loose-fitting, thin-hooded blue cloaks; of seeking hospitality in the evening in a nameless Arab village of tents whose leader, suspicious at first, welcomes you as guests of honor because the Moghaznis wore the sultan's uniform; of suddenly slowing down one's horse on a rockslide that plunges toward a stream rimmed by oleanders; of feeling the quivering flanks of the animal attempting to reach the Casbah perched on the hill as fast as possible has never known joie de vivre.

Forty years later, these images still dazzle my eyes: the marketplaces in Fez in the evening, lit by candles as if for a feast (there was no electricity in Morocco at this time); the shining eyes of the merchants, their offers of exotic merchandise; the yellow, orange, and red rug that I saw one evening in the middle of nowhere on the back of a peasant. The sunset gave it a golden tint, and a passion to possess it seized me, so strong that I not only spent all my savings but, for the first time in my life, borrowed money to buy it. When I returned to France, it seemed to me that possessing this luxury was contrary to the Gospels, so I gave it as a wedding gift to Pierre and Aline. I saw it ten years later. It was worn and soiled; their children had peed all over it. I then understood that objects have no value in themselves. They only have value to the extent that human beings want them, and only for as long as they want them. For a time, objects contribute to the sense of beauty in the human mind. Human beings give life to them. We shouldn't give such objects as presents. They become bored in the homes of others, as children do, away from their mothers, living with an indifferent nanny.

I recall the day our convoy got bogged down in a torrential downpour; the day when snow surprised us and chilled us to the bone; the day when the local kingpin, impressed by the Moghaznis watching over me, took me for a high-ranking officer and improvised a formidable *méchoui*[4] in my honor that was followed by Chleuh dances far into the night. To thank him, I gave out my whole supply of chocolate, which the Berbers ate fearfully, worried that it might be *hallouf* (pork).

What else should I mention? My stay on a sugarloaf-shaped mountain next to the monument where Sidi Ben Azza, the living marabout (mystic) of the region, lived and prayed. Standing silently with his son, while at our feet extended the Chaouia plains, where donkeys, oxen, and sometimes camels plowed. The guttural cries of the peasants, and from afar, the Muslim call to prayer. How I would love to hear them again!

One evening, I was the guest of a Rif bigshot in a village of thatched roofs, each one sporting three stork nests. I fell asleep devoured by bedbugs, while hundreds of storks clacked their beaks endlessly. Another day, I was taken for a Jew by a traveling jewel dealer because I recited the *Shema Israel* to him, and on another day, for a Muslim mystic because I didn't drink wine and knew the shahada, *"La Ilaha Illa Allah,"* by heart.

On Sundays when he wasn't too far from a city and the trails were passable, the lieutenant disappeared, leaving our group in the hands of a fat, vulgar, and debauched sergeant. Immediately, a strange rustling took hold of my comrades: at any cost, they had to find, either close by or at a distance, a joint where they could drink and have fun with women. One of them from the Pyrenees once heatedly reproached me for my contacts with the villagers: "I don't know what you do with those people. They're dirty and you'll get lice." Now, forgetting his hygienic principles, he was the first to leave in search of women. Out of twenty-two men, twenty of

4 An extraordinary meal where a whole lamb is cooked on a spit.

them, French and Moroccan, had to be evacuated at one time or another for venereal disease treatment. The two who remained healthy were Thélinge and I. Our comrades accused Thélinge of being homosexual. I wonder what they thought about me.

One Sunday, however, the lieutenant's absence set us free to go as a group and be part of a great gathering of neighboring tribes with dances and equestrian displays. Another Sunday, thanks to our geodetic triangular zigzags, we had returned to the seaside. If I remember correctly, it was December 2, and the sergeant had slipped away. Three of us decided to take off on our horses. How wonderful it was to gallop along the beach where the only imprints on the wet sand were those of our horses' hooves! It was warm, and one of us came up with the idea of going swimming. But we didn't have swimming trunks. Never mind! There was no one else around. But what about the horses? On this deserted coastline, there was no stake or ship's carcass we could tie them to, so we tied them together by the bridle, telling ourselves, "They'll pull each other in opposite directions, and they won't get very far."

Naked as Adam, we threw ourselves into the water. But hardly had we taken fifty breaststrokes beyond the big breakers on the sandbar when a frightening spectacle made us quickly return to the shore. Our horses, at a slow, regular trot, were fleeing, heading north! Back on the shore, we didn't take time to get dressed. An invisible witness to our race on the sand could have been inspired to carve a tableau in the Parthenon style: Ephebus taming horses.

Fortunately, the miserable beasts had stopped running. They were kicking each other hard, and their whinnying filled the beach. We succeeded in calming them down and separating them. One of them was seriously wounded and limping. We were going back to where our clothing lay in the sand when, from far up on a dune, an invisible witness cried out in accented French, "What are you doing there? Halt! Who are you?"

It was a customs official, a short, fat, but fearsome type, who contemplated the three of us in the nude with a condemning air. "Explain to me," he continued, "how you find yourselves indecently exposed on this beach with three horses!" We had no logical explanation to offer him. "At least tell me that you are not military men. Who is the head of your detachment?" We responded with complete silence. The head of our detachment had to be me, since I was a corporal. My uniform would have proven it, but it was lying about 200 yards away in the sand. Nothing at all on the skin I received at birth attested to the fact that I was a corporal.

"So, you refuse to answer? OK, we'll see about that. You must belong to the detachment that is camping near the wadi. I am going to send your leader a harsh report." He took out his notebook and started to write while mumbling: " . . . have identified . . . in said site . . . three entirely nude men on horseback . . . That's it, you'll be sent to prison for sure." When he disappeared, we got dressed, then returned, sheepishly, to our camp. A few francs to the Moroccan stable boy assured us of his silence. He put the wounded horse with the others. "That must have happened during the night," he said to the lieutenant the next morning, who was satisfied with that explanation and had the animal evacuated.

Despite my pranks, a friendship developed between me and the lieutenant, he a Catholic and I a Protestant. We had long conversations seated on a stone outside his tent at dusk. He showed me a photograph of his young wife and shared his joy at the birth of his first child. I spoke to him often about my religious, social, and moral preoccupations, which he generally approved of. One day, when I shared with him my disapproval of my comrades' sexual behavior, he interrupted me with a dry chuckle: "Trocmé, you really are a bit naive."

"What do you mean?" I asked.

"I'll have to be frank with you. You don't think that a normal man like me should go for months without sex, do you? I would go crazy!"

"What?" I said to him blushing. Up to that point I had accorded him my total admiration by attributing to him virtues he didn't possess. "What about your religion?"

"My religion is indulgent regarding the sins of the flesh. I go to confession and receive absolution before receiving Holy Communion."

"What about your wife?"

"How is she going to find out what I do here?"

"But you run the risk of getting a venereal disease."

"Not at all. Everywhere there are well-maintained houses where one finds willing and beautiful women. It's somewhat expensive; that's the only problem. What do you imagine I do on Sundays, for God's sake?"

I was speechless. The link of friendship being forged between us suddenly slackened. My Protestant austerity could not understand the arrangements that this man had made with God, his wife, and his conscience. I can still hear Lieutenant Tardy's snicker, but even at the age of twenty-two I couldn't approve of the double-dealing that so many men indulged in. The falseness, lying to God and to one's wife, seemed worse than the debauchery itself.

Despite this, the lieutenant continued to behave generously toward me. Whenever we went out on the same detail with the rest of the men, he let me take the lead, either on horseback or on foot, along with Thélinge, sparing us the slow advance of the ranks held back by endless minor incidents.

Taking the lead brought me three adventures I will briefly relate to conclude my account of my stay in Morocco.

One day, Thélinge and I spotted an orchard surrounded by a low dry-stone wall, and we asked the owner to sell us some oranges. He climbed up high in a tree and started to toss fruit down to us. Ten, twenty, thirty. Magnificent, juicy fruit. The oranges that we buy in the grocery store are green when picked because they must survive transportation. Taken ripe from the tree, an orange is a totally different fruit: swollen with sunlight, one might say. The man kept giving us fruit. We filled our pockets and our backpacks and, while there, ate as many as we could. We left with three oranges in each hand. He refused to take any money. "You are the guests of Allah," he declared with a hearty laugh. By entering his compound, we benefitted from all the privileges of marvelous Muslim hospitality.

Another day, alone, I asked a nomad for milk. He had me come into his tent where, to my astonishment, I found a young, unveiled woman preparing a meal for us: bread, curdled butter, and chicken swimming in olive oil. When the meal was over, the man got up, showed me five fingers, and said, pointing to his wife: "*Ouahad domo*" (five francs), and left. I found myself tête-à-tête with a resigned woman waiting for me to approach her. I put down five francs and slipped away. Outside, the man ran after me with the five francs. I refused to take them back. He seemed chagrined that I hadn't found his wife beautiful enough to make love to her.

But my last adventure was the best. M'racme is a charming, white-stoned village with roof terraces perched on the side of Mount Zerhoun, which overlooks the city of Meknès from the north. Our brigade reached M'racme, and as usual, Thélinge and I were leading the pack.

An astonishing welcome awaited us there. As we walked around the most beautiful house in the area, the owner, a heavy-set man dressed in a white djellaba, invited us to enter. He sat us down on cushions shaped like horseshoes in a kind of upper room and shared an excellent meal with us. The meal was prepared by a beanpole of a servant in baggy pants. We were stunned by so much kindness.

Toward the end of the meal, our host disappeared without saying anything. We waited in vain for his return. Tired of waiting, we started to leave. To our great surprise, the door was locked. We started knocking on the door. The beanpole with the baggy pants appeared on the other side of a barred window and made it clear to us that we were prisoners. He gloated stupidly.

Hours passed. Toward evening, our brigade arrived. They were able to liberate us. The bigshot of M'racme, our host, it turned out, was a clever rascal. Won over by the French, he didn't want to displease the authorities. He had taken us for deserters. This had happened just before the insurrection in the Rif. Legionnaires, big and blond like me, were going over to the enemy with their arms. He, therefore, had locked us up to turn us over to the police. But we also might have been telling the truth when we said we were part of a brigade arriving later in the day. So, he received us with the honor befitting officers. That way, no one, not even us, could fault him.

It was with regret that I left Morocco, and I have always dreamed of returning there. I saw at work those whom Lyautey had called "intelligence officers," young men who studied Arabic or Berber and lived alone in the backcountry guarded by a few Moghaznis. They built a residence that was open to everyone, which led the Berbers to trust them. They set up a weekly market, guaranteeing security to all who went there, built roads, helped the local leader settle disputes and maintain order, and opened schools and infirmaries.

I thought with some regret of the narrow horizon of our small Protestant parishes, with two dozen grumpy congregants on Sundays and the handful of catechumens I would have to instruct. Here a useful and marvelous future could open before me! If only there weren't the army, coercion, and weapons to deal with! For several months, I wavered between these two possibilities. I had no idea, of course, that what today we call "colonialism" would be so short-lived. Lyautey's ideology, "Show force so that you won't have to use it," his romantic vision of a chivalrous, aristocratic, and hierarchical Morocco, restored and reanimated with help from France, still held such a fascination that hundreds of young men became his disciples.

Today, I don't regret the decision I made when, in April, our return ship entered the port of Bordeaux. Human exuberance is creative. It irrigates the desert, steadies the flow of rivers, and constructs roads, schools, and hospitals, but its duration is short-lived. The pendulum swings quickly, and those who believe in politics are soon abandoned by it. On the other hand, religion builds for eternity. Regimes come and go; faith lives on. What a shame that it is so poorly served by our churches! When the hour comes when members of the churches stop proselytizing to increase their numbers, they will do good instead and accomplish what politics undertook before them out of ambition. Deserts will flourish, hospitals and schools will multiply. The truth of the Gospels will cease being a pretext for the liturgy, the sermons, and all the pointless repetitions denounced by Jesus.

7

Civilian Again

MY RETURN TRIP TO FRANCE took place without incident, except for the time on the boat when I had to intervene between a demobilized soldier from the Biribi military penitentiary in Morocco and another returning soldier. The only fault that the latter had committed was getting in front of his assailant on the steerage ladder. The aggressor was systematically destroying his victim with hard punches to his bleeding face. Every time he knocked his adversary to the ground, a circle of his obsequiously submissive admirers, who belonged to the same clique, applauded.

I entered the circle and calmly asked this nasty brute to stop. He stared at me and then pretended to box with me. I felt like a trainer surrounded by tigers. If I had turned away my attention for a second, he would have given a signal to the others, and they would have jumped me. "Get ready!" roared the leader. Having no desire to face off against him, for the first time in my military career I pulled rank, pointing to my miserable corporal stripes.

"If you hit a corporal," I yelled at him, "you can forget about getting out of the army! I forbid you to hit that guy. Do you hear me?" His face assumed the shifty gaze of a fearful, misbehaving dog, and the group dispersed. I took the victim to the infirmary.

The night was stormy; outside, the wind was howling. The boat pitched heavily. I heard, from the hammock where I took refuge, hissings and rumblings added to those of the sea. They came from the other hammocks. "Ha, you filthy monster. Do you think you're going to get away with this? Here, we're still prisoners. You're still in command. But when we land, we'll be scot-free. We'll take you on the Bordeaux wharfs. No one will be the wiser." These nasty threats lasted about an hour.

The next morning, when the ship entered the Gironde estuary, I discovered that all my gear – rifle, cartridges, cap, covers, mess kit – had been stolen. The only things I still had were the personal effects I always kept with me: my books, a clean shirt, and my precious rug that, fortunately, I had checked. I think they threw everything overboard, as there was no trace of it. They looked as innocent as possible.

I asked myself what I should do. If I denounced them, I ran the risk of sending them back to prison. If I presented myself to the Fifty-Fourth Infantry Regiment without my rifle, I could be the one who would go to prison. If I placed myself under the protection of my superiors, I would confirm these unfortunate ones in their opinion of religion (they knew I was a seminarian) and of all corporals as snitches. Furthermore, they could stab me and toss me into the ocean. I decided not to say anything.

When we were getting off the ship, I found myself not far from the leader. I went up to him and extended my hand. "You're a bastard," I said to him, "but I didn't turn you in. I'm not what you think I am." He turned away from me with a sneer and a threat.

For the few days in Bordeaux, I stayed close to my comrades and didn't relax until I got on the train for Paris. In Paris, three surprises awaited me.

The first was a 30-day leave, restricted to Paris, accorded by Lieutenant Tardy. I spent it as a civilian on Rue Jacob, in my father's apartment, where I was finally able to live in physical and moral decency.

The second was a "trick" used by the same Lieutenant Tardy that allowed me to prolong my leave. "I said that I needed you in the Geographical Services on Rue de Grenelle," he told me. "It's not true; you're much too weak in math. But you must sign in every morning. I will assign you living quarters at the Caserne des Invalides. You can figure out how to get there in the evenings. It's none of my business whether you sleep there or not."

I slept there because I wanted to make sure that I didn't get caught doing something stupid during my final months of military service. At that time, the dormitory was inhabited mainly by rats. We had to hang up everything that the rats might want to eat, so our room resembled the coatroom of a pit mine. The rest of the time, I lounged around Rue Jacob. For the first time in my life, I did nothing.

All good things must come to an end. The strings that the lieutenant was pulling were so frayed that he said to me one day, "I can't keep you any longer. I'm sending you back to your regiment. You will have to spend three months there." I turned pale thinking of the moment of truth

I would have to endure when I, the shirker, the defector, without rifle or gear, appeared before Captain Queyroi.[1]

I went to the Bureau des Invalides to pick up my orders for Compiègne. The sergeant flipped through his records. "I can't give you that document. There is no Fifty-Fourth Infantry in Compiègne! Come back tomorrow!"

The next day, he informed me: "The Fifty-Fourth Infantry was dissolved six months ago. I can't send you there."

"OK, then keep me here."

"I can't. Your mission has been terminated."

"What should I do then?"

I took all my things to Rue Jacob, where I decided to play dumb. Militarily speaking, I no longer existed. A soldier without a unit, without a company, without a leader, and without any gear no longer exists.

I wrote to the former post commander of the Fifty-Fourth Infantry at Compiègne, who kindly responded, "I can't do anything for you." I didn't want anyone to do something for me! I was forgotten, lost as far as the army was concerned. It was just what I'd always wanted.

Nevertheless, the deadline was approaching. I had finished my military obligation. I wanted to become a civilian again, but I couldn't!

I went to Les Invalides. "We have no authority to discharge you. Only your unit can do that."

"But I no longer have a unit."

"You can bloody well figure it out for yourself!"

"At least give me my orders for Compiègne, so that I can prove I'm not a deserter." They gave them to me.

At Compiègne, I went from one office to the next, from the commander of the defunct Fifty-Fourth Infantry to the main offices, from the main offices to the barracks, which were now inhabited by a battalion of balloonists. They all recused themselves. I presented them with an administrative problem without a solution!

Finally, I entered an office where I found a sergeant who was half asleep. "Discharge me," I said to him. "I'll buy you a drink." He raised an eyelid and glanced at the last page of my military orders.

"It's irregular," he said to me, "but I'll do it for you." The stamp of the balloonist company and the signature of an unaware sergeant returned me to civilian life.

1 Fortunately, this encounter never took place.

I waited a few years to receive my first draft card, which would tell me where to appear if there was a general mobilization. I waited in vain to be called up, which was lucky because, due to my own conscience and Lieutenant Tardy's counsel, I would have refused military service. All my comrades were called up, but not me. Did my name fall into a neglected category? Was it because of the balloonist sergeant? I have no idea, but since then I've been very fond of balloonists.

In the fall of that year, the Trocmé family left Rue Jacob for good and settled back into the old house in Saint-Quentin, now restored and refurnished. For sure, the old prewar atmosphere was no longer there. My sisters Louise and Madeleine had died; Robert had married Germaine; Pierre had married Aline; Yvonne and Étienne had remained in Paris for business and studies. Papa was now seventy-eight years old. Jeanne and Marie had taken control of the house, with Jeanne reigning like a queen, establishing or undoing the reputations of the sons, daughters-in-law, and grandchildren.

The beautiful furniture from the old days was replaced by furniture with a walnut finish from a period of especially poor taste. Papa could no longer maintain the standard of living we had enjoyed before the war. His fortune had been invested in a public company, created from the formerly rival cotton mills, and called the Saint-Quentin Cotton Company, which suffered from the fluctuations of the market. Maurice, who had worked so hard to reestablish the factory, would die of overwork at the age of sixty.

Papa had refused to inflate his record of war damages, but many who had lost houses or furniture had done so. As a result, we saw going up all around us, in Saint-Quentin as well as in Saint-Gobain, chalets in the place of hovels and chateaus in the place of chalets.

The government grew alarmed. In 1922, a law was passed: all war claims would henceforth be reduced by a third. Furthermore, Germany wasn't paying up its required reparations. They never would, and it was becoming obvious. That was when the dossiers of those who registered late, like Papa, who had a home in Paris, were being accepted.

Papa was summoned to the Damages Office.

"Mr. Trocmé," the arbitrator said to him, "here is your dossier. I'm returning it to you. It's much too modest. Inflate it a bit, will you."

"I called all my children together to write it up. I am claiming everything that I possessed, nothing extra at all."

"I know, I understand, but don't you see that the rules are strict. I'm supposed to reduce your claim by a third. You will be terribly wronged."

"I refuse to amend my dossier. I have always been honest, and I have no intention of changing that now."

"But Mr. Trocmé, you would not be dishonest since, in the final analysis, you would only be getting your due."

"I stand by what I said. I won't take back my dossier. Go ahead and apply your unfair reduction. If I lose out, too bad for me. There have been too many profiteers in this country. I'll serve as an example of citizenship with integrity."

That's why Papa furnished the house on Rue Gambetta so frugally.

BECAUSE OF OUR MOVE to Saint-Quentin, I finally got from Papa what I had always asked him for: permission to live at the seminary of the School of Theology in Paris at 82 Boulevard Arago.

The students who don't live there are not in the thick of things. Aside from my old friends from our Northern Group, I later discovered that the "demobilized generation" I had greatly admired (Dallière, Lestringant, Hammel) had been completely unaware of us silent rookies who listened with amazement to their discussions.

In 1923–24, this whole cohort left and was replaced by a generation younger than mine: Jacques Vernier, Jacques Martin, Georges Marchal, Marchand, André Parrot, Arnold Brémond, and others I forget.

I discovered right away how useful my military interlude had been. Far from being the youngest, I now had the advantage of being a year or two older than my classmates. In addition, I had the experience of the occupation, the evacuation into Belgium, poverty in Paris, and Morocco.

I've never had the good timing to exchange the rapid-fire word play that makes you popular, and I had a rather serious demeanor. So my nickname at the school was "Uncle Troc," whereas Roger Casalis was simply "My Uncle."[2] The students were divided into two rival groups. When it was time to elect the president of the student body, "My Uncle" won out over "Uncle Troc."

This nickname fit me well. I enjoyed it and finally began my relentless study of theology. But I never succeeded in recovering the ground I had lost during my first two botched years of study.

2 Roger Casalis (1900–1986) would serve as pastor in Le Chambon-sur-Lignon from 1927 to 1934, before being named pastor in Sainte-Foy-la-Grande, and then in Saint-Cloud.

I found the atmosphere at the school much less exciting than it had been two years earlier. The "greats" – those who, by their personality, were going to mark the church – had given way to a group of young men with less extreme abilities and personalities. It was even a bit boring under the aging reign of the great liberal masters whom I enumerated earlier, but we worked harder than we did in 1919.

I became friends with my classmates who had progressive social ideas: Jacques Vernier, who would become a missionary in Madagascar and whose brother Philippe, a future theology student I didn't yet know, would become the famous Philo Vernier, conscientious objector;[3] Jacques Martin, an intelligent, faithful friend, a courageous pacifist, and a conscientious objector;[4] and Raymond Querouil.[5]

Above all, there was Arnold Brémond, a strange fellow, or rather a stranger to this world. Slow to speak, ponderous like so many Swiss, but a poet who wrote several books and illustrated them himself, Brémond was able to see his plans through to the end. He was, during my last year of theology school, the first worker-pastor of France. He wrote to his father, an engineer in Geneva, asking him to stop sending money, and got a job as a factory worker in Ivry. He stopped living in the seminary and took a room in a poorly furnished hotel inhabited by North Africans. He was welcomed by anarchists and Communists, who had challenged him when he was making the rounds preaching: "If you are a disciple of Christ, the apostle of poverty, leave the privileged, capitalist world where you enjoy yourself and come live the true worker's life with us." The worker's life was hard at the time. There were no family benefits from the government, no health care. With his friend Janson, an anarchist, Brémond founded the "Ivry Group." It met at city hall, where great projects took shape. Instead of bringing a "bourgeois" message and doing good deeds for the underprivileged, he put a group to work. It was the workers in this group who began to organize and send their own children to summer camps in La Michaudy in the Jura Mountains, where a marvelous spirit of friendship and equality reigned.

3 Philippe Vernier (1909–1985) could not be consecrated pastor in the Reformed Church of France because he was a conscientious objector. He was tried and imprisoned several times in the 1930s. He served as a pastor in Borinage in Belgium until 1954, then at Maubeuge, and from then on was recognized by the Reformed Church of France.

4 As regards Jacques Martin (1906–2001), who was also named Righteous Among the Nations, see his daughter's biography of him: Violaine Kichenin-Martin, *Jacques Martin, objecteur de conscience, Juste et résistant* (Ampelos, 2015).

5 Raymond Querouil (1905–1988) was a pastor in Florac and then Blauzac.

Brémond kept a diary, written in an unusual style, the essential portion of which he published and later presented as the thesis for his baccalaureate degree in theology. This mimeographed thesis made a great impression at the time and inspired the first worker-priests. Brémond's work, alas, was interrupted by serious health issues: eating poorly prepared food, he picked up amoebic dysentery. We thought he was going to die. A long stay in Switzerland, in the hands of his family, brought him back to health. He finished his studies at Montpellier, where he met and married Evelyne Bruston, the daughter of a professor of Hebrew Scripture.[6] Over all these long years, he has perhaps remained my best friend.

Georges Marchal had a surprising career.[7] Looking very much like the "traditional instructor" in his way of dressing, he made himself an easy target for my fellow students. No one had yet perceived in him the eloquent pastor and fashionable man who would replace our Professor Wautier d'Aygalliers, himself a disciple of Charles Wagner, in the liberal chair at the Foyer de l'âme in Paris.

Living outside the seminary, silent, towering, and subject to brusque moments of holy indignation, there was Édouard Theis, who was also outstanding in book learning. He made all of us somewhat uneasy. I met him several times at get-togethers of the Fellowship of Reconciliation organized by Henri Roser, but we only exchanged a few words. I had no idea that one day he would be closely tied to my career. He wanted to do missionary work, and we didn't stay in touch.

At this time, Henri Roser began to play an important role in my life. He was the leader of our street-preaching group that Brémond and others had joined. They had opened a place in Aubervilliers where he preached the gospel. Rejected by missionary organizations and churches, he managed to get by on donations, scratching out a living with his young wife, whom he met during internships sponsored by Henri Nick, the brilliant pastor of Fives-Lille, who opened his arms to conscientious objectors.

One day, the Fellowship of Reconciliation asked Roser to become its French secretary. He accepted on the condition that he could spend part of his time working at the home in Aubervilliers where he helped put

6 She and her husband published an account of his time as worker-pastor: *Sur le Chemin du renouveau. Une aventure sociale et spirituelle* (Pneumathèque, 1976).

7 Georges Marchal (1905–1982) was the pastor of Foyer de l'âme, near Place de la Bastille in Paris, from 1931 to 1974.

men back on their feet by bringing them a gospel that was both profound and practical.

At the time, I had become a member of the International Fellowship of Reconciliation, and I attended the meetings where brave bureaucratic pacifists from across the Channel continuously attacked Roser, our calm giant, trying to force him to renounce his parish work. "I cannot preach a pacifism that doesn't apply to everyday life," he repeated patiently. He always won the day. He did so until 1939, when World War II broke out.

These two years of theological study were uneventful. I prepared for my exams resolutely. I refused to take part in activities with my classmates and concentrated on the Union in Clamart. I read and I thought. I conceived of the church as a friendly, egalitarian, communal group whose members offered themselves up together in practical witness to Jesus Christ. The pastor would be their brother, their inspiration, and would speak only when necessary. "I will only preach by my actions," I repeated back home in Saint-Quentin. My paradoxes made my family laugh, but I loved being taken for an eccentric. Behind this defense, I felt freer to reflect on things.

Strangely enough for a twenty-three-year-old man, I hadn't become attached, even in thought, to any young woman, and never thought about getting married. The students that I hung around with at theology school practiced a kind of Franciscanism. The Vernier brothers, along with a guy named Jean-Jacques Bovet,[8] took off on foot one summer on a pilgrimage to Assisi. At a time when only scouts camped out and hitchhiking was nonexistent (it was a post–World War II American import), this seemed extravagant. Be that as it may, we were thinking about becoming voluntary celibates to feel freer to live the life of the poorest among us, some of whom I had already met in Morocco. But Morocco didn't attract me as a missionary post: I had found there a stable patriarchal civilization at a time before slums invaded the suburbs.

What did attract our group was the world of the workers, with its Communists, its idealism, and its revolt against the church. It seemed to us that there was a misunderstanding at the origin of this revolt. We dreamed of dissipating this misunderstanding and announcing the total conversion through the Gospels. A great religious awakening would spread across Europe and the world. I didn't yet know what I was going to

8 Jean-Jacques Bovet (1905-1990) was a pastor and resister in Grasse during the 1940s. He helped rescue Jews and, in 1946, published an article on Christian responsibility for anti-Semitism.

find in the United States: a capitalist civilization in full bloom, in which Henry Ford, thanks to mass production, distributed all the material advantages of bourgeois life – cars, beautiful homes, and, already, the first refrigerators – to the workers. But enough! I'll come back to this later.

My anti-bourgeois populism prompted me to avoid the young women who haunted the theology school looking for husbands and whom Yvonne sometimes invited to our country house in Saint-Gobain. One of them, a student with Yvonne at the School for Christian Service (an evangelical school founded by Pastor Dürrlemann) named Marguerite, clearly wanted to marry the future pastor that I represented. She had a brash personality, short legs, and a waxy complexion. One day, she called me, "André, André," from the garden, where she wanted me to take a walk with her. I threw the contents of a cleaning bucket on her head from my bedroom window, which was one floor above the kitchen. I recognize today that it was a despicable and base response to her advances. If I had been less timid, I would have found other means to discourage her. She ran off screaming and crying and left the next morning.

Everything "bourgeois" got under my skin, and that included my sisters-in-law. When, in the month of August, the Saint-Gobain estate filled with mothers and children, I only had three options: hide out in my bedroom, take a walk by myself (which was not done), or read a book in the main parlor while Papa dozed off and my sisters-in-law chatted in a low voice and clicked their knitting needles.

The two Saint-Affrique sisters, Madeleine and Aline, spouses of Eugène and Pierre, set the tone. They never tired of talking about their children. Rose, the wife of Francis, deciding to play up her French side rather than the Russian, never spoke about her childhood, only about her maids. Juliette, Albert's wife, spoke little and was considered proud. Her legendary sensitivity forced her co-conversationalists to choose their words carefully. As regards Marguerite, Maurice's wife, her visits were rare and brief.

One day, in all honesty, from behind my book I very impolitely began to rail against these excellent women, all older than I was.

"Haven't you finished all this mindless chatter? You keep repeating all the same stories of maids and children, and I can't concentrate on my book!"

The knitting dropped on their laps. Four stunned faces, mouths open, stared at me, infuriated. I will never forget Madeleine's face. She was certainly the best of the four, but her facial features radiated holy indignation.

"Nothing requires you to sit here if our conversation strikes you as unpleasant."

"But I can't spend all my time closed up in my room."

"Women have things to tell one another. When you get married, your wife will be like the rest of us. I'm very curious to know just what kind of wife you will bring home."

"In any case," I replied stupidly and arrogantly, "she will not be like you!"

Madeleine was now furious because she was capable, along with Aline, of understanding how limited their conversations were. "What will she be like, then?" she asked.

Caught short, I stood up, and before slamming the door as I sometimes did, I replied: *"Pâlotte, falote, salotte"* (ugly, stupid, dirty).

These three words have remained in our family lore. From that day onward, brothers and sisters-in-law awaited, intrigued, for the "ugly, stupid, dirty" fiancée I had announced to them.

I PASSED MY FINAL theology exams in the spring of 1925 with moderate success. At that time, each professor, seeing a flock of students leaving him, kindly invited them in groups of four or five to talk about their futures. Since a few scholarships were available to good students, I decided, against Papa's advice, to do a fifth year of theology abroad. Drawn since my days in Morocco to the Middle East, I applied to the French Institute in Jerusalem and patiently awaited their response.

I got their response during an evening spent with my Hebrew professor, Adolph Monod.

"Trocmé," Monod announced with the coy smile he always wore when he had to give us a bad grade, "if you had applied in any other year, you would have had a good chance of getting the scholarship. But this year you had stiff competition from André Parrot, and it's clear that he deserves the award."

"I understand completely," I responded.

André Parrot was a young man with pursed lips, high cheekbones, and a waxy complexion, who hardly ever left his room. He spent his days bent over minuscule flash cards, like playing cards, which he filled to the brim with an illegible scrawl that only he could decipher. He was brilliant in Hebrew, Syriac, Greek, and just about everything else.

I had no alternative but to bow out.

André Parrot left for Jerusalem and then returned to the Near East for archaeological digs in Mesopotamia. He discovered the buried city of Mari, wrote a book, became a professor at the École du Louvre, then director, then a professor at the Sorbonne.

What a career I missed! But I never wanted to become an archeologist. I think now with regret, however, about the time I could have spent in theoretical study, particularly concerning the early days of Christianity. The book I published at age sixty, *Jesus and the Nonviolent Revolution*, would have commanded greater authority.

The great decisions in life are often the result of what appears to be chance. Another classmate applied for the much-sought-after scholarship to Edinburgh. All that was left was the United States, about which I knew next to nothing. I wasn't drawn to the United States either. Well, New York was worth seeing, and I received the scholarship to study at Union Theological Seminary.

Papa didn't take the news well at all. "I'm eighty years old," he said to me, "and you're going far away. There's a risk that I won't see you again."

Papa and I had developed close ties. In his youth, he had given up a pastoral vocation to help his sick father and take care of the family in which he was the eldest. I was therefore accomplishing what he had been unable to do. I often imagined that his severity toward pastors came from what he imagined he would have done in their place had he been able to pursue his vocation. Papa had been disappointed by my older brother Albert's failures and had placed his hopes in me. He became anxious whenever he saw me deviating ever so slightly from his dream of me becoming a well-loved pastor with a charming wife and many children.

As a result, America, which at that time seemed a far-away continent, frightened him. But I insisted and won out. I can still see myself in Saint-Gobain in April 1925, flipping through the catalog of the seminary. Its Tudor architecture impressed me. From then on, I was completely oriented toward that unknown future, which would, in fact, determine the rest of my life.

8

The United States

AS SOON AS the transatlantic ship arrived in Le Havre, I was caught up in a world of new dimensions that I was completely unfamiliar with. Paris's Left Bank, at that time and in a sense still today, is a small town by comparison. The pulse of London, where I had once been, already beat to another, more ample rhythm. But the transatlantic ship, *Le France*, which took me to New York, had quite another tempo.

In third class there were immigrants speaking every language: Germans, Poles, Scandinavians. In second class, where I was, there were Americanized Europeans who lived in New York or Chicago, returning from a visit to the old folks and the old country. First class, which I entered on several occasions through small doors, was filled with businessmen, manufacturers, and women in fine clothing. Their conversations were sometimes snobby, but light-hearted and funny, and sometimes sincere, broaching vast financial, political, and cultural problems I knew nothing about. These people had power and means, and I was still a long way from understanding that their competence often concealed very ordinary intellectual capacities and moral virtues.

This blast of fresh air, which would teach me to breathe more deeply, continued to blow on me during my entire stay in the United States. For the first time, my thirst for freedom was able to orient itself toward horizons other than internal ones like freedom from sin. Up to then, I had tried to escape from the pressure of my education either by moral absolutism, opposition to established rules, or by voluntary poverty.

In America, I became acquainted with the freedom that space provides. (The planet had not yet been reduced by air travel to small dimensions.) It was immense, diverse, strange. Beyond the United States, there was Asia, China, and India. Wouldn't it be marvelous to become familiar with all those countries, finally to understand what I was doing here on earth? For a long time, I believed that there was "another country" on earth happier and better than mine.

On the boat, I bonded with a strange young man who, at the age of twenty-five, wore an old-style pince-nez and a curious fedora. He repeatedly tapped its band with his right hand, as if he were afraid it might fly away. Auguste Viatte, from Porrentruy, Switzerland, was a narrow-minded, fanatical Catholic and the only Swiss I have ever known who regretted that France had not annexed his canton. Without even trying, he could have played the absent-minded, sanctimonious, reserved professor in a burlesque comedy. Otherwise, he was a perfectly charming fellow.

He spoke and understood English poorly, and that got him into some painful situations. "The young American girls to whom I teach French," he said to me one day in New York, "are very undisciplined. Can you imagine, they start laughing as soon as I enter the classroom, and they want me to give up my excellent English accent and start speaking with those terrible American nasal intonations." Later, he told me: "I am beginning to get a better grip on popular expressions. At the beginning of my stay in New York, I thought that 'watch your step,' which is written on the steps of buses, meant 'look at your change.' Now I know it means 'don't talk to the conductor.'"

Our landing in New York was the occasion of an amusing scene that could have been tragic. It was the time when immigrants, even temporary immigrants like us, could be sent to Ellis Island for the least reason and forced to stay there for weeks without being admitted or deported. Viatte presented himself to the immigration officer with his hat on his head. With his right hand, he crumpled his immigration papers; with his left, he held numerous notebooks, books, and papers close to his chest.

"Take off your hat," the agent said to him.

"What did you say?" asked Viatte with extreme politeness.

"Take off your hat when you speak to an immigration officer!" growled the American.

"I beg your pardon?" repeated Viatte, who didn't understand a word.

"Take off your hat," I whispered to him in French.

With his free hand, Viatte managed to take off his ridiculous hat, but he dropped his immigration papers on the ground. To pick them up, he put his hat on the immigration officer's register.

"You damn fool," howled the agent, "remove this hat."

Trembling and blushing, Viatte, without budging, repeated the "I beg your pardon?" he had learned on the benches of the lycée in Porrentruy.

I took his hat, and the agent, finally appeased, looked at the innocent expression of the professor, whose intentions were certainly not to overthrow the Government of the United States with violence, and affixed the signature required for admission to the sacred soil of the United States.

Believe it or not, Viatte became a specialist of American culture. He taught in several colleges in the United States, wrote books and articles, and accumulated a detailed knowledge of this vast country. However, as a Catholic, he was never able to understand that America was still a Protestant country. He attributed the country's loose morals to Protestantism. His last book attests to this.[1] Viatte showed me that, much more than language and race, religion lies at the heart of every problem of culture and civilization, at the core of these misunderstandings. We only truly understand those who have the same religion.

ON THE EVENING of my arrival in New York, I became acquainted with American doors that lock automatically and can't be opened from the outside without a key. Viatte and I took a room in a lower-class hotel at the end of the pier of the French Line. I clearly remember this hotel without an elevator. It had a sinister-looking stairwell. In the middle of the night, I felt an urgent need and went to the toilet down the hall without taking my key – and locked myself out! I called Viatte, who was snoring, then knocked on the door. He opened immediately, just as the steps of the night watchman, concerned about the noise, reached the floor below.

This ridiculous incident remains engraved in my mind because it resembled situations in my nightmares: I am just about ready to finish something but never manage to do so. Luckily, at the last minute, Viatte mercifully opened the door and saved me from appearing in my pajamas before the unpitying night watchman.

SINCE UNION THEOLOGICAL SEMINARY hadn't yet opened its doors in early September, I took a room at the International House in a beautiful area on Riverside Drive at the edge of the splendid estuary formed by the lower Hudson. Immediately, solitude encircled me as if I were in

1 Auguste Viatte, *Les Etats-Unis: La vie américaine* (Flammarion, 1962).

a rabbit hole. The rabbit hole was a small, narrow, but comfortable room overlooking the river. No breeze came through the vertically sliding window that was never more than half open, making it impossible to aerate the room fully. In the daytime, I saw only a whitish fog that almost completely hid the other bank. At night, an immense electric clock, the first one I had ever seen, lit up every minute, spelling out the exact time: "It is now 9:21 p. m." Then it faded, and an enormous "WARNERS SUGAR" blazed in the night. The lobby of the building was crawling with foreign students. There were few Americans at that time of year. I didn't reach out to anyone, not knowing how or why I would do so.

Alone, I began to explore the city: a boat tour of Manhattan, the express elevator in the Woolworth Building, which was then the tallest building in the world, and St. Patrick's Cathedral. I became familiar with the thundering elevated train, which no longer exists. I discovered the express subway, which we don't have in Paris, and the sinister expressions on the passengers' faces that don't exist in Paris either. I was surprised, shoved about, crushed, but in no way defeated. Everything was, as so often in American landscapes, larger than life. You don't "walk along" the Hudson; it "takes" too much time and is too monotonous. You don't "stroll through" Central Park; you cross it to get somewhere else. Many of the people don't even live in the city; they work or study there and return to the suburbs in the evening. New York's lack of love for itself bursts forth from its buildings. They are enormous and pretentious, on the same scale as gigantic banks, or they are shabby, ordinary, and abandoned. Riverside Church, the George Washington Bridge, and the few recent attempts at city planning have not yet succeeded in creating a New York landscape. Like the Fata Morgana illusion which, from afar, promises wonders, New York, which from the boat presents itself as a paradise, dissolves when you get close to it and, still today, only offers narrow canyons, glacial in the winter and torrid in the summer, to the traveler who dreamed of faraway continents.

In the evening, in my cell, I made tea that I drank until I sweated out the accumulated toxins of the day. Not even the exaltation that I experienced at the wide intersections of Fifth Avenue succeeded in chasing away my boredom. In New York, as in the other geometrical cities in the United States, I am bored because there is never anything to discover around the next corner, which is mathematically located so many feet from the corner where I stand.

THE SEMINARY OPENED, and I was assigned a magnificent room, number 602 on the sixth floor, on the corner of Broadway and 122nd Street. It had a panoramic view, and I could see the endless stream of cars going up 125th Street. I had a bedroom with a separate toilet and sink and a study with a big desk and an oak chair, heavy but comfortable.

I remember very little about my classes. Hebrew Scripture was weak compared to the teaching of our Adolphe Monod. The History of Religions seemed no more than a catalog next to the fiery lectures of Philippe de Félice. It was the tail end of the dying liberalism that our Parisian seminary had championed. Five years later, the theology of Reinhold Niebuhr, a Christian socialist who converted to neo-orthodoxy from fear of Hitler, would carry the day. Under Niebuhr's influence, Union Theological Seminary made a U-turn, and those students who had believed in their professors' scientific approach to theology were left out in the cold.

Fortunately, there was Harry Ward,[2] a Welshman whose English I understood, a Celt whose ironic spirit I appreciated. A Christian who had rediscovered the exigencies of the Gospels, he never failed to denounce with a hissing voice the idols of the day: prosperity, trusts (Rockefeller, Ford), the insane practice of buying on credit that led America to its financial ruin. This was 1925, the summit of the prosperity that Fordism had procured for the United States. On the point of (already) abandoning its prohibition of alcohol (only in force since 1917), America was flush with pride. It turned its back on a failed Puritanism and sought to create a civilization of happiness, where human beings adjusted to society and nature. It had rid itself of outmoded notions, such as eternal judgment, sin, repentance, and divine forgiveness, and would advance from conquest to conquest toward an ever-happier future.

Ward denounced all this, whereas Col, a disciple of John Dewey at Teachers College, where I took his classes, became its apostle. I remember with what sarcasm he put me down the day that, coming from Occupied France and Morocco and exasperated by his naive optimism, I overcame

2 Harry Ward (1873–1966) was a Methodist pastor and professor of Christian ethics at Union Theological Seminary. He was also the co-founder and first president (1929–1940) of the American Civil Liberties Union.

my timidity and raised my hand American-style. "Sir," I asked, "What about sin?"

"There is no such thing as individual sin," he responded. "Your opinion is an outworn prejudice, coming right down from medieval superstition. The only problem is your – or my – maladjustment to the society where we live."

A few years later, Hitler, benefitting from the ravages created by German students with similar doctrines, tried, like a magician, to readjust the German masses to their society as it was or, rather, as he conceived of it: the proud, insane Third Reich. The young men who surged in waves across Europe in 1939 were happy, relaxed, naive, and triumphant, all admirably adjusted to the Germanic society of which they were the products. Henceforth, all crimes were possible, since all sin had disappeared, except the sin one commits against society.

Ward's prediction about an economic depression came true only three years later. In 1925, students made fun of this prophet of doom, but I loved him. With his help, I prepared my Second Theology Master's Degree (STM) so easily that it was shameful: a 60-page paper on a subject I had been working on for several years, "The Manifestation of Religious Convictions by Alexandre Vinet." At the end of the year, I presented my thesis in English, which caused me a lot of trouble. It seems that I could have written it in French. Oh, happy America, which spares its students the sweat and anguish of terrible exams and doesn't refuse the much sought-after title of doctor for decades on end!

I DIDN'T PAL AROUND much with my American classmates for a couple of reasons. The first is that I didn't understand American English very well. It was a mishmash of sounds between the throat and the nose – at least that's what I made of it. It's true that most Americans don't differentiate very much between "Newark," which I pronounce "Niou-Ouark" and they pronounce "Nou-ork," and "New York," which I pronounce "Niou-Iork" and they pronounce "Nou-ork." Likewise, to my ear there's not much difference on the tongue of most Americans between "taxes," "taxis," and "Texas"! You had to guess, based on the context, what these unarticulated sounds meant, all of which began with a kind of groan of a cow in labor: "Uh, uh! I, I, I believe, uh, uh!"

Fortunately, I met a young guy whom I understood perfectly and who seemed to enjoy my company. I made the rounds of the city with him. It took me three weeks to discover that he was Greek and that his name was Michaëlides. Today, he is the director of a secondary school in Greece similar to the Collège Cévenol in Le Chambon-sur-Lignon.

THE AMERICAN STUDENTS, who were extremely friendly and welcoming at first, quickly grew tired of our halting English and our company. In the hallways, they passed us with a quick step and a "Hi there!" They all invariably had appointments downtown and were always on the move. Many of them paid for their studies by teaching Sunday school or holding weekend church services, but not all of them and not all the time. Their love life played a huge role in their schedules. For the first time, I heard the word girlfriend. Each one of them had a girlfriend with whom they spent evenings and Saturdays without any promises of marriage. "What a waste of time as far as their studies are concerned," I thought, and I wasn't mistaken.

I had three good friends during that 1925–26 winter. For chats, a Swiss with a nondescript personality: Marcel Christen. A gigantic, conscientious German named Petermann for profound discussions of our studies. My closest friend was Jan Kucera, a Czech who spoke slowly and in a somewhat gravelly voice. He was absent-minded, humane, and a pacifist like me. I spent many excellent afternoons with him. One Sunday evening, we went to Harlem to attend services in a black church that turned out to be half spoken and half jazz. We were welcomed with open arms because we were the only white people in attendance.[3]

There was no cafeteria in the seminary in 1925. At mealtime, students took off for small restaurants in the area – "The Little Dutch Mill Inn" or "Shipwreck Inn" – where, to save money, I ate very little, just enough to keep myself alive. Fairly often I took my meals at the International House. There I met several interesting French students: Claroué, a medical student; Teilhac, a fervent Catholic, absolutist but well bred; Desnoyers, a bragging and ambitious young man who is today the director of the French edition of *Reader's Digest*. On Sundays we took walks, following the French custom, which meant we crossed the Hudson River on a ferry and wandered through the Palisades' woods where foliage was turning

3 Later, I connected with Kucera in Czechoslovakia. As a member of the Fellowship of Reconciliation, he was condemned to prison under the German Occupation. He was sent to a logging camp under the Communists, because he had visited Jan Masaryk in prison. Masaryk was a Czech diplomat and politician who was distrusted by the emerging communist government in 1948. He was neither a Communist nor a fellow traveler.

red and would soon fall in the dry, northern wind, clearing the way for snow and winter cold.

Of course, we discussed Americans. Desnoyers envied and imitated them. Claroué, Teilhac, and Viatte, who often joined us, spoke and understood English poorly and didn't try to mingle with the people around them. Their negative mindset and the fact that, as Catholics, they felt outside this generally Protestant setting, led them to be hypercritical. I soon understood the privilege I enjoyed, by virtue of the Union Theological Seminary, of being immersed in American life. I eventually tired of their negativity, and almost completely stopped seeing them.

An extraordinary, unexpected event was about to expand my horizons and introduce me to a legendary world that, in the eyes of some, symbolized America at this time: the world of multimillionaires.

Sometime in October, I was called to the phone, and a man's voice said to me: "I am Mr. John D. Rockefeller Jr., 10 West Fifty-Fourth Street. I need a French tutor for my sons. I have been very satisfied with the tutors from the seminary over the past few years. If this is of interest to you, come see Mrs. Rockefeller." We set up a meeting, and the next day I received a pass that allowed me to enter the Rockefeller residence. Not anyone could walk in: there was an armed detective pacing back and forth in front of the door twenty-four hours a day who rang the doorbell for you if you proved yourself admissible. I entered a small parlor on the ground floor, where I underwent a second examination. If you passed, a servant led you to the elevator.

I found myself in the house of John D. Rockefeller Jr, the only son of John D. Rockefeller, the founder of Standard Oil, who was considered the richest man in the world at that time. The Rockefellers, father and son, didn't construct a French chateau on Fifth Avenue like the Vanderbilts and Pierpont Morgan. They had no desire to flaunt their enormous fortune publicly. In fact, John D. Rockefeller Sr. got into trouble with President Theodore Roosevelt, who forced him to break Standard Oil into several competing companies – in all of which, however, he was the major stockholder. He had become a symbol of predatory capitalism at the turn of the century and was immensely unpopular. He lived almost a hidden existence. His son, who had partially succeeded in having the origin of the family's fortune forgotten by multiplying donations and foundations, was a man of simple tastes. In 1925, he had already distributed $400 million to charity, a sum that has been greatly exceeded since then. Furthermore, the house on Fifty-Fourth Street had nothing extraordinary about it. It was a five-story building with wide windows, topped by a mesh cage, the children's play area.

Having no experience with the price of expensive objects, I didn't realize the accumulated value of the furniture, vases, and works of art in the immense living room on the second floor where Mrs. Rockefeller welcomed me with tea and scones. Fortunately, I wasn't alone: I was flanked by a tall red-headed American, Arthur Moor, who was quite confident. He introduced himself as the new English tutor. It was probably his presence that stopped me from dropping my teacup and spoon on the floor in nervousness.

Mrs. Rockefeller, the descendant of an old Boston family, the Aldriches, was about fifty. Her kind smile was overshadowed by a pointed nose seriously out of proportion with the rest of her face. She was much more intelligent and cultured than her husband.

The conversation was almost cut short because Moor, who was poor and had a very favorable opinion of himself, demanded that each one of us receive $200 a month. That was the salary for a full-time worker, but we only had to teach a few hours a day. Normally, the Rockefellers paid $100 a month for their tutors.

Mrs. Rockefeller explained our obligations in detailed fashion. Every day at four p.m., I would go to Lincoln School, located north of Central Park, to pick up the two youngest boys, Winthrop and David, and bring them home by bus. I could share their snacks and supper if I wanted to, but I was free at 6:30. On Friday evenings, I would take the bus that follows the Hudson up to Tarrytown, where the country home of the Rockefellers is situated and would spend the night and all of Saturday there. On Saturday evening, I would come back to New York City in the family car and be free all day Sunday.

Then Mrs. Rockefeller dismissed us, telling us she had to consult her husband because our expected salary was so high. She said she would have an answer for us in three days. I was chomping at the bit with anticipation, and was mad as hell at Arthur Moor for possibly letting such an extraordinary opportunity slip away. But the response came: Mrs. Rockefeller hired us for $175 a month. For me, it was a fortune! I immediately resolved to set this money aside and open a savings account. A marvelous project was sprouting in my head. I gathered the appropriate information and calculated that eight times 175 gave me $1,400 dollars, with which I could travel around the world, visit Tagore and Gandhi, and find in India the answers to the numerous questions I was still asking myself!

The good fortune that came my way made a great impression on many of my classmates, particularly on another Frenchman from Alsace, G., also a scholarship student at the seminary. Like most of the students, he began to look for a job to earn additional funds since the scholarship was barely sufficient. One day, as he haunted the lobby of the General Transatlantic Company, a well-dressed man came up to him and said: "Are you looking for a job? I have one for you. I am the Viscount de Rovin, an important New York City businessman. I will hire you as my secretary. I can't promise you a regular salary, but you'll receive profits from the company."

G., feeling proud of his new job, came to tell me about his godsend. I didn't pay much attention to him because we hardly knew each other. But two months later, I was called to the registrar.

"Mr. Trocmé," said the registrar, "we are concerned about your French classmate. For over a month, he has been attending classes irregularly and now isn't attending them at all, and his room in the seminary is empty. You understand that the scholarships we grant entail certain responsibilities of the recipients."

I did my best to get hold of G. One evening I found him in his room. "I know, I know," he said looking at me strangely, "but you understand, I have so much work." He was hiding something from me.

The next day, he appeared thinner than usual and wild looking. I didn't let him go until he confessed everything: "The truth is that I have no more money."

"What, no more money?"

"Yes, the Viscount de Rovin borrowed all the money from my fellowship – and hasn't given any of it back. Today, he gave me just enough to come here, spend the night, and get my things. He feeds me and lodges me in his room. We eat badly too. I'm afraid he's nothing but a sham. He's in land sales; he buys and resells. He's using me to do commercial canvassing. But I don't think his business is doing well at all. There are many fishy things about the way he lives: he borrows money, has lots of it, and never pays any back."

"You must threaten him! Demand your money or come with me to the registrar or the police."

"You don't know him," he said to me with a terrified look. "He would beat me; he already has beaten me."

"Then I'll go talk to the seminary authorities for you."

"Oh, no. I beg you. Don't do anything. He's capable of killing me and you too."

The next day, a plan, a rather daring one I recognize today, sprouted in my mind. "Tell your Viscount," I said to G., "that I wish to meet him. We'll see his reaction."

That very evening G. came back: "Listen, Trocmé," he said to me in his heavy Alsatian accent, "He wants to take you out to lunch on Sunday. Can you accept?"

"Of course," I said, delighted to see the fish take the bait.

De Rovin most certainly thought that I was another naive student like my classmate, because he came to pick me up in a Cadillac with a chauffeur wearing livery and white gloves. A rented Cadillac, to be sure, but I was not supposed to be in G.'s confidence.

Hoping to extort my scholarship money or the money I earned tutoring the Rockefeller children, de Rovin drove us to a speakeasy in the basement of a respectable-looking building on Fifty-Fourth Street. They recognized him through the peephole in the door. There was a table reserved for us. Our host ordered an excellent meal and was disappointed that I refused to taste the fine French wines he had ordered. Questionable couples around us went upstairs, and I realized that this was also a cathouse.

When dessert was served, I took the initiative: "OK, now, let's talk business," I said to de Rovin.

"Yes, that's right. Let's talk business."

"Mr. de Rovin, here is my friend, a theology student, who has come to New York thanks to a scholarship the seminary has offered him. He needs the money to finish this school year. That's the case, isn't it?" I said to G., turning in his direction.

Turning pale, G. said: "Well, yes and no. Mr. de Rovin and I are associates. We have put everything together – and we'll get our money back . . ."

"That is to say," I interrupted, "that you, Mr. de Rovin, have taken more than $1,200 from my friend, and you have no intention of paying him back."

"I beg your pardon," protested de Rovin. "What gives you the right . . ."

"If you intend to pay him back," I continued, "today's a perfect day to do so. I only accepted your invitation so we could go home with the money."

"That's a strange way to thank me for my invitation!" growled de Rovin.

"Yes, it is perhaps strange, but I am very angry at you, and the seminary authorities are also. Put the money on the table immediately, and we will leave as good friends."

"Come on, sir," he exclaimed, loudly enough for everyone around to hear him. "Do you have any idea to whom you are speaking? I am the Viscount de Rovin, Chevalier of the Legion of Honor."

I became incensed. "And I am André Trocmé," I told him, "the tutor of the children of Mr. Rockefeller who lives on this very same street. If you don't put the money on the table, I am going at once to tell Mr. Rockefeller who you are, and I will have you deported from the United States."

"Pffft! I had lunch three days ago with Mr. Rockefeller. He will kick you out of his house when he learns about the affront you subjected me to today," proclaimed de Rovin.

He was bluffing, and I knew it, but I wondered if the influence he claimed to have might eventually harm me. Furthermore, the place where we were was hardly appropriate for my moralizing.

A minute passed. I never once took my eyes off de Rovin. Then, slowly, he took his wallet out of his pocket and counted out on the table sixty twenty-dollar bills, $1,200. He made G. sign a receipt and then, looking at me with an evil eye, let loose: "Get out of here, you little shits."

He didn't have to ask us twice. We were greatly relieved to be outside, in the world of the living. I learned by chance two months later that de Rovin was expelled from the United States as an "undesirable alien."

G.'s mother took the first boat to New York and chaperoned her son. He never married and is a pastor in Alsace today.

MY TUTORING WAS A SUCCESS. Mrs. Rockefeller befriended me. As for poor Arthur Moor, he was unable to get the Rockefeller boys to like him. After a few weeks, they let him go. I never heard another word about him until one day, sometime around 1950, I ran into him. He was thin and looked wasted, chasing down jobs in New York City, surviving on private lessons. He had never married. He was, nevertheless, a brilliant guy. Certain people are marked by bad luck. He was one of them.

My duties in the Rockefeller home soon became a daily routine. I was a regular passenger on Bus #4, which still runs. The Rockefeller kids went to the progressive Lincoln School. Their parents insisted on having their sons mix with ordinary boys. With "Winnie" and David, I finally learned American English and even some slang. Sometimes we spoke French together; sometimes English. I wasn't strict with them. They were not difficult children, but they were lazy students. I was stunned by the level of work on the rare homework assignments they brought home.

They always maintained that they had too much homework to do the French lesson I was supposed to give them. Nelson[4] and Laurance, the two oldest, were even better at escaping my grasp. (Nelson was at Dartmouth College and Laurance was in high school.) I needed lures to attract them like birds, and I must have done a good job, because Mrs. Rockefeller complimented me on it. One Christmas, for example, David, who is today president of Chase Manhattan Bank, prepared a novel of chivalry in French for his mother, entirely composed and illustrated in his hand. It was more my work than his.

The last time I saw David in his stately office in the Chase Manhattan Bank, accessible only through doors guarded twenty-four hours a day by armed detectives and surrounded by walls with chevaux-de-frise, he recalled this minor event from his childhood. What David did not relate, and what I refrained from reminding him of, was the story of the leather briefcase.

Winthrop was generous. He spent his pocket money on trivialities. Once a week, he invited me to Chock Full o'Nuts on Fifth Avenue and bought us both monstrous ice cream sundaes with bananas and whipped cream called banana splits. They cost one dollar each, which in 1925 was a lot of money.

David was stingy and secretive. Going against the rule that we return directly home from school, one day he took me to the leather goods department in the big Wanamaker store. He picked out an impressive leather briefcase used by businessmen, with several pockets and locks. When it came time to pay, he said to the astonished, obsequious salesperson, "I am David Rockefeller, 10 W. Fifty-Fourth Street. Charge it to my parents' account!" The effect produced by this purchase on the Rockefeller family was disastrous. David had spent much more than his pocket money and opened a charge account in his parents' name!

4 Nelson Rockefeller (1908–1979) was the Republican governor of New York State (1959–1973) and a Presidential candidate in 1960, 1964, and 1968. He served as Vice President under President Gerald Ford from 1974 to 1977.

That evening, when I wasn't there, Mr. and Mrs. Rockefeller must have held a family meeting. The next day, on our return from school, I was instructed to go back to Wanamaker's with David and return the leather briefcase. Poor David! I'll never forget the despairing look on his young face when he recited the agreed upon phrase to the chief salesperson at the counter: "My parents believe that this briefcase is much too expensive for me." The sales personnel exchanged winks and knowing smiles, while David, red as a tomato and with tears in his eyes, stared at the ground. "It's all right," I said to David, as we were leaving. "You will forever remember this and be very proud of the education you received from your parents!"

John D. Rockefeller III, the oldest of the sons, finished college, and I only saw him rarely. Abby Rockefeller, the only daughter, had an unhappy marriage to a lawyer. The family didn't speak a lot about her. Nelson, who was exuberant and somewhat coarse, made a lot of noise when he came home from college on the weekends. Laurance was pale, astute, and had more refined tastes than the others. A precocious pessimism prevented him from being happy. Winthrop was heavy-set, active, and friendly. He later had an adventurous love affair with a film star, got divorced, and retired to a farm in Alabama. David, spoiled by his mother and more intelligent than his brothers, had already revealed a precise and ambitious character.

Saturdays at Pocantico Hills, the Rockefellers' property in Tarrytown, left me with extraordinary memories. A silent chauffeur would meet me at the train station; thanks to him, I was admitted onto the property. The elder Rockefeller had colonized a long hill about fifteen miles north of New York City. He had systematically absorbed farms, roads, ponds, villages, adding them to his own domain. It comprised several hundred acres where his chateau and other family houses were located.

Winthrop had me visit every nook and cranny of this territory on a scooter, which at the age of thirteen he handled masterfully, while he sang the praises of his all-powerful "grandpapa." One day, as we passed an impressive sunken path, sculpted with the rose-colored granite on which New York City is built, I asked Winthrop: "Your grandfather didn't just have this trench carved out for his pleasure, did he?"

"Not at all," responded Winnie in his inimitable American accent. "There once was a railroad there. It annoyed my grandfather because he wanted to extend his estate. He called his secretary and asked him: 'Who owns that railroad?' The secretary named the company. 'Oh,' replied my grandfather, 'these railroad tracks bother me. Buy the company.' He bought the company and now the tracks pass over there." With his hand, Winthrop pointed toward the east.

"My grandfather is very intelligent," he went on, pointing out a large, somewhat dilapidated white house in a grove on the property. "This house belonged to his brother William Rockefeller. He understood nothing about business. Grandfather ruined him, and now Standard Oil Company is all his. Uncle William is dead."

John D. Rockefeller Jr.'s house resembled an English chalet, with eaves in the upper rooms. It was much larger on the inside than it appeared to be. I spent my nights there in a beautiful bedroom. The windows looked out on the reddish trees of fall with the sparkling Hudson River in the distance.

The house was a silent paradise. There was a large domestic staff, but we only saw them at mealtimes. Secret stairways served each room. All you had to do was go upstairs during the day for the sound of the vacuum cleaner to stop. You were always alone in your room. Doors built into the tapestried walls were responsible for this miracle. The staff worked eight-hour shifts around the clock. They lived in the basement, where they had a living room and all the conveniences. For the most part, they were Scandinavian.[5] An evening shift functioned at night, as in a hospital.

I awakened at two one morning and decided to verify what my students had told me. I rang. The secret door opened and a uniformed maid with a starched bonnet appeared. "What would you like?" she asked. "A banana and a glass of milk," I responded just to cover my tracks. Now I had to consume this improvised meal.

The Rockefeller parents tried as best they could to conceal from their sons the enormous fortune they would inherit, just like the parents of Gautama Buddha struggled to keep from their son the knowledge of sickness, old age, and death. Each week, the sons received a limited amount of pocket money with which to buy books, notebooks, photographic film if they so desired, as well as any treats that might tempt them. Despite all these precautions, my students enjoyed their privileged position intensely. They knew that in the future every pleasure would be available to them: cars, luxurious houses, properties, farms, boats, works of art, and travel. "Papa's problem," Winthrop once told me, "is not to figure out how much

5 Nelson's son married one of the Norwegian maids who worked in his father's house.

he can spend, but to figure out how to use the extra millions that fall into his hands every morning." The "Wealth Tax" instituted by Franklin Roosevelt's New Deal didn't yet exist. If John D. Rockefeller Jr.'s fortune was as high as $1.2 billion (and that's a modest estimate), then every morning he had to reinvest $200,000 to avoid being buried under the weight of his own fortune.

Such an excess of power created a peculiar mindset in my students. Knowing that everything was or would be within their reach, they didn't passionately desire anything – except perhaps David's leather briefcase! Before the age of twenty, they were blasé and bored in all their activities: in work, because they knew they would never have to work; in recreation, because it's never a good thing at age fifteen to possess already, as was the case with Laurance, the best possible photographic equipment.

To this boredom that reigned at 10 W. Fifty-Fourth Street was added a certain carelessness regarding the domestic staff. Mr. and Mrs. Rockefeller, to set a good example, showed them the utmost politeness. But the staff simply didn't belong to the same world as they did. Let's say, to be more precise, that we tutors didn't really exist for our students. Mrs. Rockefeller watched out for me, but my students didn't, not any more than they did for two old teachers who remained in the family service until their deaths, Miss Scales and Mrs. Albertson.

Living under the roof of millionaires, I had the opportunity to repent for the troubles that we as children caused our German teachers and our maids and the little regard we French showed for poor Arabs in Morocco. The Rockefellers were right to teach their children that they were not of a different essence than the rest of humanity. This was perfectly true: their great-grandfather was a village charlatan, and their grandfather began as an office janitor. Yet I doubt that the parents were successful in this. Except for Nelson, who aspired to the presidency of the United States, and David, who is now a successful banker, their children otherwise went on to live nondescript lives as administrators of their father's enterprises.

The elder Rockefeller was very old but still alive. In the summer, he resided in Pocantico Hills and in the winter in Florida, at Ormond Beach. His millionaire's chateau stood at the center of the immense estate on Pocantico Hill. It was an Italian-style, rectangular building with a flat roof. Four gardens embellished the four façades: a French garden, an Italian garden with illuminated fountains in the evening, an English garden, and a Japanese garden. In a grotto, a drop of water fell every thirty seconds onto an enormous Chinese gong and marked the time with a mournful resonance.

One day, "Grandpa" invited me and the two boys for afternoon tea. He dominated the scene in a red armchair. The living room, which took up the entire ground floor and had windows on all four sides, was decorated in red, gold, and white, in Louis XVI style, and had an organ in the middle of the room. Grandpa spoke to us in a soft, measured voice and didn't eat anything. I remember his strange-looking head made famous by photography: the mummy of Ramesses II come back to life. He had blotchy skin and a wig of false white hair that was too well-combed to look lifelike. His body and hands were emaciated, and he suffered from a sickness that prevented the growth of body hair.

As he did with all newcomers, John D. inquired about my name, age, profession, and nationality.

"So, you're from France," he said to me. "You Frenchmen don't pay your debts. I always pay my debts."

He continued a moment later: "Young man, if you want to get rich, you must learn to pay off your debts. I am going to do something for you. Here is a dime." He took a dime out of a cloth purse that he kept in his pocket and showed me. "Promise that you will invest this money as soon as you get back home."

I promised and he gave me the dime.

"It is the way I started in life, and I became rich."

Then he inquired about my parents.

"My father is still alive," I said to him, and he gave me ten cents for him.

"Have you brothers and sisters?"

"Seven," I told him proudly.

"That's too much," said Rockefeller. "You would make me bankrupt."

A spinster who was visiting received a dime for herself and one for her dog.

Then came the time for the concert. Every week, "the best organist in New York" came to play an hour of music for John D. Winthrop, David, and I listened, sitting in our wide armchairs. I can still remember the melodies of Dvorak. The two boys exchanged winks: Grandpa had dozed off.

Nonetheless, Rockefeller was not senile. He, who without pity had manipulated men and millions, had simply given up the struggle. He had given everything to his son and now contented himself in a limited world.

He repeated to himself the few lessons that life had taught him, trying sincerely to help others succeed so they would be happy like him. Yes, the world of an old billionaire can also be voluntarily limited.

"More gasoline and higher prices, that's what we want," he told me as I was leaving.

He had a strange doctrine, and it wasn't only his. Without fully understanding, I always admired men, religious or otherwise, who believed that they had solved the world's problems because they, either by chance or by relentless work, had "succeeded."

During Christmas vacation, I had the wonderful surprise of being sent to Florida to accompany Laurance, whose lethargic temperament needed a change of scenery. There we were welcomed by Grandpa in his beautiful villa in Ormond Beach on the Atlantic Coast. The sun was shining. John D. went to church and played golf. In the evening, the governess and Laurance and I did our best to try to understand a kind of backgammon that gave the old man another opportunity to distribute his extra dimes to the winner. Laurance and I were bored stiff and didn't always behave properly.

In the morning, for example, breakfast was indefinitely delayed if the temperature in the dining room wasn't exactly as Grandpa wanted – let's say 72 degrees. He would appear on the balcony formed by the majestic staircase on the second floor and call out in a feeble voice: "Laurie, Laurie!"

"Yes, Grandpa."

"What's the temperature?"

Laurie checked the thermometer. "68 degrees, Grandpa."

The old man went back into his room and came out ten minutes later: "Laurie, what's the temperature?"

He would only come down when the central heating had set the dining room temperature at exactly 72 degrees.

One day I said to Laurie: "Blow on the thermometer; the temperature will go up." Laurie did so. Grandpa called; his grandson replied that it was 72 degrees Everyone was happy and Grandpa came down for breakfast.

In the garden, there were orange trees weighed down with magnificent fruit. Grandpa would not allow anyone to pick it. The gardeners let it fall and rot on the ground. Was it Laurie who taught me this trick, or I who taught him? By putting a piece of sugar into a hole cut with a knife, you could suck out the delicious juice from the golden orange without detaching it from the tree. It would fall to the ground, but its contents wouldn't be wasted.

Christmas evening at Ormond Beach was memorable. John D. was crowned with a golden cardboard diadem, and, like a child, he unwrapped his numerous gifts with a trembling hand. After dinner, the governess played the piano. Standing, the billionaire sang Baptist hymns in a quavering voice, tearing up, for he was very pious. I remember particularly the hymn "He Leadeth Me."

In this atmosphere, at once simple and surreal, I ended the year 1925. I pinched myself from time to time to make sure it was still I, André Trocmé, a theology student from France who had recently shared tent life in Morocco with poor nomads, who had now progressed to life with millionaires. It was also during this vacation that my romantic life suddenly reawakened. I had voluntarily put it on the back burner so it wouldn't create an obstacle to my distant goal, a life of Franciscan poverty, and my proximate goal, a visit to Gandhi.

Laurance's cousin served as the catalyst. She had come to Ormond Beach to spend Christmas vacation with her grandfather. Her name was Muriel McCormick. The daughter of John D. had married the famous McCormick of Chicago, the head of the *Chicago Tribune* and the Chicago opera. Muriel, an unattractive, heavy-set young woman about twenty-three years of age, had got it into her head that she would become an opera singer.

"She has neither the voice nor the physique," mocked Laurance. "She is whimsical, and her father has placed his millions in the balance to get her a role. It's impossible. It would be a disastrous failure. Money cannot give her the voice she doesn't have."

Muriel was rather kind to me, the only boy her age in the household at the time. She placed small gifts on the Christmas table with sweet messages for everyone. The one she offered me, accompanied by an obvious wink, impressed me a great deal. I must have been somewhat affected because Laurance teased me in the room I shared with him: "Troc, you are in love with Muriel. I am going to tell her."

I strongly denied that this was true. But I had a bad night. The absurdity of the situation appeared clear to me. "This extravagant young woman perhaps wants to amuse herself by making me fall in love with her," I told myself. "I won't fall into the trap. Furthermore, I don't love her." It was true I was unable to love her. She was too artificial for me. But I was nonetheless somewhat starry-eyed.

I told myself that a romance with a young woman of her status would be a betrayal of my ideals and my faith. She only expressed interest in my ideas as a kind of rebellion against her social milieu. In short, I only fell asleep when lucidity had replaced the unexpected turmoil I experienced on Christmas night.

The next day, in perfect control of myself, I put on an implacable face, and Muriel McCormick did the same. I repeat that I had no idea how easily boys and girls in the United States flirted with one another without it being of any consequence whatsoever.

New Year's Eve brought me an affront that completely brought me to earth. John D. had invited a famous Italian tenor, Tito Schipa, and his wife to dinner. The evening was a lot of fun. At dessert, Tito Schipa sang "O Sole Mio" in his magnificent voice. I had an animated conversation with Mrs. Schipa, a vulgar French woman seated next to me. I was clearly getting civilized! Everyone got up to have coffee. Mrs. Schipa went over to Muriel McCormick. I heard her ask: "Who is that friendly young Frenchman I was sitting next to?"

Muriel, who spoke perfect French, responded in a loud voice: "Oh, he's only my cousin's French tutor."

"Ah, I understand," replied Mrs. Schipa, who never said another word to me for the rest of the evening.

With Laurance, who at age fourteen loved to snicker in the corner, I too played the wallflower for the rest of the party. We told jokes to one another, as boys do while the important people speak seriously.

DESPITE EVERYTHING, this little incident upset my inner equilibrium, and I returned to New York less sure of myself than before. On Sundays, I went to the movies alone from time to time. I saw two silent films, one comic with Harold Lloyd, the other romantic with the typical Hollywood happy ending of that time.

Nonetheless, the poignant expression of the eyes of a cinema star remained engraved in my mind. I began to think about the happiness a man could experience loving a beautiful, intelligent, and good woman. I told myself, "Papa wants her first to be good, then pious, then intelligent. He says that beauty matters little. But I really love beauty. I can only fall in love with beauty." So, in the small restaurants where I ate my meals, I did what I had never done before in my life: I looked at young, beautiful women whose faces were attractive to me, and I asked myself, "Is she the right one, or is it the one over there?" I found faults in all of them, physical faults or character flaws.

My equilibrium was broken, not only on the romantic side but in regards to my other projects and goals as well. The Rockefellers began to allude to the 1926–27 school year, letting me know they would appreciate it if I stayed on another year. I would be able to get another scholarship at Union Theological Seminary, and I could study for my doctorate. I had heard much about the Rockefellers' social work throughout the world, and I could already see myself with a useful and brilliant future. One word from me to the Rockefellers, and I knew doors would open wide for me. The temptation was huge and obsessive. But then, I told myself, what would become of my pastoral vocation and my desire for a life of poverty? If I am called by God, mustn't I renounce the world, even if this world is a world of service to humanity?

During this period, I spent some time with the tiny chapter of the Fellowship of Reconciliation at the seminary. They debated the problems preoccupying me. A guy in his thirties named Bill Simpson had chosen the celibate life so he could live among the poor on the outskirts of New York in Passaic, New Jersey. He wanted to reform the church through a form of Christian Gandhism that matched my own quest so well I could have abandoned everything to follow him.

However, my weekends with the Rockefellers and the studies I found so interesting brought me back to a much more concrete world. Papa's letters reminded me that I was awaited in northern France to stimulate the missionary spirit among the workers. All this promised a more austere destiny for me, one that was, however, more consistent with my deepest convictions.

From time to time, I frequented the International House. When classes resumed in September, I was invited to become a member of the Cosmopolitan Club, a group I knew nothing about. I learned little by little that the goal of the club, founded by a Mr. Harry Edmonds, was to bring together foreign students at Columbia University with American students, who would initiate them into American democratic society. The club was inspired by Christian generosity, and Mr. Edmonds's activities struck the imagination of Mr. Rockefeller Jr., who built the club a kind of luxurious YMCA, the International House, on the banks of the Hudson River. It had opened only a year before I arrived in New York.

The International House held small parties, suppers, and dances. There was lots of flirting, or so it seemed to me, because the individual rooms of the men and women that occupied both halves of the building, though separated by a pitiless security staff, allowed the two sexes to meet freely in the living rooms of the "palace" and in the park on Riverside Drive.

Solicited in fall to be part of the French Club, which in turn elected officers to the Cosmopolitan Club, I had perhaps declined too quickly.

Now I suffered in my solitude. My classmates at the seminary all belonged to the club. They spoke about people and things I knew nothing about. They had activities in which I took no part. The seminary alone didn't have the milieu I needed. It consisted only of a dormitory and classrooms. I began to suffer on my lonely Sundays and regret voluntarily cutting myself off from everything outside of my studies.

My Swiss friend Marcel Christen became my connection to the International House. Sentimental but serious, he didn't worry much about his studies and spent the year going from one flirtation to another. His current companion was a Canadian student saddled with the strange name of Félicité La Flamme, and a long, pale, unattractive face. They were definitely a mismatched couple. Christen was nearsighted, ruddy, and round, a future minister; she was as Catholic as they come. This didn't prevent them from talking about marriage. Christen, who suspected the psychological struggles I was going through, never stopped telling me: "You need a girlfriend." He was absolutely right.

"There's a young woman at the International House who fits the bill perfectly," he said to me one day.

"These young women don't interest me at all," I responded brusquely. But the next day, while I was standing in line at the International House cafeteria, I saw Christen finishing his meal. He came up to me and said: "I just finished, take my place at the table." There was no choice. All the other places were taken.[6]

As I sat down, Christen introduced me to a young woman seated across from me. "She's the one I spoke to you about," he added, as he

6 In the manuscript, André's wife, Magda, wrote: "Not at all. I got to the table with my tray. There was no seat available. Christen left and offered me his place."

mumbled a name that I didn't understand. I hardly dared raise my eyes above my plate as we exchanged a few words. I took her for someone from the south of France because her Rs were a bit throaty, like those of the Catalans in Béziers. I can't remember if I thought she was beautiful, but I remember that she was approachable, simple, honest, and intelligent.

The young women at the International House all seemed artificial to me. They were constantly preoccupied with the effect they had on men. Women wore too much makeup in those days. Short hair, short skirts – the "boyish" style was the rage. It unsettled me and kept me away from them. But the woman in front of me was not made-up. Her skirt was of a reasonable length. A good sign, I said to myself.

Yet there were no real sparks between us that first day.

9

Magda

A FEW DAYS LATER, everything changed. There was a party at the International House. I was seated in the pit of the theater, when my eyes were drawn to an animated group of young women on the balcony to the left near the stage. One of them seemed to be in the center. More beautiful than the others, she had a harmonious face, a luminous forehead, dark and magnificent eyes, and a laugh that struck me as marvelous. The group was animated with pleasantries I was unable to hear.

"Is it possible," I said to myself as I left, "that this is the same person I considered so serious and preoccupied the other day in the cafeteria?"

I became sensitive to the presence or absence of the one everyone called "Magda" without knowing her family name.

From there, things evolved quickly. Christen and Félicité were members of this friendly group, as were Marguerite Soulier, a tiny French woman with curly hair, and Elizabeth Tyson, a tall blond American with blue eyes who always had a group of boys flirting with her. I learned indirectly that Magda was Italian. I saw "the Italian" (that's what I called her for lack of more information) in the hall of the cafeteria, where she was seated, daydreaming. I heard her call her friend, Elizabeth, in the small restaurant on 124th Street where I ate my meals. I could no longer evade this presence that I feared and sought at the same time.

A short time after Easter, there was an "international party" at the International House. Each country presented a skit, and I was asked to propose one for France. I wrote such a patently absurd text about a grapefruit that I refused to stage it, so I was seated in the audience.

Then something happened: the one whom I had admired from a distance appeared on the stage, dressed very simply in an Italian costume. I saw that she was beautiful, very beautiful. I'm not saying she was pretty. One can say that Magda was not pretty, but beautiful, with a classical, oval face, no make-up at all, and features animated by intelligence and goodness.

Events unfolded almost without my awareness of them. The Rockefellers gave me time off for Easter vacation. A multiday trip to Washington, DC, was organized by the Cosmopolitan Club. I learned that "my Italian" was going. "It is not because of her that I am becoming a member of the Cosmopolitan Club, but to be able to go on the trip," I told myself. Didn't I have to visit Washington, DC, before the end of my stay in the United States? This trip brought me a great disappointment and a great revelation.

I experienced disappointment on the way to Washington by train. The Italian was sitting in the middle of a noisy group. There was one person in particular, Ellis Chapburn, whose stupidity struck me as monumental. Everyone was smoking, including Magda, and she appeared agitated and nervous. I hated to see women smoking. "You're mistaken," I said to myself. "She's not the person you think she is. She's not for you, not for your poverty, not for your ministry." In Washington, we got rooms in two adjacent hotels. I was determined to visit the city, whereas many students thought only about taking walks and window shopping.

The next morning, there was a small group of students on the sidewalk: Christen; a heavy-set Swiss woman, Miss Escher; an interesting Russian, Mr. Skitzky; the Italian; and me.

From the beginning, the invisible attraction that brings together beings destined to understand each other was born between the Italian and me. Christen had come down wearing a light suit, but it was chilly. "Go upstairs quickly and get a sweater," ordered Magda. I said to myself: "She's a girl who looks out for others, not to be seen with them, but for themselves." I didn't yet know that my Italian always felt hot or cold for other people and would spend years covering and uncovering our children.

We visited the not yet completed Washington Cathedral, where I would later preach; the military cemetery in Arlington; and George Washington's country home in Mount Vernon, where, on a winding staircase, for the first time in my life, I heard talk of the Decembrist Revolt and the noble and revolutionary Russian origins of my Italian.[1]

---

1 The Decembrist Revolt, December 26, 1825, in St. Petersburg, was a failed coup d'état led by liberal military and political dissidents against the Russian Empire.

Above all, there was our evening meal in a small restaurant not far from Potomac Falls, which was still unspoiled at the time. Marcel Christen, Miss Escher, Skitzky, the Italian, and I were seated around the table. The conversation was fascinating. Skitzky was a character out of a Russian novel. He was very orthodox, very mystical, and he lived like an ascetic. He didn't want to get married so he could dedicate his life to all of humanity. Of course, this viewpoint attracted my attention. Little by little, we came to discuss God and Jesus Christ. I felt that my words aroused my Italian's curiosity. Her eyes looked straight at me, and I looked right into hers. Magnificent, intelligent eyes that radiated the diverse sentiments expressed by those around the table. She spoke, too, and then we were the only ones talking. The others became quiet; it was now a dialogue. She and I in the lamplight, and, all around, the mist of a confused world which wasn't us.

She told me about her painful childhood, her struggles to leave Catholicism and find a religion devoid of superstition.

"She's Protestant," I said to myself, and my heart jumped with joy. "She's the one who will understand me. She too is thirsting for freedom and truth. She is courageous and scorns conventions."

But Magda continued to speak: "I can't call myself a Protestant. I have never been able to declare that I believe something I'm not sure of. I prefer not to define what I believe. Human beings have superimposed too many ideas on the essential."

My heart burned within me when I realized I had found the one I had always been looking for.

I SPENT A SLEEPLESS NIGHT. This unexpected event completely disorganized my life plans. A trip around the world? I would now have to give that up. So what? Not a big deal at all. Live in poverty like Gandhi? How can you do that with a wife? My Italian had a vivid discussion with Skitzky that demonstrated the absurdity of his asceticism. She spoke out in favor of a normal, reasonable, married life. Then there was the question of my ministry. My Italian was certainly Protestant, but she remained on the fringes of faith. She was extremely critical of the church. Could she be the wife of a pastor?

I resolved to keep my distance, and interrupting my trip to Washington, the next day I took the first train to New York.

In New York, I decided to barricade my soul against the passion that filled it.

Alas, good intentions are short-lived. After a few days, I was already haunting the lobby of the International House, and I asked Christen to organize a get-together for the students who made the trip to Washington. He was happy to do so, and we agreed upon an evening to meet. When the evening came, Christen and Miss Escher excused themselves and Skitzky, who was sick, couldn't make it.

I found myself alone with Magda, whom I still called "Miss." I fought off my desire to flee. She suggested that we go see Skitzky. It was an interesting visit. We discussed problems I cared about, and Magda understood them and spoke intelligently and passionately, defending a balanced, open, and humane Christianity.

Then Magda and I left on foot and walked along Amsterdam Avenue. As soon as we were alone, a feeling of closeness, I would even say of oneness, took hold of me. It was she, I knew it, who was mine, and I hers.

Suddenly, I panicked. "If I continue," I told myself, "I am going to declare my love. I will be unable not to do so. But I'm not ready. I haven't thought about this enough. I don't want to get attached."

I mumbled an excuse: "Please excuse me, Miss, but I don't think I should ever see you again. I apologize."[2] Without shaking her hand, I walked away quickly, taking huge strides.

The minute I left her, I felt – and I thought she felt too – horribly torn apart.

I ran to my room, where I tried to gather myself and pray. "O God, what is your will? I don't want to disobey you. If this love goes against my vocation, let me know by some sign and I will give it up." Most importantly, in my turmoil I could not imagine how I would give Papa the news. "An Italian, not very Protestant, how will he react?" I asked myself. "Isn't this some crazy adventure I'm throwing myself into? Some of my friends have married women who've ruined their ministry. But this young woman is more religious than she lets on. She is very idealistic, very unselfish, and very generous." When I thought about how I had just left her, the fear of an irreparable disaster took hold of me.

"What if she too is desperate right now," I asked myself. "What kind of an ill-mannered jerk am I? What have I done? This young woman has already been very unhappy. Have I added to her misery? I have no right to do so. I must make sure that she returned safely to the International House." I made it to the Hudson River. It was after hours, but I entered

2 Magda wrote in the margin: "I didn't understand what he said to me."

the International House, where the Friday dance fires still burned brightly. I went toward the elevator: "I want to see Miss Grilli," I said to the lackey who protected the women's dormitory. "That is quite impossible, sir. You know the rules." I turned around and saw Elizabeth Tyson.

"So, it's you," she said abruptly.

"Yes, where is Miss Grilli? Did she come back?"

"Of course she came back," she said, "but she is crying bitterly. What did you do to her?"

"Could you ask her to come down?" I stammered.

A moment later, Miss Grilli was there in front of me, as if in a dream. Her face was completely distraught.

"You were thinking of me?" I asked her.

She nodded her head without saying anything.

"I have to think about all this," I told her. "I'll see you in a few days."

I left, somewhat reassured.

I GAVE MYSELF TWO DAYS, until the following Sunday. To take stock, I closed myself in my room, alone with my chaotic thoughts. Stupidly, I wrote down on a sheet of paper the "pros" and "cons" of an engagement to Miss Grilli, as if major decisions in life can be weighed on a scale. I tried to pray but couldn't do so. Finally, the scale tipped toward my heart. The opposite would have been a complete disaster.

On Sunday, April 18, 1926, after going to church, I went to the International House, where Miss Grilli was waiting for me. Curiously, I never doubted for a moment that her answer would be "yes." I must have appeared joyful, because one of my French friends, seeing me merrily climb the staircase into the International House, cried out: "What's with you, Trocmé? You look so happy!" Without even stopping, I replied: "Of course. I'm getting engaged!"

Miss Grilli was there, looking slim in her tailored suit. We walked in silence toward the ferry on 125th Street. We crossed the Hudson silently. We found a quiet little spot on the rocks.

"Will you be my wife?" I asked her. "I will be a Protestant minister, and I seek a life of poverty. I am a conscientious objector, and that could get me imprisoned and into lots of other trouble."

Only then did I realize that I hardly knew the woman into whose hands I was placing my entire destiny. But I knew I could have total confidence in her.

Miss Grilli was very tense and listened closely. She didn't say "yes" right away but started enumerating the obstacles to our marriage. "If, after listening to me, you still want to marry me," she said, "we will see." Then the one whom I knew to be so strong told me that her mother had died giving birth to her; that she was the victim of a jealous stepmother and a weak father; that she was placed as a student in a convent, became Catholic, and struggled to escape that religion; that she had been engaged to a Catholic and had just broken off with him; and that she had many health problems. As she spoke, her cheeks turned red, as they did whenever she became excited, so much so that people would tell her: "Oh, you look so healthy!" As Miss Grilli explained to me that very evening, a small increase in her temperature caused this to happen.

In hindsight, I think Magda was unwise to speak to me like this. I learned over the years that Magda often appeared anxious, tense, and desperate (that was her word for it) to those who didn't know her well. A young man whose childhood was without incident in a tranquil milieu like Saint-Quentin would be hard-pressed to understand and assimilate all the details of her unhappy lot in one hour. "I believed she was strong," I said to myself. "Now I can see that she is weak. I thought I could lean on her, but it's she who will need my support."

I was soon engulfed by the fear of lacking strength enough for two, and this fear pursued me throughout the time of our engagement.

But right now, this strong woman who had become weak was there, near me, as simple and honest as she could be. She needed me, and I was in love with her. I told her so. On the rocks of the Palisades facing the Hudson River, we came to an agreement that was sealed with a prayer I pronounced out loud. The event was celebrated in good spirits at the seminary during a small party where Auguste Viatte honored us with a poem he had composed for the occasion.

However, the first weeks of our engagement were not very happy. For a long time I hesitated to tell Papa the news. I knew it would be difficult for him to understand that I was plunging into "an adventure," as he would call it. My silence toward my father troubled my fiancée, who reproached me for it. When I finally wrote to Papa, I announced in one blow that (1) I was engaged; (2) we were getting married in the United States; and (3) after our marriage, we would return home by way of India, making a tour of the world. Our money would last until we got to India, I thought. From there we would either be repatriated or work on a boat.

This was too much for my poor father, eighty-one years old at the time! His response was not encouraging. He was OK with my engagement but was completely opposed to my getting married in the United States (what would the family think about this!). We found out later that some members of the family thought that Magda was my mistress, that she was pregnant, and that this was why we had to get married in the United States!

Papa also rejected our proposed trip around the world in the name of duty. France, he said, was in terrible need of pastors. To parade around the world as tourists when the need for spiritual leaders was so great was giving free rein to a mere caprice. Papa had always fought against any inclinations toward caprice in his sons. To confirm what he had said about the need for pastors, he had one of my former classmates, Paul Conord, write to me in the most urgent terms, inviting me to replace him as pastor in Maubeuge, since he had to leave that post.

Oh, the naivete of young Christians imbued with a sense of duty! How easy it is for those in authority to place them administratively where they can be useful! I will relate later our disappointments in Maubeuge. For the moment, I accepted coming home in September and getting married in France – a marriage in Florence with Magda's family was unthinkable. I also agreed to set up our home in Maubeuge, on the condition that I be allowed to spend a year as a worker in one of the big metallurgical factories in the region. I was given full assurance on this last point, and that removed all my hesitations. Magda and I gave up our trip to see Gandhi and Tagore and oriented ourselves toward the austere life that was calling us.

As regards Magda, there was no smooth sailing. My fiancée was exhausted. Then, as now, she never knew when to stop working. In addition to her studies at the New York School of Social Work and her tiring internships, she gave French and Italian lessons until ten pm. After all that, she couldn't sleep. All this agitation worried me greatly. We used to meet late in the International House parlor, the Duncan Phyfe Room, with its admirable wallpaper that depicted the conquest of America. When we were there alone, I tried the traditional gestures by which a young man full of passion expresses his love for the one he adores. Magda pushed me aside. In particular, she refused to let me kiss her on the mouth. My big nose, she claimed, "cut off her air supply"! She was often nervous and preoccupied with trivial things, whereas I wanted to talk about love and philosophy.

The state of Magda's health worried the nurse at the International House, the charming Miss Forsythe, who spoke to Mrs. Rockefeller about it. Mrs. Rockefeller knew about our engagement and invited us to her home to celebrate David's eleventh birthday. As a wedding gift, Mrs. Rockefeller proposed that Magda interrupt her studies, now that they were no longer as essential, and spend several weeks in a "sanatorium" in Clifton Springs, New York, to enter marriage in the best possible health.

I had to say goodbye to my fiancée, but, whenever possible on Saturday nights, I took the night train to Clifton Springs, where I would find Magda first in her room in bed and later in a lounge chair with wheels. She had to rest her nervous system completely and put on weight.

Each time I visited her, I saw some improvement. Nonetheless, inactivity was always harmful to this woman who would become my wife. As soon as she slowed down, anxieties took over. Magda literally assailed me with objections: "If you discover that I don't have the proper health or the right faith, tell me, and we will break off our engagement." I spent my time refuting her arguments, and each time I left her reassured. But, on the train going back to the city, I asked myself: "If I have to spend my life reassembling Magda's psyche while I am also in charge of a parish and the care of my own soul, how will I do it?"

The next time I visited her, Magda perceived my doubts, which she took for hesitations and lack of love, and once again she began persecuting me, testing the firm nature of my resolution.

One day, I asked to see the doctor who cared for her, and he reassured me. I thanked him for his wise diagnosis. "Miss Grilli," he told me, "is very nervous, but it's a nervousness of a physiological nature. It will never take hold of her psyche. I recommend marriage. However, you should try your best to give her an easy life, free of exhaustion. She should rest every afternoon in a lounge chair for two or three hours."

None of that was compatible with what we had both called "the life of a manual worker's wife," but it was much less frightening than the burden of a depressed spouse. Encouraged by this prognosis, I decided to accept the challenge that it posed and let myself love Magda Grilli without fear. I only became aware little by little of the immense love and boundless devotion of which she was capable.

Another stroke of good fortune facilitated the second part of our engagement. I was formally summoned to Fifty-Fourth Street by Rockefeller himself. He asked me if I was willing to take part in a trip around the United States with his family, which would extend my commitment to the Rockefellers by three months. My fiancée agreed from the outset, and I accepted. Mr. Rockefeller gave me a long list of sporting equipment that I would have to buy: high-laced riding boots, sports outfits, special shirts, even a tuxedo for evening parties in the hotels. The whole thing would have cost me more than $200. I declined. Then, Mrs. Rockefeller had an idea: she had me try on the clothing and shoes that belonged to John D. III, her oldest son. They fit me perfectly. I left on the trip dressed like a millionaire. I only had to buy my underwear. As for the black suit that I brought from France, it was OK for a tutor.

On the way, I went to kiss Magda goodbye and rejoined the caravan in Cleveland. For the occasion, the Rockefeller family rented a luxury train car, the same one used by Theodore Roosevelt on his campaign rounds. The four black staff members who took care of us remembered the president himself, whom John D. praised greatly. The train car was composed of four sleeping cabins with bunks on two levels for two people, a shower room, a dining room, and a sumptuous parlor. It was always connected to the end of the train, and it had a rather vast observation terrace, a kind of outdoor living room where Roosevelt had passionately harangued the crowds. From there, we could enjoy the countryside, while the tracks ran in the opposite direction toward the horizon.

We called ourselves "Mr. John Davidson's party." It was strictly forbidden to pronounce the name Rockefeller for fear of journalists, weirdos, beggars, crazy people, and perhaps even – you never know –murderers. In fact, our anonymity only drew more scrutiny. Hordes of journalists assailed us in every train station, trying to extract confidential information that we refused to give them. The next morning, the local newspapers ran whimsical stories on the front page about the illustrious people who had passed through town. It so happened that once a journalist called me "Miss Brocome"! I was an Englishwoman with a PhD from Oxford University. Why not? The scribblers had to write something!

Up to this point, I had only seen John D. Rockefeller Jr. rarely, at the end of the table during a meal on Fifty-Fourth Street. Now, I rubbed elbows with him every day, trying my best not to bother the family or impose myself on him. He was a small man with a modest air about him. He spoke very little but had a much steadier and richer voice than his father. He didn't at all seem like a man destined to play the major role his wealth imposed on him. No vanity, no bluff. I never heard him get angry, but he was a man of exaggerated preciseness. He made his secretaries prepare a detailed travel plan that had to be followed to the letter. The least delay provoked his displeasure. "It was not because of you or because of your health that I demanded you be well-equipped for the trip," he said to me one day. "It was because of our party. Imagine what trouble there would be if you got a cold or sprained your ankle!" In fact, when, in California, I slipped on a rock, twisted my foot, and limped for a couple of days, John D. looked at me with disfavor and spoke about sending me home!

I must remind you that this simple man had his moments of greatness. After taking over his father's affairs, he discovered how harshly workers were treated. He was a fervent Baptist who had been influenced by Harry Emerson Fosdick, an antimilitarist, social-minded Christian and an excellent preacher. The young capitalist went in person to Pueblo, Colorado, where a strike had just been quelled by force. He personally met with the union leaders, the owners of the factory, the authorities, and finally the assembled workers. On just about every point, he claimed the workers were right. He left behind him a model Workers' Business Council, which still functioned when we visited the steelworks in Pueblo in 1926. Certainly Rockefeller, having succeeded once, contented himself too easily with that success, and his sons remained, like most Americans in 1926, moderate capitalists. In Europe, they are considered reactionary.

Like everyone else, John D. had his faults. He refused the limelight, to be sure, and insisted on staying in the background. But he was hungry for approbation and compliments, as all prominent men are.

One evening, when I could hardly breathe in the cabin I shared with David, I went up to the observation terrace. I must have opened the door abruptly because John D., seeing me, had the frightened look of a schoolboy caught reading a novel when he should have been doing homework. With a simple gesture, he pretended to gather the scattered papers on his desk. I excused myself and left the room, but not without seeing what John D. was doing. He was obviously pasting into a scrapbook articles from the prior evening's newspapers whose commentaries about him bordered on delirium. The next morning at breakfast, John D. had a sheepish look on his face. Our relations, mute most of the time, were not enhanced by this ridiculous incident.

Our party included, of course, Mrs. Rockefeller, who was much livelier than her husband. She was a lover of art, an admirer of nature, and very affectionate with her sons. She was the animating soul of our group and knew how to put all the "salaried" members at ease. I won't say anything about David or Winthrop because you already know them. They photographed just about everything indiscriminately.

Besides me, there was Miss Scales, one of the old teachers in the household, who was accorded this recompense even though she couldn't take part in all the excursions because of her age, and the doctor, a heavy-set, moody guy with a difficult temperament with whom I had a few difficulties. He was responsible for the group's health and, therefore, for the success of the trip.

Our pleasures began in Colorado. Our private train car, a veritable rolling hotel, was, by prior agreement, detached from the train at certain train stations. In the mornings, we found ourselves on a storage track. The staff served us breakfast in grand style. Limousines waited for us outside. We left the train car for a few days and rejoined it further on our trip.

In this way, we visited Albuquerque and the "Indian Detour," Mesa Verde Park, the Grand Canyon, the Painted Desert, Los Angeles, Pasadena, and Santa Barbara on the Pacific Coast, where we experienced a small earthquake (I jumped out of the window of the mezzanine), San Francisco, Yosemite, the Redwood Forests, and Crater Lake. The trip ended with a week of camping at the southern edge of Yellowstone Park, amid geysers and buffalo.

During those years, Rockefeller donated a lot of money for the construction of national parks and the maintenance of those already existing. He saved a part of the splendid Redwood Forests on the Pacific Coast that had been depleted by lumber merchants. Through a third party, he was in the process of buying back the Grand Tetons and the lake at their base, an area as large as one of France's departments and the only range of the Rocky Mountains somewhat reminiscent of the Alps.

We were received everywhere in grand style. The national park directors went to great expense to organize galas for the Rockefellers: Indian dances, fireworks spectacles, and a round-up of the last herd of American buffalo. We had permission to participate on horseback in a reenactment of a buffalo hunt, but, while the herd fled, gigantic old males protected the fleeing bison by turning around and threatening to charge us.

The mobile camp in Yellowstone was also the most amusing event of the trip. Accompanied by park rangers and a large, mostly black staff, we didn't have to worry about setting up tents and preparing food. I compared this luxury camp with those I had known in Morocco. In the evenings, around the campfire, the Rockefeller boys were astonished listening to the tales of an old ranger, who remembered and described with passion the last skirmishes with the Indians and the attack on the stagecoach that he, as a child with his mother, had experienced. It ended when they seized the bandit, he said, and discovered that he was the Baptist preacher from the neighboring town! I told the boys that I had lived through similar experiences in Morocco, where the natives were the Chleuh – the Berbers of southern Morocco. That greatly enhanced my prestige among them.

MY TRIP TO THE UNITED STATES ended with a stay in Seal Harbor, Maine, where the Rockefellers had a magnificent country estate. There, one evening, I was introduced to Edsel Ford, the son of Henry Ford, whose property bordered on that of John D. Still accompanying Winthrop and David, I went rowing, fishing in the sea, and horseback riding. Then suddenly it was all over. I went to pick up Magda in Clifton Springs, and, following the American custom for lovers, we visited Niagara Falls.

A few days later in New York, Magda's friends waved to us from the platform at the end of the French Line pier as our ship slowly moved away from the quay. I felt like a dream had just ended. I regretted not saying "no" to Maubeuge, refusing the offer of a scholarship for doctoral study from Union Theological Seminary and the offer from the Rockefellers to spend another year with them. But I didn't really like America and knew that my fate awaited me elsewhere. Magda, however, had tears in her eyes. In the United States, she had found kindhearted people and the freedom she had not known in her youth. We were pressed against one another and soon were alone in the middle of the ocean with people we didn't know.

10

Maubeuge

THE MORE MAGDA AND I became aware of our shared weakness, the more a new emotion arose in both of us: our desire for each other. We were very much in love when we arrived in Paris.

My brother Pierre and his Russian wife Aline were waiting for us at the Saint-Lazare train station. A taxi dropped us off at my brother Francis's house at 15 Lagrange Street. Since 1917, the house hadn't changed – same odor, same furniture, same brother and sister-in-law, same ironic Francis, the same remarks, and the same mistakes in Rose's French. This apartment and its inhabitants remained the only fixed point amid all the changes and all the fortunate and unfortunate events that the Trocmé family experienced. Only age, little by little, wore down Francis and Rose.

Francis scrutinized Magda through his pince-nez. "You're not as ugly as you look in your photograph," he said. That was the only greeting. I shivered.

Aline took us to Le Bon Marché, where we bought an ugly wine-colored dress of poor quality that didn't look good on my fiancée. Aline insisted that Magda be "properly dressed" for her introduction to the family in Saint-Gobain.

In Chauny, Papa awaited us at the train station. He drove us, his quivering prey, to introduce Magda to her new family. When he saw the wine-colored dress that Magda was wearing, he told her: "It's good that you are wearing long sleeves." In Le Fringolet, an important family circle was waiting for us: Eugène and Madeleine, Albert, Robert and Germaine, Yvonne, Jeanne, and Marie. A small meal had been laid on an oilcloth in the dining room. The whole family, seated along the wall in silence, their heads in the half-light of the lampshade, watched us pick away at our food with our forks. "Does she even know how to behave at table?" their looks seemed to ask.

When that was over, we moved into the parlor. Magda looked out and saw the night sky dotted with lights above the immense plain of the industrial North, where we were going to live. She remarked, "It looks like the sea!" Why? Because the night before, the sea in the English Channel with its boats and shores illuminated looked like this plain. No one acknowledged her remark. Magda never knew if she said something stupid or if she said something that impressed her Fringolet hosts.

The days dragged on. Autumn gained ground, and the families returned to their winter quarters. Everyone was kind to Magda, but we both felt a chill in the air. Her zest and passion that I loved so much, her spontaneous reflections, and her nonconformism frightened the family. As for Papa, he said nothing.

The bureaucratic formalities of getting married were more complicated than we had expected. We had to procure documents from Italy and have them translated by a legal translator. "It will take at least fifty days," the authorities told us.

Magda was not happy. She was getting more and more nervous. Every evening her temperature rose to 100 degrees. Our conversations on the bench hidden in the upper part of the garden suffered from it. She spoke about going back to Italy and said she was "desperate." "You don't really love me," she said, and I didn't know how to answer her. "If I have to spend my whole life struggling against her anxious personality," I asked myself, "what will become of me?" I spoke to Papa about it, and he gave me very wise advice. "You asked for this young lady's hand in marriage. You are engaged. It's too late to back out." But there was no fervor in his response, and that chilled me to the bone.

We returned to Saint-Quentin and were married in a civil ceremony on November 10 and a religious one on the 12th. I would have enjoyed having my comrades from our Northern Group, Fabre, Cornier, and Babut, there with me. I asked Fabre, who was at the Fellowship of Reconciliation, to preside over the ceremony, but he was the only one invited. Papa refused outright to invite the others, and insisted that the old pastor in Saint-Quentin, whom I hardly knew, preside over the ceremony. This caused a scene between Papa and me. I threw the wedding invitations down the stairs, but I capitulated. Between Magda and me now, it was clear sailing. She saw how much I cared for her and stopped putting obstacles in our path. She had done so to *verify* my love and to be *sure* not to establish a household on even the slightest lie.

Nonetheless, on the night before our big day, she gave me a terrible scare. We had retired to our adjoining rooms whose connecting door was duly locked and whose key was safe in my father's pocket. Suddenly, a little white card appeared on my side of the door. It was Miss Magda Grilli's business card, upon which she had written in her big, pointy handwriting: "Who loves you for the last time!" Oh, what a bitter joke! Panic-stricken, I hammered on her door. "Is she going to run off?" I said to myself. "She is perfectly capable of doing so. What an unpredictable person!"

A calm voice answered me: "Of course Miss Grilli loves you for the last time! Tomorrow, it will be Mrs. André Trocmé who will love you."

Fabre gave an incomprehensible sermon. Magda's father came from Florence with a top hat that her stepmother had used as a soccer ball on the day he left Italy. We learned this detail later. Mrs. Grilli was jealous of Magda and furious that her husband was attending the wedding.

Cornier and Babut, who had come a great distance for the occasion, were also in the church. I couldn't resist inviting them. There had been some no-shows among the elect invited to the wedding feast and, unbeknownst to my father, I had asked my friends to replace them. This time Papa was the one to give in!

Cornier and Babut arrived late and had embarrassed looks on their faces all day long. They slipped away as soon as they could. Many years later, they explained to me why they were so embarrassed. They had come in their work clothes and after the ceremony had to go into town to buy white shirts. In addition, Cornier had to keep his back against a wall wherever he went because he had a hole in the seat of his pants!

THEN, ONCE AGAIN, the curtain dropped, and the scene changed.

On the evening of our wedding day, waiting for the train that would take us from the Gare de Lyon into Italy, my young wife and I wanted to have dinner but not in a restaurant. That was when I learned how much my wife loved picnics, which I can't stand. We landed on the steps of a stairway and nibbled on crusty, buttered rolls with ham that we had bought.

The train compartment was old and smelled like damp smoke. We didn't sleep all night. At Culmont-Chalindry, a shabby train station on our route, we looked outside and listened to cows expressing their sadness at being packed into the train next to ours.

In the morning, we were in Switzerland, where I had never been before! Oddly enough, I had explored the mountains in Africa and America before those in Europe. It was November, but the days were still marked with a dazzling brightness. There were still flowers around the attractive houses. At Thoune, interrupting our trip to Venice, we decided, on the spur of the moment, to get off at the next station. Before noon, we were at a hotel in Wengen facing the Jungfrau. We spent four extraordinary days there. Even today, recalling these days together is enough to cheer us up. Then it was Venice with its gondoliers. In Pastor Bertinatti's apartment, we found an immense corner room with a ceiling where light reflected off the water of the neighboring canal played alongside the angels and goddesses painted by a student of Tiepolo. Only the gondoliers' cries, warning of an approaching intersection, interrupted our joys. Venice was, by turns, sunny, rainy, and windy. After eleven days, we took a small hydroplane to Trieste. We got into the contraption through a hole in its top, and we rushed to portholes the size of dinner plates. An enormous woman sat between us. We couldn't see each other but we let each other know what we saw. Magda cried out, "I see a boat with red sails," and I responded, "I see the estuary of the Piave!"

From Trieste, we went on to Fiume, and from there, by boat, to Ancona. Our goal was Assisi. Marvelous days awaited us there. While the morning fog covered the Umbrian plain, Assisi, its churches, chateaus, and Mount Subasio emerged from this ocean like islands bathed in sunshine. Emptied of its summer pilgrims, the city recaptured its eternal self: women seated in front of their homes embroidering, goats passing in the hills, deserted churches in solitary meditation. We had a room in the Santa Chiara Inn, where the sound of the neighboring church's bell woke us in the morning. The dome of the church, covered with rose-colored Romanesque tiles, emerged against the dazzling fog covering the valley.

It was now my turn to be presented to the Grilli family which, for different reasons, was just as frightening as the Trocmé family. My wife became more and more nervous as the day approached. Even the weather got involved: radiant up until then, it turned bad. It was under torrential rains that I became acquainted with Florence, a sallow, gloomy, autumnal city I didn't like at all. Furthermore, Magda resumed her old habits. She got a cold and spent time in bed, while I, from a sense of duty, visited churches and museums with one of her former teachers.

As expected, the reception by the Grilli family was ice cold. Mr. Grilli came to the train station alone. But there was also an invisible spectator, Magda's former fiancé, Falkenberg, who apparently observed us from behind a column. He would never marry.

We were invited to the home of Mr. Grilli's sister-in-law, Magda's Auntie Dora, the widow of Uncle Goffredo, who had a small boarding house on the left bank of the Arno River. Every evening, there was a new invitation: the Bigiavis, the Bombicci-Pontellis, the Calosis. Magda, feeling better again, came with me each evening. The conversations in Italian, enhanced by exclamations and gestures, reverberated in my ears like cascades of incoherent sounds. They spoke French to me but tired of doing so quickly. After an exchange of banal remarks, they placed some big French book on my lap and forgot me, while Magda told stories with her usual verve. Florence was where I discovered that I had married an Italian.

The countess Bombicci-Pontelli and the Calosis were not related to Mr. Grilli but to his wife, Marguerite Grilli. They wanted to make us forget her strange attitude and obstinate refusal to see us, and tried everything, including the influence of her confessor, to bend her will. Finally, she accepted a "reconciliation" (Why? There hadn't been any quarrel!) at the foot of the altar in the Church of Saint Mark. Magda entered the church and found Marguerite. I stayed at the door in case Magda needed some help. After a while, they came outside. I was presented to Mrs. Grilli, who invited us to tea the next day in her home on Via Giusti. She received us with a stone face, gave us a cup of tea and dry cookies, and let us know, after twenty minutes of completely uninteresting conversation, that our presence fatigued her. We left with a "Phew!"

Many of the fears I had concerning my wife's character dissipated at this moment. The tales that she told of her childhood and unhappy youth had seemed so outrageous to me that I tried to place the blame on both her and her stepmother. I had also believed that by eliminating the object of her jealousy, her stepdaughter's marriage would appease Mrs. Grilli. None of this happened. Until her death, she forbade her children, Magda's half-brother and half-sisters, to see us or even write to us. Even Mr. Grilli had to write to us on the sly. Magda had exaggerated nothing: she had been the victim of a kind of madness in the mind of a woman whose life otherwise was relatively normal.

Thus Magda, alone in the world, became my wife, so much more so than other women who look back on their paternal home with regret. She identified her life with my life. She married not only a man but his career, his vocation. She did so with uncommon passion and attention because she was devoid of any temptation to look back. And I, who never loved the past, whose eyes are always riveted on the future, now had a partner whose intense sense of the present and of the human dimension of life would fill the gaps in my character. For my part, I brought Magda the security and calm that she desperately needed.

Happy marriages are not, I think, ideal marriages. Happiness comes from the lack of self-interest in the two spouses, and temperaments that complement one another. There is also the matter of equal weight. Magda and I, it seems to me, have maintained this balance. Sometimes she's the more important one – when it's necessary to *do* things quickly and well, to *dare* to undertake something, to *distinguish* between the true and the false. Sometimes it's I – when it's important to distinguish the *essentials* among fretful and secondary activities, to give our ship an unwavering steady course, and to *organize* our time.

I could only get a dim glimpse of these things when we left Florence for Maubeuge, where an impatient boss, Pastor Paul Perret, awaited us. He disapproved of our wasting a month being happy!

Maubeuge is one of the ugliest cities in France. Along the muddy waters of the Sambre River, a series of black-brick cities – Jeumont, Maubeuge, Sous-le-Bois, Hautmont, Aulnoye – extends for fifteen miles. The red smoke from the steel factories descends on the roofs, walls, and soil in a greasy crust that also penetrates the houses. Thirty-five years ago, the population, doomed to work in heavy industry (blast furnaces, steamrolling, wire drawing, foundries, glassware) and deprived of the various means of transportation that today would allow them to escape to greener pastures, rotted away in an unimaginably disgusting environment. Not that they were poor – that was our first astonishment – because you can't attract men to a job that will destroy their health in twenty years without offering them high salaries. But it seemed the people who worked these jobs weren't interested in anything but their slavish work and a tavern where they could drink until they lost consciousness.

Our work in Maubeuge was, above all, helping alcoholics. My new boss, Paul Perret, was a Swiss pastor from La Sagne, a city whose inhabitants were reputed to be frank and unpolished. He excelled in these areas.

His big, myopic eyes stared at you from behind thick, corrective lenses with a mixture of irony and severity that froze you in your tracks. The members of the parish complained about the scathing judgments of their pastor who, with a single word, could put a damper on ill-timed enthusiasm. Nonetheless, Perret ("Perretto," as Magda soon nicknamed him) had a good side as well. He was a hard worker and demanded that those around him work just as hard. His theology and social ideas were also close to mine, and he became a faithful friend. Even if those around him felt unappreciated and degraded in his presence, he never dropped them. His faithfulness to the church in Maubeuge and to its members lasted many years, right up to his death.

Mrs. Perret was an enigma. A French citizen, she was a gifted math teacher who lived in a spiritual stratosphere completely inaccessible to us. Her conversation was perfect, completely devoid of any criticism of anything whatsoever and so full of compunction and charity that she bored us to death. Every Sunday after services, Mrs. Perret invited us to lunch. She always served the same "economic ball of rice" seasoned with sermons about administering a tiny pastoral budget. This was not the spirit of poverty we were looking for, but rather a sour atmosphere created by excessively virtuous and thrifty people. She had a ravishing voice and did an excellent job of raising her four children, but never seemed happy to us. She was like a spellbound bird that her husband enclosed in a cage, every bar of which was a moral principle. We were not mistaken. Without ever admitting the cause of her despondency, every year Mrs. Perret went to Switzerland for treatment of her nervous condition.

A double disappointment awaited me on my arrival. Perretto was the general secretary of the Christian Society of Northern France (Papa was its president), which gave him control of a dozen church positions, including Maubeuge. Perretto worked hard to destroy, with his huge bear paws, all my ideas for original pastoral service.

"Take a practical training course in a factory?" he said to me on my arrival. "An excellent idea. But I checked all the factories in the Maubeuge basin. Not one is willing to hire a Protestant pastor! One of the bosses even told me, 'I would rather hire Marcel Cachin[1] than a Protestant pastor.' See what I mean?"

1 Marcel Cachin (1869–1958) was in the political office of the French Communist Party and served as the editor of *L'Humanité*, a French newspaper that, at that time, was an organ of the French Communist Party.

"I see," I replied turning pale.

"I can get you a job in an office, if you like."

"Working in an office doesn't interest me at all. I want to get experience in manual labor."

"That's what I thought. Well, do your own pastoral work; I'll put you in charge of half the parish."

I had to capitulate, feeling that I had been swindled by my father and my boss. I quickly realized the mistake I had made by putting myself under my father's authority once again. My comrades in the Northern Group were mostly from the South or from Normandy. The North meant freedom for them. For me, it was the extended family, and that family never let go of me until I left the North. Every one of our actions, Magda's and mine, was gone over with a fine-tooth comb. Each one of our conversations was reported and distorted in Saint-Quentin. In addition, my friends weren't free around me because I was the son of a boss who was in no way accommodating and whose ideas often dated back to the nineteenth century.

My second disappointment was learning that the big crisis that had made me feel morally obliged to leave the United States and assume the position of second in command in Maubeuge was totally fabricated. My predecessor, Paul Conord, announced his departure, and Perret demanded that a replacement be found before he left. I was the designated victim. Papa's moving letters, which in this regard had been perfectly honest but had been designed above all to bring back the lost sheep to the family fold and the church, were dictated by men concerned with their problems and their projects, not mine.

Be that as it may, after a week or two of adapting to our new home, I bravely got to work.

Our tasks were decreed for us beforehand by "the boss" every Monday morning in his meticulously tidy office. I say "us," because I wasn't alone. My colleague was a young woman preacher, Y. J., a former classmate of my cousin Yvonne Dumas. This pious and enthusiastic, but strange and somewhat hysterical, young woman had an olive complexion and a pair of extraordinary green eyes that served her well as regards the opposite sex. She had already sought without success to marry several pastors and told the younger girls in her church group about the eleven marriage proposals she had rejected. She lived in an apartment in the parish hall we called the Fraternité and invited me, a married man, into her bedroom – without evil intentions, I'm sure, but by some compelling need in her nature. I did everything I could to discourage her advances.

Perretto detested Y. J. as much as any serious and deeply timid man could detest a woman who gave him the eye. Our Monday morning meetings were transformed into torture scenes during which the boss interrogated Y. J. with police tactics about her incompetence, her negligence, and all the mistakes she had accumulated during the week. The poor girl lost her sassy look and broke down in tears. She wanted me to console her, but, anticipating the nature of those scenes of consolation, I refused any private meetings with her.

Perretto had also taken it upon himself to break me in. He told me what visits to make, describing in advance the type of people I would meet: dishonest, quarrelsome, bragging, jealous people; adulterers, gossips, drunks, and hypocrites. I was horrified and quickly saw how false his descriptions were. Certainly, in the proletarian milieu many vices were obvious to the naked eye. But the workers of northern France were both enthusiastic and weak. Like the people in the Gospels, they were always ready for heroism or denial. I felt my role was to incite them to heroism; Perrot believed we should denounce their denials. Our two ways of preaching, however, sometimes came together.

That is how the great bird on the open sea that I had been in New York had its wings clipped, feather by feather, until it accepted to live in a cage. I say all this without bitterness. Today I know that "a rolling stone gathers no moss." I had in me a poet and a dreamer who could have spent years collecting impressions and, little by little, lost his impact on the world. By hitching me up to a cart and shortening my reins, Perretto taught me how to pull the cart. I have pulled many carts since then, some better than others. But I still prefer mirages off in the distance to administrative committees. To each his own task.

What affected me much more deeply was the invisible wall of suspicion that the Perrets constructed around Magda. Certainly, Magda was not an orthodox Christian, and her attitude toward the church was openly critical. But she was frank, true, good, and faithful to the people around her, capable of accepting them as they were. Everyone who approached her immediately became attached to her. She became their counselor and trusted friend.

The Perrets had decided that it would be dangerous for the parishioners to get close to Magda. My wife, then, didn't even have the right to attend the women's get-togethers arranged by Mrs. Perret. Confined to the role of housewife that she never really liked, Magda fell back into the mental anguish that made our lives miserable.

I used to come home around eleven o'clock at night after my parish rounds and find my wife more and more tense just as she was getting ready to give birth to our first child. "I'll die in childbirth," she repeatedly claimed, "just like my mother." I didn't know how to reassure her.

We had wanted a modest household. The sparse furniture that we got as presents from Papa and the things we'd bought were ugly. We invited our parishioners to supper. They refused or came after they had eaten. Our conversations and preoccupations were simply beyond them.

Our first springtime in Maubeuge was rainy, muddy, depressing. One day, in a parishioner's home, I saw fresh anemones from the Côte d'Azur. They were rare then. I asked our parishioner to give me a few and brought them back to Magda with the hope that they would bring her fond memories of Italy. But she paid no attention to those poor flowers. Years later, when I told her how sad this had made me, Magda admitted that she thought I had picked them from the side of a ditch! Since then, having seen them blossom in the suburbs of Florence, I understand her scorn.

We had several arguments. Magda couldn't stand being caged in. She fled one day into the street and spoke about going off to study nursing at the Ambroise Paré Hospital.[2] She often ran a fever. Furthermore, the beginning of my ministry was difficult. Under the mocking eye of Perretto, I initiated a survey, with printed questionnaires that I distributed to Catholics and Protestants, in which I posed indiscreet questions about morality and religion. Responses were to remain anonymous, but people were distrustful and the whole thing was a failure.

One day, a good colleague my age, Marcel Heuzé, visited me with the express purpose of scolding me for not teaching pure Christianity. I realized that Perret had a big mouth and that our beginnings in ministry, commented upon by Perret to pastors and laypeople alike, caused concern for my soul and Magda's and prayers for our salvation.

You must not believe, however, that everything was gloomy in our lives. Because I arrived late for my post in December, Perret only granted us a fifteen-day vacation during the summer of 1927. I put that break

2 In the margin of the manuscript, Magda wrote: "André is wrong. It was before our marriage that I had thought about going to Ambroise Paré."

to good use by attending, alone, the famous passion play held every ten years in an outdoor theater in Oberammergau, Germany. The Fellowship of Reconciliation had established a permanent conference there during the summer. Magda insisted that I leave her in Saint-Gobain. She didn't want me to miss this opportunity. How many times since then has she sacrificed herself for my happiness or that of the children? How many times did she make me escape my fixed routine, forcing me to free myself from the tendency to confuse duty and the burden of tradition?

At the end of June, Perret left on his two-month vacation, and I immediately started to breathe. In Aulnoy, the Socialist Party organized a big meeting for peace and asked me to be one of the speakers. In my speech, I affirmed the incompatibility of the Gospels and war. The crowd was dense, and we were in a large public space. For the first time in my life, I believe that I established a sympathetic connection with the public, something I often did again later. I was the most applauded of the speakers and the press took note of this event. That got me a severe warning from the committee of the "Northern Christian Society." That's when the church, fearing the growing influence of Philippe Vernier, Henri Roser, and Jacques Martin, took restrictive measures against conscientious objection.

Another joy awaited me. In Maubeuge, as in other Protestant churches in France, we held "kitchen get-togethers," which took place in a single room on the ground floor, at once a kitchen and dining room, in the workers' houses. One of the most animated of these gatherings took place in the home of "Mother Poyard," a short, earthy, and enthusiastic woman who lived at the end of Hautmont's industrial basin, at the "Tail of the Woods," in a gray house near the Chimique, a factory that produced chemical products with nauseous fumes.

The same small group of regulars met each week at Mrs. Poyard's, but when the weather was hot, I suggested that we take the chairs outside and transform our private assembly into a public meeting. The workers returning from the Chimique stopped to listen. After a few weeks, it became their custom to do so. Soon there were about a hundred in attendance! I presented the popular, liberating, social gospel. Mrs. Poyard's sons, recovered alcoholics, gave testimony, and then we opened the discussion. Socialists, Communists, anarchists, and Catholics raised objections that I refuted politely. Several families wanted to join our church. At the end of August, however, Perret returned. He soon did everything to dampen my enthusiasm. “Just a flash in the pan,” he said to me. “These movements never last.”

It rained in the evening, and we were gathered in Mrs. Poyard’s kitchen, about fifty of us all standing up. Despite my pleas, Perret insisted on coming to test the validity of what I had told him and took charge of the meeting. It was a disaster. He made some aggressive remarks that provoked mumblings among the men and indignation from a slightly tipsy listener who tried to interrupt him. Instead of responding politely, Perret reproached him: “You’ve been drinking; be quiet; come back when you’re sober. Who’s chairing this meeting, you or me?” Grumbling, the men started leaving one by one. “C’mon, Zef, let’s go. With priests, it’s always the same way.” Ten minutes later there were no more than a dozen of us, the small handful of regulars. Perret was the only happy one. “You see,” he told me when we got back. “It was only a flash in the pan.”

“You can’t tell that man anything,” sighed Mrs. Poyard. “He’s always right.”

Despite these disappointments, my ministry was not entirely unproductive. I worked mostly with young people and the Croix Bleue.

But the Croix Bleue underwent a deplorable setback. The François family lived in the caretaker’s lodge at the Fraternité. The husband was a house painter and longtime recovered alcoholic. Mrs. François was a beautiful woman with ambition. Her husband’s sobriety allowed them to live more comfortably. She bought a piano so their only son could take lessons. Then one day they had a fight, and Mr. François walked out, telling his wife, “Since that’s the way you see it, I’m going out for a beer.” He was gone for twenty-four hours. He returned with a hatchet, chopped the beautiful piano into matchsticks, and threatened to kill his terrified wife and son.

Perretto, who always sought explanations, put part of the blame on Mrs. François – a “sensual woman,” he said – who missed her husband’s former abuse.

The tragic part was that Mr. François, when he had a few drinks under his belt, bought drinks for everyone in the house and gave away his pay to anyone willing to take it. Today’s psychologists would wonder exactly what frustrations this poor house painter with the multicolored, paint-stained clothing was reacting against!

I tried to save this poor guy by preventing him from drinking and ruining his family. When someone told me he was in a tavern, I rode my bike there and appeared next to him at the bar. He received me with demonstrations of friendship. “Ah! It’s my pastor,” he declared as he introduced me to everyone. I ordered lemonade. When Mr. François ordered a round for everyone, I objected by pointing to the sign saying that it was forbidden to serve people already in a drunken state. That led to heated arguments. Furious, Mr. François would leave, zigzag onto his bike, and take off. I would catch up to him, reason with him, and direct him toward his house.

Sometimes, with a diabolical look in his eye, he would stop in front of another tavern. “Trocmé, I’m going in here. Do you hear me? No one can stop me.” Of course, I couldn’t; he was as strong as an ox. I followed him everywhere, at least recovering the money he distributed. One day in the street when he was really drunk, he missed a turn on his bike, fell, and hurt himself badly. I helped him up and brought him home. Another day, horribly ill, he came to our house when I was out. Magda gave him coffee and put him to bed on the upper floor, where he soiled our guest room with vomit. Nothing makes you view alcohol with more horror than contact with those pathetic people who are possessed by it. They are more sick than sinful in the eyes of God.

NELLY WAS BORN on August 31. We thought we were all prepared. People didn’t go to maternity wards much in those days. Nonetheless, we reserved a room at the Ambroise Paré Hospital in Lille. Caught by surprise when the labor began, I telephoned Francis in Saint-Gobain. As soon as the obstetrician finished his work, he left Magda for other operations, which left me alone with the midwife. I watched over Magda with Frida Gardiol, her Italian friend staying with us.

Around ten o’clock in the evening, Francis and Rose arrived by car. Francis examined Magda and called the obstetrician, who had returned, a “butcher.” They exchanged unpleasant words. The “butcher” sized up Francis, left, and didn’t return.

Worried, Francis went to bed, but he returned in his pajamas from time to time to check on Magda. I’m not going to relate everything that happened. Let it suffice for Nelly to know that her mother was narrowly saved by Uncle Francis’s energy. The next morning, Magda was resting there on her pillow. Next to her, fast asleep, was a big baby who already had curly hair, a magnificent little girl we named Nelly after Magda’s Russian-Italian mother.

Perret came to Magda's bedside in a kindly and pastoral manner, very moved. He wanted to read the Bible and clumsily placed the book on top of her. Magda said to him: "Please take that big book off my stomach!"

This drama made me grow up overnight. I learned that, despite the love we have for those most dear to us, neither our wishes, nor our prayers, nor the anguish that we suffer can change the implacable course of events. I learned something else too: regardless of the love we feel for our loved ones, the healthy person instinctively enjoys breathing and moving about. Our physiological selfishness is frightening. You can't prevent yourself from considering a tragedy from your own perspective and not from the perspective of the sick one. Ahead of time, you ask yourself what you will do if the loved one dies, and already you are thinking of solutions.

I made this discovery while on my knees, praying to God to save my beloved Magda. It forced me to see my youthful, romantic hopes, as well as my belief that ordinary men could be saints, as utopian. Magda, too, taught me every day to see human beings as they are and to love them as they are and as I am, a simple man among others.

I think that many new priests and ministers suffer from juvenile romanticism. After two or three years of ministry, they become disillusioned when they discover the weaknesses of human nature. Papa himself never ceased repeating the Socratic affirmation: "First know thyself." But the church often bypasses self-knowledge. This accounts for the turn to abstract theology or liturgy or ecclesiology, or, for Communists, worship of the party. In these consoling but false doctrines, we hope to find – but won't, because they are fraudulent – the absolute charity we felt possible in our twenties.

NELLY'S BIRTH HAD OTHER happy consequences. While no doctor could explain why, it rid Magda permanently of her daily fever and regularized the functioning of her thyroid. It chased away her anguish, which only survived in the form of worried exclamations learned during her youth. Even today, in an anguished voice, Magda calls for help if she misplaces a comb. From that point forward, except perhaps when directly faced with physical suffering, Magda was the stronger and more clear-headed of the two of us in facing life's challenges.

The leaden weight of Perret's paternalism landed on us. He controlled every detail of our lives, even what Magda cooked and the contents of

Nelly's bottles. He talked about us to everyone in Saint-Quentin, where the family tribunal, composed of Papa, Jeanne the cook and household manager, and Marie the chamber maid, weighed and criticized the least of our movements.

One day, we announced to Perret that my pastoral training had lasted long enough. He was dumbfounded by such audacity! We were leaving Maubeuge at the end of the 1927–28 school year. I applied for a pastoral position in Sin-le-Noble, near Douai. Living in a cage for a year and three months had been quite enough for us.

11

Sin-le-Noble

SIN-LE-NOBLE HAD THE REPUTATION of being the most difficult ministry post in the Northern Christian Society. Founded around 1890 by Pastor Georges Boissonnas after the local Catholic priest refused to perform the funeral for a person who had committed suicide, it prospered in the hands of this masterful preacher. About fifty Catholic families became Protestant. The head of this group, old Ducatillon, who limped because of an accident in the mines, related how Boissonnas, who limped as badly as he did, tried to speak to him on the street. He fled Boissonas's approach as quickly as his disability allowed. "I knew very well," Ducatillon said, "that the day he put his hand on my shoulder, I too would follow the Gospels."

Boissonnas built a small church, where I preached for six years. He lived alone in a two-room house that served as a youth center when we were there. When he asked his friend Barde to take his place, the parents of Barde's young wife, Mercédès Walbaum (a wealthy cousin of my half-brothers), had a three-story, red-brick chateau built behind the church. "The pastor has better lodgings than the Good Lord," said the critical parishioners.

That was the presbytery where we lived from 1928 to 1934. It looked impressive with its cinder-covered courtyard where the parishioners milled about and the wild backyard where several beautiful trees were a pure joy to me. But this splendor had been conceived for central heating and two or three domestic staff. Our miserable pastoral salary wouldn't allow for any house staff, and the central heating had been taken out by the Germans during the 1914–1918 occupation. Parish activities took place on the ground floor. We lived on the second and third floors, up steep stairs. Magda had to carry the coal and the water upstairs, because the pump no longer worked.

It was during our time in Sin-le-Noble that our three youngest children, Jean-Pierre, Jacques, and Daniel, were born. Jean-Pierre and Jacques came into the world without too much drama. Perhaps they followed one another too closely, but religious scruples, combined with limited means of birth control, created an impossible choice. Either we weren't intimate with one another, which we didn't want because we loved each other deeply, or we had children one after the other. For Daniel, Magda stayed in bed for a month at Ambroise Paré before the birth by cesarean section. Then Daniel, a magnificent baby, almost died of an enormous abscess in his neck, misdiagnosed by a poorly trained nurse. As for Magda, Dr. Paucot, who operated on her, forbade her to have any more children.

Several young German au pairs came to help Magda with her difficult tasks and forced her to take care of herself. Magda had decided to eat less so her husband would be well-fed. She often only ate smoked herring when I had steak![1] These au pairs were often a problem. Lutzi, Lieselotte, and Lina the Alsatian were not satisfied with their diet, nor was the maid, Mrs. Nick. As for our children, they were superb. But they caught every bad cold that lingered in this country of miners sickened with silicosis.

Sin-le-Noble was located on the site of a former swamp. The mine constantly pumped its waters for industrial use. Sin-le-Noble forms the somewhat indistinct link between the Pas-de-Calais mining basin and the Valenciennes basin bordering the Belgian Borinage. Each pit was surrounded by a high trestle of planks and beams and marked by a conical heap of stony, sandy slag. The workers' red-brick houses, called *corons*, extended from there. The oldest ones, surrounded by a wall that allowed the police to confine and subdue strikers and their families, resembled barracks, or prisons. At the beginning of the century, the mining companies built long, gloomy streets that stretched out for miles on end. The doors and windows of each narrow house faced the street. Out back, a garden as narrow as the façade gave the miner a chance to grow a few vegetables and complete his home with a makeshift lean-to, which became the kitchen and real living space for the family.

Fortunately, after World War I, mining companies constructed actual housing projects for the workers. The detached houses, designed in

1 Here Magda wrote in the margins of the manuscript: "André was not in good shape at this time. His appendicitis operation indicated serious health issues."

English fashion, sheltered two to four families. A vegetable garden was situated in front, and the streets were wide and lined with green. Even in this pleasant setting, however, the oppression of the mining companies' paternalism could be felt. At the center of the cities rose the Catholic church, dispensary, parish hall, and private Catholic school. No one was forced to send their children to the private school, but the families that didn't show up for Mass, or whose fathers didn't sing in the church choir, could run into difficulties. A family in whose house I regularly conducted our kitchen get-togethers asked me to stop my visits. The singing of Protestant hymns wasn't appreciated by the "mine," and a nun had come to explain to the family that they could lose their low-rent lodging if they didn't look more Catholic. In fact, these people, like all my parishioners, were Catholics converted to Protestantism.

One summer, I wanted to organize the children from the big Waziers pit who hung around the streets during the summer.[2] I noticed a vacant lot with empty barracks that would have been perfect for what I had in mind. I learned that this spot belonged to the "mine." It's the policy of mining companies to buy the land whose underground resources they exploit. In fact, they are responsible for the collapse, damage, and cracks in buildings resulting from the collapse of unmaintained underground galleries no longer in use. To avoid considerable costs, they prefer owning the surface property, even if it means letting the houses collapse. That's why mining towns look so dilapidated.

In short, I approached the mining people and was received by a friendly director. He made three points:

1. Among our stockholders, we have some very influential Protestants. But, to maintain good order in the region, our administrative council has decided to entrust the Catholic Church with the education and social works that benefit the population. After all, let's admit it: the population is Catholic.
2. Therefore, we do not want a "sect" established in Waziers and won't rent you the space you would like.
3. Nonetheless, we recognize that your efforts have merit and will contribute to the moral growth of a community in need of such growth. We therefore offer your youth organization the same

2 Waziers contained several mine shafts and a church, Our Lady of the Miners, which today is listed as a World Heritage Site.

> advantages as the Catholic youth organization: free use of our sports stadium, equipment, and uniforms.

He opened a drawer and took out 2,000 francs, a considerable sum at that time. "Here is money," he said, "that you can count on as an annual subsidy for your work."

I was uncomfortable, very young, and ready to put out my hand and accept this godsend because our parish was so poor, when the director added: "I will add only one condition."

"What's that?" I asked.

"We have a period of social unrest ahead of us that might very well turn nasty. I would like you, as well as the Catholic clergy, to exercise a good influence on your parishioners and counsel prudence in your sermons. If a strike seems like a real possibility, I expect you to explain to them that their best interest lies in collaborating with their employers."

"What do you mean?" I asked. "You want them to break away from their fellow workers?"

"That they do not obey the orders of the CGT.[3] That's all."

I got up, red as a beet. "I'm sorry, sir. My job is to preach the Gospels. I can't commit to doing these things."

"As you wish," he said with a sneer, and the drawer slammed shut on the 2,000 francs.

My parishioners were not Communists. They were Socialists and friends of Sin-le-Noble's mayor, a very popular man named Foucault. He founded and still directed the Consumer and Production Worker Cooperatives. He was a generous freethinker who went to city hall wearing clogs as a mark of his refusal to accept gentrification. During our six years in Sin-le-Noble, I had the best possible relationship with Foucault, due mostly to our "Old Folks' Christmas" program.

In 1929, the economic crisis resulting from the Great Depression came down hard on the coal basin, bringing with it unemployment, starvation wages, and severe strikes. I had no other choice but to ally myself with my parishioners. I had founded a small monthly publication, *The Good Seed*, in which I tried, in the framework of our parish news, to demonstrate the social and international impact of our Christian faith. Evrard, the colleague "Perretto" had assigned to Aniche (I'll speak later about my

3 The *Confédération générale du travail* (CGT) or the United General Confederation of Labor, founded in 1922, was a trade union confederation in France that eventually became aligned with the French Communist Party.

disappointment in this regard), had a working-class background. He adopted my publication and, during elections, published a lively article in which he advised our parishioners to "Vote Socialist!" This article created one of my worst crises with the ecclesiastical authorities.

Sin-le-Noble had both the advantage and the disadvantage of being the working-class suburb of the beautiful, old city of Douai, whose bell tower, once painted by Corot, was a famous Flemish-style monument. Although Douai was second in importance to the departmental capital, Lille, and had been downgraded to the level of subprefecture, it contained a rich and conservative middle class, no less Christian, but also domineering. This group included the Deransart family.

Mr. Deransart, president of the Court of Appeals in Douai, was a typical magistrate: fat, purple complexion, small and indifferent eyes behind a thick pince-nez. His wife, the brains of the family, was equally fat, always out of breath and sweating, dressed sloppily in light, shapeless dresses, but active, affectionate, intelligent, and bossy. Deransart was also the vice-president of the Northern Christian Society. My father was the president, and I, their humble preacher.

Evrard's article exploded like a bomb in an already tense situation. The church in Sin-le-Noble had recently distanced itself considerably from the church in Douai: my predecessor, Émile Fabre, fiery in conversation as southern Frenchmen can be, was an artist whose refined tastes found few echoes among his parishioners. Therefore, he and his wife often went to Douai, where they had a pleasant group of friends who played music and practiced the arts together. My parishioners had suffered from this situation. "Mr. and Mrs. Fabre maintained a good pastoral household," said Maurice, the vice president of our parish council, "but all their friends were in Douai. Will you be like them?"

We were not like them at all! Not that we were indifferent to music and literature, but Magda and I always preferred the company of simple people despite our international cultural background that was greater than that of many pastors! Rejected by the Florentine aristocracy her stepmother claimed, Magda took after her Russian grandmother. She mingled with the Rosina Gaggiolis of this world.[4] I had my own experience with the Union in Saint-Quentin, my discovery of Christ among the humble, the Union in Plaisance and Clamart, and I was

4 Rosina Gaggioli was a poor Italian seamstress Magda met in the Union Chrétienne des Jeunes Filles who became her close friend.

comfortable with the Sin-le-Noble residents. It was the imperceptible pretensions of the middle class, their sense of superiority to our parishioners, that made me uncomfortable. We were free and intended to remain so. This attitude permitted us to experience in Sin-le-Noble perhaps the most marvelous years of my ministry.

Be that as it may, Deransart announced that he was resigning from the committee of the Northern Christian Society unless I was kicked out of that group because, in recommending the Socialist vote, I had betrayed my duties by introducing politics into the church.

Now I had everyone – Douai, Perretto, and Papa – on my back! Despite my goodwill, I could not apologize to Deransart for the mistake that had been made. I wasn't the author of the article; I didn't read it before it went to press; I couldn't repudiate my colleague Evrard.

I had a stormy argument with Deransart. I told him that I could not dissociate myself from my parishioners who were on strike and that the role of the church was to fight for social justice. He was very disagreeable, very hard, and insensitive to my pleading – typical of the magistrate he was.

Evrard backed down, however, apologized to Deransart, and promised not to repeat his actions. Deransart and I both retained our places, but *The Good Seed* never reappeared. I had made the mistake of sharing responsibilities with an unreliable colleague. Magda said that I always put too much confidence in others. That has caused me a lot of disappointments, but a lot of satisfaction as well. Despite everything, in Sin-le-Noble, for the first time in my life, I felt in full possession of my capabilities and gained self-confidence in my dealings with others.

I was aided in these endeavors by the great believer and prophet, Mr. Nick, pastor at Fives in Lille and the last survivor of the generation of the Social Christian preachers that included Boissonnas, Gounelle, Durrleman, and Aeschimann.

Nick was, above all, an artist. He had the physique, the bushy hair and mustache, the deep look in his eyes, the brilliant absent-mindedness that turned into complete presence of mind when it was needed, and the right ethics. He was a prestigious orator who read the Greek classics without a dictionary, a fiery debater about whom one wondered, "What did he mean?"

This powerful genius abandoned everything to become a disciple of Christ. He could devote himself to a human wreck until the wreck recovered fully, or spend an entire night in prayer to claim and obtain the salvation of one soul, or humble himself before a greenhorn theology student too sure of his own opinions. Nick had the gift of attracting a whole team of collaborators capable of translating his "spiritual inspirations" into the practical domain. From this group, there emerged an extraordinary initiative, the "Foyer des Frères" (Brothers' Center), with its own branch of the Croix Bleue, a beverage cooperative, and a summer camp in Aubagne near the sea. Money flowed into Nick's hands. He always had enough for those in need. He lived like a saint with the large family that his wife, who died young, had given him. The children, left on their own, both adored and criticized their father, whose great saintliness they struggled to live up to.

Most of his children – André, Pierre, Jeanne, and Paul – died before their father. He died alone, in a miserable, unheated room, misunderstood by the new generation. He was the admirer and victim of Pastor Philippe Blanc, who, called to succeed Nick, closed the cooperative, abolished his Croix Bleue, did away with popular discussions, and reduced the extraordinary revival meetings held in Fives to a small prayer circle with Pentecostal leanings. The sect members excommunicated those who didn't share their views.

But at the time I'm talking about, Fives was still going full blast. Roser, J.P. Benoit, and Philippe Vernier had all been trained by Nick. Now a widower, he was being cared for by his daughter, Jeanne, a beautiful, witty, and intelligent young woman. She had, unfortunately, married a bizarre, asexual professor, Léon James, who dominated the somewhat pretentious Federation of Christian Students. Jeanne got a divorce from her marriage that never had been consummated and returned to Fives. Magda became a close friend of hers. For the first time, I suffered from jealousy at their intimacy and learned that jealousy can destroy the most intense happiness. But Magda and I had so much confidence in each other that we let each other expand our personal horizons as we saw fit, according to our hearts and deepest inclinations. It is true that Magda always turned toward friends of the same sex, women of great value such as Jeanne Nick, Miss Matile, Mrs. Marion, and Jispa. Her friends were women of conscience with big, caring hearts, who respected our family unit.

To return to Nick, I called on him twice, both in Aniche and Marquette, in unforgettable circumstances. Located seven miles east of

Sin-le-Noble, Aniche constituted the second half of my parish before Evrard's arrival. A small Protestant community with a minuscule church and presbytery, the members eked out a living even more meager than that of our fifty families in Sin-le-Noble. Even though they worked like slaves, they were caught between their bare means and the bourgeois pretensions of a few families. "Pinko Aniche" had a Communist mayor. He returned one day from the Soviet Union and organized a town-hall meeting where Christians were requested to provide counterarguments. The Catholics recused themselves when they heard that Florimond Bonte, one of the Communists' most eloquent orators, was speaking.

I took up the challenge, but called on Nick, who in the past had helped Florimond Bonte when he was still an unknown militant worker. The big evening arrived. The communal room of Aniche was full of men in caps and suffocating cigarette smoke. I distinctly remember what the mayor and Florimond Bonte said. The former said that he observed in Russia that Communism, by abolishing competition at every level, had not only eliminated inequality among the classes but had made bad human instincts disappear. "School children no longer tell lies," he said. "Why would they? The competitive spirit has been abolished." He then described the exact methods applied in this early phase of Communism before Stalin reestablished artificial competition at the heart of state enterprises to increase production. "The so-called problem of 'sin' has been resolved in the USSR," concluded the mayor triumphantly. "The revolution pulled out its roots. What do you have to say, Christians?"

Nick spoke next. I have a detailed memory of what he said. He described Jesus as the first socialist, the friend of the poor. He contradicted the mayor and gave examples of sins, such as alcoholism and adultery, that are not consequences of economic competition. He then gave examples of recoveries made possible by the power of Jesus Christ.

But it was Florimond Bonte who brought down the house when, abandoning the traditional theme of anticlericalism and the traditional nod to Christ, he gave examples to prove that Christ had a detrimental influence on the course of history because his doctrine of nonviolence paralyzed revolutionary action. "Every time an exploited people were at the point of taking up arms to get rid of tyrants," proclaimed the gifted orator, "the deceitful message about pardon, forgiving our enemies, and having limitless patience was taught to the people by a clergy aligned with the ruling class. They disarmed revolutionary forces and prolonged the reign of injustice. Karl Marx was the first to dare to denounce religion as the 'opiate of the people.' Today, the proletariat, having become aware of these things, can finally organize. The October 1917 Russian Revolution is the avant-garde of the world revolution."

Alas, the few clumsy words I pronounced at the end in defense of non-violence hardly reached the rumbling crowd, which, to the sound of "The Internationale," had already started for the exits.

I have never forgotten this meeting. For the first time, I understood that individual conversion is not enough to resolve the issues of justice and peace. Institutions must change. Even in the hands of well-intentioned people, bad structures can lead to catastrophes. We must, therefore, draw from the Gospels an efficacious, revolutionary method of changing institutions. Even though Jesus taught this method, Gandhi was demonstrating its application. Still today, I cannot see how churches composed of self-satisfied bourgeois can become a revolutionary power in the world.

It was in Marquette, which is close to Aniche, that I called upon Nick for the second and last time. One day, I received a surprising visit from a young woman, Mrs. Roger, the daughter of the mayor of the large village of Marquette. The Socialist city council, she related, had argued with the priest about the rent for the presbytery. The bishop had forbidden Mass to be celebrated there, and the priest had left. She came to see me in the name of the city council and her father to offer me the use of the church and the presbytery: the village wanted to become Protestant! An incredible situation, like those in the sixteenth century that had permitted the conversion of entire regions, seemed to present itself once again. I went to see the mayor, and his proposals were serious. He called a meeting in the town hall. Nick chaired that meeting. All the men from the village were in the room, standing up in their caps and smoking. Nick was magnificent: he didn't use any facile, demagogic arguments that attacked Catholicism. He was too noble to stir up the Socialist crowd. He simply preached the gospel.

After the meeting, men sat around in the taverns looking at one another, perplexed, because it appeared to them that Protestantism was more demanding than Catholicism. One young man declared, "I have always thought like you, but I didn't have the words to say so."

The following week, a dozen families came to see me. We enquired and discovered that the church and the presbytery belonged to the town, and that when the Protestants and Catholics had split, the buildings had been legally assigned to the Catholics. The mayor wasn't free to dispose of them. But the mayor's office lent us a place where we could construct a church building.

That winter there was a serious struggle between the Catholics and Protestants, and our work was at stake. Every week, in the old car my brother Robert had sold me for 8,000 francs (which for me was expensive), I spent a day in Marquette, where I called on people and gave religious instruction to children. In the evenings, after dining with the mayor, I presided over a meeting that generally had between ten and thirty attendees. The Catholic reaction was terrible. The diocese, forgetting its quarrels, sent a high-powered priest to Marquette. He distributed uniforms and musical instruments to children, who paraded through the streets. The owners of the land and houses threatened to evict their tenants if they attended Protestant meetings. That would have been their ruin. They had to stop coming.

One evening after our meeting, I broke a spring on my car driving on the dreadful Marquette roads. I sought the aid of a very obliging resident who, with the help of a flashlight, began repairing my car. Lying on our stomachs, we collaborated politely. During our conversation, he discovered who I was. "Holy shit," he cried out. "You're the Protestant!" Standing up and steering clear of me as if avoiding the plague, he left me there, returned home, and locked his door. I finished the repairs as best I could, went to his closed door, and left the wire, pliers, light, and a note saying, "Thanks anyway!"

The struggle no longer favored the Protestants. A dozen people who didn't depend on the Catholic landlords remained faithful to us. There was no question of abandoning work that might one day or another take off again.

The day after the Marquette adventure and the Waziers incident, which I'll mention momentarily, Perretto appeared in the Sin-le-Noble presbytery. He announced that, because Sin-le-Noble had extended its work to the surrounding area, the board had decided to detach Aniche from Sin-le-Noble and give Aniche its own pastor. That pastor had already been named: it was Evrard, whom I spoke about earlier! This pastor came from a working-class background and would be much better adapted than I was to the proletarian milieu. In short, Aniche and Marquette were taken from me.

I felt like one of my limbs had been amputated. If I had been a few years older, I would have "raised Cain" and refused to let them take the better part of my work. But in 1931, I was only thirty years old, and I accepted this absurd decision without saying a word. Evrard, whose Baptist family was in fact from Douai, was a charming young guy, not very bright and, like all educated children of workers, petty bourgeois from tip to toe. After only one winter, the Protestant church in Marquette closed its doors, and Mrs. Roger persevered alone. I saw her from time to time at services in Douai. As for Aniche, a few years later Evrard left and the doors of its church and presbytery closed for good. That young man was too much the product of the milieu he came from.

It would be unfair to my colleagues in the North if I didn't mention the positive and deep influence they had on me. As early as theology school, we had formed the Northern Group. I was the youngest member. The oldest ones, Daniel and Robert Chéradame, Morel, and Heuzé, had served in World War I. Cornier, Ducros, and Babut were a year or two older than me. Viollier, whom I met when I got to Sin-le-Noble, was never fully accepted by the group, and it hurt him. In theology school, the group had been clearly oriented toward social issues; many of my colleagues who returned from the war were Communists. That changed under the influence of two men: Nick and Albert Aeschimann. Nick, although a Communist, was truly a great Pietist preacher. Aeschimann, a fifty-year-old pastor in Liévin, was frighteningly thin and nervous, with a penetrating gaze, and rigid viewpoints. He lived to the rhythm of prayer, faith, and zeal. This distanced us all from him, but we all aspired to be like him. According to Aeschimann, you had to be "nuts" to be a good preacher.

The second great influence on us was the "Drôme Brigadiers." Near the village of Dieulefit in the Drôme region of southern France, a group of young pastors who called themselves Brigadiers, all from the School of Theology in Montpellier, had assumed the task of reviving this former Protestant stronghold where Protestantism had dwindled a half-century before. Late nineteenth century liberalism had driven many people from churches. It was useless to go to a pastor to find God, it was said; go hunting, and you will come closer to God. The rural exodus to the cities did the rest. The Drôme, in the foothills of the Alps, was strewn with rocky peaks where the last houses of the abandoned villages collapsed.

In this climate of indifference, the Brigadiers developed a fundamentalist mystique and set up *ecclesiolae*, that is, small "faithful" congregations amid the secularized masses who now only went to church for baptisms, marriages, and funerals. The Brigadiers were relatively successful. Their "missions" were soon sought throughout France. Some of them were good orators, others good theologians. Returning from a vacation in the Midi, Jacques Babut, then a pastor in Hargicourt in Normandy, declared himself "converted" and published a declaration in which he rejected the errors of his youth, namely social Christianity and theological liberalism. He formulated the requirements for a renewed pastoral ministry.

Our Northern Group was reorganized as a sort of "Northern Brigade." It gathered its members in fervent prayer meetings and traveled to churches that had asked for retreats. Since I was the youngest of the group, I wasn't always asked to speak. A kind of triumvirate, Babut and the Chéradame brothers, organized the retreats. The first few times I participated, I understood how privileged I was, but also how uncomfortable I felt. Daniel Chéradame was generally considered the leader. Confident and authoritarian, he explained things and knew how to get what he wanted. His brother Robert, more anguished, passionate, and religious, had more spiritual power. Robert, little by little, distinguished himself as the leader of the movement, then veered toward fanaticism.

Marcel Heuzé, a former professional soccer player with a magnificent tenor's voice, raced toward his goal like a champion. Samuel Cornier was the mystic, the gentle one, the saint of the group. The son of a Salvation Army member, he was the one who led us in prayer when, on our knees, often for an hour, we sought the presence of the Holy Spirit. As for Jacques Babut, he never lost his self-control. He was a secretive fellow, intelligent, prescient, and prudent, who ended his career as the general secretary of the Reformed Church of France.

The retreats lasted four days, sometimes a week. We went as far away as Aouste, near Valence, and Marseille. But it was mainly the northern churches that called on us. We demanded that they engage in a month of spiritual preparation beforehand and proposed that "converts" sign pledges of commitment.

I must admit that this period of my ministry was unquestionably one of the most fruitful of my life. Humbled by the sincerity, total dedication, and deep faith of my comrades, whose powerful message I listened to in amazement, I recovered the fervor of my beginnings in Saint-Quentin from 1915 to 1917. It was the same openheartedness, the same willingness to let go, the same moral rectitude as before.

The decisive experience took place in Robert Chéradame's "Baby Peugeot" driving back from a retreat in Bruay. It was an illumination: whatever your state of mind, whether depressed or conceited, unfeeling or emotional, close to God or alienated, you can't eradicate the sacrifice that God, in the person of Jesus Christ, made for you. It subsists outside of you, despite you, as a reality greater than you. Therefore, have confidence!

When, many years later, I was shaken by the infidelity of human friendships – I'm talking about my friends – and by intolerable grief, the certitude that I just expressed of God's faithfulness to all people – to my loved ones tragically taken away, and to my wife and me, *independent* of our state of mind – allowed me to emerge from the darkest depths without going mad.

THE MUTUAL FEELING of discomfort between me and my comrades had to do, I think, with our different outlooks. Now entirely devoted to the conversion of souls in the Pietist manner, my colleagues would evolve in ways very different from my own and then sharply separate from one another as well. Several years later, I was alone again. I will relate these events in some detail because to me they seem typical of what can happen to a generation of believers infatuated with the absolute. They may interest readers because the fundamental problems of practicing the Christian faith hardly change, even in a rapidly changing society.

First, my religious experience in the "Baby Peugeot" already had immediate consequences in Sin-le-Noble. The parish, composed of about fifty mining families converted from Catholicism thirty-five years earlier, formed one big family of old people, adults, and children who coalesced and dispersed constantly. They came together on Sundays and remained together from ten in the morning until evening. Services, picnics, snacks, games, meetings, singing, conversations, and gossiping didn't end until ten at night. They got along well, like brothers and sisters, except when they quarreled, like brothers and sisters, over the littlest thing. Their quarrels generally lasted a long time. The offended parties grew cool and no longer came. It was the pastor's job to patch things up, to reconcile them, and he was often unable to do so. Nonetheless, these rugged people, tempted by taverns, marbles, alcohol, cockfighting, and movies, were all our good friends.[5] We were at home among them, more than in Douai, because Magda and I like what's natural.

One evening in the church's "Men's Circle," I gave a talk on the famous book by Dr. Couchoud, who maintained that Jesus Christ is a myth created by St. Paul. With arguments drawn from my former professor, Maurice Goguel, I refuted his arguments point by point. I had a spiritual revelation: If Jesus lived on earth, if he is not a myth, why do we speak of his teaching as if it were a myth? If he existed here on earth, all the words in the Sermon on the Mount would be made for us on earth. They are efficacious, and the power of God's pardon is there to erase our faults and their consequences.

I said that very calmly to the ten men present. I hadn't foreseen anything nor wished for anything, but suddenly we were all on our knees. One after the other, each of us made an unforgettable confession to God. An hour later, we rose and looked at each other with fresh eyes. The weight of secrecy, self-protection, and pride had been lifted. The spirit of God was present, and on the spot, we decided to share this extraordinary news with our spouses that very evening. This marked the beginning of the "Sin-le-Noble Revival" that lasted three or four months. I was about to discover the real power of God, a power I had never known before and have never experienced since to the same degree.

First, there was a series of reconciliations. At the end of a week, all traces of division, even between two of the most difficult women in the parish, had disappeared. Next came the morning visits. Before going to work at six, a group of men, following the direction of the Holy Spirit, went to the homes of the heavy drinkers, the rebels. Often, we hit the nail on the head. Degogny, who lived in a wooden hut and slept in a bedroom behind the kitchen, was one of the first "summoned." Even before we entered his house, he cried out to his wife to let us in: "I know who it is. It's the pastor and his friends! I've just had a vision. They've come to ask me to give myself to God. I'll be right there." Slipping on his trousers, Degogny knelt with us in front of his stunned wife.

The preaching and prayer sessions took place in kitchens. For a few weeks, I was blessed with a kind of spiritual discernment that allowed me to perceive the needs of others and act. Three remarkable examples of

5 "Movie houses," Trocmé writes, "were at the time considered places of damnation because adolescents and illicit lovers could make out in the dark."

divine direction are characteristic of these exceptional weeks of our lives: Ceccarelli, Blondel, and Célisse.

One holiday, when Magda and I were resting and I was reading aloud, I sensed very clearly that I should go visit Ceccarelli. He was an Italian miner whose adolescent children, two girls and a boy, had started attending our gatherings. He was a former drinker subject to fits of terrible anger. Magda remarked to me that we hadn't enjoyed a restful afternoon in a long time, and I began reading again. Three minutes later, the same certitude took hold of me: "Go visit Ceccarelli immediately." I once again resisted this impulse and started reading again. But when, for the third time, this interior voice told me to "Go to Ceccarelli's house," Magda got dressed to accompany me. I think it took us twenty minutes to get to his home, a detached house in the project above the railroad tracks on the road to Aniche. I knocked on the door; these houses have no bells. There was no answer.

I knocked a second time. "You see," Magda said. "No one is home. Your intuition was wrong." Before leaving, to satisfy my conscience, I turned the doorknob to verify that it was locked. The door opened onto a frightening scene. Ceccarelli held his daughter over a table. He was strangling her. Our arrival cut short his rage. His face was livid. He looked at us, released his grip, and sat down cowering in a chair. Little by little, his daughter regained her senses. They had argued over nothing. If we hadn't arrived when we did, a worse crime would have been committed. Sent by God, we had arrived at this very moment.

Since then, I have often asked myself why God doesn't more frequently send rescuers to places where a catastrophe is about to happen. Do we lack the sensitivity to hear God's instructions? Are the rescues, such as that of Ceccarelli, only the result of chance? Is it fate that sometimes creates a miracle and sometimes causes a fatality? Or does God only rarely allow a miracle as a sign of a better world so we can believe? So many questions that human reason cannot answer! But those who experience a rescue such as that of Ceccarelli can no longer doubt that there are extraordinary coincidences in life directed by the hand of God.

And now for Blondel's story. He was a railroad repairman who lived with his family in a gatekeeper's house at the railroad crossing near Donzier. His wife had begun attending our kitchen get-togethers and wanted us to invite her husband. My first visit was a total failure. Blondel didn't say hello or goodbye to me. He remained so hidden behind his newspaper that I never even saw his face.

A few days later, however, he came to one of our general meetings. But he refused to sit down. He came, he said, only because his wife wanted him to come. I can still see him standing against the wall with his arms folded and with an ironic smile on his solid, square Norman face. The next day, I went to their house to see if there was any news. His wife told me that he had said, "They're all nuts, should be locked up, all of them." It's true that, at that stage of our revivals, the prayer sessions lasted a long time and were unrelenting in their fervor. For a newcomer, the psychological shock must have been harsh. Blondel had no religious education except for a vague knowledge of Catholic catechism he had learned at the age of ten.

Nonetheless, Mrs. Blondel arrived at our house one day. "I don't know what's going on," she said. "He asked for my Bible, and ever since, he reads and reads and reads it, night and day. He doesn't say anything and no longer sleeps."

Fifteen days later, Blondel suddenly appeared at a meeting and sat down like everyone else. When I finished my talk, he raised his hand. "I want to speak," he said. I was apprehensive, but I thought this unusual incident might give me the opportunity for a good discussion. So, I told him to speak up. This is roughly what he had to say:

"If I have understood correctly, the Bible is the word of God addressed to men, and this word is true."

"Yes," I replied.

"Then Jesus Christ has come to deliver us from evil, and if we have faith, we can live like him. Is that what you believe?"

"Yes, certainly."

"Then what are we waiting for? Lately, I have resolved to follow Christ."

I don't remember anything else he said. But this unpolished man, all by himself, reading the Bible, had been enlightened by the Holy Spirit and had understood by faith the essentials of Christian doctrine. I no longer had anything important to teach him. The human soul is naturally Christian. When it accepts Christ, the union is immediate, without intermediary and without delay. Why are there so few Blondels in this world?

On one occasion, after a few months of membership in the church in Sin-le-Noble, his wife "had words" with Mrs. Delval. Blondel appeared at my place one morning, pale as a ghost.

"I've come to tell you that I'm leaving."

"Did the railroad transfer you?" I asked.

"No, that's not what I mean," he said. "I see that here as elsewhere people say one thing and do another. If we are Christian, we are all brothers and sisters, right? Well, there are some here who don't act like they are Christians. I'm leaving here."

It was impossible to explain to Blondel that there was a lot of pride in blaming everything on others. Didn't his wife have any shortcomings? He sulked with his family for a good number of weeks. Then he came back one day and said, "Our wives have patched things up."

Certainly, Blondel's absolute principles and those of so many of his colleagues who were part of our evangelical work often made community life untenable, but isn't the relativism of our older churches, where so much hidden discord stirs about, much more dangerous as regards the truth?

Célisse was the third remarkable example. The men in our group found him dead drunk in a ditch and brought him home. The next morning, I went to Waziers to pay him a visit. His head resembled that of the convict Chéri-Bibi, a well-known comic book criminal: he had a bull-neck, enormous hands, and limited intelligence. Of Flemish origin, he butchered the French language. His emaciated wife had grayish skin and was his punching bag. Piece by piece, Célisse had sold his furniture for drinking money. Although they lived in an attractive home, the interior resembled the cliché of the traditional drinker's home: in the corner on a bunch of shapeless rags slept their three frightened children.

Without expecting much, I spoke to Célisse about God.

"Doesn't exist. Don't believe it," he repeated. "How do you want me to sign up for the Croix Bleue if there's no God?" Maurice Delval had more impact than I did. "He signed up for a week," he told me the next day.

That Thursday evening in the Men's Circle, Célisse showed up. At this time in our revival meetings, we all knelt and prayed in turn. Célisse was breathing heavily and sweating like a woman about to give birth, but he knelt and, in his Northern, working-class dialect, said the following prayer, the most beautiful that I have ever heard:

> My God, since you exist, I want to thank you for what you did for me just yesterday. When I was in the cage that goes down into the mine and the shitty foreman was pissing me off, making fun of the Croix Bleue and telling me you didn't exist, you gave me the strength to

> answer him and tell him to fuck off both on the way down and on the way back up again. Amen.

Célisse never became an intellectual luminary. He was a force of nature, a kind of hurricane, powerful enough to move the sails of a windmill. He visited, prayed, convinced men in his milieu whom none of us, even the Delvals, who had never known the hell of alcoholism, were able to reach.

One day, coming out of the pit in Donziers, we were spreading the gospel by singing hymns and distributing leaflets to the miners on their way home. While I was giving a talk, a short man wearing a cap came out of a wood hut and began interrupting me in a strident tone. "Yeah, I know you, sell-outs! Paid by the priests to tell us lies. There's no God! If there was one, he would have struck me down with lightening because I told him to fuck off. After death, there ain't nothing. We'll all croak like my dog did. So, shut the hell up."

That's when Célisse intervened. Moving away from our group of friends and listeners, he went up to the guy, rolling his shoulders like the boxing champ he resembled physically. Facing this menace, the man, still mouthing off, gradually backed away. I stopped speaking, and we could all hear Célisse's thunderous voice distinctly.

"What did you say, you snot-nosed little bastard? There ain't no God? Say it again if you dare. Say again there ain't no God! You didn't see what happened to Célisse? Who got him off the booze, then? I'll show you there ain't no God!"

Slowly, with the gestures of someone getting ready to fight, Célisse dropped his jacket, and the other guy's cries seemed less clear. As he continued to insult God, I saw Célisse raise his fist. He would have crushed this despicable fellow had I not lunged forward and stopped him.

"Let me at him," cried Célisse. "He'll find out there's a God. These guys only understand violence." Maybe he was right, but I forbade him to punch our adversary, and he obeyed me. On the way home, while I tried to explain Christ's message of nonviolence to him, his forehead crinkled as he tried to understand, but he continued to repeat, "With those guys, there's no other way."

When, after six years of ministry, we left Sin-le-Noble, Célisse, his wife, and their well-groomed children came to say goodbye in such a touching manner that we have never forgotten it. After we left, he began drinking again and committed suicide in an act of despair. Today, I think that some suicides, dictated by an ardent desire to follow God and subsequent despair caused by a moral decline considered beyond remedy, are in fact purer acts than the compromises we reach between our evil habits and our belief in God's indulgence.

FOR COMPLETELY DIFFERENT REASONS, Breye's story is also worth telling. One day, in the middle of our revival, I had a visit from a distinguished-looking gentleman who said he was the pastor of a spiritualist community in Sin-le-Noble. I knew that his services were well attended. "My wife," Mr. Breye told me, "is becoming strange. She goes into the garden, hears voices, and is fearful of the terrible punishments that karma will inflict on us for our past sins." Their doctrine, borrowed from Hinduism, did in fact teach that people mount or descend in the hierarchy of the living according to the good or evil acts they have performed.

I went to see the Breye family and read the Bible with them. I spoke to them about the salvation that God freely grants us through the sacrifice of Jesus Christ. This led to an extraordinary flowering of faith. Mr. Breye, although a self-made man, was accustomed to public speaking. The religious experiences he had over his years spent preaching in the spiritualist community gave him unquestioned authority. I didn't hesitate to ask him to preside over meetings, in Waziers in particular, where we had rented a theater. These meetings continued during summer vacations. That's where Abdallah converted. He was a remarkable, illiterate Moroccan who became a man of prayer and deep faith. His mining companions soon nicknamed him "Jesus Christ" because of his beautiful face and courageous witnessing. Until his premature death from tuberculosis, Abdallah played a decisive role in the church in Douai, where he began revival meetings like those in Sin-le-Noble.

Mr. Breye's son, Armand, became my catechumen and then felt called to missionary life. He married Geneviève Pérus. With three other young men from Sin-le-Noble and Aniche, Armand Breye was the fruit of revival for the new generation.

I was always preoccupied with the church's participation in social and international life, so I oriented the energy of our converted men toward practical tasks. While the economic crisis and unemployment spread misery into the homes of the miners, I turned to our mayor, Foucault, and proposed that we organize soup kitchens where anyone could come and eat. All we had to do was gather potatoes from those who had them.

Foucault had one condition: that I get the extreme right, meaning the local priest, and the extreme left, meaning the Communist Party, to agree to take part. "The town hall will try to work with everyone at the same time," he said, "or else 'they' will play dirty tricks on us during the next elections."

The priest declined: "Our nuns do what is necessary." The leader of the Communist cell was a likable guy, but he declared that he had to consult his group. A week later, he gave me the decision that his cell had reached. "Given the present state of decomposition within the capitalist system, the Communist Party has no interest in bailing it out by works of charity. The working class must understand the rotten nature of the system of exploitation that victimizes it. Then it will rebel; that's what we're waiting for."

The mayor shrugged his shoulders, "I knew full well what they would say. Everyone's looking out for number one." I had to cancel my project. The fifty Protestant families didn't have sufficient resources to carry out this important task alone.

A few days later, hearing the jingle of a bell in the street, I went out to see what was happening. A handcart was circulating, exactly like the one we used for the Old Folks' Christmas. Large signs announced the collection of potatoes and vegetables by "Communist Rescue," which had come to help the exploited and hungry working class.

I have never been able to stomach the hypocrisy of the Communist cell in Sin-le-Noble. Yet it taught me one thing: a genuine work of solidarity should never be undertaken for propaganda reasons but only to help the beneficiaries. Otherwise, it's a treacherous weapon.

We undertook the Old Folks' Christmas in imitation of what Magda and I had seen in the United States. It's common in Europe today: Santa Claus collects goods for down-and-out elderly people. For our tiny community, it was a bold venture because there were only a few of us, and we were unknown in the region. We had to make a costume for Santa Claus. One Sunday afternoon, at least seven or eight weeks before Christmas, we dragged a small cart through the streets bordered by the interminable *corons*, knocking at each door to collect what the good people had prepared according to the leaflet announcing our project. We accepted everything: used goods, shoes, clothing, food products. We set up a sorting center on the ground floor of the presbytery. Two or three hundred packages, all well stocked, were assembled.

Benjamin Bocquillon, a tall, dark boy with a ferocious look, had agreed to play Santa Claus. However, when it came time to dress in the red outfit, he panicked and fled. One by one, all our young people backed out. We remained alone, Magda and me. Since my youth, I have always had a horror of wearing disguises, but to back out of our project at this point would have been a catastrophe. So I put on the Santa outfit and fixed the hemp beard onto my face. Magda pushed the handcart, and we began knocking on doors, accompanied by the jeers of children in the street.

The people hadn't understood why we were doing this. They asked us what business we were advertising. It was raining; we were caked with mud, chilled to the bone, and miserable. The youth from our church watched our failure from a distance and nudged one another. Without too much conviction, I approached the kids in the street, "Have you been good? Do you deserve candy or a good beating?" One group was particularly impressed. A young fellow with a dirty face whose conscience certainly wasn't clear was close to tears. Another yelled out, "Don't cry, you idiot. Can't you see it's the captain of the church?"

But all's well that ends well. Little by little, the handcart filled up, and we had to return to the presbytery to unload chocolate, biscuits, oranges, figs, old shoes, linen, socks with holes in them. We even found half a corset. Our young people came together, reassured and entertained. They soon fought over who pushed the wagon, and a victorious Santa Claus marched forth at the head of his meager battalion.

The Old Folks' Christmas was soon an annual tradition and a source of pride for the community. One Christmas Eve, in the main room of the town hall overflowing with people, I told the parable of the Good Samaritan. An enthusiastic old man cried out loudly, "That's good!"[6] when the Good Samaritan lowers himself to help his neighbor. I knew then that our call to charity was understood. When I left Sin-le-Noble, I went to see Foucault, the mayor, to take my leave. He referred to the Old Folks' Christmas and thanked the Protestants.

Our Protestant parishes often go to ridiculous lengths to teach the Gospels. To be effective, sometimes all you need is a little imagination and a sharp sense of contemporary society. It's true that today advertising and radio have reduced generosity to the level of commercial publicity. Some might say The Old Folks' Christmas would pass unnoticed in 1966, but I don't believe it, because the voluntary commitment

6 "He thought André had made up this story," noted Magda in the margin of the manuscript.

and kindness of young people impress the public much more than the actual results.

As concerns my work with international organizations, I kept in contact with the Fellowship of Reconciliation frequently enough to send two of our disabled veterans to Baden, Germany, for an international conference. Mr. Pérus and Mr. Delval were astonished by the welcome they received from former German combatants.

The "Gerhard Halle Affair," however, shook the Protestant North of France and compromised my ecclesiastical future in the area. A German Quaker, Gerhard Halle, wrote to us one day to declare that, as a military engineer during World War I, while following orders he had organized the systematic destruction of certain villages in the Cambrésis region. Regretting his acts, he wanted to visit those areas and ask forgiveness from the local population. Deeply moved to finally find a remorseful German, I organized three meetings for him: in Sin-le-Noble and Douai, where I took charge, and in Arras, where Pastor Pierre Lestringant was responsible.

The meeting in Sin-le-Noble was a great success. It was a full house. Halle spoke French and explained his psychological drama. In 1914, troops were mobilized, and he turned in his resignation as a member of the Lutheran Church. "Waging war is incompatible with Jesus' teachings," he argued. "I wanted to have a free conscience to wage war." But, one day in the trenches, doubt took hold of him. He was on the Chemin des Dames before an assault.[7] "Why am I fighting?" he asked himself. "To defend my country. But why are the French in the trenches across from me fighting? Why are they trying to kill me? To defend their country." The absurdity of these two groups of men exterminating each other for the same reason soon struck home. Nevertheless, as an officer, he didn't have the courage to refuse to carry arms and finished the war in the engineering corps.[8] "I simply followed orders in dynamiting these villages to make the enemy's advance more difficult. But my conscience reproached me for obeying such barbaric orders."

Demobilized in 1918 and back in Germany, he was called up again to suppress the Spartacist Rebellion, an uprising by Berlin workers.[9]

7 Chemin des Dames was the site of several bloody battles during World War I.

8 Gerhard Halle was a conscientious objector during World War II.

9 The January 1919 Spartacist Rebellion in Germany marked the struggle between the Democratic Party of Germany and the Communist Party after Germany's defeat in World War I.

Finally, he had the strength to refuse to obey. "Violence is a crime," he said, "a collective madness that can go on forever." He looked for a church that faithfully taught the gospel in this regard and found the Quakers. Repentant for his actions as a solider, he wanted to ask forgiveness from the French, his former victims.

Perhaps my readers will have difficulty understanding the degree of hatred for Germany that the French still felt in 1932, fourteen years after the war. The aggressive invasion in 1914, the pillaging of Belgium, the four and a half years that the *poilus*[10] spent in trenches hanging on to the ravaged French soil had left deep scars. One heard it said everywhere, "If only one German would repent for what happened. But no, not a word. They consider themselves the victims of the war. They're ready to begin all over again!"

It's true that the Treaty of Versailles, signed by German authorities, had recognized Germany's unilateral culpability in starting the war. But the German people had not confessed their guilt. Out of patriotism, they never admitted any responsibility, at least not in front of foreigners.

To my knowledge, Gerhard Halle was the first German who returned to the scene of his crimes to ask forgiveness of the French. He should have been listened to, understood, welcomed, perhaps even acclaimed. In Sin-le-Noble, in fact, people listened with emotion. He was even applauded. It was a working-class suburb. But the next day at Douai, what a dramatic evening! A tall beanpole of a fish merchant named Joly, a reserve officer who had been wounded in battle and was now president of the local veterans' union, decided to sabotage the meeting I was managing.

"This gathering is a scandal," he yelled from the back of the large town hall meeting room where he stood with a group of veterans. "You don't have a right to let a German speak here in this country drenched with the blood of our martyrs. Shut up and get the hell out of here!" The crowd began to react just as Joly had. I tried in vain to calm them down. A minority of them still wanted to hear Gerhard Halle. He managed to say a few things, but the atmosphere was so highly charged that everything he said was taken the wrong way. His painful confession only aroused cries of hatred and mockery from the majority of those in attendance. I had to end the meeting.

---

10 *Les poilus* (the hairy) is a term referring to French soldiers at the time, who let their hair and beards grow during wartime in a show of masculinity.

The next day, we were supposed to go to Arras, but the morning newspapers announced that the prefect of Pas-de-Calais had forbidden the meeting. I learned later that this had been, unfortunately, prompted by my colleague Lestringant. Frightened by the news from Douai, he didn't have the courage to cancel the meeting himself for fear of quarreling with me and losing credibility in the eyes of Halle. He found this escape hatch to wriggle out of his commitment.

Nonetheless, Gerhard Halle's tour helped Sin-le-Noble. It galvanized my Men's Circle, which, filled with faith, formed a block behind its pastor. These "uncultured" men saw more clearly the Bible's implications than the well-off, the wise, and the intelligent. I won't tell you anything about the reactions of the bourgeois Protestants of Douai, except that my pastoral career from then on was seriously compromised. They classified me among the "agitators." The secret police kept an eye on me.

As of 1930, I was once again working with the International Fellowship of Reconciliation. I was named a member of the International Council, and traveled to England, Holland, Germany, and Switzerland to attend conferences or committee meetings. It was during this glorious time that, in 1931, the pacifist Gandhi came to the second Round Table Conference in London. I didn't get to see him, but I regained all my passion for a Christian movement that practiced his method and his ideas.

If I'm not mistaken, in 1932 the "March for Peace" was held all over Europe. It was the first of its kind and very modest. In France, Philippe Vernier, Pierre Vernier, and Jean-Jacques Bovet walked through villages carrying signs and bringing people together in town squares in the evening. In England and Holland similar groups formed. In Germany, where the deadly poison of Nazism was brewing, peace activists were especially vigorous. All the national teams met near Geneva, where they were welcomed by Arthur Henderson, then the secretary general of the Conference on Disarmament, which failed miserably and actually provoked the rearmament of Germany.

I participated in the German march for two weeks. We formed a solid team of Germans, English, Americans (such as Nevin Sayre),[11] and one Frenchman (me). Every evening, in crowded halls, we addressed groups brought together by the German Peace Cartel, an organization with

11 John Nevin Sayre (1884–1977) was an American Episcopalian pastor and former missionary in China. He was a founding member of the American branch of the Fellowship of Reconciliation and served as its director from 1924 to 1935.

socialist leanings. We had enormous success in Frankfurt, where the spectators almost carried us off in triumph. In Offenbach, the organizer of the meeting, Pastor Goethe, who had both the name and head of the great writer, received us in an apartment that had been trashed by Hitler's "Brown Shirts." While being vandalized, before his telephone lines were cut, he had called the police. They arrived after the ransacking had been completed. They were working with the Nazis and issued an official police report against Pastor Goethe, finding him guilty of "disturbing public order" by calling for a meeting on peace. Naturally, our meeting was canceled.

In Heidelberg, the meeting almost turned into a brawl between Nazi and Communist youth. These youth groups came to blows every day in the suburbs of Heidelberg. Each one accused us of doing their adversary's bidding. When the meeting was over, we almost became victims of the Brown Shirts, who accused us of coming to Heidelberg to "lather us up so that later the English and French can give us a closer shave."[12] Singled out by one of them brandishing a revolver, I suggested that he kill me on the spot in front of everyone. My proposition calmed him down, and he disappeared into the crowd. The fact that I was a foreigner allowed me to escape this madman, who had already made himself famous by assassinating four Jewish people. German justice left him unscathed because it didn't dare punish the growing brutality of the Nazis.

In Reutlingen, in southern Germany, we met up with Mr. Braun, a German we had known in Douai. "It's impossible to hold our meeting tonight," he told us. "The Brown Shirts have taken over the theater where we were supposed to hold the meeting. They have sworn not to let you speak. It's better to cancel." After praying together, our group decided not to back out, and we entered the theater through the stage door. We spoke as amicably as possible to these Brown Shirts, since these young fellows were men like us, despite their collective madness. Because of my better German, I was chosen to speak first. I will never forget waiting behind the stage curtain, listening to the grumbling sounds from an angry audience. They had told me, "A little platform has been set up, get on it, and don't waste time." As soon as the curtain opened, I rushed to the platform. In a booming voice, without giving the five hundred Brown Shirts

12 The original appears in German: *"einseifen, damit später England und Frankreich uns besser rasieren können."*

time to react, I shouted the watchword of Hitler himself: *"Deutschland erwache!"* (Wake Up, Germany!).

There were a few seconds of amazement; then total silence fell over the room. Taking advantage of the silence, I tackled the problem of the day head-on: We must wake up to the threat of a second world war. I, a Frenchman, am calling for equal treatment of those vanquished in 1918. French people suffered the most cruelly in that war, but the time for pardon and reconciliation has come! "Down with all weapons! Responsible Christians today are against war and war preparations. They are conscientious objectors." My words received thunderous applause. We had won.

After me, the other orators had no difficulty making their declarations, which were warmly received. As everyone left, members of the audience were almost ready to embrace each other. The local leader of the Brown Shirts, a very young fellow, approached me.

"You have proposed exactly what our Führer has urged: justice for all, equal treatment for all, and peace."

"Yes," I responded to him, "but he didn't say it in the same manner, and why is he persecuting Jews?"

"Because the Jews are the number one enemies of peace," he responded. I was unable to change his view on this.

I have often thought about this astounding scene in Reutlingen. Hitler had succeeded in fascinating young, naive Germans with extraordinarily vicious goals. In 1940, I would once again see German soldiers surge into France. As in 1914, they came to free France of the vices that were destroying it. Their naivety reminded me of that of the Brown Shirts in Reutlingen.

Back in Sin-le-Noble, our Men's Circle, this small group of workers moved by the Holy Spirit, had spread its activity in another direction. They first contacted Nick in Fives-Lille, then Marcel Heuzé in Lens, then Daniel Chéradame, pastor in Hénin-Liétard, with whom I had been a student intern years before. Our group organized annual conferences with increasing success in all three cities. In Hénin, four hundred men filled the hall to listen to Henri Roser talk about Christian pacifism. In Lens, Arnold Brémond spoke to us about his experiences as a "worker-pastor" in a factory in the Parisian suburbs. We were on the right path. Everywhere people showed an interest, even those whom one might have considered indifferent to religious problems.

Then, at the height of our success, a series of events took place that ruined the chances for any expansion of our group and resulted in my break with my colleagues in the Northern Group.

First, there were "technical" issues. For a year, I served as pastor, not only of Sin-le-Noble, but of Aniche, Marquette, and the Douai parish, which had no pastor after Viollier left. I have already related how Perret had arbitrarily taken Aniche and Marquette from me and put Evrard in my place. But the naming of my friend Jacques Babut as pastor of Douai not only took Douai from me, which I didn't really regret, but also Waziers, where Sin-le-Noble was successfully evangelizing.

Abdallah, the wonderful Moroccan converted by Breye, was "annexed" by Douai. Célisse refused categorically to go to Douai, and the Sin-le-Noble families suddenly found themselves isolated after years of expanding beyond the limits of their township. They felt a sense of injustice which has remained to this day. I assume Babut, with his ever-present paternalistic mentality, shared the Douai congregation's fears about me. I felt that I had been judged and dismissed in a friendly manner, while the people of Douai, regrouped around Babut, had their own revival.

I should explain a few things. I was a member of the Northern Group, which met every month. During our meetings, spiritual experiences, such as forgiveness and inner purification, had taken place for years. Two very different men led the group: Robert Chéradame, an uncompromising soul, ardent and tormented; and Samuel Cornier, a man of prayer, gentle, mystical, and animated by a thirst for perfection. But after our preaching missions in the outlying areas ceased, our group ran out of steam. Robert Chéradame pushed us more and more toward greater radicalism. As a conscientious objector, he refused to do his military training and was imprisoned. But, advised by a crooked lawyer the Northern bourgeoisie found for him, he was acquitted after making amends! To explain this flip-flop he converted, a posteriori, to a "Barthian" theology that, at that time, defined human beings as sinners who cannot aspire to anything but God's pardon. Their good deeds don't count. Conscientious objection was defined by the Barthians as an act of spiritual pride. Pierre Maury,[13] a popular professor and pastor who criticized pacifism, declared, "If

13 Pierre Maury (1890–1956) was a pastor in Passy and a professor at the Faculté de Théologie in Paris. He was a friend of Karl Barth and played a major role in introducing Barthianism in France.

I throw bombs while I beat my breast, I am in God's grace, but if you refuse to kill, it's so you can have clean hands. Your pride separates you irredeemably from God's grace."

Pierre Maury presented this doctrine to the Theological Commission of the Reformed Church of France on a day when Henri Roser was unavailable. I was summoned before that same commission and found myself in front of an actual ecclesiastical tribunal presided over by Pierre Maury, defending conscientious objection in Roser's place. They didn't let me speak but made me listen to their irrevocable condemnation of conscientious objectors. This was 1932. How much water has now passed under the bridge! Since 1964, France has had a law on conscientious objection, and theology recognizes the validity of this position. The official church often lags behind public opinion.

During this troubled period that preceded World War II, Douglas Scott,[14] an English preacher involved in the Pentecostal movement, appeared. A truly extraordinary man, moderate, calm, without any theological formation, he claimed to act "solely on the Word of God," that is, the Bible. He spoke French rather well, and every church wanted him to lead their revival meetings. This, in essence, was his message: Jesus heals not only minds but bodies as well. Just look at the Bible. We must believe everything in the Gospels and, like the apostles, lay our hands on the sick to cure them. But to bring about these healings, we must receive the power from God, from the Holy Spirit. Jesus was baptized not only with water (the baptism of purification) but with the Spirit (the baptism of power). Contemplate Pentecost: the apostles were unable to do anything until they received the Holy Spirit. Then, they had the same gifts that Jesus did – healing, prophecy, spiritual discernment. Many theologians hold that these gifts were reserved for the apostles and that they disappeared along with them. They are mistaken. The Catholic Church has often downplayed individual inspiration from the Holy Spirit, and the Reformation didn't dare to follow through completely with the rediscovery of the Gospels. Those Reformers who emphasized the spirit were condemned by others as too "spiritualistic."

"But today," Scott declared, "we have rediscovered the truth. This is the great movement of renewal within the church currently spreading across the globe."

14 Douglas Roger Scott (1900–1967) was a preacher and missionary to the Congo. He introduced Pentecostalism to France.

The revival that we had just experienced in Sin-le-Noble revealed to us perspectives close to those of the Pentecostals. I decided to invite Scott to our home and get to know him. He spent three days with us. He was a simple, friendly person who showed no signs of exaltation. We went together to visit the sick. He laid his hands on them, but none of them were healed. "I am absolutely convinced of divine healing," he said, "but God may always have reasons unknown to us for not healing a particular person. My role as a believer is not to doubt, but to affirm the healing God wishes through faith." All that held together well.

One final hesitation held me back. Didn't I risk falling into a religious frenzy if I followed Scott all the way? Besides, during the Sin-le-Noble revival, I had experienced the giddiness of a mystical abyss but backed away from the edge. Let me be honest. My wife Magda, who was afraid I was losing my common sense, held me back. So, I never brought Scott to Sin-le-Noble for revival meetings. It was a good thing that I didn't, as you will soon see.

Scott led his "missions" everywhere else with surprising success. "Crippled and paralyzed people" crowded around him, coming from God knows where to be healed. During prayer meetings, both pastors and lay people "received the Holy Spirit." This happened to several members of our Northern Group. From that point onward, they gathered among themselves without informing their colleagues, such as me, who hadn't received the Holy Spirit. They subtly alluded to their experiences, implying to those of us on the "outside" that some secret disobedience might be the reason we had not received God's grace.

The catastrophe reached its peak in Fives-Lille. Nick always showed great confidence in the young auxiliary pastors who came to help him. Such was the case with Roser, Jean-Pierre Benoit, and Philippe Vernier. At that time, he was close to someone named Blanc, who is still at Fives, an enigmatic young fellow with the traits of a fanatic. Nick invited Scott to Fives, and the Holy Spirit manifested itself in some parishioners, or rather, in some of Nick's best parishioners. A circle of "true" Christians formed around Blanc, leaving Nick on the outside. For forty years, he had given the most extraordinary signs of the power of the Spirit of God, except for what the Pentecostals required: "speaking in tongues." He accepted this blow without grumbling, and for the remaining twenty years of his life, he witnessed the collapse of everything he had built. People no longer attended his "Solidarity" gatherings; his cooperative closed its doors. Blanc, on the other hand, with a small number of the "exalted," constituted the "true" church, the church of "those baptized with the Holy Spirit," the special ones who spoke in tongues!

In Caudry, the same thing happened. But Samuel Cornier, the pastor, was *among* the initiated. He died very young, leaving eight children for his wife to raise and a parish so divided that it still hasn't healed.

Likewise, in Douai, where a group of the "elect" formed around Jacques Babut, Abdallah was the prophet. The people of Sin-le-Noble responsible for his conversion were judged unworthy of admittance to the "great secret." Only a special unit of initiates was privy. What was this secret? I learned one day in Douai. Samuel Cornier had solemnly convened a meeting of the Northern Group. We were all there, including Nick. Scott was also there as the star of the group. He spoke to us very simply but urgently. "Kneel down," he said suddenly, "and ask God for his Holy Spirit. He will give it to those among you who let go of all inner resistance. Those who don't receive the Holy Spirit are hiding an obstacle within themselves, a secret forbidden by God's law. They refuse to deliver themselves entirely to the Holy Spirit."

I was quite impressed. I too wanted to "let go of all resistance." We all knelt, and the meeting lasted a long time. There were prayers, sighs, and supplications, with Scott and Cornier speaking in tongues. Then Scott began to lay his hands on us. He literally massaged the head of each of his "patients," affirming that he could feel the spiritual obstacle. "When you give it up," he told us, "something will come out of your lungs. You will spit out a kind of black mucus, and evil will leave you. Then you will speak, you will speak in tongues. It will be the Holy Spirit within you." With Scott's hands on them, several of my colleagues spoke in tongues. At least that's what Scott affirmed amid his hallelujahs. (To me, it was nothing but a few incoherent sighs. I had heard people speaking in tongues before; they spoke in well-articulated, rhythmic sentences, as in a real language.) "Hallelujah, hallelujah," cried Scott, "Our brother is blessed!" He then intoned a hymn that was sung by those "baptized by the Holy Spirit," who seemed to have passed into an ineffable, celestial happiness. As for me, I didn't dare raise my eyes to observe this spectacle, but when Scott came to me, I immediately felt that I was "outside" the common exaltation. Certainly, everything that Scott said about ceasing to resist if we are to know God is true. But what should we think about this story of black mucus that we must expectorate? I found that repulsive, and "speaking in tongues" seemed quite different to me than the thirst for God welling up within me. Scott interpreted the questions I was asking myself as resistance. He didn't push his case, and as the meeting was ending, I left. I was alone and estranged from my comrades.

From that very day, the Northern Group was split into two camps, or rather three. We all loved one another, but we no longer understood one another. The two Chéradame brothers hadn't gotten along with Scott, but they were "Barthian," and their severe dogmatism condemned non-Barthians, of whom I was one. Heuzé, Babut, and Cornier had become Pentecostals. Nick, who never succeeded in "speaking in tongues," humbly forced himself to follow them.

As for me, I was all alone, the only one in the Fellowship of Reconciliation. I was reduced to a slice of the pie in Sin-le-Noble, isolated among those who had been my intimate friends. After my departure from the North, the "Pentecostals" gained control of the men's circles and tried to transform them into revival meetings. Two years later, they ceased holding meetings because the men of the parish no longer attended. Some of Scott's disciples established new churches, as sects always do, by latching on to the coattails of already existing Protestant communities. In Normandy, they were successful and founded churches that still exist today. The Pentecostals converted many Catholics. In the North, however, they failed.

One day, I saw them arriving in Sin-le-Noble. Two young fellows who called themselves pastors wanted to know if I would collaborate with them in holding revivals in our city. When I responded affirmatively, they placed before me a text with fourteen articles "based on the Bible."

"Do you believe this?" they asked me.

"Yes," I responded. "I can subscribe to all of this, except for half an article where it states that the sign of baptism by the Holy Spirit is always 'speaking in tongues.' Nick from Fives-Lille is full of the Holy Spirit but doesn't speak in tongues. Read the Epistles to the Corinthians."

"If Mr. Nick doesn't speak in tongues," they responded, "he is not imbued with the Holy Spirit. If you don't agree with sacred scripture, we can't collaborate with you."

"May I just come to your meetings and invite my parishioners?" I asked them.

"Yes," they said. But I noticed some hesitation in their voices.

They had rented a small hall in town where they held their meetings every evening. I invited my parishioners to attend, and I joined them. We filled the hall that first evening. When the preachers asked the sick to come forward for the laying on of hands, a few obediently did so.

The next day, there were fewer people in attendance. The third day, even fewer. On the fourth evening, as I was about to enter the hall, one of the young Pentecostals barred the door. "We have concluded that the spirit of Satan is within you," he said to me. "You are the one ruining our meetings. We forbid you to enter."

I went home, but when my parishioners learned of my exclusion from the meetings, they stopped attending, and the two Pentecostal pastors had to leave town. I ask myself sometimes what would have happened if, fearing competition, I had warned my parish about the dangers of the Pentecostal movement. Twenty years earlier, Pastor Lacheret had believed it necessary to do so for the Jehovah's Witnesses. It resulted in a split in the church in Sin-le-Noble, with half of the families going over to the Jehovah's Witnesses.

The spirit of God is the spirit of reconciliation, not division. Opposition will arise, but we need not stimulate it. Faith is the true antidote to the sectarian spirit. The only thing narrow-mindedness accomplishes is to encourage the spread of sectarianism.

AFTER LEAVING THE NORTH, I once again experienced Pentecostalism at work in the Ardèche and the Haute-Loire region of south-central France. I don't want readers to criticize my colleagues. The generation that lived through the hellfire of the trenches from 1914 to 1918 could not be satisfied with half-measures. These people had wagered on faith, and they followed that faith to its limits. They had a way of reading the Bible that is lost today. Some discovered the requirement of absolute love in the Bible, and conscientious objection followed from that. Others, like the Northern Group, believed in the possibility of France's conversion. Still others, such as pastors from the rural parishes of southeastern France, sought to reconstruct the true church of Jesus Christ within the framework of the "Multitudinous Church" that brought together Christians of different and even opposed beliefs. These were the Drôme Brigadiers. Finally, there were the Pentecostals, the most radical of all, followers of Louis Dallière.[15]

Originally Catholic, Dallière was already known for his intelligence at the School of Theology in Paris when I studied there. He was clearly a leader and had a group of admirers around him all the time. In 1935, he was a pastor in Charmes, a small village in the Ardèche. After Scott passed through France, Dallière went to England to study Pentecostalism and returned to France preaching the Foursquare version of Pentecostalism.[16] Foursquare Pentecostalism differs from Scott's version in its insistence on reconstructing the original church founded on the spiritual gifts (the charismas) of the New Testament. An extraordinary prophetic movement that recalled the eighteenth-century Camisards[17] soon manifested itself around Dallière.

One day, when Dallière was on vacation in Le Chambon-sur-Lignon, I sent him a note that said: "I would like to speak with you about the events shaking the church. When can I see you?" I received the following ice-cold response: "Pastor Dallière only receives guests in Charmes, in the Ardèche. He invites you to attend meetings there." Despite his rebuff, I went there with Magda.

An extraordinary atmosphere prevailed. Pastors and lay people, seated in tiers, gathered around Dallière. Some meetings were "open." Only Dallière spoke, and he did so in a distant, monotonous tone. His doctrine seemed strange to me, abstract, intellectual, significantly different from Scott's warm sermons. Dallière constructed prestigious theories about everything he mentioned. Then, while the "outsiders" like us were invited to take a walk, the "spiritual elect" met alone. After interminable prayer sessions, they reappeared among us, their eyes rapturous with visions seen, but they didn't tell us anything. "You wouldn't understand," they said in response to our questions. My old

15 Louis Dallière (1897–1976) was a pastor in Charmes in Ardèche from 1925 until his retirement in 1962. In 1946, he founded the Charmes Prayer Union and in the same year, the Cours Isaac Homel, a Protestant boarding collège. He is considered one of the most important French Protestant figures of the twentieth century.

16 The Foursquare Church was founded in Los Angeles in 1923. It remains one of the principal Pentecostal denominations.

17 Shortly after the Revocation of the Edict of Nantes in 1685, French Protestantism experienced two waves of prophecy in what is today the Ardèche and the Drôme, then in the Cévennes. The second set off the War of the Camisards in the Cévennes (1702–1705).

friend Elie Morel was the only one who revealed a few secrets. "The seven-year-old daughter of our colleague Delord is epileptic," he told us. "They brought her here and we laid our hands on her. There were prophecies and interpretations of prophecies. She was healed. Hallelujah!" Magda and I returned to Le Chambon-sur-Lignon impressed but perplexed. Our best friends were part of these assemblies in Charmes. They appeared to be initiated into these mysteries, which were evident to their eyes but hidden from us.

A few months later, I met Delord. "How is your daughter doing? I asked him. "Healed," he responded with a joyful look in his eyes. "She doesn't have any more fits?" I asked. "Oh yes," he answered. "For two weeks, she didn't have any; now they've come back again. But she is healed! God asks us to understand her healing, even though she appears to still suffer from the sickness from which she has been healed. Hallelujah!" A year later, Pastor Delord had to put his daughter in the La Force Foundation home,[18] where she died before long. His faith in the cure was not shaken, but what did he mean by "cure"?

Dallière's brand of Pentecostalism soon manifested itself in two other forms: the refusal to baptize children and the submission of women to their husbands.

I am certainly convinced, as is Dallière, that baptizing children does not have a biblical basis. But I don't think we should divide the church because of a problem that is only a ritual. Isn't *true baptism* the conversion to Jesus Christ? Water is only a sign of secondary importance. Nonetheless, out of obedience to sacred scripture, half of the pastors in the Ardèche region refused to baptize children. They almost split from the Reformed Church of France. Only the easy-going relativism of the regional president, Pierre Rozier, prevented this misfortune from happening. Colleagues from neighboring parishes performed baptisms whenever parents wanted them.

Then, one day, Dallière announced the necessity of "wives submitting to their husbands." They must be quiet and obey their husbands, as prescribed by Saint Paul. In the Brémond household we noted a comical agreement between the poetic husband and the garrulous, authoritarian, practical wife. "Watch out, cutie pie," Evelyne Brémond cried out every time her husband came to a turn while driving their car, "There might

18 The La Force Foundation (Dordogne) has functioned as a home for hundreds of people with disabilities since the nineteenth century.

be a farm wagon coming!" One day, when the Brémonds came to visit us in Le Chambon, Evelyne was mute, her eyes lowered, her hands crossed on her lap like a good nun. Dallière had discovered that women could only be saved through their husbands' faith. Evelyne obeyed. She had subjected herself to her husband's will, as had all the women in the Pentecostal movement in Charmes. What had happened there?

In fact, the prophets of the movement were mostly women! Dallière's maid was a prophet, but his wife wasn't. So, he knelt with his maid in his office while his wife remained in the kitchen – with all due respect, of course. There were many such examples, and the movement risked turning into a matriarchy.

So Dallière resurrected the teachings of Saint Paul and decreed their application. Twenty or thirty pastoral families followed him blindly and obeyed without discussion. A few months later, Dallière tried to reestablish the episcopate. He would be the bishop, of course! Since the outpourings of the Spirit might easily become extravagant, they needed an authority to distinguish between true inspiration and demonic disorders. Naturally, that authority, too, was Dallière!

Everything ended in a kind of Catholic phase. The new episcopate was established, and Dallière dispensed divine inspiration through the laying on of his hands. He began to associate with priests, and there was even talk about his conversion to Catholicism. A young colleague, today an important person in Paris, talked about becoming a priest. They got rid of him in a hurry.

Then one day, out of the blue, Dallière announced the end of the "Charmes Movement." End of story. His disciples today still gather around him. When you question them, they still have the same mysterious air about them and say, "It was marvelous. Hallelujah!" Everything fell back into place. Dallière is a fount of knowledge and takes excellent care of the small secondary school he founded. He can teach any subject. He even prescribes the length of the girls' skirts. His wife died, and he has never remarried. He never visits other people: they must come to him. People still speak about him with admiration. "What a remarkable man! What a Christian!" His disciples still refuse to baptize children. That alone distinguishes them from other pastors. Souls thirsting after extraordinary things now go to Taizé. There, too, they cultivate secrecy; people are intrigued and look on in wonder. Taizé will have a longer life than Charmes because members practice celibacy. All sorts of transitory experiences take place there, and eventually it will become a real convent.[19]

I believe that initiatives, such as those of Scott, Taizé, and Charmes, must take place from time to time because it is right for people to try to live the gospel authentically, whether alone or in society. Their initiatives will not be lost if, soon after a period of revival and inspiration, they find practical applications for their revelations. Lacking these applications, the Spirit of God, like the sea, ebbs quickly, leaving only the disappointed remembrance of faraway bliss in its wake. Twenty or twenty-five years is the maximum duration of a new movement: the length of a generation. Then the founders of the movement grow old, and the second generation is nothing but a group of conformist imitators who occupy positions left vacant by the death of their elders. What then remains of the Holy Spirit? In fact, the Spirit of God is free and constantly at work. It inspires a generation of missionaries, of founders. But as soon as these men are in danger of becoming too important, it leaves them to fend for themselves and moves elsewhere. The Spirit sometimes calls on people like Gandhi, who aren't Christian, or like Martin Luther King Jr., whose story has not yet ended.

This doesn't mean that God has abandoned old Europe. God will come back, with or without the help of a Billy Graham – more likely without his help than with it. God will come back, perhaps even during my lifetime, or after my death, when the dead ashes of liturgicalism, ecclesiasticism, abstract theology, and all the big words emptied of their meaning grow cold. A new generation, humiliated by these failures, will thirst for a personal relationship with God. God will come back and provide churches with a new springboard. God is free, and we should never complain about the way God alternates years of abundance and years of drought in his ever-fallible church.

19 Trocmé was certainly right about Taizé, which is an ecumenical Christian monastic fraternity in Taizé, located in Saône-et-Loire in Burgundy. It is composed of more than one hundred brothers, from Catholic and Protestant traditions, who come from about thirty countries around the world. It was founded in 1940 by Brother Roger Schultz, a Reformed Protestant. Today more than 100,000 young people make pilgrimages there every year and partake in prayer, Bible study, and communal work.

12

Le Chambon

APART FROM THE MORAL SOLITUDE Magda and I encountered in the North, other signs indicated that we had to leave Sin-le-Noble. Our children were always sick. Nelly had given us reasons to worry. We had to send her, at great expense, to Switzerland, to Villars-sur-Ollon, then to Sépey near Leysin, to a home run by Dr. Auguste Rollier, a specialist who used heliotherapy to fight tuberculosis. Jean-Pierre suffered one bout of bronchitis after another. Doctor Dupas warned us, "You live in a city devoured by silicosis and tuberculosis. Except for one Belgian family, *all* our parishioners are tubercular. Your children's primary infections are difficult to overcome, and secondary ones inevitably follow. Your family doesn't have the immunity of the local people. I advise you to leave."

Antibiotics did not exist yet, and there was no reliable cure for tuberculosis. The sick were sent to the mountains, where an artificially induced "pneumothorax" restricted the use of the stricken lung.

We consulted our spiritual mentor, Henri Nick, who was greatly saddened by the situation. "You have dedicated your life to the North," he told us. "Departure would be an act of disobedience." We also consulted Nick's spiritual directors, Miss Guex and Miss Gonin, who lived in Geneva. "If God allows your children to be sick," they told us, "it's because he wants you to serve elsewhere." We set out to find this elsewhere.

It was difficult to find. Because of our commitment to the industrial regions, we didn't want to get stuck in a remote village parish, especially not one located in the mountains of Southern France. And we couldn't go to an unhealthy working-class suburb because our children needed a good climate. Then came a call from Clamart: my old friends from the Union had created an independent parish and wanted to appoint its first pastor. The idea was perfect. Clamart, on a hillside to the south of Paris, was still almost in the country. My old friends had become church elders. I hoped they would name me unanimously. Remember that during the eight years I was an official of the Northern Christian Society, I had never been named senior pastor. You could only become a pastor in the Reformed Church of France if you made a commitment in writing "not to campaign for conscientious objection." The church did not forbid a pastor from being a conscientious objector; it simply forbade him from communicating his pacifist convictions to anyone, especially young people.

Certainly, it would have been imprudent to incite young men to refuse military service, because the renewable prison sentences given to conscientious objectors demanded superior qualities that not everyone possessed. I could agree, therefore, not to discourage young men from wearing the uniform, but I couldn't silence my conviction that war and homicide are contrary to the will of God. I insisted on giving these explanations in person to the Clamart church elders, who needed to know I was a conscientious objector and would never again handle a gun.

Since Clamart and Montrouge had not yet been separated into two parishes, I appeared before the church elders of Montrouge-Clamart. My friend Albert Finet, the future founder of the newspaper *Réforme*, presided over the meeting. Finet was a royalist and a member of Action Française,[1] but loyal and respectful of others. The meeting went well. I read a declaration; a vote followed. They let me know that very evening that I had been unanimously elected.

The next day, I telephoned a certain Mr. Durand-Gasselin, president of the regional council of Paris, to give him the news. He was extremely terse. "You know, Mr. Trocmé," he said, "that all nominations are only valid after they have been confirmed by the Regional Council."

"I know, but I thought that this nomination was automatic since the pastor was named unanimously by the church elders' council."

"Mr. Trocmé, you are a conscientious objector. The confirmation of your nomination has not been finalized. In fact, I can tell you ahead of time that it is highly unlikely."

1 Action Française was an influential right-wing, anti-republican group in France during the first half of the twentieth century.

"But how is that possible?" I exclaimed. "I am willing to sign the required oath if I am permitted to add certain explanations that leave no doubt about my position as a conscientious objector and the testimony I must offer to the truth. I gave these explanations to the Montrouge-Clamart council, and they were satisfied with them."

"That's not the issue, Mr. Trocmé. What matters is the decision reached by the national synod."

"When is the regional council meeting?" I asked. "I'd like to explain myself."

"It meets tomorrow," responded Durand-Gasselin, a former military officer. "If we find it appropriate to hear your testimony, I will notify you. But it is highly unlikely."

I awaited a summons that never came.

The next day, I decided to attend the council meeting anyway and showed up at the French Protestant Center on Rue de Clichy. I sat down in the antechamber. Around nine o'clock, the council members arrived. Most of them recognized me. After all, wasn't I the son of an outstanding and respected layman, Mr. Paul Trocmé, a son who had perhaps "turned out badly," but his son nonetheless? Some council members were even my former university classmates who had made their way up the Protestant establishment.

When Durand-Gasselin arrived, he made an angry gesture. "I didn't summon you," he said to me. "I know," I responded, looking him directly in the eye. "But I'll stay here until I am heard." A quarter-hour went by, and the door opened. Fifteen or so gentlemen received me standing. They never asked me to sit.

Durand-Gasselin questioned me in his curt officer's voice: "Mr. Trocmé, we have only one question to ask you, and we ask you to respond only by "yes" or "no," without adding a word. In the event of a war, would you enlist and defend your country? Yes, or no?"

"I refuse to respond to such a question with a simple yes or no without giving an explanation. I have here one typed page that I read to the Montrouge-Clamart church elders' council. I would like to read it to you, and then I will answer your question."

"Only one page? Show it to me. Gentlemen, what do you think?" Fraternal heads nodded. Mr. Gounelle offered me a pale smile of encouragement. "Go ahead and read," said Durand-Gasselin. I read my document calmly and slowly, but inside I was trembling.

When I finished, Durand-Gasselin said: "And now, Mr. Trocmé, I repeat my question. In the event of a war, would you defend your country, yes or no?"

"You heard my declaration," I replied. "The answer is no!"

"Very well," Durand-Gasselin said ferociously, "your nomination to the post in Clamart will not be confirmed. You may leave now."

Overwhelmed, red with anger, and indignant, I responded, "Gentlemen, it seems to me that at a moment when you take responsibility for such a decision, we should be able to say a prayer together!" Fifteen mouths opened half-way; fifteen looks began to drift around the room. But Mr. Durand-Gasselin, sensing the ridiculous nature of the situation, quickly brought things back to order. "Mr. Paul Gounelle, would you like to say the prayer?" Mr. Gounelle said the prayer. He was old and his voice quavered. He asked God to bless his church and to lead the young, stray pastor back to the right path. I was that young pastor.

At that point, I left. They didn't even say goodbye. I found myself in the street, shown the door by the Reformed Church of France. I didn't suspect that it would take another world war and the shame of collaboration with the conquering enemy to cast doubt into the hearts of the good patriots of 1914. For them, France had been right and would always be right. France's cause was God's cause. How then could a Christian doubt France's cause by refusing to bear arms?

Turned out by the Reformed Church of France! Where to go now? I began to regret that I hadn't accepted the offer from the Fellowship of Reconciliation several years earlier. Lilian Stevenson and Nevin Sayre had asked me to become the secretary of its French chapter. I had refused when I was at Sin-le-Noble but had spoken to Sayre and Stevenson about Henri Roser who, rejected by the church, was living from hand to mouth in Aubervilliers, a community northeast of Paris, where he worked as a nondenominational evangelist. Roser had accepted the position and henceforth divided his time between Aubervilliers and the Fellowship of Reconciliation.

I had no other choice but to return to Sin-le-Noble. Yet I had already announced my departure.

I then turned to the Central Society of the Reformed Church. Mr. Benignus, the secretary general, received me cordially and a few days later, Magda and I presented ourselves at Thonon-les-Bains, on the banks of Lake Leman in Geneva.

They welcomed us warmly in the small church. A second church in Evian that I would also serve was even more miniscule. The theological test they had me take satisfied the departing pastor, Mr. Bordreuil, a fundamentalist, as well as the English ladies who directed the evangelization work in the Haute-Savoie region.

When I declared that I was a conscientious objector a spontaneous empathy flowed between me and the council. Despite my position, on the evening of that memorable Sunday, after a closed session, the church council (Thonon did not have a sovereign elders' council) announced that I was nominated, and that the Central Society generally ratified its decisions. They accompanied us to the train station in a procession. In the night train that took us to Paris, Magda and I rejoiced. If our children coughed, we could take them in an hour to a place high in the mountains, bathed in sunlight, like Villars. The countryside too was so beautiful, and the people were less unpolished than those of Sin-le-Noble.

As soon as we got off the train the next morning in Paris, we brought our good news to Mr. Benignus. He greeted us with a strange look. When I said to him, "I've been named," he interrupted me with a peremptory "No."

"But I had unanimity," I declared.

"Less one voice, and an important one: Miss Gander, the hardware store owner, who plays a preponderant role in the parish. She opposes your pacifism but didn't have the presence of mind to vote no. After your departure, she telephoned Pastor Henri Westphal of Lamastre. The Westphals have property on the banks of Lake Leman, near Thonon. Mr. Westphal is a moderate man who can direct the two difficult parishes of Thonon and Evian. I let Miss Gander know by telephone that I named Mr. Westphal."

I left there like someone who had been hit on the head with a bludgeon.

There we were, shown the door by the church and the Central Society to which I had belonged until then. Perhaps it was only justice. Consecrated a pastor before the stupid synodal ruling concerning propaganda for conscientious objection, for eight years had I believed myself to be *in* the church, whereas Henri Roser, Jacques Martin, and Philippe Vernier, my best friends, saw themselves refused pastoral consecration. Henri Roser would only be consecrated at fifty, after World War II. A disgusted Jacques Martin went into business and had a difficult life. They have only just granted him consecration at the age of sixty. As for Philippe Vernier, he was forced to emigrate to Belgium, where they granted him consecration and the title of pastor. He didn't come back to France until after the war.

While waiting, only one thing remained for me to do: play dead, that is, embed myself in Sin-le-Noble. They wouldn't dare expel me from there!

That's when I received a letter from my friend, Pastor Roger Casalis, who was leaving a village in the Midi region named Le Chambon. There, with some other friends, he had tried to implement a rural group like our Northern Group.

He had to leave his position for health reasons. The elders refused to give him a car, and he no longer had the strength to make the rounds on his bike. This refusal showed him that he wasn't very popular. He wanted to leave but had a hard time finding a replacement.

Magda and I went to Le Chambon, after stopping in Die, where they were also looking for a pastor. Die, situated in the region called the Drôme, was a small southern city at the bottom of an alpine canyon. Everything there had a musty smell. An old woman, Mrs. Coursange, invited us into a living room with furniture covered with sheets and the shutters closed. "Are you for or against the Brigadiers of the Drôme?" she whispered in my ear. She didn't know, poor thing, that the Brigadiers were passé. The big questions now were, "Are you for or against the Pentecostals?" and "Do you oppose the baptism of children?" I responded to her evasively because her question had horrified me: "for," "against," it was the old French Protestant South with its eternal, rancid-smelling doctrinal disputes.

Le Chambon was not, as I had believed, in the Midi. The Midi stops sharply at the bend of a torrent, the Eyrieux, that we had followed by car upriver from the Rhône River. Its high valley, after crossing a forest of pine trees, suddenly opened onto "the Plateau."

The Plateau, where we were to spend seventeen years of our life and where our children would grow up, is an undulating plain, situated at a mean altitude of about 3,300 feet above sea level. Its hills, crowned with a uniform forest of pine trees, are often cut by a low cloud ceiling in winter. The strange impression of being on a plain disappears as soon as you move about by car or on foot. A complicated network of small, brown, bubbling streams zigzags through the meadows, then squeezes into a rocky run before emptying into a much larger valley – all on a human scale with the scenic quality of a great, ever-renewed national park. In clear weather, the elegant stretch of extinct volcanoes emerges on the horizon: the Lizieux, in the form of an embrace; the Mézenc, in the shape of a policeman's hat; the Gerbier de Jonc, as its name indicates, resembling a cone-shaped haystack.

The village of Le Chambon is ugly. Building façades of gloomy granite alternate with the dirty yellow or gray stucco of old-fashioned hotels. The church appeared immense to us – uncomfortable, with five hundred seats, but with large windows that let in floods of white light and sometimes a ray of sunlight.

The house had walls three feet thick and small windows that opened toward the southeast, the type that let in sunlight only until noon. The house had been dug from rock. On the ground floor, at the back of the kitchen cabinets, water seeped through the porous stone. But the garden was so beautiful. A series of terraces towered above a mountain stream, the Lignon River, that rumbled in winter and was reduced to a trickle in the summer. The whole setting seemed heartbreaking to us because we arrived during a violent storm, and the interior of Pastor Casalis's presbytery was messy, dreary, and tasteless. This building had been the winter home of the Count de Fay, whose coat-of-arms – a stag and two palm leaves – was roughly hewn into the granite above the main entrance.

That Sunday, I preached in the spacious church. The parish's welcome struck me as lukewarm. It took me a long while to understand the caution, not to say the congenital distrust, of the peasants. I had always promised myself not to become a country pastor, seeing myself as better suited for the city and its problems. However, I had no alternative but to apply for the position. I returned to Sin-le-Noble and soon learned that the group of church elders had preferred me to the other candidate. The administrative problems had been rectified by my old classmate René Herdt, the regional president, who had, on his own initiative, named me "temporary" for a year, thus excusing me from the oath not to campaign for conscientious objection. Le Chambon was mine for the taking, and I took it. Miss Matile, an important member of the council of elders, insisted on my nomination despite my ideas. The national council named me on a temporary basis.

In September 1934, after our unsuccessful vacation to La Bourboule, the Trocmé family set off for Le Chambon with four still very young children. While we had central heating installed in the presbytery (I laid down this one requirement), we settled in Miss Matile's home, then a boarding house. It cost us a fortune, because the people in Le Chambon didn't exercise the same hospitality as people in the North did. On the contrary, here they practiced the tourist industry.

Le Chambon had a thousand inhabitants living in town and another two thousand dispersed among the surrounding farms. There were only 124 Catholics, but the influence of the Reformed Church was undermined by a strong, sectarian Darbyite minority and a Salvation Army post.[2] Only three families prided themselves on being cultured: Doctor Riou and his wife; Mrs. de Félice, an old, rich, eccentric landowner; and Miss Matile, the founder of a children's boarding house. Mr. and Mrs. Darcissac, very devout teachers, at least had the distinction of being eccentric, but their horizon was limited to the Plateau's regionalism. Mrs. Marion, a pastor's widow who ran a small boarding house, was active in the parish but said little.

By autumn, the weight of this conservative peasantry oppressed us. These peasants seemed to have nothing in common with the farmers of my native region, Picardy. In our eyes, the Plateau was hostile territory. It had difficulty providing for a peasantry that knew spring, summer, and autumn, though especially winter, which lasted nine months of the year. A peasantry that went about repeating, as if it were the pinnacle of human wisdom, the local saying: "Nine months of winter, three months of misery." A peasantry that knew lean times and did anything and everything to get by. A peasantry that smelled of manure, pigs, cabbage, potatoes, and the Scotch broom with its bitter odor that they burned sparingly in their cook stoves in winter. Its flowers that cover the embankments and the threshold of the forest look as if they are on fire like the sun in June. From working lives spent close to the earth, these peasants had even taken on the color of the granite stone they extracted from the ground to construct their uncomfortable farmhouses.

They knew life and death, especially death. Burial ceremonies played a huge role in their somber existence. They conceived of youth as "something that will soon pass," adulthood as a period of hard and disappointing work, and old age as the time for settling their affairs with God, if they hadn't in the interim sunk into secret alcoholism. For them, the truth was found in the past – "before 1914." The truth, for them, was "Moussa Berteran" (Pastor Louis Bertrand), who represented the ultimate in virtue and faith. "Ah," repeated the old timers from the

2 Followers of John Darby (1800–1882), founder of the Exclusive Brethren. About a thousand of the people living in and around Le Chambon-sur-Lignon in 1940 were Darbyites.

days of Mr. Bertrand, "the pastor made the rounds, and the church was full on Sundays, but today, what can you expect?" This "what can you expect?" expressed at once a complaint against the present and an admission of definitive, irreparable powerlessness. The present was only the subject of complaints, while the future was loaded with fears. The exodus of the young toward the cities did the rest. Those who stayed were headed for death, and the pastor was charged with the task of helping the village die.

Yet the village was growing. Forty years earlier, a pastor from Saint-Étienne, Louis Comte, had organized the village's first summer camps called "Children on the Mountains." Some residents of Saint-Étienne and rich Protestants in Valence, originally from the Plateau, had rediscovered the land of their fathers and built country houses around the village to spend the summer there. For several weeks in July and August, the village came alive, and the church was full. Shop merchants and hotel-keepers came out of their torpor and worked in a frenzy to make enough money for the year. The small, ruddy-faced country women became boarding-house maids and sported white aprons. August 15 was the high point; that's when the church's annual social service bazaar was held in the courtyard. Immediately after, the rains returned, the "season" was finished, and the shutters closed. Everything was back to normal, which is to say autumn's sleep and winter's death. Those whom summer had made rich concealed from the poor the extent of their earnings, adding their complaints to those of the peasants about the weather, their poor health, and their impending death.

It was, nonetheless, in Le Chambon, from 1934 to 1944, that Magda and I were truly happy for the first and last time of our lives, despite the war that lasted five years. In 1934, Magda, at thirty-three years of age, had reached the height of her energy. The young, thin, feverish girl had disappeared and given way to a vigorous plant that the severe climate of Le Chambon caused to bloom. After the birth of Jean-Pierre, she had even gained too much weight. The caesarian section she had undergone to give birth to Daniel had left her exhausted. Le Chambon made her forget her fatigue. I now found her prettier: a classic beauty, strong and ardent as ever.

Photographs from this period of Magda surrounded by her four children confirm this. Mrs. de Félice told me something once that I will never forget: "Your wife possesses three qualities that one rarely finds in the same person: beauty, intelligence, and goodness." It was true. Magda radiated Florentine elegance. Her glances, sometimes searing with indignation, sometimes tenderly anguished for her loved ones, corresponded perfectly with her husky and staccato Italian voice. Her words, often reflective, passionate, or comical, but always original, kept her children, her husband, and our family helpers from getting bored. Her former anxiety now only revealed itself in her obsession with details. This made us all suffer, but for the privilege of living with such a generous, intelligent, energetic, and unselfish woman, I gladly put up with the exhaustion caused by her incessant agitation.

In Le Chambon, Nelly quickly overcame her health crisis. She began to put on weight and grew strong. She inherited her mother's hair, but blonder and wavier, and magnificent eyes, hazel rather than brown.

Jean-Pierre finally emerged from his childhood lethargy. He dropped the "What?" he famously said whenever he woke from his daydreams. He soon had to wear glasses that concealed the extraordinary look he had in his eyes: deep blue and always turned inward. He thought a great deal, worked hard in class, and began early to write with talent. I felt very close to him. It seemed like we were brothers, though he was more gifted than I was – in music, for example. His mother made sure he had every opportunity to develop his talents, such as through music and drawing lessons. He quickly excelled in these two arts.

Jacques was a lot slighter than Jean-Pierre, who, like his sister, was sturdy. We always found "Jacquot," a deft climber, on walls, trees, tables, and furniture. At the beginning of our time in Le Chambon, he climbed on the back of a chair and began to suck – God knows why – on a curved hook fixed to the wall. The chair slipped and Jacquot, who was perhaps three years old, remained suspended by his mouth as the hook pierced his cheek like a fishing hook. Nelly heard him moaning. She entered the room and had the intelligent idea of holding her brother up as she cried for help. We had to turn him to his side to free him without tearing off the corner of his cheek. The only mark that remained from this incident was a dimple still visible today on his adult cheek.

Underneath his outgoing disposition, Jacquot was a worrier like his mother and, like his father, a timid soul who withdrew at the slightest touch, the least criticism, or an unexpected visit. At these moments, he escaped to the back of the house or threw himself under the table. He was the most spoiled of our children, and his affectionate nature – tender, religious, and idealistic – and his trusting blue eyes and delicate features earned the attention that visitors to our home lavished on him.

Daniel was completely different. A big fistful of dark curls fell over his round, jovial, ruddy face. Never sick, muscles galore. Beautiful brown eyes that looked you straight in the face. We were convinced that he would be a child without any problems. Perhaps we were too convinced. In my childhood, I too had suffered because of my cheerfulness and physical vigor. Everyone thought I was free of problems. Still today, my brothers tell me, "Pierre always had a complicated nature. But you never had any problems."

WE HAD FOUND a depressing presbytery whose main entrance porch was cluttered with dusty rubbish. Under Magda's magic hand, everything was transformed. We suspended a swing from the beams; an iron lantern forged by our village blacksmith, Mr. Jouve, added style. We repainted the dirty gray shutters green. The dining room took on a new look. We had arrived with almost no furniture, but that room needed very little because its walls were lined with handsome wooden cupboards that reached all the way to the wooden ceiling. Since we now had central heating, we removed the blackened stove from the fireplace and made wood fires in the winter. The fireplace walls painted, in faux red brick, added a bright note at the end of the long, gray room. We ordered an old-fashioned grandfather clock from the village jeweler and daubed the casing to make it look antique. Our newly countrified family grew up to the beat of its pendulum and the striking of its bell.

In the dining room, three French windows with deep embrasures (the walls were a yard thick) opened onto a terrace. White tulle curtains softened the severity of these openings and captured the morning sunlight. Nothing blocked our view of the green meadows and woods in the summer or the white snow in winter.

A secondhand furniture sale in Lyon soon brought us a rustic buffet that fit perfectly between the two windows. We garnished it with multicolored crockery. A medieval-style iron chandelier with diamond-patterned holes cast geometric light on the walls. A small pedestal table fit into one of the embrasures; the windowsills were covered with geraniums and green plants. Two parakeets in a hanging cage annoyed us during our meals with their untimely cries. Best of all was the table: long, with four massive legs in the rustic Spanish style, on which

Magda put a light beige, Basque-style oilcloth with multicolored stripes. This table became the symbol of our family. We ate there; the children did their homework there; we made our drawings there. When there were too many adults around the table for meals – Magda invited people all the time – the children moved from the large table to a small, low table made by the carpenter, and sat on stools appropriate to their size.

When I left my office – a long, dark room accessible only by a narrow door cut through the thick wall – I contemplated my family bustling about in the dining room. Bursts of happiness and pride rose in my heart. "What have I done," I would say to myself. "What have we done," I would say to Magda, "to be so happy!" I didn't know then that I was at the high point of my life and that major events would wreak havoc in a few years.

The best time of the week was Monday, my day of rest. I began exploring the roads of Le Chambon with great pleasure. With those of our children not yet in school, we spent our leisure time strolling through the woods. Unfortunately, it wasn't long before I started to have serious back pain. Stiff as a board in the morning, I could only get my flexibility back by walking a lot. But the more I walked, the more I suffered from lower back pain. It would torment me all night and the following morning.

One day, I could no longer walk at all. A farmer found me doubled over, seated on a slope a mile from the village. He harnessed his mule and took me home on a sleigh. I underwent treatment at Aix-les-Bains, where the specialist declared that my vertebrae were compressing the nerves that controlled my legs. "Avoid walking too much. Use a car, and things will get better."

So, I went to Lyon with Mr. Eyraud, the car mechanic from Le Chambon. He advised me to buy a used Citroën C4. It struck me as luxurious but would pass for an old jalopy today. From then on, I made the rounds in my car. That cost me my reputation: I was no longer considered a new Mr. Bertrand because I no longer stopped at the corner of a field to speak with peasants who left their work for a moment to greet me.

For the family, the C4 was a source of countless pleasures because the Plateau is the ideal region for car rides. With our children – whom, I admit, we allowed occasionally to skip school (on their birthdays, for example) – or alone with Magda, we explored all the small roads in the surrounding areas. "Where do you want to go?" I asked my passengers. "To Scotland, to Auvergne, to the Midi, or to the Vosges Mountains?"

And it was true! Within a half-hour, without rushing, we found ourselves in unexpected and magnificently varied landscapes.

"Scotland" was Mont Mézenc, with its high, desolate plateaus and its view which, on a clear day, went from Mont Blanc to the Puy de Sancy and from the hills of the Velay to the Montagne Noire – about a fourth of France. It was also the lakes of Issarlès, and Saint-Front, with its strange granite sanctuary that resembled a Breton chapel. The area has other things in common with Brittany and Scotland, such as its granite cottages and the mysticism of its Celtic population.

Auvergne meant the Massif mountains of the Meygal region, with its volcanoes covered with forests; the village of Monedeyres and its church, outlawed by the diocese because of a stubborn heresy described by Jules Romains in *Cromedeyre-le-Vieil*; or it could be Le Puy with its Romano-Mauresque church, the Saint-Michel d'Aiguilhe chapel, and the ring of chateaus that surround it, with the Polignac Tower looming over them all. Auvergne was also the incredible eagle's nest of Borée, a sleepy village since the twelfth century on the steep north side of Mézenc. One evening we saw, from the cross of the Boutières that towers over Borée, the sun set gloriously, and, in the opposite direction, the moon rise, eclipsed by the shadow of the earth. We were between the two, and we waved our arms to see if the shadow of our movements was visible on the moon!

The Midi was the chateau of Rochebonne, a ruin perched on sheer rock, flanked by a waterfall bordered by meadows and old pine trees where you can hear the cicadas sing. The Midi was also the Eyrieux valley, with its cypresses and peach trees blooming in the spring. I especially remember the steep gorge that descended toward Aubenas, where we found olive groves before getting to the Pont d'Arc, a natural bridge crossing the Arizona-like canyon of the Ardèche.

Finally, the Vosges was La Louvesc and its spur covered with tall, dark fir trees topping the Rhône Valley. There we visited the sanctuary of Saint Jean-François Régis, the Jesuit apostle, emulator of Saint François de Sales, who, in the seventeenth century, tried with gentleness to reconvert the Huguenot plateau to Catholicism but failed to do so.

During excursions, we had lunch at the stroke of noon, an omelet or cabbage soup in some small country inn we chanced upon. If the weather was nice, we sat at the edge of a woods, where we got a great view of a canyon, read a book, or chattered away. It was thanks to the C4 that Magda and I experienced the heights of marital happiness, on getaway day trips with just the two of us. In the evening, we were back with our four rambunctious children. The au pair was relieved to see us. Mrs. Eyraud dried her hands on her apron and went home. When she was there, we knew that all would be well during our absence, and we left without any worries.

MY BEGINNINGS IN RURAL MINISTRY were far more encouraging than I had dared to hope. As mentioned, I had quickly acquired the reputation of being a "new Mr. Bertrand," and I had heartily enjoyed these long walks through the countryside. Each pathway – whether to La Bruyère, Les Tavas, Romière, La Suchère, or Les Eyrauds – first ascended sharply as it exited the ravine where Le Chambon was built. When I reached the top of the hill, I had to overcome my shortness of breath, stumbling a little on the uneven pebbles. What a reward, though, when you reach the Plateau. In clear weather, your gaze extends around twenty-five miles, up to Mézenc. In winter, my heavy boots made the snow squeak on the ground, as the branches, under the sun's heat, swayed sharply while unburdening themselves of the weight of accumulated snow and ice. In the fields where I walked to arrive more quickly at an isolated farm, springs gurgled as they broke through the frozen soil. On the horizon, the woods extended in the silvery fog. The silence was so absolute when I stopped that only my accelerated heartbeat broke it, along with a dog barking in the distance.

Often the fog engulfed the snowy countryside as I returned from my meetings or visits in the evening. I didn't want to get lost, because my tracks were quickly covered if the wind we called *la Burle* began blowing. I was never fully reassured until the ravine of the Lignon River abruptly opened at my feet and I heard the water, which let me know which direction to take. I tripped my way through the snow until, through the fog, I could make out the frame of an illuminated window. Then I knew I would soon be home and that the last steps through the sleepy village were nothing but the prelude to my arrival at the presbytery door, where I shook the snow from my boots.

I entered the dining room, where eight arms embraced me, "Papa, Papa!" They were never indifferent, the four enthusiastic lights of my life. Jacquot and Daniel each took hold of one of my legs and sat on my feet so we could play "elephant's paw" as I tried to walk. Jean-Pierre encircled my waist and put his "hairy helmet" under my arm. Nelly strangled me with both arms, and I still had one free arm to caress her beautiful, silky hair or pull on her blond braids. Mama would stop what she was doing for a moment to observe this dizzying spectacle. And I, formerly such a lonely man, was now like a tree covered with branches and fruit, in a word, content. Sometimes, I told them the story of the "little beast," which I made up as I went along; sometimes the little beast became an enormous beast.

In spring, the landscape changed. The waterlogged meadows became impassable and were covered with flowering salsify.[3] Suddenly, in mid-May, the late-arriving mountain springtime rushed upon us and a few cherry and other fruit trees hastily blossomed at the edge of the woods. In June, the golden Scotch broom burst forth on all the slopes like puddles of sunlight. An unbelievable variety of low grasses bloomed in the meadows. Then, very quickly, summer came – with its tourists and its artificial life. The peasants disappeared from church services for three months: haymaking, harvest, and the potato season came one after the other. The pine forest crackled in the heat. Our children swam in the basins formed by the levees along the Lignon River. In mid-September, the early frosts turned the leaves of the beech trees reddish-brown, and winter began again with its alternating periods of snow, thaw, wind, fog, and the smell of burning Scotch broom. There certainly were "nine months of winter and three months of misery," that is, of relentlessly intense work.

My work among the peasants soon proved to be depressing. In their eyes, I was the worried city dweller who tried hard – "Why?" – to change things that always remained the same, the inevitable return of work and family events.

The parish functioned according to several well-established traditions: Sunday services, the gathering of young people on Sunday afternoon; two "local get-togethers" during the week; catechism on Thursdays. "You will have time to read, study, and write," my predecessor, Roger Casalis, had told me. "It's a big parish, but not very demanding."

After two years, I was dying of boredom. In the North, I was accustomed to speaking simply to uncomplicated people. But in Le Chambon, I quickly perceived that my words didn't have the same meaning as in the North. When, in the North, I pronounced the word "God," I brought on a revolution. Amid slavery, poverty, and work in the mines, God appeared as a liberator. But here, God was nature, destiny, the unknowable, whose fortuitous strokes arrange births and deaths, health and sickness,

3 An edible European plant belonging to the daisy family.

sunshine and frost. Faith consisted in bowing before its arbitrary decrees. That was religion. This religion, sometimes coupled with frugality, made people hesitant to call the doctor. "What do you expect?" said the old-timers who dominated the area with their secular wisdom. "All will die in their turn."

If I spoke about Jesus Christ in the North, about his cross and his redemptive power, this signified the recovery of alcoholics, reconciliation between enemies, the conversion of atheists. In Le Chambon, an old Protestant territory, generations of pastors, Darbyite preachers, and Salvation Army personnel had announced Jesus Christ and certainly had reaped a harvest. But what were the fruits of their teaching? A sentimental, religious emotion, to be sure; a less crudely fashioned family life, yes; but how would a "born-again" peasant be distinguished from all the others? Working in the fields was the same for them all. Good fortune came either to the workaholics or the evildoers. It didn't necessarily come to the meek, or to the dreamers who preferred the Bible to their pickaxe. As far as women were concerned, between their poultry yards, households, pigs, gardens, and children, they were all, by forty years of age, worn down by incessant fatigue. "Don't lose heart" was, for them, their entire religion.

I was struggling in a world that thought it understood my teachings but was unable to grasp what I was saying. If what I was saying had to do with the parish, things became even more complicated!

In the North, the poor, little Protestant parishes, lost among the de-Christianized masses, appeared as havens of grace for all the walking wounded, despite their fights and relapses. Those who, one day, met true friends at a religious service and found true devotion and God's marvelous forgiveness there, could no longer do without it. The church of Jesus Christ was their home and true family. In Le Chambon it was entirely different. Everyone was Protestant, so that distinction no longer meant anything. We could certainly note a remarkable sociological fact here: the rarity, if not to say the non-existence, of divorce. Except for that, Le Chambon resembled any other sample of humanity. There were honest people and crooks, misers and generous folks, idiots and clever fellows. Hovering over the entirety of this small world was an enormous mediocrity, the terrible and oppressing tyranny of "the village's opinion." The Darbyites, a virtuous sect, cast merciless judgments on all those not holding their beliefs. Everyone dreaded these criticisms.

There were judgments "from the left," formulated in the two or three cafés frequented by men and young people. They said "prayers" for us "revivalists" – that's what they called us – that contained three times more slander than the prayers they accused us of saying for the salvation of drinkers and people leading sinful lives.

The "penguins" also formed public opinion. I am the one who thus labeled this group of stupid, unemployed boys. Always on the corner of the town's intersection, they turned their shameless faces toward every passerby – pastor or adolescent, old man or young woman. They observed them from a distance, looked them over closely, mumbled some insidious remark in the local dialect as they passed by, and hurled vulgar pleasantries in their trail as they left. Nothing escaped the judgment of the "penguins," especially things Christian. They fouled, mocked, and destroyed everything Christians dared hope for. As soon as one of my catechumens began to hang around with the "penguins," he ceased greeting me, as was the custom in the village, affected a mocking air, and scorned believers. He was too afraid of the "penguins" to free himself from them. The "penguins" also reigned on the sports field. It was said that their Sunday matches ended up in isolated country bars, where there were lots of young girls and the wine flowed freely.

Everything concerning sexuality at that time on the Plateau was still considered unimaginably vulgar. There was no real idea of engagement to be married in Le Chambon. A strange kind of Puritanism deemed that engagement had an indecent character about it. Yet they let Mother Nature arrange things. Parents pretended to be ignorant of their children's dating behavior. "Oh, I know very well that on Sundays, she goes over there, on the side of the mountain, with him!" they would say.

Then one fine day the crisis would erupt. The girl was pregnant. Her parents shrieked and shed tears. They soon stifled the scandal by going to find the pastor. "I've come to see if you will marry us," said the girl or the boy, blushing. They rushed to settle things. The bride wore a tailored suit, not a white dress. Oh, those shabby women's suits altered to disguise the young bride's expanding waistline! After the wedding, the young couple tried to find lodging, most often on the floor above their parents. The baby's arrival settled everything; everyone was reconciled around the crib.

I soon noticed that the pious people, those who came to church – perhaps forty couples and as many widows and older, single ladies – were unfortunately no more considerate or generous than the rest of the population. Admittedly, the opinions expressed in the bars and by the "penguins" went too far. By underscoring the defects of the "revivalists," they excused their own faults. But the "practicing Christians," who formed a sacred shield around the pastor, received his visits most frequently, hosted the local meetings, and nodded their heads in agreement when speaking about the sins of the "worldly," were not without sin themselves. In the country, everybody knows everything, and the pastor knows nothing. He needs years to find out what's really going on and understand the silent allusions and the shrugs when his every effort to do something new fails.

Unable to change the old folks, I put all my efforts into working with the young, especially the men. When we arrived, seven or eight girls and three or four boys made up the entirety of the parish's youthful members. When we questioned them about their occupations, there were downward glances and smiles. Half jovially and half impertinently, one girl dared to say to us, "Me, I watch over the cows." It was true, of course, but it was hardly the whole truth. That was our first lesson in how to talk to the villagers: no direct questions. It was much better to beat around the bush for a quarter-hour before inquiring, discretely, if, perhaps, one never knows . . . The person in question that day was Lucie Héritier, a tall, upright young lady who never disappointed us. She refused to speak in front of others. What she did was none of their business.

I divided my youth group in two. During the week I met with those from the village who played soccer on Sundays. They thought they were ahead of the curve because they attended the advanced classes in the village school. Two of them became teachers, the others, shopkeepers and coffee shop owners. I never got anywhere with them. They were a sneaky group. The worst among them controlled their betters, preventing them from becoming Christians by making fun of them.

Those from the countryside were completely different: rough on the edges, slower, believers. Their leader was Henri Mandon, who had lost his father and was already mature and responsible for a farm and his three younger brothers and sisters. He later directed the first farming school in Le Chambon and established a rural cooperative. With him were a dozen younger boys who, little by little, discovered their faith. A repentance movement began, and prayer meetings took place. I believed that the movement would spread to other young people. I even hoped for a revival, but I quickly perceived that the divisions between the different milieus were such that nothing would move beyond the tight circle of rural youth. Nonetheless, they had formed a group of intimate friends. Their conversions were sincere and solid and they gave the church its most enthusiastic members.

To overcome their insularity, I decided to widen their horizons with a trip. We rented a bus and, on Pentecost Sunday, loaded it with forty boys and girls to visit the Museum of the Desert, in the Midi.[4] We spent the night at the YMCA in Nîmes. The old folks in our church soon accused me of squandering money that "could go to the poor" – though it never would have. For fear of the Darbyites' criticism, most of the "local groups" forbade their children to travel, even though it was free. A fund-raiser organized in the spring had covered the expenses beforehand.

From every indication, the village needed to breathe! Previous pastors had tackled the problem, in particular, Charles Guillon. When he became secretary of the worldwide YMCA in Geneva, his former parishioners elected him mayor of Le Chambon. Mr. Guillon, a savvy politician, pursued the prudent policy of "defending the town's interests," which meant expanding tourism and modernizing the roads and water distribution. My conversations with him were disappointing. He responded evasively to my proposals. He didn't want to take responsibility for anything that might undermine his political situation in the village.

Before explaining how the village began to breathe, I must relate my quarrels with the regional synod of the Reformed Evangelical Church.

PARADOXICALLY, THE PROTESTANT CHURCH of France was still split in 1934. We belonged to the so-called "evangelical" synod, while two or three of our colleagues were from the "liberal" synod, which meant they didn't endorse the Apostles' Creed when they were consecrated. In our region, the "liberals" were also on the left politically, whereas the "evangelicals" were more conservative. In the large towns, such as Saint-Agrève, Annonay, and Tournon, the reactionary middle class could express itself in proper French and played a preponderant role in the regional synod. This group looked unfavorably on

4 Le Musée du Désert was founded in 1911 inside the birth home of the Camisard leader, Pierre Rolland, on the Soubeyran farm in the Gard region. In the history of French Protestantism, "The Desert" is the period from the revocation of the Edict of Nantes in 1685 to the Edict of Tolerance in 1787.

my arrival in Le Chambon. Certain members of the regional council wanted to rattle me by refusing year after year to lift my temporary status. The situation became more complicated when my friend and protector, René Herdt, left Saint-Agrève and the regional presidency. That was when the Croix-de-Feu (Cross of Fire) movement was spreading like wildfire.[5]

It's hard to imagine today what the political climate was like in 1936. In Germany, Hitler had come to power. His troops had reoccupied the left bank of the Rhine River, demilitarized since the 1918 Treaty of Versailles. France, abandoned by its former allies, had not dared to react. The Front Populaire government did nothing,[6] hoping that Nazism would be merely a flash in the pan. Then, several former combatants from 1914–18 were moved by the appeal of the very handsome, Catholic, and likeable Colonel La Rocque. He was not a fascist, but fascist practices rubbed off on the movement: blue shirts, parades with torches, the straight-arm Roman salute. Christian symbolism had been mobilized for the Cross of Fire. The fire was love of the fatherland; it was the fire of the trenches; it was devotion unto death to the nation's cause.

In our synod, this meant the elimination of any element considered dangerous: pacifists, socialists, followers of Gandhi. Although I avoided any politics in my preaching, the bourgeois who spent their summer vacations in Le Chambon were irked by my pacifist sermons and tried to get rid of me.

This issue exploded during the synod in Annonay. Elections to the regional council were taking place. An official list presented by the outgoing board left the Croix-de-Feu regional candidates in a good position. The vote was by secret ballot, but ordinarily the candidates nominated by the outgoing board were elected by a strong majority. The voting took place and then the counting. What a surprise! The peasant delegates, always silent during these sessions but constituting the majority of the synod, traditionally found themselves on the left because of their longtime Huguenot opposition to the government. The Croix-de-Feu candidates irritated them with their impassioned declarations, so the peasants crossed out their names on the list and voted in large numbers – for me!

5 Croix-de-Feu (1927–1936) was a right-wing political party founded by World War I veterans that espoused ultra-nationalistic views. It was led by François de la Rocque. It had anti-Semitic and fascist overtones and was dissolved by the Front Populaire government in 1936.

6 The Front Populaire was an alliance of French left-wing movements during the interwar period.

I was not a candidate but was known to be on the left! I was elected a member of the regional council in the first round.

"We have to invalidate this election!" cried the Croix-de-Feu members. "Mr. Trocmé is only a temporary pastor. He is not eligible." They were probably right. No organization grants eligibility to temporary personnel. But they could only invalidate my election if a legal document allowed them to do so. They therefore consulted the synodal regulations. They found an article that declared auxiliary and voting pastors ineligible, but the category of temporary pastors had not been anticipated by the legislators. Did it exist statutorily?

The synod was unable to nullify my election, so I soon occupied a seat on the regional council where, along with my colleagues, I had to regulate the situation of the region's pastoral staff – that is, my own situation.

Ecclesiastically speaking, this was the most prosperous period of my life. In 1938, due to the successful efforts of Marc Boegner, the two churches (the evangelical and the liberal) merged and incorporated the former "free churches." The venerable Pastor Debard of the Free Church of Saint-Étienne agreed to be president of the new thirteenth region, which included fifty-two churches and large cities like Clermont-Ferrand, Saint-Étienne, and Roanne, for a year. Everyone began to breathe more easily. At the end of the year, Debard withdrew, and as we were great friends, he publicly designated me as the man who, in his opinion, had all the qualities needed to become regional president. If I had accepted, today I would perhaps be an important person in the church. But I was staggered by Mr. Debard's proposal. Fearing I would be absorbed by administrative tasks for which I had no liking, and wishing to keep my hands free because I could sense the war approaching, I categorically refused this nomination, despite the urging of my colleagues.

Ever since, I have often asked myself if I made a mistake that day. Perhaps I should have tried to organize myself better and concentrate more on the concrete, administrative, ecclesiastical aspect of things. Our region might very well have behaved better during the occupation. I would have had a seat on the national council of the new Reformed Church and brought a touch of Christian pacifism to it. As it was, I sat for several years as a delegate of the national synod, where, I must admit, I felt alone and miserable.

But no, that day I slammed the door on any "career" in church governance. I got the reputation of a "difficult" pastor because this decision allowed me to continue to speak my mind. I would later pay for my independent spirit with a demotion.

"Who then, in your opinion," the regional council members asked me, "should be the regional president?" I designated Pierre Rozier, the spokesman for the bourgeois conservatives of the region. If he was sympathetic to the Croix-de-Feu, he was prudent enough to keep it to himself. He wanted to be president, that was clear, and I knew it. "Pierre Rozier likes administrative tasks," I said. "He is the one you should appoint."

I acted to some degree out of cowardice, it's true. Pierre Rozier lowered his eyes, assumed false modesty, moved his small, white hands about, said a few innocuous words, and asked to be free of any parish commitment. He lived in Valence, outside the region, because he owned a family house, and from there he could travel more easily by train to Saint-Étienne and the northwest part of the regional territory. He was elected. Twenty-six years later, he still holds the same position.[7] Rozier never made any serious blunders; he never compromised himself; he worked to bring together the Pentecostals and the rest of the pastoral corps. That was his most remarkable contribution as president. With a wave of his small white hands, he got rid of all the pastors who caused problems. He was always in agreement with those who spoke forcefully but avoided difficult decisions, letting those in a higher or lower echelon take that responsibility. At the national council in Paris, his presence sometimes provoked smiles. He was a terrible bore and, instead of supporting us, blabbered a lot and ranted against everything going on in Le Chambon because he was afraid of being held responsible for our mistakes. Thanks to his good offices, in Paris I acquired the reputation of a difficult, undesirable anarchist. This reputation, always accompanied by a nod to my "prophetic" temperament, followed me until the day I arrived in Geneva at the age of fifty-nine! No French parish of any importance would dare take on such a dangerous pastor. I don't, however, consider myself a dangerous person, except to Pierre Rozier, who never thanked me for installing him in the presidential chair. On the contrary, he was always afraid to discuss things with me because of my towering height (he was tiny), my trenchant observations (he never

7 He retired in 1967.

gave his views on anything), and my steady gaze (his eyes fluttered from left to right). I like Pierre Rozier, but I don't take him seriously, and he knows it.

NONETHELESS, UNTIL 1943 I remained popular in the thirteenth region, and that favored the founding of the École Nouvelle Cévenole (the future Collège Cévenol). After dropping the plan to bring a new industry to Le Chambon, some of us came up with the idea of establishing a small secondary school there.

Doctor Cambessédès, a faithful summer resident, envisaged the school as a kind of "home" for children with delicate health. Mr. Guillon thought about organizing a type of YMCA camp like those in the United States. He showed me his plans: in the winter, its premises could serve as a school.

Mr. Charles Schmidt, a library inspector, was then renting an apartment on the Luquet farm.[8] It was in a room of this apartment, which today serves as the school's office, that our dreams took shape. An elementary-school inspector, Mr. Liquier, joined our deliberations. We didn't want to compete with the public school's advanced classes that were directed by Mr. Darcissac. We would therefore be secular, but Protestant and international in spirit. We sought a way of expressing the old Protestant "left-wing" worldview that was still so alive in the area. I insisted that we teach pacifism.

But how could we realistically implement these ideas?

I began looking for a man enthusiastic enough to create a small academic program. The letters I addressed to Albert Meyer, professor at the exclusive École des Roches in Normandy, and other Protestant teachers produced no results. However, I convinced a young college graduate, Pierre Duflo, to come to Le Chambon. He asked me where the school was located. I showed him the annex that had recently been built behind the church, in spite of the village's skepticism. It was an inelegant performance hall that could be divided into three smaller rooms by using wooden panels.

Mr. Duflo asked me where his salary would come from. "The students will pay tuition," I told him. "But where are the students?" he inquired.

8 Mr. Schmidt's daughter married Daniel Isaac, the son of the Jewish historian Jules Isaac, a dominant figure in Christian-Jewish relations in post–World War II Europe.

"We'll have the children of the pastors from the surrounding area and those of Miss Matile's boarding house," I answered.

He left, saying he had to think things over. Indeed, there was a lot to think about! From Paris, he wrote to me, "I consulted my friends; your project is insane, not at all viable."

Everything was at a standstill when, one day, Guillon said to me – and in this way at least played his part in the founding of the École Nouvelle Cévenole – "There is always your friend Theis, whom I just saw in Vézénobres, near Nîmes. He has been in America, Madagascar, and Cameroon. He is a conscientious objector like you and is bored to death in Vézénobres. Go see him."

I went to see Édouard Theis, my old university classmate, in Paris. He hadn't changed from the old days: huge, quiet, enigmatic, sometimes falling asleep in the middle of a conversation, but very cultured, intelligent, capable of strong passions and great friendship. He was gifted with incredible perseverance when it came to pursuing a goal he had undertaken or promoting ideas he considered just. Theis had a university degree in the humanities that included Latin, Greek, and French literature. His wife struck me as even more enigmatic: silent, fatigued, and overwhelmed by a bevy of seven girls, who seemed to be raising themselves on their own.

The Theises came to see us in Le Chambon. They were given a tour of the property and left without a word. It's a lost cause, I said to myself. Then Theis wrote to say, "I'll come if you can get me a financial guarantee from the church."

At the 1937 regional synod, I presented my school project and asked to be granted a "half-time pastor" as an assistant. Fortunately, the financial allotments for Le Chambon surpassed by far the cost of one pastor's position. My request was granted, and starting in the fall of 1938, Edward Theis served in Le Chambon as a half-time, second pastor. After several relocations, the family settled very comfortably in the house called La Guespy (the wasp nest) belonging to Théodore de Félice. The little school that would become the Collège Cévenol opened its doors in the annex behind the church.

The walls were so thin, the teachers disturbed one another as soon as they raised their voices. At the beginning there were only four teachers and eighteen students. Theis, the only salaried staff, taught French, Latin, and Greek. The students who could afford tuition assured him of a half-salary. Between classes, he served the farm areas of Les Tavas and Romières. Three women taught other modern languages. Magda taught Italian, Mrs. Theis, an American, taught English, and Miss Hoefert taught German. She was a refugee who had left Austria after the Anschluss. She was half-Jewish and lived as an au pair in Miss Matile's home. For the sciences, the students crossed the street separating the church from the public school and took classes from the competent Mr. Soubeyrand. This had been arranged by Darcissac, director of the advanced classes and secretary of our parish. "It's all to the advantage of the public school," he said. "It increases our numbers." But he refrained from talking about it with the academic authorities.

13

War Again

THE BEGINNINGS OF the École Nouvelle Cévenole in 1938 and 1939 proved difficult because of Theis's and my pacifist ideas. Our advantage was that we supported each other. War loomed on the horizon, then broke out in 1939. At the time of my nomination, the church council of elders had accepted the idea that I would act as a conscientious objector in the event of war. They remained loyal in defiance of the frightened church authorities. Trouble came from elsewhere. Theis expressed his views categorically; his sermons were heavy-handed and often clumsy. I said the same things but more gently, making them easier to swallow. More than any other group, Theis attacked the rich, against whom he held bitter grievances: a Protestant millionaire had caused his father's death by brutally firing him from his job as secretary of the YMCA in Paris. The summer residents took a dislike to Theis and told me about it. I defended him to the best of my ability because I was the reason he was there. As a result, I shared his unpopularity.

Unfortunately, I was soon dropped by my best friends, in particular Miss Matile, who had gone all out to support my nomination in 1934. She was about forty-five when we arrived in Le Chambon. She had a lively intelligence, beautiful gray eyes, and an impressive forehead. After serving as governess for the Morin children in Doctor Riou's boarding house, she founded the first children's boarding house in Le Chambon, Les Genêts, on the Côte de Molle. Her educational methods were not to everyone's taste. She had a reputation for being extremely strict. She smeared burning medication on the chest of offending students, for example. This wasn't dangerous, but it did sting for a couple of minutes. Some of her former students greatly admired her; others couldn't stand her. She remained unswayed. Persuaded that she loved and was loved in return, she spoke of "my Chambon" and "my children" with an infectious enthusiasm. She was a pacifist, a member of the League of Mothers and Educators for Peace, and brought together the ladies of Le Chambon, such as Mrs. Riou, Mrs. Darcissac, Mrs. de Félice, and Magda, to talk about peace. Magda was deeply attached to her. Often, when I returned home late from my visits to parishioners, the young au pair told me, "Madam Trocmé wants you to know that she went to Miss Matile's house." They read good books together and discussed them at length.

In her will, Miss Matile left her house to the social services of the Chambon church, and Les Genêts became an old-age home. The public health service later added a rest home to it. Several years after the war, Miss Matile died in Sanary, southern France. Her body was brought back to Le Chambon. She had imagined that her former students would come and pay homage. Alas, her tomb has been completely abandoned. How's that for gratitude?

AS HITLER BECAME MORE and more brutal and threatening, most French pacifists abandoned a position founded on feelings rather than principle. The Anschluss of Austria, the humiliation of the Munich Agreement, and Hitler's betrayal of Czechoslovakia all sparked anguish and justified anger. Pacifism had to be established on something other than confidence that the Germans would remain peaceful. Only those who rejected all violence possessed this "something other." Once you definitively refused war as an option, you could persevere in peace, despite everything, by obeying God and believing in the miracle of love, even in the presence of unrelenting, diabolical forces like Nazism.

One would have to experience "spy-phobia" and the hysterical fear that seizes wartime crowds to understand the isolation that we suddenly encountered and why it was so dangerous for us. When, the following year, Mussolini declared war on France, we found the following sentence written in chalk on our door: "Go back to Italy with your Italian wife, you *Boche*, and leave us the hell alone." Without saying anything, we erased the insult with a wet rag. It was not the right time to protest. Public opinion didn't support us.

Hitler, with his violence and lies, certainly did everything to turn world opinion against him. Having lived through World War I, I struggled against a growing temptation: Go to war? No way! How could I kill innocent people? But shouldn't I have taken advantage of my knowledge of German to infiltrate Hitler's entourage and assassinate him before it was too late, before he cast the world into boundless catastrophe? The fear of separating myself from Jesus Christ, yes, a kind of perseverance in the midst of expanding darkness, kept me a pacifist. It was also the urgent needs of my ministry in Le Chambon, which became more and more engrossing.

During the anguished summer of 1939, Hitler, demented and malevolent, took Austria and Czechoslovakia and threatened Poland. The news of the Hitler-Stalin pact and the invasion of Poland struck us as absolute catastrophes. I still remember Daladier's somber voice, transmitted by loudspeaker in the main square in Le Chambon, announcing that France and England had declared war on Germany. A few days later, in Lyon, military ambulances crawled out of the hangars where they had slept during the interwar years. They moved through the streets like an interminable funeral procession of cockroaches. I saw them as a sinister sign marking the end of civilization. "All these men are going to die for nothing," I told myself. People accosted each other and asked: "Now, do you believe in the devil?" The invisible master of lies, violence, and death had plotted everything.

Summoned for military service, Henri Roser, Philippe Vernier, Pierre Vernier, and Jacques Martin refused to wear the uniform and went to prison. I waited week after week to get the call and meet the same fate, but nothing came.

I INSERT HERE TWO LETTERS written by André Trocmé. He wrote the first in early September 1939. He would have mailed it had he received his draft notice. The second was written on October 16, 1939, to Marc Boegner, president of the national council of the Reformed Church of France, to clarify his position.[1] *—Ed.*

Le Chambon, September 1939

Dear Sir:

I have just received my orders to report for duty.

I have a strong desire to serve my brothers and risk my life for them in a time as tragic as this one. However, I will not follow these orders,

1 These letters were hidden in the attic of Mrs. Marion's house in Le Chambon and found in August 1974, two years after André Trocmé's death in August 1972.

because to do so would put me in the morally impossible position of disobeying the divine commandment, "Thou shalt not kill."

I am a minister of the Christian religion. My life is consecrated to Christ, to whom I owe everything. I cannot, therefore, be part of a national army, either as a combatant or noncombatant (chaplain, stretcher-bearer, or medic), at a time when, in obedience to that country's command, the army is charged with the formidable duty of killing.

On the other hand, I would be happy to serve the martyred people of the bombarded cities and villages with all my strength as a worker, stretcher-bearer, or civilian medical assistant.

I would like to place myself in harm's way and give my life as have those who made the sacrifice of theirs.

I know that this constitutes the crime of insubordination, and I am ready to undergo the punishment prescribed by law and, as a condemned person, to carry out any task and run any risk to come to the aid of my suffering fellow citizens.

Yours sincerely,
André Trocmé

October 16, 1939

Mr. President:

I am sad and astonished by the contents of your October 4 letter. You state in that letter that you find me in error (in my interpretation of Scripture and in my interpretation of Christian doctrine). And yet the Oxford Ecumenical Conference, where you were a vice president, abstained from making a similar judgment. It considered the three attitudes of Christians toward war equally possible and worthy of respect.

Although you affirm that I am in error, you nonetheless did not conclude that I had to leave my position immediately, which would have been logical, since the presence of a conscientious objector in the Christian pulpit during wartime constitutes *par excellence* support for conscientious objection, whereas the imprisonment of the conscientious objector would undermine his authority.

You say that I have tendered my resignation to the council of elders of my church. Kindly allow me to set the record straight. I did not submit my resignation. I offered to resign if the council judged that this was preferable for the peace and honor of the church. The council of elders refused my offer.

Finally, you invite me to submit my resignation definitively the day I am called up to service. You thereby ask me to recognize before God and his church that the vocation I have received is incompatible with the pastoral vocation, and that divine truth, to which I bear witness, is opposed to what the church teaches. If the church judges me in error, it is up to the church to indicate this by giving me notice to cease my ecclesiastical functions (this is the opinion given by Mr. Rohr in his report to the Synod of Saintes). One cannot demand that a sincere person disavow the truth he believes. It is impossible for me to submit my resignation, all the more so at the time when God asks me to carry out the unique and indivisible vocation that I have received from him. At that moment, I will be more than ever the pastor of the church in which I was consecrated.

I have before me the text of a report addressed to Christian churches last July with a cover letter signed by you and the other members of the Provisional Committee of the World Council of Churches. Here is the wording of paragraph 6 under headline III:

> Churches must maintain the integrity of Christian fellowship between those who differ, for reasons of conscience, in their understanding of their duty as regards participating or not participating in war. Churches must cultivate understanding of diverse opinions and try their best to react against the tendency to identify Christian pacifism with antipatriotic politics. They must demand from the state that none find themselves deprived of their civil rights, nor of the exercise of any of their rights to religious freedom because they refuse, for reasons of conscience, to participate in the use of military force.

President Boegner, I know you are doing your best to prevent the state from depriving me of my rights to religious freedom. I know too that you do so with great courage. Therefore, I cannot understand why, at the same time, you seek to deprive me of my right to religious freedom within the church. How can the church demand from the state what it refuses to give its own pastors?

In conclusion, allow me to express my sadness and astonishment at seeing the hateful word "propaganda" again in the regulations from the Synod held in Saintes, while three brave servants of Jesus Christ are suffering for their master.[2] It seems to me that we should have more respect for those who, also for reasons of conscience, are suffering for their country.

You know very well, President Boegner, that the grave question God has placed before your conscience and mine cannot be resolved by an administrative rule about "propaganda." What is at stake here is the honor of Jesus Christ and of God. Our Christian church must declare itself today on the use of violence. It is God himself who demands this by way of our present ordeal.

Let us keep an entirely respectful attitude toward each other. Let us at least practice our Christian solidarity before the world, above and beyond any other solidarity. To act otherwise is to divide the church; it is to sin grievously against the divine unity to which the church bears witness here on earth.

Yours sincerely,
André Trocmé

FRANCE DIDN'T NEED ME YET. She had her quota of soldiers dug in at the Maginot Line or playing boules in their useless garrisons. Whereas Germany wiped out Poland in three weeks, the few weak French offensives in Lorraine only managed to occupy a few German villages serving as a buffer zone to the Siegfried Line. The "phony war" settled in. Since we had four children, I was classified with men aged forty-seven (even though I was only thirty-nine in 1940), the so-called "protected," who would only be called up as a last resort. Roser had intentionally failed to mention his four children. He was therefore called up, and his refusal to show up carried a heavy prison sentence. In my case, police headquarters in the Haute-Loire region had automatically issued a report on my family situation when I moved to Le Chambon.

Winter was difficult but eventful. Refugees surged toward Le Chambon, either from Central Europe, Paris, or eastern France, in anticipation of the military encounters they feared. Two of these, Miss Pont and Miss Grétillat, who feared bombings and had resigned from the Collège Lucie-Berger in Strasbourg, were useful to us. Miss Pont became co-director of the Collège along with Theis. She complemented him with her pedagogical experience and meticulous mind. Miss Grétillat taught mathematics. This solved the problem of the advanced courses formerly

2 In fact, there were four: Henri Roser, Phillippe Vernier, Pierre Vernier, and Jacques Martin.

taught in the public school, now completely off limits to all children from private schools by order of the Academic Inspector.

Several families of summer residents spent the winter as well in Le Chambon. The fresh air, good food, and safety made the stay worthwhile now that their children were able to continue their secondary education here. As a result, there were forty students in the École Nouvelle Cévenole during the 1939–1940 school year.

FROM THE PULPIT and while visiting our parishioners, Theis and I continued to express our convictions clearly. We could not contest the right – or the duty – of the state to resist a monster such as Hitler. The literature that we received from the American Fellowship of Reconciliation along the lines of "Keep America Out of War" seemed completely out of touch with reality. We couldn't overcome evil by pretending that it didn't exist. Rather, we found a way of resisting Nazism without killing human beings in daily obedience to the gospel of peace. Our viewpoint earned the opposition of several Protestants who heard our sermons.

There was Mr. Barbier, for example, from the Barbier boarding house, the husband of a courageous woman who, in emulation of Miss Matile, earned the family's livelihood by maintaining a children's boarding house while he, a ruined, depressed manufacturer, roamed the countryside with his dog. Barbier accused me with such virulence, both verbally and in letters of denunciation, that my freedom was soon endangered. There was also Pastor Paul Schmidt, brother of Charles Schmidt, the friend with whom I launched the École Nouvelle Cévenole. Paul Schmidt was the general secretary of the Protestant Association of Elementary Education. Attracted by the idea of absorbing our school into his association – fortunately, ours was in secondary education – and thus gaining importance, he settled down for the winter in Le Chambon. Since we knew about his reactionary ideas, we didn't give him control over our affairs. He became one of our most dangerous detractors, never ceasing to announce to all Protestantism the imminent ruin of the school, a poorly managed enterprise whose founders demoralized young people through their bad example.

Luckily, Paul Schmidt had little authority in French Protestantism. More dangerous was the hostility of Mr. Anstett, an Alsatian native and professor of French at the lycée in Lyon. Like many people in France with

German names, he wanted to make others forget his Germanic roots by flaunting his extreme nationalism. His knowledge of German got him mobilized in the Army's Counterespionage Corps. He soon created a dossier denouncing me. Didn't I have a German mother, pro-Communist sympathies (my "General Information" file had followed me from the North), and pro-German sympathies as well (the Fellowship of Reconciliation and the Peace March)? He spread rumors everywhere that I was an undercover agent for the fifth column, a spy for Germany whose function was to disrupt the nation's will to resist by spreading defeatist rumors. His actions, combined with the diabolical propaganda of the "Traitor of Stuttgart,"[3] who inundated France with alarmist news, stirred up ill-feeling and doubt. In the minds of simple people, my opposition to the war led them to compare me to this traitor.

Our most powerful adversary was Mrs. Bertrand. Daughter-in-law of the old pastor, Louis Bertrand, who had been so popular in Le Chambon, this woman, about thirty-five years old in 1939, had launched a scout troop in Le Chambon. The troop included children of peasants, townspeople, and tourists. She became very popular and didn't hesitate to denounce the lukewarm patriotism of the current pastors. When Paul Reynaud, then Minister of Armaments, set up the campaign called "Victory Steel," Mrs. Bertrand, despite the opposition of the pastors, made use of the naive zeal of the scouts and sent them from farm to farm to collect old pieces of metal that she piled at the end of the train station platform. From there they would be transported to the foundries. Theis and I didn't think that this paramilitary activity was appropriate for Christian youth, but Mrs. Bertrand stood up to us, and we had to let her do as she wished.

In May 1940, we would meet Mrs. Bertrand by chance in Paris. The Germans had broken through the frontline in the Ardennes. We expected a huge, pitched battle like the Battle of the Marne, a battle that would save France. Theis and I had gone to Paris because we wanted to offer our services to the International Red Cross.

Seeing us, Mrs. Bertrand said, "Ah, I see that, like me, you have come to Paris to get your affairs in order!" At the time, "to get your affairs in order" meant withdrawing your money from the bank and fleeing south. This very act aggravated the collective panic that led France to its

3 Paul Fredonnet, dubbed the "Traitor of Stuttgart" by the French press, was an extreme right-wing French journalist executed for treason at the end of the war.

defeat. No money in the banks meant no credit for the state or for anyone else. Every man for himself! Crowds surged in the streets; government employees left their posts at the mere thought of undergoing bombardments like those in Rotterdam. Stupidly, Theis and I had thought we were going to the site of the battle and its suffering. Clearly, we and Mrs. Bertrand didn't understand one another. The "Victory Steel" ended up rusting on the train station platform in Le Chambon, while Mrs. Bertrand, like most of the patriots, would become, through the actions of Philippe Pétain's Vichy government, collaborators with Adolph Hitler and enemies of Britain, once again called "Perfidious England." All this accomplished through patriotism, of course.

But in 1939, the "phony war" had completed its dirty work over the winter, and the French people were still guardedly hopeful. Things went exactly as Hitler had planned: with Poland wiped off the map in three weeks, France's and England's war against Germany lost its immediate objective. The warring countries could sign a peace treaty over the corpse of Poland. Certainly, we were worried to see the Maginot Line stop at Luxemburg. Memories of 1914 and the violation of Belgian neutrality by German armies haunted the French people. No French government had dared complete the fortifications on the border facing Belgium for fear of upsetting this small, friendly country that wished to remain neutral. The King of Belgium offered endless demonstrations of caution for fear of angering Hitler, who was always looking for any pretext of alleged anti-German "chaos" to justify wiping out his defenseless neighbors.

When Hitler invaded Belgium and Holland on May 10, the French and the English were, sadly, hardly surprised. It was 1914 all over again. Secret conversations among the Dutch and Belgian chiefs of staff had already taken place, and the French and British armies immediately began moving north to help these two small countries defend themselves. What is still astonishing today is the fact that the Allies extended their forces along an immense front without understanding that they ran the risk of being cut off from their rear guard and thrown back to the sea. But political considerations demanded that Belgium and Holland be defended. It was not the news of German aggression against Belgium that spread panic, but the news of the destruction of Rotterdam, an open city,[4] by aerial bombardments. In one fell swoop, terror cast hundreds of

4 That is, a city declared to be unfortified and undefended and, therefore, by international law, exempt from enemy attack.

thousands of civilian refugees onto the roads. Low-flying German planes fired mercilessly on the Belgians and French. In the Ardennes, German armored vehicles moving at forty miles an hour broke through the Allied front without fear of separating themselves from their home bases. The Allied armored vehicles only drove twenty-five miles an hour and were accompanied by infantry soldiers who slowed down their advance.

The panic that followed the bombing of Rotterdam was indescribable: Holland emptied into Belgium, Belgium into northern France, northern France into Paris and, a week later, Paris descended upon Central France and the Midi. Soon refugees flooded into Le Chambon. They related scenes of horror they had witnessed and of which they were victims: cities on fire, roads cluttered with cars that had run out of gas, crowds furiously demanding to pass, ditches into which all types of vehicles – horse-drawn, hand-pushed, motorized – had toppled, no longer able to advance. Scenes of panic and violence unfolded: everyone wanted to board the last trains or get an automobile or a bicycle. Families were dispersed and children lost as German planes machine-gunned the crowds along the roads. A woman coming from Belgium related how, getting up from the ground after a German plane had passed, she discovered that the child she had covered with her body had been killed underneath her by a bullet!

The craziest rumors circulated. The Germans, people said, had found the means of using water for fuel. They filled the tanks of their vehicles at the village fountains, threw a few pellets of something into their tanks, and charged ahead. In fact, the Germans had organized their Panzer Divisions so that refueling vehicles could come alongside the tanks as they sped to the front line. The British and French troops, separated from their command, mingled with the civilian population in flight and retreated in disorder. They didn't dare clear a path by firing on their compatriots obstructing the roads. The Germans, for their part, were not hampered by such scruples: they fired on the masses of human beings, cleared the passage, and went forward without slowing down.

Such stories moved me, of course. I remembered 1914, which began with a great defeat in Belgium, and I imagined, like all French people, that the "miracle of the Marne" would happen again.[5] Meanwhile, I was

5 The "miracle of the Marne" refers to the strategic victory for the Allies that proved to be a critical turning point in World War I. Paris was saved from capture and the "Schlieffen Plan" for a quick German victory was torn to tatters.

sheltered in Le Chambon while my ninety-five-year-old father, as I would learn later, was back on the roads fleeing in his old car driven by Jeanne, one of his household helpers. They hoped to reach La Rochelle, where my brother Pierre lived – and eventually managed to get there safe and sound.

Now was the time, I told myself, to prove that conscientious objectors were neither cowardly nor egocentric. Why not become an ambulance driver for the International Red Cross? I talked to Theis, and toward the end of May we traveled to Paris. We went to see Marc Boegner, the head of the French Protestant Church, who directed us to the representatives of the International Red Cross. It was true. The Red Cross was hiring ambulance drivers for what was still being called the frontline. Iron gray uniforms, international statutes, rights recognized by the two involved armies, risks identical to those of the combatants: just what I wanted. The International Red Cross welcomed us cordially and asked the French army to free us from our military obligations. The International Red Cross was a Swiss organization whose neutrality was covered by that of the Helvetic (Swiss) Confederation, and their statutes prohibited them from accepting commitments from non-Swiss and non-Swedes drafted by their national army.

This was the recruitment office's response: You can hire Édouard Theis. He has eight children and can't be drafted. But you cannot take André Trocmé. He only has four children and will be called up soon. I went home crestfallen, certain that Theis would leave without me. But he backed off immediately. It's true that with eight children, he had more to do than add another victim to the general butchery that would ultimately end the war. As for me, now declared eligible, I prepared myself to refuse the expected call. I was far from imagining what would happen – the imminent capitulation of France! On June 22, 1940, the armistice was signed in Compiègne in the famous "Armistice Train Car" where Germany had capitulated in 1918. At first, I experienced a feeling of gratitude for Pétain. He had ended the useless massacre. But my relief was replaced by shame when I learned that the French government would continue to exist, only thanks to Hitler, in the form of a protectorate south of a demarcation line. In the disorder of my thoughts and the contradictory news we were receiving by radio, I imagined that the army had capitulated in France and the government, taking refuge in Algeria, would continue the struggle against the Nazi monster with the English. Thus, the conscientious objector who refused to kill wished for the continuation of an armed battle that the Maréchal, our head of state, had abandoned. How ironic!

Pétain soon announced his policy of "collaboration" with Hitler. The great majority of French people, guided by a blind confidence in Pétain, the World War I hero of Verdun, followed the new state leader. In Vichy, out of 600 members of Parliament, only eighty opposed the new regime. Its institutions would be modeled on those of Italian Fascism. In Le Chambon, just about everyone sided with Pétain. With sad surprise, Theis and I found ourselves alone once again. All our friends – Dr. Riou, Dr. Le Forestier, Miss Matile, and the families from Saint-Étienne and Lyon who owned villas in Le Chambon – hung pictures of Pétain in their living rooms. He was the father, whose children, crushed and humiliated by an unexpected defeat, needed him to restore their destiny. What astonished us most was the change in our ferocious nationalist enemies. Ansett, Barber, Bertrand, and Paul Schmidt outdid one another in spitting out their hatred of the English, now guilty of having dragged France into an insane war. The death knell had sounded for the parliamentary system, rotten with Socialism, Communism, and pacifism, that had led France to the tomb. Everyone praised the authoritative regime inaugurated by Pétain, a strongman who could deal peer to peer with Hitler and Mussolini and bring back France's lost honor. People underscored Hitler's supposed moderation: he hadn't annihilated France and, unlike the way he had treated Poland, now wanted to work with France as a partner worthy of respect.

In no way did Theis and I agree with this opinion, though politics played a much greater role with Theis than with me. André Philip, a Protestant, Socialist deputy from the Rhône region, a brilliant orator and friend of the Jewish Socialist Léon Blum, had taken refuge in Le Chambon with his family. His wife and children moved into La Guespy, on the floor above the Theis family, where he strongly influenced my co-pastor. Léon Blum soon became the scapegoat responsible for France's defeat. André Philip had already organized political resistance to Pétain's regime and now courageously declared himself in solidarity with Blum.

My hostility to the regime had different sources. I still esteemed the courageous old man who dared to shoulder responsibility at the hour of defeat. Nevertheless, better informed than the average French person about Italy and Germany, countries I had visited, I had a premonition that Fascist pressure would soon be brought to bear on us. I was, therefore, on the lookout! Miss Hoefert and Theis had translated and published an excellent, short German work entitled *Village on the Mountain*, a diary of a German pastor persecuted by the Nazis. This became the bedside reading of our parish. We knew that Pastor Niemöller and a few colleagues had begun to resist the racist Nazification of the church by founding the Confessing Church at Barmen. We sought our inspiration in the example of these men whose principles were profoundly rooted in the Gospels.

Theis and I were the only conscientious objectors who had not been jailed since the beginning of the war. We published a small postcard silhouetting the Tower of Constance and the word "Resist."[6] On it we sent a monthly message of encouragement to all our friends connected with the Fellowship of Reconciliation, a missive consisting of biblical verses with a statement immune to censorship. It was therefore natural that our objector friends flocked to us when their prisons suddenly opened in June 1940 after the Germans arrived. Mrs. de Félice had already welcomed Claire, the wife of Henri Roser, and Henriette, the wife of Philo Vernier, and their children. We tried our best to help them, but it wasn't easy. They believed they had lost everything in Paris and in Belgium and were, like many refugees, unconsciously jealous of our happiness. We had lost nothing! We did not suffer! In addition, we were officially recognized, licensed pastors with a large parish. Our church was packed every Sunday, especially since the arrival of the refugees. At first, we did not suspect that our good friends were troubled by such feelings. Little by little, we came to this realization.

Henri Roser arrived first, completely exhausted. As the Germans approached Rambouillet, the authorities opened the prison where he was serving his sentence and cast him onto the street without money, severely weakened by his confinement. The entire population left the bombarded city of Gien. Roser got something to eat in a restaurant whose owner had gone mad and served him a light meal.

Then one day, Philo and Pierre Vernier arrived at our Chambon home. They too had been liberated by distraught jailors who, as the Germans

6 Situated in Aigues-Mortes, the Tower of Constance was used as a prison for the Huguenots who refused to convert to Catholicism after the revocation of the Edict of Nantes in 1685. Marie Durant (1711–1776) was held prisoner there for thirty-eight years. She is said to have inscribed the word "Resist" in the stonework with a knitting needle. She refused to convert to Catholicism.

arrived, had abandoned their wives and children. These panics were the savvy work of the "Traitor of Stuttgart," who, as the Germans advanced, simply picked up the telephone book, contacted a few important figures, especially government employees, and told them, "We will string you up in the city square because we know about your hostile activity against the German Reich." In Le Chambon, Théodore de Félice, warned in this manner, disappeared one morning into Switzerland and didn't return until after the German occupation ended.

The Vernier brothers experienced extraordinary ordeals and were separated from one another by the fleeing mobs. Philo had been arrested by the French police. His prison clothing and shaved head gave him away. Imprisoned again, he was threatened with death. The flight of the police saved his life, but he was caught by the Germans, suspected of spying, imprisoned again and almost shot. Forgotten once again by his jailors, he found an old bicycle without a handlebar in the corner of a wall. A broomstick did the trick. It was on this unlikely vehicle that he arrived one morning in a state of unbelievable exhaustion. His brother Pierre, nicknamed Piot, soon joined him, and we welcomed them with all our hearts. We had in our home at that time a young Alsatian au pair named Marie-Louise. She was pious and not terribly gifted, but honest and good. The first evening, Piot, just out of prison, fell in love with her; she was taken by his magnificent blue eyes. They were soon married and had many adventures. When their farm in the Midi didn't work out, he became director of the first farming school in the countryside of Le Chambon. They now live in Les Castors in Le Chambon with their numerous offspring. Piot is a vocational teacher at the École Nouvelle Cévenole.

In 1940, the arrival of Roser and Philo appeared providential to me. It seemed that Le Chambon, with the help of men like these two, could fulfill its mission as a "village on the mountain," a citadel of nonviolent resistance. I wanted to put them to work immediately, but they were worn down by months spent in prison. Moreover, their legal status was far from clear. None of the three had been formally pardoned for their offenses. None of the three wanted to be "picked up" by the police and reincarcerated, because, under Pétain, the old legal system was still in force. As a result, they lived almost clandestinely, and I couldn't assume responsibility for exposing them. To my great chagrin, they believed that my hesitations came from the fear that I might compromise myself by associating with them. For their part, once they learned that their own occupied regions had not been destroyed, they quickly thought of returning home, Roser to Aubervilliers, where he had evangelical work, and Philo to Belgium, where he was a pastor. They wrote to the judicial authorities to inform them of their situation and their presence in Le Chambon but never received an answer.

On top of that, American ladies from the Unitarian Church, animated by great good will, arrived in Le Chambon. They were persuaded, as we were also, that the war was not over and that we had to save as many children as possible by sending them to America. This idea did not seem as good to us as it did to them. We were tempted for a time to separate ourselves from our children but finally rejected their kind offer. The half-American Theis family sent their three oldest girls, Jeanne, Jacqueline, and Louise, to the United States.[7] The Rosers were also tempted to go, the more so since the International Fellowship of Reconciliation offered to pay for the trip and the family's stay in America. At the time, Henri Roser was one of its secretaries.

This issue caused an incredible scene between us, one that still causes Magda and me great pain. We went to see Henri and Claire Roser so we could discuss the situation with them and help them make the right decision. The Unitarians' offer was magnificent, and the future of the Roser family was otherwise terribly somber. If they returned to Paris, they would be in a German military zone, cut off from the International Fellowship of Reconciliation, their only financial resource. Roser could be incarcerated again at any time. That day, we appeared to them as the incarnation of the "Tempter," the devil himself. They were struggling to find the path of the most austere obedience to their faith. That meant Aubervilliers, perhaps prison. We weren't aware of their anguish. After they had asked repeatedly for our advice in the past, they now concluded that we "came to corrupt them, push them into disobedience!" There was a deluge of unjust accusations! They reproached us for intruding into their private life, for interfering in a problem that only concerned them. We had not suffered! We didn't understand the situation of a prisoner and his wife. We were ashamed to associate with them. We refused to allow Henri into the pulpit of our church, etc. In short, we left there aghast, with our friendship shattered, without ever understanding the roots of so much bitterness.

7 Pastor Theis's wife, Mildred, was American. In addition to the three girls named by Trocmé, the Theis family also sent their twins Marguerite and Françoise.

Many years later in Paris, Claire Roser was perfectly charming toward Nelly, whom she almost considered her daughter. But she was obviously struggling with a subconscious impulse of jealousy toward us. This impulse reappeared twice. When we were passing through Paris, we wanted to see Claire. She was about to have such a serious operation that her husband wouldn't leave her room at the Diaconesses' Hospital. Henri, anticipating our still unexpressed intention, let us know that Claire *could not bear* our visit, nor could he. He begged us to refrain from coming.

It was just before our arrival in Versailles in 1950, and we were delighted at the prospect of working with Claire and Henri. But that proved impossible. An invisible barrier separated us. Henri was always perfectly friendly when we met him in Versailles or in Paris at the Fellowship of Reconciliation. But we had to face the facts: Claire could never forgive us. For what? We still don't know to this day.

All this is so strange! In my life, 1940 marked the beginning of a whole series of painful discoveries about human nature. Being a person of faith did not ensure being easy to live with. On the contrary, men of great faith who dared to do what others were fearful of doing probably became touchier than others. Ever since, I have renounced a former dream: to establish a community where pacifists could practice their convictions. Pacifists, sadly, are much too difficult to live with.

Despite my sad observation about the difficulties caused by friends who are extraordinary in faith and spirit, I don't at all regret living my entire life among them. I have often been ashamed of my own lack of faith when faced with their example and faithfulness. In 1940, for example, I was ashamed that I hadn't gone to prison. I was still unaware of the other forms of courage and service that I would be offered.

As for the conscientious objectors, their fate was decided in 1941 in a strange way. The judicial authorities informed Roser, Philo, and Piot that they were granted total remission of their sentences. (Philo, however, was bothered on several occasions after the war and served jail time twice.) Why were they released from prison? They only learned much later. Hitler, in the conditions of the armistice that he imposed on France, demanded that all French people who helped him to victory be liberated, including conscientious objectors!

At that moment, the poor conscientious objectors were totally misunderstood by their own country, which imprisoned them as traitors, and the enemy, which took them for allies.

Lately, reading in the magazine *Match* the story of the 1917 riots that almost brought about the mutiny of French troops who refused to go to the frontlines, I was able to assess the profound reasons for the anger of the masses against pacifists. Is it not treason to refuse to fight when all others are "doing their duty" to "save the imperiled homeland"? Only loyalty to a supranational cause, like the kingdom of God, or humanity, can justify disobedience to the laws that govern a human society fighting for survival. Today, however, the possible annihilation of all life by the H-bomb has changed the meaning of the word "survival." A nation whose every inhabitant could be annihilated by nuclear weapons would not survive. Erased from the earth's surface, it would no longer know either honor or dishonor, victory or defeat. It would have simply ceased to exist.[8]

ON SUNDAY, JUNE 23, 1940, in the church of Le Chambon-sur-Lignon, André Trocmé read the following proclamation to his parishioners. It had been written by Trocmé and his co-pastor, Édouard Theis.[9]

Brothers and Sisters:

Yesterday, the president of the Protestant Federation of France gave a speech on the radio.[10] We wish to add our voices to it. In his address, Mr. Boegner calls on the French Protestant Church to humble itself for the sins that have led our people into the situation where they now find themselves.

Just as in Israel's moments of great distress, our time now is one of humiliation. Let us all ask pardon for whatever responsibility we bear for the current general catastrophe. Let us ask pardon for the sins we have committed and for those we have allowed to be committed. Let us ask

8 The following words were later inserted at this point in the manuscript: "1967 – Alas, the masses have become accustomed to atomic danger and, twenty-two years after the end of the war, the new generation has learned nothing. It has fallen victim to the same errors, the same reactions of collective defense, and the same righteousness as the preceding generations. I no longer believe that "mutually assured destruction" can be prolonged indefinitely. One day, a vapid, foolhardy person will show up to press the fateful button of the atomic bomb to save the ideal he champions. The masses will follow suit . . . and die."

9 André Trocmé did not include this document in his memoirs, and it does not appear in the French edition of the memoirs. We include it because of its personal and historical significance as perhaps the first nonviolent protest against the German-Vichy alliance.

10 In 1940, Pastor Marc Boegner was both the president of the national council of the Reformed Church of France and the president of the Protestant Federation of France.

pardon for our complacency, for our lack of courage that made moral recovery impossible in the face of threatening storms, for our lack of love when faced with the sufferings of others, for our lack of faith in God and for our idolatry of money and power, also for all the feelings unworthy of Christ that we have tolerated or sustained in our own hearts. In a word, let us ask pardon for our shared sin, which is the only real cause of these nameless misfortunes that have descended upon us.

Let us all humble ourselves before God as individuals, as heads or members of a family, as citizens, as Christians, as pastors, as church elders, as group leaders, as unionists, as faithful members of the church. It is from God that we beg forgiveness for our personal sins, for the sins of our people, and for the sins of contemporary humanity and our current church, with which we are united. It is from God alone that we seek spiritual recovery.

Nonetheless, we must avoid certain ways of humbling ourselves that would constitute disobedience to God.

First, let us not confuse humiliation with discouragement; let us not think and tell those around us that all is lost. It is not true that everything is lost. Gospel truth has not been lost. It will be freely proclaimed from this pulpit and in all our church gatherings and family visits. The Word of God is not lost, and it is precisely in the Word of God that we will find all the promises and possibilities of spiritual revival for ourselves, our people, and our church. Faith has not been lost. A genuine humbling of the self doesn't weaken faith; it leads to a more profound faith and a more fervent desire to serve God.

Secondly, let us not humble ourselves for the faults of others in the spirit of bitterness and resentment. Lately, during our pastoral visits, we have heard numerous complaints: complaints by soldiers about their officers, by officers about their soldiers; complaints by bosses about their workers, by workers about their bosses; complaints by the rich against the poor and by the poor against the rich; complaints by pacifists against patriots and by patriots against pacifists; complaints by believers against unbelievers and by unbelievers against believers. Everyone accuses everyone else, trying to dodge their own responsibilities by blaming their fellow citizens and foreigners. We have forgotten that God alone is able to judge and measure individual responsibility. We do not believe that this type of humility is fruitful or capable of preparing for the reconstruction of our country and our church.

Thirdly, as we humble our hearts, let us not humble our faith and our convictions founded on the Gospels. Although we have not made good use of the freedom we have been given, let us not renounce our freedom on the pretext of humility, becoming slaves who bow down in cowardly fashion before the new ideologies. Let us not have any illusions: the totalitarian ideology of violence has recently acquired enormous prestige in the eyes of the world because, from a purely human point of view, it has succeeded marvelously.

To humble ourselves is not to acquiesce to such a doctrine. We are convinced that the power of this ideology is comparable to the authority of the beast described in the Apocalypse. This doctrine is completely anti-Christian. For us, it is a question of conscience to affirm this today, as it was yesterday. Christians have given their lives to fight against this doctrine. To humble ourselves for our sins of the past is not to kowtow to this ideology today. It is by giving our lives to Jesus Christ in the service of his gospel and universal church that we will practice fidelity and true humility.

To our appeal for Christian humility, brothers and sisters, we would like to add a few recommendations in the name of our Lord, Jesus Christ.

First, as of today, let us abandon all division between Christians and all bickering among French people. Let us stop labeling one another with scornful terms: right-wing, left-wing, peasants, workers, intellectuals, proletarians, or landowners. Let us stop blaming one another for wrongdoings. Let us begin again to have confidence in one another, to greet and welcome one another, recalling at each encounter, as the first Christians did, that we are all brothers and sisters in Jesus Christ.

Next, having rid ourselves of distrust and hatred, as well as the political passions that breed them, let us decisively gather around Jesus Christ, the leader of the universal church. Let us adopt, as the source of our thoughts, obedience, and actions, his gospel and nothing but his gospel.

Finally, let us understand that returning to gospel obedience will obligate us to break with the world and the way of life we have accepted until now.

Formidable pagan pressure will be exerted to make us and our families passively submit to totalitarian ideology. If they don't succeed in immediately making us yield our souls, they will at least want us to yield our bodies. But as Christians, it is our duty to arm ourselves with the weapons of the Spirit and combat the violence brought to bear upon our consciences. We call upon all our brothers and sisters in Christ so that none of them will agree to collaborate with this violence, and, during the coming days, with the violence that will be directed against the English people.

To love, to forgive, to do good to our adversaries – this is our duty. But we must do so without abdication, without servility, and without cowardice. We will resist whenever our adversaries demand that we act in ways opposed to gospel teaching. We will do so without fear, but also without pride and without hatred. This moral resistance is not possible without a clean break from the inner bondage that has dominated us for a long time. A period of suffering, perhaps even of famine, is coming upon us. We have all lived, more or less, according to the cult of mammon, in the egotistical comfort of small families, with easy pleasures, laziness, and the bottle. Presently, we are going to be deprived of many things. We will even be tempted to try to escape unscathed, to take advantage of what we have left, even to dominate others. Let us abandon our pride and our egoism, brothers and sisters, and our love of money and our confidence in material possessions. Let us learn, today and tomorrow, how to rely on our heavenly Father, waiting for our daily bread and sharing it with our brothers and sisters, whom we must love as ourselves.

May God free us from our anguish as from false certainties; may God give us peace that nothing and no one can take away from God's children. May God console us in our grief as in all our struggles. May God deign to make all of us humble and faithful members of the church of Jesus Christ, of the body of Christ, in the expectation of God's kingdom of justice and love, where the will of God will be done on earth as it is in heaven.

14

City of Refuge

1940: FRANCE, EUROPE, and the world sink into war.

For me, it was the second time. I had already experienced this drama. I didn't know exactly what was lying ahead because history never repeats itself. I couldn't predict the future, but I knew it would be dreadful. I had my family to protect and my parish to guide. I had to stick to my beliefs, and I feared my own weakness. The incidents with Henri and Claire Roser had deeply humiliated me. In a sense, Roser had "tried" to go to prison by not declaring that he had children. I had children too and had declared them. As a result, I was not drafted into the military. The problem of loyalty to my beliefs remained. One way or another, I had to bear witness, but I didn't yet know how.

Later, I tried to explain to the "purists" that we do not decide to be nonviolent or truthful in advance as if we had an outline, a moral blueprint to follow automatically. Events appear almost always as a series of little, unexpected problems we must solve one at a time. We choose between two alternatives, one of which, in the final analysis, appears closer than the other to the laws of Jesus Christ. In that moment, one is sure of nothing. If the choice is the right one, if it does not conceal a hidden interest, it will open onto new possibilities and new opportunities for service. It will also present new problems and demand new options. That's how I would describe our often-hesitant march, step by step, through the darkness of the Second World War.

In 1938, when Édouard Theis and I founded our independent secondary school based on the practice of nonviolence, we had already made our choice. Now we had to continue. But it wasn't as simple as that. Viewed from the outside, the École Nouvelle Cévenole was flourishing:

18 students in 1938, 40 in 1939, 150 in 1940, and because of the influx of refugees, 250 in 1941, 300 in 1942, 350 in 1943!

Two problems immediately cropped up: Who would teach at the school and who would be included in the student body? Paul Schmidt, who wanted to take control of the school to make it a traditional Protestant establishment, wanted only Protestant teachers and students. Certainly, there were Protestants among our finest teachers, such as Miss Pont and Miss Grétillat, Mr. Braemer, Mr. Tissot, and later the famous philosopher Paul Ricoeur. But we also decided to hire foreigners, and if they presented themselves, Jewish teachers as well. As a result, we had Miss Williamson and Miss Maber (threatened with incarceration in internment camps by the police because they were English); Mr. Hano, a brilliant humanities professor at the Lycée Henri IV in Paris, dismissed from his position by the Pétain regime because he was Jewish; and Miss Hoefert, who was half-Jewish.

What a great environment, you might say! Yes, if everyone in Le Chambon had agreed with us. But people outside the school, such as the Schmidts, Bertrands, Barbiers, and Anstetts, spoke out against the Jewish teachers and called for an end to "the scandal." They trumpeted their demands from the rooftops, exaggerating all the unavoidable little incidents that arise in any teaching institution. "Can't you see?" they proclaimed. "This will never work with men like Theis and Trocmé." The school, I replied, was not yet on solid financial or pedagogical grounds.

Furthermore, what was this school? The three contiguous rooms of the church's annex had been too small for quite a while. To help, Theis had rented Les Genêts on the Côte de Molle from Miss Matile, as well as a dreary, abandoned building across from the railroad station from the Saigne family. That wasn't all: classes were held throughout the village, sometimes at the Pension Barraud or the Pension Charra, sometimes in basements or unheated attics. One entire winter, Magda had her Italian classes in a bathroom. The students were supposed to remain in place while the teachers galloped from one spot to the next, wasting the least amount of time possible. They always had "their tongues hanging out" and ran "like poisoned rats," the Chambonnais said.

When a new arrival asked the local train station master, "Where is the École Nouvelle Cévenole?" he responded truthfully with a broad gesture, "It's everywhere!"

The first serious problem arose from inside the school: the question of saluting the flag. Once in power, Pétain adopted the exterior trappings of Fascism. His portrait had the place of honor in the classroom. He ordered that every morning before classes, public and private school principals hoist the colors on a flagpole erected in the courtyard. The students, lined up at attention like soldiers in units, saluted the flag while raising their right arm in the typical Fascist manner.

Our history teacher, Pastor Henri Braemer, a traditional old-style patriot, heartily approved. It was an order; we had to obey. Furthermore, it gave France "a soul," and France "needed one." After discussing this matter, Theis and I said no to saluting the flag. "But they will close the school," groaned the pessimists among the teachers. "Too bad," declared the directors.

Braemer insisted. The confrontation was difficult. Darcissac, the director of the public school, whose courtyard was only separated from the church by the road going down toward the bridge, found the solution. "I'll put the flagpole from my school in the courtyard," he said, "at the edge of the low wall that separates it from the street. Forming a half-circle on the inside of the courtyard, my students will salute the flag. The students from the Collège can form the other half of the circle in the street. That way there will be only one ceremony." "All those who wish to salute the flag may do so," declared Director Theis.

For a few weeks, Braemer, with a small group of our students, saluted the public school's flag from the street. Then – we're in France after all – his zeal petered out, as did that of the public-school students. Saluting the flag became a weekly ceremony. Then the custom died out, and the state was unable to impose any sanctions.

Thanks to little acts of civil disobedience like this one, more comical than dramatic, the Pétain regime soon lost control. Several months later, the members of the French teaching corps, as a body, refused to take an oath to the head of state, knowing Pétain couldn't punish everyone. If only he had taken advantage of the nation's emotions when he first took charge of Vichy!

The same thing happened with *La Légion*, the association of World War I veterans that supported the "Savior of Verdun," Maréchal Pétain. "*Maréchal, nous voilà!*" (Marshal, here we are!) sang the legionnaires. In the spirit of its founders in 1940, the Legion was expected to control local administrations, keep an eye on public opinion, report the lukewarm and the traitors, who were then sent to internment camps ("political re-education camps," as they were called by Vichy).

Those who had not fought from 1914 to 1918 could also become members of the Legion, and they were by no means the least enthusiastic. When the Legion became less zealous, a man named Darnand,[1] one of Pierre Laval's collaborators,[2] infiltrated the group and created the Milice, modeled on the German SS. Its brutalities in much of France rivaled those of the Gestapo.

In 1940, the Legion presented itself to us in Le Chambon in sheep's clothing. The sheep they were after was Mr. Fay, the treasurer of our parish, a severely wounded veteran of World War I (with one arm and one leg missing), a good, peaceful man and an officer in the *Légion d'honneur* order of merit. "Join the Legion," he was told by the regional government offices. "You'll be named local leader. What a great role you will have in the nation's recovery."

Mr. Fay came to see me. "There is an unconditional oath of obedience to the Maréchal's orders," he told me. "As a Christian, can I accept this assignment?"

"To the extent that the orders you receive are not contrary to the will of God," I answered. Mr. Fay followed my advice. When he became the local leader, he very quickly refused to denounce his fellow citizens or control public opinion. "God forbids me to do that," he protested to his superiors. They were unable to counter his objections.

The Legion's failure allowed other forms of conscientious objection to develop in Le Chambon-sur-Lignon. Those who didn't dare resist openly refused nonetheless to denounce fellow citizens. In this way, the spirit of resistance gradually nourished in the École Nouvelle Cévenole spread to the entire parish.

I've already mentioned that when I was named pastor, I duly alerted the church elders that I would refuse to bear arms if I were drafted. Without approving my views, they accepted my right to hold them and openly promised to support me come what may. They remained perfectly loyal to Theis and me. When resistance to Vichy was necessary, however,

1 Joseph Darnand (1897–1945) was a right-wing political figure and a decorated French soldier. In 1943, he became the de facto leader of the Milice, Vichy's paramilitary police force. He was executed after the war in October 1945.

2 Pierre Laval (1883–1945), a former prime minister, would become Vichy prime minister in 1942. After the war he was tried and executed for treason.

soon after our refusal to obey racial laws, the parishioners became frightened. The first peasants willing to take Jews into their homes were Darbyites, who did not belong to our cultural association and whose doctrines outlawed any political involvement.

Our church elders followed their example, hesitatingly at first, but gradually with conviction.

On August 1, 1941, the parish openly said no for the first time. The week before, the town hall gave us an order from the government: "August 1, the anniversary of the Legion's founding, is a national holiday. Clergymen will have the bells of their churches rung at full peal for fifteen minutes starting at noon." It was the price we had to pay for the favors that the state accorded to churches.

I showed the order to Amélie, our tiny concierge, who worked in our home from time to time. "It goes without saying," I told her, "that you will do nothing of the sort, even if someone tries to make you do so." Amélie understood completely. She was a Darbyite at heart.

On August 2, I encountered Amélie in the village. The bells of the Catholic church had rung resoundingly, while those of our church had remained silent.

"Well, Amélie, did everything go well yesterday? No incidents?"

"Fine, Mr. Trocmé. No problems."

"No visitors?"

"Oh, yes, two women from the villas in the hills. You know, women who were all made-up."

"And?"

"They came looking for me. 'You're not ringing the bells, Amélie? Today is a national holiday.'"

"'The pastor didn't tell me to,' I told them."

"Well, given your pastor, that's no surprise. Hurry up, Amélie. It's already noon. It's an order from the Maréchal."

Amélie recounted these events with a sly, little smile.

"And how did you respond?" I asked her.

"I told them, 'The bells don't belong to the Maréchal, they belong to God. We ring them for God; otherwise not.'"

"Bravo! And what happened?"

"They ordered me to open the door for them so that they could ring the bells since I wouldn't do it. I defended my church! I told them I would not open the door and they had no right to enter without the pastor's permission. I stood firmly in front of the door. Wait, I'll show you." Amélie stationed herself squarely in front of me as she had before the two women, her short arms courageously spread wide apart to defend her church.

"How did everything end, Amélie?" Once again, she smiled mischievously.

"Oh, as you know, yesterday at noon, it was raining buckets. I was sheltered under the beam of the heavy door. They were in the courtyard. Soon they were drenched and left."

Nothing had happened, Amélie had told me, since the bells had not rung. Her courageous resistance was nothing to her, hardly worth mentioning. If, like pulling teeth, I hadn't drawn it out of her, I never would have known this story, so worthy of the Huguenots of old, who were unable to recant because they didn't know how.

Amélie died a long time ago. As for the two "ladies," you already know one of them – Mrs. Bertrand. Fifteen months earlier, she was collecting scrap metal intended to defeat Hitler, but now Pétain could claim her as his collaborator. There's no escaping patriotic conformism.

All might have gone well in Le Chambon during the war if we hadn't gone looking for foreign refugees – political refugees from Central Europe, Spanish Republicans, and above all, Jews.

Right after France's surrender to Germany in 1940, Magda and I had to face the problem head-on. As night fell at the end of an exhausting day, a German woman rang at the door of the presbytery. She was soaked from the rain. A Jew, she was fleeing the German advance. We gave her a place to sleep for the night and decided that we had to find shelter for her in Le Chambon. We turned first to the French Jews who had taken refuge in the area. They told us that by protecting German Jews, we would be endangering French Jews, who at that time still had nothing to fear. We went to the mayor, Mr. Guillon. "Absolutely no Jews here," he ordered. "I have already been threatened with death by the 'Traitor of Stuttgart.' This woman must leave."[3]

Magda's insistence had no effect. We had to obey. The poor woman spent the night in our home. She had left her shoes to dry at the oven door and they were burned to cinders. The next morning, we went

3 Trocmé may be correct here in saying that he spoke with Mr. Guillon, but others claim that Guillon had already resigned as mayor and gone to Switzerland. In that case, those words would have been spoken by his replacement, Mr. Grand.

into the village to find shoes. We found some, and the Jewish woman disappeared, leaving the memory of our naivety and foolishness on our consciences. We never heard another word about her, but we resolved henceforth never to reveal our secrets to those in authority.[4]

A few days later, Mr. Guillon left for Switzerland, as more Jews began to arrive in Le Chambon. The first ones to come were French, very fine people, very rich, forced out of their businesses, their factories, their jobs. They had a lot of money and didn't hesitate – any more than other refugees – to pay high prices for farm products. Their spending helped to augment the insufficient official rations.

It didn't take long for competition between rich refugees and the poor village population to create a painful tension. Le Chambon was not alone in this regard. The Vichy press denounced the Jews, blaming them for the black market. Public opinion, always stupid, turned the Jews into the scapegoats needed to explain the suffering people endured.

Nonetheless, Le Chambon was "at peace" on its mountain, while sinister rumors came to us from the Midi. Tens of thousands of foreigners, penned up in camps named Gurs, Argelès, and Les Milles, were living in frighteningly dirty, destitute conditions. Although we were in the South, the Gestapo already had inspectors organizing deportations of political suspects to Germany in the so-called "Free Zone" during the last months of 1940. Families were separated without pity. A Protestant group, the Cimade, led by Madeleine Barot, had succeeded in placing a few courageous social workers in the camps. Likewise, the French Red Cross and the American Quakers were trying hard to get help into the camps in the form of food and clothing. All this, while we in Le Chambon had everything we needed and were living in peace.

I convened the church elders. I pointed out our privileged situation, the ease with which they could carry out the pastoral duties of our parish during my absence. We had Édouard Theis, half-time pastor; Henri Braemer, pastor at the Collège; and Mr. Poivre, a retired pastor. I proposed that they send me as "an ambassador" to an internment camp to distribute food and other forms of help the parish would donate.

Édouard Theis agreed, and they consented to appoint me, but they asked me to investigate the camps first. I left for Marseille, on the first leg of my trip, to meet with a Quaker delegation from the American

4 In the manuscript, Magda adds: "This was when the issuing of false identity cards began."

Friends Service Committee, including Burns Chalmers, currently head of the Quaker enterprise in Washington, DC. We have remained good friends. He advised me not to go to the camps. "We already have several organizations there, and this could be awkward," he said. "You tell me that you come from a mountain village that still enjoys some degree of safety. Let me explain our problem. Together with the doctors and the French officials who direct the camps, we try to deliver medical certificates to the largest possible number of adults, declaring them unfit for work (at this time, deportation meant forced labor). If we don't succeed in saving the father, we try for the mother. If the parents are deported, we take charge of the children. We then get permission for the internees declared unfit for work to reside outside the camps. It is very difficult to find a French village willing to run the risk of receiving such compromised adults, adolescents, or children. Do you wish to be this community?"

The unexpected task was there before me. "But these children must be lodged, fed, and instructed," I said. "Who will take care of all that?"

"Find the houses and the instructors," Chalmers replied. "The Quakers and the Fellowship of Reconciliation will support you financially."

Burns Chalmers's promise was not forgotten when the United States entered the war in 1941. The Americans had long since left French territory. Nevertheless, with the help of Guillon and by channeling the necessary funds through the Ecumenical Council then taking shape in Geneva, the Quakers, the Fellowship of Reconciliation (thanks to Nevin Sayre), and the Congregationalists secretly provided for the housing of children and adolescents and for scholarships to the Collège. Courageous emissaries carrying money crossed the border clandestinely. Many were arrested. One of them was executed by the Germans.

Back in Le Chambon, I pulled off an easy victory with the church elders. They were relieved to know that their pastor was staying put. I called on my cousin, Daniel Trocmé, son of Henri Trocmé (headmaster of the prep school École des Roches), to open the first children's home. Until then, he had been an instructor at the École des Roches, which had been relocated to the southwest of France.[5] Without knowing it, I had signed my beloved Daniel Trocmé's death warrant.

5 Daniel Trocmé (1912–1944) was, as of the fall of 1940, instructor of mathematics and physics at L'École des Roches. From 1937 to 1940, he was an instructor of physics, chemistry, and natural sciences at the Lycée Chateaubriand in Rome.

Daniel was a true product of the École des Roches. An intellectual with rather vague ideas, often absentminded, he was totally devoid of selfishness and animated by a rigorous moral conscience. Poorly prepared to run a home for teenagers, he nonetheless came through admirably. We had rented a former children's boarding house in bad shape on the slope of the Côte des Barandons, two miles from town. The students had to rise early to get to school on time. Most local children, including our own, had adopted the oldest of the village's shoes, wooden clogs, which kept them warm in winter. But for the children of the Barandons boarding house, the trip was too long and the clogs too heavy. The shopkeepers hadn't stocked any shoes for a long time. As a result, Daniel spent part of his nights patching up shoes with bits of car tire so his children could attend class the next morning.

The Maison des Barandons, renamed Les Grillons (The Crickets), wasn't the only home for long. I had written to Switzerland requesting help from the International Civil Service. Rodolfo Olgiati, who had added the Secours Suisse aux Enfants (Swiss Children's Welfare Agency) to his other activities, turned up one fine morning in Le Chambon. He was enthusiastic about the idea of a city of refuge and founded La Guespy. Soon thereafter a third home, Faïdoli, opened. Its first director, Mr. Bohny, was a teacher from Basel, a former member of the civil service who became our friend and did an admirable job.

Later, we had a visit from Tracy Strong Jr., whose father was secretary general of the YMCA. At Charles Guillon's urging, I had been invited to take part in a YMCA "mission" to Hungary. This was just before the war, in 1938, and we were received, almost officially, by Count Teleki, nephew of the prime minister. Following this trip, Tracy Strong Sr. had asked me if I might one day be willing to become the international secretary of the YMCA. At the time, the idea greatly appealed to me. I accepted, in theory, but the war put things off until later. When I saw Tracy Strong Sr. again in Geneva in 1945, he told me that I was too old (I was forty-four) and that the YMCA's work in prisoner camps had enabled them to find future secretaries who had shared the tragedies of the camps. They were better able to lead the postwar YMCA. We know today that the postwar YMCA's "social program" produced few results. Will the YMCA ever recover from the poorly understood crisis of secularism it is still entangled in today?

Tracy Strong Jr. had come to Le Chambon to inspect the Joubert camp. Modeled on American summer camps, it was already under construction on the banks of the Lignon River. There were wooden cottages for dormitories, with a permanent central building to accommodate the administrative offices, dining hall, and recreational rooms. Marc Varilhac, son of the mayor's secretary, was promoted out of the blue to foreman of the camp and learned skills for his future entrepreneurial career on the job. I can still see myself visiting the construction site with Tracy Strong Jr. "Mr. Trocmé," he said suddenly, "I am very impressed by what I see here, and I will recommend that my church (the American Congregationalists) work with you as soon as the war is over. Right now, we must leave France because the United States will soon enter the war. But when the war is over, we will help your church. What would you suggest?"

This conversation took place just a short time before Pearl Harbor.

"If you want to propose something useful to your friends," I told him, "propose that the United States send a 'youth ambassador' to Le Chambon, a pacifist and a member of the Fellowship of Reconciliation, so the ambassador's ideas correspond to ours."

My proposal didn't fall on deaf ears. When I traveled to the United States in 1945, a man named Clark from the American Board of Congregationalists, under the auspices of Nevin Sayre, took the trouble to come from Boston to New York solely to meet me. The next day, in a coffee shop, I was introduced to a young couple ready to come to France as "ambassadors." The husband, who had just gotten out of a Civilian Public Service camp (alternate service during the war for conscientious objectors), was named Howard Schomer. One of the first American "fraternal workers" in Europe, he played a major role in Le Chambon and at the Collège.

Tracy Strong Jr. also encouraged Student Aid (coming from the Universal Federation of the Associations of Christian Students and, therefore, from the YMCA) to rent the Hôtel des Roches and house students from the internment camps. Professor Legal of Montpellier, then Mr. Pantet, and finally Daniel Trocmé directed this house. It was the scene of a tragedy I will relate later.

Next, it was the Cimade's turn. They rented the Coteau Fleuri, a large boarding house located in Les Tavas. Our friend Françoise Perrotte, a former evangelist from the North, ran this house, which sheltered men, women, and children, all snatched from the claws of the Gestapo.

At the end of 1941, seven houses for refugees were functioning at full capacity in Le Chambon. Like a rolling snowball, refugees and those taking care of them arrived, increasing the workforce at our school, the public school, and the annex, as well as boosting attendance at Sunday worship.

In the church on Sundays, you could hear our hearts beating. Theis's and my sermons were anxiously awaited events. Some people reproached Theis for insisting too much on "Thy Kingdom Come" of the Lord's Prayer, which the followers of Vichy, as well as the Third Reich's spies who made a point of attending, found offensive. At our services we often proposed principles of resistance and obedience to the Gospels that most Protestants adopted with great courage.

In the streets of Le Chambon, believers and nonbelievers, Christians and Jews, reformed Protestants and Eastern Orthodox Christians intermingled easily. The real problem concerned relations between the local country folk – upset in their daily habits, overwhelmed by the refugees that they confused with tourists, shocked by the loose conduct of the Collège's students – and the city dwellers, who, in their turn, were irritated by the sluggishness and hesitations of the peasants.

The traditional neighborhood meetings had long seemed outmoded to me. Bible study groups saved the situation. Today, unfortunately, thirty years after my arrival, everything is back to normal in Le Chambon: Sunday school, local meetings, back to square one. None of the reforms stuck. It is routine that kills the church. Typically, the pastor arrives at exactly 2:30 p.m. at a low-ceiling farmhouse and spreads his books on a large table pushed off in a corner. Before beginning, he scrutinizes the faces of fifteen to twenty old-timers (they look old when they're forty) lined up on benches. He indicates a hymn, intones the hymn, sings the hymn, almost as a solo, with the accompaniment of several quavering, off-key voices. He reads the Bible, offers some Bible commentary, tries to catch a furtive glance, a curious, and often emotional but soon lowered look from an impenetrable listener, ends with a hymn, a prayer, another hymn. He shakes the callous hands of those leaving and sits down with his hosts to have a cup of ersatz coffee and a slice of pound cake while listening to the dreary local news – sicknesses, infirmities, accidents, deaths, regrets about the past, detachment from the present, worries about the future. "Let's get out of here," he says to himself, "before night and fog descend on us!" The pastor must shuffle through the snow or wade through the mud as he takes a detour across the meadows to reach the houses of old-timers unable to leave home. He commiserates with them. The sweat from this effort freezes quickly in the poorly heated kitchens where the sick person, seated on a wobbly chair, maintains a mediocre warmth by shoving broom twigs into the stove while exchanging monosyllables with his pastor.

During the war, all this tradition was replaced by weekly Bible study, directed by lay refugees. Every two weeks, those responsible gathered in the church. Under the pastor's direction, they discussed two questionnaires. The goal was to elicit spontaneously from the participants themselves a valid interpretation of a chosen biblical text. With highly skilled people such as Suzanne Bidgrain (former secretary of the Universal Federation of the Associations of Christian Students), Miss Pont, Mr. and Mrs. Poivre, and Mrs. Cambessédès, discussions quickly became animated. The participants then dispersed to thirteen different districts and redid their Bible lessons, making them accessible to ordinary people, sometimes even eliciting discussion from the people involved. These Bible studies were a great success. The participants doubled in number and younger people joined. Never had the parish lived a more intense spiritual life. Even more importantly, the prayer that rose from these groups was fervent, practical, and tangible. It was here, and not elsewhere, that we received from God answers to the complex problems of sheltering and hiding Jews. This is where we devised our nonviolent resistance. Nonviolence is not a theory superimposed on reality; it's an itinerary that we explore day after day in communal prayer and in obedience to the directives of the Holy Spirit.

Our parish flourished, but sadly, I only heard reproaches from my church elders. The peasants are like that. They complained that they "no longer see their pastor." The elders whined: "The lay teachers will never be able to replace him." In fact, they saw me more often in their districts than in the past, but the Bible studies were weekly instead of monthly, and the pastor couldn't be everywhere at the same time. The grumbling continued. "Our pastor is taking care of tourists and young people. He's abandoning the sick," they murmured. It's true that I visited the sick less often, those who took between fifteen and twenty years to die. But Miss Verdeil covered these visits well. Our earthy evangelist, she moved about repeating in her southern French accent, "Old-timers, I love them. Why wouldn't I? I have the soul of a butterfly, despite my slightly weighty appearance." What an admirable assistant and how easily she adapted to our region! While I devised, organized, and renewed, she faithfully continued her acts of kindness on behalf of the old and the sick. She scolded them in a friendly manner, wrested a smile out of them, and they loved her too.

IN 1942 THE POLICE NETWORK began to tighten around Le Chambon. That spring, Maréchal Pétain paid an official visit to the department of the Haute-Loire. There was a stampede. All the motor vehicles in Le Chambon received fuel vouchers for the occasion. Local people and tourists went to Le Puy-en-Velay, our provincial capital, to wave flags in tribute to the Maréchal. I still remember Dr. Le Forestier's enthusiasm. He absolutely insisted that I accompany him and was astonished and scandalized when I refused to do so.

At the beginning of the summer, the prefect of the Haute-Loire region, Mr. Bach, sent me an apology. He had not convinced the Vichy authorities to let the Maréchal come to Le Chambon and witness the admirable works of French Protestant youth!

The "admirable works" of the young people were, of course, the Collège (still no fixed location), the homes for refugee children, the YMCA Camp Joubert, and several male and female scout troops under the excellent direction of Naho, alias Pierre Brès, the school's physical education teacher.

The prefect's letter continued in the following manner: "To compensate for missing the Maréchal, you will have an official visit on August 15 [if my memory is correct] from Vichy's Youth Minister, Mr. Lamirand. I know you are eager to make this a memorable visit."

Theis and I were devastated. For two years, we had done our best to keep our youth free of government influence. Vichy had immediately tried to regroup all youth into the blue-shirted "Compagnons de France." With their Fascist salute of the flag, their bugles, parades, social activities, workcamps, and cult of homeland and the Maréchal, they resembled the Hitler Youth too closely to succeed in France. Catholic and Protestant scouts soon demanded their autonomy. The state capitulated, but it still generously subsidized youth movements to control them better.

In Le Chambon, we taught pacifism and were opposed to all totalitarian systems. We had decided to oppose Lamirand's visit when, from "on high," we were made to understand that the decision was out of our hands. The "on high" was Jean Beigbeder, nicknamed "Owl Eye" (he was almost blind), an important scout leader. He came from Paris to tell us he would take care of things. There would be a banquet in the Joubert camp, an official procession down to the sports field in Le Chambon where all the different groups would assemble, then a welcome in the church followed by a prayer service. "It will be magnificent," Beigbeder told me. "Besides, Lamirand is a good guy, you'll see."

We were cornered, but things worked out our way, not Lamirand's. The so-called banquet turned into a very simple meal served from the meager rations granted us by official supply regulations. I was seated next to the minister. "It's better like this," the "good guy" Lamirand said to me with a laugh. "It's more in line with the Maréchal's spirit, more patriotic." He was dressed in a superb navy-blue uniform loosely copied from German uniforms.[6] His laugh sounded forced because, despite rationing, he was accustomed to official spreads.

The "procession" was greeted by a sullen village. I was in Lamirand's car. No flags at the windows, no one on the sidewalks; the people had complied with their pastors' wishes. Lamirand was astonished. Surrounded by the prefect, the subprefect, and the mayor's assistant, he got out of the car at the sports field. The pastors didn't follow him: they didn't want to be involved in a public demonstration. No parade had been planned. Hundreds of inquisitive children crowded around him, hoping to shake his hand: "Bonjour, Monsieur!"

"Bonjour, bonjour," responded Lamirand, surprised and charmed by so much "spontaneity." Pierre Brès gave a short talk, recalling Romans 13 and the respect due to those in authority. In the commotion, Lamirand responded with only a few words. It seems he had prepared a long speech that he felt obliged to retract.

He then went to the church, where the pastors awaited him. Since Theis and I had refused to preach before the authorities, Marcel Jeannet, a Swiss pastor and president of the local church government, spoke. How picturesque: a Swiss pastor officially welcomed the representative of the French government. He did well, was brief, and recalled the position of the church: obedience to the state, but on the condition that the state not coerce the church into infringing on the law of God. I was seated next to Lamirand. I passed him a hymnal and showed him the verses. Awkwardly, he tried to sing. The poor man! And his day wasn't over yet.

6 In fact, it was the prefect, Robert Bach, who wore the official-looking uniform. As Pierre Sauvage's *Weapons of the Spirit* 1987 documentary shows, on this day Lamirand wore an elegant tweed jacket, riding pants, and high leather boots.

As we left the service, a dozen of the older students at the Collège, among them several future theologians, approached Lamirand and read him a document, asking him to take note of it. Here are the contents of that document to the best of my recollection:

> Dear Minister Lamirand,
>
> We have learned about the scenes of horror that took place three weeks ago in Paris. French police, on the orders of the occupying powers, arrested all the city's Jewish families in their homes and confined them in the Winter Bicycle Stadium.[7] Fathers were snatched from their families and deported to Germany, children brusquely taken from their mothers, who met the same fate as their husbands. We know from experience that the decrees of the occupying powers are quickly imposed in non-occupied France by the French head of state, who claims they are his own spontaneous decisions, and we fear that these measures inflicted on the Jews of Paris may soon be applied in the Southern Zone.
>
> We want you to know that there are several Jews among us. But we don't distinguish between Jews and non-Jews. That would be contrary to the teachings of the Gospels. If our comrades, whose only fault is their birth into a different religion, receive a deportation order or are required to list their religion in a census, we will encourage them to disobey these orders, and we will do our best to hide them.

Mr. Lamirand turned pale and responded: "These questions are none of my business. Address them to the prefect." He got back to his car as fast as he could.

The prefect was furious. He knew very well who had inspired this text and turned to me: "Pastor, this day was supposed to be a day of national harmony. You are sowing division!"

"There can be no question of national harmony when our brothers are threatened with deportation."

"Indeed, I have already received such orders, and I will carry them out. The foreign Jews who live in the Haute-Loire are not your brothers. They belong neither to your church nor to your country. Furthermore, they are not being deported."

7 On July 16 and 17, 1942, in Paris roughly 9,000 French policemen arrested over 13,000 Jews (men, women, and children), most of whom were held in the Vélodrome d'Hiver, an indoor bicycle arena. 12,884 of these persons were eventually deported.

"What's going on then?"

"My information comes directly from the Maréchal himself, and the Maréchal doesn't lie. The Führer is an intelligent man. Just as the English have created a Zionist home in Palestine, he has ordered the resettlement of all European Jews in Poland. There they will have land and houses. They will lead the life that best suits them, and they will cease to contaminate the West. In a few days, my staff will come and identify the Jews living in Le Chambon."

"We don't know what a Jew is. We only know men."

(Now menacingly) "Mr. Trocmé, you had best be wary. Seven of your fellow citizens write to me regularly about your subversive activities. Until now, I haven't paid much attention, but I'm aware of what's going on. If you're not careful, you'll be the one I'll have to lock up. A word to the wise should suffice."

He returned to his car.

There you have it! No one knew in 1942 exactly what would happen to the Jews who were deported. We learned about Auschwitz, Dachau, or Maidanek only *after* the liberation. Nazi Germany created such terror among Germans themselves that no one among those who knew dared utter a word. They didn't dare believe it. They didn't want to believe it, for fear of being sent there themselves. Where? To the death camps, the gas chambers, the crematoriums.

Therefore, we knew nothing, but what we did know was that it was wrong to turn over a brother who had entrusted himself to us. No one in Le Chambon in 1942 would agree to do that.

HERE I INSERT a short excerpt of a sermon André Trocmé gave in his church in Le Chambon on Sunday, August 16, 1942, a few days after Georges Lamirand's visit. After describing the roundup of Jews in Paris on June 16, he added:

For several days now, these same measures are being enforced in our Free Zone where foreign Jews are hunted.[8] It's a disgrace for all of Europe that these acts, which we had thought relegated to the bygone past, can still take place, and that we, the French, haven't acted against such barbaric practices.

8 The mass round-up of foreign Jews organized by Vichy in the Free Zone took place ten days after this sermon.

The Christian faithful should get down on their knees and ask God's forgiveness for their failures and current cowardice. Let us pray to God to inspire our leaders – who authorize such excessive measures in our country – to seek more moderate, lenient, and humane advisors.

I tell you this because I can no longer remain silent. I do not say these things in a spirit of hatred but with sadness and shame for humanity and our country.

HOW MANY JEWS were in Le Chambon in the summer of 1942? Not that many, perhaps a hundred, or 150 at the most. We knew them all. Several farms sheltered many of them. The others were divided between the village and the seven refugee houses. We had two in our home: Monsieur Colin and Madame Berthe. Mr. Colin came to us one morning with a warm letter of recommendation from Pierre Vernier, then the manager of a farm near Sanary. Pierre Vernier was a good friend, so we took Colin into our home and treated him like a brother.

His real name was Cohn. He came from Berlin and was a cabinetmaker. About thirty-five years of age, prematurely old, with a jaundiced complexion, already bald, and very likeable – a bit too much sometimes – his sudden flashes of anger revealed a rather egotistical nature. In our house, he became a handyman. We certainly had no need for his services, but to occupy his time and give him a sense of purpose, we asked him to make furniture for us. Our children liked him and joked around with him.

Mr. Colin worked in the huge attic of the old presbytery, where he also fixed up a hiding place in case the police came to search the house.

To get a ration card in his name at the mayor's office, I had to falsify his foreign-national card. With very light scratching, Cohn became Colin. Mr. Vérilhac, the mayor's secretary, groaned audibly when given such suspicious papers. At first, he even refused to serve us. "Come back when you have other papers to show me," he declared in a loud voice to the frightened supplicants in his office. The presence of a denouncer among those in earshot would have sufficed to get the suspect deported. Admonished by the pastor, Mr. Vérilhac changed his attitude. He learned to look the other way when necessary. He was even grateful to receive false papers that allowed him to tell the Vichy police on inspection tour: "Nothing to report," meaning "no Jews in the township."

A few months later, Madame Grünhut (Green Hat) turned up. She was a fifty-year-old Jewish woman who had escaped from Karlsruhe, Germany. She looked very Jewish and spoke with such a strong accent that we simply buried her papers in an iron box in the garden and asked Darcissac, the director of the public school and secretary of the parish, to give her a completely new identity. She became Alsatian and Aryan, of course. Darcissac, a great photographer, became a specialist in forging false papers.

I have forgotten Madame Grünhut's assumed name. At home, we called her Madame Berthe and asked her to do the cooking. She was grouchy and clumsy. The smell of burnt food hovered constantly in the house. "We only have potatoes and root vegetables," we told her. "Boil them but don't burn them." She responded crabbily, *"Si ch'ai, che fais, si ch'ai pas, che fais pas"* (If I have, I do. If I don't have, I don't do). This expression became proverbial in our home. It meant: "If you give me butter, I will prepare good meals, but if there's no butter, I'll burn the food."

Don't believe for a moment that life was sad in the presbytery in 1942. On the contrary, this was the happiest year of our lives. Dr. Le Forestier, after living for a year as our boarder and filling the house with whimsy, banter, and joy, married the ravishingly beautiful Danielle Vérine. He lived at Côte de Molle in a lovely villa but came often to visit us. Pierre Brès and his no less beautiful Dutch spouse were also among our friends.

Nelly, an enthusiastic scout, was fourteen, with thick braids and a healthy body. At twelve, Jean-Pierre was interested in everything. He took piano lessons from Mrs. Manchon, Theis's sister, who considered him extremely gifted. He thought deeply and came back from a sojourn in Leysin in love with poetry and the mountains. Jacques, ten, was affectionate and overly sensitive, an enthusiastic but difficult student. The time he spent with Aunt Annette in Geneva did him a world of good. Daniel, oh Daniel, was no problem at all. He was stocky, realistic, played with marbles, and fit in perfectly in the village. Who could have foreseen what was to come?

The house resonated with songs, cries of joy, sometimes with disputes. Magda, overworked and undernourished, took in boarders. There was a famous trio of them: Vivien, Mélèze, and Ondine. Those were the nicknames of the three young women whose names I forget, except that of Catherine de Seynes, the one called Vivien. They helped somewhat by setting the table.

HERE I INSERT A LETTER written by André Trocmé in January 1943 to his older brother, Robert. Prudently, André addressed the letter to "Simone." The letter describes the Trocmé family's life during this unusual time.

Your January 13 message touched us deeply. I have little taste, alas, for the inter-zone cards where we can only write a few words with trivial news.[9] Today I'm able to write you at greater length, and I'm delighted to do so. If I have time, I'll compose a short account of the Chambon Trocmés.

Worries: first, health. The children are fine, very well in fact. Their parents, less so. Magda, always overworked, for reasons I'll tell you about in a moment, is very thin. She has trouble eating and is aging so quickly that we became worried about the future. A medical consultation in Lyon, however, has reassured us that there is nothing dangerous in this rapid aging. She needs less fatigue, less nervous tension, and more rest. She's unable to find a maid. The refugees pay a fortune and snatch them up.

Now even I am beginning to crack. Terribly overworked, my mind went blank in the pulpit the Sunday before Christmas, and I was so mentally exhausted that I had to cancel all meetings for a week. Ten days in Dieulefit after Christmas with Magda put things back in order. But, having barely returned to Le Chambon, I was pinned down by the old lumbago I had gotten rid of three years ago, and I spent two weeks barely able to walk. All this is a warning because it's tied to obvious burnout. The death of my friend Samuel Cornier, the pastor in Caudry who left nine children behind, greatly upset me. I must find a way out of this whirlwind. But, practically, that's impossible.

So, you see, nothing but work, and never a quiet moment in a house always full of people coming and going.

Next, financial worries: In January, I started making 2,000 francs a month (before that I earned less). The cost of living here, according to the people arriving from elsewhere, is about twice what it is in Paris. Certainly, we are privileged: we have potatoes, a little butter, skim milk,

9 During the occupation, the authorities permitted family correspondence from one zone to the other (Free/Occupied) on formal printed cards where one filled in information—about one's whereabouts, one's health, one's needs. No writing was allowed between the lines.

some meat, and even food coupons! But the coupons are not always redeemable, and we must buy everything at illegal prices. We spent 24,000 francs – yes! – to get our stock of potatoes. They aren't that expensive anywhere else in France. We spent just about the same amount on winter firewood, which you can get at half that price in neighboring townships, but we can't find any way of transporting it. Our peasants, overwhelmed with cash offers from the refugees and the students at the Collège, have completely lost their minds. Our budget is totally unbalanced. We are consuming large portions of our capital. If that weren't enough, Magda is killing herself working: she is giving twenty-four hours of Italian lessons a week and has three boarders, not to mention the refugees.

All this gives us a lot to worry about. We know that others are in a similar predicament, but we want to escape this quandary and with it the sense that we are throwing capital, health, future, and household harmony down a bottomless hole simply to survive. On a short trip to Valence, Magda saw Yvonne, who is in the same boat. It seems that getting food supplies today is much more difficult in the south of France than in the north.

That covers the material side of things. Here's the moral side: you may be aware that this summer we were able to help about sixty Jewish refugees in our home. They were hidden, fed, saved from deportation, and often taken into safe territory. You can imagine what struggles with the authorities and real dangers that created for us. We were threatened with arrest and underwent long interrogations. Today, thanks to the occupation, we appear to be reconciled with the authorities. But because our deeds have become known and spread to Périgueux by way of Saint-Étienne, Jews, by the dozens, by the hundreds, have come to Le Chambon. My normal ministry has been completely shut down. Usually, in the summer, our dining room serves as a waiting room for ten to fifteen people a day. Now it's a waiting room all year long.

I've described the atmosphere. You already know the setting: 3,300 parishioners of whom 2,000 are peasants, 700 live in the village, and between 500 and 600 are from outside the area. Of these: 160 Central European refugees, adults, children, students in six different homes; 300 students at the Collège (the Pourtalès and the Turckheims, members of the Protestant aristocracy, sit on the same benches as our young peasants); about thirty instructors, fifteen or so directors of boarding houses, of music, conferences, singing, and four scout troops. There is a preparatory school of theology, a workshop for professional development, and soon there will be an agricultural school. Everyone passes through the presbytery, but we no longer know everyone by name. The school has been *too* successful. There would be 400 students if we were able to house them all, and these are not refugees but students whose parents have entrusted them to us to be educated.

Compared with most other churches, we are spoiled when it comes to staff. About twenty future pastors serve here as leaders, presiders, and monitors. We have thirty-five youth staff and twenty Bible study group leaders. Our local men's groups have about two hundred participants, with fifteen staff who give lectures every two weeks on "the individual, the family, and the Christian community."

Since November I have had a secretary who takes care of my mail and financial affairs and gives me a hand with practical tasks. The outstanding generosity of our friends has granted me this luxury which is, in fact, a necessity, since it's thanks to him that my mail is finally up to date and I can write you such a long letter.

What has become of our family life in this whirlwind? We are rarely alone with our children. All of us find this painful. Magda and I tenaciously hold on to our Mondays together and still manage to read a good number of novels to each other, but on Mondays the children are in class, and in the evening we are exhausted! A month's vacation compensates us for these disappointments. Yet, since we must take it before the "summer vacation season," we only have the children with us for two weeks. Nonetheless, our little ones make the most of every experience. They are learning the great lessons of life while they are young. Every day, they see passing before them new dramatic situations as well as interesting and original people – a musician, a famous historian, an inventor, an artist.

André

TWO WEEKS AFTER Lamirand's visit, the first bolt out of the blue interrupted our euphoria. One Saturday evening during the summer of 1942, automobiles followed by police cars and motorcycles appeared in the market square. Policemen got out, stationed themselves everywhere in the village, and set up headquarters at the mayor's office.

I was soon called to the mayor's office, where I found myself in the presence of a senior civil servant, police chief for the department. There was none of the politeness that characterized Lamirand's visit. The chief was brutally direct:

> Pastor, we know in detail about the illegal activities you've been involved in. Several Jews – whose names I know – are hiding in this town. I have an order to take them to headquarters for a police check (he lied; it concerned deportation). Everything must take place in orderly fashion. You will give me the list of these people and their addresses, and you will advise them wisely, so they don't try to escape.

"I don't know the names of these people," I replied to the police chief (I did not, in fact, know their real names), "but even if I had the list you request, I wouldn't give it to you. These people came to the Protestants of the area seeking refuge and protection. I am their pastor, which means I am their shepherd. The shepherd's role is not to denounce the sheep confided to his care."

"Pastor," replied the chief, whose tone became hostile, "what I told you is not advice but an order. If you oppose the authorities, you are the one who will be arrested and deported. I will hold you responsible for all unacceptable resistance to the laws of your country. Furthermore, the Jews are not members of your flock. They are foreigners, suspicious types, and black-market peddlers. You are not responsible for their well-being. If you refuse to give me the list, at least give me a note in your handwriting advising them to submit voluntarily to the head count to which they are subject."

"I refuse to give them advice that endangers their safety."

"OK, it's settled. I will give you until noon tomorrow, Sunday, to make up your mind. If you disobey the orders, you will be arrested, along with your accomplices. Furthermore," (he let out a menacing laugh), "your resistance is futile. You have no idea of the means at our disposal: motorcycles, cars, radios. We *know* where those you protect are hiding!"

When I returned home, I sent for the scouts: "Go quickly and warn so-and-so, on such and such farm, that they have to flee tonight."

This warning set into motion a kind of "battle plan" we had put in place soon after Lamirand's visit. It called for dispersing the Jews "into nature," some going into Ardèche, the neighboring department, and the others hiding in the woods.

That same evening, I had a visit from a trembling Mr. Grand, the deputy mayor, to whom Mr. Guillon had left all the difficult tasks. He begged me to capitulate. "It's my own safety and my family's that's at stake; I am threatened with arrest tomorrow at noon," he pleaded. "I am too," I responded, "but sometimes we have to say no to injustice."

The next morning, Sunday [August 30], was one of the "great days" in Le Chambon during the war. Emotion and curiosity had brought out a huge crowd. The church was packed. Many people were unable to get in. Theis and I, convinced that we were going to be arrested at noon, read a declaration from the pulpit, the text of which should be somewhere in my papers. We urged our listeners to obey the law of God rather than men. Our aim was to hide those who had come to our church seeking refuge. We must exercise in their favor "the right of sanctuary" established in the Hebrew Bible for innocent people being persecuted.

When we left the church, emotions were high. The congregation said farewell to us. But nothing happened.

Nothing happened because during services something had happened at the mayor's office. Summoned in haste, the municipal council (a delegation appointed ex officio by the government), of which our evangelist, Miss Verdeil, was a member, had met. They were surrounded by policemen with machine guns in hand. At the command of the police chief, the council signed an "appeal" to the Jewish refugees, entreating them in no uncertain terms, to keep the peace, to report to the mayor's office that same afternoon and submit obediently to the scheduled head count.

A rather funny census! Two or three buses were already stationed on the main square to take the Jews away. The writer of the appeal was Mr. Monjot, one of the summer teachers and a boarding house director, whose text began with the baffling and characteristic words: "Indisputably comprehensible measures . . ." What cowardice! What lapses of conscience can fear and conformism generate, as this text sadly attests.

Luckily, none of the Jews summoned by the municipal council showed up at the mayor's office. Then, toward the end of the afternoon, the police ran wild.

First, they searched the village houses, demanding everyone's identity papers, opening cupboards, going down into basements, going up into attics, and knocking on walls to see if they rang hollow. They were often polite, sometimes rude – but they found no one.

The next day, the police searched the farms in the surrounding areas. I have often asked myself if this two-step operation was the result of awkwardness or already the sign of an unwillingness to carry out these orders. This second day didn't produce any results either. The police returned empty-handed. The villagers related the adventure of a lieutenant, dressed in a brand-new uniform, who, in searching around a farm, stepped on rotten boards covering a manure pit. A very foul-smelling rescue followed. The farmers washed his things and comforted him with coffee. The adventure had turned from tragedy to comedy, and the anxiety of the first day was replaced by an ironic and friendly welcome reserved for "those decent fellows who opened Pandora's box of miseries." "Come on in," the farmers said. "Have a drink with us! Sit down. Jews? What would Jews be doing in these parts? Have you ever seen one? I've heard they have hooked noses."

EVERYTHING WENT WELL, except for Mr. Stekler. He was a nervous Austrian lawyer, the brother of Miss Stekler, an enterprising elderly Protestant who lived among the rich as a governess after the racial laws chased her and her brother from their country. Convinced that he didn't have enough Jewish ancestry to merit deportation, Stekler stayed at home, where the police nabbed him. Two empty buses were stationed in the main square. In one of them, looking pitiful, was Stekler. A menacing policeman prevented anyone from going near him. Very few people knew the timid Stekler, but several people of good will, seeing him so overwhelmed, approached, hoping to give him a small package.[10] The policeman, at first unyielding, finally agreed to pass on the object. "We can bring things to Mr. Stekler," echoed within the presbytery. Young people took care of spreading the news to the entire village. Soon there was a parade, a demonstration, around the bus. Disconcerted by such obvious signs of affection, the police discovered that the supposedly guilty man they held (spy, black-market peddler, whatever) was perhaps not a criminal after all. Their weakened opposition soon turned into complicity. Pyramids of objects – woolen clothing, shoes, food – piled up

10 Magda adds on the manuscript: "Our Jean-Pierre was the first, bringing him the chocolate he had gotten with his ration card."

on the bench next to Stekler who, with weak handshakes and tearful eyes, thanked his friends and benefactors.

On Monday evening, the bus took Stekler, alone, to his destiny. The village was ashamed of letting him leave. But two days later – oh, what a triumph – Stekler reappeared, free as a bird, smiling and struggling to carry all the packages that had been given to him.

What had happened? At the prefecture, they pointed out that according to German law Stekler was "Jewish enough" to be deported. But according to Vichy law, which was a bit more liberal, Stekler was not Jewish.[11] They had to release him.

Thus ended "the great round-up" in Le Chambon during the summer of 1942. Or rather, not quite. The police remained in the village for three weeks. In the morning you could hear motorcycles backfiring. They were going to "surprise" a nest of Jews tired of living like woodsmen. It was in vain. The farms on the Plateau had dogs that barked even at distant sounds. For centuries in this wooded country where silence reigns, people have known what was going on. The "nest" was always empty when the police arrived. Furthermore, the police were influenced by public opinion and no longer believed in their mission.

About that time, Étienne Grand, son of the mayor of Le Chambon and today an architect, had a strange encounter. He was leaning back against a tree, reading, when a policeman passed by. From a distance, Étienne heard: "Psst, psst." He continued reading.

"Yo, over here," the policeman called, a bit louder.

Étienne raised his eyes. The policeman performed a strange pantomime: with a gesture, he signaled to Étienne to "buzz off." Étienne had no idea what the man meant. Uncomfortable, the policeman came closer: "Go away," he said. "I didn't see you."

Étienne inquired, "You didn't see me? What are you talking about? What do you mean?"

"I'm looking for Jews," he replied. "If you don't take off, I'll have to arrest you."

"But I'm not Jewish," exclaimed Étienne, and then he realized that because of his dark complexion, large nose, and thick lips, the worthy police officer had mistaken him for a Jew.

11 This statement is incorrect. One was more likely to be identified as Jewish under Vichy law than under German law.

"Oh! You're not Jewish," cried out the relieved cop. "So much the better, because I don't like the work they make us do."

The "conversion" of the police succeeded so well that in the months after the Germans occupied the "Southern Zone," a mysterious voice on the telephone would issue warnings. It probably came from Le Puy: "Beware tomorrow morning."

That was all it took for us to put our well-developed plan, "Disappearance of the Jews," into action.

15

Imprisonment

IT WAS IN THE FALL of 1942, I think, that Commissioner Praly arrived in Le Chambon-sur-Lignon. The German government's Compulsory Labor Service had led many French young resisters to hide out in Le Chambon and other isolated rural areas in France.[1] Advertised at first by Vichy as a voluntary replacement for the poor French prisoners of war held in Germany, the Compulsory Labor Service soon showed its true face: it was meant to replace drafted German workers in factories across the Rhine. By going along with it, French workers helped the German war effort. Some naive Frenchmen left voluntarily in the beginning, but prisoners of war only dribbled back into France. Soon the Germans made the work mandatory. This caused massive resistance. Young people disappeared from their hometowns and showed up in the mountains, where they lived in small groups under false names, often demanding food from the local population.

Alerted by the Germans, the Vichy police, often composed of lukewarm gendarmes, soon doubled in strength with the addition of Joseph Darnand's fascist Milice. Their task was to flush out and arrest those who had gone underground.

It so happened that many of the young, armed with hunting rifles, resisted with force. A guerrilla war ensued. Only much later did the Allies parachute in equipment, explosives, and arms to the so-called *maquisards*.[2]

1 Created under laws and regulations of Vichy, between June 1942 and July 1944, the *Service de travail obligatoire* (Compulsory Labor Service) forced hundreds of thousands of French workers to go to Nazi Germany and work as laborers for the German war effort.

2 The *maquisards* were members of the *maquis*, the rural French Resistance guerilla bands of young Frenchmen who preferred to live "in the bush" than go to Germany as forced laborers. Eventually they were armed, and they harassed the Milice and the German occupation troops.

Commissioner Praly's mission was to spy on the Jews and the *maquisards*. He was lodged in the Hôtel des Acacias, across from the train station. He was young and handsome, and chosen because he was Protestant. He flirted with the girls in the village, bought drinks in the cafés, and got all the information he wanted. Every evening, he went to the post office and mailed off a thick, sealed envelope that denounced all of us. His presence endangered our security.

One day, I bumped into him in the street. He spoke to me sternly about the Hôtel des Roches, "a dangerous den of Jews and anti-patriots." I reproached him for his work as an informer. He responded in a frivolous manner: "We all do what we need to do to survive."

In the summer of 1943, a young man, completely out of breath, barged into the presbytery. "Mr. Trocmé, someone has just assassinated Praly!" I went as fast as I could to the Hôtel des Acacias, where I found a very pale Praly on a stretcher that nurses were about to put into an ambulance. "You've been involved in a dirty business, Mr. Praly," I told him. "What a punishment! But God will forgive you if you ask for forgiveness now." Praly said nothing as he lowered his eyelids. He bled to death on the way to the hospital in Le Puy.

He was the victim of four *maquisards*,[3] who were infuriated by the danger he was causing the Resistance. They arrived on bikes, and two of them asked to see Praly. He got up from the table and came to meet them in the hall of the hotel. They drew their pistols, riddled him with bullets, then calmly got back on their bikes and rode off. I never learned their names.

This made things worse for us. Suspecting the local police of half-heartedness, the Milice increased its own investigations and frequented the Café Chalaye to get information. Suspecting the Milice of half-heartedness, the German Gestapo engaged in often bloody raids with the help of the military police and, later, auxiliary units of the Waffen-SS commanded by Colonel Metger. Since the landing of Allied troops in North Africa in November 1942, all of France had been occupied, and the myth of Vichy's independence yielded to harsh reality. Nonetheless, many collaborators, fearful of Communism, maintained their faithfulness to Vichy.

3 The number of *maquisards* involved in the murder of Praly is disputed. Some source say it was two, some three.

In February, Theis, Darcissac, and I were arrested. Why? I found out later that they suspected me of arming the *maquisards* who killed Praly. The authorities no longer believed I was sincere when I claimed to be nonviolent. In their eyes, it was a pretense. At that time, I had no direct connection with the *maquis*. Only my actions toward the Jews could have made me suspect.[4]

My arrest took place on the evening of February 11, 1943. When I returned home from a day of visiting parishioners, Magda met me at the door. "André," she said, "there are policemen here who want to talk to you." I understood immediately what it was about. For months, Magda had kept a suitcase packed for me in the event of my arrest. When nothing happened, she had unpacked it.

Going into my office, I found two police officers: a commander and a lieutenant. The commander was dignified and had the look of a funeral director proceeding with the grim formalities. He spoke with a Corsican accent and introduced himself as Silvani, head of the departmental police. Then he went on: "Mr. Trocmé, I have been charged with a task that is painful for me to fulfill. I am obligated to arrest you. You will be assigned to a supervised residence. You will not be mistreated. Don't try to flee because it would be useless; the village is surrounded. Believe me that I regret having to do this. Until now, I have only arrested criminals. Today I am being forced to arrest an honest man."

As soon as Magda, who was prompt in her decisions, knew what was happening, she did three things: she set the table for dinner and invited the commander and his lieutenant to eat with the family;[5] she sent someone to warn the village that I had been arrested; and she repacked the suitcase for me.

Our dinner was dismal. The children, dumbfounded, looked at the officer, who hardly ate anything. "I don't have the heart to eat," he repeated, looking down at his plate. I ate copiously, not knowing what was going to happen. "Why shouldn't I eat," I said to the commander, "I have nothing to reproach myself for. But tell me why I am being arrested."

"I have no idea; I know nothing about it; I can't tell you anything," he responded in a gloomy tone. During this time, behind doors, Mr. Colin

4 This was August 6, 1943. André Trocmé was arrested on February 11, 1943 and released a few weeks later on March 16. He had been back in Le Chambon for several months before Praly was assassinated on August 6th. Trocmé didn't go into hiding until later that month.

5 It was customary to invite to dinner whoever was in the presbytery at mealtime.

was on edge and kept wondering, "Will it be over soon? Can I come out of my hiding place?" What a strange thing – the police never even asked us if we were hiding Jews.[6] They hadn't been given that specific order!

In the village the announcement provoked immediate reactions. While we were eating, the doorbell rang constantly as our parishioners came to say goodbye to me with tears in their eyes. We embraced and they put precious, little packages into my hands. "To take along with you," they said. Biscuits, chocolate (whose taste we had forgotten), warm socks. The two officers were wide-eyed as they watched this parade. Seeing the two officers through the half-opened door, our parishioners didn't dare to express their thoughts aloud. But they whispered to me, "This is a bit much, isn't it? What wrong have you done?" The most touching present was a roll of toilet paper on which Suzanne Gibert [André's goddaughter] had scribbled in pencil the Bible verses for the following week.

This was followed by goodbyes which, I must say, were heartbreaking. Would we see one another again? It was impossible to know in such tragic times! On the inside, I was calm, almost joyful. It was the moment I had been expecting for a long time, the moment when I would be called upon to bear witness to my deepest beliefs.

A front-wheel-drive Citroën took me into the night. I had no idea where we were going.[7] "First, we are going to pick up your colleague, Theis," said the commander, who sat next to the driver. "Then we must find the director of the public school, Darcissac, who has fled. We have orders to arrest all three of you."

Theis, overwhelmed, sat next to me. They drove us to the school where the Darcissac family lived. Commander Silvani told Mrs. Darcissac, "Advise your husband to give himself up. Fleeing will make people think he's guilty. If he is guilty of nothing, let him come forth to be arrested!" Of the three of us, Darcissac was certainly in the most danger because he was making false identity cards.

Mrs. Darcissac was persuaded. She told them where her husband was hiding, and he surrendered without any resistance. He was extremely depressed and so fearful he could hardly speak.

6 Magda notes on the manuscript: "At that time, we had Mr. Colin, Madame Berthe, and two young French, Jewish, female boarders who were students at the Collège."

7 Here Magda wrote in the manuscript: "I accompanied André in the police car to the end of the village. As we left the house, a group of friends lined both sides of the street, and Miss Stekler suggested that everyone sing Luther's hymn, 'A Mighty Fortress Is Our God.'"

They took us to police headquarters in Tence for the formalities.[8] Then the convoy of five or six cars headed toward Le Puy. On the way, Silvani turned toward me and Theis – Darcissac was in another car – and tried to reassure us. "Things will change," he said. "You won't be here for long." We tried hard to believe him.

Sometime around 1955, Magda and I saw Silvani again. He was now a colonel in Algeria, commanding a regiment of "Harkis" fighting for France.[9] He was in great spirits, after having been extremely worried when France was liberated because of his collaboration with Vichy. Always an optimist, Colonel Silvani, in his strong, petty-officer, Corsican voice, rolling his "r," announced the upcoming pacification of Algeria. This time, I didn't try to believe him![10]

We got to Le Puy around midnight and were put in empty barracks, where we slept in uncomfortable military beds. They were very polite to us.

But not the next morning. At six, rough voices awakened us, "Let's go, get up in there. Faster." We were soon taken to the train station in a paddy wagon. Two policemen we didn't know, one of whom was from Martinique, guarded us. They wanted to handcuff us. We objected by pointing out our professions and promised not to flee. The petty officer signaled that they should leave our hands free.

When we changed trains in Lyon, I encountered the "look" that law-abiding people have for criminals, a look that is quickly turned away and indicates fear, scorn, and self-righteousness. "Since he is a prisoner, he has done something wrong. He's not a person 'like us'!" We were placed in a reserved car and forbidden to talk to anyone. The police officers addressed us familiarly with *tu* and wouldn't answer our questions. Darcissac was crushed; he felt rejected and dishonored. Theis was mute. I tried to lighten things up with a few pleasantries.

In the evening, after taking several different trains, we arrived in Limoges. They put us up at police headquarters. A captain met us with the same coarseness reserved for criminals. "Since these people have been arrested, they are therefore guilty." That was his reasoning! "Pastors and a

8 Tence was the capital of the canton that Le Chambon-sur-Lignon belonged to and where police headquarters were situated.

9 "Harkis" were Algerian soldiers who fought on the side of the French during the War of Independence in Algeria.

10 Marginal note by Magda: "After the German debacle, fearing reprisals, Silvani asked André to write a letter certifying that he, Silvani, had arrested him with decency and 'all due respect.' André did so, but in Algeria Silvani seemed to have forgotten this detail."

teacher," he hissed with contempt. "Nutcases, that's what you are! Where will we find vice lurking next? Tell me, what have you done? Admit it! Black market, fraud, perhaps?"

"We don't know," we responded. "Perhaps we were arrested for having tried to save Jews from being deported!" His furor increased, "Jews! Ah, that's a good one. That no longer surprises me! You're complicit in their conspiracies! They're the ones who have led France into the abyss. Well, now you are going to pay for your misdeeds against the Maréchal!"

Voilà! He was sincere but so narrow-minded. We nonetheless begged him to let us go to church services the next morning, Sunday. He refused. "That's the last straw," he said. "Insipid ceremonies, to top it off!" That was the day I modified my cosmogony. Until then, I had believed that there were two powers fighting for control of this world: God and the Evil One. Henceforth, I believed there was a third power influencing our world: Stupidity.

We were, however, able to inform my former classmate, Limoges' Pastor Chaudier, that we were at police headquarters. He came to see us. He was friendly, but ill at ease and circumspect. We felt that even he didn't think we were innocent.[11]

The next morning, they didn't take us to church services but rather to the camp in Saint-Paul-d'Eyjeaux in a paddy wagon. Silvani had promised us a "supervised residence," perhaps even a hotel! What a painful disappointment!

Our "residence" was in a valley, in low, wooden, gray barracks surrounded by two high rows of barbed wire. From watchtowers, sentinels armed with machine guns surveyed the camp and the surrounding area, as one would expect at a concentration camp. On the other side of the barbed wire was an administrative building where they booked us after taking our fingerprints and photographing us from the front and in profile, as they do with criminals. From that point onward, we were referred to by our prisoner numbers. We had lost our true names.

"What a somber Sunday," murmured Darcissac, alluding to a popular love song.

For the first time, I ached with fear. We knew what concentration camps were. What if this were one? What if it were the antechamber of a German concentration camp? When we entered the no man's land

11 Later, Albert Chaudier (1901–1984) redeemed himself by his Resistance activities. He had been the star in preaching at the School of Theology, a born orator.

between the two rows of barbed wire, we saw about thirty men (out of the 500 or so in the camp), dressed in old military overcoats, with waxy faces. The sight of them filled us with anguish.

"Who are you?" cried out the wise guy among them. "Poor bastards like the rest of us, I hope."

"Yes," we yelled back, "just like you. Two pastors and a teacher!" The inmates burst out laughing. "Ha, ha! That's just what we needed. We have a priest and a rabbi but no pastors until now! Teachers too. There's no lack of them." The welcome we received from these good people was magnificent. The food was awful. But despite the thinness and jaundiced look of the inmates, a spirit of merriment, zaniness, and marvelous camaraderie reigned in the camp.

We soon learned that our fellow prisoners were the cream of the Communist cells in Southwest France. Some had been interned as early as 1939 at the time of the Hitler-Stalin Pact. Among the other inmates, there were several Socialists and a few Catholics, all guilty of acts of resistance or simply opposition to the Maréchal. Some of them proudly went by their Resistance names.

Saint-Paul-d'Eyjeaux was a "re-education" camp, not a forced labor camp. Our days passed in idleness because they had long ago given up attempts to "re-educate" such "tough" inmates.

Camp life would have been bearable without the presence of snitches, who reported everything said in the barracks to the director, and the food, mostly rutabagas, salsify, and Jerusalem artichokes, which eventually weakened even the most robust constitutions. We nonetheless joked around a lot in the camp. Under the guise of crude pleasantries, we continuously exchanged political news. Because we were wary of the snitches, we communicated in undertones, on the run. Under the cover of banal jokes yelled from one end of the barracks to the other, we bonded through information whispered at close range. Our morale was good. We survived on our illusions.

Where did our information come from? From radio receivers kept in tin cans that clever comrades constructed with the help of wire and contraband lamps smuggled in by the rare prisoners who worked outside the camp or got them when they went to the dentist.

We had the latest news from the BBC. That's how we learned one evening about the capitulation of the German army in Stalingrad. We let loose. The whole camp broke out in song, shouted at one another, congratulated one another! Remember that most of our comrades were Communists. For them the victory in Stalingrad had a double meaning: it announced the imminent end of Fascism and the coming victory of Marxism.

Those weeks spent in the camp amid Marxists had a decisive influence on me. Because of my theological training, the failure of the "Revival Movement," and the abstract nature of Barthian theology, I no longer believed that my stubborn fidelity to Christ's message could vanquish evil during the dark night of history we were living through. Our arrest and the network of pitiless police repression seemed to demonstrate the uselessness of the Gospels in this world.

But our comrades thought differently. They believed that they possessed an efficacious means of putting an end to evil on earth. Furthermore, they believed that the "big event" was coming. Hitler represented the final convulsions of a dying capitalism, which for them was the incarnation of evil. They were experiencing a type of apocalypse. Stalingrad was the harbinger of the fall of Babylon. Crushing Fascism would mark the beginning of the Messianic Age.

I remember one of them, a teacher, walking with great strides into the barracks and declaring with firm belief, "The proletariat is healthy, free of the gangrene that eats away at the exploiters. When the exploiters have disappeared, everything will fall back into its natural order. Then we will see the world of the workers, where competition, rivalry, jealousy, violence, lying, and war, having become useless, will disappear."

For them, this world free of evil was at hand. We only needed to defeat Hitler and his henchmen, Mussolini and Pétain. All means were justified to reach this end, not only Stalin's war and his deceit surrounding the Hitler-Stalin pact, but also the guerilla warfare of the *maquis*! Sabotaging railroad tracks, telephone lines, or factories working for the enemy; setting up ambushes; killing isolated "Krauts," preparing insurrections – that was the hard but necessary work of the moment. Anyone who refused to do this work was a coward, an accomplice in evil. Sometimes you had to "take out" these accomplices so they could no longer fool the people. Then the end would come. "Then and only then," our comrades said, "will we be able to love and practice nonviolence with you." We responded that we had to love God, as absurd as that might seem, right now. Love and pardon right now.

When we first talked with our comrades, they were scandalized: "Refuse to kill, refuse to lie – that's complicity with the enemy," they said. "That's the eternal sin committed by Christians, the opium of the people. It has prevented history's evolution!"

You can imagine that these conversations were widespread in our barracks. It became an intellectual center visited by inmates from other barracks, who sat on our beds to hash things out.

I can hardly remember the names of my comrades today. To do so, I would need Theis's and Darcissac's infallible memories. Some were very young and had already paid personally as heads of the *maquis*. Others were fathers of families, responsible for Communist cells, who had acquired the experience of a pastor or a teacher. Yet others with gray hair hoped to reach the Promised Land.

Only a few of the prisoners were vulgar or brutal. The other inmates considered them two-faced and untrustworthy, and avoided them. In our barracks, there was also an old man in a gray shirt, somewhat secretive, very Catholic, and well-groomed in his person and his affairs to the point of meticulousness. His religious faith, like ours, led him to resistance. We were very close to him.

One subject of astonishment among our comrades was the abundance of packages Theis, Darcissac, and I received. Theoretically, we had a right to one package a month, but the camp director, a man of goodwill, allowed some leeway. He even allowed visits! A visiting room made it possible for inmates to see their families. They sat together on benches lined up against the walls under the surveillance of armed guards. Together again, couples embraced. I called that "love on the bus." The expression stuck.[12]

Magda came often, loaded with supplies of food from our parishioners, who were moved by our fate. Her packages had been searched by the police at the train station in Saint-Étienne. They wanted to confiscate them. She had pleaded, protested, affirmed that it was not black market, and indicated that they were for Pastor Trocmé, whose name was becoming known and respected by railroad workers inclined toward resistance. Oh, my wonderful France! How I learned to love

12 Magda notes on the manuscript: "The benches were up against the walls of the narrow barracks. 'Love on the bus' took place seated on these benches, one's back against the wall, while the armed guards walked back and forth between the two rows of benches."

those people who, in the simplest ways possible, argued with the police, took risks, even the risk of letting Magda through! One of the railroad workers had been Darcissac's student.

The mail brought us more packages. As a result, the shelf that we made above our cots looked like a grocery store. There was much more than we needed, so we shared it with the comrades in our barracks and beyond.

"We never knew that pastors were so rich," marveled our companions, emaciated by forced fasting which, for some, had lasted years.

"We are not rich," we told them. "These are presents from our parishioners. They are quite fond of us!"

"I'll be damned," exclaimed one of them. "I'm the head of a cell in Béziers and I've never gotten anything from my comrades. So that's how it is where you come from?" he said with a glimmer of admiration for Christians apparent in his tone.

"Yes," we responded, "but we have a particularly good parish."

How beautiful that good parish appeared to us from a distance! We didn't know if we would ever see it again. We suddenly understood all the affection, faithfulness, and capacity for dedication hiding behind those lowered eyes and hesitant words of Le Chambon's peasants. During our absence, and even because of the emotion caused by our absence, the parish never fell apart. On the contrary, it had never shone more brightly. Pastors visiting Le Chambon and resident lay people outdid one another in devotion. To be sure, the patriotic sermons of old Pastor Poivre caused a stir; I'm not sure he was in complete agreement with us.

HERE I INSERT a letter written to the three prisoners by Dr. Roger Le Forestier that accurately describes "the particularly good parish."

Dear Friends:

We are thinking of you, and your presence in our thoughts allows the work of the parish and of Christian charity to move forward. The church in Le Chambon isn't like the dove of the Holy Spirit. It's a duck . . . a decapitated duck that advances automatically.

Yesterday evening, our men's get-together in the Molle Circle was very animated. Daniel Trocmé, the day's speaker, and I presented news about your life in the internment camp, which was received with great emotion and sympathy.

This morning, Mr. Poivre preached on Herod and John the Baptist. Temporal power will never silence the voice of God speaking through the prophets. Undoubtedly, Poivre wishes to join you. We sang "A Mighty Fortress Is Our God" and "Don't Feel Sorry, Zion." The priest in Le Chambon, if interrogated, would have said, "You did everything that could be expected of you," and expressed deep sympathy for the three of you. Furthermore, I have learned that all of French Protestantism has heard about what happened to you. Some are indignant that the church and Christians are once again persecuted; others place their hope in God, whose mysterious ways lead to the salvation of the faithful. Catholics also have their martyrs, including the head chaplain of the French Scouts. The Jews as well: such as the personnel of Oeuvre de Secours aux Enfants.[13] Have courage and determination; God is at work.

When I left you, I went to Vichy with Daniel Trocmé. The following day, a Tuesday, I met with Mr. Cadot's chief of staff at the police headquarters in the Ministry of the Interior. I submitted the letter of introduction on my own official stationery that I had read to Darcissac in abbreviated form: "I request a meeting regarding the arrest of three friends. They are two pastors of a parish with 1,200 members and the director of a school with 460 students, and fathers of eight, four, and three children." As a citizen of Le Chambon, a Protestant, a friend, and a family doctor, I was obligated to speak in your favor. The conversation was polite and diplomatic. I spoke as a Protestant and a Chambonnais.

I used several well-turned phrases: "You have struck at the heart of French Protestantism"; "You are going to give the palm of martyrdom to my friends, who do not desire it"; "Their liberation cannot be conditional because men of God form a single block and preach the gospel and divine law, which transcends all human law"; "You have been poorly informed by agents who are strangers to Protestantism and to the community of Le Chambon." Finally, I asked that a "serious investigation be made, not by anonymous informers but by public figures." I have learned that Prefect Bach also asked for an inquiry, which was carried out recently.

Indeed, the state police had reports drawn up long beforehand from informers' tips, anonymous letters, and superficial inquiries on five

13 Oeuvre de Secours aux Enfants (OSE) was a Jewish children's welfare organization founded in Russia in 1912. It moved to Berlin, then to Paris in 1933, and again in 1940 to avoid the Nazis, to Vichy and then Montpelier. It was active in placing Jewish children on the Plateau, thanks to Madeleine Dreyfus and André Chouraqui, who worked in the Garel Network.

"persons of interest," who were then arrested on charges of "pacifism, conscientious objection, helping persecuted people, and connections to international humanitarian groups (Quakers in Geneva and the Red Cross)." There was you three from Le Chambon; two others from elsewhere. They expected to find "misguided charity, political intrigue, and Gaullism," but instead they found "love, faith in God and in the church of Jesus Christ."

Therefore, I advise you to remain in the camp, where you have mature men of conviction to save through faith. Here there are only women who have already been saved and numerous children whom we will care for with tenderness and perseverance.

Our friends in Le Chambon, too numerous to name individually, join me in sending our faithful and affectionate friendship in Christ.

Roger Le Forestier

IN THEIR TURN, *the three prisoners sent two messages to their parish in Le Chambon on Sunday, February 14 and Sunday, February 28. The first, transmitted by telephone from Limoges, perhaps by Pastor Chaudier, has not been preserved. Here is the text of the second.*

Philippians 1:1–14

Dear Brothers and Sisters:

We are more convinced each day that God himself led us to Saint-Paul-d'Eyjeaux. You know that for several years your pastors have wanted to leave their easy lives and bring the gospel to those who suffer. Today, God has fulfilled this wish much better than we could have if our plans had been realized. Every day, thanks to the grace of God, we have long and fruitful conversations about the Gospels with people from all walks of life. They listen to us and have confidence in us because we are here with them and share their fate. Last Sunday, our small section was overflowing with men who listened to us sing, pray, and speak, many with tears in their eyes. Therefore, don't pity us, brothers and sisters. Your prayers have already been answered. Continue to protect our wives and children as you now do with such affection. We thank you all for your gifts. We are loaded down with them and share our joys with others. We are without worries about the church. In Le Chambon as well, hasn't God prepared everything by giving each one of us responsibilities so that the church, for the glory of God, will continue to render witness and augment God's influence, above all for the disadvantaged among us?

André Trocmé, Roger Darcissac, Édouard Theis

ONE MORNING, WE LEARNED that an "important person" interned in the barracks next to ours, whose real name we didn't know, had escaped. The BBC had already announced his arrival in London.[14]

Here's how the extraordinary escape happened: every night, for weeks, a tunnel was dug under the wooden planks of the barracks next to ours. No one knew anything about it. Just imagine this engineering feat carried out in silence between two nightly rounds by armed guards. It was several yards deep and fifty to a hundred yards long. How was it possible to hide the excavated dirt with tin cans? How was it possible to avoid being denounced, even involuntarily, by the indiscreet and the talkative?

The success of the operation was only possible because the thirty inmates in that neighboring barracks abandoned any hope of personal profit to help the "important person" escape. All the risks they ran were unselfish, even though there were dungeon-like cells in the camp where prisoners were mistreated and beaten. No one wanted to compromise the success of the enterprise by thinking of himself.

How was de Gaulle informed in London? I have no idea. I only know that a plane from the Free French Army awaited this "important person" at some distance from the camp, and that the next morning he was free in London. *Free* and no longer under the constant menace of death by deportation that weighed on the rest of us!

When we got word of the Soviet victory in Stalingrad, the whole camp had sung, and inmates shouted to one another. Now we had a good laugh about the camp police's lack of insight regarding the prisoner's escape. They blamed the Alsatian guard. He was arrested right after the escape and thrown into a dungeon. He maintained that he never saw anything, even though the tunnel's opening was only a few paces from his watchtower!

"We had to grease his palm; we gave him a bundle," our comrades confided to us. "There was no other way! Wouldn't you have used the

14 This important person was the philosopher and mathematician Jean Cavaillès. He was shot by the Germans in 1944.

same trick? Against people like that (they meant the Vichy clique), you use any means necessary. Without that money, that 'important person' would still be here!"

Against such evidence, we had no answer.

NO ANSWER, EXCEPT TO preach the gospel. Theis was the one who began leading services in the camp. I'm more flexible than he is, more adaptable, perhaps. I enjoy interminable discussions with friends. Silent, ponderous, somewhat Lutheran, Theis said to me one day, "We have to offer Protestant services." Skeptical, I accompanied him to a meeting with the director. He received us politely. "I can't refuse you," he said, "since I authorized the priest to say Mass. But no one shows up even though nearly everyone in the camp is nominally Catholic. In your case, as far as I know, besides you three, there is only one other Protestant!"

That sole Protestant was a funny guy with a long, pointy nose whose nickname in the camp was "Knife Face." If I remember correctly, he was from La Rochelle. He hung around us only to take part in the food windfall coming from Le Chambon. That aside, he had no other religious beliefs.

"We'd like to try anyway," we responded.

"OK, I'll free up a room for you in the barracks. You're on for next Sunday."

The room was small. We also had the use of a blackboard. With his beautiful handwriting, Theis copied a few hymns on the blackboard and posted a notice on the announcement board in the middle of the camp. Darcissac managed to recreate the melodies by humming a few notes. I agreed to give the first sermon and chose the famous passage on faith in Chapter 11 of Hebrews: "Faith is the assurance of things hoped for, the conviction of things not seen."

When the time came, there were twelve of us. Theis took care of the liturgy, which was received with appropriate seriousness. I did the preaching. It seemed to affect our audience profoundly. Darcissac taught those present the hymn about faith: "Faith makes the strongest walls tumble before our eyes; faith opens all locks and wins all battles." Our friends sang at the top of their lungs.

After the benediction they all remained and began discussing the big question. "The things we hope for, that you spoke about, are they for this world or the next? If they are for this world, we're with you. As for the other world, we know that there's 'something beyond,' but it's too vague, too far off. It doesn't interest us."

"It's 'on this earth as it is in heaven,'" we responded. The discussion was fascinating.

"You're gonna do your thing again, right?" one of them asked.

"Yes, next Sunday."

"Next Sunday is too far off! Do it every evening. We'll show up."

We feared being banned if we attracted too much attention, so we compromised and made it three times a week. We posted another notice on the announcement board. The results were astonishing. The next time, there were twenty of us. The barracks was full. Then there were forty. There wasn't enough sitting room; half of the crowd listened from outside through the open window. The "Protestant thing" was the event of the week. The camp leadership became alarmed. "What on earth could they possibly be saying that would arouse the enthusiasm of those materialistic unbelievers?" they wondered. They sent a police officer. He sat in the first row, said nothing, took notes, and gave his report to the camp director.

Since the camp was supposed to re-educate its incarcerated lost sheep by convincing them of the ultimate wisdom of the head of state, Philippe Pétain, it was dangerous to discuss "Christianity and Marxism." We had to find another way. "Continue to talk about Jesus Christ," our friends suggested. "That will make them happy! But if we talk about Karl Marx, that will cause problems, and our meetings will be prohibited. So we'll say Pétain instead of Marx. They'll never know the difference."

That's what we did, and "they" didn't know the difference. After the sermon and hymn, we held discussions. I used my authority to interrupt the conversation when it went beyond what caution demanded. The police officer zealously took notes. Clearly, he was impressed with the re-education program led by these two excellent pastors.

We discussed Marxist revolution versus nonviolent revolution, but the police officer never caught on. After a week, the entire camp, returning from meals or going to the laundry, sang or whistled "Faith makes the strongest walls tumble before our eyes." That made the barbed wire separating us from the newly verdant countryside seem less insurmountable.

The end of our stay in Saint-Paul-d'Eyjeaux was as surprising as our arrest. One morning, about five weeks after our incarceration, Theis,

Darcissac, and I were summoned to the administrative building, the one situated at the camp's entrance.

"Pack your bags," the guard told us. "You're moving out."

"That's it for us," we told one another as we gathered our possessions. "They discovered what we're doing. Now, they're prohibiting our get-togethers and deporting us."

"Gentlemen!" said the employee who received us behind a makeshift counter. It was the first time we were ever addressed by anything other than our prison numbers. "Gentlemen, I have good news. You're free! The train for Limoges leaves at ten o'clock. Hurry up!"

We were astonished. He went on: "I know nothing about why you were arrested or why you are being released. To be released from custody, kindly sign these documents."

Filled with joy, I had already picked up my pen when Theis stopped me. "Wait a minute, André, did you read this page?" It was a mimeographed declaration that said, in effect: "I, the undersigned, swear fidelity to the person of the Maréchal of France, the head of state. I will obey, without discussion, all orders given to me by government authorities regarding the safety of the country, etc."

"We can't sign such an oath. It's against our conscience," we declared.

"This is a political re-education camp!" he replied. "No one can get out without declaring allegiance to the head of state.

"It's contrary to the Bible to swear allegiance. Besides, we wouldn't be doing it sincerely."

"What?" cried the director, bursting forth from his nearby office. "This oath contains nothing against your conscience. The Maréchal wants nothing but the good of France!"

"We disagree with the Maréchal on one point. He turns the Jews over to the Germans. We are opposed to this practice. If we go back home, we will certainly continue to disobey orders received from the prefecture. How can we sign then?"

The director turned red with anger. "You refuse to sign! That's insane! It's the first time this has happened! All those freed before you have signed. I'm no longer astonished that you are here. Dangerous anarchists, that's what you are! You know as well as I do that the Jews harm us. They are filth we must get rid of! But wait a minute," he noted in a confidential tone. "Let's be reasonable. I appreciate your courage. However, you have wives and children. Sign. It's a simple formality. No one will know what you do once you leave here."

"If we sign," we responded, we'll have to keep our oath. We can't pledge to carry out unjust orders."

"Have it your way!" he roared. "You will rot here indefinitely, or maybe the Germans will deport you. That'll be a different matter entirely! Take these men back to their barracks," he ordered the guard.

Of the three of us, Darcissac alone signed. "I'm afraid of losing my position," he said. "I'm a government employee." He was at once sheepish and joyful. He had been so frightened. Now he was free. It's true that, unlike Theis and me, he didn't have a spiritual vocation to remind him, "It's for *this* that I have called you!"

Returning to the barracks, I was sick at heart. You slowly get used to fear; you even resign yourself to it. But you lose hope quickly! For ten minutes, I had been free in my imagination. Now, once again, the horizon darkened. How would it all end? Deportation? A concentration camp in Germany? Would I ever see my loved ones again? Yet, an inner voice kept telling me: "It is for *this* that I have called you. Obey."

I obeyed without hesitation, but I felt like I had just committed suicide.

HERE IS THE TEXT of a letter that André wrote to Magda that same day, March 15, 1943.

My Darling,

We were liberated. Our bags packed, buckled up, and ready to go. We were at the camp's exit. Darcissac was freed.

But we refused to sign the document I've copied below, so we were sent back to the camp. We await a decision from Vichy about our liberation. Of course, we fear a negative one. We are here, then, probably indefinitely. So many contradictory feelings in my heart! The sudden, immense joy about coming home mixed with sadness at the thought of abandoning the work we had just begun; the moving farewell scene in the barracks that Darcissac will describe for you. There we were at the gate with our ration cards and our tickets in our pockets. Then, suddenly, the news: "You, Darcissac, you may go. You two remain here." I kept a straight face, but my tears were ready to flow. In my imagination, I was already holding you in my arms, and the children as well!

If I wasn't anguished about your health, this would be easy. But I am endlessly worried about you, especially now that Jispa has departed.

Don't worry about my health or my state of mind. Both are good. I'm doing my duty. Perhaps this was God's plan so that our fellow inmates could see that we firmly believe in what we preach.

This means more inconvenience for those who have helped in the past. Once again, they must approach Vichy. You must let Pastor Boegner know immediately. Explain to him that my refusal is in no way a mark of opposition to the current regime – not more or less than it would be to any other regime. It's a refusal to swear any oath whatsoever, in accordance with the Gospel's commandments.

If I made this commitment, I would be obligated to keep it. I could never do that. I cannot enter into any such agreement with any authority or human organization. Hug the children for me and explain all this carefully to them.

Here's the document I refused to sign:

> I, the undersigned [name]
>
> Having been released from the monitored residence of Saint-Paul-d'Eyjeaux (in Haute-Vienne), certify that the camp commander has informed me I must solemnly pledge to support the new social order, respect the work and person of the head of state, the Maréchal of France, and avoid involvement in any anti-national activity. If I violate this agreement, I will be subject to legal proceedings, as well as any new administrative measures taken against me.
>
> Saint-Paul-d'Eyjeaux, [day, month 1943]

I made this declaration:

As a Protestant minister, I cannot enter into any such agreement, regardless of the social order. But I can pledge to respect the person of the Maréchal of France.

HERE IS AN EXCERPT *from a letter written by Albert Chaudier, also on May 15, 1943, to Pastor Marc Boegner:*

They had packed their luggage and said their goodbyes when they were informed that the police inspector had to hold them until Vichy had ruled on the new situation created by their refusal to sign the loyalty oath.

Darcissac, director of the public schools in Le Chambon, has been freed. He is in my home right now. Tomorrow I will go to the regional prefect's office and clarify the spirit of our friends' refusal. Thus, if he is consulted, he will be able to approve their release.

Our two colleagues are once again interned in the camp. This is particularly difficult after experiencing such hopes for liberation, but they accept their fate with remarkable serenity as they fulfill their lively and interesting ministry in the camp, most notably by holding Bible studies.

We await the decision, which could come quickly or be delayed.

I think it would be appropriate for you to use your authority to explain the justifications to Vichy.

IN OUR BARRACKS, our return was met with cheers, "You're free. Bravo!" There wasn't an iota of jealousy among our comrades.

"No – we refused to swear an oath to Pétain!"

"What? It can't be true! You're completely nuts. We know you must sign that rag, but it's meaningless. It's a 'signature extracted by force,' that's what it is. Everyone who was liberated before you signed it. It didn't prevent them from working in the Resistance."

One of our comrades, who kindly helped me put away my things, added, "If I were you, I would have signed with both hands, and then, two days later, I would have blown up the railroad tracks." He was a railroad worker.

"Can't you see that your Christian thing won't work? Revolution by nonviolence, by not lying! That might work if we were dealing with decent human beings, but not with these swine! 'I won't sign your paper,' you said! Now they'll never let you go. You must fight fire with fire. Otherwise, there's no way of winning."

Depressed, we kept quiet. Darcissac had said his goodbyes to us with the encouraging words of a healthy person leaving the hospital room after visiting someone condemned to death.

"I just signed my own death warrant," I kept telling myself.

The next morning, after a bad night, Theis and I were again called to the administrative building, where the director received us. He couldn't have been more friendly. "Gentlemen, I have good news for you," he said. "I received a telephone call from the office of Pierre Laval. I was ordered to free you immediately." We were thunderstruck!

"But we can't sign the loyalty oath."

"I've been ordered to free you without your signature," he said. "You must know people in high places. But hurry up. The train leaves at ten a.m., and I don't want a lot of commotion in the camp. Go get your luggage in the barracks!"

We left without further ado.

"What?" asked our comrades.

"Free!"

"You signed?"

"No, without signing!"

"Holy shit!" cried out the friend I spoke with the night before. "Your Christian thing does work on occasion." He couldn't get over it, nor could the friendly group who helped us pack.

Before leaving our friends, we formed a circle, hand in hand. All very moved, we sang, *"Ce n'est qu'un au revoir, mes frères"* ("Auld Lang Syne"). I never saw these good people again. Most of them died after being deported, including the little Catholic man with the blue shirt. How cruel! One day, however, I met a Socialist from Saint-Étienne named Fromage, who in the camp had sported a much more valiant *nom de guerre*. He had been released a few days after us and had also refused to swear the oath to Pétain. The director simply took it into his head to override the oath. We had made a breakthrough in the methods of a totalitarian regime.

The Saint-Paul-d'Eyjeaux camp didn't survive for long after our liberation. Fearing, justifiably, the Vichy bureaucrats' laxity, the Gestapo came one day and deported everyone to Germany. No one ever returned.

Who was responsible for our release? After France's liberation, several people bragged about doing so. Marc Boegner told me one day, "I went personally to see the Maréchal." Prefect Bach, asking me to testify on his behalf after the war at his trial for collaboration with the enemy, wrote, "I was the one who got you liberated. I asserted your innocence to Pierre Laval."

All of this is probably true, but I learned two other reasons that get still closer to the truth. First, our arrest had become common knowledge in England. It was the first time Pétain had arrested Protestant pastors. The BBC, using this for propaganda, proclaimed, "You can see clearly that Pétain is in the pay of Hitler. He maintains that he is free and well-disposed toward the church; in reality, the persecution of the church has begun in France, as in Germany, on the orders of the Führer."

Laval liberated us to placate England. In 1943, after Stalingrad, we could feel the tide of war changing. The fact that the second order for our liberation came from the office of the head of state and was executed so urgently seems to indicate that it was caused by political reasons. Humanitarian motives don't come about so quickly!

The second reason was perhaps the fear that our presence in the camp would cause unrest. The director might have signaled this to Laval. If that was the case, the Gospels have demonstrated their efficacy in the modern world, even among the Communists.

HERE I INSERT two letters written on March 18, 1943, by Marc Boegner to Magda and André Trocmé.

Dear Madam,

I had just written to you when I received a letter from Mr. René Bousquet,[15] informing me of his instructions for the release of the three internees, and a second letter from Mr. Chaudier explaining the circumstances under which my colleagues were authorized to leave the camp.

I immediately wrote to Bousquet to explain the religious reasons behind your husband and Édouard Theis's refusal to sign the oath and begged him to stand by his original decision to release them. I sincerely hope he will respond to my second request with the same goodwill that motivated his first response.

Given this new situation, I will wait to see what happens before deciding on a trip to Le Chambon.

Pastor Marc Boegner

My Dear Colleague,

I have just learned of your and Édouard Theis's release. I want to let you know how delighted I am. You have certainly begun a beautiful ministry in Saint-Paul-d'Eyjeaux. If you had stayed there longer, you would have established a close relationship with a group of men whose only previous contact with Christianity was negative and blasphemous.

15 René Bousquet (1909–1993) was the secretary general of the Vichy police from May 1942 to December 31, 1943. He was assassinated shortly before he was to be tried for his decisions during the Vel d'Hiv roundup of July 1942.

Your parish, the Collège, and the church need you. I am grateful for the way things worked out. I can say with some satisfaction that the secretary general of the police acted responsibly regarding the requests I made on your behalf.

You need rest, and Mrs. Trocmé needs to recover her strength. Do what you consider reasonable in the current situation, but I strongly urge you not to throw yourself into new activities. If you have any proposals about new activities, do not hesitate to send them my way.

Kindly relay everything I have told you to Theis, as I am too busy today to write to him separately, and am leaving for Nîmes tomorrow.

Pastor Marc Boegner

FROM LIMOGES, WE SENT a telegram home with the good news. We expected a huge turnout at the train station, but there was nothing. Marcel Jeannet, president of the local council of elders, who had officially replaced me during my absence as head of the parish, had given the instructions, "Absolutely no demonstrations," so as not to alarm the police. The Chambonnais grumbled but stayed home. I still think today that such a nonviolent demonstration would have favorably impressed the authorities.

The following Sunday was a different story. In our sermons, Theis and I related our adventures, and Darcissac said a few words. Standing, the congregation sang "Faith makes the strongest walls tumble" in emotional voices I will never forget. Everyone embraced us. A photograph I've saved depicts the "Three Musketeers" leaving the church together that morning.

16

In Hiding

DURING THE FEW WEEKS I was absent from Le Chambon, other pastors had enough time to exert their influence. The older Mr. Poivre was a beneficial presence. His only error was to confuse patriotism and religion and to encourage the parish to favor armed resistance.

The problem was Pastor Jeannet, who was supported by Pierre Rozier, president of the regional council. By nature, Rozier detested risk, anything that might cause tension and disputes or "threaten the peace of the church." I have esteemed men who, for theological reasons (I'm thinking of Henri Braemer) or politics (like Professor Anstett), have disagreed with my positions. They had convictions. In Rosier's case, it was nothing but prudence. "You're going too far," he told me. "Le Chambon, with its Collège Cévenol and its unrest, is creating problems for me." He was incapable of passionate involvement in the plight of the refugees. Moreover, the Jews who had arrived by way of the Collège Cévenol caused difficulties in the thirteenth region.

Marcel Jeannet, a Swiss evangelist, became Rozier's tool. Years earlier, I had spoken wholeheartedly in favor of Jeannet's consecration as pastor. He had acted courageously and behaved congenially. Now, however, he became disagreeable. I only understood much later why this had happened. Because he was a friend and a good pastor, I had asked him, a bit naively, to replace me during my two absences from Le Chambon. Alarmed by the way I ran the parish (he considered my direction chaotic and was a stickler for order in administrative details), he began to dream, as I found out later from his brother-in-law, of replacing me as pastor. He would thus become the spiritual leader of the Plateau, where Le Chambon was the most important church community.

My return from Saint-Paul-d'Eyjeaux, then from the Drôme, where I spent a few long months in 1943 and 1944, and the goodwill I enjoyed in the parish were for him a double disappointment. He reacted by blowing the least little negative incident out of proportion, then recounting it to Rozier, who transmitted it to the national council, thus raising fear among the church's leaders. His behavior led to the minor drama I'll describe now.

In 1943 (or was it 1942?) I went as a delegate to the national synod in Alès.[1] The Confessing Church in Germany had long before spoken out against racism. The Reformed Church of Holland had just made a courageous public statement on the subject. As Germany tightened its grip, the Reformed Church of France urgently needed to take a public, unified stance.

According to church rules, five delegates were required to present a motion to the synod. Along with a handful of other delegates, I composed a motion that the church protest firmly against racial persecution, protect victims of racism, and oppose any laws that violate biblical teaching.

At the age of forty-one, what a naive child I still was! I should have yelled out my motion in the open session, like a blast from a canon! But I believed it was more polite to show my text first to Mr. Boegner. He read it, raised his eyebrows, and said: "This is very important, very interesting! I'll take care of it!" He walked away with my motion. I stood there dumbfounded, incapable of reacting. As soon as the session began, Boegner spoke: "Certain colleagues are troubled by the situation of the Jewish refugees. This is a very serious question that deserves our full attention. I request a closed session with verification of the delegates' credentials at the entrance. We don't want the press who are here to interpret the decisions we make in tomorrow's papers."

Fair enough, I said to myself, unable to smell a set-up.

That evening the closed session took place. The atmosphere was tense and dramatic. Boegner spoke. He listed all his personal efforts to intervene on behalf of the Jews. He had already divulged a letter he had written to the leading rabbi in France. Generous and vague, the letter had established Boegner as a great resister. He had taken personal steps with Maréchal Pétain, "all tied to the idea of tolerance" and "committed to

1 In fact, it was on May 8, 1941.

doing everything to avoid deportations." This included intercessions with the National Council of the French State that he belonged to. In short, Boegner had done everything that needed to be done.

"But we want the entire church to commit itself," I objected. "The church is hesitating; it sends contradictory messages from different pastors, parishes, and regions. We must call upon all Protestants to protect the Jews."

"That's madness!" replied Boegner. "You will only bring down the thunder of Hitler's Germany on the Reformed Church of France, that small flock I shepherd. We must consider above all the 'physical survival of French Protestantism.' And that's my business. Trust me." He then demanded an immediate vote. Except for two or three votes, one of which was mine, the vote of confidence was unanimous. No one had even read my statement.

This event cast a pall of suspicion over my relations with Boegner. I was furious at being conned and ashamed of the Reformed Church of France's silence, which lasted almost to the end of the German occupation. Neither Boegner nor Pétain ever succeeded in saving a single Jew. Only in specific parishes, where individual pastors stood firm, as in Lyon, Grenoble, Marseilles, in the Cévennes, and in Paris with Pastor Bertrand, did the church's courageous voice resound.

When, in 1946,[2] at the General Assembly of French Protestantism, Boegner read a long report on "French Protestant Resistance during World War II," he delineated the steps he had taken with Pétain. He congratulated the Cimade (which richly deserved it) and acknowledged parishes that had acted courageously. Le Chambon-sur-Lignon, which, according to Jewish organizations, had housed and saved between 2,500 and 3,000 Jews, was not named.[3] Le Chambon-sur-Lignon, with its progressive ideas, its nonviolence, its "tragedies," as Pierre Rozier would say, hadn't been a good example for other parishes.

The tragedy – the first real tragedy in Le Chambon-sur-Lignon – struck the Maison des Roches, the home set up at the Hôtel des Roches. I wrote previously that Student Aid sheltered roughly twenty-five refugee students there. Some of them already had their baccalaureate diploma or its equivalent. All of them were preparing for exams with the books available. Only

2 The meetings were held in Nîmes from October 2 to 26.

3 Records show that Boegner did in fact congratulate the Cimade and notably its house, Coteau Fleuri, in Le Chambon-sur-Lignon (which therefore was mentioned).

a few of them were Jewish.[4] Professor Legal, after running the house on a volunteer basis for a year, returned to Montpellier to teach law. Mr. Pantet, the former director of the Asiles de Lemé in the North, who had taken refuge in Le Chambon-sur-Lignon, succeeded him, but he soon begged me to replace him "for health reasons." In fact, Pantet was afraid, because trouble was brewing in Le Chambon. My cousin Daniel Trocmé accepted this difficult position at a time when the forays of the Milice and the Gestapo were increasing. At that time, for example, the Hôtel du Lignon housed about sixty German officers and soldiers on R&R after fighting on the Eastern Front. From time to time, we heard German military music in the marketplace and on the streets. It provoked a good deal of mockery among the villagers because the bandmaster had an enormous paunch. During one concert, Dr. Le Forestier, who tried to drive his car along the street, made the director back up little by little until he freed the main street of this bulk.

A German chaplain, a very strange character, also cracked down on the village. He claimed to be a member of the Confessing Church, but it didn't prevent him from hunting down Jews. "It's a scandal that the Jews, who take up too much space in this country, swim in the river at the same time as the Aryans," he declared to me. "From the pulpit, you should forbid them to swim in the river, especially when there are German soldiers in the water."

Since I refused to intervene, he decided to do the policing himself. He chased all the young people with darker skin – there are many in France – and let it be known they were Jewish. The students took off when they saw him coming and went back after he left.

Who denounced the students of the Maison des Roches? Was it he? French collaborators? Were some of the students involved in the Resistance?

In any event, one morning, Suzanne Heim, a student living in the Grillons, came to the presbytery distraught, crying out: "The Gestapo have surrounded the Maison des Roches. They are arresting everyone!"

Magda was always courageous – I still wince when I think of the risk she took. She decided to ride her bike to the Maison des Roches.

Here I yield my pen to Magda because on that day I was out of town.

4 Others were also refugees. Some were from Luxembourg, whom the Germans considered deserters.

[MAGDA WRITES] Suzanne told me that Daniel had been arrested by the Gestapo that morning at the Grillons and then taken to the Maison des Roches. The children had told him: "They're coming to arrest you; go out the back door and run into the woods!"

"I can't do that," he responded. "I'm responsible for the Grillons and the Maison des Roches!"

What was I to do? The Maison des Roches was over a mile from town. I took my bike and, once I got there, somehow managed to get into the kitchen. The Germans must have mistaken me for one of the household staff. I tried to enter the dining room, but a hoarse, German voice ordered me not to come any farther.

The students were seated, lined up against the wall. Daniel Trocmé was with them. Against the other wall, the Gestapo soldiers stood holding their machine guns. I think there were five of them. I sat down in the kitchen. One by one the students passed through on their way to be interrogated in the next room. What sadness! Some came back distraught; they had perhaps been beaten. While passing, they whispered hastily, "Here's my mother's address," or "Here's my fiancée's address," or "There's a gold watch in my night table," or "Send the money that's in my room to my home." It was heartbreaking.

Suddenly, eggs appeared. Eggs? Eggs were a rarity, yet the members of the Gestapo were given two each, as were the staff and I. The students received their ration of bread and water. Someone had a great idea: instead of using big pitchers of water, we used only small glasses, which allowed us many more visits and chances to talk briefly with the prisoners. I approached Daniel, who said to me, "Go quickly to the Hôtel du Lignon (the German soldiers' quarters) and let the German officers know what's going on. Tell them that the Gestapo is here. Try to save us by reminding the officers that, a few weeks ago, one of my students saved a German soldier who was drowning in the Lignon River."

I left the house. That wasn't difficult, but how would I re-enter later?

Fortunately, I speak German. When I got to the Hôtel du Lignon, I had a hard time reaching the officer I sought – the one who had been there the longest. I was afraid I would deal with an officer who had just arrived and knew nothing about the rescue.

The sentinels and officers were surprised but intrigued by my bizarre request and my insistence. Finally, they led me into an office with two officers. One was young, the other much older.

"How long have you been in Le Chambon," I asked them.

"That's none of your business," one responded.

"Then I can't ask you anything!"

Surprised, they told me when they had come here. "Then you know about the soldier who was drowning in the Lignon River and was saved by a student from the Maison des Roches?"

"Yes, of course!"

Then I asked for their help: "Gestapo soldiers are arresting the students in the Maison des Roches. Come, speak to them, tell them the story of the rescue. They are holding innocent people! Save them!"

"What the Gestapo does is none of our business."

"You are officers. You should know what 'honor' is. I am a woman, and I ask you only to tell them the truth, to confirm that what I say is true!"

"Go ahead, then. We'll follow you.

"No, I'll wait for you."

"But you have a bicycle with you."

"I'll go on foot and push my bike."

We took off together, to the curious looks of the passersby. Why was Mrs. Trocmé taking a walk with two German officers?

As we left the village, we met two young women from the Christian Union that I directed. They were riding bikes.

"Will you lend us your bikes? It's urgent." Stunned by fear, they gave them to us. The Germans and I followed our path, all three of us riding women's bikes, with me in the middle.

Silence. A heavy and painful silence.

So I spoke: "Why are there so many massacres in the Clermont-Ferrand area? That only gets the inhabitants worked up!" There had been raids and shootings after students from the University of Strasbourg arrived in Clermont-Ferrand.

"This is a war! Every German soldier killed deserves to have French hostages killed in return!"

It wasn't working. I had to be quiet or change the topic. I decided to change the topic. "Don't you think it would be better to send the Gestapo to the Russian Front instead of having them do the work they do here?"

The younger officer's eyes flashed. Amused? Surprised? Approval? Who knows? The older one responded, "They have all already been to the front!"

Once again, silence reigned. This time it was heavier and more painful. When we arrived at the Maison des Roches, I was not readmitted. The two German officers went inside. I then said that I was Daniel Trocmé's cousin, and I needed to talk to him. I thought it wiser to say I was Daniel Trocmé's cousin than Pastor André Trocmé's wife. They told me to come back in two hours.

I returned home without knowing what had happened at the Maison des Roches. I was no longer a member of its household staff!

At noon, the oldest of my sons, Jean-Pierre, who was only thirteen, wanted to accompany me to the Maison des Roches. There was nothing I could do to dissuade him. He came along on his bike "to protect me."

Trucks stood in front of the home. The students stood in single file. Daniel was first in line. A soldier was beating a young Jewish boy with leather straps. Only after everyone left did I learn that the straps were phylacteries!

The German soldier screamed, *"Schweinejude! Schweinejude!"* (Jewish pig). Daniel Trocmé said to me, "Only the Spanish student who saved the German soldier and is not Jewish was released. Tell my parents that I'm leaving. Don't worry. You know I love to travel!"

The prisoners got into the trucks, and the trucks left. Jean-Pierre was green with rage and on the verge of tears. He clenched his fists. "When I get older," he said, "I will get my revenge!"

"You know what your father says about pardon and reconciliation," I told him.

"Yes," he said, "but what I have just seen is too horrible."

Those of us still remaining spoke with the Spanish student who had been released. We looked around for the addresses and the money left by the students, but the Germans had taken everything. Anything of value in the bedrooms had disappeared.

[André resumes] Only three of these young men returned from the camps.[5] Daniel, who was first incarcerated in a prison in Moulins, never had the chance to explain himself. He was *verjudet* (considered Jewish) by the Gestapo because of his strange name, his knowledge of

5 On the number (nineteen including Daniel Trocmé), the fate, and the identity of those arrested at La Maison des Roches, see Gérard Bollon, *"Contribution à l'histoire du Chambon-sur-Lignon: Le foyer universitaire des Roches et la rafle de 1943," Cahiers de la Haute-Loire* (1996): 391-421. See also Patrick Henry, *We Only Know Men: The Rescue of Jews in France During the Holocaust* (Catholic University of America Press, 2007), 63.

German, and his insistence on defending the residents of the Maison des Roches. He spent time in several of the most treacherous concentration camps.

A few months later, his brother, François Trocmé, the director of a factory in the southwestern part of France, had his hands blown off as he attempted to remove an explosive device from a machine. In the hospital, he was visited by German officers who congratulated him for saving his factory that was now working for Germany. François had wanted to refuse to see them. He hadn't done that to help the Germans. Then he thought about Daniel and agreed to their visit.

"What can we do for you?" they asked him.

"Find my brother, who was deported to Germany, and get him out of his camp," he replied.

"It will be difficult," they answered. "But we'll try."

At the end of spring 1944, we received the following news: "The inmate Daniel Trocmé died on April 4, 1944, at two o'clock in the morning in the concentration camp in Majdanek, Poland."

Majdanek, like Auschwitz, became infamous for its gas chambers and crematoria. Thousands of Jews were murdered there.[6] We have every reason to believe that this was the fate of the "Jew" named Daniel Trocmé.

Several weeks after his death, the Gestapo made another enquiry at city hall in Verneuil, where Daniel was born, trying to verify if he was Jewish. The Gestapo did things backwards!

THE NEWS OF DANIEL'S DEATH plunged me into deep despair in the spring of 1944. I had written to his parents, Eve and Henri, to tell them that I thought Daniel had been arrested instead of me.[7] He had just taken over the Maison des Roches when he was arrested. There wasn't enough time for a file on him to appear in the Gestapo's records. I also told his parents that I reproached myself for bringing him to Le Chambon.

I wrote to them again, blaming myself once more for Daniel's death. They were sublime. "You were aware of our son's lack of certitude regarding his faith. He was still trying to find himself," they responded.

6 Majdanek was a death camp on the outskirts of the city of Lublin in Poland. It functioned from October 1941 until July 1944. Roughly 78,000 people were murdered in Majdanek, around 59,000 of whom were Jewish.

7 Records suggest that Daniel Trocmé was arrested and deported not because he was sheltering Jews or connected to André Trocmé but because the Germans considered the Maison des Roches a home of (future) armed resisters.

"He found what he was looking for and gave his life for it." Such admirable people, who loved their son deeply!

A few months later, as the Allies advanced into Normandy, Eve took refuge with her husband under the bridge on the campus of the École des Roches in Verneuil. It had been transformed into a shelter, and its entrances and exits were sealed by sandbags. Suddenly, she collapsed on her husband without a sound. She had just been killed by a piece of shrapnel.

One Sunday morning a short time later, Henri Trocmé was walking beside a highway on his way to church in Verneuil when he was struck by an American jeep and killed.

Oh, the somber, absurd, and black night of war!

LET ME PICK UP the narration of the year 1943 where I left off.

Sometime in July, I received a strange visit. A young *maquisard* came to inform me that my life was in danger. "I'm a double agent," he said. "I pretend to work for the Gestapo, but I furnish them with false information. This makes me privy to what their agents are saying. The other day in Valence, they decided to put a price on your head. They are going to kill you."

"Kill me?"

"Yes. Here's how the system works. The Gestapo gets the French police to offer suspended sentences to criminals so they can work for the German secret police. If the French police arrest someone, the Gestapo claims him. They change his identity, and he reappears in another part of France. His mission is to make troublesome people disappear."

"That explains the recent attacks on respectable people," I exclaimed.

"That's exactly right," the young man responded. "In this way, the Gestapo avoids anti-German reactions. No one knows the motives for an absurd assassination."

"You say that I'm going to be assassinated?"

"If you don't go into hiding, yes!"

Never had I been faced with such a moral dilemma. My conscience told me, "It's precisely for *this* I have called you," and I feared yielding to the cowardice of going into hiding. What about the example I tried to set? Wouldn't this be seen as a sign of panic?

I discussed the problem with Magda. Perhaps I spoke to others about it. In any event, word got around, and several people came to see me.

I am convinced that Jeannet alerted Rozier, and that Rozier, who didn't like responsibilities, told Boegner about it. It wasn't Boegner who paid me a visit, but Maurice Rohr, Henri Trocmé's first cousin from the École des Roches and vice president of the Reformed Church of France.

"We have already had enough misfortune with the arrest of Daniel Trocmé and the students in the Maison des Roches," he told me. "What good will it do to add another martyr to a list that's already too long?"

"It will serve as an example," I told him. "I have preached nonviolent resistance. I am obligated to remain at my post until the very end."

"The parish is already upset," Rohr told me. "You have a price on your head. You know how these executions happen. They take you for a car ride and then your corpse is found at the edge of the woods. Or they storm into your house during a meal, and the Gestapo henchmen spray the whole family with machine guns. Are you stubborn enough not only to let yourself be killed but to run the risk of your wife, children, and boarders getting killed or wounded?" Rohr then gave me some recent examples of such killings.

"No," I said.

"Do you actually believe," he said, "that your parish will remain nonviolent if you are assassinated?"

"I'm afraid they won't," I said.

"Be reasonable then. Disappear for a time, even just a few weeks. The BBC has announced that the Allied landing will take place this summer. It would be insane to put yourself in greater danger. We need you alive, not dead."

The Reformed Church agreed to continue my salary for Magda and take care of all my expenses while I was in hiding.

I let myself be convinced, but to this day I'm not sure I did the right thing. During my absence, there were no more arrests in the village, but the underground resistance took a turn I didn't like. I also ask myself if my children, who, like all children, were idealists and believed until then that their father was a hero, didn't "lose their faith" in me because I went into hiding. Perhaps they even lost their faith in nonviolence and, to a certain degree, their faith in God. These questions still haunt me today. What will I say to God, and what will God say to me?

There was nothing dramatic about my disappearance. Our family left one Sunday morning on a bicycle excursion. We managed to borrow some bikes that were still in fair condition, which was increasingly difficult.

Somewhere between Le Chambon and Saint-Agrève, Mr. Lespet, a hardware dealer in Lamastre, picked me up. What a courageous man! As night fell, I arrived at the Lamastre presbytery. Our friend Henry Estoppey was replacing Pastor Minssen for a few weeks. He put me in a room I couldn't leave. Fortunately, I had books, my dear books.

In Le Chambon, of course, my absence was noted, but Magda was never questioned by the Gestapo. In Lamastre, Estoppey obtained food stamps for me. Thanks to Darcissac's handiwork, my name was now Mr. Béguet. A new identity card showed a man without mustache wearing tinted glasses. It was difficult to recognize me.

When Minssen returned from his vacation, he was not happy to see me and asked Lespet to find me another hiding place. Furthermore, some young Protestant girls from the stocking factory recognized me one day at the presbytery window, where I imprudently had gone to get some fresh air.

One evening, I was driven in Lespet's car to a farm in Chamos, several miles from Lamastre. From the nearby hills you could see the village at the bottom of the valley.

This change of residence was prudent. Estoppey had a visit from the Gestapo in Intres, his parish, where they thought I was hiding. They searched around, found no one, and lost track of me.

I spent a few long weeks with the Ranc family in Chamos in a kind of attic attached to the house. The Rancs were unsophisticated and good people. The husband was a prisoner in Germany; his parents lived there with his young wife and a little boy. We spent the evenings cracking chestnuts. In a time of famine, they constituted the staple diet of the Ardèche people. Due to lack of exercise and the chestnuts, I gained a few pounds that I have never managed to lose.

In the daytime, I took walks in the pine forests, which were crackling with sunlight, without running into anyone. The Rancs told their neighbors that I was a depressed gentleman. I looked the part in my dark glasses. But gossip will have its way, and Lespet, deciding I was no longer safe, had me move once again.

This time, it was to an isolated bourgeois property, half farm, half villa, between Lamastre and Vernoux. It belonged to Miss P., or rather to her parents who lived in Paris. Mr. P., a major entrepreneur, was earning millions constructing enormous cement bunkers for the Germans along the Normandy coast, the so-called Atlantic Wall.

Not knowing which side would pull off the victory, P. played both sides. He encouraged the Ardéchois Resistance and allowed the *maquis* to stock weapon reserves on his rural property. A strange atmosphere! How distant I was from the great ideological battles taking place in Le Chambon. I suffocated morally.

I suffocated even more because Miss P., who might have been between thirty-five and forty, made me work, even though I was paying for room and board. She treated me as a boss would treat the hired help and sent me to watch over the goats, milk them, and make cheese – the famous, delicious Picodon cheese.

I carried a book with me in my pocket, but it was impossible to read. Goats are vagabonds, and if you don't run after them, they get lost. I tried to attach them with rope I carried in my pocket, but they bleated miserably and stopped eating.

In the evenings, I tried to read in my room, but it wasn't heated. I shivered from the cold and slid under the covers. That made me fall asleep. So, I asked Miss P. for permission to spend the evenings in the parlor. The parlor was a large, sad-looking room with a fireplace. She tolerated my presence with a petulant air.

These evenings soon became unbearable. Sometimes, I tried to initiate a conversation, and she responded in monosyllables. At other times, she tried to be more intimate, asking me to bring her a cushion, or a blanket, or to care for her as if she were my sister or . . . something else.

I was so uncomfortable with her attitude that I wrote to Magda about it. I couldn't correspond directly with her. A raid on our home or simply a monitoring of her mail would have revealed my whereabouts. For this reason, we had a "mailbox," meaning a third person who changed the envelopes. This system worked well, but it took time!

One day, I saw my courageous Magda arrive. To throw off the police, she had come by way of the Eyrieux valley instead of passing through Lamastre. On her bike! Crossing the departmental route, she had pushed her bicycle along the dried-up stream bed. She was exhausted but already had a plan.

We would spend a night together in the Rhône Valley on a farm with a brave family. The next day, a mechanic from Die, Mr. Brunel, would pick me up and take me to an isolated boarding house in the Drôme Valley.

That's how things worked out. Sadly, I hardly saw my dear wife when I was moved into the "chateau" in Perdyer, the home of Mrs. Deloche, and a real boarding house. We ate well because Mrs. Deloche was an excellent cook who didn't hesitate to pay the necessary price to the local peasants. Never, even before the war, had my stomach been feted like that, and I gained even more weight. Yet I still appeared rather lanky.

To everyone in the house, I was "Mr. Béguet." This time, those who knew my real name held their tongue. I didn't go to Sunday services in Châtillon for fear of being recognized. I had discussions with Mr. Tamar, a heavy-set Jewish man who, like me, was hiding in Perdyer. He had an argumentative nature. If I said to him, "It's a beautiful day," he would reply, "No, Mr. Béguet, it's not a beautiful day, it's a very beautiful day!"

HERE I INSERT *two letters written by André Trocmé during his time in hiding. The first accompanied a draft constitution for a sort of "third order" for Protestant men, and the second was his 1943 Christmas message to his parishioners in Le Chambon-sur-Lignon.*

October 20, [1943]

Dear Brother Dreyer:[8]

Here are the fruits of almost two months of reflection during which I asked God to show me what the men in Le Chambon and, more generally, what all men in our church need: to develop discipline and openly serve others.

The goal of our men's get-togethers this winter will be to establish the "Order of the Servant" of Le Chambon.

Read and think deeply about what I have written. Show it to two or three men who you're sure will understand and, perhaps, observe it. Correct what doesn't seem right. Pray to God. This, I think, is the beginning of something great. I sincerely believe that God has inspired me to do this. If you agree, send the pages back to me. Let me know who wishes to join you in this endeavor.

The little chains are a new and inspired way, I think, of avoiding the Croix Bleue–type of commitment and the YMCA or scout-type badges. Our men must remain discreet but conscientious. The chain will let people know who belongs to the order and who does not. If you agree, talk to Chabrut and ask him to print numerous copies of these four pages (about 2,000 or so) in small format on high-quality Bristol vellum paper. Order

8 The Dreyers lived in Le Chambon. The husband picked up the refugees when they arrived at the train station in Le Chambon; his wife taught mathematics at the Collège Cévenol.

the chains at Silas Gonthiez's, the Protestant jeweler in Tarbes. Check with my wife. He puts announcements in religious newspapers.

The chain should be made of inexpensive white metal. Make sure it has a heavy enough link to differentiate it from the chains with medals that Catholics wear, but make sure it's thin enough to avoid hurting the neck. The clasp can be inexpensive.

Christmas 1943

Message to My Church

Dear Fathers, Mothers, Brothers, Sisters, Sons, and Daughters in Jesus Christ,

I write to you this December 12 Sunday morning from a lonely place, while you are all gathered for services. It has been four months since I have attended religious services, except for those on the radio. You can understand, then, that thinking of our well-attended church this morning, I feel a surge of nostalgia for you.

What I have learned over these lonely months is that human beings are nothing if separated from God's love for them. As soon as I leave the orbit of the church, the place from which I announce God's love and where we try to live in the warmth of that love, I am no longer anything. I have come to understand much better now the loneliness of prisoners – and yet my lot is so much better than theirs. Their solitude comes from the fact that no one really cares for them. If some misfortune befell them, no one would look after them in the great deluge of misfortune that inundates the world today. Human beings are egotistical animals. Like other animals, they spend their life looking for food. Then, one day, they disappear without leaving a trace. They have worked hard. They go to great pains, but it's all meaningless.

Yet, as soon as God distinguishes some of these from thousands of others, even millions, as soon as God calls out their names, these people become living souls. Their lives have value and a goal. They must respond to God's love by loving God in return, trying to illuminate the lives of others by showing that God is love.

That, my friends, is precisely how you have been, for more than nine years – my fathers, my mothers, my brothers, my sisters, my sons, and my daughters. How often have I heard from your mouths words of encouragement and love which immediately conferred on my life all its meaning. That's what the church is: a place where human beings mutually support one another in Christ by repeating to each other, "God loves you. You are not lost. Hold your head high!"

All of that, my friends, you already know. Then I ask myself why some of you still voluntarily keep your distance from the church. When one is cold, one gets close to the fire! Yet a fire burns in Le Chambon, a great fire of love, aflame in the hearts of those whom God has pardoned. Why do you not come toward the fire? Why do some of you, who live less than 200 yards from the church, prefer to die out in the cold?

Perhaps it's my fault. Perhaps I, your pastor, your shepherd, haven't borne witness to God's love for you. In my solitude, I have thought a great deal about the past. I have assessed what was lacking in my nine years of ministry among you. Overwork, fatigue, the continuous rush of these months of war, days going by too quickly, all this meant that I was perhaps unable to find the few minutes needed to say to each of you what you were waiting for: "Raise your head; God loves you."

In my thoughts, each day, I make many visits to you. As soon as I return, I tell myself, I will visit so-and-so and give him a message from God. Then I start to doubt. If I return, will I be able to do a better job than in the past? Won't I, once again, be busy with the concerns of those poor souls who come to me and crowd my office?

I prefer to write to you today. You know well that your pastor loves you, in God's name, with all his heart. It is not his heart that was frozen over, but yours, at least sometimes.

I think of the woman who traveled 180 miles to be part of the "spiritual days" and left full of joy, just like the merchant who found a pearl of great value. I wonder with anxiety if it's your soul that is already frozen, dead from the cold to the point of no longer needing the warmth and the light of God's love!

Kindly pardon me, my "indifferent" friends, for addressing you first in this Christmas message. I am also thinking of those who are at the heart of the church: the church elders, those responsible for charitable works, members of all our individual groups, those who attend services regularly, members of our Bible study groups, and the men holding vigil groups. But all those have already found God and are in good hands. The Good Shepherd is above all preoccupied with the sheep that are not in the fold. Let your pastor be like the Good Shepherd. Let him worry about you, my former catechumens, the young men who don't go to the YMCA, the scouts, or even church services. I fear that your souls may suffer eternal death. If your souls are already dead here on earth, how will they be resurrected in the afterlife?

I am thinking of Christmas and now want to turn toward those who, in the absence of their pastors, have sensed within themselves the call to be shepherds. There are two fewer pastors in Le Chambon, but I know that forty or fifty have risen to replace them. I want to tell them, "Friends, prepare your feasts. Organize Christmas as it should be. But don't forget the essentials. You are surrounded by many of your brothers, in the country and in the village, who are cold, so cold that they are about to die. The essential is that you cease being aloof, drop your egoism, your grudges, and allow the love of God to flow freely from your forgiving heart upon all those you visit during the Christmas season."

Don't be afraid to dig deeply, to ask important questions, to heal wounds, and if necessary, to clean out the abscesses. Dare to be courageous, a true disciple of Christ in your own family and to those you visit.

I was dismayed to learn that some of you, perhaps misled by the political situation, have fallen out of charitable relations with others, including our enemies. I am afraid that our church may lose the fine reputation for pacifism that it acquired during these last war years. How do you think you can carry the message of divine mercy to others when thoughts of vengeance against our adversaries and those who have supported them are in your hearts? May our church become, through you, in 1944, the home where all people come to take courage at the call of their name by the very voice of Christ, who has forgiven them.

As regards your solitary pastor, he too will soon return to the church that he greatly needs. On that day, he will rise, full of joy, to the sound of the voices of those who for nine years have constituted his spiritual family – his fathers, his mothers, his brothers, his sisters, his sons, and his daughters in Jesus Christ. They always revealed God's love to him with words of pardon, love, and encouragement.

HERE ANDRÉ TROCMÉ RESUMES *the description of his life in hiding in the Drôme near Dieulefit.*

Two of my children even visited me. Jean-Pierre came in the middle of winter. I took him into the hills where we had a snowball fight and played Indians. Then Jacquot came. He was troubled by my situation and also wasn't doing well in school. I told Magda I would homeschool him, and we were very happy together.

Mrs. Deloche set me up in an immense bedroom with a beautiful wooden ceiling and exposed beams. I suffered from the cold even though there was a stove. Moreover, there were mice. Jacquot and I decided to raise a litter of them (they were so adorable) in the galvanized iron tub we used for washing ourselves. The baby mice couldn't get out of the tub because the edges were curved. We made them a cardboard house, but they all died quickly. I think they missed their mother.

Jacquot attended school using the name Jacques Béguet and studied math with a Jewish man living near the chateau. I made him do his homework, but we had fun telling lots of jokes to each other, especially those with plays on words. Despite my isolation, I led a carefree life in Jacquot's company!

However, once when I picked him up in Lyon, I almost fell into the hands of the Gestapo and lost my life. I was supposed to meet him at the house of our friends, the Paillots, in Villeurbanne near Lyon. On the trip there, everything went well. We spent the night there. On Sunday morning, the day of our return to Perdyer, we rose early. If I remember correctly, the train was supposed to leave at 8:30 for Valence.

Not early enough, because I only had a few minutes to pick up Jacquot's luggage in the checkroom where Magda had left it the night before. I had the baggage stub.

When we got to the Lyon-Perrache station, I left him at the top of the station's high stairway. "Wait for me here," I said. "I'll be right back." I started running toward the checkroom situated in the left wing of the long station.

I heard yelling behind me. I didn't pay it any mind, oblivious to the fact that it was aimed at me. I continued running. Suddenly I found a German soldier in front of me. His face was flushed with anger, and he pointed a rifle at my chest. Behind me was another equally threatening German soldier.

Frightened and ignorant of the reason for this rough treatment, I surrendered. They let out guttural, inarticulate shouts and made me back up one step at a time. I encountered an obstacle and fell backward, right into the open back door of a paddy wagon. They picked up my legs and threw me inside, slamming the door and locking it from the outside.

Slowly getting my wits together, I sat on the bench and tried to assess my position.

1. As absurd as it appeared, I had been arrested simply for running. The arrest had nothing to do with the fact that I was on the Gestapo's list.
2. They were going to interrogate me and send me to prison.
3. My papers said "Mr. Béguet." I didn't know what city was listed as my birthplace. I would need to lie to maintain my new identity. I had never foreseen such a stupid arrest. My false papers were only to prevent the French police from seeing my real name, which would have required them to turn me over to the Germans. I also needed a ration card with a name that wouldn't denounce me.
4. I decided that I couldn't lie. That would be "tempting God," another slide toward the types of compromise my vocation as a pastor forbids. I would tell the complete truth. "My name is not Mr. Béguet. I am Pastor André Trocmé." This decision calmed my conscience. After all, if God had just caught up with me, as he did with Jonas, and destined me for sacrifice, I couldn't easily "buck" him.
5. But what about Jacquot? He would not see me return and would never find his way back to the Paillot family. I knew his hypersensitive temperament. He would be terrified. I had to get a message and the baggage stub to him.

Through the small, barred window at the back of the paddy wagon, I hailed the sentinel guarding me, in German, of course. What luck that I spoke German!

"*Psst – Hören Sie mal*" (Listen up).

He paid no attention to me. I persisted, and this time he came toward me.

"My son, a twelve-year-old, tall and blond, is waiting for me with our luggage in front of the station. Will you kindly fetch him? I must tell him where to go, since I've been arrested."

The sentinel was skeptical and called the non commissioned officer, to whom I made the same request. I must ask the captain," he said.

I waited a long time before the captain arrived. I explained my situation to him in detail.

"You're lying to me," he said. "Why were you running?"

"I was late for the train for Valence and was running to the baggage claim. Here's my baggage stub; you can verify it."

"You were not trying to escape the round-up?"

"What round-up?" I answered naively.

"Didn't you notice that the station was surrounded by police?"

"No, I was in a hurry."

"You broke through the police barrier without realizing what you were doing? That's highly unlikely."

"It's true, though."

"OK, we'll find out right away. Take the prisoner to the front of the station," he ordered the sentinel. "If it's true that his son is waiting for him, bring them both back to me. If not," he added with a threatening look in my direction, "if you try to fool the German police, your number is up! Don't try to escape, or you're a dead man."

They let me out of the paddy wagon. The sentinel planted the barrel of his gun between my shoulder blades. "Get going," he said. I walked like an automaton toward the front of the station. "I only hope that Jacquot is still there," I said to myself. He was there, and he welcomed me from afar with gestures of relief.

"There he is!" I said to the sentinel. Seeing the German soldier behind me, Jacquot thought at first that I had asked the soldier to help us with the baggage. Magda, who had more nerve than anyone, had once done that in Valence. "I was making him useful," she said to me when I reproached her.

"I've been arrested, Jacquot," I said to my son, who then saw the rifle pointed at my back. "Let's go. We must appear before the German officer."

"Papa, Papa, what's going to happen to us?" he exclaimed. Overwhelmed and terrified, we returned to the captain.

He looked at the blond, handsome boy in tears. He was deeply moved. "You were telling the truth," he said to me.

"Go ahead," he said to the sentinel. "Take this man and his son to inspection. Stay next to him until he passes through the ID check. Don't let him flee. Get going." Then he turned and saluted me! "*Danke schön*," I responded and left without further ado.

The sentinel placed us in a long line of travelers passing inspection. From a distance, you could see an officer seated at a table. He looked closely at the documents the travelers handed him and consulted a directory of suspects, comparing the photographs of the suspects with the faces of the passengers.

"My troubles aren't over," I said to myself. "I have false papers. I've already told them that Jacquot is my son. The name on his papers is

Trocmé – a suspicious name – and mine say Béguet. It'll be hard for me to lie. I must avoid this inspection. But how?"

The line moved slowly. The people complained about missing their trains. My sentinel began chatting with his buddies in a group a short distance from our place in line. Soon, the sentinel fell behind us as the line progressed. "If we can get behind that cement column, we'll be out of his view," I thought. "Let's try it and see if he reacts." I knew that the exit for travelers getting off the trains and going into town was behind the column. "Jacquot," I murmured to my son, "do exactly what I do slowly and without running. Be ready with your luggage in hand."

"OK, Papa." For a moment, the sentinel stopped looking at us. I left the line and took five steps. That was enough to get behind the column. Jacquot followed me.

The soldiers didn't react. "Let's leave the station with a group of travelers," I said to him. Slowly, calmly, we exited without any problem. The ID inspection was only for those traveling, not for those returning home.

We went down the staircase and climbed onto a waiting tram. Fifteen minutes later, we were at a church service on Rue Fénelon, where Juliette Paillot worshiped. I picked up the hymnal and sang as I had never sung before. It was Sunday and I was free. I had come close to death; I had already accepted death. But now I was free, without having to lie! The only time, perhaps, in the history of the Gestapo, that a prisoner, arrested and already in the paddy wagon, walked away with the ID papers that would have damned him.

Who saved me? My son, whose tears touched the police officer. God, certainly, after a strange set of circumstances that began with my late morning departure, continued with my careless running, but ended in this church. "God doesn't want me to die now," I told myself. Juliette was astonished to see us and let us stay a second night. The next morning, one of her sons scouted the train station. He came back with the news: "It's all clear; you can go now." That evening, we were in Perdyer.

THIS STRANGE STORY has an epilogue no less strange.

A few years ago, in Petit-Lancy in Switzerland, I received a visit from a history professor who was trying to reconstruct the history of the Resistance during World War II. He asked me to recount my war experiences. "What's the story," he asked me, "about your arrest in the early part of 1944 at the Perrache train station in Lyon?"

"How could you possibly know this story?" I asked him. "No one knows about it."

"You'll never believe it!" he responded. "I'm working with the recovered archives of the Lyon Gestapo. They recognized you from your photograph, but it was too late to catch you. You had already escaped. How did you pull that off?

I told him the story of the cement column.

"You certainly kept your cool!" he exclaimed. After your escape, they discovered who you were, and the officer who let you slip away was held responsible. According to the archives, he was sent to the Russian Front. That's where they sent negligent officers to punish them."

I hope that my nice, unwitting liberator wasn't killed on the Russian Front. He didn't deserve such a fate simply because the tears of a boy moved him.

DURING MY LONG DAYS in Perdyer, I edited the manuscript of a book that I entitled *Dare to Believe*, written for secular teachers like Paillot, with whom I discussed it. It would never be published. Indeed, the "secular teacher" mentality, anticlerical and naively convinced of its rationalist atheism, had practically disappeared by the end of the Second World War. Problems of efficiency replaced those of rationality. The technological revolution and the success of Marxism in so many countries had given prominence to the notion of "historical evolution." Believers and nonbelievers alike wondered what, in the end, was the goal of human activity. Progressive Christians, who wanted the Gospels to be efficacious and procure peace and justice on earth, and the Marxists, who by then were only materialists in their economic theories, reached an agreement. The fears the Marxists had about alienation and religion, which deprived human beings of the will to transform the world, subsided little by little.

17

The Resistance

THE ALLIED LANDING IN NORMANDY cut short my stay in Perdyer. As soon as the news broke, the *maquis* came out of hiding and proclaimed the Fourth Republic (de Gaulle's republic) and their loyalty to the government in exile in Algeria. They no longer obeyed Vichy, whose administration, nevertheless, continued to function. It still had to provide salaries for government workers, food stamps, and security passes until the war officially ended.

In areas tightly controlled by the Nazis, Vichy held firm. Elsewhere, there was excitement and confusion. The *maquis* appealed to two very different groups: the *Armée secrète* (Secret Army), which had Gaullist tendencies, and the *Francs-tireurs et partisans français* (Snipers and French Partisans), or FTPF, which had Communist tendencies.

The "Communist" *maquis*, the most active group, resurrected the old revolutionary term "patriot." Their operations bordered on recklessness: ambushes of German detachments, attacks on moving German vehicles, the use of bazookas parachuted in by the English, and the sabotage of railroads and bridges with a new, easy-to-transport explosive called "plastic" because it looked like pliable dough.

Such activities exasperated the Germans, who believed that their adversaries were Communist terrorists. They fled in fear, and their own propaganda claimed they would be tortured and imprisoned if they fell into the *maquis*'s hands. That's why their crackdowns were so savage.

Their heinous acts gained notoriety in Vercors, on the Plateau des Glières, and in the battle of Mont-Mouchet in the Massif Central, where Jacques Monod, a Protestant professor I knew, was slain with his unit by the Tatar Legion, which was composed of Soviet prisoners of war of Asian origin. The Germans released them, put them in SS uniforms, and turned them into executioners in France. If they had been sent to the Eastern Front against their compatriots, they would have betrayed the Germans or deserted.

When the news of the Allied invasion broke on June 6, 1944, I resolved to return to Le Chambon with Jacquot to take part in the liberation activities we hoped for. The Rhône Valley was occupied and tightly guarded by the Germans, who were moving troops from the South toward Normandy, where the battle was raging. Mr. Brunel, the garage owner in Die, transported us in his car. He obtained a safe-passage document for us from the *maquis* that was inspected at several Resistance posts before we reached the no man's land on the outskirts of Livron, just inside the Rhône Valley. He didn't dare go any further because the Germans took potshots at all nonmilitary vehicles.

We did a few miles on foot, taking an indirect route that bypassed the main north–south highway, which was full of military vehicles. We slipped into the Livron presbytery, where my colleague Vermeil lived. He welcomed us warmly.

"The Germans blew up the bridge on the Rhône," he said. "We must take a ferry. It's in German hands. They don't let anyone through without a special security pass signed by the *Kommandantur*!"

"That's hardly encouraging," I replied.

"Don't worry. You must be from Livron to get this pass, but I have friends in city hall. Give me your ID cards. Mr. Béguet and his son, Jacques Béguet, innocuous names. I'll give it a try."

We spent the night in Vermeil's house. The next day, he brought us a superb security pass from city hall with the *Kommandantur*'s stamp. I no longer have it because as soon as I got back into the zone controlled by the Ardéchois *maquis*, I destroyed it for fear of being taken for a collaborator by some FTPF fanatic.

The ferry crossing went off smoothly. Around nine a.m., we got to the departmental train station in La Voulte-sur-Rhône. To our surprise, the local trains were running. This was one of the contradictions that characterized this strange time. Some sectors of daily life fell apart; others kept functioning normally.

We entered the stationmaster's office. He recognized me right away and welcomed me in a reassuring manner.

A German military train had broken down a few hundred yards to the north of the station on the tracks along the right bank of the Rhône from Nîmes toward Lyon. Every five minutes or so, someone knocked at the stationmaster's door.

"Gentlemen," said a German with a strong accent, "*Wasser bitte. Durstig! Soif!*" [Water, please. We are thirsty!]. In a mix of French and German, he explained that the train would be blocked there for hours because the tracks had been blown up by terrorists. "*Terrorist! Boum, boum! Alles kaput! Kommunist! Pas bon! Tac sur le train–die Geleise gesprengt! Nicht vorwärts! Malheir, la guerre!*"[1]. I didn't let them know I could understand German.

The stationmaster explained the situation. "They think, with some justification, that the *maquis* is coming from the hills, those steep slopes that tower above the railroad tracks. They conscripted local peasants to guard the rails every fifty yards, but the tracks get blown up anyway!"

"How is it possible?" I asked.

"We railway workers are the terrorists. The service teams that repair the tracks under the supervision of the Germans bury plastic explosives and blow up the tracks even before the first repairs have been completed. The Germans have been blocked here for four days. They aren't clever enough to figure out our game!"

When Germans came to exchange cigarettes for water, the stationmaster welcomed them without bitterness, like a good father receiving his adult children.

WE ARRIVED IN LE CHAMBON as evening approached. What a reception! Mama, Nelly, Jean-Pierre, Daniel, Jispa, Madame Eyraud, the whole village. The church overflowed on Sunday. We could see the light at the end of the tunnel.

"How can we be so happy? What have we done to deserve this?" I asked my spouse one day as I looked around the big dining-room table at my family, together again. If only Magda wasn't so thin! She was exhausted from malnutrition, overwork, and enormous responsibilities. With Jispa's help she had run the household well and represented her husband during his absence. How tall, affectionate, full of life, and handsome my children were!

1 "Terrorists! Boom, boom! Everything is destroyed! Communists! Not good! Tack, tack, tack. The rails were blown up! The train can't go forward! Catastrophe, the war!"

I didn't regret coming home, even if it put me at risk. Furthermore, I must have been divinely inspired to return. I soon learned that the Germans had come back in full force to the Drôme Valley, raided Perdyer, and arrested several "patriots" and Jews, whom they executed. They raided Vassieux-en-Vercors using parachutes and gliders, and massacred hundreds of Resistance fighters and civilians.

I certainly found Le Chambon changed after my ten-month absence. The *maquis* no longer hid. Young people paraded in the streets with sub-machine guns, in mismatched uniforms: caps, belts, jackets, and military pants they had acquired.

There were more refugees than ever. The Cimade had organized an "underground railroad" (named in honor of the one that smuggled American slaves to freedom) that allowed Jews to cross the Swiss border. Older teenage girls escorted them. Furnished with false papers, families set out on trains. They were forbidden to speak lest their accent give them away to informers. They spent the night in hospitable rest houses, like the Abbey of Tamié, the Protestant presbytery in Annecy, and the Catholic presbytery in Douvaine located very close to the border. The priest put a thick cement pipe under the barbed wire. Those being persecuted crawled through. On the other side, they were in Switzerland!

In the beginning, the Swiss authorities often sent the refugees back because they didn't have visas. Sent back, they often fell into the hands of the German police and were deported. Eventually, thanks to public opinion, this situation improved. Refugees whose names were given in advance to the Ecumenical Council were granted asylum, meaning they had the right to live in special camps in Switzerland. Mr. Guillon, the former mayor of Le Chambon, was responsible for these lists.

The underground railroad worked remarkably well, so well that Jews escaped by the hundreds: between 2,500 and 3,000 through Le Chambon alone.[2] The village became known: the more refugees left, the more arrived. During my absence, Magda, with the courageous help of Simone Mairesse, spent her time placing new arrivals with farming families.

2 It is almost impossible to nail down the exact number of Jews hidden on the Plateau during the war. Contrary to what André Trocmé says here, Le Chambon was never conceived of as a stage on the way to refuge in Switzerland. As regards the number of Jewish refugees on the Plateau between 1939 and 1945, see Muriel Rosenberg's recent *Mais combien étaient-ils?* (Le Cheylard: Editions Dolmazon, 2021).

Édouard Theis had left Le Chambon a few days after me in the summer of 1943. He didn't return until the liberation. Along with André Philip's wife, Mireille, he played a role in politics and in the evacuation of Jews. One day, Mireille bravely left Switzerland buried under coal in a locomotive. Couriers constantly shuttled back and forth between Savoie, L'Ain, and Switzerland.

Other fugitives used smugglers, local peasants who knew the mountain passes and charged high prices. Disgusted, Morel, the young pastor in Devesset and a seasoned mountaineer, became a smuggler who charged nothing. His pied-à-terre was Pastor Chapel's presbytery in Annecy. I mention him because of an unlikely episode that reveals the odd mentality of that time.

A Jewish family entrusted Morel with their safety. One elderly family member with a weak heart suffered a heart attack during the crossing and died. Morel had to return to the French side of the border. The irresponsible Jewish family was furious and sued Morel in the Vichy courts for "reckless homicide." Morel was imprisoned as he awaited trial. It took great cleverness on the part of the tribunal to keep the Gestapo ignorant of a trial taking place right under their noses, but the judges managed to acquit Morel. I found the same intense, vibrant atmosphere in Le Chambon. But not everything was so great. Old pastor Poivre and Henri Braemer had, in fact, replaced me for sermons, but officially, Marcel Jeannet was my replacement. His disappointment at seeing me return, which meant he had to go back to his little parish in Le Mazet, was palpable. In his opinion, I carried adventure in my suitcases, and that meant trouble. He let me know what he thought of me.

As for my other friends and colleagues, they were now converted to de Gaulle and the Resistance, as if they had never thought otherwise. The whole village, including the students, was sliding toward violence.

I wasn't surprised to learn that our old friend, Léon Eyraud, was at the heart of a left-wing cell, having abandoned his Christian faith a long time before.

Or that André Bass, a Jewish lawyer from Paris, tried to establish a Jewish *maquis* recruited from the hundreds of Jews hidden in the area.

Or that at the request of Simone Pévenage Mairesse, who lived in Mazet and was involved with the Resistance, the villagers collaborated in everything short of assassination.

There was also in Le Chambon a unit of the Gaullist-leaning Secret Army. Its leader was Commander Fayol, a Jew from Marseille with a truly noble character. He tried to get me to join. When I refused for reasons of conscience, he nonetheless remained my friend and came to see me often. And why not? We both had moderate views. I thought it was insane to attack German soldiers; that only provoked reprisals. He agreed completely. Perhaps, in Le Chambon, that was how we had avoided the fate of Vassieux!

The Saint-Agrève and Lamastre *maquis*, which belonged to the FTPF and was largely composed of agitators, reproached the Secret Army for its inaction, requisitioned whatever they thought they needed, and assassinated forty-five Frenchmen suspected of "secret dealings with the enemy." Most of these Frenchmen were innocent.

The FTPF arrived one day in Le Chambon to requisition the entire inventory of a tobacconist named Fay. It caused such a furious reaction among the people of Le Chambon that things nearly degenerated into a shootout between the Secret Army and the FTPF. I intervened forcefully that day to get the FTPF out of town.

Another time, the FTPF almost unleashed a murderous raid on the Germans that would have resulted in the destruction of Le Chambon. The *maquis* of the surrounding area included young people from Le Chambon and students. They liked to parade around the streets with their guns, wearing scraps of military uniforms. Everyone was duly impressed, including my sons. It was only normal.

What wasn't normal, however, was the visit I received one day from a delegation of future theologians who lived in the Genêts. "All the theologians are going into the *maquis*," they told me. "We will form a Christian *maquis*, so we want to have a communion service every day. Will you lend us a chalice and a communion plate from the church?"

"I'm afraid that's impossible," I told them. "How do you reconcile the Last Supper with your desire to kill Germans?"

"We are convinced that God is ordering us to do so," they responded.

They left and went as far as La Bruyère, where they camped. They had trouble getting supplies and began requisitioning what they needed on the local farms. "It's for the defense of the country," they said.

"You're just a bunch of small-time thieves," grumbled the farmers they threatened at gunpoint.

Only a few of the future theologians resisted this movement and remained in Le Chambon. Others returned after a few months, sheepish and disillusioned. War didn't grant them the great self-liberation they vaguely sought in the sacrifice of their lives. Had their preachers misled them?

During these troubled weeks, Darnand's Milice and the German troops weren't idle. Our plateau remained under a double threat: from the west, where the Germans with the support of the Tatar Legion were still firmly entrenched in Le Puy, and from the east, all the way into the Rhône Valley. The German command could no longer tolerate the increasingly bold incursions of the *maquis* on the roads or railroads that interfered with the free circulation of their troops.

In the east, the Milice, spurred on by the new regional prefect,[3] engaged in raids intended to intimidate the *maquisards*. The goal was to sow terror that would leave them paralyzed. One of these terrorist acts was particularly despicable and, by its useless cruelty, caused such indignation in the countryside that it was attributed to the "Krauts." Yet the authors of this atrocity were Frenchmen who belonged to the Milice. Sadly, there were few differences between the Milice, the "French Gestapo," and the German Gestapo itself.

Here's what happened: A large and well-armed group of *miliciens* showed up at a farm in Lizieux and fiercely demanded to know where the *maquisards* were. "There are no *maquisards* here," said the two old people who lived on the farm. "There are only our two brothers who work in the fields. They are not involved in any politics. You wouldn't do them any harm, would you?"

"No, no, rest assured," responded the two *miliciens* with loud laughs. "But we are hungry. Give us something to eat!"

Thinking that they could win them over with a good meal, the two old people took out everything they had: sausage, salt pork, butter, and cheese, whose taste the city dwellers had forgotten. The *miliciens* gorged themselves. When the meal was finished, they brandished their weapons and invited the old people out for a little walk, not too far behind the farmhouse.

Behind the farmhouse lay the corpses of the two brothers, who had already been assassinated by the *miliciens* before they entered the farmhouse. The men had never belonged to the *maquis*.

3 Vichy had replaced Prefect Bach, who was judged lukewarm.

After such crimes, hatred against the "Krauts" burned more intensely. The number of those joining the *maquis* increased wildly, but they were unaware of their weakness in the face of German troops.

A field situated near Devesset, outlined at its four corners by flashlights, provided English planes a place to parachute in light arms and military equipment at night. The Allies even parachuted in a uniformed English officer to assume command. Although he spoke French well, he was not favorably received by the Secret Army or the FTPF and had to settle for an adviser's role. We learned later that, because the British and Americans feared a Communist insurrection, they refrained from sending the *maquis* more powerful weapons such as mortars and heavy machine guns. This enabled the Germans to inflict bitter losses on the Resistance. Because of the inferiority of the Resistance's weapons, mainly revolvers and bazookas, combat between the *maquis* and German troops always ended badly for the *maquis*.

This explains what happened on the national highway between Le Puy and Saint-Étienne, nine miles north of Le Puy. Impatient with Commander Fayol, a group of overanxious members of the Secret Army ambushed a German convoy. Among these tough guys was a tender soul, our friend "Lieutenant La Morlière," whose real name was Gaudelette. Mrs. Gaudelette was a super-patriotic woman who voluntarily sent others to their death. Her husband, a peace-loving, antimilitaristic reserve lieutenant, had no desire to join the *maquis*. His wife considered his lack of enthusiasm dishonorable and cowardly, and she tormented him until he joined. He took his handsome uniform out of camphor, the one he had put away after the 1940 debacle, and became Lieutenant La Morlière.

He wouldn't remain so for long. No sooner had he joined the *maquis* than he was led, against his will and egged on by his wife, into the expedition near Le Puy. There was hardly any combat at all. As soon as the Germans had endured a few rifle shots, they responded with bursts of heavy machine-gun fire. The *maquisards* disbanded immediately. There was only one casualty: Lieutenant La Morlière, killed instantly. The Germans left his body on the road and prohibited anyone from burying it. This tactic served as a warning to those who might think about another ambush.

The deflated *maquisards* returned to Le Chambon. Mrs. Gaudelette rushed to our house. She was crying hysterically. What a strange conversation ensued!

"I was the one who sent him to his death," she cried out. "I alone, do you understand! He didn't want to go. He was a tender-hearted soul. I accused him of cowardice and forced him to sign up. He wasn't sold on the idea. Oh, what's going to happen to me and the children? I need him. Do you understand? I need a man. You're not going to leave him lying there on the street, all alone, are you? I know that you liked him, Mr. Trocmé, and he liked you too. You must perform a funeral service for him! You'll bury him, won't you, Mr. Trocmé?"

"You know that the Germans are firing on sight at all civilian cars and have forbidden anyone to touch your husband's corpse," I objected.

"I know, I know! But you will go anyway, won't you? God will protect you. I know it! You're not a coward. Unfortunately, my husband was a coward. Oh, how right you are to be nonviolent!"

I promised her I would go, and she left. I was sick at heart. "It's now or never to prove that I don't practice nonviolence because I'm a coward," I told myself. "Burying a friend is a peaceful act *par excellence*. Yet to disobey the strict orders of the Germans, to walk into the lion's den, at best to get arrested while there's a price on my head, would be absolute madness."

But I felt that I had it way too easy in Le Chambon, while others were risking their lives. I also needed to show the "tough guys" who reproached me for my ten-month abscence that it wasn't fear that had sent me into hiding.

Magda was indignant and tried to stop me from going. Jean-Pierre, who loved me greatly and whom I loved tenderly, clenched his fists, and cried out, "It's unjust. She has no right to ask that of you. It will only cause two deaths instead of one."

The most difficult part was finding a car. The village where Gaudelette was murdered was twenty-eight miles from Le Chambon in a rough area. Prudence dictated that I return before dusk. I didn't have any more gas vouchers. I would have to depend on a friend to take me. Mr. Grand, the mayor, looked at me like I was insane. "I have my family, my responsibilities as mayor. It's a useless risk," he said. Le Forestier couldn't do it; neither could Mr. Sagne. Everyone excused themselves, as in the parable, while I descended the rungs of social dignity.

"There's always Eyraud, the gangster," people told me. "He's got balls!"

Eyraud was the wayward son of our dear housekeeper, Mrs. Eyraud. He had already done time in prison and managed to get by thanks to some nervy black-market deals. Too cunning to join the Resistance, he was nonetheless clever enough to steal gas cans from the German army motor pool on the outskirts of Saint-Étienne and sell the spoils from these glorious expeditions to the *maquisards* for a good price – the price of the life he had just risked.

Eyraud had a front-wheel-drive Citroën. As soon as I told him about my project, he accepted. "I won't pay you," I told him. "It's for Gaudelette."

"You can't leave a man to rot on the road," he said. "We'll go tomorrow."

The next day, we tied two bicycles onto the roof of his car and left, using back roads and driving prudently. At the crossroads, I got out, scanned the horizon, and indicated to Eyraud that the way was clear.

When we were a few miles from the national highway that goes from Le Puy to Saint-Étienne, we hid the car in the woods under fallen branches and straddled our bikes.

When we got to the combat area, which we easily recognized from the description we had been given – a turn in the road lined with trees – there was nothing: no dead body, no German patrol, only a dry spot of blood. We hurriedly crossed the road to the village.

"A French officer was killed a few days ago on the road," we said. "Do you know where his body is? I'm a pastor and I've come to bury him. He was Protestant!"

"Do you think our priest would leave a Christian like that without burial?" exclaimed the people in the village. "He said a Mass for him! We didn't know he was Protestant. We'll take you there. He's in a family vault. We all chipped in for the casket."

"But the Germans had prohibited anyone from touching the corpse!" I said. "What you did was dangerous."

"The Germans, the Germans. The Germans can go fuck themselves with their prohibitions! We are men here, not savages!"

We went to the cemetery and improvised a small funeral service. At my side was Eyraud, the gangster, with his hat in his hand, and a few people from the village. Under the stone was Gaudelette, who hadn't wanted to die.

I often think about Gaudelette, the village priest, and the courageous people in the village. I think about my excellent German family and my good Swiss parishioners,[4] who are so fearful, so humbly submissive to the law, no matter where it comes from or what it commands, whatever it

4 Trocmé wrote these lines in the 1960s, when he was the pastor of Saint-Gervais in Geneva.

dictates. Would they have had the good sense, mingled with humor and courage, to boldly disobey an infuriated enemy that had lost all sense of moderation during the weeks in which they sensed defeat? And I, who had made such a mountain out of this expedition, returned in Eyraud's car, almost laughing. How would the Nazis ever defeat such people?

Gaudelette's body was taken to the cemetery in Le Chambon after France's liberation. He lies under a stone cross beside another tomb that means so much to us.[5]

THE THREAT FROM THE EAST overtook us in a dramatically different way than the threat from the west.

One morning around nine, some foolhardy *maquisards* showed up at the presbytery. "Mr. Trocmé," they said, "the Germans are coming back up the Eyrieux Valley in force. They burned Le Cheylard and massacred the residents. They are closing in on Saint-Agrève. We are leaving to fight them. We must evacuate the village to save the inhabitants!"

This news was correct, although greatly exaggerated. Stories about the destruction of villages by fire and the slaughter of communities were common at the time. Le Chambon was plausibly the next target. In town, I met with the mayor, Mr. Grand, and two local doctors. We all agreed to send scouts from house to house to warn the inhabitants. By noon, the village was empty. Magda and the children went into the woods, as did others. We awaited the arrival of the Germans.

In the evening, Magda returned to the village so I wouldn't be alone.

I went into the village and saw a group of *maquisards* in a heated discussion with Dr. Le Forestier. "He has refused us the use of his ambulance to get to the Front," they complained when they saw me. "The battle is raging in Saint-Agrève, and we need to get there immediately. If we go by foot, it will take us two hours!"

"My truck carries the insignia of the Red Cross in big letters so it can be seen by aircraft," replied Le Forestier. "According to the Geneva Convention, it cannot transport either soldiers or arms! Furthermore, I am the doctor for the *maquis*. If there are wounded combatants, I must fetch them, and I'd be without my ambulance. Get out of here."

"The doctor is right," I told the *maquisards*. "Those are Red Cross rules."

"We don't give a shit about the Red Cross. Give us the keys!" cried the men, as they shoved the doctor.

5 Jean-Pierre Trocmé's tomb.

"What's going on?" interrupted a voice speaking in heavily accented French. It was an English officer I had never seen before, fighting his way through the crowd in his khaki uniform with a beret marked "para."

"This man is a spy, a traitor," yelled someone, pointing at Le Forestier. "Kill him!"

Pale with anger, the officer pulled out his revolver and pointed it at Le Forestier's chest. He was going to shoot.

"Don't do that!" I cried out in English. He turned around. "This man is not a spy; he is our village doctor."

I explained the situation to him, but the English are slow to get the picture. "He refuses to go into combat! He's a coward. I'll arrest him," he exclaimed.

"He is not refusing to go into combat. He's a doctor who must be ready to care for the wounded," I responded.

"He's right on that score, but I'll arrest him anyway," he protested. "If there are any wounded, we'll come get him, and he'll go pick them up."

There was nothing else to say. The Englishman was in command.

At that point, I suggested a middle ground to the Englishman. "Have him confined to my house, the Protestant presbytery. There will be no need to watch over him. He won't try to escape. Right, doctor? You'll give me your word of honor not to escape?"

"I give you my word," said Le Forestier, and I was authorized to take the "prisoner" into the presbytery my family had evacuated.

I took another walk in the village and learned that there was a battle in Saint-Agrève and that they needed Le Forestier and his ambulance immediately.

I raced to the presbytery and called out, but no one answered! There was no Le Forestier! He had broken his promise. I was furious.

I quickly went up the Côte de Molle. It was four p.m., and I found him at his house, on the balcony, relaxed, surrounded by his wife, his sister-in-law, and his children, having tea. Out of breath, I yelled, "You shouldn't have done that to me. It's happened! They're asking for you and your ambulance in Saint-Agrève. There are wounded fighters."

"I'm not going."

"What do you mean, you're not going? This time, it's your duty to go. You're not afraid, I hope!"

"No, but I'm not going, after the way they treated me! Prisoner of the *maquis*? Me, one of its founders! That English jackass would have shot me as a spy if you hadn't intervened!"

"Precisely," I said. "Since I got you out of that situation, I'm now asking you to go to Saint-Agrève."

"No, Mr. Trocmé, I'm staying right here. I don't give a damn about their wounded or their battles. Furthermore, I don't even believe that there is a battle."

He remained steadfast. I came home dejected.

The strangest part of all this is that Le Forestier was right. There never was a battle in Saint-Agrève. Therefore, there were no wounded.[6] It was nothing but panic that had created these imaginary events, which had grown worse as the rumor spread. In fact, the Germans had been on their way to Le Cheylard, where previously they had burned many houses and shot several men, but they suddenly turned right toward the Rhône Valley. We will never know why.

That same evening, the *maquisards* returned with their tails between their legs, with no great adventures to relate. The relieved inhabitants came out of the woods and prepared dinner in their homes. As for Le Forestier, he still had to prove that he wasn't a coward. He would do so soon, with tragic consequences.

6 There was nevertheless a strafing by the German troops on July 16, 1944.

18

Tragedy

IT WAS DANIELLE LE FORESTIER who came one day asking for assistance. "Roger is determined to help two *maquisards* in Le Puy get out of prison. A sympathetic guard transmitted their letter to him."

I went to see Le Forestier, who was in a state of worried excitement. "We're dealing with a family," he said. "They were arrested by the new prefect. If they remain in prison, the Gestapo will seize them. We must get them out before it's too late. Some *maquisards* want to storm the prison. That's insane! I'll drive there and intercede with the prefect. I'm a doctor; I have gas vouchers. Do you want to come with me?"

"Certainly not," I told him. "Your project is reckless! Go to Le Puy by car? The Germans shoot all civilian cars on sight, even doctors' cars. You'll never make it back."

"I have the Red Cross sign on my car," he said. "They'll let me through. I have been constantly accused of cowardice since the Saint-Agrève affair. I am no longer informed about the meetings of the Chambon Resistance Council I founded. They want to take the list of council members that I keep in my home from me. I hid it, though. They'll never find it. If you won't come, I'll find someone else!"

Then he left. "He's lost his mind," I told myself. "He'll come back to his senses. It's insane to keep a list of members of the Resistance in his home." One of the Resistance's absolute rules was never to keep a written list of members. When possible, they even avoided learning the real names of their own contacts.

Despite his wife's entreaties and those of his best friends, Le Forestier left for Le Puy, accompanied by two young *maquisards* – two culpable idiots, as you'll see.

Danielle Le Forestier managed to visit her husband in prison and gave me the following account of his arrest.

Le Forestier arrived safely in Le Puy and parked his car in front of the town hall, thereby winning the first part of his gamble. He then went into the prefect's office and demanded the release of the prisoners. The prefect, however, was intractable.[1] After a fruitless discussion, Le Forestier left the office and returned to his car. There he was ambushed by the Gestapo, who were looking for its owner. He was struck, knocked to the ground, and had two of his teeth broken. His face was horribly swollen. This took place in view of the two *maquisards* Le Forestier had left to watch the car. They were sitting outside at a café and witnessed his bloody arrest without intervening.

What had happened? A fatal coincidence. The Gestapo was on alert because, while Le Forestier was in the prefect's office, robbers had held up one of the city banks and carried off several million francs. Were they bandits? Perhaps. There were many people who took advantage of these turbulent times to commit crimes falsely attributed to the *maquis*. Was it a crime committed by the local maquis that needed cash? This was more likely, because such operations – against city halls, for example, to get ration cards – were necessary for the *maquis* to survive.

The police in Le Puy, including the Gestapo, were on alert. It didn't take long to find a car parked in front of the prefect's office and to search it. Behind the back seat, they found a loaded revolver that the two *maquisards* had hidden without telling Le Forestier. He had warned them, "Above all, no arms. That's how we will succeed!" On that day, Le Forestier, a Christian and a doctor, wished to practice nonviolence and act by persuasion. But his acolytes betrayed him twice, first by disobeying him, then by slipping away without helping him. They returned to Le Chambon and spread the sad news.

And what happened to Le Forestier? He was brought before a German military court and accused of plotting against the German Army. The evidence: a loaded revolver! The prosecutor, a certain Colonel Metger, requested the death penalty for "disobeying driving restrictions and carrying forbidden weapons." Le Forestier orchestrated a magnificent defense. He insisted that he did not know about the gun, but he couldn't prove that he had been accompanied. He related his actions before the prefect and offered a moving witness for Christian nonviolence. "We

1 The two prisoners survived. They were never deported by the Gestapo.

refuse to obey unjust laws; we hide Jews; we disobey your orders. But we do so in the name of the Gospel of Jesus Christ," he declared.

The presiding judge was the commander of the Le Puy area, Major Schmähling. He was an officer in the reserves, a high-school teacher, and a fervent Catholic. He believed Le Forestier's testimony and barely got him acquitted.

As compensation, he asked Le Forestier to make a "voluntary commitment" to work in Germany. "There are no more doctors in our bombed-out cities," he told him. Grateful to Schmähling for saving his life, Le Forestier signed. Before he left for Germany, Danielle managed to see him. It was heartbreaking, but he had been acquitted.

She would never see him again.

APPARENTLY, DURING THIS terrible two-month period that preceded liberation, the divine blessing that had allowed us to sneak through the cracks until then was taken away from us. Thereafter, circumstances seemed to turn against us.

All the victims during these tragic weeks perished senselessly. Le Forestier, the village's "utter fool"[2] – the least scheming person, the most idealistic – was the first victim. Manou Barraud was the second.

Situated at the end of the village on the road to Tence, the Barraud Boarding House was a joyful place for young people to meet under the indulgent eye of old Barraud, a Swiss carpenter, former artisan, and disappointed missionary, and Mrs. Barraud, a remarkably intelligent, practical, and good Alsatian woman who worked night and day to keep her family alive.[3]

The two oldest girls were beautiful and always had boys hanging around. Gaby was engaged to a theology student, who later dropped her. Manou was very young but claimed to be engaged to a *maquisard*, a student from Lamastre who proudly carried a revolver.

"Papa! Mama! Come quickly to the Barraud Boarding House! Manou is dying. Her fiancé killed her!" That was the summoning shout we got one afternoon from our own Jean-Pierre. When we arrived at the

2 It was with tenderness that Magda gave Le Forestier this name (*puro folle* in Italian).

3 Georgette Barraud, née Hoffmann (1893–1984), a teacher, met Émile Barraud in Zambia, where they were both missionaries. They settled in Le Chambon in 1936. He was a cabinetmaker, and she founded a children's boardinghouse, called Beau Soleil, where she welcomed Jewish children during the occupation. She and her daughter, Gabrielle (1922–2011), have been named Righteous Among the Nations in Jerusalem.

boarding house, Manou was dead. A few moments earlier, bragging to Manou about his promotion to weapons bearer, he had aimed his revolver at her. "Don't do that!" cried Manou. "Don't do that."

"Don't worry. There's a safety latch."

The shot was fired, piercing the girl's stomach. She died a few seconds later of an internal hemorrhage, after crying out to her fiancé, "You killed me!" Mrs. Barraud caressed the frighteningly pale forehead of her daughter. The bewildered "fiancé," not comprehending what he had done, tried to excuse himself by endlessly explaining. We had to quiet him down. It was a senseless tragedy, but it couldn't be undone.

Manou's burial took place two days later amid a large crowd of villagers, refugees, and *maquisards*. The Barrauds were admirable. Manou was buried in the cemetery against the wall that opens onto the sports field where, just a few days earlier with Nelly, Rolande Lombard, and a group of other girls, she had played basketball in her baggy, short red pants, coached by Pierre Brès, the gym teacher.

Manou's death had many consequences, one of which was that members of the *maquis* were no longer allowed to carry arms in the village.

Coming back from the cemetery, Magda and I said to each other: "If something like that ever happened to us, we couldn't bear it." Truer words were never spoken.

Of course, Magda and I thought about our own children.

Nelly would soon be seventeen, had two thick blond braids, and an enthusiastic look about her. She was a conscientious scout with an athletic body and was an excellent student at the École Nouvelle Cévenole.

Jean-Pierre was always thinking. I remember his inward, secretive gaze, his drawing, and his music. His body had suddenly begun to grow, so that at fourteen he had the shoulders and strong legs of a man. He was also a good scout and a good companion, with lots of friends.

Jacques was blond, thin, handsome, and growing like wildfire. He was a fervent scout and wanted to become a pastor. Later, he would accompany Captain Haldimann of the Salvation Army in his summer evangelical campaigns.

Daniel, the one without problems – or so we thought – had brown and laughing eyes under his wild mop of hair. He was stocky, resourceful, always on the move, but rebellious against all regimentation, and lazy in class.

But, above all, Jean-Pierre! Nelly and Jacques, the only children we still have, won't hold it against me if I explain in detail the place Jean-Pierre occupied in my life. At this time, Nelly already had a well-defined personality. She was "organized," as she said; everything was orderly in her world. She was intelligent, didn't get bogged down in complicated problems, and lived in the real world. She and I were already great friends. I could count on her, and she could count on me. But we didn't confide in one another. She was a blend of Magda and me, but she looked like the Trocmés, so I called her "Trocmette" when I was in a good mood, and "Aunt Pauline" when she got up on her high horse. She never forgot when I was strict with her. I prevented her, she tells me, from participating in skiing excursions organized by Mr. Barraud, which I don't remember, and from going to "home parties" that "those women" organized unbeknownst to the school, where dancing was forbidden – which I do remember. I didn't want to give the young Protestants in the village an example that would have encouraged them to attend the more licentious dances held in cafés, though I don't ever remember having been too strict.

And my Jacquot? We had our faith in common, our vocation, which at the time seemed very solid, our not always realistic idealism, and our enthusiasm for people. But also, our disappointment when others didn't understand us. Jacquot was more vulnerable than I was. As a child, he drew back when touched. This exaggerated sensitivity, which sent him into alternating highs and lows, forced me and Magda to warn him about the dangers of too much excitement. We had all around us examples of students at the Collège who had succumbed to harmful excesses. On our advice, Jacquot became neither a pastor, nor a missionary, nor a member of the Salvation Army. I think it was better this way. The discipline of a life in business forced him to keep his feet on the ground. He needed that – provided, of course, that the inevitable callousness of such a life did not destroy the purity and candor of his youthful faith.

But Jean-Pierre! He resembled me. He was my alter ego. In him, I recognized the same sluggishness in physical movements that everyone criticized when I was young. Jean-Pierre's "What?" when he was preoccupied has remained famous in our family. He also had my complexion, solid body, nearsightedness, and manner of thinking. I'm not a deep or quick thinker. On the contrary, I have difficulty grasping ideas clearly, and my memory is mediocre. But suddenly, after months, even years, my ideas flow: ordered, settled, and clear, nourished by a treasure trove of readings and past experiences I thought I had completely forgotten.

I love to think. Only rarely am I at peace, which I am granded by God as a gift. Soon, from deep inside me, all the problems resurface: life, death, love, faith, liberty, truth, justice. I construct hypotheses that collapse as soon as I find the weak point in my argument. The site is always under construction. From time to time, however, after lengthy, fruitless reasoning, a heavenly flash illuminates me like a foretaste of eternal beauty or a glimpse of rock-solid truth. That's all I need. I often give the impression that I'm too sure of myself, because I don't share my doubts with others. If only they knew what it costs me to think through these problems, they might confide in me and we could search together.

At fourteen, Jean-Pierre was already a deep thinker. I knew it; I felt it. But he had the reticence common to his age and confided few of his reflections to his parents. He had older friends and discussed things with them. He had a close friendship with a seventeen-year-old Jewish fellow, Francis Meyer, who joined the Liberation Army and was killed in Alsace. Magda and I guessed Jean-Pierre's thoughts from his school essays that were returned to us full of corrections in red ink in Miss Pont's handwriting. She didn't appreciate his style. But we, his parents, felt the emotion and maturity of the descriptions and ideas in these compositions.

Jean-Pierre often repeated a sentence that for me has remained enigmatic: "There is something that prevents me from being happy." I never dared ask him what he meant, for fear of forcing my way into his fourteen-year-old soul. Perhaps I should have done so.

Jean-Pierre blossomed at the piano and already played Beethoven and Chopin. Under his fingers, Chopin's music was striking. As events in France grew somber, his playing became more poignant. His music teacher, Mrs. Manchon-Theis, told me one day, "He is exceptionally gifted. He already has the sensitivity of an adult. He will be a talented artist if he is willing to work. Perhaps even a composer!"

One day, after listening to him play while I was in the kitchen, I came up behind him and placed my hands on his broad shoulders. "Jean-Pierre," I said to him, "You are my oldest son. One day, you will succeed me; you will continue what I have done. You will do a better job of it than I did, at least in certain areas. I can count on you, can't I?"

Jean-Pierre didn't say anything. He began playing the piano again. I felt like caressing his shock of straight hair, which was at the level of my lips. Such moments are rare between a father and his son.

Then came that terrible day.

We were returning, on August 13, 1944, from the Bois du Genest, a home a mile from the village, where Magda and I had gone to make peace between Mr. Beutler, Jean-Pierre's friend who gave us a portrait of him in pencil, and a nurse from the Swiss Children's Welfare Agency. A stupid business, because these two pigheaded Swiss fought and reconciled regularly over trifles they considered important. We stayed with them to share "the reconciliation cake." Magda wanted to go home. I insisted, alas, that she stay. Details, I tell you, insignificant details, make and unmake human destinies.

As we returned with Jacquot, Magda – what a strange intuition – repeated the sentence that she had already said at the Beutlers: "I hope I get home in time!"

At the presbytery, everything was quiet and sunny. I didn't go inside, but went straight to the church, where I was expected for a meeting. I was halfway down the alley that forms the shortcut between the Rue de l'Eglise and the Rue du Temple, when I heard Jacquot's voice – Was it a voice or the cry of a wounded child or was it I who cried out? I no longer know.

"Papa, Papa, come quickly! Jean-Pierre has hanged himself!"

On the upper floor, on the right before the open bathroom door, there were already several people gathered. I moved them aside. Jean-Pierre was stretched out on the ground in his bathing suit, smiling, but dead. "I just took him down," said Magda in an expressionless voice, as if she too were dead. "He was so heavy! He attached a cord to the flush-water tank on the wall above the toilet. I don't know how I did it. He's still warm! Go get a doctor quickly. Perhaps he is still alive."

But Jean-Pierre was dead. I touched him. He was no longer breathing.

"That must be what happened," the evidence told me. "That, and nothing else. There's nothing to be done." The same sense of inevitability that filled me when, at nine years of age, I saw my mother lying dead on the side of the road. The same beloved body, but dead. A void, nothing. My son!

For a moment I revolted against the evidence. I was on the point of saying, "Leave, all of you." I wanted to lie on top of the body, as the prophet Elijah had done on the son of the widow of Zarephath.

But no, that would have been to tempt God! And the memory of all the failures of the Pentecostals prevented me from acting out my wishes. Often, since then, I have reproached myself bitterly. Mouth to mouth resuscitation for several years now has brought back asphyxiated, drowned, and hanged people. If I had only known. People didn't talk about that method then. They talked about heart massage, using the hand on the open chest. That worked sometimes. If only Le Forestier had been there!

Precious moments passed as we awaited the arrival of Doctor Riou. The warmth was leaving the large, well-proportioned, and tanned body of my son.

Riou arrived and from the first glance was negative. "I am going to proceed with an intracardiac injection," he declared. It had no effect: Jean-Pierre was physiologically dead. I left in a friend's car to get Nelly, who was camping at Saint-Front Lake.

From that moment on, everything is confused in my memory. I must have fallen into a frightening state of shock. Jean-Pierre had committed suicide. That much was clear. But why, why, why? His last day had been so cheerful. At noon, he had been making jokes at lunch.[4]

MAGDA WAS ADMIRABLE during this horrible time. On the day of the burial, the casket was carried by Jean-Pierre's friends, led by Olivier Hatzfeld, his history teacher. The six of us who remained – Magda, Nelly, Jacquot, Daniel, Jispa, and I – held hands. A profound nausea gripped my stomach.

The tomb was covered with flowers from our beloved fields in bunches held together by multicolored ribbons that children's hands had tied. Magda kept repeating, "My poor little one! My poor little one! If only I had been there. I should have been there. I had a sense of foreboding. Going off like that, all alone, all alone, without a goodbye."

She cried, but I couldn't.

The next day, when we went to the cemetery, Magda began to detach the multicolored ribbons from the bouquets.

4 Here, the family has redacted from the manuscript Trocmé's report on the last hours of his son's life, and the explanations of Doctor Riou, who concluded that Jean-Pierre's death was an accident and not a suicide. The explanation is that Jean-Pierre was acting out the famous poem by François Villon, "La Ballade des pendus" (Ballad of the Hanged), when he slipped and accidentally hanged himself.

"What are you doing?" I asked.

"I'm taking the ribbons for the poor refugee girls who have replaced the young men deported from the Maison des Roches," she replied.

Then I understood that she would heal more quickly than I would. She hadn't lost her awareness of the outside world. I had.

I lost faith in the God of my childhood. It is said that despite the sad experiences we might have, we never forget the religion of our childhood if we learn it from our mothers. What did my mother tell me? I no longer know, but I knew then that "the Eternal One is the one who protects me." An invisible, paternal presence never left me. The heavens were caring. The will of God was carried out on earth for those who obeyed God. An image that my mother had placed in our childhood room depicted an angel watching over two children on the edge of an abyss.

What about my mother's death? A later explanation allowed me to see it as God's will. How many times did I hear my father say in 1914, "Fortunately, your German mother is dead! She could never have lived through such a rift between our two countries and our two families." After the fact, I too came to rationalize my mother's death.

But Jean-Pierre's death . . . Stupid, no other word for it. That wasn't the case for Gaudelette's sacrifice! Jean-Pierre wasn't even the victim of an imbecile, like Manou. Absurd! Our visit to the Beutlers, our tardy return. Jean-Pierre had been his own victim, the victim of his imagination.

Absurd, too, were the terrible consequences of all this on our children and my ministry. Nothing positive. Nothing but nothing. Playthings in the void, that's what we are.

I lost my faith, or at least my confidence in a God who follows me and protects me from all evil. We were subject to absurd, chaotic circumstances. That's what life is. Without knowing it, I had joined Camus and Sartre, who were still unknown at that time.

"God will give me an answer," I told myself in the beginning, walking in the woods. "I will have a vision," and I began calling out loud, "Jean-Pierre, Jean-Pierre," but I met no one and had no visions. Jean-Pierre had disappeared, disintegrated along with his thoughts, his music, and the poems he carried within him.

I could no longer pray, because my prayer was either met by an angry God who told me: "It's because you went into hiding and were afraid of death that I took your son instead of you," or it got lost in the void. I didn't pray for a long time. I was incapable of having a dialogue with a

God who remained silent or elsewhere, in a world completely different from the one where I struggled. For my mental health, I stopped praying.

How did I come out of it? I didn't. Still today, I carry my son's death within me. I am like a fir tree whose top has been chopped off. Fir trees never grow back their tops. They remain shorn. They grow outward, perhaps. That's what I did. I thought less and threw myself into action. Under a scar that the years have thickened little by little, an incurable wound bleeds deep inside: total resignation before the void where I'm headed, along with all those around me.

But I decided to go on.

The following Sunday, I preached from the pulpit. It was a terrible test, but I preached the gospel. Oh, not the gospel of childish confidence, but the harsher, barer gospel of the wager, a gospel turned toward the future for which, if necessary, one was ready to sacrifice the present. A gospel founded on a prophetic promise, an unlikely historical event, the resurrection of Christ. In Christ, all live.

Little by little, a different God from the one at my mother's knees was revealed to me. "I am in prison," I told myself. "I can see nothing, but between two of the stones of this tomb, a tiny crack is opening, a crack in the form of a cross. The fissure is Christ! From now on, the cross is the only image for an obtuse, suffering man subjected to the absurd demolition of the traditional God. No longer a protective God, or an all-powerful God, but a God totally immersed in the suffering of the creation. A God whose origin and future we do not know, but a God who identifies fully with my nothingness and my hopes."

What about Magda and my children?

During a short vacation spent away from the presbytery at Camp Joubert, I still couldn't measure the damage that Jean-Pierre's death did to them. The children played and laughed. We didn't want to restrain them.

But after!

Magda, the woman I love, my physical and spiritual spouse, was stronger in the short run than I was. Never did she brush up against the abyss, as I did, where one loses, if not one's reason, at least one's reason to live.

"Jean-Pierre never had his life," she repeated. "He should have had his life." Magda loves life, not only her own, but also the life lived by others. She truly loves other people, above all the wounded and the crippled. Magda woke up from this crisis bleeding to death, like me, in her faith.

Neither prayer, nor communion service among the faithful, nor hope in the eternal – nothing that had come to life for her during our early years in Sin-le-Noble now seemed possible. She moved away from the church, from the church community, and from her husband as pastor. This has been the cause of painful tensions between us, and I reproach myself for the reprimands that, in the heat of difficult discussions, I threw in the face of my courageous spouse.

Nelly might be the one who came through it the best. She was seventeen, had lots of male and female friends, and possessed an incredible vitality that kept her afloat. But I often wonder whether the pessimism she has exhibited since then was caused by our family catastrophe.

Jacques was the most visibly wounded. He admired his older brother and was somewhat envious of him. Now that Jean-Pierre was dead, it seemed to him that life was no longer worth living. "I'll do what Jean-Pierre did," he said in his despairing moments. Once, after being scolded, he tried to throw himself out of the window. We caught him by the wrists! It was only when he attended the Quaker-run Westtown Prep School in West Chester, Pennsylvania, that Jacques recovered. He came back to us a little too sure of himself for our liking, a bit of a braggart. His wife, Leslyn, full of good common sense and vitality, and the birth of his children, I think, completed his healing.

And Daniel? On the surface, he was still the joyful jokester we had always known. But he started to display some strange tendencies. He, who had always been so sociable, began to complain about having no friends. We lost control of a whole segment of his life. He refused to join the scouts. At eleven, he was still marked by his brother's death.

WE NEVER TOOK THE TROUBLE to rectify the gossip, whether hateful or pitiful, regarding Jean-Pierre's death. At least on the surface, we kept our heads high and our mouths closed. We were satisfied with Doctor Riou's conclusions.

We also decided not to talk too much to the children about their brother's death. Their lives had to continue as normally as possible. School, vacation, teaching, and religious meetings continued as before.

Perhaps I was too silent. I should have taught my children the basic tenets of faith. They must have been struggling with problems too weighty for their young moral consciences. How happy those parents who, naively confident, transmit a simple faith to their children, a faith which perhaps doesn't coincide perfectly with reality but puts the next generation on a path that leads to inner peace. Unless it doesn't . . .

It was after Jean-Pierre's death that we came to know him through the discovery of his secret notebooks. We learned that he considered himself the "head of an island," and recognized his right to cloak his thoughts in mystery. That's how adolescents are. They must conceal themselves to affirm themselves and thereby escape the grasp of their parents, brothers and sisters, and teachers.

We knew that Jean-Pierre was a musician. We did not know he was a poet and an artist. The drawings we found were simple, but the energy of the lines in two or three of his landscapes was striking. The same is true of his poetry. It appears that he began to write poetry during his stay in Switzerland in the winter of 1942–43 when he was twelve.

One of his poems astonished us. It's the story of a shepherd who goes into the mountains with his sheep on a Sunday. He goes higher and higher and, suddenly, the poem stops. Then Jean-Pierre writes, "Don't cry over the shepherd; he's with God." Was it a poetic coincidence, an omen, or even a premonition of the great poetic ecstasy that took him away one Sunday? A poem that you want to relive, imitate, even recreate so well that it also carries you off to death!

Jean-Pierre never spoke to us about his faith. We were moved to find in his handwriting a meditation on Good Friday entitled "Night." Its profound sadness ends with a profession of faith, underlined in red: "The night no longer matters, when we put the lamp on top of the bushel."

It is this quotation that we had engraved on the long stone bearing two granite crosses that covers his remains and those of Manou Barraud, against the wall that separates them from the sports field where they so often played.[5]

This posthumous discovery of our Jean-Pierre helped staunch the terrible wounds people caused us by the rumors that he was a budding juvenile delinquent! A juvenile delinquent? This secretive boy who, at thirteen, read the Bible to the old women at the lower end of town and prayed with them, replacing his father who was not there to do so? "He was our friend," they mourned, as did Mrs. Vey, the baker. These tributes increased our sense of loss, even as they assured us that someone like him could only be with God. Today, we are just as sure of it.

5 André and Magda's ashes and those of their son Daniel, and Jispa's, are now under the same stone.

19

Liberation

HISTORY CONTINUED its relentless march alongside the events of our personal lives. History played with the life and death of millions of men and women. It sent the Jews, sheep without shepherds, to the gas chambers, and the civilians of Hamburg, Dortmund, and Dresden to the furnace of incendiary bombardments where they were vaporized in flames.

Le Chambon lived through several astonishing weeks.

Returning from the cemetery after burying Jean-Pierre on August 15, 1944, Darcissac said to me: "I know that this has been a terrible day for you, but you should know that the BBC announced that the Allies have landed in the Midi."

From this day forward, the Germans, caught between two armies, began to evacuate the south of France. They did so without panic. Their admirable discipline contrasted with the 1940 stampedes of the Allies.

As Germany's hold loosened, the boldness of the *maquis* increased. The last 120 German occupants of Le Puy received the order to fall back to Saint-Étienne and Lyon. On the road, they encountered a swarm of *maquisards*, far too great a number for the Germans to resist. The sides exchanged fire. A Trocmé cousin, Jean Rist, from the École des Roches, was killed. He was the only casualty. The Germans capitulated.

They were taken to the outskirts of Le Chambon and put into an imitation chateau at the Pont de Mars on the Lignon River. French police guarded it. What a strange turn of events! They were the same police officers who, a few days earlier, followed Vichy's orders. Sensing the tide turning, they now guarded the prisoners they would have obeyed earlier. Since these prisoners were held in my township, I automatically became their chaplain!

It wasn't an easy task. These 120 Germans were accused of horrible crimes. Public opinion was incapable of nuance. The most compromised Vichy collaborators were now the most enraged against the "Krauts." They had to seek revenge, not only for the suffering they bore but for their cowardice and guilty consciences. A few months later, in the streets of Saint-Étienne, German prisoners were attacked by enraged mobs. Two were lynched. The bodies of forty-five massacred prisoners were found in a well in Ardèche.

Our policemen, fortunately, did their best to resist the demands of the hotheads, who would have willingly executed the 120 prisoners. My visits contributed to their security but didn't make me popular.

I went, nonetheless, and asked to see their leader. It was Major Schmähling, who gave me the details of Le Forestier's trial. "He's in Germany now," he told me. "His wife will see him again."

They remained polite, even obsequious, and saluted me, clicking their heels and sarcastically calling me "*Herr Pfarrer*" (Reverend Pastor). "The war isn't over yet," they claimed. "Our Führer has more tricks up his sleeve. First, a strategic retreat; then a secret offensive that will cast everyone into the sea. Just like Dunkirk, ha-ha!"

They didn't humble themselves in my presence at all. I offered to come on Sunday afternoons for a religious service. "That's very kind of you," said Schmähling. "I'm Catholic, but I'll give the order and everyone will come." Although he was a prisoner, in the eyes of his men he was still their leader.

When I arrived the following Sunday, a guttural command resounded throughout the camp. The men dropped what they were doing and found their place in line as they would have for a maneuver. Marching four by four, they entered the hall and remained standing. "In the name of the Father, the Son, and the Holy Spirit," I said.

Only then did they sit down on the benches.

I had asked Captain Neunkirchen, a very tall, thin man, to read the liturgy in my place. It was the Lutheran liturgy, with responses and spontaneous chants, which I didn't know. He did an excellent job. I learned later that Captain Neunkirchen had commanded the military police and arrested many resisters. He would have arrested me if he had had the chance!

Preparing my sermons for the Germans took a lot of work. Unlike my usual way of proceeding, which consists of giving sermons using lots of detailed notes, I had to write out my entire text and ask Miss Hoefert to translate it into German. I then read her clear handwriting to the prisoners.

Since my visits to the German soldiers were unpopular among the French, above all among the *maquisards*, I decided to give the same sermon in French on Sunday morning that I preached to the Germans in the afternoon.

I don't think my sermons were ever discussed more thoroughly. I recall that I wrote a kind of catechism lesson, beginning with the Ten Commandments and ending with the justice, truth, and nonviolence that we can always practice because of the forgiveness of sins that God offers us through Christ. I severely condemned war.

My "exaggerations" displeased the *maquisards*, who appeared everywhere once the Germans disappeared from Le Puy. They showed up in scruffy bunches, with their weapons in shoulder holsters, to attend church services. I had to get angry to make some of them leave their guns in the church courtyard before entering the house of God.

They didn't like my sermons. "Go tell that to your German friends," they said when I insisted on justice, nonviolence, and the forgiveness of sins. "The Bible is true in theory, but in practice, with 'those kinds of people,' only brute force counts. Think about Oradour."[1]

"You're right," I responded. "This afternoon I will read the very same text to the Germans." That silenced them.

The Germans didn't like my sermons either. "We're not the ones you should be preaching to," they objected. "Tell it to your friends, the Communists. To justify their revolution, they have spread a doctrine of violence throughout the world based on the idea that the end justifies the means. The Germans are honest and courageous. They believe in God and have shed their blood to save Europe from the 'red plague.' You'll see what happens when we are no longer here to protect you from Communism!"

When I spoke to them about Oradour, they shrugged their shoulders and refused to believe it. *"Das ist blöde, lügnerische Kriegspropaganda"* (That's nothing but stupid, lying war propaganda), they said, shoving aside the Allied leaflets I handed them.

1 On June 10, 1944, a German Waffen-SS company wiped out the village of Oradour-sur-Glane, massacring 642 civilians, including women and children.

Thus, from time to time, the most frightening crimes are committed on both sides by those solidly convinced of their innocence and of the one-sided guilt of their adversary. Such conviction authorizes all excesses: "Against people 'like that,' everything is permitted!"

The German prisoners were malnourished and complained about it. They had, up to that point, unconsciously inflicted the harshest deprivations possible on the country they occupied through their requisitions and systematic rationing. Butter and meat had been reserved for the troops or left the country on trains for Germany. We were all emaciated. A photograph of Magda taken at the time revealed the silhouette of a skeleton. The Germans were fat with pink complexions.

My arguments didn't satisfy their stomachs, so I decided to do something. I suggested that several people chip in to buy them grapes, which we had in abundance. It was September 1944. Furthermore, on Sunday, I brought a few members of the church with me, several of whom spoke powerfully about nonviolence in front of the German soldiers, who were taken aback.

My distribution of grapes made me unpopular. Once again, the "tourists" in the village began to murmur that I was a "Kraut" after all.

When we were liberated, the Germans were sent to regular prisoner of war camps. Schmähling, Neunkirchen, and Colonel Metger, the commander of the Tatar Legion, were tried for war crimes. Metger was condemned to death, with good reason; Schmähling and Neunkirchen were acquitted. They had only half-heartedly obeyed orders and had decided to help some people, many of whom testified on their behalf. Schmähling was even the guest of the city of Le Puy many years later. An artist, he brought several of his beautiful watercolors. His efforts on behalf of the city were greatly appreciated.

I'LL FINISH LE FORESTIER'S STORY. His wife never heard a word from him. The war ended. All the prisoners returned, but Le Forestier didn't come back. Since he had not been deported but had signed a voluntary commitment to serve as a doctor in Germany, we expected him any day.

Then someone suggested that he may have been a victim of the massacre of Saint-Genis-Laval. Leaving Lyon after a night of drinking, the Gestapo police had entered the cells of Fort Montluc Prison very early in the morning and haphazardly selected men, women, and children, who were taken to an abandoned farm in Saint-Genis-Laval. In the farm's main room, the Germans slaughtered them with machineguns and piled up their bodies. Then they sprinkled gasoline on the pile and set it on fire. The neighbors heard the screams of those unfortunate ones who had not been killed by machine-gun fire.

Danielle went to see the prefect of the Rhône Valley. He showed her eighty small sacks containing remains. "There were eighty-five victims," they told her. "But this is all we have. The other remains are unidentifiable." Danielle examined every sack, one by one, and found nothing. She was ready to breathe a sigh of relief, when, in the last one, yes, the very last one, she discovered a button from an article of her husband's clothing with the name of the tailor in Montpellier and cloth from his undergarment. Le Forestier, the happy-go-lucky guy, the carefree one, the *puro folle*, had suffered this horrible death.

Danielle tracked down some of her husband's former cell companions. "He could have escaped between Le Puy and Lyon," they told her. "One or two prisoners succeeded. They wanted to take your husband with them. But he told them, 'I gave my word of honor to work in Germany. Because of that, my life was saved. I must keep my word.' At Montluc, he was admirable, joyful as a child, singing hymns, and reading the Bible. Everyone loved him."

How did he get sent to Montluc? I learned the story many years later from Schmähling himself, whom I visited in Germany after the war. I was a speaker for the Fellowship of Reconciliation and gave a talk one night in Cologne, in one of the few public halls that survived the bombings that destroyed the city.

At the end of my talk, members of the audience approached me. "Don't you recognize me," one of them said. "I'm Mr. Nethe. I'm Jewish. Thanks to you, I was hidden in Mrs. Eyraud's house. Then the Cimade got me into Switzerland. I lucked out! Mrs. Eyraud wrote me that two days after I left, the Gestapo raided her house!"

"I congratulate you, Mr. Nethe, for surviving."

"Here," he said blushing. "When I saw your name on the poster, I said that must be Pastor Trocmé from Le Chambon. I've brought a small package I would like you to give to Mrs. Eyraud as a token for all she did for me. Oh, you understand," he said while clearing his throat, "I'm a manufacturer of women's lingerie, somewhat elegant lingerie, but . . . maybe a pastor wouldn't . . ."

"Oh, I'll be happy to take it to her," I responded.

At that moment, a tall silhouette inserted itself between Mr. Nethe and me, clicking its heels. "Neunkirchen," a tiny voice pronounced, as the body of a giant bowed from the waist down. "Mr. Neunkirchen!" I exclaimed, "Captain Neunkirchen! What are you doing here?"

"I'm from Cologne, and I came to hear you speak. I want to congratulate you on your excellent talk."

I remembered that Neunkirchen had been the former head of the military police that hunted down Jews and resisters with the same relentlessness.

"Mr. Neunkirchen," I said to him, "I almost forgot to introduce you to Mr. Nethe. He's German like you, but he's Jewish. Your task was to arrest him and deport him to the gas chambers."

The two men shook hands. They were visibly uncomfortable, especially Mr. Neunkirchen.

"Ah! Those were terrible times, Pastor Trocmé," he said. "We knew nothing. You believe me, don't you? We knew absolutely nothing about extermination camps."

"I want to believe you, Mr. Neunkirchen. But it remains true that if the church of Jesus Christ hadn't hidden Mr. Nethe and if the Cimade hadn't gotten him under the barbed wire into Switzerland, he would be dead like the other six million people of his faith."

"I know, I know," said Mr. Neunkirchen, completely overwhelmed.

I saw these two men again several times. Whenever I spoke in Cologne, they were in the audience. Neunkirchen once arrived with twenty young people; he was a retired teacher who now taught night school. "I tell my students they must come hear you," he confided to me, "because you are right."

Believe it or not, Mr. Neunkirchen, a former member of the German police, became a member of the Versöhnungsbund, the German branch of the International Fellowship of Reconciliation, and Mr. Nethe, who has forgiven him, did as well. They have even become friends and came to hear me together.

All this takes us away from the Le Forestier tragedy, you might say. But it doesn't!

When we first met in Cologne, I told Neunkirchen, "I would really like to meet with Schmähling. Do you have his address?"

"He lives in Munich. Here's his address," the old captain replied.

A few months later, when I was in Munich with Magda on a lecture circuit, we went to see Schmähling one afternoon. He lived in a building that had been half destroyed by the bombardments. We rang the bell. He opened the door. After a short hesitation, he recognized me: *"Ach! Pfarrer Trocmé. Ja natürlich, kommen Sie doch herein!"* (Oh, Pastor Trocmé. Yes, of course, come in!) He and his wife were having their afternoon coffee and invited us to share their cake.

"I came to ask you two questions, Mr. Schmähling, that I could never answer. Here's the first: You knew that Le Chambon was a nest of resistance activity. There were Jews there, and also the *maquis*. Certainly, your police did some harm to us, but why didn't you ever send a punitive expedition against us, as the Germans did in so many other places?"

"Mr. Trocmé," he said, "it's difficult to say. You know that we had the Tatar Legion in our area under the command of Colonel Metger."

"I remember. Sadly, they made themselves famous on Mont Mouchet.[2]

"Yes, Colonel Metger was a gung-ho guy who insisted that we intervene. I always told him, 'Let's wait.' But toward the end of the war, after I heard the declarations of Le Forestier, a Christian who explained clearly why you were disobeying us, I believed he was sincere. I'm a good Catholic, you know, and I understand these things. 'This type of resistance,' I said to Metger, 'has nothing to do with the violence you can repress with violence!' I therefore strenuously opposed all interventions with our troops. It's perhaps for that reason," said a smiling Schmähling, "that I became your prisoner."

"Perhaps," I responded. "But, if that's the case, why weren't you able to save Le Forestier?"

"To save Le Forestier, I had to fight against other officers and put myself on the line. 'I am sure this man is not dangerous,' I declared at his court martial, and I commuted his punishment to voluntary service in Germany."

"So, what happened?"

Schmäling reflected, with clenched fists and tears in his eyes, "Those Gestapo *Schweinehunde* (bastards) must have sent a message to their colleagues in Lyon. When Le Forestier got there, he was taken out of the line of people going to Germany and thrown into Fort Montluc Prison. That's what happened."

2 In May and June 1944, a series of battles took place on Mont Mouchet, located on the border of the French departments of Cantal, Haute-Loire, and Lozère, between the Germans and the *maquis* of Mont Mouchet. The Germans defeated the *maquisards*: 238 French were killed and 180 wounded. In revenge for earlier losses, the Germans pillaged several of the surrounding villages and executed 100 hostages.

"That's what happened," I robotically repeated.

"That's why," Schmähling continued, "I still wake up with nightmares. I still see this beautiful young woman and her two children who came begging me before taking leave of her husband. She had confidence in me. I promised her that he would return. What must she think of me now?"

"She hasn't forgiven you," I had to tell this poor major, who today was an old, retired teacher.

Danielle Le Forestier, who was indeed very pretty, returned to her home city of Cannes. Many men, dazzled by her beauty, asked for her hand in marriage. She never remarried, however, but worked courageously to raise her two sons.

THE LAST ARRIVAL of "refugees" in Le Chambon was particularly moving: the French and foreign survivors of the "phantom train," which came from Marseille. What was this "phantom train?"

At the time of their orderly retreat from the Midi, the Germans decided to take the political prisoners with them. They put them into several trains, most of which arrived at their destination in Germany. Among them was the train that transported my friend, Marcel Heuzé, a pastor in Marseille who, like me, was too much of a friend to the Jews. He died in 1945, just days before his concentration camp was liberated.

Only one train never arrived in Germany. During the night it stopped several times, waited at length on the sidetracks, was pushed backward and forward as the car bumpers clanged. The Germans guarding the prisoners weren't worried about the situation. They had been through this before.

At dawn, the train was suddenly stopped in a rock cut and surrounded by a swarm of *maquisards*, who cried out, "Hands up! Give up – you've had it!" The mechanic and the conductor of the train, in cahoots with the railroad workers, had diverted the train and taken it close to Annonay, in the area controlled by the Resistance. After a quick exchange of fire, the Germans surrendered, except for one young man who emptied his clips before dropping to the ground, shot in the thigh.

Le Chambon welcomed about fifty of the survivors, all stunned by their unexpected liberation. Among them was the young, wounded German, whose hair reminded me of a fox. He was taken to the Enfants à la Montagne house, which the *maquis* had transformed into a field hospital.

Two days later, they came looking for me. "There's a young German prisoner who won't let us bandage him or operate on him. He refuses all food and has a terrible fever. If he keeps this up, he'll die. You know German; come and talk sense to him."

I went there and did, in fact, find a kind of wild young fox. He had red hair and green eyes and the frightened expression of a trapped animal, ready to bite.

"Na, na, was ist denn los?" (Let's see, what's the matter?), I said to him in my most paternal tone, but hearing his own language only made him curl up tighter on his bed.

I spoke to him for a long time without getting any answer. "You've happened on good people. They are going to heal you. They will do you absolutely no harm." When I told him, *"Sie haben ja Vater und Mutter zu Hause"* (You have a mother and a father at home, don't you?), his red mop of hair swayed from side to side, and I realized that I was dealing with a very young boy, perhaps a child.

Then, suddenly, his anguish overflowed. He began to tremble and sob. In a broken voice, he managed to say this: "I know why you are saying all that. You want to trick me. You're a Communist. I know it. I have fallen into the hands of Communists. If I take your food, it will be poisonous. If I let you inject me, it will make me crazy. They explained all this to me at home. I must not capitulate. I should have died. I have been a coward, a coward!" I touched his shoulder, and it jolted. "I am not a Communist; I am a pastor." I spoke to him the best I could about a loving God. I read some verses from the Bible and prayed. He gradually stopped trembling. Finally, I put my hands on his red hair to give him a blessing.

"So, you think I can let them take care of me?" he asked. "You think I can eat?

"Of course," I responded.

At the door I went to open, the friendly faces of the *maquis* nurses were already there to help.

The young fox was quickly tamed. His wound healed, and he was soon hobbling on crutches in the courtyard. As with so many others, the liberation took him away, and I never heard from him again.

In 1966, I was in Algiers at the house of Pastor Blanc, director of the Christian Aid Committee for Algeria. I was introduced to his mother-in-law, Mrs. Boeykens.

"Are you the same André Trocmé whom we received in our home in Brussels in 1917?" she asked me.

"Yes I am," I responded. "I can still see your husband with his square, red beard. He was the president of the YMCA on Rue Ernest Allard."

We were evoking pleasant memories of World War I!

"Is your husband dead?" I asked.

"Sadly, yes, Mr. Trocmé. Our oldest daughter was a courier for the Resistance. The Germans knew about it. She escaped from them, but they arrested my husband. He too was marginally involved."

"What happened?"

"They deported him. I was also arrested and thrown into prison in Marseille. I never saw him again."

"And you?"

"I was in the 'phantom train.' You know, the one that the railroad workers turned over to the *maquis*!"

"I know this story very well," I told her. "Some of the survivors came to Le Chambon. One of them was a young German with red hair, wounded in the leg. Did you see him?"

"I think so. He wanted to kill me."

"Tell me about it, Mrs. Boeykens!"

"After the exchange of fire, the German guards surrendered, and the *maquisards* cried out, 'You can get out of the train now!' I went into the corridor, and there was a young German, wounded in the thigh, lying in a puddle of blood. When he saw me, he made a sign for me to come to him, which I did. Then he aimed his gun at me and said, 'I'm going to kill you.' I was barely able to throw myself on top of him and disarm him. He was crazy, really crazy."

"Yes, crazy with fear and hatred, Mrs. Boeykens. It didn't stop him from almost killing you, but he was just a poor young child who had been brainwashed by the Nazis!"

How many lives have been cut short in wartime by "crazy" people like him?

And for what reason? For nothing.

ONE DAY IN SEPTEMBER 1944, General Jean de Lattre's army entered Le Chambon in rapid-gun carriers and a few tanks with raised hoods. Out of these tanks there emerged helmeted men with drawn features and distant looks in their eyes. Many were North Africans. Having survived tough battles in Italy, they smilingly accepted the kisses young women blew their way, the hurrahs of the men and children, and the flowers thrown in front of them. They appeared blasé, almost indifferent.

For us, it was the end of our anguish. Certainly, I looked upon this spectacle with pleasure, but something in me was dead. It was my son, who wasn't there to witness it. I had already lived through the 1918 liberation in Belgium. I was seventeen years old then, with a bright, young soul. A bitter disillusionment followed my hours of enthusiasm. I knew that the days following victory were deceptive, and I wouldnt be deceived. But there was something else: I already felt cast aside by the waves of the ambitious survivors who wanted to take advantage of the rising tide. I felt that a page had just turned and that André Trocmé, now forty-three years old, had just lived the most difficult and useful years of his life. I had to turn this page courageously, forget this past as we had all forgotten 1914, and live today to lay the foundation for tomorrow, which was already fast upon us. As a Christian, I knew that political liberation was not the kingdom of God.

Like the froth of a wave, all those whom the war had brought us were carried off by the liberation.

First, the *maquisards*. The politically astute de Gaulle engaged them by the tens of thousands in the Rhine Army to counter the danger of Communism. He also needed them among the Allied forces to represent France when it came time to settle scores.

The liberation also carried off the refugees, the Jews in particular, who had promised to "build the Collège Cévenol" in gratitude of the shelter they found on the Plateau. Then, more modestly, they agreed to create the "Daniel Trocmé Scholarship." But they fled like a flock of sparrows as soon as they could.[3] The last ones to leave, ashamed of the behavior of their fellow Jews, took up a collection that brought in 9,000 francs.

Carried off, too, were many teachers at the Collège who had come to teach during the war years. The children's homes closed their doors, one

3 Right after liberation, many surviving Jews turned their backs on this traumatic chapter of their lives in order to go on. As one, Joseph Atlas, states in Pierre Sauvage's documentary *Weapons of the Spirit* (Le Chambon Foundation, 1989): "The Jews, for the most part, appeared to forget their benefactors. I left for South America. I forgot Le Chambon. I forgot it deliberately because I was emerging from a nightmare. The Chambonnais might have been hurt by that. They might have thought we didn't fully appreciate their hospitality. Such was not the case; their hospitality remained very close to my heart, but I had to absorb, understand, and surmount the tragedy that the Jewish people had lived through."

after the other, cutting the enrollment at the Collège in half. The poor teachers didn't know where to go. The village emptied. It was November in Le Chambon once more, with two-thirds of its shutters closed and its landlords eagerly awaiting the next year's tourist season. Was it worthwhile keeping the Collège open?

Far away from us, toward the Rhine, the liberation had already stopped. We thought the war was over, but it would last yet another year, until the fall of Berlin.

One day, near the bridge on the Lignon River, I met Professor Anstett from Lyon. Anstett was a parishioner of Pastor de Pury. He distinguished himself by his astonishing political shifts.

In 1940, he was drafted and became a member of the Military Intelligence Service. He denounced me as an enemy sympathizer and demanded my arrest. But at the time of the 1940 armistice, he did a U-turn and came to Le Chambon in an Armistice Commission vehicle, serving as an interpreter.

From 1941 to 1943, as an enthusiastic supporter of Maréchal Pétain, he obstinately refused to greet me. He considered me a spy, first in the pay of the English and then of the Americans. He may have been responsible for my arrest. When his children met me in the street, they spat on the ground and sang "La Marseillaise."

In 1944, he became a resister and was "shocked" by my pro-German sympathies.

Now, after the liberation, he came toward me near the bridge with a smile on his face and his hand extended toward me.

"Mr. Trocmé, I have come to ask you to forgive me. I was mistaken about you. You are the one who was right!"

I shook hands with him. "Thank you for your apology," I told him. "Everything is forgiven, but I wish you had apologized sooner."

"I was obsessed, Mr. Trocmé," he responded.

"What astounds me in your case and that of many of our colleagues," I told him, "is the continuous, opportunistic change of convictions. I'm sure it's unconscious. For my part, when I was very young, I had the privilege of becoming a believer in nonviolence. This put me in opposition to all violence and kept me from making many errors. I was:

> opposed to the anti-German hatred prevailing in France in 1918. For this, I was branded a Communist in 1927.

> opposed to nascent Nazism in Germany. People claimed I was a French propagandist come to hoodwink the Germans.
>
> opposed to the run-up to the war. I was accused of complicity with Hitler.
>
> opposed to the war in 1940. You denounced me as an agent of the fifth column, then as a clandestine Italian Fascist because of my wife.
>
> a resister against the German occupation and Vichy's subjection to Germany. You denounced me as an English agent, then American, then Jewish, then Communist again.
>
> opposed to the retaliation against German prisoners. Once again, I was considered a 'Kraut in disguise.'

"I was simply trying to be a good Christian. It was public opinion that fell from one kind of violence into another, from one form of collaboration with evil into another."

"You're right," Anstett said. "Now I fully understand your course of action. But I was obsessed. You disgusted me. De Pury was the one who helped me understand." De Pury was his pastor, a Swiss disciple of Barth. His courageous words landed him in Fort Montluc, where the Gestapo imprisoned him although he was a citizen of a neutral country.

20

The Collège Cévenol

SEPTEMBER 7, 1967, LOCARNO, SWITZERLAND.

At sixty-six years of age, I pick up the pen hesitatingly, because nothing I write about now will be like the preceding events. In 1944, I was only forty-three years old, yet I had already lived the essential years of my life. Everything I now mention has been the consequence of, or a commentary on, discoveries made during the war years, namely that the practice of Christ's gospel is not only possible for an individual believer but also for a group of determined believers.

The church of Jesus Christ, whose face we often seek in vain in our traditional parishes, is nothing but this group of men and women who take the risk of acting out their faith day in and day out in accordance with Jesus Christ. This constantly renewed adventure, whose outcome can't be known in advance, is made possible by the daily directives God gives to those who listen and strive to obey.

Obedience is always imperfect. Errors of judgment, behavior, and orientation are so frequent that the secular world sees nothing special about believers. They are less exciting and appear less effective than the political and military celebrities who dominate the news.

I have certainly known a small number of extraordinary men born to be saints or leaders. When they are disciples of Jesus Christ, these men arouse the hesitating crowd. They form disciples and acquire a following. Personally, I have never possessed their power of attraction. I am not aware of ever having been a leader. I have always doubted, not God, but myself. This lack of confidence paralyzes me when I have the chance to exercise a true leader's powerful influence. On the contrary, every time the Holy Spirit inspires me to undertake an adventure, I seek reassurance by associating with men I trust, not because they are exceptional, but because I'm not. I need their competence and wisdom to obtain the results I want.

To build the Collège Cévenol, for example, I would have gotten nowhere without Édouard Theis. He has all the qualities I lack – along with certain shortcomings I don't have. I'll speak first about his qualities. He has a wide-ranging vision and is enterprising. He works tirelessly to reach his goals, indifferent to money and devoid of personal ambition. He doesn't need to be admired or popular. He is fully committed to the tiresome, everyday tasks that fall to the director of an establishment.

Theis dared three things I never would have envisioned:

1. He wanted to locate the Collège Cévenol at the foot of the Peybrousson Hill, with its back against the communal woods. I had proposed a much less grandiose location nearer the village.
2. He knew how to set up and maintain contact with the newly formed Ecumenical Council of Churches in Geneva and with the APIDEP, an international Protestant loan association.[1] In 1944, they lent him one million French francs at his own risk, an enormous amount of money at that time. A Geneva banker, Mr. Sauter, was alarmed during his visit to Le Chambon in 1945 when he realized there wasn't even a responsible legal association backing his loan. The only guarantee offered to the lenders was the land we had just bought: a field of uncertain worth where cows were still grazing.
3. After the war, Theis proposed a large establishment with dormitories, an idea that frightened me because of the communal problems that always arise in boarding schools. I preferred to continue housing students in the children's homes in and around Le Chambon and to limit the Collège to teaching, as had been done until then.

Theis was strongly opposed to the children's homes because he felt the proprietors' main interest was making money. Nor did he trust their pedagogical abilities. He had spent many lean years during his youth and wanted the Collège open to all serious students, even those unable to pay. Thanks to his persistence, as long as he was director, the Collège managed to give scholarships to all worthy students whose parents applied for them.

1 This organization, Association protestante internationale de prêt, loaned the funds necessary to start the Cimade's home called Coteau Fleuri.

After the liberation, Theis showed up one day with one million francs from Geneva hidden in his belt and bought the Peybrousson field. But he had to pay back the Geneva bankers. That's when we remembered our American friends.

Theis had married an American and taught for a while at the College of Wooster in Ohio. I placed a lot of hope in the Rockefeller family. Theis and I had both worked for them as French tutors.

I said earlier that Tracy Strong Jr., then secretary of the worldwide YMCA, had visited us in 1941 before the break between Germany and the United States. He had promised us support after the war. "America must send us a 'youth ambassador,'" I had suggested to him at the time. My proposition hadn't fallen on deaf ears.

Moreover, Theis and I were both active members of the International Fellowship of Reconciliation. Throughout the war, the Fellowship of Reconciliation (FOR) and American Quakers sent money for the refugees. We counted heavily on their aid, particularly on that of their secretary general for America, A. J. Muste,[2] and that of Nevin Sayre, secretary of the International Fellowship of Reconciliation, both of whom procured generous gifts.

We hitched our wagon to a star. Theis left first and spent four months in the United States. I was not far behind him and spent another four months across the Atlantic. What a strange and extraordinary trip! I hadn't been in the United States since 1926. I was exhilarated by the transformation it had undergone in the last nineteen years despite the war: millions of cars, neon lights, a superabundance of everything, and all of it inexpensive. This incredible prosperity formed a cruel contrast with a Europe that was exhausted, miserable, ruined, and neglected after World War II.

But before arriving in the United States, I paid a heavy toll. The French merchant fleet had been destroyed. The ship *Le Normandie* had burned in New York harbor due to the negligence of the American workers who had transformed it into a troopship. France was completely isolated from the world. I had to request the right to travel on one of the American Liberty Ships. These were rather small ships, mass-produced in the United States to fill the gap in the Anglo-Saxon fleet caused by German submarines. On these ships, the American armies crossed the

2 Abraham Johannes Muste (1885–1967) was a naturalized American citizen from Holland, a pastor, a militant socialist and pacifist, and leader of the Fellowship of Reconciliation.

Atlantic, docking in England, and then went on to North Africa, and finally to Italy and Normandy.

The Liberty Ship I managed to board in Le Havre transported American troops to Boston. They were an exuberant mixture of discharged soldiers of all races and branches of service celebrating the end of a war, which, for many of them, had been a rather pleasant adventure. These men put all Europeans in the same bag, friends or enemies, German or French, who troubled the world's order from time to time, then called on peaceful and generous America to help. These GIs seemed completely ignorant of the suffering endured by civilian populations that had been chased from their homes, starved, and bombed. They believed they had brought a jumble of democracy, bathrooms, hygienic food, and peace to these civilians. In short, although it was forbidden, these joyful guys gave themselves over to endless and noisy games of craps that devoured all the money they had saved in the military.

Our crossing would not have lacked charm if the few French civilians on board had had a place to sit. We had hammocks where we could stretch out but not sit down because the ceilings were too low. On the deck, there were coiled ropes, a few small deck shelters, and the ship's railing, but the soldiers grabbed these areas first. Thus, the civilians' days were spent standing. Since the sea was rough and the boat small, you had to hang on to the sides while shouting out snatches of conversation.

Fortunately, there was a dining hall. We had the right to eat American army rations. What unheard-of luxury: real coffee, an endless supply of white bread, various cereals, milk in rectangular cartons, butter, sugar, chocolate, oranges, grapefruits, meat. Unbelievable but true.

The first two days, I left the dining hall with a sandwich and fruit in my pockets, because I was so accustomed to leaving the table hungry. Then I realized that I no longer ate between meals and abandoned my squirrel-like habits. But I remained scandalized by the GIs waste of food. They had the bad habit of leaving half of their food on their plates, and the ship left in its wake excessive garbage that the seagulls and porpoises attacked.

Between meals, I tried to sit discreetly in the empty dining hall to read or write a bit. My game was discovered by the American officers, who ejected me because I was a civilian. The space was reserved for them. I learned to remain standing or reclining for the ten-day ocean crossing.

I had a minor adventure that showed me how all armies resemble each other. I became friends with the chaplain on board. He gave me as a gift one of the Bibles that the army distributes free of charge to all its soldiers. I was looking forward to attending Sunday services when he called me in and said: "I'm sick. Do you want to replace me?" (He had a bad case of the flu.) I accepted with pleasure. What an unbelievable opportunity to speak to American soldiers after speaking to German prisoners of war and French *maquisards*! I prepared my sermon and included a lot about non-violence and conscientious objection. I was soon ready, even though my English had seriously degenerated after nineteen years on the shelf. Then, on Saturday, the ship's captain summoned me. He was a disagreeable officer who talked down to me: "I understand that you intend to address our troops tomorrow, Sunday."

"I agreed to replace your chaplain," I responded. "He's sick."

"There will be no religious service this Sunday," he said. "American army regulations forbid civilian clergy to preach to troops."

"But these men have been discharged," I responded. "They belong to many different churches."

"That's none of your business! This ship is a military transport. I'm its leader. I am ordering you to be quiet!"

I never have luck with the military, regardless of its nationality. They can smell my pacifism a mile away.

Our Liberty Ship landed in Boston one fine fall day. I still see myself strolling in the central park of that old city, looking for a hotel. I also see myself the next day, on the train to New York, admiring the magnificent red and gold American fall foliage and the cheerful white houses, packed tightly around the yacht harbors, wherever there was an opening in the immense forests stretching along the New England coast.

Nevin Sayre received me in New York in the FOR's narrow office on Broadway, not far from Union Theological Seminary, where I had spent the 1925–26 academic year. His welcome was cordial, as was that of A. J. Muste. Certainly, they were happy that the FOR had maintained its presence in Europe during the war. For the Americans, the war had just ended with the atomic destruction of Hiroshima.

But the United States was already turning its attention to the defeated nations, Germany and Japan. The American pacifists had learned over the course of five years of war to prefer their enemies to their friends. A few weeks later, on the Pacific Coast, I was dumbfounded to hear Donald

Soper, the famous English pastor, declare at the FOR convention: "We waged this war for the French, whom we don't like, against the Germans, whom we do like!"

"That's not pacifism!" I wanted to cry out. "Pacifism has nothing to do with your political or sentimental preferences!" But I remained riveted to my chair. If I had protested, no one would have understood.

Nevin explained that our Collège was not of real interest to a movement primarily dedicated to conscientious objection. However, he had organized lecture tours for Theis and me throughout the country, all the way to the West Coast. The FOR would pay all expenses for the trip and, in exchange, would pocket the speaker's fees we received, but I was authorized to keep any special gifts I might be able to raise.

The Rockefeller brothers arranged a meeting for me with the secretary of their Charitable Funds Organization the day after my arrival in New York. This man invited me to lunch in one of the distinguished clubs where New Yorkers do business. I spent an hour eloquently explaining our Collège to him – our Collège that was born of extraordinary circumstances, dedicated to peace, and in need of a huge sum of money to pay for the land, classrooms, and dormitories.

The poor fellow didn't understand. "Who sent you?" he asked. "Your government? The French Protestant Church? Your board of trustees?"

"We have no board of trustees – not yet" I responded. "We haven't been recommended by anyone" (in fact, the Reformed Church of France had a jaundiced view of Theis and me and considered us a couple of snipers ready to skim off American funds to the detriment of official channels). Our only bargaining chip was that twenty years earlier, we had been students at Union Theological Seminary and French tutors of the Rockefeller boys.

"OK, that's fine," said the secretary as he rose from the table. "I'll speak to the Rockefeller brothers. You'll have their response in three days."

Three days later when, for the first time, I was the guest in the "Prophet's Chamber" at Union Theological Seminary,[3] my alma mater, I received a short message from the secretary: "The Rockefeller brothers have just given a gift of one million dollars to the Ecumenical Council of Churches for the creation of study centers in the Geneva area (the

3 The "Prophet's Chamber" at Union Theological Seminary is the room offered to important former students.

Bossey Center). For the time being, they are no longer funding projects in Europe." Mr. Boegner, president of the Ecumenical Council of the Protestant Federation of France, which was being organized at the time, had gotten there shortly before us and obtained the gift.

Despite the hospitality I enjoyed during each of my later trips to the United States, the president of Union Theological Seminary, Mr. Pit Van Dusen, Theis's fellow student, never accorded me the honor of addressing the student body. Correctly or incorrectly, as a member of the FOR I was considered a representative of "liberal, social, and pacifist theology." This theology had dominated the interwar years until the conversion of its leading scholar, Reinhold Niebuhr, to a typically American, pragmatic neo-Calvinism that taught young soldiers that individuals can conduct themselves morally, but society cannot. Society must choose between two evils – either let Hitler continue his destructive path or wage war against Hitler. The lesser of the two evils, obviously, was to wage war against Hitler, because Christians, as responsible citizens, had to be willing to get their hands dirty.

Such a theology had no trouble reducing to rubble the humanitarian arguments of many American pacifists, who had asserted that "if the United States and the other democratic nations had treated Germany more humanely in 1918, the rise of Hitler would not have happened," and maintained that "nonviolence is an infallible method that leads one's adversary to repent and reconcile with you!"

Having just escaped from the inferno of war, I could have effectively countered this neo-Calvinist argument, but Van Dusen never gave me the opportunity for a public discussion. He allowed me, however, to post a sign and meet students in the lobby. Groups of five, six, and sometimes ten, some of whom had heard of the FOR, joined me while larger groups met elsewhere.

Niebuhr himself pontificated. The students followed him and shook their heads in pity for those pacifist "has-beens," like Muste and Nevin Sayre, with whom I was now associated.

The wound caused by the disdain of the Rockefellers and the Union Theological Seminary was somewhat healed by my meeting with Mr. Clark, a representative of the American Board of Congregationalist Churches, who came all the way from Boston to meet me. He invited me to a restaurant and reminded me that in 1941 I had requested an American 'youth ambassador' for Le Chambon.

"We have chosen this ambassador from a good number of candidates. He is a conscientious objector recently released from a Civil Public Service camp. He has just gotten married."

He introduced me to a young couple. The man was thin, elegant, with slightly Asian features; the woman was blond and dressed in bright colors. "Typically American," I said to myself.

"They don't speak French but claim to have studied it." American style, I thought.

"They will arrive in Le Chambon next fall," Mr. Clark said. "Their names are Howard and Elsie Schomer."

I asked myself: "What will they find in Le Chambon next fall? Will the Collège still exist? The owners of the hotels where we found refuge during the war have taken steps to get rid of the Collège. Where would it go?" But I refrained from telling Howard and Elsie Schomer about the cold sweats I was experiencing.

In Chicago, in a large, dreadful train station, I met Theis. If I remember correctly, he introduced me to the first automatic lockers I had ever seen. Theis was pessimistic. He had just finished a lecture tour that hardly covered his expenses. I told him we would combine our resources so that neither of us would appear more successful than the other. Would I have better results than he did?

I don't remember the exact outcome of my lectures, except that I encountered unexpected obstacles. Nevin recommended that I "dramatize" our nonviolent resistance against the Nazis, but how could I explain to pacifist Americans, who had just emerged from an exhausting struggle with Roosevelt and "his war," the frightening moral tragedy that we in Europe had barely survived? They couldn't believe that Nazism was *evil*. Many were Quakers who professed a kind of Rousseauian belief in the fundamental goodness of human nature. They objected: "Couldn't you speak to those Nazis and awaken that small, inner voice that exists in all human beings?"

"We couldn't approach the Nazis," I responded. "They ruled over us and created a reign of terror with the Milice, which was composed of French collaborators. The anti-Jewish laws were written in stone, and political persecutions were frighteningly cruel."

"There's a misunderstanding between you and them," replied my good friends. "You had to tell them the truth, the whole truth, about love, as Christ and Gandhi did. You would have disarmed their hatred. Why did you lie?"

"We had to give the Jews and members of the *maquis* false identity papers. Otherwise, their real names would have been revealed to the people issuing the ration cards they needed, then to the French police, then to the Gestapo. Their real names would have sent them to their death."

My friends shook their heads with pity: "If you had only told the whole truth to your adversaries, everything would have worked out well."

The second, almost insurmountable problem was how to explain what French Protestantism was. In the USA, the "average man" is Protestant. If anyone asked me, "What is your denomination?" and I responded "Reformed," they said: "Ah yes, in our city we have a small "Dutch Reformed Church." If I said "Presbyterian," they spoke about John Knox, and if I spoke about Calvin (most of the people I spoke with hardly knew who he was), they only knew of "a Swiss fanatic who sent people to hell through double predestination."[4] So, I ended up telling everyone, "I am a French Huguenot." They answered me, "But all the Huguenots left France because of persecutions and fled to Switzerland, Germany, Holland, and America. You can't be a Huguenot, because France is an entirely Catholic country." Then I had to try to explain that in the mountains and the countryside, poor Huguenots subsisted, and I represented them.

One day in Baltimore, in a professor's big library, I tried once again to interest a sympathetic but skeptical audience in the Collège Cévenol. Among all the gilded titles that decorated the somber book bindings, I saw the words "The Camisards" shining forth. I jumped up and opened the book. It was an eighty-year-old publication, written by an American traveler named Taylor who had visited the Protestant region of Les Cévennes.[5] "Here they are!" I cried out, "the people I'm talking about! The Huguenots, the Camisards, it's the same thing! An American knew about their existence. He visited their descendants. Look!"

Their heads came closer, and the book passed from hand to hand. Its yellowed pages had photographs of the old peasants in 1880, bearded, wearing felt hats, somber looking, closely resembling the American colonists. "There's the photograph of the church in Le Chambon where I'm pastor," I exclaimed. "And the farm in Mazel where Désubas,

4 Many people don't know that Jean Calvin was French.

5 Charles Taylor, *The Camisards* (Marshall, Hamilton, Kent & Co., 1893)

the preacher, was arrested before being condemned to death. There's Désubas's bed!"[6]

The disbelief of my auditors vanished. Finally, I had cited an authority worthy of confidence because he was American! He had a home and an identity; he didn't relate "hoaxes." That evening, I won the match, because the professor in question was none other than the brother of my new friend, Carl Sangree.

LET'S GO BACK a few weeks. I had returned to New York with the $4,000 I'd collected. This allowed us to reimburse the bankers in Geneva and become owners of the Peybrousson acreage, but didn't give us any funds to build even wooden huts on our land.

It was the very end of my trip. The next day I headed back to France. I was sadly packing my bags in the "Prophet's Chamber." They consisted mostly of cardboard boxes containing clothes and shoes people had given me. Mentally, I calculated that the trip had been a failure.

"Our dreams have ended," I was telling myself when someone knocked on the door.

"Come in," I said wearily.

A very impressive-looking man and woman entered. He was short with rough features and spoke little; she was slender and livelier.

"We attended one of your meetings the other day," they told me. "We want to know how we can help you." I had heard this at least fifty times. I knew that most of the time it signified a rather vague goodwill which normally ended with some advice like, "You should go see Mr. So-and-So at the Ecumenical Council . . . or the Protestant Federation. He will surely be able to help you!" However, the modest air of the two people I was talking to made me think that perhaps, like so many other Americans anxious to travel (and help suffering Europeans, of course!), the Sangree couple had come to ask for a position at the Collège.

"What do you know how to do?" I asked.

Carl Sangree responded very modestly, "I am the pastor of a Congregationalist Church, or rather I was a pastor in West Cummington,

6 Mathieu Majal, known as Désubas (1720-1746), was the pastor of Désert en Vivarais et Velay. He was arrested on December 11, 1745, in Mazel near Saint-Agrève, and executed on February 1, 1746, in Montpellier. His tragic fate failed to provoke a revolt, but was the subject of jeremiads that were still well known in the twentieth century.

Massachusetts, but had to relinquish my position because I got divorced to marry Florence, whom you see here with me. I don't know French and I have never taught. In my youth, I was a football coach."

"Alas, we don't play American football in Le Chambon," I interjected. "What about you, Madam?"

"I was the administrative director of Northfield School for Girls, but I gave up my position to marry Carl. I know how to keep the books," she added.

"We already have an accountant," I responded.

"Well, in that case . . ." said Mr. Sangree, and they got up to leave.

As she stood near the door, Mrs. Sangree pronounced the words that changed everything: "There is one thing I didn't tell you, Mr. Trocmé. During the war, Carl and I opened a small home in West Cummington for Jewish refugees who had fled the Nazis. It was your concern for the Jews that struck us in your talk the other evening. To feed the refugees, we developed certain fundraising methods that may be of interest to you. We formed small committees of students in New England schools. Perhaps we can revive these groups to help the Collège Cévenol."

"Ah, that's quite another story! That's very interesting," I exclaimed. "Come, let's all sit down."

Over the following hour, our friendship with the Sangrees was born. It continues to this day, a friendship that enabled the Collège Cévenol to take flight.

We decided that I would not take the ship the next day but remain with the Sangrees for a month to develop a plan for the Collège. It wasn't until the next morning that I started to ask myself some questions about the Sangrees. Had I committed myself too soon? Could I trust this pastor who had been dismissed by his church? Fortunately, the feedback I gathered that morning from Muste was positive, and the next day I took off in the Sangrees' car. They sat in front and I in the back with Chippy, their dog, a huge, hairy animal far too affectionate for my taste. We drove to Massachusetts. I was their guest at High Hollow, a stylish old farm the Sangrees managed on a wooded hill that overlooks Cummington that has since hosted many people associated with the Collège.

I discovered Northfield School for Girls, where Mrs. Sangree was still known to everyone and where I often spoke during my itinerant years, as well as Mount Hermon School, an institution for boys, Northfield's twin. Both were created by the famous evangelist Dwight Moody on his family property. Hundreds of missionaries discovered their vocation in these parts. Mrs. Sangree took me to Smith College, "the best college for women in the USA," she said with pride. I have since discovered that every American educational institution proclaims itself "the best in the USA," at least in one field of study.

That's where my troubles began. I had spoken to the Sangrees about a "Collège." But in the United States, a college is a four-year university that prepares students for a diploma they call a bachelor's degree. I spent a long time grasping the difference, then trying to make them understand that the French baccalaureate only guaranteed entrance to the university. I insisted, however, that the Collège Cévenol was much more advanced than a US high school and deserved the title of college or lycée without being a university. I had to prove, among other things, that the *bachot* was a difficult exam.

Disappointed to learn that we were not what Americans call a college, the Sangrees showed me some prep schools. These were private establishments, often very expensive, that prepared students for entrance into American colleges. Some of these schools practiced new educational methods on a large scale: manual labor, agriculture, visual arts, and music. I was blown away by the combination of deliberate rusticity (barns made into dormitories) and unheard-of luxury. In one of these institutions, students had their own rooms with separate study and shower. The director explained that an authentic Oriental rug covered all floors to give each student a sense of beauty. In the evening, dinner was held at small tables by candlelight. Students, dressed in tuxedos, were obligated to speak French, German, or Spanish with the language teachers dining with them.

For my part, I tried to explain our schools to the Sangrees: classrooms with high, cold windows that smelled of chalky blackboards and students' soiled aprons, the dreary dormitories of the boarding schools, the barking of the monitors, and detentions. I spoke of the enormous effort we made in Le Chambon, in frightening material circumstances, to abolish such a climate and create an atmosphere of trust between students and teachers, to bring about the exchange of ideas, and to speak about God, Jesus Christ, and pacifism in a spirit of mutual respect and freedom. How difficult it was for them to understand!

In one of these prep schools, during a later visit, I met a French student about twelve years old, who must have come from a wealthy family capable of paying for this expensive education.

"You should talk to your compatriot," the French teacher told me confidentially. "It's not working out. He doesn't fit in. We don't understand his attitude."

"What's not working out?" I asked.

"He makes fun of everything. He makes wisecracks to his teachers and comrades. Is that what they do in France? Here we don't do that. *It is not done.*"

That was my initiation into the terrible conformism of Americans! But in the present case, could I condone this typically French attitude that forces all of us to be on the defensive: teachers against students, students facing the sarcasm of their teachers, the unbearable, humiliating teasing that I always suffered from my schoolmates?

In America, *it is not done*. People trust you. It is precisely this trusting spirit that I wanted for Le Chambon.

After about two weeks, the Sangrees had almost understood what I was trying to explain to them. The Collège Cévenol was an *adventure*. You could count the number of Protestant *collèges* in France on one hand, and they were all in cities. Rural lycées didn't exist in France. The Collège Cévenol was the first and only one of its kind, the first coeducational school where boys and girls lived side by side.

Furthermore, the Collège Cévenol was nothing but a handful of pacifist pastors and teachers, animated by a deep faith, but without money, buildings, or any backing. This word, *bâtiment* (building) was about the only word that Carl Sangree came to understand in our language, but he repeated it for twenty years with such persistence that this word alone sufficed both to convince his compatriots of the necessity of helping the Collège Cévenol and to justify our own enthusiasm.

It was therefore decided in the Sangrees' car that, for the start of classes for the 1945–1946 school year, the Collège would simply be provisionally lodged in barracks. We left for Washington, DC, to ask the American Military Administration to give us a certain number of barracks. Unfortunately, the day before our arrival, sales of these buildings had been frozen. They were henceforth reserved for GIs returning from war and flocking to universities. Exporting them was forbidden.

On this snub, I left the United States, still with only $4,000, the exact sum needed to pay back the million Swiss francs. But I was encouraged by Sangree's promise: "We will come to Le Chambon next year. In the interim, find some wooden buildings. We'll try to find the money to pay for them."

On my return to the "Prophet's Chamber" in New York, I had another pleasant surprise. My former boss, Mrs. John D. Rockefeller Jr, invited me to her home. I visited her the day before my definitive departure. She looked much older but was as friendly as ever. She insisted on giving me a check for $1,000. "My family doesn't want to take on any responsibility for your Collège," she said (Were they distrustful of our pacifist position?), "but I know how much you have struggled during the Occupation and how many of the essentials you are lacking. Here is $1,000 for you, your wife, whom I know, and for your children. Do with it what you want."

A thousand dollars! What a godsend! At the end of the war, we had no clothing or shoes. After I left Mrs. Rockefeller's home, I hastened to buy things for my family. I decided, however, to give half of this unexpected gift to the Collège. That raised the sum I had collected to $4,500.

When I returned to Le Chambon a few weeks later, I naively related this story to the Collège committee and proudly handed them the $4,500. I was later accused by the school accountant of stealing $500. Never have I more regretted giving $500 out of my own pocket to the Collège, money Mrs. Rockefeller never intended for the school.

THE SECOND LAUNCH of the Collège in 1945 was much different from the first. Time and distance have allowed us to forget the wounds and worries that accompanied it. The heroic period of the occupation was long over. Now, only a few teachers huddled around Theis and Trocmé. Most had disappeared with the refugees. The ones who stayed returned to a somewhat normal life and forgot the tormented past.

In the spring of 1946, I was invited to participate in the first international meeting of the Fellowship of Reconciliation in Stockholm. I trembled, knowing I would meet Germans for the first time since the end of the war.

I remember with sadness my first contacts with Germans after World War I, even with those who called themselves pacifists. Their implausible notion of justice, their ignorance of the suffering Germany had inflicted on others, and their sense of entitlement and national pride seemed unbearable to me. That mentality had prepared the way for Nazism and World War II.

What would I find in Stockholm?

There I found, in the extraordinary atmosphere of the FOR, a few Germans I already knew. Among them was Wilhelm Mensching,[7] a pastor who, by a strange turn of events, had succeeded my grandfather in the pulpit of a small church in Petzen, in Schaumburg-Lippe. (Other pastors occupied this pulpit in between.) Mensching was an admirer of Gandhi and had remained faithful to his Christian pacifism, refusing to do the Hitler salute, and brushing aside all collaboration with Nazism. The Gestapo had often threatened to arrest him, but the tacit support of his parishioners protected him. He was safe and sound, smiling and persistent, relating tales of other German resisters: Professor Herrmann and his wife, condemned to a fortress for listening to the BBC and helping Jews. This double crime got them locked up in a fortress instead of a concentration camp, from which they never would have returned; Father Metger, who was shot because of his opposition to Nazism; Hermann Stöhr, my friend, who was decapitated in Berlin for being a conscientious objector.

In my resistance tales, I evoked the names of Daniel Trocmé and Roger Le Forestier. I was astonished to learn that, probably for the first time in history, Christians in the heart of both camps had fought on the same front and against the same enemy – deadly violence in all its forms. Until World War II, the church could only offer the world the pathetic spectacle of Christians divided into antagonistic, patriotic armies dying heroically for these opposing causes and receiving blessings and encouragement from the divided church – a church charged with preaching the truth of one God, father of all human beings.

My snooping (curiosity is perhaps my most remarkable natural gift) led me to discover in Sweden the prefabricated buildings the Collège needed. These attractive, comfortable houses could be assembled in a few days anywhere in Europe by Swedish specialists. All you had to do was pay, and the buildings weren't expensive. In any event, we had no choice. France had forbidden all construction until bridges and

7 Wilhelm Mensching (1887–1964) was a missionary in Africa and the pastor in Petzen from 1920 to 1952. He also directed the International FOR. He and André Trocmé were both nominated for the Nobel Peace Prize in 1950. He has been recognized in Jerusalem at Yad Vashem as Righteous Among the Nations.

factories had been rebuilt. The only way to bypass the law was to import building material. I returned to Le Chambon with the documentation and informed the Sangrees. They telephoned back, "Buy!" The money wouldn't come from France (which was forbidden by the Currency Exchange Control), but rather in US dollars paid directly to Sweden.

Theis soon left for Sweden. I should have gone with him. My idea was to erect a bunch of "houses" on our campus (just like the one Theis later lived in), arranged in little "family compounds" under a teacher's direction. Unfortunately, Theis ordered long, dull, military-type barracks for the boys' residence that still embarrass us today. Thrifty and unimaginative, Theis had underestimated American generosity. When the Sangrees arrived that summer, it was too late to modify the style of the buildings. Moreover, the buildings hadn't arrived yet. The Sangrees threw up their hands in disbelief when they saw cows grazing in the Peybrousson field.

Suddenly, the fog cleared. In August, one month after the Sangrees' arrival, the Swedish panels, accompanied by an installer, were unloaded at the train station. They had arrived by way of our sluggish, narrow-gauge railway, which became the object of student mockery: they named the student newspaper *Ça file doucement* (it moves slowly).

On low quality film, the Sangrees recorded what happened next. As in Gulliver's Island of Lilliput, the hands of dozens of children aged twelve to eighteen took hold of these panels, raised them up, loaded them on trucks, transported them, placed the trusses in the locations prepared earlier to hold them, bolted the panels, and painted them. All this under the direction of the Swedish installer, who didn't speak a word of French, English, or German. Everything went smoothly. On October 1, the miracle was complete. The Collège moved into barracks that were half dormitories, half classrooms, and our director, Édouard Theis, settled into a wooden bungalow with his family. From there, he could oversee the first steps of his brainchild.[8]

Even miracles come in threes! The first miracle was our friendship with the Sangrees. The second was the barracks, and the third would be the Luquet farm – or as Carl Sangree called the place, "Lucky."

When they arrived, the Sangrees were shocked by the drastic situation in which we found ourselves. Although the barracks housed five or six classrooms and fifty boarding students, the Collège, with an enrollment of 350 students, couldn't function.

8 Note by Magda in the margin: "His *collège*; not one of his daughters!"

"Perhaps there's a farm for sale nearby," repeated the Sangees, "even if only a dilapidated building that puts a roof over our heads." We looked around. The owners of Luquet, a farm whose land was adjacent to our field, wanted to sell. Providence at work! But they were asking for a million and a half francs, and the Sangrees had bled themselves dry for the barracks and even found themselves in debt. We were stuck.

Then one day, out of the blue, a bigwig from the Presbyterian Church in the United States showed up in Le Chambon eager to perform an act of charity. We explained our dilemma.

"I think I can help you," he said. "How much does 'Lucky' cost?"

"A million and a half francs – six thousand dollars."

"Six thousand dollars? That's exactly the amount my church gave me to do charitable work in Europe. Done deal!"

A few days later, we purchased Luquet. Theis and Miss Pont had their offices there, and the school's secretary as well. The barn was used for a gymnasium; the stable became our mess hall (and still is today). In the other wing, we set up all the classrooms we still needed.

That's how the Collège Cévenol passed from a chaotic, wartime adventure to an institution. But before becoming an institution, we had to go through many crises, some difficult.

Three principles inspired our conception of the school. The first, our evangelical faith, required us to remain attached to the Protestant parish of Le Chambon rather than establish a second parish for "privileged" students and teachers. Secondly, we were Christian pacifists. This caused a lot of hostility toward us, but also much deep devotion. The third was our intention to provide a serious curriculum and excellent teaching that would rival the state-run lycées and make it possible for a high percentage of our students to receive their baccalaureate diploma.

We soon encountered hostility from the peasant population. They were convinced that we pastors were making money from this enterprise. In their opinion, we had abandoned them in favor of a new category of tourists. The aged and the sick in the country could never get enough visits from the presbytery, despite the dedication of our parish assistant, Miss Alice Verdeil.

Some of our most noteworthy professors came to the Collège because of the radical nature of our thinking. These teachers made us what we are today: Paul Ricoeur in philosophy, Howard Schomer in history, Mr. Tissot in math, and André Hano in the classics. Technicians and pedagogues, our teachers, men and women, dedicated themselves entirely to their students. There is an African American still teaching in Le Chambon. I met him on a train in California and hired him on the spot: Tom Johnson, who spent his career with us. Races and nationalities didn't matter at the Collège. Theis knew how to give everyone an equal opportunity to develop their individual talents. He didn't micromanage.

I was president of the administrative board and usually found myself deluged with initiatives from Theis or some other teacher. I recall the day when the teachers – after unsuccessfully begging the board to make all salaries equal, from that of the director down to the kitchen help – confronted my refusal. I considered their proposal romantic and unreasonable. They announced that they themselves had created a common fund into which they had put their salaries, which they would distribute without regard for diplomas or age, only for the number of children in each family.

This proposal caused the first great crisis in the faculty. Certain teachers, less unselfish than their colleagues, refused to join the common fund. Their example created tensions. They were soon followed by others. Those pushing for the common fund vividly reproached the board's neutrality in the affair.

"If you had decided, as a board, in favor of equal salaries, we would not be in conflict today."

"Can you really demand," I asked them, "that others in your situation make the same sacrifice you make because of your beliefs?"

This crisis could have led to the Collège's demise. Instead, it created permanent tension between the board and the teachers, often concerning financial matters and the determination of salaries, that caused me great grief and contributed to my decision to leave the Collège in 1950.

Conflicts are relatively easy to solve when their cause involves rival *interests*. We reach a compromise, unless, as happened during the colonial period, we go to war out of self-interest. But at least the motives are clear. *Ideological* wars, which we used to call religious wars or crusades, are more serious because all those involved believe they must give their life for the survival of truth or of the church they are defending against the devil. *Racial* and *national* wars are often like ideological wars: China against the United States, the yellow race or black race against the white race.

But *conflicts of conscience*, even if they don't end up in war or murder, are the most dreadful of all, because all parties believe themselves obligated to defend someone's honor in a courageous and impartial manner. To capitulate is to become an accomplice to calumny. To maintain the truth is to collide head-on and break with one's best friends. Just think about the Dreyfus Affair![9]

This is precisely what happened at the Collège. The director of the boys' residence was accused of wrongdoing. One third of his colleagues believed him guilty and demanded his dismissal. The other two-thirds judged him innocent and expelled the opposing third from the faculty. This incident lasted over a year and ended with the departure of the school's director and founder, Édouard Theis.

Theis was replaced by Roland Leenhardt,[10] a pastor from neighboring Tence who died suddenly after a year and a half at the helm.

The Collège set out to find a new director, eventually appointing Pierre Gagnier, who arrived in September 1967 to take charge of his duties.

Pierre Gagnier is elegant, distant, precise, and won't let himself be pushed around like Leenhardt.[11] Can he hire and keep a faculty as conscientious and capable as the Collège had in the past? The reputation of the Collège has been seriously damaged, but its American friends, frightened by the crisis, are already regrouping. They had heard only one side of the story and hadn't understood the real drama. They believed that Theis was the victim of a plot. Now they are talking about building a gym and boarding quarters for the boys. All well and good, if they rebuild the original spirit of the Collège Cévenol.

As for me, I have high hopes for the new director. After years of degeneration, during which I saw the scandal of a school "dedicated to peace" in the throes of a civil war, I learned to speak of the Collège Cévenol in a more detached fashion, as a solid, secondary, Protestant establishment, situated in a good climate, doing a great service to families who have

9 In 1894, a Jewish army captain, Alfred Dreyfus, was wrongfully convicted of treason for allegedly selling military secrets to the Germans. When the evidence began to point to the guilt of another army officer, the affair split the nation into two opposing camps. In July 1906, Dreyfus was rehabilitated by a civilian court of appeals, but the Army didn't proclaim his innocence until 1995. Dreyfus was imprisoned for 1,517 days on Devil's Island in (then) French Guiana.

10 Roland Leenhardt (1913–1966) was the pastor in Tence from 1939 to 1945 and director of Protestant schools in Madagascar until 1963. He has been recognized as Righteous Among the Nations at Yad Vashem in Jerusalem.

11 Pierre Gagnier (1909–1988) was the pastor in Lozère in Nice from 1941 to 1953, where he and his wife saved Jews from the Nazis. Both have been recognized as Righteous Among the Nations at Yad Vashem in Jerusalem. He directed the Collège Cévenol until 1970.

children with health and psychological needs. But the visionary period has long passed, and I'm beginning to resign myself to that reality. In any event, I remain president of the civil society that owns the land, buildings, and furniture of the Collège. I call the board together from time to time to take care of legal formalities.

IN RELATING THE CRISES experienced by the Collège Cévenol, I have succumbed to the sadness that engulfs me when I discover the accumulated ruins of my life: the emotional ruins from the accidental death of my mother; the material ruins of the house where I was born in Saint-Quentin; the family ruins after the deaths of Jean-Pierre and, later, my son Daniel;[12] the ruins of an educational enterprise begun in faith and joy that ending up being just another institution.

What remains today of the Union in Saint-Quentin, the Union in Clamart, of Sin-le-Noble and its Men's Circle, of the farming school in Le Chambon, Eirene in Morocco, Saint-Gervais-Philippeville in Algeria? Nothing, or almost nothing: only the memory of inspired moments in the company of a few friends filled with faith, plans, and confidence, many of whom are dead, old, or elsewhere. But I shouldn't complain. Most of my colleagues at the School of Theology in Paris have experienced far worse tragedies than I have. Many of the spiritual awakenings that flourished twenty years ago have gone dormant due to the small number of French Protestants and their limited financial and intellectual resources. Moreover, the popularity of the ecumenical movement has resulted in marriages between the younger generation of Protestants and Catholics. If only these were good Catholics! But no, the children of the generation led by the prophetic spirit have mostly abandoned religion. They are absorbed by the "affluent society," carried away by the pleasures of an overly facile life with no vision whatsoever.

I would, therefore, be wrong to complain, because the Collège Cévenol is still standing and vibrant. Its presence prevented a decrease in the population of Le Chambon, a municipality that, thirty years ago, was discouraged and defeated. New people arrived ready to replace those who, old and worn out, withdrew one by one. The form of the Collège changed, but the educational program we established has survived and

12 On January 17, 1962, at age twenty-eight, Daniel committed suicide in the mountains above Denver, Colorado, where he lived and worked.

thrived: an international Christian education for peace. In the end, the right ideas always gain acceptance despite human mediocrity.

At the foot of the Peybrousson hills, "permanent structures" rise as witnesses to the Collège's best years: a vast and graceful classroom building, an elegant and cheerful girls' dormitory; carpentry and mechanics workshops; different types of houses with youth rooms ready to welcome teachers and their families; and the library, set in the Luquet barn thanks to the generosity of Robert Pettengill, who remains an exceptional American friend.

Then, there's "Coco's Shelter," a kind of guitar club on the ground floor of the old farm, where generations of students have come to blow off steam. There's also the stadium, with its regulation cinder track encircling the soccer field, and a tennis court built by Carl Sangree with the help of several student summer campers.

What about the Collège's spiritual life? There are Wednesday morning services, when the entire Collège heads down the hill into the village, with the director and the teachers leading the way into Le Chambon's church. They hear a teacher, pastor, or student offer them substantive words of exhortation in full and frank language. For me, those services symbolize the Collège's solid faith in its first years. Getting back up that hill is more difficult, especially when the road is icy, but this weekly exercise builds character.

There are weekly meetings with the older students, where a director, pastor, teacher, or student raises one of the great contemporary problems – justice, racial equality, war, peace, the meaning of the church, nonviolence – before opening the floor to an often heated discussion. What a marvelous path this forges in the minds of tomorrow's adults! Evening services in the different buildings frequently provoke strong reactions from the skeptical, but this is where many young, disoriented students find faith and meaning for their lives.

All this is only possible thanks to a team of extraordinary teachers, each unique, from the scout leader to the conscientious objector, from the dreamer with his head in the clouds to the meticulous scientist, from the Jew wounded by the Holocaust to the African American welcomed as a full-fledged colleague, from the incessant researcher to the calm and conscientious worker, all united in the same conviction: to participate in building a better world, one where lying and hatred have been banished.

For years, the team worked enthusiastically under the direction of Édouard Theis. He was aided by two energetic female directors – Miss Pont and Mrs. Lavondès – who interpreted his unspoken wishes. This blend of teachers, workers, monitors, and cooks characterized the Collège Cévenol. Some people judged the school an insane enterprise doomed to failure, but others understood that it was an inspired adventure capable of reviving Christianity for French and European Protestant youth. Despite the tensions and conflicts inherent in communal life, everyone helped each other, and all pursued a common goal. I still meet, in Europe and America, former students of the Collège, who for the most part, have an unforgettable, positive memory of it.

As for me, from 1946 on I was excluded from the inner circle. My pastoral duties made me a receptacle for complaints and constrained me to silence. I was constantly on guard for fear of being dragged into the coterie that, for several years, gravitated around Édouard Theis, only to break away from him suddenly and join the opposition.

For this reason, I couldn't have any friends other than my wife, who showered me with friendship. There were never any secrets between us. I could count on her just as "night watchmen count on daybreak."[13] This rich friendship with my wife perhaps prevented me from looking for other friendships that might have let me integrate myself more fully into the Collège community. My ministry kept me at a distance and allowed me to avoid getting dragged into quarrels between tightly knit groups at each other's throats, but it didn't spare me enmities or misunderstandings that I often only grasped later. Naive confidence is the best passport in life, if not for businessmen, at least for pastors.

I COME NOW TO the de Seynes affair, which goes back to 1947, right after the war. For the second time in my life, a worried and embarrassed regional president approached me. The first time, it had been Paul Perret in Sin-le-Noble, who took the parishes of Aniche and Marquette away from me to install a man more qualified to communicate with the workers – Pierre Evrard, who turned out to be a complete failure.

This time, it was Pierre Rozier. Yes, him again. "Certainly," he said to me, "the work in Le Chambon has progressed extremely well." Whose fault is that? I said to myself. "Theis should dedicate himself entirely to

13 Psalm 130.

the Collège." The regional council (from which I had been expelled[14]) decided to give "me" a second, full-time pastor. They had already selected a remarkable man, an ex-banker from Paris, the son of a good Protestant family. After the death of his wife, he had felt called to become a pastor at the advanced age of forty. This man was so remarkable that he only needed a few months of study to earn his degree in theology and prepare for his pastoral duties. As a former banker, he would put the finances of the Chambon parish back in order.

"I had no idea that our finances were out of order," I responded to Rozier. "The parish regularly meets the target date set by the synod and even supports neighboring parishes." I had proposed to the council of elders in Le Chambon that we always reach our goal by November 30, a month before the end of the fiscal year, which we had. The council members, as well as the pastor, provisionally covered the gap if contributions were late. This system worked so well that there was always some surplus rather than the usual deficit.

"I know, I know," responded Rozier (who might have heard some council members complaining), "but, in the final analysis, your finances aren't done according to the rules."

"Ah, yes, the rules," I replied in a mocking manner, which, in turn, exasperated him.

"Yes, but listen," replied Rozier. "Mr. de Seynes is a man of such stature that it would not be right for you to be his superior. Given that you asked to be reduced to half-time, we are proposing that de Seynes become president of the council of elders."

"Twelve years of ministry in Le Chambon, twenty years of pastoral service," I thought. "The church was full; the parish was growing, our work with youth was bursting with energy; we had two pastors instead of one. Yet, they place me under the authority of a man without any pastoral experience?" Rozier probably thought: "Trocmé must be brought back into line. He's a fanatic, a dangerous man who causes too many problems." I could see on his face the fearful reaction typical of him. On this day, however, I didn't get angry. On the contrary, I discovered in this degradation a door that opened onto another future.

The Fellowship of Reconciliation had asked me to become one of its secretaries. I responded with a qualified yes. "I must remain in Le

14 Magda adds in the margin of the manuscript: "Rejected because of the committee's fear when André was in hiding; fear of being compromised by André's courage."

Chambon for a few years to consolidate the Collège. I can only become a part-time secretary of the FOR," I explained. But the regional council's decision freed me. "Perfect, perfect," I said to an astonished Rozier. "This is coming at just the right time. The FOR has asked me to become a secretary. So, I'll become a part-time secretary for the FOR with residence in Le Chambon. On half-salary, of course, like Theis has been up to now. De Seynes will be the main pastor in Le Chambon." Rozier left happy.

De Seynes arrived in April 1948. I could immediately sense, with some bitterness, how things would play out. After twelve years, I was the old pastor. The parishioners reproached me for "not making enough home visits." In fact, during the war, my time had in part been devoured by the refugees – out of sight, out of mind. When the war ended, I started my home visits again and even organized "neighborhood missions," during which I spent the night in parishioners' homes. But the peasants nodded their heads and repeated, "Mr. Tro-que-mé prefers the tourists to us poor peasants," and I could tell that my reputation had worn thin.

But now de Seynes, a widowed gentleman with three children, was our pastor. Soon the council of elders enjoined us to vacate the presbytery by October 1, 1948 ("our presbytery," the house where we had spent twelve years of joys, struggles, and suffering). Did the fact that de Seynes was a millionaire, who could have easily extended his stay in an excellent hotel or rented an expensive house, ever cross the elders' minds? There were so few lodgings available for people of modest means like us – and we too had three children. Did anyone think about that? We had to clear out.

Of course, there was the Schnerb villa, closed since the war, which had served as the *maquis* headquarters for torturing collaborators. Its owner, a Jewish woman from Saint-Étienne, had lost her son and no longer came there but refused to rent it out. We had to get the president of the Jewish community in Saint-Étienne to intervene and emphasize what I had done to help persecuted Jews during the war to get her to finally say yes.

For the first and last time in our lives, we lived in an almost new, cheery home, with large windows that opened all the way out. We only stayed there a few years before moving to Versailles, where we would live for ten years in a "luxurious slum" before our departure for Geneva, where we then lived at 30 Avenue du Plateau, which wasn't a dump but also wasn't the most comfortable situation.

The Schnerb house had one very good thing going for it: this bright house took us away from the obscurity and sadness that weighed on us in the old presbytery, where every room recalled the life and death of Jean-Pierre.

Magda bore her pain courageously. I often fell into a melancholy state, sustained only by the faith that, as pastor, I preached from the pulpit, in local gatherings, and at the deathbeds of my parishioners.

A country parish is composed of old men who nod their heads and draw you to thoughts of death. I was dead, too, but only forty-seven years old. The Schnerb house and my partially itinerant ministry kept my mind off these dark matters.

By snatching me away from my somber thoughts, the Schnerb house and the FOR helped me to begin over again. There were people to reconcile, Europe to reconstruct, and America, suddenly so close and overflowing with generous and constructive optimism. I set about my work. I had lost my joy (I no longer sang or played my accordion), but I acquired the courage of a mature man.

In any event, de Seynes was not doing well. He was a likable fellow, so elegant that everyone who met him, me included, felt clumsy and ordinary. But his sermons were conventional; they too were "well-bred." As the peasants say, "A new broom sweeps well." They flocked to church for a few weeks – until Christmas. After that, their ranks thinned out. He had been ordered to reorganize the parish's finances, so he never let a service go by without asking for money. This made the peasants uneasy, and, for the first time in ten years, triggered a major deficit at the end of the fiscal year.

Then de Seynes's work pace slowed. At Easter, he was exhausted, and the parishioners began to grumble. Oh, not so much against him, but against me, who, now only a part-time pastor, overloaded "the poor Mr. de Seynes" with work during my absences from the village. "You are no longer our father," one of the church elders said to me. "You can't be a part-time father."

My friendship with Howard Schomer also rapidly deteriorated. He was close to de Seynes. Schomer always preferred distinguished men; it was one of his faults. The state of de Seynes's health worried him: the pastor no longer left his office; he smoked and smoked; his hands trembled; he was declining quickly.

Schomer lived in Mrs. A.'s boarding house. Mrs. A. was furious with me (whom she had once highly praised) because I called the police one day to strike fear into some hooligans who, late one evening, had entered the Schnerb villa while Magda and I were away. They had pushed Jispa down because she objected to their attempt to harass two young women boarding with us. One of Mrs. A.'s grandsons was part of this group that was causing a scandal by busting into young women's boarding houses. No one had yet dared report them.

This event also caused some painful tension between Theis and me. Theis wanted me to apologize in front of the Collège's assembled student body for calling the police. "What you did is not the action of a nonviolent person," he claimed. I refused to humiliate myself. My call to the police immediately put an end to the activities of these well-respected students. They might have become thugs had I not stopped them.

Schomer came to the house and made a big scene, reproaching me and Magda for the way we were raising our children and for overloading de Seynes with parish work. Silent, we took the hit.

Then, at the beginning of September 1949, de Seynes asked me to come to the presbytery. I thought it was to arrange the details for his pastoral consecration, which was to take place in Le Chambon before a large gathering in November. But I was mistaken. I found my colleague drowning in a sea of smoke, nervous and despairing.

"I must share some shocking news with you: I will not be consecrated pastor in November, and I'll be leaving Le Chambon."

"What?" I already saw myself being blamed for this sudden departure.

"For months, I have been torn between two feelings – the desire to remain faithful to my vocation, which is solid, and my growing attachment to a woman. But now I've decided. I'm going to marry again!"

"Congratulations," I told him. "This is good news for everyone. Why would your remarriage make you leave Le Chambon?"

"This woman is Catholic, very Catholic, and the church authorities on Rue de Clichy in Paris consider a Catholic marriage incompatible with the exercise of my pastoral ministry. I asked to be consecrated to banish the temptation of marriage. But that didn't work. I am going to remarry and leave the ministry. Please keep this under your hat, I beg you!"

I did so. Pierre Rozier came from Valence to see me. We decided that, to avoid a scandal, de Seynes would "disappear from the scene" without fanfare, without any farewell gathering. We would say it was for "health reasons."

A week later, he left for good. I remained there, tight-lipped, once again entirely responsible for the parish, subject to the parish's opprobrium, a true scapegoat.

"Mr. Trocmé killed him," the parishioners murmured. Theis, the Collège, Mrs. A., and Schomer, who were all ignorant of the facts, chanted the official version: "Mr. de Seynes, exhausted by work in a parish that's too heavy a burden for one person, abandoned by Mr. Trocmé, was obliged to offer his resignation. Mr. Trocmé kept raising the bar for him." In fact, for several months, de Seynes hadn't done much at all. I was the one who did his work and mine, plus that of the FOR!

Weeks and months went by. I was the only pastor in Le Chambon while, at the same time, I traveled all over Europe, burning the candle at both ends. Theis and Schomer filled in for me during my absences. One Sunday I had just returned from Finland. After five nights spent on boats and trains so I would be on time for one of my evening get-togethers, I arrived early in the morning to be in the pulpit at 10:30 a.m. Schomer came to see me with his hand extended.

"André! Forgive me. I've been unfair to you."

"Oh?"

"I was just in Paris on business and went to visit de Seynes."

"Oh."

"What did I discover? He hardly let me in the door. He was holding a big reception with a good number of elegant people. It was his engagement dinner. Do you know who he's marrying? A Catholic woman! That explains everything."

"I knew all about it," I told him.

"You knew it and said nothing?"

"I promised to say nothing about it."

"Everyone thought that de Seynes was ill and that it was your fault. He's in excellent health."

"I know."

"That's terrible! Everyone reproaches you for causing his departure. 'A secret disagreement between our pastors,' they say."

"I realize that."

Little by little, the news of de Seynes's marriage became known in the parish – like most secrets, which eventually become known. Some people looked me in the eye again and shook my hand warmly.

But the damage had been done. You can't climb back up such a steep incline. Sooner or later, I had to leave Le Chambon.

De Seynes's successor was Christian Mazel,[15] who called himself "liberal." In America, a liberal is someone who has expansive ideas and is open to progress. In French Protestantism, the word "liberal" has a precise meaning: you reject the doctrine of the Trinity and do not recite the Apostles' Creed. In a sense, I too am liberal, but not in the same sense as Mazel, Theis, or Ducros, who all have a rather dry conception of faith. I am inspired by my master, Wilfred Monod, who, free of doctrinal conformity, remained communicative with Protestants of many different beliefs during the age of "Pietism."

To tell the truth, I still don't have a clear idea of why Mazel was considered "liberal," unless it meant that he suffered from the narrow-mindedness of the churches in the south of France where he was raised and that he loved to proclaim his attachment to liberalism. A few years later, his reputation earned him a promotion to the pulpit of the Oratoire du Louvre in Paris.[16]

Whatever the reason, Rozier named Mazel to Le Chambon as a gift to me. "He will fit well into your milieu," he said. He wasn't mistaken. Right away, Mazel and his wife became close to the teachers, many of whom were their age. His preaching was interesting, ornate, a bit facile, but it reached its listeners better than de Seynes's gloomy homilies.

Mazel and I got along well. Considering his ultrasensitive nature – he was easily hurt – we made a good team. He was the most affectionate of my numerous colleagues.[17]

AT THIS TIME, I made a serious mistake with my children. Nelly had already left home, but Jacques and Daniel remained. I should have taken charge of their religious education and prepared them myself for confirmation.

Why didn't I do it? For two reasons. My status as half-time pastor didn't give me the right to offer a class in religion; the stationary pastors (Theis, Mazel) oversaw that. It would have been strange for me not to entrust my children to my colleagues. Also, I followed the general

15 Christian Mazel (1919–2013) remained pastor of Le Chambon until 1960, when he went to the Oratoire du Louvre in Paris. Later, he was editor-in-chief of the journal *Évangile et Liberté*.

16 Situated across the street from the Louvre, the Oratoire du Louvre is the most prestigious Protestant church in France. Napoleon gave it as a gift to the Protestants in 1811. Today, it is known for its liberal teaching.

17 Magda notes on the manuscript: "Mazel was the full-time pastor, André was half-time; and that created no problems at all."

opinion among pastors that their children, after attending Sunday school taught by their father and receiving religious education at home from their father, might be "immunized" against the religious teaching of that same father. It was better, as a rule, to entrust the adolescents to a colleague.

This was a tragic error on my part. My children suffered as "the sons of the boss," not only the "boss of the parish," but even more, the "boss of the Collège." Parishioners and teachers expected them to set perfect examples and study hard. This was not always the case. Theis, and later Mazel, did not always treat them benevolently and, as theology instructors, were too narrow and dogmatic for Jacques's and Daniel's taste.

I was naive enough to think that if my children didn't like their religion teachers, they would naturally accept my opinions, which seem so obviously right to me. But they didn't. My children certainly admired their parents but found us a bit "crazy." We led an exhilarating but fatiguing life, not one they wanted for themselves.

If I had given them their religious instruction, I might have been able to put things in their proper place, but I only realized that when it was too late, after we moved to Versailles. They would have loved to be pacifists and conscientious objectors but didn't feel they had the strength. I understood them: it was difficult to imagine Jacques, with his tense nervous system, in prison for his convictions, or Daniel, with his earthy temperament, leaving the beaten path for high adventures.

Sometimes I wonder if the way Magda and I identify Christianity with conscientious objection discouraged our boys. Feeling incapable of following in their parents' footsteps (if only they understood that their parents are not extraordinary people!), they concluded that they didn't have faith. I'm speaking mainly of Daniel, who said openly, "I don't have faith." Nelly and Jacques were different. Nelly's beliefs are close to those of her parents, or rather, close to Magda's. As for Jacques, he married a churchgoing woman and regained his spiritual equilibrium through membership in the church.

But in Le Chambon, my children were bored with Theis and played tic-tac-toe during Mazel's lessons. It's strange that Mazel is now in demand as a catechism teacher in Paris!

21

House of Reconciliation

WE LEFT LE CHAMBON in 1950. The International FOR, Nevin Sayre, and my committee obligations required us to live somewhere more accessible than Le Chambon. When we lived there, I had to get up at 4:30 a.m. and drive to Saint-Étienne on foggy, icy roads to catch a 6:30 train to Paris. I would arrive in Paris between noon and 1 p.m., only to leave again at 6 p.m., arrive in Saint-Étienne between midnight and 1 a.m., and drive back to Le Chambon, where I'd arrive between 2 and 3 a.m. It was an impossible and dangerous life.

Where would we go? We couldn't find anything to rent around Paris. We had hoped to occupy a small apartment belonging to the Eyrauds, a Protestant family from Saint-Étienne, located at the Marché Saint-Honoré in the noisy center of Paris. A detached house situated in the suburbs of Château-Malabry disgusted us completely. We thought of Jacques Martin, who lived for a while in a large old house in Versailles belonging to one of the Monods, well-known Protestants. He had turned it into a hostel for pacifists, internationalists, and researchers of every stripe. But we couldn't get this house: after serving as a kindergarten, it had just been sold. After that, we looked for big houses that functioned as adult boarding homes and had leases for sale.

In the Parisian area, commercial properties were overpriced. The price of a boarding house for lease in Saint-Germain-en-Laye made us recoil. Unless the predecessor had made a very bad deal and couldn't find anyone to buy his business assets, you simply couldn't find what you were looking for.

While exploring real-estate agencies, I came upon the Lycée Agency in Versailles and asked my standard question, "Do you have boarding house leases we can buy?"

"Yes," replied the employee, and she showed me possibilities for 10 and 15 million francs!

"That's too expensive for me."

"There's a boarding house called Le Calme on the Rue du Général-Pershing, but I wouldn't recommend it. It's far from the center of town, so nobody wants to stay there. The current proprietor wants two million francs. He's drowning in debt. You could get it for less."

My ears perked up. "Can you drive me there?" I asked.

"Don't waste your time. This sale doesn't interest us. Head on up there, if you want, but the house is in shambles."

I decided to go alone, on foot, to Le Calme. It was a mile from the real-estate office, and the second half was uphill. Yes, it was out of the city, in the woods. The Rue du Général-Pershing was still narrow at that time and had large, decrepit properties along it. At the top of the hill, I could see the tower of what appeared to be an eighteenth-century chateau. An outmoded gate opened onto a large park full of litter, but the house, square with large windows and a Mansard roof, was noble. What a marvelous surprise!

Trembling, I went up to the proprietor, Mr. Vrinat. Yes, he and his mother had run a boarding house for children for seven or eight years. Then everything went wrong – there was a scandal and the boarding house had to close. Vrinat wanted to maintain it as a family boarding house but couldn't make a go of it. He wanted to sell his lease: two million francs. "That's nothing," I thought to myself.

I offered him one million francs; he compromised at 1.5 million, and we sealed the deal. A few days later, we signed a lease in a lawyer's office in Sceaux. The owners were two unpleasant brothers who fought in front of us.

It was an unexpected bargain. The house was dirty; there were leaks in the roof; the garden was full of rubbish and wooden shacks built and sold by Vrinat. But what an impressive setting and so much space: an immense living room, a long kitchen, a good-sized dining room, and a large office on the ground floor. On the upper floor, there were three large rooms (capable of housing thirty-five people in bunk beds), a study and an extra small room, a shower, a toilet (alas, old-style, without a flushing system), and a chapel – that's what we called a large, round room situated in the tower where we set up a wooden cross between two immense windows.

I was so pleasantly dazzled by my find that I decided to play a trick on Magda. I told her that I had found lodging but that it was pretty run down. When we arrived in Versailles to visit the place, I pointed from the window of the taxi to a real dump, which has since been destroyed. Magda, who always saw the bright side of things, blurted out, "It's not that bad at all. You'll see. We can fix it up nicely." But the taxi didn't stop. It went on to the right place, and Magda began to cry out, "André, you're crazy. It's a chateau, way too beautiful for us!"

In fact, it was a small chateau, with its terrace overhanging the drive, its park with big trees, its tower, its aristocratic dignity – kind of like the old Saint-Quentin house, dignified, large, but in bad shape.

"Think of the job we'll have! What if we don't find a cleaning woman?"

In the end, Vrinat gave us his lease for one million francs and some of his furniture for 500,000 francs. We needed sheets, blankets, and tables for the dining room. I ordered trestle tables, like the ones I had admired in the conference center in Bièvres. The beds and the mattresses were already there, though in bad shape, along with some wardrobes and dressers. We bought garden furniture for the big living room and dozens of rustic chairs at the Bon Marché. In a few weeks, the house was ready to welcome its first groups.[1]

I had dreamed for a long time of setting up a center like this for the FOR and of testing a new method of evangelizing. Pastors, I told myself, always present themselves as beggars. They ask for money; they knock on doors; they ask to be admitted. People give, but reluctantly. What if pastors, instead of always asking, were able to *offer* something like hospitality? Schomer had shown me the way by opening the Acceuil Fraternel (House of Welcome) in Le Chambon. Many American colleges have a guest house. The Quakers, who are discrete evangelists, have hostels in London and Washington. Thanks to the Quakers, we learned how to run seminars in Le Chambon. Men and women of all perspectives came together to freely discuss justice, peace, and God.

For ten years, our dream was reality. Instead of running all over Europe and America preaching to the choir, I had a home where my audience members were invited to visit me. The "House of Reconciliation" became the flagship, a symbol of pacifism in Europe and in the Parisian region. Men whom I could never have reached otherwise – Claude

1 The first group was headed by Dean Dupré and Chaplain Max Adams from Macalester College in St. Paul, Minnesota.

Bourdet, Edmond Michelet, and Jacques Madaule – spoke there.[2] Thanks to this marvelous setting (alas, appearances are important), such people took the FOR and its message seriously.

Our technique was simple: above all, hospitality. Entire groups arrived in crowded buses of between forty and forty-five people. Since we had bunk beds in the dormitories, we could accommodate groups of this size. Sometimes the groups had their own program. They were Christian tourists, often Catholics, who took advantage of our incredibly low prices. Sometimes they asked us to organize meetings with such and such a group of French people. Sometimes they organized their own meetings or small conventions. Youth groups spent the weekend at our place.

When we were not the organizers of the get-togethers, our contribution was threefold: house, feed, and inform our guests about the FOR's work. Our short, informational talks took place at the table, where we also invited questions. Many people who had never heard of nonviolence listened for the first time to this good news and never forgot it. The House of Reconciliation, as well as the Collège Cévenol and the summer seminars we started in Le Chambon with financial help from the Quakers, served as major ways of recruiting new members to the FOR.

Magda and Jispa threw themselves headlong into this backbreaking project and, in a few months, completely transformed the huge house we had found in such a sad condition. We removed ten cubic yards of trash from the gardens with the help of crews from the International Volunteer Service. They also dismantled the foundations of the old wooden shacks. White curtains brightened up the windows, flower beds bloomed, and the lawns were carefully mown. Later, after the street was enlarged, twenty climbing rosebushes decorated the railings, arousing the admiration of passersby.

There was so much work to do inside the house! First, the correspondence and finances. We couldn't afford to pay a full-time secretary. What's more, the secretary would have had to know French, English, German, and Italian. A German woman, Mrs. Hinzmann, and then a French woman, Mrs. Campguilhem, gave us a hand. Every month, an accountant came to help us with our books kept in French francs, English pounds, American dollars, and German marks.

2 Claude Bourdet (1909–1996) served in the Resistance and was deported. He cofounded the Movement for Disarmament, Peace, and Freedom. Edmond Michelet (1899–1970) also served in the Resistance and was deported. He was named Righteous Among the Nations. Jacques Madaule (1898–1993) was a professor, writer, and specialist of Paul Claudel's works.

The mimeograph machine was always rolling. Some volunteer workers created more problems than they solved, and the atmosphere in the office was sometimes tense, even inflammatory. So, I left the office completely in my wife's hands and found refuge in the second-floor study, where I prepared my lectures. My presence in the office would have only complicated matters and caused more tension.

Then there was the housework: cooking for up to forty-five people and keeping the whole place clean. A real challenge to one's sanity! No woman from town stayed very long. We had inherited from Vrinat a couple who lived in the concierge's lodge near the front gate. He had advised us to get rid of them because the woman was bossy and dishonest. Whoever remembers the conditions in the Parisian area after the war will understand our problem. We had rented unoccupied premises. The occupants of the lodge had no right to be there, and we refused to have them pay us rent for fear that they would settle in for good. The police refused to evict them. But I found a way to get them out. Next to our house, the owners had another dilapidated, unoccupied house. I had the prefecture requisition this house and offer it to the couple. This new lodging allowed them to leave our property – which didn't prevent them from stealing electricity from us by plugging a pirate line to our meter!

We looked for a family of caretakers – a handyman to work during his free time and a woman to cook for our groups and help in the house. We spoke with a Protestant lawyer working with combat veterans. Unfortunately, he stuck us with a crook named S., a swindler and liar, who used my car when I wasn't there and had a bad influence on my sons. His wife was a wreck, overwhelmed by problems with her children. They had hardly settled in when we realized the catastrophe. We had to move heaven and earth to get rid of them.

Finally, the Quétiers arrived. They became our good friends. Mr. Quétier was a police officer, very dignified, an active and honest handyman. His wife, a near-illiterate woman from Brittany, had grown up as a maid in an inn and could do everything. She was an excellent cook and housekeeper – when she was in a good mood. When she wasn't, Magda and Jispa had to put up with her sulking and prolonged strikes caused by a word she had misunderstood or demand for a higher salary. We paid her an hourly wage for her work, while her husband took care of the heating and garbage in exchange for their lodging. Their lodging became upscale when the highway department, after widening the street, built them a brand-new, attractive lodge.

Our association with Mrs. Quétier began rather dramatically. She had just started working, when a German group announced its arrival. It was a choir from the banks of the Weser River, under the direction of a music professor. Mrs. Quétier simply refused to cook for them.

"My brother was tortured and murdered as a *maquisard* by the Krauts. There's no way I'm going to serve the Krauts now." It was futile to tell her that we were talking about adolescents who hadn't taken part in the war. Nothing would persuade her. She went back into her house. We had to improvise simple meals, and I explained to the Germans what had happened. They were devastated. They had never heard about the suffering inflicted by the Gestapo in occupied countries. "But we weren't the ones who did it," they repeated, "and we didn't know about it." They were sincere.

When their time to leave came, the director of the choir had a touching idea. He grouped his singers in a half-circle around the lodge, which had its doors and windows closed, and began softly singing some well-chosen songs.

A head appeared at a window upstairs, then two; then the window opened, framing Mrs. Quétier. The director gave a short speech in French and, speaking for the group, expressed the remorse that these young people felt at the thought of the crimes committed by Germany. Then he took out a bouquet of white flowers. "In homage and with respect for your brother," he said to Mrs. Quétier, who came down to accept it.

As you might expect, Mrs. Quétier was deeply moved. We never again had to ask her permission to have any group in the House of Reconciliation. She became our capable and friendly coworker, except for the occasional lapses in goodwill that I mentioned earlier.

During our years in Versailles, two painful disappointments obscured the joy we otherwise experienced from offering hospitality and spreading the message of peace.

The first, which we expected, was caused by the French Reformed Church's attitude. I had no reason to complain about my colleagues. At least those belonging to the western suburbs of Paris were friendly. They had organized a "pastoral group" and invited me to join, but I could only attend their meetings on occasion due to my constant commitments.

I was disappointed, rather, by the coolness of my former friends in the Northern Group (Babut and Ducros). The former was absorbed by administrative tasks for the national council of the Reformed Church; the latter had become pastor of the Oratoire du Louvre and president of the Social Christian Movement and had completely "forgotten" his membership in the FOR. He remembered it only when he wanted to send his daughter to England. Things went better with Henri Roser. Wasn't he the president of the French FOR? But for reasons explained earlier, our friendship with his family was beyond repair. I never sensed his support for our work, either at the annual FOR conventions taking place at our House of Reconciliation or at our International Volunteer Service meetings.

I gradually lost what little remained of my confidence in the courage of my pastoral colleagues.

Protestantism is a democracy. Whereas the Catholic or Anglican priest must satisfy his bishop, who listens too easily to complaints but can also defend the priest against his parishes, the Protestant pastor is named by the parish, especially by its council of elders. He *must* therefore "succeed" in the parish. That means satisfying the administrators in place.

The misunderstanding arises out of the concept of the "good shepherd." For the pastor, the "good shepherd" is, before anything else, a prophet who remains faithful to the Gospels, a redresser of wrongs, a good teacher, an awakener of moral consciences. For the parishioners, the "good shepherd" is an omnipresent, friendly, comprehensive, compassionate, and helpful being.

Young pastors, recently graduated from theology school, throw themselves into their ministry with enthusiasm. They attempt to "awaken" the first parish given to them. A few succeed. The great majority lack both the eloquence and the charm to do so. Their experience ends in failure. If the young pastor is a bull in a china shop, the authorities give him a bad grade, and his reputation follows him the rest of his career unless he makes amends. If he wants to avoid quarrels, he will adapt himself to his situation. The prophet in him fades away; he becomes a conscientious, timid ecclesiastic. Sometimes the "bull in a china shop," after making honorable amends, applies his energy to the service of the synod. These will be tomorrow's bishops.

For my former comrades at the School of Theology, I arrived in the Parisian region with the reputation of a pacifist and a conscientious objector. This did not work in my favor. But Roser had that same reputation in spades and was head of the Popular Mission. To be fair, however, the Popular Mission is not a synodal organization, and its agents are recruited among progressive pastors. Roser's only parochial experience in fifty years of ministry was in a small, dying church in the heart of Paris.

I was reputed to be a "misfit," in part deservedly, because I didn't identify with any of the "fashionable" movements that came one after another: the Drôme Brigade, Pentecostalism, ecumenism, and Taizé, for example. This led to my estrangement from those colleagues who threw themselves into these movements – and returned from them ten years later ready to jump on the bandwagon of the next popular movement.

For Babut, I'm sure, I was "the one left behind" from the Northern Group that he abandoned to join the Pentecostals, then to become regional president, and finally secretary general of the church. My reputation suffered from the absurdities that wartime refugees in Le Chambon and Pierre Rozier spread about me.

When a French pastor assumes a post in Paris at the end of his career, it proves that prudence has become his ruling quality. As a result, even though I presented myself as a lecturer on postwar problems in the annual circular sent to all Parisian pastors, it was only rarely, and with strong recommendations of caution, that I was invited to speak before limited groups of young people and catechumens. My lectures offered a unique view of postwar Germany, Europe, countries on the other side of the Iron Curtain, the United States, and Israel. This was well before pilgrimages to Israel, Franco-German meetings, and trips to Russia or the USA became fashionable.

Pastor Marcel from Saint-Germain, for example, asked me to speak to his catechumens so that he could contradict me the following Sunday. He didn't invite me to stay as he demolished my ideas.

This could all be attributed to was pastoral prudence, of course, but also to a profoundly reactionary mindset in the parishes around Paris. Paris was "the end of the career" of the French Protestant functionary. Who goes to Paris to finish a career? The bureaucrat who has kept to the straight and narrow, who was never the object of a disturbing report by his superiors. It is that bureaucrat, civilian or military, often retired and decorated, who sits on the Parisian councils of elders. How could a friend of mine even suggest to his council of elders that they invite Pastor Trocmé, a conscientious objector, an enfant terrible in the Reformed Church, a pastor without a parish, associated with a suspect group called the FOR?

The most unlikely rumors spread: Americans (friends of the Collège Cévenol and the FOR) were paying me a fantastic salary (which made my colleagues jealous). In fact, I tried to keep my salary at the exact same level as that of my colleagues, but I couldn't get my colleagues to believe me, no matter how often I told them. It was also rumored that I had bought the "Versailles Château" with American dollars and was leading a "chateau life."

None of these rumors kept them from sending us their scout troops or parish youth groups on the weekend. These youngsters complained about the lack of comfort and were more difficult than the foreigners.

The Protestant parish of Versailles received me coolly. My fellow student Henry Minssen, a gentle, sickly man who always showed me affection, came to welcome me. Minssen had housed me in his presbytery in Lamastre during the war when I first went into hiding. He explained that some people in the parish considered my arrival catastrophic.

Our relations with his parish, however, were normal. On Sundays, when I was there, I went to services with Magda and Jispa, whenever they weren't overburdened with work at the house. Minssen's sermons were always interesting but often sad. His colleague Arnold Ullern, a zealous man, often clumsy, and heir to a Pietist tradition, frequently made appeals for conversions which were lost in the cocoon-like atmosphere of the petit-bourgeois audience.

The council of elders consisted of several important bourgeois who remained from the time when Versailles had many Protestant millionaires associated with "high Protestant society." Some of them wanted to impress Versailles's reactionary Catholics by assuming an authoritative, conservative stance that humiliated their pastors. Some of them had even formed "a Barthian study group" because they underestimated their pastors' theology. In short, those were the people who considered my arrival in Versailles catastrophic.

We got along well from the beginning with the newly formed Catholic left, the Popular Republican Movement led by Georges Bidault that emerged from the Resistance with Christian Socialist tendencies. Discouraged by the collapse of their early idealism, they decided to make common cause with Socialists who were anti-Communist and fervent antimilitarists to create a new party, the Unified Socialist Party.

We had a lot of difficulty maintaining our position of nonviolence. After Magda and other women created the group "Women's

Responsibility in the Atomic Age," we were under pressure from the left and the far left.

I was constantly asked to add my signature to declarations and protests. These were valuable, of course, but their political intentions could hardly be missed. I learned to recognize the characteristic frenzy of people caught up in politics. Often animated by noble ideas at the beginning, they inevitably become associated with others with less pure ambitions. Political commitment doesn't happen without the formation of political parties, clans, and groups, with all their compromises, schemes, and horse-trading. I had seen all that with the "Combatants for Peace," which soon became the "Peace Movement." My refusal to sign "The Stockholm Appeal"[3] put me in a bad light with my best pacifist friends (Philo Vernier, Francis Bosc, Étienne Mathiot). It was clear, however, that they were only protesting American atomic weapons. No one mentioned what Russia was preparing.

When the Algerian War broke out, things became even more delicate. As a person committed to nonviolence, I couldn't support either the organized terrorism of the Algerian nationalists from November 1, 1952, onward, or the police and subsequent military repression by France. The Catholic left, epitomized by Abbé Boudouresques and Abbé Davezies, and followed by Pastor Mathiot, had sided with the insurgents. The National Liberation Front (FLN) wasn't content with waging guerilla warfare in Algeria.[4] They also organized attacks in France. We were asked to hide members of the FLN. It was difficult to know whether they were innocent people being tracked down by the French police or terrorists hiding out the day after an attack. Some people were scandalized by our refusal to practice this type of resistance.

On the other hand, we passionately joined the courageous campaigns led by Robert Barrat in *Témoignage Chrétien*,[5] a Catholic journal that emerged from the Resistance and, without any problem at all, went way beyond the mediocre declarations in our Protestant journals.

3 This was a petition against nuclear arms, launched in the spring of 1950, by Frédéric Joliot-Curie and the World Movement of Partisans for Peace.

4 The National Liberation Front (FLN) is a nationalist political party in Algeria. Its armed wing engaged in a fierce struggle against French authority during the war in Algeria.

5 Robert Barrat (1919–1976), a journalist and an editor of *Témoignage Chrétien*, supported Algerian independence and was a conscientious objector. On April 11, 1958, with Trocmé, Lanza del Vasto, and others, he gained entrance into the Marcoule Factory to protest nuclear weapons.

In defense of Protestantism, it's true that the Protestant minority in France is politically divided and that the left doesn't have enough supporters to fund a left-wing Protestant newspaper. *Témoignage Chrétien* has the support of numerous, enthusiastic, left-wing Catholics and has flourished since World War II.

In a separate category of publications, the *Cahiers de la Réconciliation*, edited by Henri Roser and *La Revue du Christianisme*, edited by Maurice Voge, lacked neither insight nor courage. Maurice Voge lost his job for his courageous, if somewhat clumsy, push for Algerian independence.

THE VERSAILLES COUNCIL OF ELDERS watched the growing influence of the House of Reconciliation with dread. My two colleagues did their best to improve the situation. I was even invited to speak to the council. I explained the nature of the FOR, as well as conscientious objection and nonviolence. My colleagues sometimes asked me to replace them when they were sick or absent.

The winter of 1955 (or was it 1954 or 1956?) was remarkable. My sermons were well received by the parishioners, and I was invited to give four sermons on topics of my choice. Many people came to my first sermon – and to the second as well. However, I did something that had irreparable consequences when I told the congregation, "My brothers and sisters, next time I intend to examine, in the light of the gospel, certain problems raised by the war in Algeria."

The next day, Minssen telephoned to reproach me for my "blunder."[6] The vice president of the council, a certain Mr. H. (director of a Barthian group) had threatened to resign if I gave the announced sermon.

"Couldn't you simply change the topic?" asked Minssen.

"Mr. H. has no idea what I am going to say. I merely announced that I would examine certain problems raised by the war in Algeria in the light of the gospel."

"Mr. H. is convinced that you will put the *pieds noirs* on trial and is opposed to politics in the pulpit."[7]

---

6 Magda's marginal note: "André is mistaken. He didn't telephone. He came to see us. I received him; André wasn't home. I was astonished to have a 'pastoral visit.' But that wasn't it. He came to tell us that he was feeling much better and would be able to take over again in the pulpit. André would no longer have to be bothered. It was only after many questions from me at that moment, and, later, from André, that the truth emerged."

7 *Pieds noirs* were people of French and other European descent born in Algeria during the period of French rule (1830–1962).

"I will not do politics in the pulpit. That's all I can tell Mr. H. He should trust me. I would like to talk to him."

Despite his refusal, I went to see Mr. H., who was distant but polite. I quickly discovered that he was the president of a company whose principal business was in Algeria. As a good *pied noir*, he felt attacked and wounded by all those who doubted the legitimacy of the "French presence" in Algeria. I reassured him and told him about my many travels to North Africa and my respect for the settlers, who belonged to a bygone era.

"It's too soon to liberate the Algerians," he said. "We can't do it for another fifty years."

"In any event," I reassured him, "I have no intention of speaking about these things from the pulpit. I will speak about certain problems that confronted Jesus and his disciples and how Jesus reacted to these problems, which are not without analogy to the problems facing us in Algeria."

We left one another, I hoped, on good terms.

But a few days later, Minssen called me back on the phone. "The council of elders met. They want you to change the subject of your sermon or not lead the service."

"I won't lead the service," I told him.

That's what happened. I was never again invited to preach in Versailles. However, a few weeks later, I met Ullern, the other pastor, in the street. He was extremely cordial.

"Did you know that Mr. H. resigned from the council of elders?" he asked.

"It's the first I've heard. I knew he had threatened to do so if I preached about Algeria, but since I withdrew . . ."

"Your forced withdrawal provoked reactions in your favor from several elders. H. felt himself targeted, and, being touchy, he quit."

"I regret causing this dissension," I said.

"Don't regret anything," replied Ullern. "Everyone was tired of H. He was a real dictator. We made him vice president to quiet his endless objections, but it didn't pacify him. On the contrary, you did us a big favor."

Yet Ullern also never asked me to continue the lecture series. That was over for good.

These little tragicomic conflicts with the Versailles parish would have been easier to bear if we had been fully supported by the International FOR committee in England.

Don't get me wrong. What I am going to relate now in no way detracts from the admiration I feel for the great leaders of the FOR: Henry Hodgkin, one of its founders; Mathilda Wrede, noted for her work in prisons; Leonhard Ragaz, an ecologist and advocate of religious socialism; Henri Roser; Muriel Lester; A. J. Muste; and Nevin Sayre. They will remain, in the history of twentieth-century religious faith, people of extraordinary stature. They dominated their historical moment by their courage, their faithfulness, and their ability to forgive. The small flaws, often comical ones, in each of them take nothing away from their exceptional prophetic value. Nevin Sayre was, and will remain, a true friend for us, a constant, reliable support even during the extremely difficult times that the committee put us through.

From our very first contacts, this committee was a disappointment.

Why is it that my idealism always causes me to look for a country or an organization that is freer, more tolerant, and closer to the truth than the one in which I find myself? My *Sehnsucht* (nostalgia) certainly comes from my melancholic youth when, after the death of my mother, my family that was too self-righteous, too sure of itself, too critical of everything, suffocated me. At that time, I thought that Germany, with my Schwerdtmann relatives' warm spontaneity, must be the ideal place.

My first liberation came in the Union in Saint-Quentin during World War I, when I saw with my own eyes comrades repenting, finding peace, helping one another, sharing everything. I have never lost this vision. All my life I have remained a pilgrim looking for another such "union." There was the Clamart Union, then the Northern Group, where we experienced hours of supernatural inspiration. But "unions" disperse or change their nature. I've described the bitterness caused by the breakup of the Northern Group because of Pentecostalism. Then there was Le Chambon, with its Bible study groups and nonviolent resistance during the war years. But after the war this exceptional group in Le Chambon dissolved.

There was also the Swiss Children's Welfare Service. Amid the shame that war brought, I imagined Switzerland as a better country that had learned to replace saber-rattling and disgraceful collaboration with philanthropic activity. Today I live in this same Switzerland, and all I can say is that it is no better or worse than any other country.

I also passed through a pro-American phase. My first trips there never disappointed me. American FOR groups emerged from a difficult period of resistance and from time spent in Civilian Public Service camps. They spread across the globe in generous mutual aid campaigns and enjoyed an intense, marvelous life under the inspiration of Nevin Sayre and, above all, A. J. Muste.

I was so impressed by the Quakers that I thought about becoming one. I sometimes regret today that I didn't take that step when we were in Versailles. Then I was so taken by the example of the Mennonites that I copied their methods for supporting conscientious objectors when I founded Eirene.[8]

But each time, as the first positive impression gave way to a fuller understanding of the place, I had to recognize that all human milieus resemble one another. The best ones distinguish themselves by an obvious disinterest in money and by magnanimous activities; the excellent ones by their profound humility and their capacity to forgive and (something much more difficult) to forget. But the Tarpeian Rock is near Capitoline Hill.[9] Here I discovered that climbers who think they are near the summit are often animated by pride or jealousy that approaches hatred. When that comes from people who profess to be nonviolent Christians, it leaves a burning wound.

I discovered this situation in 1948 when, after being named European secretary for the International FOR, I went to London to receive instructions from the secretary general, an English Quaker named Percy Bartlett. He received me icily, refusing to turn over the correspondence dossiers of the European members of the FOR. They were indispensable, if he and I were to coordinate efforts.

When I asked him for the addresses, he handed me a box of file cards dating from before the war. It certainly was not his fault. The war had broken off all relations between England and the Continent, and most of the addresses, I soon learned, were no longer valid.

But why not simply explain the situation to me? I quickly discovered that Percy was afraid of me and jealous. His bad temperament was common knowledge among the English members of the FOR and created

8 With the help of the Mennonites, Trocmé founded Eirene as an "International Christian Service for Peace" in Morocco during the war in Algeria. Volunteers taught modern ways of farming in addition to teaching the illiterate how to read and write. It was a destination for conscientious objectors. Today, Eirene is a strong organization providing services in many countries.

9 The Tarpeian Rock is a steep cliff on the south side of the Capitoline Hill, just above the Roman Forum, used in ancient Rome as a site for executions. Convicted criminals were flung from the cliff to their deaths.

a deep division within the International FOR, where he served as secretary general. Percy was an employee of the English PTT (Post, Telegraph, Telephone) and a conscientious objector during World War I who had became a Quaker. He was intelligent but not well educated: he agonized, as only the English can, over his lack of a university degree. He was the secretary of the London Union of the FOR, and at the beginning of World War II, he became interim secretary of the English FOR. Percy moved to general secretary of the International FOR when Henri Roser was not available. The English committee promoted him to get rid of a difficult personality. I only learned all this ten years later, when he resigned.

In France, Belgium, and Switzerland, his ignorance of the language relieved me of all problems. But not in Germany. Percy didn't know German, but Germany was a major preoccupation of its former enemies. I knew German, and my lectures drew large audiences. My views on Nazism and the need for reconciliation were received as more legitimate than those of the Anglo-Saxons. But Percy named as his secretary a woman from Cologne, an ex-Nazi anxious to show off her credentials and her perfect knowledge of English, who pulled the wool over the eyes of the Americans and the English.

It was the same in Italy. Magda, at first alone, then with an Englishman named Hogg, and later still with Nevin, established the first FOR group in the country. Percy, through several English expatriates in Rome and elsewhere, tried his best to organize some young, English-speaking Italians who wanted to obtain grants to study in America. They had no real interest in the movement.

Magda, the Italian, lost no time making friends with some of the most noble pacifists of Europe: Aldo Capitini, Balboni, Tassoni, and later, Danilo Dolci, who together formed the Italian pacifist movement. Admittedly, their Christianity was somewhat unorthodox, but the real problem was that the "Quaker-leaning" factions in Rome didn't even know this group existed. Percy refused to recognize the group and questioned its validity. He made the FOR committee dismiss the request for affiliation by the remarkable professor from Pérouse, Aldo Capitini, a confirmed pacifist and founder of civic cultural centers throughout Italy, on the grounds that his views were not Christian enough. Capitini was a disciple of Tolstoy and Gandhi. He was born Catholic, but what church in 1950 could house his pacifism?

In Switzerland, the movement was squashed for years. Percy let its directorship rotate among a few sympathetic Quakers, who made no headway with the dominant Protestant confessions, who weren't interested in the Quaker message sullied by "theological liberalism." We were at the high point of Barthianism in the church.

After several years, it was clear that the few friendships Percy maintained in Germany had little to do with the movement that had recruited men like Martin Niemöler, Heinz Kloppenburg, and Hans Iwand. After the Versailles movement opened a door into Holland and *Kerk en Vrede* (Church and Peace) joined the FOR as a bloc, Percy confined himself to paperwork and Scandinavia, a region he kept as his private preserve.

Percy deluged me and Magda with accusations, generally in the form of malicious and false rumors. We learned one day in London, for example, that we had acquired the house in Versailles for ourselves, thanks to American money, and were renting it out at a very high price to the FOR, while maintaining a family boarding house for our own profit. How could we have bought, for a million and a half francs, a property that at that time was worth 30 or 40 million francs, in one of the most elegant neighborhoods in the area?

Percy also knew that we had borrowed the American money and that I was sweating blood and tears to pay back Nevin Sayre with the money I earned on my lectures in the United States. He was also fully aware that we had to supplement our modest salary from the FOR to help our children, who were students in the USA, by taking in boarders in our own third-floor apartment. An accountant looked over our books every month. But Percy convinced the European committee that our center should have been *bringing in* money to cover the modest rent.

So, one day in London, we quit! Nevin Sayre caught up with us in the street. We were both crying from humiliation and desolation.

In the United States, I had spoken little with Nevin about my concerns. When we saw him in London, he recommended that I react as a Christian. Fortunately, his confidence and the immense joy I got from lecturing and raising funds, which I gave to the FOR after I had paid my Versailles debt, largely compensated for the grief the European committee caused me.

By his adroit manipulations, Percy kept his collaborators in a state of constant inferiority. In his eyes, we were only "itinerant secretaries."

When we requested a budget for a secretary-typist, he replied, "Do your own correspondence," or "Send me all the correspondence. You don't have the right to correspond directly with the national movements and their members."

Excluded from all the committees that made major decisions (policy, finances, youth, personnel), we were never invited to present our own proposals. We spent a good part of the time taking walks while others were working. The committees were poorly informed about the work we were doing, and at the final plenary session we were presented with irrevocable decisions that often did not correspond to the current situation in certain countries.

"You know nothing about business," Percy scoffed. Yet, I thought to myself, as president of the Collège, I managed complex issues and significant sums of money. But it's better not to say certain things out loud for fear of committing the sin of vanity. Behind Percy stood the English FOR, the motherhouse of the entire movement that was founded in 1914.

In 1914, when faced with German aggression, England first adopted a law of universal conscription (it has since been abolished). Such a compulsory law made people question all the traditional civil liberties in England, which until then had used only voluntary soldiers. Many Englishmen, for diverse reasons, but mainly religious ones, became "conscientious objectors." During World War I, they were severely punished with prison terms; some died because of their steadfastness.

This attitude went hand and hand with a certain philosophy used to justify it – not only religious but political. It generated a humanist tendency along Gandhian lines, but much more simplistic: "If our country behaves correctly toward other nations, those nations will respond by acting correctly. If this doesn't happen, it's because the politics of our country is *wrong*, and the other country is in the *right*."

In the late 1930s this fallacious attitude caused former Labour leader George Lansbury, as a representative of the FOR, with Percy Bartlett as his manager, to make personal visits to heads of state such as Mussolini, Hitler, Stalin, and Roosevelt. They were received with open arms by each leader, only to be told, "We're not at fault. My people are treated unjustly. If other nations were reasonable, we would have peace."

The next obvious step was to conclude that the English government, in which Labour was the opposition party, was wrong. They took that step.

During World War II, there were many English conscientious objectors (around 60,000). The majority accepted work in civil defense or agriculture. A small number of intractable objectors preferred prison. But the government, wisely refusing to make martyrs of them, sent the obstinate radicals straight home, where their situation was embarrassing.

When the war was over, the English FOR concentrated its efforts on abolishing corruption, which they considered the absolute evil. All other problems – colonialism, world federalism, the United Nations, inequality among races and peoples, voluntary service – were left in the background. They were like the Pietists, who consider all activity not geared toward the salvation of souls offensive to biblical teaching.

In the European committee, the English branch of the International FOR was all-powerful. The members of the committee appeared only every other year at the council meetings. The American FOR provided the world organization half or more of its finances. Formerly the patrons of the movement, the English furnished a part of the finances, but they were the home team and still exercised a veritable dictatorship through their secretary general, Clifford McQuire. McQuire was a member of all the influential groups. The purse strings of the organization were tied and untied according to his judgment. I often clashed with him, but he was an upright person, a brilliant orator and organizer, in a totally different class than Percy. He was a man without any reason to be jealous or fearful.

The only questions that Clifford asked his "employees" – that's how he treated me – were very simple: How many conscientious objectors are there in France (or in Italy and Switzerland)? How many contributing members do you have (full members who have committed to being conscientious objectors or sympathizers)? How many local groups are there? In many cities in England, a Protestant country, the FOR has groups that are almost "sects," they are so numerous. Clifford pouted about the "lack of progress" regarding our statistics and our finances. It was useless to try to explain to him that:

1. Our conscientious objectors were punished with repeated sentences of two years in prison and had to give up all semblance of a normal life.
2. In traditional Catholic countries, believers waited for instructions from the church, but the church teachings supported the notion of a just war.

3. In countries with a tiny Protestant minority, the conscientious objector, usually either a Protestant or a humanist, could only serve as a rare example of almost superhuman faith and courage.

Nothing worked! "A national movement comes of age the day it can pay for a salaried secretary general!" was Clifford's response.

Our bank accounts and statistics were skimpy. Germany, Holland, the Scandinavian countries, Switzerland, all between 50 and 100 percent Protestant, corresponded directly with London. We Latin countries (France, Italy, Belgium, Spain) were struggling with a Catholic Church that upheld the idea of a just war and condemned conscientious objection, and with a state that crushed all attempts to refuse military service with consecutive prison sentences. These sentences forced objectors to renounce everything – career, marriage, friendship, and future. We faced a state that considered all propaganda for conscientious objection criminal activity, and a vacillating Protestantism that began to vote half-heartedly for the recognition of conscientious objection while continuing to ostracize conscientious objectors.

Under these circumstances, how could we have possibly made public the list of contributors? The Algerian War opened a lot of eyes, woke up the Catholic conscience, and finally, when it was over, led to the concession of a shaky statute for conscientious objectors, who are now required to do public service twice as long as military service.

We tried to explain all this to the English. It was a waste of time. The divide between us and them became greater, and Percy did nothing to bridge it.

What should we conclude from all this? Enlightened by my encounters with the great founders, I believe that I touched the true church of Jesus Christ on earth, the one in which we love and understand each other and forgive one another. It is also true that the founders, as people, were exceptional men and women of remarkable intelligence, charity, and prophetic vision.

There were, however, lesser men, conscientious objectors who thought they had solved all problems because they refused to kill their neighbors in wartime. All problems: the problems of race, of class, nations, and languages. They proceeded in their own provincial way, intolerant of those who didn't think like them and didn't speak their language.

They obviously preferred those who knew English well and became exasperated with those who, like Henri Roser, spoke English poorly.

Such people, wherever you find them, but especially when they're involved in generous, charitable work, cause problems that are difficult to resolve. Unconsciously jealous of those who solve difficult problems, who accomplish the impossible because they have the gift of enthusiasm and the ability to work with others, these people compensate by a fanatical attachment to form, finances, and administrative rules. They take great pleasure in dismantling and deflating the projects of the pioneers.

After World War I, the English FOR had quickly become a recognized institution. How could things have happened otherwise in a country where the right to conscientious objection was recognized, practiced, and professed by a public fundamentally respectful of the individual conscience? Free of other battles to wage or sufferings to endure, the English FOR began to recruit members and figured that we could do the same. They held the International FOR in their hands. They founded a youth committee – ah, the charming get-togethers of young people I attended in England where young people played games!

But they were scandalized because France, Belgium, and Italy were unable to send delegates to these meetings. It was the time when French, Italian, and Belgian youth members were serving repeated, pitiless prison terms.

So many small-minded men run institutions. They institute rule after rule, losing sight of the enormous problems confronting them.

MANY TIMES I PROPOSED that we divide the countries into three categories:

1. The Protestant countries (England, the United States, Holland; soon Germany, but sadly, not yet Switzerland) where freedom of conscience is traditionally recognized and where the FOR can operate without violating rigorous laws. In these countries, I said, we could expect an organized movement with numerous members and a paid secretary.
2. Countries with a Catholic majority (France, Belgium, Italy, Austria, Spain, and Latin America), where you must obtain permission from the Catholic Church to disobey draft requirements.

While waiting, amidst a thousand pitfalls, the movement, which is illegal, can only assume a semi-clandestine character since it encourages insubordination. Let me add that since then, thanks to two Catholic FOR secretaries (Jean Gros, a Frenchman, and Hildegarde Mayr, his Austrian wife), the Catholic Church counts a growing number of conscientious objectors. France and Austria, having discovered that conscientious objectors do not all belong to far-out sects like the Jehovah's Witnesses, have accorded conscientious objector status to these courageous young people. (Though when I first proposed this, we weren't there yet, and misunderstandings between the English and those of us on the Continent continued. The craftiest among us on the Continent inflated the statistics and announced the existence of "local groups" – in Austria, Germany, and even Italy – when there was hardly a handful of sympathetic souls when an FOR speaker came to town.)

3. The third category would be non-Christian countries, and those behind the Iron Curtain, places where freedom of conscience doesn't exist or where the word "conscience" itself, meaning the capacity of the individual to oppose customs and laws in the name of his or her personal convictions, has never been recognized.

Nothing has changed in this regard since I left the FOR seven years ago, except one thing: the adoption of a statute for conscientious objectors in France, Germany, Austria, and to some degree, Belgium. Switzerland, Italy,[10] and Spain are still lagging behind.

This new situation has allowed churches to accept conscientious objectors – but with some delay. It wasn't their synods that made the case for the objectors in the firmest possible way, but a few courageous individuals like Henri Roser and Louis Lecoin, an anarchist whose hunger strike won over public opinion, which only reacts to the shock of sensational events.

Churches now recognize the legitimacy of conscientious objection. Our movement is legal and well-established, and people like Jean Lasserre, named secretary of the French-speaking nations, can work independently from the Anglo-Saxon committees. He is paid by the French, Belgian, and French-speaking Swiss movements.

10 Note from Magda: "Italy formally accepted conscientious objection in 1971, shortly after André's death on June 5, 1971."

As I turn my back on these committees and their desiccating administrative sessions, forgetting the moral solitude they left me struggling in, I will now briefly relate my travels – or, to avoid being tedious, the most colorful facts that marked them.

After our great sorrows, travel was the healing medicine I needed. Pastors spend their time confronting sickness and death. When they are young, they go toward the future with youth groups. But after forty, they lose their youth, and, having suffered much, they can no longer play or sing. The crippled, the sick, and the dying remain. The perpetual defeat of humanity by sickness and the infrequency of "triumphant deaths" lowers the morale of pastors who want to hope, believe, and construct a future.

I explained above why I found myself pushed aside during the establishment of the Collège and how much I suffered from that. When I left Le Chambon in 1950, I resigned from the presidency of the administrative council of the Collège and asked Mazel to replace me. Wasn't he the new pastor of Le Chambon and already a member of the council?

But things between Mazel and Theis were not going very well. Theis treated him as he had treated me, presenting him with faits accomplis and keeping him uninformed. Mazel didn't react the way I did. He rebelled, demanded an accounting, and clashed with Theis. Furthermore, he was just as touchy as Theis, and soon things between the two men got even worse. Mazel resigned.

Although I was living in Versailles, they asked me to assume the presidency again, which I did, moved as I was by the marks of friendship that Theis and others had shown me since I lived far away! But the Collège never again became my spiritual home. I was alone with Magda and Jispa.

22

Conclusions

EUROPE WAS IN RUINS – literally, but more importantly, morally and spiritually. The formerly occupied countries licked their wounds as their liberation erased the nightmares of collaboration. In the aftermath, all the French discovered that they had been resisters; they glorified the *maquis* and hoisted de Gaulle to the heavens. It was difficult to speak about nonviolence when everyone was convinced that the Allies had chased the Nazis from France by holding a pistol to their heads.

But we could still talk about nonviolent resistance in Le Chambon. Certainly, there had been armed resistance: the American landing in Normandy, Stalingrad, and the Russian victory. However, there were also Christians who refused to obey for reasons of conscience. They were no less conscientious objectors than those who preferred prison to murder. These Christians also refused to practice other evils – injustice, lying, and political and racial persecution.

In the small French Protestant community of Le Chambon, where everyone knows everyone else, we were modest about our nonviolent accomplishments. We would have been considered braggarts if we had done otherwise. Didn't others resist as well? That Salvation Army man and that pastor, didn't they get deported and murdered? Aren't you alive? Keep quiet! I was quiet and stuck to generalities and theoretical topics. History will judge, I thought. We hadn't worked for human recognition.

But in Germany and Italy, there was no reason to keep silent about our experiences. When I gave my first lectures, Italians and Germans were in a tragic situation. By temperament, Germans are credulous when it comes to their government and have an innate respect for the *Obrigkeit* (the powers that be). Between the two World Wars, the Germans I met, even the members of our pacifist movements, couldn't believe that their emperor could have been at fault. Where there were errors of judgment, bad luck, or treason, they were likely to blame the Jews and the Communists.

The foundation of Nazism was this absurd proposition: Germany is innocent; the Germans are good, victims of the aggression and hatred of their jealous neighbors. The Hitler Youth were taught these ideas (one of my cousins helped start the Hitler Youth in Göttingen and was killed at the beginning of the war), as were members of the Compulsory Work Service and the Brown Shirts. The Germans felt a masochistic pleasure in voluntarily dissolving all associations not linked to the state, even the FOR. Our organization had no reason to exist since the state did everything better. Then came the war.

In 1946, during my first trips to Germany, no one among my best-intentioned auditors seemed capable of a reasonable analysis of the war's causes. "We were attacked," a deaconess in Singen declared publicly. "We had to defend ourselves."

What about the campaign in Russia, where an entire people refused to let themselves become subjugated? "It was the diabolical power of Communism," they replied. "Why didn't they support our Führer. He would have prevented the frightening triumph of Communism!"

The police state, the Gestapo, the concentration camps should have opened the Germans' eyes. "We had no idea whatsoever about the concentration camps," they declared with their hand on their heart.

"Even when the people of Weimar saw long lines of detained men and women arriving?" (Weimar was where the Buchenwald camp was located.)

"They told us they were ordinary criminals, and we believed them!"

We believed them! We believed them! What a difference between France and Germany! The French distrust everything the authorities tell them. The Germans seemed to have a blind confidence in them.

"Didn't you notice that among your fellow citizens certain people, because they were Jewish or liberal, suddenly disappeared?"

It was an embarrassing question that many simply didn't answer. The most courageous among them would say: "We knew there were camps, but, even in our own families, we didn't talk about it for fear of being denounced and sent immediately to those camps."

I spoke earlier about the obsession with denunciation that paralyzed the best among them, even before the war. During the war, any doubt at all was considered a betrayal of the Fatherland. Because they had to save Germany, they went along with the Nazi party and remained as inconspicuous as possible.

Hitler's suicide and the unconditional surrender of Germany cast this naive people into a state of indescribable collective stupor.

I paid a visit to the surviving members of the German FOR. They received me as best they could. I slept on couches in refurnished basements of burned-out buildings. That was the second time I stayed with them; the first time I had to beg for the "advantages" that the French, English, and American Occupational Forces offered. Foreign civilians were forbidden to eat the rations given to the starving population. I had to eat in the officers' mess hall – me, a pacifist, – and sleep in the hotels reserved for them. In the evenings, we held our meetings clandestinely because the Germans were now afraid of the occupying authorities, after being fearful of the Gestapo.

As the years rolled by, however, faces lit up, and the initial depression yielded to a more accurate view of things. Freedom of the press, the Nuremberg Trials (at the beginning, Germans thought the charges were made up), and contacts with the outside world allowed public opinion to correct itself. Politically, there was a right, a left, Christian Democrats, Socialists, Communists. Their opinions clashed but without threatening freedom of expression. But this only came about slowly, as a few examples will demonstrate.

I was traveling with a well-intentioned German who had agreed to drive me to Hamburg. From his refusal to speak, I could tell that he still considered me an enemy. He was obviously thinking about something. Crossing the southern suburb of Hamburg, we saw nothing but piles of ruins on all sides. The road was almost impassable.

Suddenly, my driver stopped and pointed to a hill of bricks and twisted scrap metal on the left. It was all that remained of a large apartment building. "My mother and my sister have been buried there for two years! It's the work of your friends, the English, models of Christian civilization!"

It was terrible, undeniable. I said nothing. Before long, he drove on.

I decided to risk a few remarks. "Hitler began these methods in 1940. There was Rotterdam, Coventry, London. "

"Never did the German people make other people suffer as greatly as other people have made us suffer," replied my driver. I understood that no discussion of this issue was possible. This man had succumbed to the ruthless accounting system used by opposing groups of humanity to justify their mutual destruction. When he tallied it up, the debt owed by the Germans was small change, while that owed by others amounted to billions.

This made me think of the Germans' refusal of responsibility after World War I. Some claimed in 1923, for example, "We have never inflicted on others the type of famine that is imposed on us even now. The French are purposely not reconstructing their devastated regions to prove that the Germans are barbarians." I remembered that the Armistice border in 1918 passed through France, while German territory was intact. I compared the ruined northern cities of France with the beautiful German cities left standing and filled with gardens. Perhaps it took the crushing defeat inflicted on Germany in 1945 for the Germans to fully learn what war entails. Germany was crushed, many of its cities destroyed. Hildesheim and Nuremberg, beautiful, museum-like cities were leveled – 40, 60, or 80 percent destroyed. I cried over the destruction of so much beauty, but, I must admit, I had a cold stone deep in my heart, a lack of pity that I still feel. They *had* to learn.

They did in fact learn. I can now talk to Germans the way I do to other people. The barking of neo-Nazis and irredentists[1] no longer reaches them. Even the *Wirtschaftswunder*, the extraordinary economic rebirth of West Germany (with massive aid, it must be said, from the USA and American banks that have invested in Germany the millions they count out parsimoniously to other nations) doesn't give the Germans illusions of superiority. They work hard, absorb refugees from East Germany, rebuild their cities, and find leaders of good quality. They have not become again that exalted and dangerously mystical breed that destroyed Europe twice in thirty years.

My second story takes place in Petzen, in a railroad workers' shack. The old man had been confirmed by my grandfather and remembered him well. He gave me a souvenir of his confirmation that included a picture of my grandfather. It was an intimate, familial setting. I remember the sharp, bitter taste of thin, buttered slices of black bread accompanying the coffee, the embroidered cloth on the oval table, the sofa where I sat as their special guest, and the sugary blandness of the enormous *Zuckerkuchen* (sugar cake) ordered from the bakery in my honor.

1 People advocating the restoration of any territory formerly belonging to their country.

Wilhelm Mensching presided. He was already old, bent over, with a sickly complexion, but his burning religious fervor kept the flame of faith alive in the hearts of his parishioners. He understood these people. He was one of them. He would soon leave his version of the Collège Cévenol, the *Freundschaftsheim*, behind him.[2] The conversation was freewheeling, but then we touched on a sensitive topic: Why did the Germans only oppose Hitler with such sporadic resistance, even within the Confessing Church? I knew that the Confessing Church had rejected the notion of racial distinctions for doctrinal reasons: they believe that salvation comes from grace alone, not from belonging to a certain race.

"Luther distinguishes between religious duties and civic duties. We must serve the prince. God wills his authority. Believers who confess their evangelical faith must also serve the state faithfully as functionaries, teachers, and soldiers. It's their duty."

"But the state committed crimes. Why didn't you protest the concentration camps?"

"We had no idea they existed," was their answer.

"Were we really ignorant of their existence?" suggested Mensching.

There was silence. Then an old man, a peasant, began to speak. He hesitated. He was afraid.

"Don't tell anyone what I'm about to say," he said. "No one. I don't want any problems. But I discovered something." (This was 1949, four years after the fall of Hitler.)

"What!" cried out the people in the room.

"Yes, near Porta Westfalica there was a camp. I went there a few times to deliver coal. I passed two guard posts with my cart. They searched me. In the camp, I saw men wearing striped convict clothing. They looked sallow and emaciated. The guards spoke to them brutally. One day, I saw twenty of these men, loaded down with sacks of stones, walking round and round to the howling of a police officer. When one of them fell, they made him stand by kicking him."

"You never said a word about any of that," cried out those in attendance.

"That's right," responded the old man. "When I left the camp, they threatened me: 'If you say anything at all about what you've seen here, we'll find out, and we'll get you and put you in the camp.'"

---

2 "Friendship House," a "peace school" he founded at Bückeburg in 1948.

"What was the name of this place?" I asked.

"Dora," he responded.

Dora, where Daniel Trocmé, Philippe Cambessédès, and so many others were held; where, in a secret underground factory, the V1s and V2s were developed;[3] where prisoners were forced to witness hangings accompanied by music or face death themselves if they refused. I related what I knew. My German friends were floored.

A young woman then spoke up, "I was a member of the Nazi Youth," she said. "I spent a night with my friends in a tent in the woods near Dora. We heard cries, horrible human cries, of people being tortured. When we returned home, we spoke to our parents about it. They were terrified and forbade us to talk about it to anyone."

Now, three years later, those sealed lips opened. "We knew something, yes, we knew something," the adults confessed, looking down at the floor.

If we want the words "Christian civilization" to have meaning, we must completely revise religious education. Merely teaching the Ten Commandments waters down sin, reducing evil to a handful of infractions against personal and familial propriety. This must be corrected. We must teach young people that conformity and fear are the most serious sins. They led to the stoning of the prophets and the crucifixion of Christ. They allowed Christian nations to wage endless wars without realizing their guilt. Nonconformity for reasons of conscience is the first duty of Christ's followers.

The next most serious sins are complicity with injustice, exploitation, humiliation of others, silence in the face of shameful actions by our society. When human beings liberate themselves from the "what will others say about me" syndrome to champion the rights of those without voices, they will be ready to practice the other Christian virtues of purity, goodness, patience, and forgiveness. Woe to those who begin with laxity! They will end up as cowards and miss the gospel's liberating power.

CHÂTEAU DE PERDYER, July 17, 1968

I'm writing from the big, second-floor room on the "Jacques Martin side" of the Château de Perdyer. It looks exactly like the room adjacent to the one on the "Mrs. Deloche side" of the house where I spent the winter

3 The V1 missile, once launched, flew until it ran out of fuel and came crashing down and exploded. The V2 rocket was a long-distance weapon that could travel at the speed of sound.

of 1943–44. Right now, I'm on vacation on the "Martin side" for three weeks with Magda. Back then I was hidden under the name of Béguet on the "Mrs. Deloche side."[4]

Opposite the chateau, on the left, is the picturesque Lambert farm (Pépé and Mémé Lambert are still alive) that Jacquot visited when I gave him Latin and German lessons and he went to the village school. Also, opposite the house is the conical, yellowish mountain called the Piémard. It would be ugly if the finest grapevines in the country didn't garnish its foothills. Everything is the same – Mrs. Deloche is still here; the Lamberts are too. The battles of 1943–44 are over; today peace and prosperity are everywhere. The mountain roads that the *maquisards* traveled secretly are filled today with hundreds of boy and girl scouts, in small groups without adult leaders, tranquil, sure of themselves, disdainful of the "old people" we have become. Our colorful adventures have faded with the passing of the years.

The countryside has shrunk too. When I walked through it then, it seemed immense, mysterious, and threatening because of my uncertain future. It's just a short drive to shop in Die, where I didn't dare show my face during my eight months in hiding. Yesterday we went to the Archiane Cirque, a grandiose, solitary cul-de-sac that I found threatening in the past. Back then, the village of Archiane was half in ruins and on the verge of disappearing. Yesterday, cars were parked in single file at the entrance to the refurbished village. Every house in decent shape has been turned into a cheap-looking, outdoor refreshment stand. Like grasshoppers, clusters of tourists and boy scouts scarf up everything that can be sold – fake-colored postcards, fake antiques, and fake orangeade. Now civilized, Archiane has lost its silence and majesty, like the monuments that too many tourists have admired and photographed.

ENOUGH STERILE MUSING. I'm still here, at least provisionally. The death of my son Jean-Pierre is an insurmountable obstacle, a darkness I refuse to examine further for fear of suffering and questioning myself too much. Since his death and that of my other son, Daniel, and even, I now realize, the death of my mother, I have learned to live with gloom and hostility, coolness and indifference, the absurd and

4 The large house referred to as the Château de Perdyer was divided into two parts. One belonged to Eva Deloche, the other to her first cousin, the same Jacques Martin who appears in these memoirs.

the inevitable. I'd call these forces fate if I had to invoke a name. I feel suspended over a void that licks my feet, grabs me, and tries to drag me into nothingness.

Suspended by what? My faith. But not a naive faith filled with statues of angels and Christ or marvelous examples of providence. Providence has spoiled me at times, but more often has abandoned me when I needed it most for my children. No, the faith that holds me suspended is a wager in which the will plays a huge role. I have learned to turn away from the absurd and attach myself to that which must be, which will be.

Why should there be peace one day? Why should truth carry the day? Why should justice triumph? I don't know. I find no proof in the past, present, or foreseeable future of humanity. In my opinion, the major obstacle isn't human wickedness but rather human stupidity, the herd instinct, our immeasurable naivety.

Given these circumstances, why do I have faith? Probably for two reasons. The first, that in my youth, I received a sober religious education, without embellishments, that life's hardships have not disrupted. And second, I am naturally melancholy and pessimistic about people, life, and myself. Disposed to introspection, I couldn't have survived if I hadn't made the wager of faith. Moreover, my faith has always been global in perspective. I have not only wagered on the existence of God, but *also on the possibility of goodness on earth* ("Thy will be done on earth as it is in heaven"). The theoretical existence of God is of no interest to me.

My faith affects every realm of my life: society, church, family, children, parishioners. There's a certain *practical* aspect to my ministry, even though I am hardly a practical man. If my ministry can't be translated into facts and acts, it doesn't interest me.

That's why I have treasured my contacts with the FOR. There I discovered the only spring of living waters in this world that satisfied my thirst. When I was very young, I was disconcerted by the ease with which so many believers separated their lives into watertight compartments. Some compartments contained faith, consolation, virtue, generosity, and lack of self-interest. Others were reserved for careers and businesses, or familial, civil, and national obligations: here, every man was for himself. Collective, narrow interests, monumental national pride, partisan politics, and murder were the rule. For me, it was impossible to maintain this dichotomy and believe. If I had been able to do so, I would have become a good soldier, cruel, ready to die and to kill. Or, as a politician,

I would have become a disciple of Machiavelli because I am interested in crowd behavior and know something about it. As a businessman, I would have become cunning and sly, *furbo*, as they say in Italian. I would have passionately desired riches, perhaps even stolen.

As a believer, I had no choice but to renounce all that: cruelty, ambition (even ecclesiastical ambition), riches. Yet, even as I suppressed my passions through faith, they continued to swarm within me. But they no longer endangered my faith. I dominated my sexual passions, for example, by recognizing that my love of beauty, truth, and purity was completely incompatible with these guilty indulgences.

To be completely honest, there's another reason for my faith. Since childhood, I have lacked self-confidence. Why? Once again, because of my upbringing. Papa's look was the look of God. He was, if not too pure, at least too strict to envision sin. Iniquity infested me. I didn't like to work hard (doctors later informed me that this situation was due to a glandular problem), but I nonetheless dreamed of being a hero. I loathed the verse: "He who is faithful in little things will also be faithful in big ones," because I wasn't faithful in the little ones, even as I aimed for the big ones. In retrospect, I was remarkably conscientious for my age. At the time, however, it seemed that "good students" – my brother Pierre and cousin Yvonne, for example – surrounded me. Only Étienne, who was skinny and a poor student, reassured me. My reaction was to treat him as an inferior – another sin. In short, I was in bad shape when I approached adolescence and its sexual torments. I was heavy, ill-at-ease, with puffy features. I had unconditional admiration for those with self-confidence. For years, I blushed when people looked at me because I felt their gaze could perceive all the sins gnawing at my soul.

It was faith that saved me from this psychic malady undermining me. I didn't realize right away that I was saved. I was never able, like the young members of the Saint-Quentin Union, to proclaim that I had experienced a sudden conversion brought about by an encounter with Jesus Christ. No, I was saved because, underneath the sick person I have just described, the being I have become was slowly developing into someone robust, joyful, and hopeful for the future.

To keep that being alive, to avoid falling back to my pre-Christian self, I had to drink from the only spring that could satisfy my thirst: the waters of the absolute. I had to pitch my tent in faith and frequent those whose triumphant faith embraces all of life. They became my models.

They were my brothers and sisters, even if their personalities didn't suffer from the morbid weakness I still suffer from today.

One last reflection: These "great" ones I knew, these "giants of faith" – the Cérésole brothers, A. J. Muste, Danilo Dolci,[5] Philippe Vernier, to cite only a few (I never met Gandhi) – had the power to generate disciples, admirers, and imitators of every stripe. I am intentionally using this vulgar word because their disciples were often bearded, vegetarian, wearing sandals, and dressed in bizarre ways. The disciples of the "giants" have often succumbed to utopian ideas. Refusing to see the world as it is, rejecting the idea that man is often stupid and cruel, they imitate the exterior signs of poverty and nonviolence by adopting strange clothing and eating habits. Their eccentricity does nothing to promote the causes they believe in.

Perhaps there is a place in this world for practical, nonviolent people who understand human frailty. Even as they take their inspiration from the "giants," they see their own limitations and understand the absurdity of trying to be angelic when they are still beastly.[6]

These nonviolent people, idealistic and practical at the same time, are my models. Martin Luther King Jr. was the most accomplished of them. He has my highest admiration. Henry Hodgkin, Mathilda Wrede, Leonhard Ragaz, Pierre Cérésole, A. J. Muste, Muriel Lester all died without their hopes becoming reality. In 1968, a few of the erratic cornerstones among the founders of the FOR – Friedrich Siegmund-Schultze, John Nevin Sayre – are still alive but diminished by sickness. What do they all have in common? Faith, such as I defined it earlier. Faith in the possibility of goodness on earth.

It was in Bad Boll, in the institution left by Johann Christoph Blumhardt and his son Christoph Friedrich Blumhardt, that I understood the power of these people's faith.

The year before, the reunion of the founders of the International Fellowship of Reconciliation took place in Denmark. Several of my friends from the School of Theology in Paris were invited. Cornier, Fabre, Roser, Bresch. They came back "converted." No one remembered me; I had been too timid to talk.

5 Danilo Dolci (1924–1997) was an Italian social activist who became one of the leaders of the nonviolence movement in Italy. He is often referred to as the "Gandhi of Sicily."

6 Trocmé is referring to Pascal's famous statement: "Man is neither angel nor beast. The problem is that those who try to act like angels end up acting like beasts."

Their enthusiasm soon cooled. For Cornier, Bresch, Ducros, and many others, the FOR was nothing but an episode in their life. For Fabre (who edited the *FOR Notebooks* for a while but soon ceased all activities), Roser, and me, the FOR became our life. Roser sacrificed everything for it, as did Jacques Martin and Philippe Vernier. Roser, a voluntary preacher in Aubervilliers, after being refused pastoral consecration because he was a conscientious objector, became secretary of the FOR (even secretary general for a while). He served with a Catholic from Vienna, Kaspar Mayr, as his assistant. They maintained their modest office in Paris on the Rue de Provence until the Second World War.

At first, I didn't sacrifice anything for the FOR. We lived at 30 Rue Jacob in Paris. I was a student. My father's rules were so strict that I wouldn't have thought of straying from them. At the Union in Plaisance and then in Clamart, I became another person, a "leader," as they say today. But neither at home nor at the School of Theology, where I met my friends who had fought in Verdun, was I anything more than a heavy-set and timid boy, totally lacking in self-confidence.

In this frame of mind, I went to Bad Boll. The "great ones" were absent, but Ragaz, Roser, and an English deputy, Sir Walter Ayles, were there. They tried not to bring up the First World War, which had just ended. Some wanted to pass over the question of responsibility for the war and war crimes that had been so divisive during our initial ecumenical meetings. Many pacifists refused to accept this facile solution.

I, who had lived through the occupation, protested against this tendency right away, so they formed a commission for "war crimes" and asked me to give a report. I clumsily tried to plead for charity, for pardon that didn't overlook the truth.

The rest of the time I listened, dumbfounded, and took notes. I heard the defense of authority, biblical knowledge, sociological competence, lived experiences, the "crazy" ideas that were mocked in my home or at the School of Theology in Paris. I learned suddenly that I was not crazy or alone, but that in every country, in opposing camps, the same thoughts, the same Spirit descended upon men and women who didn't know one another. This struck me as bordering on the supernatural.

By the way, I have had these supernatural "encounters" throughout my career. In truth, I have never converted anyone at all to Christian pacifism, but during my life as an itinerant lecturer I have recruited, stirred, and brought together isolated individuals who already carried within them belief in pacifism.

Most men and women behave like pacifist *gentlemen* and *ladies* in their private lives (they haven't killed, stolen, or hurt anyone) but cannot even conceive of nonviolence in their public lives. They make no distinction between police action and war, certain that their party or their country is right. Another small number of men and women seem to understand the vanity of collective pride and the absurdity of war. They are pacifists by reason and by instinct but don't know how to translate this knowledge into action.

Almost always, this second group of men and women are isolated, just as I was isolated until I joined the FOR. They become discouraged, doubt themselves, shrivel up, and cease acting. If they are religious, their pacifist convictions take the form of mysticism. Like people from the East, they believe they have resolved the problems of the world by renouncing their personal desires and illusions and finding inner peace.

Then, one evening, they attend a lecture by a visiting Christian messenger of peace, who declares with simplicity:

1. The Sermon on the Mount is practical and efficacious.
2. If Christ's disciples today really believed in Christ and his teaching, they could bring about individual, social, and political transformations of incalculable dimensions.
3. Disciples of Christ should not fear rejection or suffering. God offers solutions to the problem of this world.

The "unwitting pacifists" begin to question. Contradictions suddenly appear absurd, and the conversation with the visitor, after the lecture, continues past midnight. The next morning, very early, the visitor, a tireless pilgrim, catches a train or a plane to be "parachuted" into another city, where the scenario begins again, until the day when pacifist cells are formed in his wake. They defend conscientious objectors, struggle against the atomic bomb, work with "protest groups," but never cross the line between peaceful action and violence.

A painful break with the partisans of violence often occurs. The two groups reunite when the violence, either verbal or physical, has run its course and its partisans realize that in the final analysis, violence is ineffective.

From crisis to crisis, the political pendulum swings, from right to left, from left to right. The extremists always lead the way. They tear up the streets and smash the shop windows. The "politically neutral" always close their eyes and "wait for it to pass." They get out while the getting is good. Meanwhile, the nonviolent, never neutral, never violent, maintain contact with their friends and enemies, correct falsehoods, and join forces with all those fighting for justice, truth, and peace.

Epilogue

Patrick Cabanel

DEATH PREVENTED ANDRÉ TROCMÉ from finishing his memoirs, which don't go beyond the 1950s. In a note at the end of the manuscript, Magda summarizes what the rest of his memoirs might have included:

1. Travels across the world, including those in Tunisia, Algeria, and Morocco (hot spots) and experiences during the war in Algeria. We were in Algeria on May 13, 1958.[1]
2. The founding of Eirene.
3. Laying the cornerstone for Freundschaftsheim in Bückeburg.
4. His pastorate in Geneva at Saint-Gervais Church.
5. A training school for diesel mechanics in Skikda (Philippeville) in Algeria.
6. Ecumenism between Saint-Gervais Church and the Catholic Cathedral in Geneva.
7. The growth of our family with twelve grandchildren.

This final segment of André Trocmé's life was rich and busy. There are several accounts of these final years in books about André Trocmé in French and English.[2] I will nonetheless say a few words about them.

As recounted in this book, right after World War II, Trocmé remained a half-time pastor in Le Chambon. His other half-time appointment was as the European secretary of the International Fellowship of

1 Eighteen days of violence in Algeria, beginning on May 13, 1958, caused a political crisis in France and brought Charles de Gaulle back to power after a twelve-year absence. This is often referred to as the Algiers Putsch or the Coup of May 13, which marked the collapse of the Fourth Republic and the founding of de Gaulle's Fifth Republic.

2 See, for example, Richard P. Unsworth, *A Portrait of Pacifists: Le Chambon, the Holocaust, and the Lives of André & Magda Trocmé* (Syracuse University Press, 2012).

Reconciliation. In 1949, he worked full-time for the FOR with his wife Magda as co-secretary, drawing only one salary. In 1950, the couple settled in Versailles in a rented house that became the House of Reconciliation, also known as the *Moulin de la Paix* (Mill of Peace).

From there, André and Magda became globetrotters for peace and nonviolence, traveling throughout the world to spread the International FOR's ideas, to raise money and, as André says in his memoirs, to move beyond the death of their son Jean-Pierre. The former pastor who was so passionately involved in Maubeuge and Sin-le-Noble, then in Le Chambon, was now an "ambassador" for worldwide Christianity. It would take too long to list all the trips undertaken separately by André and Magda. I will mention, however, Magda's trip to India in 1949–50, which resulted in her *Journal d'une pacifiste aux Indes* (Diary of a Pacifist in India).[3]

At the same time, André became a representative of left-wing Christianity, actively involved in the fight against nuclear weapons and for the independence of Algeria. In 1959, with Alfred Kastler, he founded the French Federation Against Nuclear Weapons. The two men sent a letter to the president of France in May 1959, asking him to postpone France's acquisition of the atomic bomb. "We think moral progress alone can answer the questions posed by technical progress," they wrote. "Moral progress is always the fruit of decisions by the moral conscience, a reaction against the fatalism of evil."

Even before the war and decolonization, the Trocmés had turned their attention to Algeria. Their first trip took place in 1953, when they also traveled to Tunisia and Morocco. This was followed by a six-month stay in 1956 to organize literacy classes for Algerian women. On a visit two years later, they witnessed the Algiers Putch, and André wrote an opinion piece about it in *Le Monde*. In 1957, at the invitation of Willem Visser't Hooft, André and a group of German Mennonites founded the Association of Eirene ("peace" in Greek) for the purpose of sending conscientious objectors to Morocco, Algeria, and other areas to undertake humanitarian work on the model of Pierre Cérésole's International Civilian Service, which had been founded four decades earlier.

3 Nicolas Bourguinat, "Une enquête dans l'Inde indépendante. Magda Trocmé, une pacifiste parmi les disciples de Gandhi en 1949–1950," *Source(s)* 8–9, 2016, 157–183, and Magda Trocmé, "Parmi les disciples de Gandhi: journal d'une pacifiste aux Indes (octobre 1949–février 1950)," *Source(s)* 8–9, 2016, 185–267.

André once again became a pastor on May 1, 1960, this time in Saint-Gervais parish. He remained there for ten years. The only offer he had received in France was for Saint-Véran, a tiny parish high in the mountains, the kind normally reserved for beginning pastors. A German cousin living in Geneva and member of the Saint-Gervais parish alerted André to the open position, and he was named to it.

In 1963, André and Magda created the Saint-Gervais-Philippeville Association, which allowed the parish of Saint-Gervais to support the establishment of a school for diesel mechanics in Philippeville, Algeria (now called Skikda).

André's last ten years were marked by a tragedy, the death of another son, Daniel, in 1961. These years also brought satisfaction on many levels: the implementation of a statute for conscientious objection in France and the liberation of imprisoned conscientious objectors; the publication in 1961 of his book *Jésus et la révolution non-violente* (Jesus and the Nonviolent Revolution),[4] a work he considered highly important; the publication of a collection of parable-like short stories, *Des Anges et des ânes, contes de Noël et d'autres temps*[5] (Angels and Donkeys: Tales for Christmas and Other Times).

In May 1964, in Florence, he participated in a posthumous tribute to the historian Jules Isaac,[6] who lived on the Plateau Vivarais-Lignon during the 1940s. In 1971, the Yad Vashem Institute in Jerusalem awarded André Trocmé the Medal of the Righteous Among the Nations, an honor hardly known at the time. He was proposed for the Nobel Peace Prize twice, in 1950 and 1955. When he learned of the honor from Yad Vashem, he felt that the award should have gone to the entire village of Le Chambon or that he should have at least received the award in Le Chambon so that all the residents could participate in the event. He wrote the following letter to Anny Latour,[7] a historian of the French Jewish resistance, concerning this matter:

4 André Trocmé, *Jésus et la revolution non-violente* (Labor et Fides, 1961); *Jesus and the Nonviolent Revolution* (Plough Publishing House, 2014).

5 André Trocmé, *Des Anges et des ânes, contes de Noël et d'autres temps* (Labor et Fides, 1965); *Angels and Donkeys: Tales for Christmas and Other Times* (Good Books, 1998).

6 Jules Isaac was an important Jewish historian, celebrated for his tireless work in Christian-Jewish relations and his key role in the formulation of the Catholic Church's *Nostra aetate* during the Second Vatican Council.

7 She had just published *La Résistance juive en France 1940–1944* (Paris: Stock, 1970).

> Why me and not the many humble peasants of the Haute-Loire, who did as much and more than I did? Why not my wife, whose behavior was much more heroic than mine? Why not my colleague Édouard Theis, who shared responsibilities with me? I can only accept the medal of the "Righteous Among the Nations" in the name of all those who dared help our unjustly persecuted brothers and sisters, at the risk of their lives. Despite everything, I still feel guilty about what was not done.[8]

A few weeks later, less than two months before his death, André Trocmé reunited his family in Lucinges, an estate near Geneva, for his seventieth birthday. He read this message:

> Two things have happened to me in my life.
>
> At the age of seventy, I am taking stock of my life. I admit that I have not altogether won the wager I made because I never learned to love people as much as I wished. I am a man, a bit coarse, sometimes a little too enthusiastic, sometimes a little angry. I never learned to love others as I wanted, but I did learn two things.
>
> Above all, I discovered that God loves me. I did not know God well, but I now know that God knows me and loves me. That was a wonderful discovery.
>
> Then I discovered something else. To show me that God loves me, God sent me someone filled with tremendous love, so awesome that I have symbolized it with a crown, a love as red as blood, a burning love. [André places a crown of red roses on Magda's head.] In addition, my Italian lady was beautiful. She resembled a certain lady immortalized by Leonard da Vinci. [Here, André takes out a 18x20 cm framed reproduction of *The Virgin, the Baby Jesus, and Saint Anne* from the Louvre. He places next to it a picture of the same size of Magda holding baby Nelly on her lap. The resemblance between the two Florentine beauties is extraordinary.] Besides beauty, she had this tremendous love!
>
> Now I would like to say something to my grandchildren.
>
> First this: I want you to believe in love. Even when you experience

8 This letter was cited by Patrick G. Henry, *La Montagne des Justes* (Editions Privat, 2010), 40. Trocmé succeeded in having the ceremony moved from the Israeli Embassy in Bern to Le Chambon-sur-Lignon, where it took place in the Protestant church at the time of his funeral. Magda was named Righteous Among the Nations in 1986.

discouraging moments in your life, I want you to continue believing in love. It is the most beautiful thing that exists. Not the stupid love you hear about in songs today, not sex, but true love. The love that Magda Grilli has shown me my whole life.

Secondly, I want you to wager on love. I want you to try at your age what I tried when I was sixteen and tell yourselves that it is worthwhile to spend life loving others.

And thirdly, when you are discouraged, when you have no more to give, when there's no more love in your heart, I want you to begin again like the two little boys on the beach when the tide swept away their sandcastle. They made a new castle, even though they knew that the tide would return and carry off their masterpiece once again.

There. I've said everything I wanted to say to you.

Acknowledgements

Having read André Trocmé's memoirs, published in 2020 in French, Patrick Henry and Mary Anne O'Neil offered to translate them into English. This book is the product of their efforts. As the daughter and granddaughter of André and Magda Trocmé, we honor and thank Patrick Henry and Mary Anne O'Neil for their unfailing devotion to documenting this extraordinary period of time in world history.

Nelly Trocmé Hewett, daughter
Katia Trocmé Blackburn, granddaughter

As translators, we wish to express our gratitude to three friends who made our translation possible. Nelly Trocmé Hewett not only offered us the opportunity to translate her father's memoirs but also explained numerous references to people, places, and events that we could never have understood without her. Katia Blackburn spent countless hours formatting the text for both Nelly and us and made it possible for us to communicate with each other. Dr. Culley Jane Carson edited every chapter. Her excellent knowledge of French and English vocabulary and style saved us from many inaccuracies and greatly improved the readability of our text.

Patrick Henry and Mary Anne O'Neil

My thanks go to Gérard Bollon, François Boulet, Christophe Chalamet, Nelly Trocmé Hewett, and Pierre Sauvage.

Patrick Cabanel

About the Editor

Patrick Cabanel, a professor at École Pratique des Hautes Études, is a French historian specializing in the history of religious minorities and French resistance to the Holocaust.

About the Translators

Patrick Henry is professor emeritus of philosophy and literature at Whitman College. He is the author of five books. Mary Anne O'Neil is professor emerita of French, Spanish, and world literature at Whitman College.